THE REVOLUTION TO COME

The Revolution to Come

A HISTORY OF AN IDEA FROM THUCYDIDES TO LENIN

Dan Edelstein

PRINCETON UNIVERSITY PRESS
PRINCETON & OXFORD

Published by Princeton University Press
41 William Street, Princeton, New Jersey 08540
99 Banbury Road, Oxford OX2 6JX

press.princeton.edu

ISBN 978-0-691-23185-3
ISBN (e-book) 978-0-691-23184-6

British Library Cataloging-in-Publication Data is available

Editorial: Priya Nelson and Emma Wagh
Production Editorial: Jenny Wolkowicki
Jacket design: Haley Jin Mee Chung
Production: Danielle Amatucci
Publicity: Alyssa Sanford and Kathryn Stevens
Copyeditor: Maia Vaswani

Jacket images: Adobe Stock / Shutterstock

This book has been composed in Miller Text

Printed in the United States of America

10 9 8 7 6 5 4 3 2 1

This book is dedicated to the Stanford Summer Humanities Institute (SHI) students who participated in my "Revolutions" class from 2011 to 2024. Thank you for your questions and insights, for skipping July 4 festivities to attend the lecture, and for your renditions of *La Marseillaise*!

CONTENTS

INTRODUCTION

Come the Revolution

AS WORKERS FLOWED out of a factory one afternoon in New York City, a communist organizer harangued them from a soapbox on the sidewalk. A crowd gathered to hear him out. "Comrades," the organizer cried, "are you not tired of laboring for another's gain? Why don't your wages reflect the real work you do each day? Don't you deserve a better deal than this?" A few people cheered in assent. "Then, comrades, join us in our fight for the Revolution! Come the Revolution, the rich will cease to steal from the poor. Come the Revolution, the workers will own the factories. Come the Revolution, everyone will eat strawberries and cream!" Then a small voice piped up in the crowd: "But what if I don't like strawberries and cream?" The organizer stared coldly at the questioner and responded: "Come the Revolution, everyone will *like* strawberries and cream."

This joke was told to me by my father, who heard it from his (very conservative) high-school history teacher during the McCarthy era. The joke seems to have originated during the 1930s, when it featured in a vaudeville show.[1] While obviously anti-Communist and counterrevolutionary, it offers a window on the history of revolution. For starters, it draws our attention to an important difference in how revolution has been understood over time. If this joke were transposed to the streets of New York in the 1770s, it would make little sense. No American colonist fighting the British would have imagined that their taste in fruit or dairy could possibly be affected by the outcome of the war. The organizer's answer to the worker's question becomes funny only after a certain moment in history, once "revolution" had acquired a different meaning than it had, say, in 1776.

But the joke also sheds light on this more modern understanding of "revolution." "Come the Revolution, everyone will like strawberries and cream"—if we strip away the frivolity of this punchline, we are left with a basic claim that reflects what many actually believed. Come the Revolution, everyone *should* come to an agreement: differences in opinion will disappear, especially about subjects less trivial than fruit. The Revolution will not only improve people's lives but should reflect a consensus about what the good life is. Put simply, come the Revolution everyone should agree that strawberries and cream are our just dessert.

Of course, what makes the joke funny is that things do not turn out that way. Come the Revolution, people may agree on some things, but never on all. In most societies, these disagreements are not a problem: we don't expect politicians from different parties to have the same views on issues. Pluralist democracies, by definition, recognize a plurality of opinions. But revolutionary governments do not share this commitment. As Trotsky observed in 1924, "In the last analysis the party is always right. . . . [N]o one can be right against the party."[2] If the Party decrees that everyone will like strawberries and cream, that is what right-minded people must do. The sinister implication of the organizer's answer is that those who do not like strawberries and cream will be forced to—or face the consequences.

In the slapstick manner of vaudeville comedy, then, this joke connects the modern belief in unhampered progress and the assumption that reasonable people will reach a consensus on all things with the threat that failure to do so will be met with political violence. It does not offer any explanation for how or why these ideas and practices go together. That is the role of history, not humor. But the joke helps to frame some of the great mysteries of the modern age. How and when did revolutions become seen as the solution to social problems? What prevented them from playing such a role in earlier times? And why did political movements rooted in optimism and humanitarianism often lead to oppression, incarceration, and death?

These are some of the questions that I address in this book, which offers a history of the idea of revolution. To be clear, it is not a history of revolutions in general, though many appear in the following chapters. The revolutions that I discuss are primarily here to illustrate how the idea of revolution evolved (or did not) in the midst of political changes. The later chapters also trace how the modern idea of revolution—an idea that emerged, I argue, only in the mid-eighteenth century—shaped the actual course of subsequent revolutions, starting in 1789.

In some respects, this book resembles other intellectual histories, in that it charts the changing meaning of a concept across an extended period of time. I track "revolution" from Thucydides to Lenin (and a bit beyond), paying close attention to how historians, philosophers, and politicians used language. Most obviously, I focus on the word "revolution" itself, but also on a host of others, across many languages. Where this book differs from comparable endeavors, however, is in the fact that the concept of revolution was primarily fashioned by its critics. Indeed, from the Peloponnesian War to the American Revolution, revolution retained a sulfurous odor. With few exceptions, revolutions were widely condemned as destructive events, to be avoided whenever possible. The primary sources for this period, accordingly, are almost entirely negative.

To modern ears, these accounts of revolution cannot help but sound conservative. In a sense, they are: their authors believed that conserving the state in its existing form was a good in and of itself. But it would be a mistake to call them "conservative" in our contemporary sense. That label derives its meaning from its antithesis, "progressive," and before the eighteenth century, there were no progressives. That is, the idea that history was gradually but persistently driving humanity toward a more reasonable and just future was not to be found before around 1700. (I suggest below that Christian ideas of providentialism and millenarianism rest on a very different theory of history.) Earlier writers who warned against revolution were conservative not because they opposed progressives but because they did not have a progressive option. Conserving the state was the only reasonable objective of political thought. Even when revolution appeared inevitable, as it did to Whig politicians in the 1680s and to their American descendants in the 1770s, it had to serve the purpose of stabilizing the state.

Once a progressive theory of historical progress became available, by contrast, writers could advance a more favorable view of revolution. And that is precisely what happened: at the very moment when French thinkers began promoting the idea of historical progress, they also turned the meaning of revolution on its head. Where it had previously been seen as a divisive and dangerous phenomenon, these (literal) progressive thinkers portrayed revolution as the gateway to a new and improved future. It is only from this point onward in the historical record that we start to find an abundance of positive accounts of revolution.

This disparity in our primary sources for revolution—overwhelmingly negative from Thucydides to Hobbes, very often positive from Turgot to Khomeini—leads directly to the thesis of my book. How we think about revolution is ultimately conditioned by how we think about history. People who believe that history is progressing toward a better future are more likely to place their trust in a revolution. Those who, conversely, assume that future societies will face the same problems that they always have in the past will likely view revolutions with skepticism. To understand how the meaning of revolution changed throughout history, we must examine competing accounts of human time.[3]

If the joke about strawberries and cream would have mystified American revolutionaries, it was because they still accepted the historical vision, with its attending fears, that ancient Greek political thinkers had fashioned. A good example of the staying power of Greek ideas can be found in John Adams. In 1787, as delegates to the Constitutional Convention were preparing to leave for Philadelphia, Adams was in London, representing the United States as the ambassador to Great Britain. While there, he published a work that advocated for the kind of balanced constitution that the delegates ultimately adopted. This text, *A Defence of the Constitutions of the United States*, offers a surprisingly dark take on revolution: "Human nature is as incapable now of going through revolutions with temper and sobriety, with patience and prudence, or without fury and madness, as it was among the Greeks so long ago."[4]

It might seem ironic that Adams, one of the leading revolutionaries of 1776, should express these reservations about revolution in 1787. To some extent, the circumstances had changed. Now it was the young republic itself that was under threat, notably by internal turmoil such as the veterans' uprising in Western Massachusetts (known today as Shays's Rebellion). And Adams was possibly more cautious in his views than other American statesmen. What's telling is where Adams found support for his fears—"among the Greeks so long ago." In the Preface to his *Defence*, Adams listed the many revolutions, and their respective body counts, that had dotted a sixty-year interval of Greek history. He singled out one in particular for its savagery: the uprising on the island of Corcyra (present-day Corfu). This episode, famously recounted by Thucydides in his history of the Peloponnesian War, still filled Adams with dread two thousand years after the fact:

> Every kind of death, every dreadful act, was perpetrated. Fathers slew their children; some were dragged from altars, some were butchered at them; numbers, immersed in temples, were starved. The contagion spread through the whole extent of Greece: factions raged in every city.[5]

This famous account of revolution loomed large in ancient political thought. Greek and Roman philosophers and historians perpetuated Thucydides's chilling account of revolution, and their warnings passed on into medieval and Renaissance texts. From this vantage point, the joke that after the revolution everyone would like strawberries and cream simply would not compute. Revolutions were more likely to bring about death and destruction than universal harmony.

But why was a future filled with delicious treats out of the question? The ancients' negative outlook on revolution rested on a monochrome vision of human history. Empires rose and fell, cities flourished and declined, and strange twists of fate continually surprised us. But the basic stuff of human life and society remained the same. "To examine human life for forty years is the same as to examine it for ten thousand years, for what more will you see?" asked the Roman emperor Marcus Aurelius in his *Meditations*.[6] For all its unexpected turns, history was a hamster wheel, powered by one unchanging constant: our flawed human natures. It was difficult to envisage a fantastic world to come, because the past and present were mirrors of the future. There was no reason to believe that the problems confronting humans today would disappear tomorrow, as the source of our problems lay within us. Or as Adams put it: "Human nature is as incapable now . . . as it was among the Greeks so long ago."

But there was another thread tying Adams and other political writers to their classical predecessors. Ancient Greek thinkers had also drawn political conclusions from their observations—and in some cases direct experiences—of the horrors of revolution. The best way to avoid such catastrophes, they argued, was to design a state in a way that reduced the risk of revolution. Since revolutions typically pitted one social group against another, the best constitutions should rest on some sort of power-sharing agreement. This kind of agreement was not one of opinions: the ancients never imagined that a wealthy landowner and a poor artisan would agree on substantial matters. It was rather a compromise, a distribution of power. Different social groups would fill different roles in the state and exercise different functions. This was the theory of the "mixed" or "balanced" constitution, which Adams recommended in his *Defence*.

The most canonical expression of this constitutional theory came from Polybius, a Greek who spent most of his life in Rome, during the apogee of the Roman Republic. Polybius's theory is sometimes dismissed as derivative, but his reworking of Plato and Aristotle introduced important revisions. Where his predecessors had focused on balancing the interests of rich and poor, Polybius paid equal attention to the distribution of political powers across institutions. In so doing, he established the theory of a well-balanced constitution. This is the theory of "checks and balances" that the American Founding Fathers so eagerly embraced.[7]

Polybius also proposed a new contender for the title of best constitution: the Roman Republic. By applying categories from Greek political thought to the Roman constitution, he combined the foundations of Western political science with the most storied case study in Western history. This Polybian synthesis shaped how political theorists in Italy, England, France, and the American colonies understood republican government, well into the eighteenth century.

Finally, Polybius described the passage from one form of government to the next as a recurring cycle. Monarchies gave way to tyrannies, before aristocracies replaced them, only to degenerate in turn into oligarchies. These were overthrown by democracies, which lapsed into mob rule, until eventually a single leader emerged, starting the cycle anew. Here was the grueling circle of history: false hopes and false starts, punctuated by bouts of oppression and destruction. The only way out was to adopt a balanced constitution, on the model of the Roman Republic. By merging the best of monarchy (a strong executive), aristocracy (a wise legislative), and democracy (a fair judiciary), states could withstand the inevitable slings and arrows of political fortune.

The Roman Republic eventually collapsed, in one of the most analyzed sequences of events in history. But its failure did not invalidate Polybius's theory, in the eyes of his followers. Like Plato before him, Polybius had recognized that all states must eventually fall. The republic lasted almost five hundred years—not a bad run, by either ancient or modern standards.

The collapse of the Western Roman Empire, another five hundred years later, posed a greater threat to the longevity of the Polybian synthesis. Polybius, who wrote in Greek, was largely forgotten in the West for the next millennium. Some of his ideas persisted thanks to other writers, most notably Cicero, who adapted them in his treatise *On the Republic*. But even this classic Latin work was largely lost after the fall of Rome, to be recovered only in the nineteenth century. If it was remembered at all before then, it was largely thanks to Augustine, who quoted and attacked Cicero at length in *The City of God*.

In that book, written as the Western empire was teetering on the verge of destruction, Augustine also outlined one of the most influential Christian theologies of history. In one important way, Christianity upended the classical perception of history as an endless cycle of hubris and humiliation. The awaited Second Coming of Christ gave a direction and purpose to history. Apocalyptic predictions about a thousand-year reign of saints even foreshadowed, in the eyes of some historians, the modern idea of revolution.

But if we look more closely, the impact of Christianity on the classical framework for thinking about history and revolutions was surprisingly minimal. This was in no small part thanks to Augustine himself. Divine history had a clear structure, with a beginning (Genesis), a middle (the Crucifixion), and an end (the Last Judgment). But human history, Augustine argued, was much messier. Indeed, until Christ returned, human affairs would continue to be determined by our sinful nature. There was no divine message to be found in the rise and fall of cities or empires. Fortuna—a pagan goddess who was kept on under new Christian management—continued to rule, capriciously, over the sublunar world.[8]

The classical phobia of revolutions also persisted, thanks to the lingering memory of Roman history in the medieval world. The final hundred years of the Roman Republic, recounted by Sallust, Cicero, Livy, Appius, Plutarch, and many others, reinforced the impression that republics—and, to an even greater extent, democracies—were messy, turbulent regimes, which invariably resulted in death and revolution. This impression became even stronger with the translation of ancient Greek philosophers, Aristotle in particular, who gave popular governments bad press. The recovery of Polybius was a slower affair: only by the end of the fifteenth century could Western Europeans engage with his political ideas. His analysis of the Roman Republic as the best possible constitution was an immediate hit. Machiavelli was so impressed that he included it almost word for word in his *Discourses on Livy*. Translators had to render the unusual Greek word that Polybius had used to describe the cycle of governments—*anacyclōsis*. No doubt recalling the circular motion of Fortune's wheel, a popular medieval motif, they settled on "revolution."

From the sixteenth century onward, then, the idea of revolution was doubly indebted to classical political and historical thought. The word itself was closely connected to Polybius's vision of the "revolution of governments" (*politeiōn anacyclōsis*), as attested by the popularity of equivalent phrases in Italian, French, Latin, and English. Political writers praised constitutions that balanced monarchic, aristocratic, and democratic elements as the greatest safeguard against revolution. English jurists in particular touted their own constitution as a worthy successor to Rome's, since its unusual combination of clergy and aristocracy in a single chamber of parliament (the Lords Spiritual and Temporal) gave it the appearance of combining the three "pure" forms of government. This entirely coincidental resemblance between the medieval English constitution and Polybius's ideal type had an outsized influence on the revolutions that rocked England and its colonies between 1642 and 1776 (the subject of part 2 of this book). The lure of the well-balanced constitution proved hard to resist.

This constitutional model was especially attractive to Westerners who had received a classical education. English, French, and Italian political observers were often more familiar with Roman history than with their own. They studied the science of politics in Plato, Aristotle, Polybius, Cicero, and Tacitus. The great modern authors, such as Machiavelli, Bodin, Grotius, Hobbes, Locke, Montesquieu, and Rousseau, also drew extensively on classical sources, even when challenging their conclusions. While some Protestant sects espoused millenarian beliefs that exhibited similarities with later revolutionary movements, any attempts to act on these beliefs were short-lived and soon forgotten. Most Europeans continued to view revolutions as dangerous gambles that, if truly unavoidable, should be curtailed as quickly as possible. Defenders of republican government typically argued that the only good that could come from a revolution was the establishment of a well-balanced constitution, as the Romans had done after overthrowing their last king.

How did it become possible to think about revolutions differently? Some historians have pointed the finger at Christian apocalypticism, but it is hard to see how it could have played much of a role. The overwhelming majority of modern writers and politicians who pushed for revolutionary change showed little interest in, or even knowledge of, millenarian currents. Just because there are resemblances between historical phenomena, or because one came before the other, does not mean they are connected.[9]

What's more, these fringe millenarian beliefs were not the only historical visions that challenged the monochromatic view of history favored by the ancients. As the recovery of classical knowledge peaked in the seventeenth century, some observers began to wonder whether modern accomplishments in the arts and sciences did not rival, or even surpass, those of their ancient forerunners. A quarrel broke out between defenders of the two camps, the Ancients and the Moderns. The stakes of this quarrel can seem petty. Was Racine a greater playwright than Sophocles? Did Homer ever nod off? But other questions led to a heightened awareness of the gradual changes that occurred over millennia. Time itself became a variable in these debates. Many discoveries—the compass, for example—happened fortuitously, almost as a simple matter of time. Modern societies had a built-in advantage over ancient ones. Time was an agent of cultural change.

It was in the context of such arguments that the modern theory of progress emerged. This theory would be put to many uses, including Western imperialism, though at first modern Europeans mostly measured themselves against their ancient counterparts. The theory of progress also rested on a very different logic than Christian apocalypticism. Its proponents did not posit a moment of rupture (*kairos*) before which all would be the same, and after which all would be transfigured. Instead, they argued that progress was a gradual process that took place over long stretches of time (*kronos*). What drove progress was reason, not revelation. Over time, human knowledge became perfected through trial and error, and the accumulation of discoveries.[10]

As the modern theory of progress grew in popularity over the eighteenth century, a new concept of revolution emerged alongside it. In this progressive account, revolutions were the escalators of history, leading human societies to higher levels of development. Enlightenment *philosophes*, Voltaire in chief, were soon describing moments of cultural upheaval as "revolutions:" the Renaissance, the Reformation, and the Enlightenment itself. These "cultural revolutions" were mostly wondrous affairs, when the human spirit revealed its potential. The successes of the philosophes' powerful allies—Frederick II in Prussia, Catherine II in Russia, Gustav III in Sweden, Joseph II in Austria, and Turgot in France—subsequently led them to dream of enlightened rulers launching political revolutions under the banner of reason.

It is here, even before the French Revolution, that we find a radically novel and positive understanding of revolution, one that inverted the negative and destructive model of the Ancients. At the heart of this concept lay a new attitude toward the future. For the Moderns, the future was a terra incognita that could not be charted by means of the experience and knowledge of the past. When a Frenchman awoke after a seven-hundred-year slumber, in Louis-Sébastien Mercier's best-selling novel *The Year 2440* (published in 1771), the world around him was unrecognizable. A political revolution, inspired by Catherine and led by an enlightened French king, had wholly rationalized Church and state. All the social and political problems of eighteenth-century France had been resolved, to everyone's satisfaction. Presumably, everyone now liked strawberries and cream.[11]

The modern idea of revolution rested on the belief that all humans would eventually recognize the rightfulness of rational progress. This view was best summarized by Condorcet, ironically, in a text he wrote while on the run from the revolutionary government in 1793. Since Bacon and Descartes, he observed, scholars had made tremendous progress in almost every field, from physics and politics to epistemology and economics. In the eighteenth century, a new generation of philosophes "propagated" this new knowledge, which in turn began to shape public opinion and influence statecraft. Superstition, prejudice, and error were slowly swept away by this tide of reason, or rather, Condorcet clarified, by this "revolution." Eventually all people—and in a near future, all peoples—would be freed from their traditional shackles, and could bask in the light of truth, as discovered by the great minds of science or philosophy, and reflected by their propagators.[12] This Enlightenment narrative was not original to Condorcet, but had been expressed in various places throughout the eighteenth century, most notoriously in the *Encyclopédie*. A graphic illustration of its structure even featured on the frontispiece of Voltaire's 1738 presentation of Newton's philosophy (see figure 0.1). The divine light of truth passes through Newton's mind and is reflected in Emilie du Châtelet's translation of the *Principia*, before illuminating Voltaire's text.

Along with the other philosophes, Condorcet insisted that the freedom individuals gained from the Enlightenment was the freedom to think for themselves. *Aude sapere*, or "dare to know," is how Immanuel Kant defined the Enlightenment for his German readers, borrowing a tag from the Latin poet Horace. Don't believe what a theologian or a book tells you to think, Kant admonished his readers: "Use your own understanding."[13] But the philosophes assumed that by thinking on their own, people would end up thinking like the philosophes. Just as Newton had discovered the invariable laws of gravity, reason should similarly lead us to discover the invariable laws of economics, politics, morality, and legislation. There were not two sets of laws of gravity; why should social and political issues have more than one correct solution? The Physiocrats, a group of economists and philosophers with whom Condorcet was associated, took this theory to its logical conclusion, arguing that there was a "natural and essential order of political societies," applicable to all places, at all times.[14]

The enlightened faith in progress thus left little room for dissenting views. On some topics, such as religion and law, the philosophes retained a more modest epistemology.[15] But there was a heady thrill to the thought that Europeans were making strides toward the rational restructuring of

FIGURE 0.1 Voltaire, frontispiece to *Elémens de la philosophie de Newton* (1738). Wikimedia Commons, public domain.

the world. Those who disagreed with the advocates of progress were likely still under the influence of superstition, prejudice, and error.

In this way, the modern theory of progress encouraged, if it did not necessarily impose, an anti-pluralist outlook. Its technocratic undercurrent was already visible during the Enlightenment. "The philosopher is a gentleman (*honnête homme*) who always acts in accordance with reason," reads a famous definition of the philosophe; "Graft a ruler onto such a philosopher, and you will have the perfect ruler."[16] Enlightened progressives could be surprisingly intolerant of contradictory views, since they presumed that all right-minded people must eventually come to the same conclusion. When that failed to happen, it was easy to surmise that the dissenters were not right-minded and possibly deranged. "Whoever fails to seek truth ceases to be human, and should be treated by fellow humans like a savage beast; and once truth has been discovered, whoever refuses to follow it is insane or morally evil." This was the conclusion reached by Denis Diderot, the affable and worldly editor of the *Encyclopédie*.[17]

To be fair, Diderot himself later recognized the limitations of this view. In a wickedly self-critical dialogue, his interlocutor asks him, "Are virtue and philosophy for everyone?" before answering his own question: "Imagine a wise and philosophical universe; you must admit that it would be miserable as hell."[18] To the ancients, this modern outlook would have seemed more mad than sad. The very reason why Greek philosophers had recommended mixing constitutional forms was because they recognized that wealthy and poor rarely agreed on fundamental "questions of equality and justice."[19] This assumption was shared by later republican thinkers, including the framers of the US Constitution. James Madison defended the bicameral structure of Congress as the best way to manage the inevitable diversity of interests and opinions in the young republic. "As long as the reason of man continues fallible, and he is at liberty to exercise it, different opinions will be formed," he insisted. It was ludicrous to attempt to give "every citizen the same opinions, the same passions, and the same interests." The ultimate source of discord, for Madison, was the same as for Aristotle: "the various and unequal distribution of property."[20] Only the wealthy liked strawberries and cream.

Of course, the philosophes did not go around executing those who failed to seek the truth or to follow it. They assumed that such failures were fluke occurrences. Their veiled threats of legitimate violence against "enemies of the human race," as Diderot castigated his imaginary opponent, were generally little more than rhetorical flourishes, aimed at marginal groups—"savages," pirates, brigands, and tyrants. Most other humans, being rational, would eventually get with the Enlightenment program.[21]

But this trust that public opinion, when properly guided, would converge on the correct answer faced a serious test in 1789. The early events of May–June followed the Enlightenment script of revolution almost to a T. Unlike their American counterparts, the ringleaders of the newly proclaimed National Assembly eagerly identified their political struggle as a "revolution." They cast off the classical phobia of revolutionary anarchy. Their revolution was "pure," even "bloodless." It marked another step in the general progress of humanity toward a more just future.[22]

Not everyone saw the events of that summer in this way, as the early trickle of emigration demonstrated. And the storming of the Bastille sullied the deputies' self-image of a nonviolent struggle.[23] But the greater threat to the Enlightenment ideal of a progressive revolution came from its supporters. Soon it became clear that the revolutionaries held markedly divergent views about the kind of future the revolution was to deliver. Public opinion did not converge around a single "natural and essential" way forward. Instead, it splintered.

These divisions among revolutionaries were doubly problematic. From an Enlightenment perspective, they were unforeseen. Progress was supposed to bring consensus. The only logical explanation, for each group, was that the others were wrong. Error, superstition, and prejudice clearly had not vanished overnight.

But adding to this surprise and sense of superiority was the fact that these viewpoints found institutional support at different levels of government. In Paris, members of certain districts advanced openly democratic ideas about how the new government should be founded. Representatives at the municipal, departmental, and national levels rejected these views, believing that affairs of state should principally be left to those with greater experience and wealth. Because all these officials exercised different functions (e.g., local policing vs. national legislation), the splits in public opinion translated into fractures of political power. Officials engaged in a series of standoffs: districts against municipal government, municipal government against national representatives, national representatives against departments.[24]

Divisions among political players were of course nothing new. In eighteenth-century France, royal power was regularly challenged by the *parlements*, or high courts. A century earlier, the English Parliament had fought a war against the English king. In both cases, opposite sides invoked rival interpretations of sovereignty to justify their claims, and brandished competing accounts of constitutional history. In these cases, however, political arguments were largely about the *past*. What was the correct interpretation of constitutional traditions? After 1789, each side claimed a privileged knowledge of the *future*. Proponents of a mixed or democratic government argued that their side was clearly superior because humanity was progressing in that direction. Since history could not advance in multiple directions at once, anyone who disagreed with your views was not only wrong but (in the new language of 1789) a "counterrevolutionary."

Another major difference with earlier political conflicts is that, after 1789, opposite sides tended to view each other as illegitimate. The *parlementaires* may have clashed with the king, but they never questioned the legitimacy of royal power. It took the English members of Parliament two civil wars before even contemplating the removal of Charles I. By contrast, French revolutionary rivals routinely decried each other as usurpers. The radical districts questioned the legal standing of municipal and national representatives, who in turn rejected the districts' actions as groundless and despotic. When they were not ad hominem, these attacks typically stemmed from mutually exclusive understandings of how to exercise popular sovereignty. Who should have the vote? What should they vote on? What was the appropriate kind of government for popular sovereignty? Because the revolutionaries could not agree on these fundamental questions, they ended up challenging the legitimacy of their opponents.

At various points during the French Revolution, the political situation resembled that described by Lenin in his famous essay "The Dual Power." Just as the Paris Commune of 1871 drew on a different theory of government and sovereignty than the French National Government, Lenin argued, so too did the Petrograd Soviet and the Russian Provisional Government.[25] In fact, the Paris Commune of 1792 had stood in almost the exact same relation to the French National Assembly in August and September of that year. Each questioned the legitimacy of the other, and did not fully recognize its authority. In place of the happy consensus promised by the modern progressives, the modern revolution delivered discord, and pushed its supporters toward violence.

Some may wonder how modern the French revolutionaries really were. The liberal politician Benjamin Constant would blame the Terror on the

Jacobins' proclivity for ancient republics. If the French Revolution was conducted, as Marx memorably put it, "in Roman costumes and with Roman phrases," was it really modern at all?[26]

This question should not be dismissed lightly. In some respects, the French were even more obsessed with antiquity than their American counterparts. Not only was their own schooling equally grounded in the classics but they pushed the parallels with Greece and Rome further than the Americans. French revolutionaries bestowed on their children (or themselves) classical names: Anacharsis, Brutus, Gracchus, Minerva, or Mucius were not uncommon. They portrayed their politics with classical allegories: Hercules slaying the (aristocratic) hydra was a popular motif, divine allegories paraded through revolutionary images, and references to classical politicians peppered revolutionary speeches.[27] They even turned to antiquity for social and political models: Marat wished to bring back the office of dictator, others sought to model national education on the Spartan example, and Saint-Just looked to Rome for republican institutions.[28]

But the French brought something else to this store of classical learning. The republic that they dreamed of establishing was not simply an improved version of the Roman precedent, as the English and Americans had sought. They fused classical ideas with the naturalizing politics of the Enlightenment. Indeed, for every allusion to ancient history in a revolutionary speech, there was an appeal to nature and natural law, as well. This naturalizing trend was already visible in many of the political theories of the French Enlightenment, most notably Physiocracy (Greek for "the rule of nature"). It also aligned with the late-Enlightenment emphasis on historical progress, which was assumed to lead in the direction of reason and justice. For Condorcet, it was the discovery of "the true rights of man" that marked an important step on the road toward progress. Accordingly, the revolutionaries could be both classically minded and historically progressive at once. The "natural republic" that they envisaged had never yet materialized in human history. Robespierre, who modeled himself on Cato the Elder, could also gesture toward a remarkable future when the French will have "fulfilled nature's wishes."[29]

The promise of a natural republic to come led the French to make political decisions that would have been heterodox in America. Perhaps their most shocking one occurred in October 1793, when the Convention suspended the constitution that the French had just ratified and declared a "revolutionary government" instead. The stated reason for this suspension was the ongoing war against both civil and foreign enemies, though there is evidence that the Jacobins also feared losing their majority. Either way, they opted for dictatorship, at least "until peacetime."

This proclamation of a "revolutionary government" had lasting ramifications for the modern idea of revolution. For its opponents, it came to stand for the worst excesses of the Terror. When Napoleon Bonaparte seized power in 1799, he deftly and repeatedly used plebiscites to legitimize his rule. While he minimized popular participation in government, he promised to protect individual rights. These promises often fell flat in France, but Bonaparte articulated the basic liberal compromise: limit the exercise of popular sovereignty; prevent the electoral fighting that had plagued the Directory (the regime, based on the 1795 constitution, that Bonaparte had overthrown); and pose as a defender of individual liberty. Historians are right to highlight the authoritarianism of Bonaparte's regimes, but he also made important contributions to the establishment of liberalism, especially outside of France.[30]

Indeed, it was under this liberal guise that revolution caught on in other countries. In Haiti, revolution was liberal in a pointed sense, as it sought to prevent the re-enslavement of Black citizens. Unfortunately for them, this emphasis on civil freedom largely came at the expense of political rights. In Spanish America, revolutions doubled as wars of independence, bringing military leaders to political prominence. As Bonaparte before them, they usually promised a stable government with limited political participation in exchange for rights protections. Revolutions in southern Europe sought a greater role for representative government, but struggled to succeed in the era of Restoration politics.

In some respects, liberalism can seem like a return to classical politics. Liberals liked to speak about the separation of powers, and placed high hopes in constitutions. But this resemblance is limited. For many liberals, constitutions were a source of hope because they signaled admission into the modern world. After 1815, many Europeans found Restoration politics outdated, and a liberal constitution marked the way forward. Unlike their classical predecessors, liberals did not regard revolution as a last-ditch measure to be attempted only in the face of the most oppressive tyranny, but as a means of historical progress.

Even their conception of constitutionalism departed from classical ideas. Liberals no longer concentrated on the proper distribution of powers across political bodies. Their primary goal was to secure individual rights. Securing these rights was viewed as the proper objective of modern politics, and what distinguished "the liberty of the moderns" from that of the ancients (in Constant's famous distinction). This objective was not incompatible with the concentration of power in a single executive. Many liberals hailed from the military, and many generals rose to the top of republics, where they accumulated power. It was the Napoleonic formula.[31]

Elements of classical political theory certainly remained present among liberal thinkers. But after 1789 one finds few Polybians of Adams's strain. The French Revolution reconfigured the entire political spectrum, to the point that even conservatives acknowledged that no return to the status quo ante was possible. A writer and aristocrat who emigrated during the Revolution (and later served as minister of foreign affairs), François-René de Chateaubriand compared 1789 to the Rubicon: once crossed, there was no going back. The revolution transformed the very meaning of "conservative." As Prince Tancredi Falconeri famously remarked in *The Leopard*, Giuseppe Tomasi di Lampedusa's novel about the Risorgimento in Sicily, "If we want everything to stay the same, everything needs to change."[32]

Precisely because the liberals endorsed the modern doctrine of progress, they found more formidable challengers among more radical progressives. If the revolution really was a portal into a new and improved age, why should the liberals have the final say in human affairs? Surely there were more things in this heavenly future than were dreamt of in liberal philosophy. Progressive writers sketched out remarkably detailed blueprints of a better world to come. While they disagreed on the minutiae, their collective musings imparted to their readers a sense, bordering on certainty, that the perfection of politics and society was within reach. The theorists themselves quarreled incessantly, but consumers of their work, which often assumed literary form, came away with visions of communes dancing in their heads.[33]

This mobilization of the imagination had powerful political effects. First, it fueled a growing discontent with liberals. The French Revolution of 1830 led to the fall of the Bourbons, but how different was the reign of Louis-Philippe? The July Monarchy was hardly the glimmering future that progressives craved. Second, the distance between the present state and the desired future continued to expand, as industrialization worsened labor conditions and socialist projections grew more elaborate.[34]

This yawning gap posed a problem for progressives. All were committed democrats: it was the only form of government fit for a rational and just future. But could democratic governance really navigate the treacherous way between the messy now and the perfected future? Compounding this problem was the current state of the people. How could the poorly educated, economically beholden, and ideologically oppressed masses be trusted to govern their way to the promised land to come?

Faced with this dilemma, progressives looked more favorably on the solution improvised by the Jacobins in 1793. Perhaps some temporary measure like the revolutionary government could bridge the social and political gap between present and future? There was at first some queasiness about endorsing dictatorship. But by 1848, Marx was calling a spade a spade and calling for the "dictatorship of the proletariat."[35]

It was an ingenious phrase, combining the progressives' democratic commitment (were not the proletariat the majority?) with their need for a tactical solution. But what did it really mean? How could a broad swath of the population act as a dictator? The Paris Commune of 1871 offered a tantalizing glimpse of how to square this political circle. Democratically elected, autonomous councils could administer affairs locally, and elect delegates to coordinate with other communes at a federal level. Power would flow from the bottom up, with power mostly concentrated at the lower levels, in the working class. In this way, progressives could have their socialist cake and eat it, democratically, too.

It was this same theory, inspired by the short-lived Paris Commune, that underpinned the rallying cry of the Bolsheviks some forty-five years later: *All power to the soviets!* (*soviet* is the Russian word for "council"). The 1917 February Revolution had led to a tense standoff between the Petrograd Soviet of Workers' and Soldiers' Deputies, and a Provisional Government. When the Bolsheviks toppled the latter, political power was supposed to return to the soviets throughout Russia. As it turned out, however, the political solution that Marx and Lenin had discovered in the Paris Commune was reversible. Political power could be anchored in local councils, with minimal coordination and control from above, as intended. But it could also end up concentrated at the top, and distributed downward only in crumbs. Structurally, the political organization looked the same. The 1936 constitution of the Soviet Union could formally announce that "the Soviets of Working People's Deputies . . . constitute the political foundation of the U.S.S.R." (art. 2), and that "all power belongs to the working people of town and country as represented by the Soviets of Working People's Deputies" (art. 3), when in practice power was closely guarded at the top. The "dictatorship of the proletariat" turned out to be a dictatorship *tout court*.

Concentrating power among the upper echelons of the Party, however, did not resolve all political challenges. How was the Party, "the vanguard of the working people" (1936 constitution, art. 126), to determine policy? Again, it rested on a reversible organizational structure. In principle, policy votes were determined democratically, by party members. *Bolshevik* in Russian means "majoritarian," and originally identified the voting bloc that won an electoral majority at the 1903 Congress of the Russian Social Democratic Labor Party. But after the Bolsheviks seized power, most important decisions tended to be made by a small group of leaders. After 1928, many were made by a single one.

The rise of revolutionary authoritarianism is one of the most striking features of twentieth-century revolutions, many of which can be metonymically identified with a single name—Stalin, Mao, Castro, Ho Chi Minh, Pol Pot, or Khomeini. The ability of these individuals to wield so much power is often credited to personal qualities (e.g., charisma) or flaws (e.g., megalomania). But the fact that so many different revolutions arrived at the same outcome suggests that something beyond personality must be at play. Ideology is one suspect, but there is minimal ideological continuity between a Stalin, a Pol Pot (who knew little Marx), and a Khomeini (a Shia cleric).

What all these revolutions do have in common, by contrast, is a faith in the role of revolutions in history. All subscribed to the modern viewpoint that revolutions are the vehicles of historical progress. Most of these revolutionaries will have disagreed about what constituted "progress," but therein lies the key. Even within a single revolution, disagreements about its goals and methods abounded. The existential problem with modern revolutions, as the French discovered in 1789, is that no natural consensus emerges about (in Lenin's words) "what is to be done." The splintering of opinion produces factionalism, which in turn leads to power struggles. In the absence of a robust and trusted institutional structure for resolving these differences, revolutions can teeter back and forth, and ultimately collapse.

Entrusting extensive power to a single person, therefore, was a way to fix a structural problem with modern revolutions. In the end, someone has to decide what the revolution stands for and how to achieve it. Just as Hobbes had argued that a single ruler was needed to define laws and religious doctrines in a kingdom, modern revolutions crave a Red Leviathan to settle disagreements about what "revolution" actually means.

This fix, however, is not without costs. If modern revolutions do not deliver a consensus about the right way forward, this does not mean that modern revolutionaries have given up on the idea that a right way forward exists. "There can be no solution of the social problem but mine," asserted Shigalov, the ideologue of the secret revolutionary society in Dostoevsky's *The Possessed* (published in 1871–72).[36] The revolution cannot stand for one thing and its opposite. Trotsky and Bukharin could not both be right. There can be only one correct path forward.

The Red Leviathan thus serves a double purpose: to determine what is right, and to decide who is wrong. There is a causal relationship—again, structural rather than ideological—between modern revolutions and internecine violence. For classical revolutionaries, disagreement was a feature of society. The reason why they put so much care into balancing the constitution properly was to manage disagreements, not to eliminate them. For modern revolutionaries, by contrast, disagreement was a bug, a symptom of error, prejudice, superstition, or something more nefarious still—counterrevolution. Indeed, strong was the temptation to label one's political opponents not merely wrong or misguided but counterrevolutionaries. From the French Revolution onward, it was a temptation to which revolutionaries often succumbed.

Anti-pluralist, the modern doctrine of progress could also turn murderous. In modern revolutions, political differences were often settled in blood. What else could one do with counterrevolutionaries, real or imagined? The French called their opponents "enemies of the human race," so unnatural was it, in their minds, to go against the revolution's progress. "Enemies of the people," "saboteurs," and other slurs accompanied later counterrevolutionaries to their deaths.

Looking back on the revolutionary regimes of the past century, it is hard to imagine anything comparable recurring today, at least in the West. Our commitment to democratic governance is more established; the appeal of radical and violent ideologies has lessened; by many measures, there has been an overall improvement in living conditions; and our culture maintains a vivid memory of past revolutionary tragedies. At the same time, thirty years after the end of the Cold War, "revolution" is no longer a scare word. From socialists to nationalists, "revolution" once again conveys a certain excitement—no more politics as usual, enough with this corrupt system, and so on. At an ideological level, these "revolutionary" programs have little in common with past ideologies. But the structural challenges with modern revolutions remain. We are stuck in a vicious circle: democracy, as it is currently practiced, fails to deliver the social changes that many desire, both on the Left and on the Right. But a revolution that did away with our constitutional structures could produce an even worse outcome. Whether dissatisfaction with the present regime ultimately leads to revolution in the future is hard to predict. But we can be sure that, come the next revolution, not everyone will like strawberries and cream.

Revolutions are complex events that stretch out over years, if not decades. It is no wonder that historians tend to study them one at a time, often focusing on particular moments or issues in a single revolution. The comparative study of revolutions, by contrast, is a topic that has attracted the attention mostly of social scientists. Their primary concern has been to explain why revolutions occur in the first place, though they also propose various models for how revolutions unfold.[37]

As an intellectual history of revolution, this book might look like a strange hybrid of these two approaches. I compare many revolutions over a long stretch of time, but do not seek to propose an overarching account of what causes revolutions. I deal with the kind of corpus normally treated by social scientists, but as a historian. For these reasons, much of the social-scientific literature on the topic is not particularly relevant to this study, except perhaps in one important way. Some social scientists might call into question the very premise of this book—namely, that ideas about revolution play any role whatsoever in the outbreak or course of revolutions.

A fundamental premise of much social-scientific research on revolutions is that political thought is mostly irrelevant. As the sociologist Theda Skocpol observed,

> Most theorists of revolution tend to regard the political crises that launch revolutions as incidental triggers or as little more than epiphenomenal indicators of more fundamental contradictions or strains located in the social structure of the old regime. . . . An assumption that always lies, if only implicitly, behind such reasoning is that political structures and struggles can somehow be reduced (at least "in the last instance") to socioeconomic forces and conflicts.[38]

This materialist conception of society, where all that *really* matter are "socioeconomic conflicts," has a venerable genealogy. It was Marx himself who called for a "revolt against the rule of thoughts," and sought to "liberate [people] from the chimeras, the ideas, dogmas, imaginary beings under the yoke of which they are pining away." For Marx, the ideological clashes between political rivals were ultimately a red herring. The real reason why revolutions broke out was because tensions between social groups with opposed economic interests had reached a boiling point. These tensions were most likely to explode when there was a major historical shift underway in economic production. Hence, the rise of the bourgeoisie as an economic powerhouse set it on a collision course with the feudal aristocracy. As it rose to power, it also produced an ideology that justified its claims: "The class which has the means of material production at its disposal, has control at the same time over the means of mental production, so that thereby, generally speaking, the ideas of those who lack the means of mental production are subject to it." We should not let ourselves be fooled, Marx insisted, about the causal relationship at play here. Economic relations generate culture and political ideas, not the other way around.[39]

Marx's emphasis on historical materialism, which he opposed to philosophical idealism, has had a long legacy in social-scientific methodology. In a broad sense, his claim that changes in economic relations have major political effects is hardly controversial. Economic trends have a major impact on elections (recall James Carville's slogan for Bill Clinton's 1992 presidential campaign: "It's the economy, stupid"). But Marx's argument is much stronger: he insisted that *only* material considerations have an impact on political events, and that ideas and culture are merely smoke and mirrors deployed by the ruling class to stay in power.[40]

There are a number of reasons why we might call into question the complete dominance of economic conditions on political events. First, social scientists have yet to agree *which* socioeconomic conflicts are determining. After all, states can be unbalanced in many different ways. Is it the growing economic inequality between capitalists and wage laborers that inevitably produces revolutions, as Marx and others believed? Or is it interstate conflicts that lead to domestic unrest? Maybe demographic shifts are the source of rebellion? Or do ill-timed efforts to modernize the economy bring down the state? All of these accounts are plausible, but they cannot all be correct. And it is hard to argue that "only socioeconomic conflicts determine political outcomes" if the socioeconomic conflicts in question are unspecified, and possibly vary from case to case.[41]

Secondly, why is it that massive socioeconomic tensions very often do *not* result in revolutions? History offers many examples of states that survived terrible economic conditions without any major political upheaval: in modern times alone, consider Great Britain in the Victorian age, the United States during the Great Depression, or India since independence. Why do socioeconomic tensions sometimes produce revolutionary upheavals and sometimes not?

A third problem with the materialist approach is that it treats politics as a pale shadow of socioeconomic relations. Political thought, in this model, can never be autonomous: modifications of economic forces produce new political claims, not vice versa.[42] But is this empirically true? England, for instance, witnessed a massive economic expansion in the eighteenth century.[43] As I detail in chapter 6, however, English political and constitutional thought remained remarkably stable between 1689 and 1789. Whigs and Tories alike upheld the vaunted principles of the Glorious Revolution, principles that they proudly traced back to Polybius and Cicero. There is little in Sir William Blackstone's *Commentaries on the Laws of England* (1765–69) that reflects the new economy of the expanding British Empire. Montesquieu recognized that commercial activity distinguished modern republics from their ancient precedents, but his constitutional theory of the separation of powers barely takes this economic difference into account.

Conversely (and fourthly), there are clear cases where the line of causation runs from political ideas to economic practices. Consider the idea of a free market, one of the pillars of the capitalist economy. This idea first began to circulate in Jansenist circles as a response to a theological question: Can sinful practices still have a positive effect for humanity? These debates took place in the late seventeenth century, long before any government in Europe had actually attempted to liberalize its economy. The various laissez-faire efforts that followed were all driven by intellectual theories, not the other way around.[44]

Finally, there is a certain irony to Marx's insistence that economic conflicts will invariably unleash a political revolution. By the end of the nineteenth century, the promised revolution had failed to materialize. Had socioeconomic tensions diminished? Hardly: the Belle Epoque, or Gilded Age in the United States, was a time of growing social inequality. So why hadn't there been a revolution? Marx's greatest disciple offered a rather unorthodox answer: Lenin argued that party operatives needed to inculcate a "political consciousness" in the proletariat—that is, by spreading *ideas*. The first successful Marxist revolution was brought about by a political party that ignored Marx's relation between socioeconomic conditions and political thought.[45]

None of the above is meant to imply that economic tensions play no role in the outbreak or course of revolutions. It is highly unlikely that there will be a revolution in Switzerland, at least as things stand. Ideas of revolutionary change will have little purchase in the absence of major hardships. But hardship alone does not seem to be a sufficient condition for revolution. Sometimes it is the "epiphenomena" that push a society across the revolutionary threshold: it took a video of the Tunisian street vendor Mohamed Bouazizi setting himself on fire to spark a revolution in Tunis. Socioeconomic conditions in Tunisia were terrible, but they had been terrible for decades. The same holds true for Egypt, which experienced a revolution shortly thereafter.[46]

The goal of this book is not to resolve the mysteries of revolutionary causation, even if it seems obvious to me that, at least after 1789, the *idea* of revolution clearly played a part in triggering future revolutions. But my broader methodological claim is that political questions have a degree of autonomy from economic conditions. This autonomy is far from complete. As I explain in the following chapter, the very idea of a balanced constitution emerged as a political solution to the socioeconomic conflicts between wealthy and poor in Greek city-states. But as it was developed by later thinkers, notably Polybius, the theory of balanced government—alongside its loathsome opponent, revolution—acquired a logic of its own. Polybius's idea of checks and balances was not only intended to mitigate class conflict. It also served to prevent ambitious individuals *of any class* from gaining excessive power and subverting the constitution.

What's more, changing economic conditions had little impact on the success or failure of this political framework. In part, this is because it was so capacious: no matter the forms of economic production, the net result has been remarkably stable across history. There have always been a wealthy few and many poor. This is one reason why the American founders, as I detail in chapter 7, still found the Polybian framework so effective. The material conditions of the eighteenth-century American colonies differed greatly from those of republican Rome, but that did not upend how people thought about political structures. Because these ideas also had the imprimatur of antiquity and the hallowed British constitution, they were all the more difficult to displace.

And when this political model was ultimately displaced, it was not because of new economic conditions. It's true that Turgot, one of the most important theorists of modern progress, was also an economist who as minister championed the liberalization of the grain trade. But the doctrine of progress that he first articulated in 1750, while still a theology student at the Sorbonne, was not influenced by innovations in economic theory or practice. His political masterpiece, the *Memorandum on Municipalities*, is similarly driven by the progressive imperative to rationalize, not by his economic experience. If anything, the economic foundations of the *Memorandum* are backward facing: Turgot recommends that voting power be proportionally allocated based on the size of property holdings (see chapter 8).

This book ultimately makes a fairly moderate and commonsensical plea: We should take ideas seriously, perhaps not as seriously as the German idealists whom Marx pitilessly mocked, but more seriously than some social scientists. And we should recognize that changes in political thought are not only occasioned by external events (socioeconomic or other) but can come about through intellectual debates. The world of ideas is not impermeable to the world outside, but it is not just a play of shadows and light either.

PART I

Fortune's Revolutions

CHAPTER ONE

Revolution in Ancient Greek Thought

JUST AS THE rape of Helen split the Homeric world in half, a revolution tore apart the Hellenic world. Or so suggested Thucydides, who began his history of the Peloponnesian War in an unlikely place: the Greek city of Epidamnus, on the Illyrian coast (modern Albania). The conflict began, he tells us, when the Epidamnian commoners overthrew the aristocrats and banished them from the city. The exiles then partnered with local tribes to fight back. Both sides in this civil war subsequently appealed to other, greater Greek powers. The commoners allied with Corinth, and the aristocrats with Corcyra (modern Corfu). What started off as a minor affair on the distant margins of the Greek world quickly spiraled into a multistate conflict. But the cascading effect didn't stop there. Soon the Corinthians and the Corcyraeans were also at war, with each side appealing to the Athenians, one of the two Greek superpowers. The Athenians ultimately sided with Corcyra, but their limited engagement was seen as a violation of their treaty with Sparta, the other superpower. And so, like the butterfly flapping its wings in Brazil and causing a tornado in Texas, the revolution in Epidamnus brought about a thirty-year war between Athens and Sparta, engulfing the entire Greek world.[1]

As with the butterfly effect, the initial role of the Epidamnian revolution may well have been incidental, a happenstance trigger that did not determine its outsized results. Thucydides himself argued that the real cause of the Peloponnesian War lay elsewhere, in the existential threat that Athens, the rising power, posed to Sparta, the established hegemon. But it is significant that a minor revolution could even be imagined as leading to such a massive conflagration. This reasoning reflected the deep-seated fear among the Greeks of the destructive and destabilizing force of revolution.

It was not an idle fear. The bloody clashes between Athenian and Spartan confederacies paled in comparison with the civilian unrest the war unleashed. The war itself had a revolutionary quality, as proponents of popular government aligned themselves with Athens, the best known of Greek democracies, while wealthy citizens sought aid from the Spartans, who supported oligarchic regimes.[2] Popular and oligarchic leaders alike used the war to advance their domestic agendas, even betraying their cities to Athenian or Spartan forces (respectively). Revolution was the driving force of the war.

The Barbarity of Revolution

The terrifying results of this division soon became visible on the island of Corcyra. It was here that the political differences within the state produced the worst of all revolutions described by Thucydides, one whose ferocity would haunt later generations, all the way down to John Adams. The war between the two Greek superpowers severed the city-state in two. Some Corcyraean aristocrats, who had been captured by the Corinthians during an earlier naval battle, were freed so that they might flip the island's allegiance from Athens to Sparta (Corinth was one of Sparta's allies). The returning prisoners launched a revolution, massacring many of the pro-Athenian, popular leaders. But their success was short-lived, and the commons (*dēmos*) soon regained control of the island. Fearing a Spartan attack, their repression of this oligarchic revolution was unprecedented: "There was no length to which violence did not go." Revolution upended everything: laws and private honor, even the bonds of kinship, were overturned. Thomas Hobbes, who translated Thucydides into English, had the Corcyrean revolution in mind when he sketched his grim portrait of the state of nature. Revolution produced temporary insanity: words lost their meanings. A French critic would similarly comment that the "fanatical" revolutionaries of 1789 had produced a "reversed language" (*langue inverse*).[3] Social values were overturned: revolution turned Greeks into barbarians. Or rather, it revealed how their vaunted civilization was little more than a thin veneer over our common barbarity: "Human nature, always rebelling against the law and now its master, gladly showed itself ungoverned in passion," Thucydides glumly observed. Finally, and most dangerously, revolution was a contagious pathogen, spreading from state to state, with levels of violence and retaliation escalating as each city outdid the last in brutality.[4]

If the revolution at Corcyra elicited such a lengthy and grim analysis by Thucydides, it was because of this horrific revelation. The war itself had shown that great powers are more likely to follow self-interest rather than justice when dealing with their antagonists. All sides might appeal to fairness and formal treaties, but in the end the victors dealt with the vanquished in the way that suited them best. Internally, however, justice, fairness, and trust still prevailed. How could society subsist otherwise? There could be no trade, no alliances, no empire if different parties and individuals did not uphold their obligations. Maybe justice was impossible to achieve in war, where there were no impartial judges, but surely in a state that had its own laws, and recognized authorities, the situation was different?[5]

Corcyra proved the contrary. The real war was not between the Athenians and the Spartans, but raged within every single city, pitting the wealthy few (*hoi oligoi*) against the many (*to plēthos*). And these class struggles were more than battles for political dominance. They distorted and destroyed everything. Political leaders did not merely seek to advance their party's cause, but were driven by personal ambition (*philothymos*) and a will to rule (*archē*). A race to the extremes ensued: whoever proposed the most violent, the most uncompromising measures was sure to find favor. There was no room for moderation (*sophrosyne*). Oaths, contracts, and alliances lasted only so long as they were useful. Accordingly, no one trusted anyone else anymore. Hobbes transposed this nightmarish vision onto his state of nature, but in some respects it was worse than that. The state in revolution was a perversion of the state, a social hell in which the trappings of society remained in place only to mask the unbridled violence and greed (*pleonexíā*) that really governed human affairs.[6]

What made this dystopian vision all the more terrifying was its ever-present threat. Corcyra was not an aberration, it was the new norm.[7] No one could now ignore the depths to which humans can sink. Later generations would be foolish to assume that they were immune to such horrors. "The sufferings which revolution entailed upon the cities were many and terrible, such as have occurred *and always will occur*, as long as the nature of mankind remains the same," intoned Thucydides. In the darkness of revolution, there was a sobering lesson of history to be gleaned. We can always count on humans to act abysmally; revolutions give us leave to leave our senses. It was this regularity of human affairs that made history useful in the first place: "an exact knowledge of the past," Thucydides proposed, could offer "an aid to the interpretation of the future, which in the course of human things must resemble if it does not reflect it." If there was a point to the study of history, it must be to discover how to avoid the fate of Corcyra.[8]

East and West

Was Thucydides's phobia of revolution simply a predictable response to political change? Or was there something more specific about the Greek world that prompted this anxiety? From a comparative angle, the Greek experience was uncommon. Unlike most other peoples in the ancient world, the Greeks were accustomed to a variety of political regimes. Tyrannies, oligarchies, and democracies all rubbed shoulders, and could even follow each other in the same city. In Thucydides's Athens, the tyrant Peisistratos had followed Solon, a democratic reformer, in the sixth century BC. Revolution was frightening because the risk of regime change was so real.[9]

It is not that the Greeks alone could conceive of the rule of the one, the few, or the many. If Herodotus is to be trusted, the Persians had once considered the merits of different constitutions, and even considered "the rule of the multitude," or democracy.[10] But while they might contemplate other regimes, the Persians never actually experienced any form of government besides monarchy. Regime change, as opposed to a change of ruler, was a hypothetical question, not a present danger.

The particularity of the Greek anxieties around revolution come into clearer view when compared with a related Chinese concept. The modern Chinese word for "revolution," *geming*, derives from an ancient term that described dynastic shifts.[11] One of its earliest and influential uses was in a commentary on the *Yijing*, or "Book of Changes," written between the first century BC and first century AD by a Confucian scholar. In a famous passage on the hexagram 49, this scholar wrote:

> Heaven and earth undergo their changes, and the four seasons complete their functions. Tang and Wu made revolutions in accordance with the will of Heaven, and in response to the wishes of people. Great indeed is what takes place in the time of change.[12]

This was an extremely influential passage that would be quoted repeatedly in the centuries to come. It refers, first, to Tang, the founder of the Shang dynasty (*c.*1600–1046 BC), who overthrew the last Xia ruler. According to tradition, Tang had justified his seemingly rebellious actions by claiming that he had received the mandate of heaven, or *tianming*: "For the many crimes of the sovereign . . . Heaven has given the charge to destroy him." Tang had also invoked the people's suffering under an unjust ruler as an added reason for his actions.[13] But this appeal to popular consent did not mean that the authority for Tang's uprising came from the people. It was Heaven's mandate that the Xia dynasty should fall, which is why this "revolution"—literally, the change of that mandate—was deemed "great." A similar story was told about Wu, the founder of the Zhou dynasty, who claimed to be "executing respectfully the punishment appointed by Heaven" by deposing the last Shang ruler, around 1046 BC.[14]

Scholars associated with the School of Naturalists, which combined the theory of the five elements with that of yin and yang, interpreted these dynastic shifts as part of the natural passage of time. The shift from one dynasty to the next corresponded, in this view, to the alternation of the five phases: "The dynasty of the Shun ruled by the virtue of Earth, the Xia dynasty ruled by the virtue of Wood, the Shang dynasty ruled by the virtue of Metal, and the Zhou dynasty ruled by the virtue of Fire," declared the founder of this school, Zou Yan. The fall of one dynasty and the rise of another could be violent: both Tang and Wu had raised armies to overthrow the reigning kings. But where Fortune, or *Tyche*, in the Greek universe was a chaotic force, often acting without rhyme or reason, *geming* participated in the orderly system of changes that structured time for the ancient Chinese. It was a "half-scientific, half-political doctrine," the Sinologist Joseph Needham observed. The suffering of the people factored into this doctrine as an omen of pending change: "When some new dynasty is going to arise, Heaven exhibits auspicious signs to the people."[15] The philosopher Mencius would go so far as to assert that rulers who did not serve the people could be deposed:

> The people are of supreme importance; the altars of the gods of earth and grain come next; last comes the ruler. That is why he who gains the confidence of the multitudinous people will be Emperor. . . . When a feudal lord endangers the altars of the gods of earth and grain, he should be replaced.[16]

But none of these political changes affected the nature of the regime: monarchy succeeded monarchy. The incorporation of *geming* into a naturalistic theory made it a necessary, even positive, event. For many Greeks, by contrast, revolution was an abomination, an upending of the regular order, during which all values were turned upside down.

Philosophy against Revolution

Thucydides's historical lesson was also a political one. If revolutions reopened Pandora's box, the purpose of political philosophy must be to design a government that was as resistant to revolution as possible. The canonical example of such a government was Athens's rival, Sparta. As

Thucydides himself acknowledged, Sparta "at a very early period obtained good laws, and enjoyed a freedom from tyrants which was unbroken; it has possessed the same form of government for more than four hundred years."[17] The lasting power of the Spartan constitution made it an object of envy and admiration (even if Sparta, too, feared revolution at home).[18] For a government to remain the same for a long period of time was perhaps the greatest sign of its strength and prudent design. Novelty was frowned upon in the ancient world. The Athenians, in particular, were regarded as suspiciously innovative, and by extension, prone to revolution.[19]

The secret to the long-lasting Spartan constitution lay in its idiosyncratic design. Aristotle described it as a combination of different constitutional forms. Sparta had two kings (monarchy); a senate, or *gerousia* (aristocracy); and a small council of five magistrates known as the Ephors, who were elected by all citizens (democracy). The effect of this mixture was to ensure that everyone felt included in the political process: "If a constitution is to be preserved, all the sections of the state must wish it to exist and to continue on the same lines," Aristotle noted about the Spartan constitution.[20] The superior design of its constitution may have been Sparta's secret weapon. The war that was sparked by a revolution would be concluded by one, too, Thucydides observed, referring to the political turmoil in Athens.

For there was in Athens "a sort of seam hidden beneath the surface of affairs, as in a piece of iron," as Plutarch later phrased it.[21] This was the seam between rich and poor, and it was the Athenians' Achilles heel. The problem was not that democratic governments made poor decisions, but rather that "faction [was] dominant in the city," and the Athenians "fell the victims of their own internal disorders."[22] Just as in Corcyra, personal ambition and private interests came to dominate the general welfare of the state. Twice toward the end of the Peloponnesian War, following military disasters, elite Athenians conspired to overthrow their city's vaunted democratic constitution. The first of these revolutions occurred in the aftermath of the ill-fated Sicilian Expedition, when the Athenian fleet and army were devastated. In response, a small group of Athenians briefly rose up in 411 BC to install an oligarchic government.[23]

This new regime, called the Four Hundred, did not last long, but Athens's subsequent defeat at the hands of Sparta, a full seven years later, led to a much more noxious brush with oligarchy. The victorious Spartans encouraged wealthy Athenians to establish an oligarchic government, which became known as the Thirty Tyrants. The Thirty enacted a campaign of brutal repression, targeting democratic sympathizers, or even anyone whose property they coveted. If Corcyra highlighted the horrors of a revolution by the demos (or commons), the Thirty showed that oligarchic revolutionaries could be just as bloodthirsty. "If anyone thinks that more people than is fitting are being put to death, let him reflect that where governments are changed these things always take place," reasoned the Thirty's ringleader, Critias. The oligarchs simply had to kill more people because they had more enemies. One in twenty Athenians perished in the space of eight months. Eventually, the Thirty's rule was overturned by a group of exiles, and democracy was restored.[24]

These events shaped Greek political thought in profound ways, in large part because they had a direct impact on the foremost Athenian philosophers, Socrates and Plato. For both men, the revolution of the Thirty was personal. Critias was a first cousin of Plato's mother, Perictione. Her brother Charmides was also a close associate of the Thirty.[25] In addition to these family ties, there were intellectual ones: both Critias and Charmides were Socrates's students, and feature in Plato's dialogues. This meant that Socrates himself was implicated in the rule of the Thirty, even though he refused to collaborate with them.[26] All the same, his familiarity with the tyrants cost him dearly. The exiles who restored democracy passed an amnesty law, protecting all Athenians (except for the Thirty and their closest associates) from prosecution for actions undertaken during the oligarchy. While no known mention was made of his ties to Critias during Socrates's trial, it is likely for these connections that he was tried and executed, a mere four years later. The youth whom he had allegedly corrupted was responsible for horrific attacks on his fellow citizens. By lashing out against Critias's erstwhile teacher, the Athenians could find some measure of retribution. Socrates was an early victim of revolution.[27]

The central question of Greek political philosophy is typically understood as *What is the best constitution?* But this was another way of asking how to avoid the worst of all political fates—namely, revolution. Plato made this point explicitly in *The Republic*: "Is there any greater evil we can mention for a city than that which tears it apart and makes it many instead of one?"[28] In addition to witnessing revolutionary violence—both Critias and Charmides died fighting the pro-democratic exiles—Plato had also observed firsthand the fundamental instability of political regimes. The impermanence of all things was an axiom of his political thought: "Not even a constitution such as this will last forever," Plato has Socrates proclaim, apropos the ideal city dreamt up in *The Republic*. Other, less perfect regimes were even more likely to fall apart. Oligarchies invite revolutions by reducing the common people to poverty and leaving them with nothing to do. Democracies are just as unstable: Excessive freedom makes the people ungovernable. The wealthy class inevitably pushes back, leading the masses to elevate a ruthless leader as their defender. Plato's account of how democracies fall echoes the manner by which Peisistratos became tyrant of Athens in the sixth century BCE.[29] For the Greeks, every revolution was a social revolution.[30]

For Plato, like Thucydides, the political ground was always shifting under our feet. This was the stuff History was made on: the ebbs and flows, the rise and fall, the revolution and restoration of regimes. Uncertainty and surprise were the only constants in life. Such was the wisdom of Solon, which he shared with the vainglorious Croesus, king of Lydia: "Human life is ever subject to all sorts of vicissitudes. . . . [T]he future which is advancing upon every one is varied and uncertain."[31] In the political realm, such instability was reason enough to try and pause the dizzying dance from one constitution to the next. But lurking in the interstices between regimes was the even greater threat of violence. Plato did not need to spell out, as Thucydides had, what kind of death and destruction one could expect from revolution. His Athenian readers knew its effects all too well.

What was to be done, then, to prevent revolution and its attending evils? Plato developed Thucydides's political insights more methodically. Those states that had avoided regime change, like Sparta, had successfully combined elements of different constitutions into a single mixed government. With a direct nod to Sparta, Plato recommended this model in his late dialogue *The Laws*, arguing that all successful political systems must combine aspects of monarchy and democracy.[32] This defense of a mixed government, and the particular fascination with the Spartan constitution, would become central motifs in political thought for centuries to come.

The Fairness of Inequality

The most important theorist of mixed governments was Plato's student Aristotle, who came to a slightly different conclusion in his *Politics*. Barring uncommon cases, Aristotle recommended "a good blend of democracy and oligarchy." The best way to achieve this blend, he suggested, was to grant citizenship to all free inhabitants, thereby making participation in the deliberative and legislative assembly democratic. But there should also be restrictions, based on property qualifications, on eligibility to elected offices (or magistracies), making executive power oligarchic.[33] His justification for this "middle form of constitution" was that it stood the greatest chance of preventing future revolutions: "since where the middle class is numerous, factions and party divisions among the citizens are least likely to occur."[34]

The ancients' predilection for combining governmental forms rested on a principle that is deeply foreign, even abhorrent, to modern sensibilities. They considered social inequality to be not only inevitable but *fair*. It was inevitable because, as Aristotle noted, "We see that all the cities are composed of households, and then again that of this multitude some must *necessarily* be rich and some poor."[35] This observation concerned only the inequities among citizens, and did not take into account those who were truly at the bottom of the social order—the enslaved. The ancient acceptance of inequality was, by today's standards, shockingly broad.

But social inequality was more than just a stubborn fact. Reflecting a common view, Aristotle argued that the unequal distribution of wealth and honors was also equitable. This argument might seem puzzling, given he claimed that "justice is equality."[36] In fact, these two positions were not contradictory, as Aristotle identified two types of equality. On the one hand, there is the equality of numbers, or "arithmetic equality." If a landowner pays a worker one drachma per bushel of olives, then it is only fair that he pay his other workers the same amount. On the other hand, if the landowner wants a sculpture, and solicits two bids, one from the famous Praxiteles and the other from a young local artisan, it would be fair if Praxiteles charged more. The principle here is what Aristotle calls "equality of value," or proportional equality. Just as one statue is more valuable than one bushel of olives, so too some artists, teachers, athletes, soldiers, and goods have greater value than others. In this regard, justice is equality, but, Aristotle adds, "only for those who are equals."[37]

There were important political ramifications to these two concepts of equality. Obviously, democracies favored the former. In Athens, all male citizens of age were considered the same for the purposes of attending and speaking at the assembly, serving on juries, and standing for most elected offices. In the famous constitutional debate recounted by Herodotus, the proponent of democracy Otanes affirmed that "the rule of the multitude has in the first place the loveliest name of all, equality" (*isonomia*).[38] Oligarchies, by contrast, assumed that only those of equal status should be treated equally. It would not do, accordingly, for lesser citizens to rule over their betters. In a full-blown oligarchy, only the wealthy enjoyed the rights of citizenship.

Aristotle identified these rival conceptions of equality as the main source of political tension and revolution. "Party strife is everywhere due to inequality," he asserted, "where classes that are unequal do not receive a share of power in proportion . . . the motive for factious strife is the desire for equality."[39] This desire for equality went both ways. In a democracy, the wealthy resented being governed by men of lesser merit (in their esteem). In an oligarchy, it was the reverse, and the poor found it unfair that they were treated as unequals.

There was no rational solution to this conundrum. Everyone recognized that in some cases arithmetic equality should hold, whereas in others, such as military strategy, what mattered was equality of value. Even the Athenians elected their generals, rather than choosing them by lot. But there was no consensus about which type of equality should prevail in a state. The unfortunate result of this stalemate was often revolution. Unable to solve the problem by persuasion or logic, Greek citizens resorted to the force of arms.

Aristotle's proposal to mix constitutional forms was an attempt to strike a political compromise. "The proper course is to employ numerical equality in some things and equality according to worth in others," he concluded.[40] In this way, citizens might feel equal to one another in the assembly, while allowing the wealthy to occupy the elected magistracies. He chose, characteristically, a middle way, but his moderation was pragmatic.

The powerful attraction that mixed constitutions exerted over the following centuries derived in large part from this belief that they alone could defuse social tensions and prevent revolutionary outbreaks. But both this attraction and belief rested on a specific historical outlook, one in which social inequality was understood as an inevitable and constant factor of human life. The ancients would have concurred with Marx and Engels's pronouncement that "the history of all *hitherto* existing society is the history of class struggles."[41] But they would have added: "as will be the *future* of all societies." There was no escaping the iron law of social inequality or the painful toll that social strife took on lives and property. And the projection of this iron law into the future informed political thought. The skillful design of a constitution was an attempt to hold back the ruinous floods of history, and maintain the state and the status quo for as long as possible.

The immutability of human affairs inscribed in this view may seem rather alien and depressing to our modern eyes, but it also encouraged a proto-liberal mindset that is more familiar. Many accounts of liberalism trace its modern origins back to the sixteenth-century Wars of Religion, when it became brutally evident that confessional differences were here to stay.[42] The stubborn fact of religious disagreement led philosophers, rulers, and theologians to begrudgingly adopt a pluralistic outlook. Catholics and Protestants might view each other as heretics, but for the sake of political stability, they agreed to tolerate those who sought salvation through a different faith. This was still only a proto-liberal mindset, as it did not view religious diversity as a *positive* feature of life. In other words, this toleration was not a philosophy that "allow[ed] people to choose a conception of the good life, and then allow[ed] them to reconsider that decision, and adopt a new and hopefully better plan of life."[43] It was a truce among former foes. Still, acknowledging that there was and always would be a diversity of beliefs, and that none could ever eliminate the others, was an important precondition for the liberal embrace of pluralism.

It was this same proto-liberal, merely tolerant attitude that we can identify in classical political perspectives.[44] Oligarchs and democrats, so often at each other's throats, each compromised in the name of political stability and regarded the other as admissible members of the polity. It was a very limited form of pluralism, which could swiftly devolve back into violent confrontations. The lethal retributions of the Thirty Tyrants on democratic supporters is a case in point.

This early classical expression of pluralism bears only an indirect relation to the later development of liberalism. Indeed, it would be centuries before Europeans went from merely tolerating religious or social differences to fully embracing a pluralistic society. Classical ideas about social differences contributed only marginally to that process. But the pragmatic kind of toleration that they encouraged had an impact on political thought by its thwarting of *anti*-pluralistic tendencies. Already in antiquity, we find plenty of examples of such tendencies, from the monotheistic cult of the pharaoh Akhenaten, who imposed the cult of Aten over all other gods in Egypt, to the self-deification of Caligula, who replaced the faces on the statues of the Roman gods with his own. Many religious movements, especially at their inception, sought to command universal adoration, by force of arms, if necessary. Pluralism does not come naturally: we arrive at it only after exhausting other options. Greek experiences of civil strife offered an empirical antidote to any such fundamentalist fantasies in the political realm. Greek philosophers did not daydream about a time when rich and poor would see eye to eye, or when the rich and poor would be equal. Rather than pursue such outcomes, they focused on balancing the competing interests of rival social groups.

This ancient focus highlights a crucial contrast with modern thinkers. Where classical philosophers derived constitutional principles from the irreducible divergence of social views, their modern, Enlightenment counterparts would base theirs on the future convergence of public opinion. This projected resolution of differences was a property of the modern view of history in terms of gradual, rational progress. Because the ancients did not think consensus was possible, they aimed to prevent revolutions; for the moderns, revolution would bring consensus in its wake.

The Distribution of Powers

If class struggles are what tore states apart, the Greeks also recognized that some parts of the constitution were more vulnerable than others. Demagogues subverted the constitution by manipulating the citizens' assembly (the *ekklēsia*): "These men cause the resolutions of the assembly to be supreme and not the laws, by referring all things to the people," Aristotle warned. In this way, demagogues could stir up revolution, and turn a democracy into a "tyrannical form of monarchy, because their spirit is the same, and both exercise despotic control over the better classes."[45] The many poor could use their majority in the assembly to tyrannize the wealthy minority.

The deliberative assembly was the key to almost every constitution, Aristotle asserted, because it exercised "the sovereign power" (*to kúrion*). It could pass laws that changed the property qualifications for office, or even eligibility for citizenship. Other institutions had different functions. Justice was meted out by juries, typically chosen by lot from a pool of citizens (at least in democracies). Elected officials (including military generals) oversaw the administration of the state and the conduct of war. Noticing this same pattern across a wide variety of states, Aristotle concluded that these were the three main parts of every constitution: "the body that deliberates about the common interests," "the one connected with the magistracies," and "the judiciary." Essentially, he identified what would come to be known as the legislative, executive, and judicial aspects of state power.[46]

The tripartite division of governmental powers played an important role in the history of revolution, through its connection with the ideal of a mixed constitution. This connection was not always present: a "pure" democracy like Athens had a citizens' assembly, a pool of jurors, and magistrates. Even in Aristotle's preferred "middle constitution," the property qualifications for elected officials might be higher, but the basic political institutions remained the same.[47]

But states that mixed constitutional forms more elaborately, such as Sparta, could end up with a different set of institutions altogether.

Lycurgus had established a council of elders, or senate (*gerousia*, from *gerontes*, "elders"), which Plutarch claimed was his most important innovation: the Senate had "an equal vote with [the kings] in matters of the highest importance, brought safety and due moderation into counsels of state."[48] Here was a different model of constitutional design, one that did not simply rest on a compromise between social classes. The Spartan example pointed instead in a different direction, toward a dynamic structure that could respond to a variety of political threats. The Senate prevented Sparta from lapsing into either a democracy or a tyranny; it was an especially effective institution for preventing revolution.

By the time Plutarch was writing, there would be another, even more renowned exemplar of a mixed constitution, one in which legislative power was also divided between a senate and a popular assembly. As Lycurgus before him, Romulus, the legendary founder of Rome, had established a council of elders, or senate (from *senex*, "elderly"), which Plutarch regarded as one of his chief achievements as well. Its value similarly came from its role in stabilizing social relations. Thanks to the Senate, Plutarch wrote, Romulus "inspired both classes with an astonishing goodwill towards each other, and one which became the basis of important rights and privileges." It was on the basis of the Roman state that Polybius would soon articulate his foundational theory of constitutional design and compose a new chapter in the history of revolution.[49]

The First Languages of Revolution

It is easy to picture John Adams ensconced in his ambassador's residence in London reading Thucydides, Plato, Aristotle, and Polybius, and finding their lessons about revolution to be as relevant to the American states as they were to the Greek. The lasting familiarity of these ancient authors may be explained, in part, by the clarity of their thought and language. But what language, exactly, was Adams reading? We know that he owned editions of classical Greek texts in the original, often with Latin-facing translations.[50] He also had English and French translations of these same works. But when Adams encountered Greek historians or philosophers in any of these languages, he would have read something different than we do today. Indeed, none of these authors spoke of "revolution."

Adams himself, of course, was no stranger to the word "revolution." He had, after all, just participated in one. And like all British and former British subjects, he was familiar with what was simply called "the Revolution" in eighteenth-century England, or what we now know as the "Glorious

Revolution." Adams could also put two and two together. The horrific events at Corcyra clearly had something in common with the revolutionary threats that preoccupied him. When he read Thucydides's account of the atrocities committed in Corcyra, he had no difficulty relating them to the "butchery of thousands upon every revolution."[51]

But when and how were the massacres at Corcyra identified as a "revolution"? Today, the question might seem trivial, a mere matter of semantics. As he was writing in Greek, Thucydides himself obviously did not use the term "revolution," which comes from Latin. Modern translations almost invariably describe the incident at Corcyra in familiar language: "so bloody was the march of the revolution," reads the standard English version.[52] Like Adams, we also easily recognize the results of revolution in the terrors detailed by Thucydides.

SEDITIO

But this was not always the case. Earlier readers are likely to have pictured events differently. When Hobbes translated this same phrase, he opted for "sedition," rather than revolution. He was not alone, as this word choice was typical for all English, Latin, French, and Italian translations of Thucydides, at least before 1800. It is the translation that Adams would have read in his bilingual Greek-Latin edition of *The Peloponnesian War*, which referred to the *seditio* in Corcyra.[53]

A sedition is a different beast than a revolution. The term encodes both a value judgment (negative) and a specific point of view—that of the legitimate authorities looking down on those who unlawfully threaten their power.[54] Seditions had a popular dimension in an age when "popular" was rarely a positive attribute. Disgruntled veterans or hungry crowds who rose up in anger did not describe their actions as "seditions." To apply this label was to speak the language of the power in place.

Since seditions were by definition illegitimate, their ultimate goal was irrelevant to those who used the term. Whether the insurgents demanded a different ruler or government, or simply wanted to pillage and burn, it was all the same: sedition was the name assigned to the violent means, regardless of the ends. Samuel Johnson, in his *Dictionary of the English Language* (1755), gave "turbulent" as a synonym for "seditious," which makes etymological sense, as "turbulent" described the actions of the crowd (from the Latin *turba*, "crowd").[55] In this respect, a sedition was unlike a revolution: its primary focus was not regime change. Conversely, genuine attempts to topple the government were conveniently amalgamated with bread riots, tax rebellions, and other kinds of popular violence, all thanks to the language of "sedition."

The ideological baggage carried by "sedition" did not stem entirely from medieval and early-modern rulers and their proponents. The term's history can be traced back to Roman times, when authors similarly used *seditio* to describe the uprisings of the disaffected plebs. Just as internal strife, for Greek philosophers, was the ultimate threat to the state, so too for Livy *seditio* was "the one poison, the one bane in powerful states which made great empires mortal." Writing the early history of Rome with the civil wars of the late republic in mind, Livy repeatedly described sedition as the gravest danger for the state.[56]

As these examples suggest, the words we choose to describe events shape our understanding and judgment of them. Framing political troubles as "seditions" essentially ruled out any favorable understanding of regime change and promoted a conservative outlook that portrayed change in general as negative. This outlook was not only the result of translation but tracks the meaning of the terms originally employed by ancient Greek authors. If anything, the word that Thucydides had used to name the horrors of Corcyra, and that Plato gave to the worst evil that could befall a city-state, was even more terrifying. That word was *stasis.*

STASIS

Stasis was the specter haunting ancient Greek political thought. It bequeathed to *seditio* and its vernacular equivalents the primary meaning of social conflict and violence. Not every stasis led to regime change, nor did it aim to. But the actions designated by stasis were overwhelmingly bad: violence, pillage, death, and destruction were its four horsemen. Sometimes stasis exploded into full-blown civil war, and many authors associated the two. But it could take less all-consuming forms; one historian even described it as "an everyday phenomenon." When the Greek historian Appian wrote a history of the late Roman Republic, he saw stasis in the incessant fighting that consumed Rome onwards from the murder of Tiberius Gracchus.[57]

For Plato, stasis was the problem that political philosophy must try to solve. In *The Republic,* he described it as a kind of political malady that derived from internal division.[58] It was stasis that Plato witnessed when his relatives oppressed their fellow citizens who favored democracy. In the case of the Thirty Tyrants, however, they also ushered in a different constitution, replacing democracy with oligarchy. Was this, too, part of stasis? When Plato turned to the question of regime change, he adopted a different vocabulary. Again, modern translations typically gloss over this difference. In book 8 of *The Republic*, Socrates asks, "Is this the simple and unvarying rule, that in every form of government revolution takes its start from the ruling class itself?"—but the Greek term rendered here by "revolution" is actually the verb *metabállō*.[59] This was a more neutral term, composed of the verb "to throw" and the prefix for "beyond." Regime change, for the Greeks, occurred when a constitution "moved past" itself, into another form. Political revolution was a type of metamorphosis.

The conceptual distinction between revolution as violent uprising (*stasis*) and revolution as regime change (*metabolē*) would last for centuries. This lasting separation was largely due to Aristotle, whose *Politics* became the textbook of political philosophy in the West, after its incorporation into Christian thought.[60] As with Thucydides and Plato, modern translations make Aristotle sound much more familiar, rendering his arguments with contemporary language. Book V of the *Politics*, where Aristotle discusses regime change, is usually rendered as treating "the number and the nature of the causes that give rise to revolutions in constitutions." But Aristotle retained Plato's terminology. While recognizing that social turmoil (*stasis*) was often a prequel to regime change (*metabolē*), Aristotle also noted how these two phenomena could occur independently: "Revolutions in constitutions [can] take place even without factious strife [*stasis*]."[61] A democracy can slowly slide into an oligarchy or even tyranny without fighting in the streets.

How and when did these separate categories become fused into the single phenomenon of revolution? Evidently, they remained apart in Western political thought for a long time. Roman writers retained the idea of regime change without political violence. Livy described the rule of the Decemvirs who took over Roman government for two years to establish new laws as a "mutation" of the political regime (*mutatur forma ciuitatis*).[62] This term would become the preferred Latin translation for *metabolē*. When William of Moerbeke translated Aristotle's *Politics* in the thirteenth century, he rendered *metabolē* as "mutation" (*mutatio* or *transmutatio*), and *stasis* as "sedition" (*seditio*).[63] Later translators followed his lead, thus perpetuating these conceptual differences. In 1438, the Florentine chancellor and scholar Leonardo Bruni offered a humanist upgrade for Moerbeke's medieval Latin, but kept these key terms.[64] The Latin lexicon for revolution remained unchanged well into the seventeenth century.[65]

This same pattern held for translations of Aristotle into French, Italian, and English. In the oldest known French translation, from the fourteenth century, Nicole Oresme wrote of the "transmutations and corruptions of governments." He also rendered *stasis* as "sedition."[66] The Renaissance French translation by the scholar Louis Le Roy adopted the same terms, as did the earliest translations into Italian.[67] The first English translation evoked "the changes happening in publicke Estates," and warned of "seditions."[68] Only during the actual age of revolutions did translators start to identify Greek terms with their modern name.[69] John Adams in fact possessed the first translation of Aristotle into any language that described the rotation of regimes as "revolutions," though he himself would have first studied the Greek philosopher in an earlier edition.[70]

The heavy armature of Aristotelian terminology helped preserve the classical outlook on revolutionary change for nearly two millennia. "Mutation" retained the Greek notion of impermanence: no regime was impervious to change over time. Paired with "sedition," mutation was something to be avoided, to the extent possible. When Coluccio Salutati, Bruni's predecessor as chancellor of Florence, discussed in 1400 the "mutation" (*mutatio civitatis*) from the Roman Republic to the empire, he channeled the fundamental conservatism of ancient philosophers: "It is better to bear all ills rather than risk the dangers that come with change." His reasoning was that history is fundamentally unpredictable: "There never was anyone possessed of power so great or prescience so divine that a political revolution [*mutatio*] unfolded according to his intention."[71] Like the Greek philosophers before him, Salutati evaluated revolution from the viewpoint of historical change. Since change was mercurial and unreliable, it was dangerous to place any trust in the "mutations" of political regimes.

The key takeaway for the history of revolution is that the word "revolution" was nowhere to be found in this Aristotelian tradition. As this tradition overlapped to a considerable degree with the broader field of political science in the West, this absence is most glaring. The emergence of revolution as a term employed by political thinkers, and as a distinct concept, cannot be located within the primary channel of Western political philosophy. So where did it come from? Why could Adams describe the uprising in Corcyra as a revolution? As the following chapter shows, it took a different Greek thinker—and a different Greek word—to produce our concept of revolution.

CHAPTER TWO

Rome, Polybius, and the Revolution of Governments

come se il cielo, il sole, li elementi, l'uomini fussino variati di moti, d'ordine e di potenza da quelli che erono antiquamente.

—MACHIAVELLI, *DISCORSI*, BK. 1, "PREAMBLE"

REVOLUTIONS IN THE ancient world did not always turn out badly. The city-state that conquered the Mediterranean world owed its government to a revolution. The last king of Rome, Tarquinius Superbus, was insolent and violent, or so the story went. He shared these traits with his son, who raped the virtuous wife of a Roman officer. Lucretia, as she was named, informed her family of the deed before stabbing herself to death, a scene later immortalized by countless artists. Holding up the bloody dagger she had used, Brutus, a family friend and leading citizen, led an uprising that resulted in the expulsion of the Tarquins and the end of monarchy. In its place, the Romans established a republic that lasted nearly five hundred years.[1]

It fell to a Greek, Polybius, to first reveal the secrets of the Roman Republic's longevity. Writing during the republic's apogee, both in terms of its military supremacy and the strength of its institutions, Polybius analyzed the Roman state through the lens of Greek political philosophy. He concluded that Rome offered the best example of a well-balanced constitution, on par with (if not surpassing) Sparta. It was a momentous pronouncement, placing Polybius at the start of a long tradition of Roman enthusiasts, who looked to the state established by Brutus as the ideal republic.

But his importance does not end there. Through his analysis, Polybius merged the dominant Greek framework for thinking about politics with what would become the best known and studied example of an ancient republic—namely, Rome. This Polybian synthesis—revised and extended over the ages by Cicero, Plutarch, Machiavelli, Marchamont Nedham, Bolingbroke, Montesquieu, John Adams, and many others—influenced political thinkers down to the eighteenth century and beyond.

Polybius's place in the history of constitutionalism has long been acknowledged, but scholars have paid less attention to one of its most important features. It was a distinctly *anti*-revolutionary tradition.[2] The Roman Republic was admirable above all for the fact that it had avoided revolutions for nearly half a millennium. This anti-revolutionary bent was not lost on Polybius's early-modern admirers, who readily accepted the Greek phobia of revolutions and pessimistic vision of history. The eventual collapse of the Roman Republic only reinforced this basic point: revolutions were among the worst disasters to befall a state. Ironically, it was thanks to revolutionaries in England and the American colonies that the Polybian synthesis received its most fervent defense. And it was the *rejection* of this synthesis that shaped the modern sequence of revolutions. The intellectual history of revolution is thus doubly intertwined with the ideas and reception of the Greek historian of the Roman Republic.

The Fortune of Global History

Born around 208 BC, Polybius was the son of a military and political leader from Megalopolis, a city in the Peloponnese located halfway between Sparta and Olympia. The city was part of the Achaean League, a powerful federation of Greek city-states that Alexander Hamilton would later admire and hold up as a model for the United States.[3] At various points, the Achaeans had been allied with the Macedonians, the other major power in the Greek world. Though greatly diminished since the time of Alexander the Great, the Macedonians remained a military force to be reckoned with. They clashed repeatedly with Rome, fighting a third war in 172 BC. The outcome was determined by the Battle of Pydna (167 BC), where the consul Aemilius Paullus defeated Perseus of Macedon, paving the way for Roman rule over the Hellenic world. The conquest of Macedonia brought the Romans so much wealth that they did not need to pay taxes for over a century. For himself, Aemilius reserved only Perseus's private library. He gave it to his two older sons, who had distinguished themselves in the war. It was around this time that the Romans developed their infatuation with Hellenism, much to the displeasure of traditionalists such as Cato the Elder. Soon wealthy Roman families were sending their sons to schools in Athens and collecting Greek books and statues.[4]

They also collected Greeks, including a thousand Achaean hostages, to ensure the league's loyalty to Rome. Among these hostages was Polybius, who became tutor to the consul's son, Scipio Aemilianus. The Greek teacher and his young Roman friend may have pursued their studies by reading Greek books from Perseus's former library. Scipio was also the adoptive grandson of Scipio Africanus, who had triumphed over Hannibal at the Battle of Zama (202 BC), bringing the second war against Carthage to an end. Polybius later accompanied his friend and tutee during the third and final Punic War, personally witnessing the younger Scipio's capture and total destruction of Carthage (in 146 BC).[5]

Those familiar with the name Polybius today likely associate it with political ideas about a well-balanced constitution. But Polybius was first and foremost a historian, closer to Thucydides than to Aristotle. His *Histories* offer a riveting account of the Punic, Gallic, and Macedonian Wars, which he presented as a world war, the first of its kind. Never before, he argued, had events on both ends of the known world—essentially, the entire Mediterranean basin—formed "a connected whole." "The affairs of Italy and Libya," he explained, "are involved with those of Asia and Greece, and the tendency of all is to unity." The conclusion of this global history was no less interesting than its interconnected parts. Within a span of fifty-three years, Rome emerged as the unrivaled master of the Western world.[6]

Polybius also intended his history to serve for the instruction of future statesmen, such as his own student Scipio Aemilianus, who was the youngest consul ever elected. "The study of history is in the truest sense an education, and a training for political life," he proclaimed at the outset of his work. One of the lessons that history taught was how to ward off the "vicissitudes of fortune," or more precisely, "fortune's revolutions." Indeed, the term that Polybius employed here was *metabolē*, the same that Aristotle had used to describe regime change. Fortune's revolutions threatened military and political leaders alike.[7]

Thucydides offered an obvious model for Polybius's endeavor, as he had similarly written his history "for those inquirers who desire an exact knowledge of the past as an aid to the understanding of the future," which, he added, "in the course of human things must resemble if it does not reflect it."[8] Both historians also shared a particular concern for the destructive power of revolutions. Where Thucydides began his account with the revolution in the small city of Epidamnus, Polybius started his with the hostile takeover of Messina, a city on the eastern tip of Sicily, by mercenaries from neighboring Campania. Just as Athens and Sparta came to blows over a conflict on the margins of the Greek world, Polybius suggested that a minor skirmish on the edge of the Roman Empire drew the two western Mediterranean superpowers, Carthage and Rome, into a war that with interruptions lasted 120 years (264–146 BC).[9]

The Cycle of Governments

But Polybius also considered revolution from a more theoretical angle. He interrupted his historical narration to explain, in book 6, why the Roman Republic withstood so many internal and external threats to become the dominant Mediterranean power. To support his argument, he sketched out a general theory of regime change. It is this theory that, centuries later, redefined how modern observers wrote and thought about constitutions, as well as revolutions.[10]

Polybius readily acknowledged that most of his political ideas were inspired by earlier authors. Like Plato and Aristotle, he identified six types of government, or rather three pure forms and their corrupt counterparts.[11] The pure forms were kingship, aristocracy, and democracy, which degenerated into tyranny, oligarchy, and ochlocracy ("mob rule"), respectively. Like his predecessors, Polybius also argued that all six forms of government were unstable, and (following Plato) that their inevitable decline followed a predictable pattern.[12]

But he introduced a critical twist to the Platonic account of regime changes. In *The Republic*, Plato had described the descent from the best form of government to the worst as a gradual slide, with each stop along the way marking a downward step. Aristotle had criticized this analysis, faulting Plato for assuming that constitutions could deviate only from one form to another, say, from democracy to tyranny, when in fact "revolutions also occur the other way about, for example from democracy to oligarchy." What's more, Aristotle contended that Plato had not taken his own theory to its logical conclusion: "According to him tyranny ought to change into the first and best constitution, for so the process would be continuous and a circle [*kúklos*], but as a matter of fact tyranny also changes into tyranny," as one tyrant can succeed another.[13]

Polybius stuck with the Platonic idea that a given form of government (say, aristocracy) naturally devolves into only one other (for Plato, timocracy). But he also took Aristotle's criticism on board, and turned the overall pattern of regime changes into a cycle. In the Polybian version, then, each pure form still collapses into its evil twin: kings give way to tyrants, aristocracy descends into oligarchy, and democracy leads to

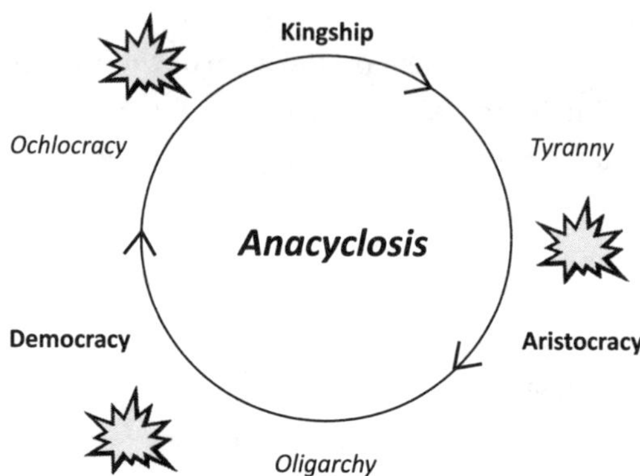

FIGURE 2.1 The Polybian cycle of governments and revolutions.

ochlocracy. But when we get to the bottom, we go back to the top: mob rule is replaced by a new king, and the cycle begins anew.

Polybius needed a word to describe his repetitive, circular pattern. He settled on an uncommon one: *anakuklōsis* (usually transcribed as *anacyclosis*).[14] Anacyclosis was a repeating circle, an endless cycle of change. As we will see, it was from this word that our modern term "revolution" derives. But the original meaning of *anacyclosis* was quite different. It did not refer to individual regime changes, but to the overall cycle through all six constitutions.

Not every regime change, moreover, was accompanied for Polybius by what we would today think of as a revolution. As Aristotle before him, Polybius maintained a distinction between regime change (*metabolē*) and political violence (*stasis*).[15] In his model, the degeneration of a pure form of government into its corrupt counterpart did not entail violence. Aristocracy simply slipped into oligarchy, for instance, once rulers were chosen for wealth or power rather than virtue. It was only the passage from one of the corrupt forms to a new pure form—e.g., from tyranny to aristocracy, or oligarchy to democracy—that involved a revolutionary uprising (see figure 2.1).

Polybius also shared his predecessors' views on the futility of revolutionary violence. Lives and property were destroyed, but for what? A corrupt government might be replaced with a better alternative, but it, too, would soon decay, and we would be no better off in the long run. The Polybian cycle was grim: we lurched from one false hope to the next, saving ourselves from bad regimes only through costly revolutions. The anacyclosis of governments captured a tragic vision of history.

There was, however, an exception to this dismal rule. The only way to get off the Sisyphean hill of human suffering was to establish a government unlike any of these six types. Again, Polybius took his cue from earlier authors who had extolled the mixed Spartan constitution as exemplary. But he now offered a more contemporary ideal: the Roman Republic. Polybius claimed that the Romans, like the Spartans, "combined all the excellencies and distinctive features of the best constitutions." Their two consuls, elected yearly, had inherited the role and functions of the Roman kings. The Senate was an aristocratic institution, since membership was reserved for the wealthiest and most honorable citizens. Finally, as the consuls and officeholders were elected by the Roman people, who also tried all capital crimes, Polybius recognized a democratic element in the Roman constitution.[16]

The Distribution of Powers: Checks and Balances

Polybius retained the traditional Greek assumption that tensions between social classes (in Rome, between patricians and plebeians) was the primary source of political strife and revolutions. He also accepted social inequality as fair, and projected it far into the future. But he partially reframed the balance between rival social groups as a balance between the different powers of government.[17]

This was Polybius's most innovative and far-reaching contribution to political thought. In fact, some of the specific powers that he attributed to different institutions live on today in the United States Constitution. The consuls enjoyed powers that are still vested in the US executive branch: they were commanders in chief of the military and the "supreme masters of the administration," who "see to the execution of its decrees." Polybius called attention to how the Roman Senate had the power of the purse ("control of the treasury"), as well as some legislative power. And in the people rested the highest judiciary power, as they constituted "the only court to decide matters of life and death," similar to our modern juries (see table 2.1).[18]

Some might object to this comparison on the grounds that Polybius ignored a key principle of modern constitutional thought: the separation of powers. This principle is often used to distinguish modern constitutions from their classical precursors. Allegedly elaborated in the seventeenth and eighteenth centuries, mostly in relation to the English constitution, it was widely embraced during the age of revolutions, and from there became a touchstone of modern constitutionalism.[19]

Table 2.1. The Distribution of Powers in the Roman Republic according to Polybius

	Powers		
Institution	Executive	Legislative	Judicial
Consuls	Commander-in-chief Responsible for administration Foreign affairs Law enforcement Public expenditure	Summon and preside over legislative assemblies	Military justice
Senate	Foreign affairs Appointment of generals	Power of the purse Appropriation Decrees	High crimes Arbitration
Plebeian Assembly	Declaring war	Lawmaking Veto power (tribunes) Approving treaties	Courts (popular juries)

On these grounds, Polybius and other classical theorists are often written off as irrelevant for modern debates. It is true that in Polybius's analysis, governmental powers were not so much separated as distributed (as evident in table 2.1). There was a kind of power sharing among institutions, each of which reflected a different constitutional form (monarchic, aristocratic, democratic). For some modern scholars, this model smacks of antiquated ideas about mixed government and unequal social orders. What relevance could it possibly have to the US Constitution, which clearly separates governmental powers and does not traffic in the mixing of forms?

But constitutional theory is not the same as constitutional practice. The American case, which I discuss more thoroughly in chapter 7, is illustrative. The Americans were fond of invoking the separation of powers doctrine, as formulated by Montesquieu. Following the French sage, the framers of the Constitution granted legislative power to Congress, they entrusted the executive power to the president, and they placed judicial power in the courts.

But was it really that simple? In the *Federalist*, James Madison acknowledged that no one actually believed that governmental powers should be "wholly distinct and separate." In his view, Montesquieu "did not mean that these departments ought to have no partial agency in, or no control over, the acts of each other." Rather, what Montesquieu really meant was that "where the whole power of one department is exercised by the same hands which possess the whole power of another department, the fundamental principles of a free constitution are subverted." It was fine, in other words, for the Constitution to grant the president veto power over legislation (art. 1, sec. 7), or to let the Senate serve as a court for impeachment cases (art. 1, sec. 3). After all, Madison pointed out, many state constitutions, such as New Hampshire's, "mix these departments in several respects."[20]

If this is the true meaning of "separation of powers," how different was the account offered by Polybius? By emphasizing the distribution of powers, Polybius too clearly meant for specific powers to remain separate. Only the Roman Senate could appropriate public funds; only a jury of the people could sentence Roman citizens to death (as Cicero found out the hard way). At the same time, different institutions had "partial control over" one another's acts. The Plebeian Assembly could overturn a senatorial decree, or refuse to ratify a peace treaty negotiated by a consul; the Senate could withhold funds for military operations, or replace a consul's generalship at the end of his term. To borrow Madison's expression, no department enjoyed the whole power of any other, but they all exercised partial control over one another. As the political scientist Isaac Kramnick concluded, "What the Constitution created was much more of a mixed government of shared powers, much more a government of checks and balances, than of a separation of powers."[21]

The doctrine of the separation of powers thus rests on an abstraction that has rarely, if ever, been enacted in practice. The main reason for its impracticality is that it fuses a plurality of discrete powers into a single bundle. Even the US Constitution refers to "*all* legislative Powers" in the plural (art. 1, sec. 1), acknowledging that there is more than one such power, before indeed granting a share of said power to the executive branch (in the form of presidential veto). But this is precisely the distributive model that Polybius had admired and described in the Roman Republic. He certainly knew, from Aristotle, that the functions of government could be grouped into three general categories. But the art of designing an effective constitution lay in determining how to distribute discrete powers across multiple institutions, not in allocating to a single institution the entirety of one category.

This difference between focusing on the distribution of powers and focusing on their separation brings us back to revolution. Montesquieu's main concern lay in preventing a government (specifically, the French monarchy) from becoming despotic. In this regard, he did not even mind if the legislative and executive powers of government were combined, so long as the judiciary remained independent.[22] But Polybius, like earlier Greek theorists, had a broader objective, which was to prevent *any* regime change or revolution. The slide into despotism (or tyranny, in his model) was certainly one danger, but not the only one.

For this reason, Polybius identified a mechanism that was more sophisticated than Montesquieu's simple prohibition of combining all three powers. Under ideal circumstances, the different institutions of the Roman Republic worked in concert: for instance, the people might declare war, permitting the consuls to lead the troops, so long as the Senate funded the effort. But it was in less than ideal situations that the true genius of the Roman constitution appeared. Here is how Polybius described the state's special design:

> When one part swells up, and belligerently seeks to overpower the others, the mutual interdependency of all the three, and the possibility of the pretensions of any one being checked and thwarted by the others, must plainly check this tendency: and so the proper equilibrium is maintained.[23]

The Roman constitution, in short, was self-correcting. It did not simply consist of static blocks but was dynamic, in perpetual motion, as its constituent parts acted and reacted on and against each other. Paradoxically, this motion created the greatest prize of constitutional design: stability. Where Plato and Aristotle had emphasized the blending or mixing of constitutional forms, Polybius drew on the lexical register of balance (*isorropía*).[24] The best constitution was "accurately adjusted and in exact equilibrium."[25]

While the classic image of balance is a scale with two equal weights, that is clearly not what Polybius had in mind.[26] For starters, there were *three* distinct powers in the Polybian "system" (*systema*). As he reminded his readers, the threats to a constitution were not regular, but could appear all of a sudden. It was *time* that constitutions had to guard against—fortune's revolutions. The brave men who overthrew a tyrant might be successful in governing the state aristocratically, but their offspring would exhibit vices that undermined their authority, causing their own downfall. Democracies might similarly function well at first, but gradually the people became licentious, and mob rule ensued.[27]

The creation of political stability in Rome was a balancing act: each order must be prepared to respond to the others if and when they "swell up" (*exoidéō*). At the end of book 6, Polybius sketched out a future scenario in which the constituent parts of the republic failed to block those who "expanded beyond their rightful place," and destroyed the balance.[28] This failure to keep the different parts in check would lead to a constitutional crisis and a revolution into some other political form.

To achieve the desired equilibrium between parts, then, any excessive movements had to be actively countered. Each power must "hinder" (*kōluō*) the others, Polybius wrote. The only way to avoid revolutionary violence was to put a "halt" (*epistasis*) to the ambitions of factions. The counterrevolutionary purpose of Polybius's theory was embedded in the very terms that he used: *epistasis* was the cure for *stasis*.[29]

It is in our own terms, however, that Polybius's insight becomes more familiar: here were the "checks and balances" that led to a stable constitution. The historian David Wootton has even pointed out how this specific phrase may have originated in readings of Polybius.[30] Already in 1654, Marchamont Nedham, who applied Polybius's theory to the constitution of the short-lived English commonwealth, argued against granting both legislative and executive powers to Parliament, as there would then be "no manner of balance or Check . . . reserved upon them."[31] In a 1701 treatise, John Toland admired how the constituent parts of a balanced government "are a mutual check and balance on one another's oversights or encroachments"—practically a direct translation of the above quoted passage.[32] Toland clearly had Polybius on his mind, as two pages later he noted how mixed government "is by Polybius and many Judicious Politicians among the Ancients esteem'd the most equal, lasting, and perfect of all others."[33] Polybius's eighteenth-century English translator, Edward Spelman, also paraphrased his constitutional theory in these same terms. Looking back from the fall of the Roman Empire, Spelman blamed Caesar for removing the "Check from the other two Orders"—namely, the Senate and the people—and thus leaving Rome vulnerable to attackers whom it had "often vanquished, and always despised, while the Ballance of all Three was preserved."[34] Finally, it was John Adams who popularized our current expression of "checks and balances" (in the plural), in a text brimming with plaudits for Polybius, the *Defense of the Constitutions of the United States*.[35]

And it was this theory to which Madison appealed in his own *Federalist* essay on "checks and balances."[36] "Ambition must be made to counteract ambition," he concluded, again paraphrasing Polybius book 6. His concept of "partial control" was possible only when powers acted upon and against one another, rather than lying separate. The American solution for preserving the Constitution over time, and staving off revolution, came not from Montesquieu's reflections on the English constitution, but had its origins in Polybius's study of the Roman Republic.

Divided Sovereignty

There was, however, a distinctly classical twist to Polybius's theory. If the different institutions of the Roman Republic could withstand one another's incursions, it was because none of them ruled supreme. In most constitutions, Aristotle had remarked, sovereignty (*to kúrion*) was vested in a single institution, typically the legislative assembly.[37] But in Rome, each of the constituent parts could be seen as supreme. Viewed from one angle, Rome was a monarchy; from another, an aristocracy; from yet another, a democracy.[38] The Roman Republic was not a hybrid state, composed of the scattered pieces of the pure forms of government. It was all three of them at once. Following Polybius, Cicero would call Rome a "triple state" (*triplex rerum publicarum*).[39] Sovereignty did not reside in one social group and one political body, as Aristotle had taught. Each facet of the Roman Republic was sovereign (*kúrios*) over certain aspects of government.[40]

By dividing sovereignty in this way, Polybius created a backstop for the checks and balances that kept the constitution in good working order. It was an original and unorthodox claim, which attracted great criticism. In the sixteenth century, Jean Bodin rejected the premise that sovereignty could be divided, insisting instead that "the type of state of the Romans in the age of Polybius . . . was entirely popular."[41] But precisely because Polybius retained the older Greek assumption that mixing constitutional forms was the only way to strike a balance between social classes, he could recognize different groups and different political bodies as sovereign at the same time. Hence, the Roman patricians enjoyed sovereignty over those affairs that the Senate oversaw, whereas the Roman plebs were sovereign on judicial and other matters.

Dividing sovereignty was thus a crucial factor in designing the state to withstand revolutionary changes. These overlapping but partial claims to sovereignty were the forces that maintained the balance of distributed powers. Each part might desire to overwhelm the claims of the other two: the people could rise up against the patricians; the patricians could repress the people; a mighty general might seize dictatorial power. But each part was also aware that it had a rightful claim only to a portion of sovereignty, and by extension, over a specific set of powers. None could legitimately claim power over the whole. More than just the distribution of powers, it was this division of sovereignty that allowed the Romans to escape the eternal return of anacyclosis.

Modern constitutional thinkers, from Bodin to Carl Schmitt, have habituated us to think of sovereignty as indivisible. But as late as the eighteenth century, this idea of divided sovereignty remained vital for definitions of a balanced constitution. Even in the American Revolution, its lingering presence is still evident in the Constitution of 1787.[42] The persistence of this idea also highlights how the French Revolution ushered in a dramatically different situation. While the French revolutionaries advanced rival definitions of sovereignty, theirs were all-encompassing and mutually exclusive. Classical revolutionaries sought to divide sovereignty in order to establish a government that withstood the tests of time. Modern revolutionaries would fight one another for the full exercise of sovereignty to bring about historical transformations.

Toward Republican Virtue

There was a third, less noticed dimension to Polybius's account of the Roman constitution, which proved equally influential. In addition to constitutional structure, he also emphasized the staying power of Roman "customs and laws" (*éthi* and *nómoi*) to maintain the probity of private lives and to keep "the public character of the state civilized and just." He praised Roman funeral rites for their salutary effect on attendees. He recommended their draconian laws against bribery in public elections (laws that would soon fall into disuse). And he underscored the effect of Roman religion in promoting "a scrupulous fear of the gods," thereby ensuring that the Romans honored contracts, kept their word, and behaved lawfully. Polybius did not believe that men were angels: "Every multitude is fickle, and full of lawless desires, unreasoning anger, and violent passion." But that is why, he continued, "the only resource is to keep them in check by mysterious terrors and scenic effects of this sort."[43]

The successful balancing act that the Romans had accomplished with their constitution was thus not the only secret to their political longevity. There was a hidden restraint that kept the play of constitutional forces within acceptable bounds. Historians of political thought tend to credit later republican writers, such as Machiavelli and Rousseau, with this cultural emphasis on customs and laws for maintaining virtue among citizens. But it is a theme that Polybius developed at length, in the same book (if in a later section) that would attract so much attention after it was rediscovered in the late fifteenth century. This theme, too, formed part of the Polybian synthesis.

Foreshadowing these later writers, Polybius already showed how the two main elements of the Roman political order—its constitution and its customs—served somewhat different purposes. He recognized that the Roman constitution was particularly well suited for conquest and growth, since unlike the similarly balanced Spartan constitution, Rome's could sustain a virtuous cycle of conquest and plunder. It was a distinction that Machiavelli repeated in his *Discourses*.[44]

But customs and morals helped Rome fend off revolutions on a different, longer time scale. Nothing could of course prevent the eventual degeneration of the republic. As Polybius noted, it must eventually succumb to some external misfortune or internal decay. The Romans came close to annihilation after their devastating defeat at Cannae (216 BC). Had Hannibal pressed on to Rome, the republic may have been done in by external aggression. There was only so much one could do to fend off fortune's deadly messengers.

But Hannibal represented a rare type of threat to Rome. More common was the sort of internal corruption that Polybius had identified as the hidden motor of anacyclosis. And virtuous customs and laws were what could postpone the inevitable revolution that would overthrow even the best of all political orders. Their importance is evident, albeit negatively, in Polybius's final prediction for how Rome would ultimately fall. The aristocrats would continue to grow exceedingly wealthy from the spoils of military victory, and compete ever more fiercely for the honors of public office. Aristocracy, in other words, would degenerate into oligarchy, and the traditional respect for customs would be lost. But competition for the favor of the people would make the latter arrogant, and they in turn would claim the power of kingmaker, before demanding "to have all or far the greatest [power] themselves." They would make a play, in other words, for total sovereignty, against the constitutional laws of the state. In the end, there would be another revolution (*metabolē*) and Rome would descend into mob rule.[45] Polybius did not describe what would happen next, but his own model of anacyclosis suggests a return to monarchy. All told, he was not far off.

Polybius's entire political philosophy, from constitutional design to political culture, thus had one overarching goal: avoiding revolution. But there was an exception to this general rule. The Romans, after all, had avoided the repeated horrors of revolution through a revolution of their own.[46] Some states, like Sparta, had found more peaceful means of achieving a similar end. But the revolutionary escape from anacyclosis was a likelier scenario for others. The Polybian model thus allowed for one, and only one, positive model of revolution. If a revolution led to the establishment of a well-balanced government, and put the cycle of political regimes on hold, it was a laudable achievement, to be praised and emulated by others.

Cicero: Liberalizing the Roman Constitution

Polybius's flattering vision of the Roman Republic was well received by his hosts. A century later, Cicero staged his own political discourse, *On the Republic*, at the home of Scipio Aemilianus, Polybius's friend, who also served as the author's mouthpiece. Cicero/Scipio openly acknowledged Polybius's influence on his political ideas. But he was writing under different circumstances. The Roman republican constitution no longer appeared as the best possible political achievement. The hostility between the popular and aristocratic parties (*populares* and *optimates*) was at an all-time high. As consul, Cicero had staved off a populist conspiracy by Catiline to overthrow the state. After his consulship, he was exiled by a resentful tribune of the plebs, Clodius. Ever since the destruction of Carthage, the last threat to Rome's Mediterranean hegemony, the corrupting power of money had known no limits. "At Rome anything could be bought," sighed Cicero's contemporary, Sallust.[47] The severe laws against election fraud that Polybius admired had fallen by the wayside, as ambitious politicians bought their way to power. The civil war between Marius and Sulla featured atrocities that rivaled those of Corcyra: "The war ruined everything," declared the Greek historian Appian, writing in the second century AD.[48] His gory account of the civil wars that racked the late Roman Republic helped shape the narrative that, far from constituting an ideal form of government, republics such as Rome's were prone to collapse and destruction.[49]

The specter of revolution was thus very real in Cicero's time. And the Romans continued to view revolution as a terrifying disaster, as had the Greeks. For Livy, internal dissension was the "ultimate evil to befall the state" (*ultima publicorum malorum*), worse than war, famine, plague, or anything else that angry gods might unleash.[50] The main Latin expression that Roman writers used to describe revolutionary endeavors was "novelty," or literally "new things" (*novae res*). Priding themselves on their respect of tradition (*mos maiorum*), Roman political writers found such talk of a "new" political order abhorrent. Catiline had sought to stir up the Roman people's desire for "something new" (*novis rebus*), by which he meant murdering the leaders of the Senate and burning down the city.[51] Livy identified Manlius Capitolinus, whose epithet reflected his brave action defending the Capitol from the Gauls in 390 BC, as the prototype for the "revolutionary" class traitor.[52] For the ancients, new things were a bad thing.

Cicero insisted even more than did Polybius on the necessity of virtuous morals for preserving the republic. Republican thinkers in the Renaissance and Enlightenment would likewise emphasize the centrality of virtue: it was the "spring" of republics, Montesquieu proclaimed.[53] But the well-balanced constitutional order continued to exert its appeal as well. Cicero celebrated the Roman Republic's mixture of governmental forms, as well as their equilibrium, in terms similar to Polybius.[54] Each pure form of government can easily slip into "a certain depraved form that is a close neighbor to it," he wrote. This instability might seem chaotic, but it followed a pattern: "Remarkable indeed are the periodical revolutions and circular courses followed by the constant changes and sequences in governmental forms," he remarked, echoing Polybius. (Cicero did not actually use the word "revolution," since *reuolutio* was not a classical Latin term, as the following chapter explores.) The only way to escape this cycle was to create "a well-regulated mixture" (*moderatum et permixtum*) of all three, as the Romans had done.[55] The effort to moderate and mix a state's government would remain a central political—and revolutionary—objective until the late eighteenth century.

Cicero's political masterpiece vanished soon after the fall of the Roman Empire, and was recovered only in 1819 in the Vatican Library. It was primarily known until then through extensive quotations by Augustine, in *On the City of God*. While Augustine did not quote the passage where Cicero renders Polybius's account of the cycle of governments, he did include a later quote where Scipio describes the ideal of a well-tempered government in musical terms: "So also is a State made harmonious by agreement among dissimilar elements, brought about by a fair and reasonable blending together of the upper, middle, and lower classes, just as if they were musical tones."[56] In such indirect ways the Polybian synthesis continued to resonate long after the Roman Republic had fallen.

Before leaving behind the Roman reception of Polybius, it is worth underscoring an important contribution that Cicero made to the theory of the well-balanced constitution. For Polybius, there was no evident connection between such a constitution and political freedom. The freedom (*eleutheria*) enjoyed by the Spartans, for instance, was only indirectly related to their own balanced constitution, in the sense that its robustness helped protect them from invasion.[57] This was a traditional Greek understanding of freedom: to live as an autonomous people, independent from foreign rule. To the extent that freedom was attached to a particular regime, it was not to the mixed, but to the pure, democratic constitution. The great Athenian leader Pericles, in the famous funeral oration reported or reimagined by Thucydides, referred to "the freedom which we enjoy in our government," which he explicitly identified as a democracy.[58] Cicero acknowledged this tradition, but argued that purely popular regimes were excessively prone to the "fury and license of the mob," and pursued equality to the point of inequity.[59] Only the tempered (*temperatus*) constitution, he insisted, which combined elements of all three pure types, "offers a high degree of equality, which is a thing free men can hardly do without for any considerable length of time." The long-term stability (*firmitudo*) that this constitution offered was ultimately of secondary importance.[60] This Roman identification of political freedom with a balanced constitutional order would become a defining feature of this theory in the centuries to come. In modern times, only the English constitution, Montesquieu would remark, had freedom as its primary goal.

CHAPTER THREE

How Translations of Polybius Transformed Political Thought

WESTERN POLITICAL THEORY was forged in the crucible of revolution. Fears of violent class conflict, anxieties about regime change, distrust of human nature, and the difficulty of establishing a balanced constitution—these were the problems that revolutions uncovered, and that philosophers struggled to fix. There was just one thing missing: the word "revolution" itself. From Thucydides and Plato to Cicero and Livy, no ancient writer used this term. So where does it come from? And how did its adoption affect the ideas that "revolution" came to designate?

If the word "revolution" was unknown in antiquity, its emergence is still tied to ancient texts. As the present chapter shows, "revolution" became a technical term of political thought only after the rediscovery and translation of Polybius in the fifteenth century. The word itself, of course, predates this moment, and its prior history helps explain why various translators across Europe independently settled on this term to render an unusual Greek term: *anacyclosis*.

Substituting "revolution" for *anacyclosis* had a major impact on how political theorists came to understand revolutions. From a complete cycle of regime changes, revolution became a singular event, combining social violence (*stasis*) with the transition from one regime to another (*metabolē*). While revolution remained the principal political problem to avoid, this new name was more neutral than the terms it replaced. This neutralization in turn paved the way for the next act in the history of revolution: its transformation during the Enlightenment into a positive goal.

The Wheel of Fortune

The earliest translation of Polybius's *politeiōn anacyclōsis*, as we saw in the previous chapter, was arguably Cicero's description of "the periodical revolutions and circular courses followed by the constant changes and sequences in governmental forms," in *On the Republic.*[1] Cicero employed two quasi transliterations of *anacyclosis*, referring both to the orbit (*orbes*) and the circuit (*circumitus*) of regime changes.

As it so happens, the text that preserved much of Cicero's work (though not this particular passage), Augustine's *On the City of God*, also contains the first extant use of the word "revolution." Following its etymology (from the verb *reuoluo*, "to roll back"), Augustine employed the word to describe a rotating motion.[2] He attached no political significance to the term, nor would anyone for centuries (*The City of God* was completed in 426 AD). But "revolution" was now available in Latin, and would soon enter vernacular languages.

It was in this physical sense of movement that "revolution" first appeared in French, English, and Italian. One of the word's earliest and most common usages was in astronomy. The medieval *Romance of the Rose*, composed in the thirteenth century, referred to the "revolutions . . . of celestial bodies."[3] Thanks to this association with the heavens, "revolution" could also be used to indicate a sudden change of circumstances. In the English translation of the *Romance* (possibly by Geoffrey Chaucer), the narrator writes, "It is of love, as of fortune, / that changes often . . . A fool is he that whole her [Fortune] trust, / for it is I that am come down / through change and revolution!"[4]

Many historians have pointed to this connection with astronomy as the origins of the political meaning of "revolution."[5] But in fact, the more important semantic association was with the goddess Fortuna. Underpinning this association between fortune and revolution was one of the most powerful symbols of the medieval period, Fortune's wheel. The popularity of this image can be traced back to a sixth-century text by Boethius, *The Consolation of Philosophy.*[6] Boethius was a Roman senator and consul, later accused of treason by the Ostrogothic king Theodoric. While in prison awaiting execution, he composed a dialogue between himself and Lady Philosophy, who criticizes him for "entrust[ing] yourself to Fortune's dominion . . . What, are you trying to halt the motion of her whirling wheel?" Fortune herself is then given a voice to celebrate her "sport": "I turn my wheel on its whirling course, and take delight in switching the base to the summit, and the summit to the base." The examples that she

FIGURE 3.1 The Wheel of Fortune, Carmina Burana manuscript. Bavarian State Library, Munich, *Codex Buranus*, Clm 4660; fol. 1r. Wikimedia Commons, public domain.

provides are all of "the overthrow of prosperous kingdoms by the random blows of Fortune."[7] A powerful politician who had himself fallen from power, Boethius infused the symbol of Fortune's wheel with a distinctly political meaning. Later representations of her wheel typically illustrated its movement with images of rulers past, present, and future, describing their circulation in terms of their ruling status (see figure 3.1).[8]

By the fourteenth century, authors were referring to these turns of Fortune as "revolutions." It was after a description of Fortune's wheel, which can "whirl down, and overturn / who sits highest," that the English *Romance of the Rose* spoke of "change and revolution." The Italian humanist and novelist Boccaccio also made "Fortune's revolutions" (*Fortuna revolutionibus*) a theme of his biographies of great men, many of whom were unfortunate kings.[9] The "revolutions" of Fortune's wheel were rarely revolutions in our current sense, but the predominance of this image and its association with this term may explain why later translators all reached for the same word to render *anacyclosis*. And the staying power of Fortune as the ruler of our fates perpetuated the classical conception of history as both providential and mercurial well into Christian times.[10]

But revolution was still not closely associated with the idea of regime change. Historians who have argued for the astronomical origins of "revolution" typically point to Copernicus's *On the Revolutions of the Heavenly Spheres* (*De revolutionibus orbium coelestium*, 1543) as the model for political usages of revolution. In fact, Italian chroniclers were already using *revoluzione* in the fourteenth century to describe political uprisings that resulted in regime change.[11] The historian Ilan Rachum has accordingly suggested that the word started off as "something of a . . . Florentine slang," and was for that reason shunned by political writers like Machiavelli, who would "consider it too coarse, lacking refinement, or below the standard of an acceptable literary vocabulary." Eventually, though, the term made the jump from local Florentine histories into philosophical studies of politics.[12]

How, when, and why did *revoluzione* graduate from local Florentine histories to philosophical studies of politics? Rachum suggested that it was the publication of the first Italian dictionary in 1612, the *Vocabolario degli Accademici della Crusca*. As we will see, however, "revolution" had already been adopted as a term of art in multiple languages by that time. What's more, there is little evidence that the Italian terms *rivoluzione* or *rivolgimento* were really "too coarse" for political writers to employ. If Machiavelli avoided the word in his *Discourses on Livy* (written *c*.1517), he used it in *The Prince* (written *c*.1513).[13]

The Early Reception of Polybius Book 6: Machiavelli

The reason why political writers (as opposed to, say, historians) tended not to use "revolution" is more likely because they had another, more established language for describing political change, which was Aristotelianism.[14] A century before Machiavelli, the chancellor of Florence, Coluccio Salutati, had described the transition from the Roman Republic to an empire as a kind of "mutation" (*mutatio*), precisely the term that translators of Aristotle had used for *metabolē*.[15] These writers needed a reason to replace this canonical vocabulary with different terms.

And they found such a reason in Polybius's sixth book on political thought. Thanks to translations of Polybius's *Histories*, political writers encountered an alternative to the Aristotelian account of political change.

Not only did Polybius's approach appeal to them conceptually, it also gave them a new term to work with.

From late antiquity until the fifteenth century, Polybius was known in western Europe only through secondary sources. The revival of Greek in fourteenth-century Italy, and increased contacts with Constantinople, led to the recovery of forgotten manuscripts. Polybius's *Histories* were rediscovered in stages. The first two books of the *Histories* were translated into Latin in 1418–19 by Salutati's successor as Florentine chancellor, the humanist Leonardo Bruni. A more thorough translation of the first five books was published in 1473, at the behest of Pope Nicholas V, renowned bibliophile and patron of the arts.[16]

How the sixth book became known is more mysterious. The earliest references to it appear at the start of the sixteenth century.[17] The Florentine patrician and humanist Bernardo Rucellai, in whose gardens Machiavelli and other scholars would gather, discussed book 6 in a work composed sometime before 1504.[18] In a 1506 commentary on Aristotle's *Politics*, the French humanist Jacques Lefèvre d'Etaples (who had traveled extensively in Italy and knew Greek), also mentions Polybius book 6, but addresses only the mixed nature of the Roman republican constitution, not the broader political theory.[19]

The first discussions of *anacyclosis* appeared around the same time in works by the French political writer Claude de Seyssel and Machiavelli. As we will see, there are good reasons to consider these authors together, despite their political and geographical differences. Seyssel, writing a defense of monarchy for the king of France, stuck closely to the Aristotelian language of political change.[20] Machiavelli provided a lengthy paraphrase and at times quasi translation of Polybius book 6 in the *Discourses on Livy*, but he, too, did not speak of revolution.[21] Instead, he offered a transliteration of *anacyclosis* as a circle: "This is the cycle through which all states that have governed themselves or that now govern themselves pass."[22]

What's mysterious about this early engagement with Polybius is that neither Seyssel nor Machiavelli could read Greek, and at the time no translations of book 6 were available in print. In the 1950s, the historian Jack Hexter advanced an ingenious theory to solve this riddle. Drawing on evidence that Seyssel employed a Byzantine scholar, Janus Lascaris, to translate other Greek texts into Latin for him, Hexter concluded that Seyssel must have asked the same for Polybius, and that a copy of this translation (which exists in the Vatican Library) must also have made its way into Machiavelli's hands. Lascaris was indeed well connected to the Rucellai circle, which is where Machiavelli most likely learned of Polybius

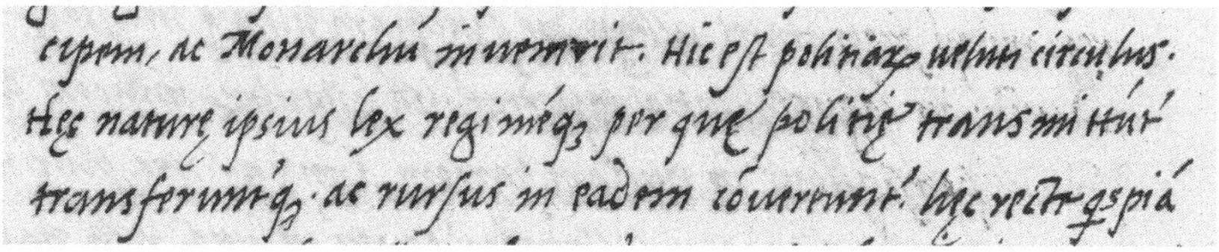

FIGURE 3.2 Lascaris's manuscript translation of Polyb. 6.9.9–10. MS Biblioteca Apostolica Vaticana 2968, 4v.

book 6.[23] This thesis initially attracted a great deal of skepticism, but new evidence in its favor has emerged.[24] Even further support can be found by comparing Machiavelli's own paraphrase of Polybius with the Lascaris translation. Indeed, unlike most subsequent translators, Lascaris had simply provided a literal transcription of *anacyclosis*: "This is the quasi circle [*circulus*] of governments," he wrote (see figure 3.2).[25] Machiavelli's *cerchio* (the Italian word for "circle") was the obvious choice for rendering Lascaris's *circulus* into Italian.

This first wave of Polybian reception did not greatly affect the terms of political thought. Like Seyssel, Machiavelli ended up adopting the traditional Aristotelian language of regime change, repeatedly invoking "the mutation of states" and "seditions." He likely picked up these terms from translations of Aristotle, or from Aristotelian writers.[26]

But there was more to Polybius than his constitutional ideas. Machiavelli may also have derived some of his ideas about republican morals and virtue from him. Here the line of intellectual transmission is murkier. As his title indicates, Machiavelli's *Discourses* were largely a commentary on Livy's *History of Rome*, which was the canonical source for the history of the early Roman Republic. Many of the stories about Roman virtuous actions recounted by Livy continued to fire the imagination of republican writers well into the eighteenth century. The famous account of Mucius Scaevola, who when taken prisoner by the Etruscan king Porsena placed his hand in a brazier to demonstrate the fierce determination of Roman soldiers, so inspired a young Jean-Jacques Rousseau that he nearly burned his hand on a plate warmer when reenacting Scaevola's gesture.[27] Republican thinkers discovered other key features of republican virtue in Livy as well. Machiavelli took to heart Livy's story of how Numa Pompilius pretended to receive counsel from a goddess in order to "to inculcate in [the Roman people's] minds the fear of the gods." He learned from this example that "the sacredness of promises and the sanctity of oaths were a controlling force for the community scarcely less effective than the fear inspired by laws and penalties."[28] Machiavelli's signature republican argument, on the advantages of citizen soldiers over foreign mercenaries, was also a topic that Livy touched upon, and that Machiavelli developed in the *Discourses* with examples from Roman history.[29]

That Polybius also addressed these topics may seem coincidental, or of indirect relevance. After all, Livy drew on Polybius in his own *History*, and may have been struck by how Rome's political culture had impressed a Greek observer. But could Machiavelli have rediscovered any of these ideas directly in Polybius? His strong views on mercenaries certainly mirror Polybius's equally negative opinions. Machiavelli first voiced these views in *The Prince*, in a chapter that mostly cited contemporary examples. Of the sole two ancient examples, one concerns Carthage, and most likely came from Polybius's detailed account of the mercenary war that Carthage fought at the close of the first Punic War. Machiavelli could have read this gory account in the published Latin translation of the first five books of Polybius's *Histories*.[30]

In *The Prince*, Machiavelli's focus was entirely on the unreliability of foreign mercenaries, a point that Polybius makes repeatedly in his first books.[31] When the same topic comes up in the *Discourses*, however, Machiavelli voices the complementary case—namely, that "Men fighting in their own Cause make good and resolute Soldiers." Only among "the natives of [his] country" can a political leader find the "attachment and devotion" necessary to "maintain [the] commonwealth."[32] This positive claim echoes another passage from Polybius book 6, where he contrasts the Carthaginian mercenaries with Roman citizen soldiers, underscoring the latter's superiority: "Even if the Romans have suffered a defeat at first, they renew the war with undiminished forces," he argues, "for, as the Romans are fighting for country and children, it is impossible for them to relax the fury of their struggle; but they persist with obstinate resolution until they have overcome their enemies."[33]

It is difficult to know whether Machiavelli was familiar with this particular passage in Polybius, as it does not feature in Lascaris's translation.[34] It would, however, feature in all the print translations that appeared from 1540 onward, and the text itself would have been in the Greek manuscript copies of the book 6 extracts circulating at the time.[35] Some of Machiavelli's friends could read Greek, and may have discussed these later passages with him. There are in fact other arguments from this section of book 6 that closely resemble Machiavelli's claims in the *Discourses*.[36] The tradition of political thought that emphasizes the need for a well-balanced constitution, the importance of virtuous customs and laws, and the danger of future revolutions may more accurately be described as Polybian rather than Machiavellian.[37]

The First Print Translations of Polybius Book 6

Polybius's influence expanded rapidly once translations of book 6 came out in print. The first published extracts concerned Polybius's discussion of the Roman military.[38] This middle section of book 6 attracted a great deal of interest in the sixteenth century. But the political sections were hardly ignored. A race ensued to translate the rest of book 6, as the rush of new translations in the 1540s suggests. Only now did "revolution" emerge as the term of choice for interpreting Polybius's political thought.

The very first print translation into any language of the passages detailing Polybius's political thought is one that has escaped the attention of previous scholars. It is tucked away in a curious book published in 1540 by the Venetian printer Francesco Marcolino.[39] This book presents itself as an Italian translation of the Venetian humanist Giovanni Battista Egnazio's *De Cæsaribus libri III*, a series of short historical vignettes about every Roman emperor from Julius Caesar all the way up to (the Habsburg) Maximilian I.[40] Buried at the end of this work, however, was another short text: "Two Fragments from the *History* of Polybius, on the Diversity of Republics, Translated from Greek into the Vulgar Language," as the full title indicates. Marcolino took credit for the idea of including these fragments, and promised to deliver a translation of the remainder of Polybius's *Histories*. (As far as I can tell, none was published.)

Whoever he was, Marcolino's anonymous translator inaugurated the tradition of rendering *anacyclosis* with a Latinate equivalent: "And this is the revolution of republics."[41] It is telling that the translator used the older form *rivolgimento*; this was the term typically employed by earlier Florentine historians.[42] Its repurposing here hints at an awareness of the preexisting vernacular term. Marcolino himself picked up on the originality and importance of this new expression. In his dedication to Piero Strozzi—who three years prior had led the "revolutionary" Florentine forces seeking to overthrow Cosimo I de' Medici at the Battle of Montemurlo—Marcolino wrote that "no-one better than you has understood and seen the causes of the revolutions of states."[43] This last phrase, *rivolgimenti delle republiche*, would prove extremely catchy, as we will see.

In short order, two additional translations of book 6 appeared in print, both in 1545. One was in French, by the renowned scholar Louis Maigret.[44] He had already published a French translation of books 1–5 three

ſeigneur ſeul cruel, & effrené. Voila doncq' la
reſolution des choſes publiques comme en fa-
çon de cercle: c'eſt auſsi le naturel departemẽt
par lequel elles ſont changées, conuerties, &
par le meſme ordre & certain de rechef remi-
ſes. Leſquelles choſes ſi quelqu'vn veult dili-

FIGURE 3.3 Louis Maigret's 1545 translation of Polyb. 6.9.9–10. Bibliothèque nationale de France.

years prior.[45] His subsequent work was dedicated entirely to the extracts from book 6. His rendition of *politeiōn anacyclosis* was somewhat odd (see figure 3.3): "Here is the resolution of the republics as if in a circle."[46] This translation is not completely absurd: *résolution*, in sixteenth-century French, had a meaning of "resolving" logical difficulties.[47] One can plausibly imagine an interpretation of Polybius that viewed the passage from one regime to the next as a kind of musical "resolution" of the conflicts within each. But it would be a remarkable coincidence if Maigret had chosen to translate *anacyclosis* with a word that was one letter removed from "revolution," the term employed by almost every other translator. Was "revolution" so novel, in this political sense, that a confused typesetter substituted a medial *s* (i.e., *ſ*) for a *v* (or *u*)?

Luckily, there is a way to test this hypothesis. Seven years later, in 1552, Maigret published a revised edition of his 1542 translation of books 1–5, adding to it a translation of book 6. And here we find a corrected version of this passage: "Here is the revolution of governments."[48] (see figure 3.4). This time, there is no doubt about the word chosen to translate *anacyclosis*: Maigret had clearly corrected a printing error.

The same year that Maigret published his translation, the humanist Lodovico Domenichi published the first complete Italian translation of Polybius in Venice.[49] Domenichi's translation would be reissued at least three times, and remained the standard Italian translation for nearly two centuries.[50] Domenichi offered a wholly different translation from the Marcolino, but followed the trend of rendering *anacyclosis* as "revolution:" "This is the revolution of republics in a quasi circle; this is the natural order in which they mutate and revolve, and return anew to the same order."[51] A notable feature of Domenichi's translation is that it activated

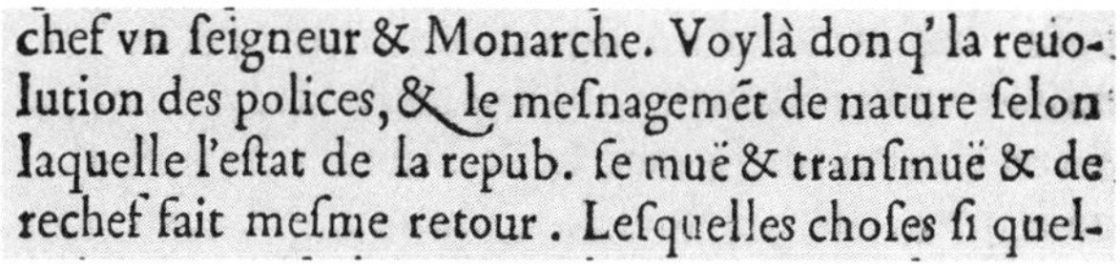

chef vn ſeigneur & Monarche. Voylà donq' la reuolution des polices, & le meſnagemēt de nature ſelon
laquelle l'eſtat de la repub. ſe muë & tranſmuë & de
rechef fait meſme retour. Leſquelles choſes ſi quel-

FIGURE 3.4 Louis Maigret's 1552 translation of Polyb. 6.9.9–10. Bibliothèque nationale de France.

"revolution," using it as both a noun and a verb ("si riuolgono"). "Revolution" also spread throughout the text: where Polybius had used the Aristotelian *metabolē* to describe changes of government, Domenichi referred instead to the "revolutions of republics."[52] Revolution was becoming a technical term in political thought.

Domenichi's translation had particular importance for the dissemination of Polybius and "revolution" in Italian. But scholars across Europe soon had access to a full Latin translation as well. In 1549, the Protestant theologian Wolfgang Musculus published a reedition of an older Latin translation of books 1–5, to which he added a new translation of book 6. This edition proved very popular: it was reprinted four times over the next sixty years.[53] Musculus, too, rendered *politeiōn anacyclosis* in "revolutionary" terms: "Here is the revolution of governments, here the natural order according to which governments mutate and are transformed, and revolve back to their origins."[54] Like Domenichi, Musculus mobilized "revolution" as a verb, though employed the classical Latin verb *reuoluo* (in the passive voice, *reuoluitur*). Musculus was not quite as eager as Domenichi to extend the semantic range of *revolutio*: when Polybius used *metabolē*, he fell back on "mutation."[55] But in his index, Musculus did refer more generically to the "revolutions and mutations" of constitutional forms.[56]

By the middle of the sixteenth century, then, Italian, French, and Latin translations of Polybius all expressed his political thought in terms of "revolution." For the time being, this translation was limited to Romance languages (Spanish had to wait until 1789). The German translation by the classicist Wilhelm Xylander, published in Basel in 1574, opted for the verb *verändern* (to change).[57] This was a missed opportunity, as "revolution" entered the German language only in the eighteenth century.[58] A Dutch translation (1640) by Johannes Vennekool similarly did not include the term.[59] Tellingly, neither participants nor contemporary observers appear to have used "revolution" (*revolutie*) in reference to the events of the Dutch Revolt (1566–1648). It was only in the late seventeenth century that historians began speaking of the "revolution" in the United Provinces.[60]

The Latin translation by the Huguenot philologist Isaac Casaubon (1609) overshadowed these earlier ones, and did the most for Polybius's reception throughout Europe. It featured the Latin side by side with the Greek original. Thanks to this soon-to-be standard edition, Polybius "was read and studied . . . as perhaps never before or after."[61] To some extent, Casaubon's translation confirmed Polybius as a "revolutionary" theorist: "This is the cycle in which governments revolve," he wrote.[62] Unlike Musculus, however, Casaubon did not use the neo-Latin term *reuolutio*, only the classical verb *reuoluo* (again in the passive voice). By this point, the newer political meaning of *reuolutio* as a political concept had arguably rubbed off on the older verb. Casaubon also framed Polybius's theory in more traditional Aristotelian language. His Polybius was significantly less revolutionary, but by that time it did not really matter: revolution was out of the bag.

Spreading "Revolution"

How can we tell whether these translations played a role in disseminating the new political understanding of "revolution"? There is, first, a good deal of chronological evidence to prove this point. Before Latin and vernacular translations of Polybius book 6 became available, even authors familiar with his text (either through direct access to the Greek original, or through secondhand knowledge) rarely used the term "revolution." To Machiavelli and Seyssel, one can add the example of the Florentine statesman Donato Giannotti. His 1531 *Della repubblica fiorentina* discusses the Polybian cycles of government, and even follows Polybius in singing the praises of mixed government in republican Rome. But he does not speak of revolution, sticking with "the mutation of the state."[63]

After the flourishing of translations in the 1540s, however, mentions of Polybius's political thought tended to be accompanied with "revolutionary" language. In some cases, the word simply appeared in citations (or paraphrases) of the famous passage on *politeiōn anacyclosis*. The Venetian humanist and senator Sebastiano Erizzo, in his *Discorso dei governi civili* (published 1571, written earlier), alludes to this passage in terms that combine Domenichi's translation and Machiavelli's paraphrase: "And this is the revolution of governments in a circle-like movement."[64] In France, Louis Le Roy, a professor of ancient Greek at the Collège de France, wrote a political treatise in 1575 that referred to Polybius repeatedly, and lifted the passage about the "revolution of governments" from Maigret's French translation.[65] "Revolution" even made its way deep into rival territory. An Italian priest, Antonio Scaino, published a popularization of Aristotle's

Politics in 1578, which to the usual discussion of seditions and mutations added mentions of "revolutions in cities."[66] Scaino referred to Polybius book 6 in his commentary, and discussed Polybius at length, along with "civil revolutions," in an essay on the Roman Republic appended to his discussion of Aristotle.[67]

It is often claimed that "revolution" first featured in a book's title in the seventeenth century.[68] In fact, it was already there in the sixteenth century. When Bernardino Corio's 1503 history of Milan, which initially did not include any mention of revolution, was reprinted in Venice in 1554—shortly after the two Italian translations of Polybius had appeared in that same city—the editor added a new title page that described the book as detailing "the revolutions of almost all of Italy."[69] In 1570, the Estense court historian Giovan Battista Pigna published the first volume of his *Historia de principi di Este*, whose title page announced that it covered the period between the "revolutions of the Roman empire" and 1476.[70] And a decade later, Valerio Sale, a jurist from Bassano, published a study of political government whose subtitle highlighted its focus on the "revolutions of states."[71]

But the clearest evidence that the Polybius translations were central to the diffusion and adoption of "revolution" as a political concept can be found in the success of a particular phrase: "la revolution des polices" (Maigret), "la rivolution delle Republiche" (Domenichi), "politiarum reuolutio" (Musculus). These different expressions, in multiple languages, all reflected the fundamental idea behind *politeiōn anacyclosis*. Like genetic markers, we can use them to analyze the dissemination of Polybian thought and of the political language of revolution.

We have already encountered examples of this phrase in texts by Marcolino, Domenichi, Scaino, and Sale. In the second half of the sixteenth century, it became a common Italian phrase. "So many revolutions of states in Italy," one reads in the continuation of a 1557 translation of Venetian history by none other than Ludovico Domenichi, Polybius's translator.[72] The "revolutions of states" was listed as the topic of an imagined speech by Cicero in a collection of orations.[73] Giovanni Botero, in his famous 1596 book on reason of state, also addressed the "revolutions of states."[74] Indeed, it was under this form that "revolutions" typically featured in works of political thought, including Ciro Spontone's *Dodici libri del governo di stato*.[75] When the *Vocabolario degli Accademici della Crusca* (1612) defined "revolution" as "a feature best attributed to governments," it did not "prepar[e] the term for its new role in political discourse," but rather enshrined a usage that had already imposed itself.[76]

Finally, the impact of these Polybian translations is evident in the emergence of a new historical genre: the "revolutions in *X*," where *X* was a place name. This genre first flourished in Italy with histories of revolutions in Bohemia, Capri, Catalonia, and Naples appearing between 1620 and 1647.[77] So common was this practice that when the Italian count Alessandro Senesi published a translation of the French historian Pierre Matthieu's *Histoire des derniers troubles de France* (1594), it seemed normal to change the title to *Historia delle rivolutioni di Francia* (1624).

Rewriting Polybius

Because Polybius wrote in Greek, the reception of his work differed from that of other forgotten classical works. When Poggio Bracciolini rediscovered Lucretius's *On the Nature of Things* (*De rerum natura*) in a German monastery in 1417, the shocking ideas that he and others read there did not require a new language to be expressed.[78] Bracciolini knew Latin, as did all scholars of his day, and as they would for centuries to follow. While Greek eventually became de rigueur for advanced studies, most readers still encountered Greek texts in translation. The words that translators chose were therefore of particular importance. Polybius's idealized description of the Roman constitution did not change too much when rendered in Italian, French, Latin, or English. By contrast, the decision to translate *anacyclosis* as "revolution" proved fateful. For the translators, it must have been an obvious choice, as they appear to have hit upon this term independently, likely owing to the familiar image of Fortune's revolutions. But this "natural" translation in fact transformed the original meaning. In Greek, *anacyclosis* referred to the overall cycle of regime changes. It did not describe the particular changes between regimes—for example, the passage from oligarchy to democracy, or tyranny to aristocracy. But as the above examples show, writers immediately began using "revolution" to refer to singular events as well. The "revolution of governments" (*politeiōn anacyclosis*) became the "revolutions of states" (*rivolutioni degli stati*).

This difference might seem negligible, yet it had oversized effects. To start with, "revolution" soon displaced the Aristotelian vocabulary of political change, to the extent that, by the eighteenth century, even translations of Aristotle's *Politics* used "revolutions."[79] This displacement, in turn, had further consequences. "Revolution" was more neutral than "mutation" or "sedition," the traditional jargon of Aristotle's translators. It did not imply the corruption of a pure form into a mutant other. Nor did it cast political resistance as an illegitimate, treasonous affair (to this day, a "seditious conspiracy" is a federal crime in the United States: see 18 U.S. Code § 2384). In the context of Polybius's thought, "revolution" was still something to be avoided, and for a long while the historians and political observers who employed the word kept it at a prudential distance. But unmoored from its point of departure in Polybius, "revolution" could be put to other uses by innovative authors. A new vocabulary opened up new possibilities in the history of ideas.

CHAPTER FOUR

The Misfortunes of History

The future's uncertain and the end is always near.

—"ROADHOUSE BLUES," *THE DOORS*

WHO WAS THIS Fortune who caused revolutions? The Greeks named her Tychē, and the Romans made her a goddess, Fortuna. Sometimes she blindly bestowed gifts from her cornucopia. But she also had a moral streak, striking down the overly ambitious or successful. After his astounding victory over Perseus of Macedon at Pydna, the consul Aemilius Paullus turned his thoughts to the reversals of fortune that were bound to follow such good luck. As if on cue, two of his younger sons died in rapid succession. One of his older sons, Scipio Aemilianus, who also fought at Pydna, similarly reflected on the vanity of earthly triumphs when his army destroyed Carthage, some twenty years later.[1]

It is Polybius who recounted Scipio's lament, told to him as they stood together watching Carthage burn. Scipio feared the jealous and senseless Fortune who gave with one hand and took away with the other. But Polybius deemed Tychē capable also of great deeds, not just senseless actions. In the fifty years that had preceded the destruction of Carthage, "Fortune made almost all the affairs of the world incline in one direction, and forced them to converge upon one and the same point," he announced at the opening of his *Histories*. To him, the supremacy of the Roman Republic in the Mediterranean world was fated.[2]

For Polybius and his contemporaries, Fortune encapsulated both the unexpected and the unknown, thus concealing a profound ambiguity. Were some events simply destined to occur no matter what? Greek mythology was replete with stories about fate, from the Moirai ("Fates") to Achilles and Oedipus. Zeus himself, Aeschylus had Prometheus exclaim in a play, "cannot escape what is foretold."[3] But did some events happen for no reason at all, and simply by chance? Natural disasters and human errors were unavoidable, but not necessarily meaningful. In that case, the study of history and philosophy could only temper the impact of such accidents, by revealing the method to Fortune's madness. But there was no total science of the future. Whether intended or accidental, Fortune's revolutions eventually caught us all off guard.

When the Roman emperor Constantine converted to Christianity in 312, Fortuna was one of the most worshiped goddesses in the pagan pantheon. Young men dedicated their first beard trimmings to her; women prayed to her during childbirth; Fortuna brought health, safe travels, and most importantly, success (i.e., "fortune"). As the purveyor of material prosperity, she seemed unlikely to survive the conversion of the empire to Christianity. Augustine mocked the idea of a divinity who is "sometimes good and sometimes bad." What kind of goddess is that? If Fortune is simply chance, then "there is nothing to be gained from worshiping her." If she is more than chance, then one should worship the God who is acting in her stead.[4]

Where Fortuna oscillated between destiny and chance, Christianity swung the pendulum strongly toward the former. The fate of humanity had been sealed with the creation of Adam. The Coming of Christ was foreordained from the beginning of time. Everything now pointed toward the Second Coming, and the Final Judgment. There was no "good fortune" anymore, only salvation. Divine providence ruled the world.

And yet somehow Fortune survived the bonfire of the pagan idols. Augustine himself was partially responsible. Earlier theologians had claimed that human affairs reflected divine providence in a fairly transparent fashion. For the early Church historian Eusebius, Constantine's conversion of the Roman Empire was a manifest expression of God's plan, and announced the final age of the world. But this literal reading of human affairs had its problems. What was one to make, for instance, of the dreadful sack of Rome by the Visigoths in 410? For three days, they pillaged the city, looting and murdering the inhabitants. If the world was entirely governed by providence, how was one to explain such a catastrophe? Why had God allowed the capital of the world and the epicenter of Christianity to be ransacked?[5]

This was the catastrophe that led Augustine to embark on his magnum opus, *The City of God*. Against Eusebius and others who believed they could read God's intentions directly in the course of events, Augustine argued that such events were, for the most part, meaningless. Far be it from the bishop of Hippo to question divine providence, or the belief that the entirety of history unfolded according to God's plan. But we humans were just fooling ourselves if we believed that our puny minds were capable of discerning the structure of this plan. Just as a mosaic pattern seems chaotic and illegible when viewed up close, the divine order made sense only from a God's eye perspective.[6] We should not read too much into human affairs, as they tell us little about the divine order.

Augustine further argued that in the current age of humanity—the age after Christ's birth and death, but before the Second Coming—we shouldn't really expect much order at all. Human history, during this strange intermission, was stuck in a holding pattern. Kings and emperors ruled over peoples like God over creation, but they were mere simulacra of the true Lord in Heaven. What happened on earth between now and the end times was but "a succession of miseries" (*series calamitatis*).[7]

Augustine thus deftly combined an overarching order of sacred history, stretching from Genesis to the Apocalypse, with the more chaotic and haphazard sequence of secular history. Sacred history was like the general theory of relativity: it unfolded in a predictable fashion across great expanses of time. Secular history was closer to quantum physics: it was quirky, unpredictable, and did not clearly align with its divine counterpart. It was this duality that made it possible for later authors, such as Boethius, to incorporate into Christian doctrine the older, pagan deity of Fortune. Fortune might even do God's bidding by reminding the powerful that their days were numbered.[8] But she returned as a capricious agent of apparent chaos, less to be worshiped than feared.

Progression before Progress

Providence is not the only historical innovation that has been credited to Christianity. Some have argued that Augustine developed a doctrine of progress that would not have been out of place among Enlightenment philosophers. Augustine recognized that humanity had come a long way since the Fall, noting "the many great arts invented and exercised by human ingenuity."[9] But this was not a novel observation. Pagan philosophers and historians had long surmised that humans once resembled animals, and that we developed our cultural and technological sophistication over time. These classical observations about human progress, however, reveal a markedly different understanding than what we find in the modern doctrine.[10]

A first difference is that the bulk of human progress, for the ancients, had occurred before recorded history even began. According to Cicero, it was these preliminary advances that had made civilization possible in the first place: "What other power [than speech] could have been strong enough either to gather scattered humanity into one place, or to lead it out of its brutish existence in the wilderness up to our present condition of civilization as men and as citizens[?]" he queried in *On the Orator*.[11] By exchanging ideas with one another through speech, humans had progressed beyond the state of beasts (*fera*). But this argument that human progress is what produced civilization in the first place did not entail any hierarchy among existing civilizations, or between earlier and present ones.

In other cases, authors did own that progress might still be ongoing. For instance, Lucretius argued that "even now some arts are being perfected, some also are in growth." While this argument sounds similar to the modern idea of progress, it was in fact also an extension of the belief that most improvements had happened before the start of civilization. Lucretius introduced his argument by noting, "The world is young and new, and it is not long since its beginning." Like Cicero, Lucretius located the bulk of progress during a time before there were any records, beyond those that "reason offers us as traces."[12]

During these primitive times, however, we do find Lucretius describing a process that resembles the modern doctrine. How did early humans discover "ships and agriculture, fortifications and laws, arms, roads, clothing, and all else of this kind," he wonders. It was all a matter of time, and by dint of experience:

usus et impigrae simul experientia mentis	the practice and experience of an active mind
paulatim docuit pedetemptim progredientis	by degrees taught progress step by step.[13]

Here we find two of the primary features of modern progress: gradual improvement ("paulatim . . . pedetemptim progredientis"), which is brought about not by acts of genius but mere trial and error ("usus et . . . experientia").[14] Was Lucretius a modern, then?

There was still an important difference: he did not project progress indefinitely into the future. Indeed, this entire section ends with the suggestion that progress had literally peaked:

namque alid ex alio clarescere corde videbant	as they saw one thing after the other grow clear with their minds
artibus ad summum donec venere cacumen	until arriving at the summit of the arts.[15]

The difference here with the modern idea is that progress, for Lucretius, is not endless. It tends toward a goal, which once reached it does not surpass. Cicero made a similar argument in an essay on rhetoric: at first, sculpture and painting had been fairly primitive, but with later artists "everything has been brought to perfection."[16] As the historian E. H. Gombrich commented a propos this passage, "The classical view [of progress] comes quite legitimately to the idea of a final stage beyond which the tool can no longer be perfected."[17]

Modern writers may have discovered in the ancients the concept of gradual improvement, but what was missing was the idea of continuous *future* change. The claim that humanity had progressed from a primitive stage to present civilization—and may even have some growth areas left—was still fully compatible with the classical viewpoint that future civilization would be, mutatis mutandis, no different than it is now. What made the modern idea of progress so distinctive was the belief that future progress was unrestricted, and that the world to come could be radically different than the world at hand. That belief is not to be found in antiquity.[18]

These encomia for human progress, moreover, were counterbalanced by historical accounts that portrayed the passage of time more negatively. Most famous was Hesiod's myth of ages, which offered an opposite spin on the march to civilization. In this narrative, which later authors frequently copied (most famously, Ovid), our happiest age was our first, the age of gold. Our current, miserable age of iron was defined by the metal used for war and hard labor.[19]

While this pessimistic narrative had a mainly symbolic value, it did reflect a conservative outlook common in antiquity. Authors might acknowledge progress in some areas, while still emphasizing the importance of continuity and tradition. For instance, Aristotle recognized how "in general all the arts and faculties" had improved over time, and that "the laws of ancient times were too simple and uncivilized." But he also warned against change for its own sake: "It is a bad thing to accustom men to repeal the laws lightly." This veneration for tradition was also common in Roman times, as is evident in their emphasis on the "ways of our ancestors," or *mos maiorum*.[20]

Apocalypse Soon

If Christianity did not introduce the modern idea of progress, any more than classical philosophers did, what about the idea of a privileged historical period at the end of time? Many scholars have noted similarities between Christian apocalypticism and modern theories of an end of history.[21] It was not simply that Christians believed the world would end: Stoic philosophers had already imagined a fiery conclusion to the universe. Rather, it was the ways in which Christian theologians drew out these end times that provided rich fodder for the historical imagination. The key source text here was the Book of Revelation, the sanctioned expression of Christian apocalypticism (along with certain Old Testament prophecies). One passage in particular proved highly influential. John of Patmos, the book's supposed author, wrote that there would come a time when Christian martyrs "came to life and reigned with Christ a thousand years. The rest of the dead did not come to life until the thousand years were ended."[22] This reference to a thousand-year reign *before* the Last Judgment gave rise to various currents of "millenarianism," the belief that a new millennium would someday dawn on earth, ruled over by Christ and the saints. In one particularly notorious reading of Revelation, Joachim of Fiore, a twelfth-century monk and theologian, interpreted this coming age as a great utopia when justice would prevail on earth.[23]

There is undoubtedly a kind of revolutionary power to apocalyptic thinking. In 1534, Anabaptists took control of the German city of Münster, proclaimed the imminent return of Christ, and redesigned society according to Old Testament practices (they notably reintroduced polygamy).[24] A century later in England, a group of fanatical Puritans proclaimed that, following the death of Charles I, the fifth age of humanity had arrived, when saints would rule the earth. They took their name, "Fifth Monarchy Men," from the prophecy in the Book of Daniel, which described four historical empires, and announced a fifth and final kingdom come.[25]

When Christian millenarians participate in revolutions as historical actors, it clearly makes sense to study what apocalyptic thinking contributed to the course of events.[26] But it is another matter altogether to suggest that Christian millenarianism shaped the thought of revolutionaries who, unlike the Anabaptists or Fifth Monarchists, showed no prior interest in apocalyptic beliefs. Are Robespierre, Fourier, Marx, Lenin, and Mao really the descendants of Joachim de Fiore? Are the political utopias of modern times just secular revisions of the Christian millennium?

The parallels between these different movements are certainly intriguing. But a closer look at the intellectual history of revolution points to serious problems with this line of descent. First, there is no evidence that Christian millenarianism directly influenced later ideas about revolution. Well into the eighteenth century, political observers continued to view threats to established rulers as the machinations of Fortune. On occasion, there were popular warnings that political troubles announced the end times, but most writers rejected such responses as naive.[27] Outbursts of millenarianism did not fundamentally challenge the Christian distinction between Fortune and providence. To paraphrase this chapter's epigraph, the end might be near, but the future was always uncertain.

A second problem with this claim is chronological. Its defenders posit that the full imaginative and political potential of millenarianism was unleashed at the very moment when Christianity was losing ground as an all-encompassing cultural framework. Consider the French Revolution, which was the first to embrace revolution as a positive force, capable of propelling humanity into a new age. When asked, in 1794, to define the end goal of the revolution, Robespierre declared that it was "the reign of eternal justice."[28] This statement may recall Joachim's description of the new millennium. But what could explain the resurgence of this vision at a time when Joachim had been largely forgotten, and Christian millenarianism had lain dormant for a hundred years?

This problem only becomes greater when twentieth-century revolutions are considered, particularly those that took place in non-Christian societies. How could Chinese Red Guard students pursue a Christian millennium? Even if we assume that they had inherited a millenarian vision from Marx (hardly a Christian fundamentalist himself), why would a secularized, unacknowledged religious belief in the kingdom of God have struck a deep chord among a people with little familiarity with Christianity? Culture and ideas are not transmitted from one generation or people to the next like family jewels; every act of transmission is also an act of transformation. And ideas do not persist for all time in the ether. In the absence of actual Christian millenarians, or of individuals who were directly familiar with their beliefs, there are few compelling reasons to credit apocalyptic ideas with determining or even influencing modern revolutionary thought.

One reason why the parallel between Christian millenarianism and modern revolutions has proven so seductive is that we have a hard time imagining where else revolutionaries might have found their ideas about a glorious, just future. If not in apocalyptic thinking, what was the source? We will see in chapters 8 and 9 how a major eighteenth-century shift in historical thinking, unrelated to apocalyptic visions, laid the groundwork for both a utopian conception of the future and a new understanding of revolution. While some still view Enlightenment doctrines of progress as fundamentally deriving from Christian providentialism, their origins and organization in fact have little in common with earlier religious cosmologies.[29]

There were also other, non-Christian references that offered glimpses of a time out of time. Hesiod's pessimistic myth of ages had already been appropriated in antiquity to produce a happier outcome: the return of the golden age, a motif that Virgil famously adopted to celebrate the reign of Augustus.[30] The dream of a new golden age remained popular up until the French Revolution, when it became a commonplace description of current events.[31] Like the Christian millennium, the golden age was associated with justice, in the figure of the goddess Astraea. Classical references such as these were common in literature, art, theater, and opera, and nourished people's imaginations far more than Christian apocalypticism. Robespierre is more likely to have had Virgil's pastoral visions in mind than Joachim de Fiore's saintly millennium.

There were certainly strains of Christianity that rejected the prudential and Fortune-fearing mindset of pagan historians. And the sway of this classical mindset waxed and waned over the centuries. But despite rejecting so many other features of pagan culture, Christianity proved surprisingly accepting of its main historical outlook. For this reason, Christian authors perceived political revolutions in much the same way, as dangerous events to be avoided. The rediscovery and reappraisal of classical texts, starting in the late Middle Ages, reinforced this perception and provided a welcome remedy to their frequent repetition: the well-balanced government.

PART II

Constitutions and Revolutions in the British World, 1642–1787

On ne peut jamais quitter les Romains.

MONTESQUIEU, *DE L'ESPRIT DES LOIS*, 11.13; 1:185

LOOKING BACK ON the English Civil War and the regimes that followed, John Locke observed a trend:

> This slowness and aversion in the people to quit their old constitutions, has, in the many revolutions which have been seen in this kingdom . . . still kept us to, or, after some interval of fruitless attempts, still brought us back again to our old legislative of king, lords and commons.[1]

Locke knew that the English were not incapable of envisaging other constitutional models. The Levellers had pushed for a government without a king or House of Lords; on these points, the commonwealth of 1649 delivered. Over a century later, in 1776, another Englishman, Thomas Paine, similarly imagined a government without a king, or even much executive power at all. But in the end, these were, as Locke put it, "fruitless attempts." Oliver Cromwell became Lord Protector in 1653, a position soon to be hereditary, making him a king in all but name. A Stuart monarch, Charles II, regained the throne in 1660, and reestablished the House of Lords. Paine's vision for the federal republic also lasted about ten years, before the Constitutional Convention replaced it with a government that featured a strong executive office, and both an upper and lower chamber of Congress. The pull of the "old constitution" was hard to resist, indeed.

Locke's observation was meant to be reassuring. He himself was writing to defend the legitimacy of revolution against a supposedly tyrannical king. His patron, the Earl of Shaftesbury, was leading an effort to depose Charles II, who had blocked Parliament's attempts to remove his Catholic brother from the line of succession. Locke wanted to reassure his readers that the next revolution would not conclude as the last had, with a series of ill-fated and short-lived governments. In the end, Shaftesbury's attempted revolution did not get off the ground, but the "Glorious Revolution" that ultimately replaced James II played out as Locke had predicted. It recalibrated the rights and duties of England's "old legislative of king, lords and commons," rather than ushering in a new constitution.[2]

These "three British revolutions" were among the most prominent that the Western world witnessed between 1600 and 1788. They were not the only revolutions of this period, and as we saw in the previous chapter, there was an entire genre of "revolutions in *X*" that thrived in the early seventeenth century. But these British revolutions are of particular interest for what they can teach us about the evolving meaning of "revolution" itself. They also publicized the term and its political implications in detailed and elaborate ways. The execution of Charles I sent chills down the spines of European monarchs and was still invoked as a precedent during the trial of Louis XVI in 1792. The Glorious Revolution established a form of government that became an object of fascination for political writers not only in the British Empire but also on the Continent. And the American Revolution met with great enthusiasm across Europe, particularly in France, where the young republic, its constitutions, and its statesmen were fêted.[3]

Given the outbreak of the French Revolution a mere six years after the Treaty of Paris confirmed American independence, 1776 and 1789 are typically clustered in the same "age of Atlantic revolutions."[4] In this account, the British revolutions are viewed as the progenitors of modern revolutions.[5] Due to their overlapping personnel, claims, and even documents, it can be difficult to disentangle the American and French Revolutions. But this confusion may also be misleading, as it encourages historians to project causal relations where there may be none. Events that happen in close proximity may be intertwined, but their synchrony can be coincidental. Still, given the outbreak of revolutions around the globe after 1800, it is hard to resist the impression of a single tidal wave, swelling in the American colonies, cresting in France, and then breaking across Europe, the Caribbean, and South America.

But what if there were in fact two waves, converging briefly in the late eighteenth century, yet stemming from different places and traditions?

Rather than the precursor to the French Revolution, the American Revolution might best be understood as the culmination of an English political process—the last Polybian revolution, as it were. It displayed traces of the next wave, whose rise had begun before 1776. When Thomas Paine announced that "the birth-day of a new world is at hand," he was speaking the language of modern revolutionaries. But this modern spirit was hardly an American invention, nor was it widespread in the colonies.[6] It was a rumbling that came from a different historical process gathering speed in France and in England: the rise of the modern vision of human progress. This vision had some proponents in the embryonic United States, but it ultimately had a minimal impact on political thought across the Atlantic in the 1770s and 1780s. The Americans remained deeply committed, like their English predecessors, to Polybian assumptions about history, constitutions, and revolutions. The modern wave that rippled across the American Revolution left but few lasting marks.

There is another reason to study the three major Anglo-American revolutions together, which is the particularity of England's "old legislative of king, lords and commons." At the time Locke was writing, no other European constitution could be described in these terms. For contingent reasons, the English constitution bore an uncanny resemblance with the ideal Polybian state. This resemblance could be contested and would be interpreted in different ways. But it certainly contributed to the reception of Polybius and other proponents of a balanced constitution (such as Cicero and Machiavelli) in England. And it may also have been a reason why the English and their American brethren found it so hard to "quit" this celebrated constitutional model.

CHAPTER FIVE

An Eccentric Constitution (1642–60)

AT FIRST GLANCE, the reception of Polybius in England mirrored the French and Italian cases, albeit with a slight delay. English writers swiftly adopted "revolution" as a technical term for describing regime change. On occasion they retained the original Polybian sense of *anacyclosis*, in reference to the full circle of governmental transformations. "Revolution" could thus describe both the events that led Charles I to lose his kingdom (along with his head), and those that brought his son, Charles II, to the throne in 1660.[1]

But there was one crucial difference to how Polybius was read in England. Unlike those of most other European countries, the English government already resembled the Polybian ideal of republican Rome. Recognizing this resemblance might require some squinting. But superficially at least, political power was divided in England among a king, the Lords, and the Commons. This arrangement was unusual, since many other European states that had a parliament or estates general separated out the clergy and the nobility.[2] In France, for example, the estates general combined *three* distinct estates, not including the king. The clergy was also represented in England, but it was folded into the House of Lords (whose full name is the Lords *Spiritual* and Temporal). This apparent merger of the first and second estates into a single chamber of Parliament led to much debate over the respective places of the clergy and the king in the English constitution. Was the clergy a distinct estate of the realm? Was the royal office part of a tripartite constitution, or did the king plane above the three estates? There were countless disagreements over these issues, and perceptions varied over time. But the loose resemblance between the

Polybian ideal and the English reality conditioned some observers to recognize a well-balanced mixture of monarchy, aristocracy, and democracy in their own political system.[3]

This identification first became prominent in Tudor England. In 1559, the year after Elizabeth acceded to the throne, the bishop and constitutional scholar John Aylmer described how:

> The regiment of Englande is not a mere Monarchie, as some for lacke of consideracion thinke, nor a meere Oligarchie, nor Democratie, but a rule mixte of all these, wherein ech one of these haue or shoulde haue like authoritie. . . . The King or Quene, which representeth the Monarche. The noble men, which be the Aristocratie. And the Burgesses and Knights the Democratie. The verye same had Lacedemonia.[4]

As Aylmer's last reference indicates, this analysis of the English constitution likely drew on Aristotle's account of the Spartan ("Lacedaemonian") regime, in book 2 of the *Politics*.[5] It was largely thanks to Aristotle that the ideal of a well-balanced constitution had been perpetuated in the late medieval period. Aristotle's major Christian interpreter, Thomas Aquinas, did not openly advocate for a mixed constitution, but pushed for "tempering" the power of kings by means of aristocratic councils, established laws, and even popular elections.[6] His vision of a tempered monarchy, as opposed to a genuinely mixed constitution, proved tenacious. Even Claude de Seyssel, one of the earliest European theorists to draw on Polybius's political ideas, still claimed that the French monarchy was merely "restrained." The nobility controlled military offices, thus presenting a check (*frein*) on royal overreach, and the judicial offices were all filled by high-status commoners, who could in turn check the aristocrats.[7]

In France, there was never any question that the constitution was monarchic, tempered or not. But the English constitution was more ambiguous. The rediscovery of Polybius helped those who would depict it as a mixed form. There is evidence that Aylmer, who knew Greek, was familiar with Polybius.[8] The bishop John Poynet similarly insisted, in 1556, on the advantages of mixed government: "Where the mixt State was exercised, there did the Common-wealth longest continue."[9]

By the turn of the century, English writers were drawing explicitly on Polybius's account, if not always in a positive way. In a treatise supporting James I's accession to the throne in 1603, the historian Sir John Hayward noted, "Polybius saith that [the Roman republican constitution] was mixed; the consulls represe[n]ting a monarchie, the senate, an aristocracie, & the c[om]mon people a democracy." He did not concur with

Polybius's celebration of this model, arguing that Rome "atteined the highest pitch both of glory and greatnes vnder emperors," whereas during the republic, "it neuer inioyed [ten] yeeres together free fr[om] sedition."[10] But he admitted that Polybius's view was widely accepted, notably by Cicero and Dionysius of Halicarnassus.

Book 6 of Polybius's *Histories* was translated into English only in 1633, by Edward Grimeston.[11] Up until the Civil War, few writers addressed the political ideas laid forth in this text. Polybius was read mostly for his historical account of the Punic Wars and the organization of the Roman army. Grimeston's translation did, however, introduce a subtle novelty. Rather than translating *politeiōn anacyclosis* as "the revolution of states," he opted for "the revolution of Governments." It was a phrase that soon caught on, as England experienced its own unprecedented revolutions.

The Battle for the Constitution

On August 4, 1642, the English Parliament issued an unusual declaration: "We, the Lords and Commons, are resolved to expose our Lives and Fortunes for the Defence and Maintenance of the true Religion, the King's Person, Honour and Estate, the Power and Privilege of Parliament, and the Just Rights and Liberties of the Subjects." This statement might not seem out of the ordinary, but for the fact that it was found in "A Declaration to Justify Parliament's Proceedings and Resolutions to Take Up Arms." The enemy that Parliament was taking arms up against was the king.

If Parliament was tying itself up in knots—going to war with the king to "defend and maintain" him—it was due to a constitutional crisis. Many disagreements about the nature of the English constitution stemmed from its peculiarity, compared with those of most European states. Others had surfaced in the wake of the Protestant Reformation. The reason why Charles had recalled Parliament, in 1640, after eleven years of personal rule, was to pay for war against the Scots, who had rejected the Anglican Book of Common Prayer and excluded bishops from their Church.[12] The twenty-two bishops in the English House of Lords also attracted Puritan ire, both for ecclesiastical reasons and because they cast the decisive votes blocking key bills from the Commons.[13] These bills sought to curb the royal prerogative, notably by obliging the king to call a session of Parliament at least once every three years (the Triennial Act), and by abolishing the Star Chamber, an extraordinary court used by the king to suppress political and religious dissent. Determining the monarch's proper exercise of executive power would be a lasting challenge in the Anglo-American constitutional tradition.

Due to the bishops' unwavering opposition to these and other measures, the Commons ultimately passed a bill excluding them from the House of Lords (in June 1641). That such a measure was not regarded as a drastic constitutional alteration further highlights the peculiarity of English government. Because the lords both temporal and spiritual sat in the same house, the bishops could be removed without visibly modifying the constitutional framework.[14] There would still be an upper chamber without high-ranking clergymen. By contrast, in France, such a move would have completely reconfigured the estates general, reducing them from three to two.

The so-called Clergy Act had little chance of passing in the House of Lords, but the bishops overplayed their hand, and in January 1642 twelve of them were imprisoned in the Tower of London on charges of treason. Suddenly, Charles's legislative wall crumbled, and Parliament could now pass a slew of bills that redefined and restricted his power. Charles responded by brazenly invading the House of Commons on January 3, 1642, to arrest five opposition leaders, including John Pym. But the latter had received advance warning and escaped. His plan having backfired, Charles left London and prepared for war. Parliament followed suit, and that August was ready to issue its declaration to take up arms.[15]

By that time, however, many members of Parliament had decided that the majority had gone too far. In the *Grand Remonstrance* presented to the king in December 1641, for instance, Pym had claimed for Parliament the right (among others) to vet appointments to the royal council. Some members felt that such measures intruded on the king's prerogative, and ultimately switched sides. For his part, Pym insisted that the conflict with Charles was due to "a malignant and pernicious design of subverting the fundamental laws and principles of government."[16] Both sides, in other words, accused the other of violating the constitution. Crucially, no one suggested—at least, not yet—that the constitution itself should be altered. Supporters of Parliament remained as wedded to their conception of the English constitution as the Royalists did to theirs. If armed conflict proved inescapable, it would ultimately be ill-suited for resolving this interpretative dilemma, as Parliament would discover.

It was in this context of king and Parliament heading to war, each clinging to the English constitution, that one of the most intriguing and Polybian declarations was issued. In June 1642, a pamphlet appeared under Charles I's name, entitled *His Majesties Answer to the XIX Propositions*. The king did not write it and may not even have read it in full. So he may have missed a critical passage, which has been described as "the most influential [statement] ever made on the nature of the English government."[17] Penned by Sir John Colepeper, a member of Parliament who had recently crossed over to the Royalist side, it described the English constitution in a Polybian fashion, as the perfect balance of monarchy, aristocracy, and democracy:

> There being three kindes of Government amongst men, Absolute Monarchy, Aristocracy and Democracy, and all these having their particular conveniencies and inconveniencies. The experience and wisdom of your Ancestors hath so moulded this out of a mixture of these, as to give to this Kingdom (as far as humane Prudence can provide) the conveniencies of all three, without the inconveniencies of any one.[18]

In addition to this classical argument about the need to blend or mix different forms of government, the *Answer* also emphasized how the different powers of government should be distributed. To the king belonged the power "to resist Invasion from abroad, and Insurrection at home." We can recognize in this description key features of what would soon be called "executive power," and what Polybius had already attributed to the consuls (most notably the role of commander in chief). The House of Commons had the power of the purse ("the Levies of Moneys"), as had the Roman Senate for Polybius. This fiduciary responsibility has traditionally been an aspect of legislative power. The House of Lords enjoyed "a Judicatorie power," and as the aristocratic house of Parliament, provided "Counsell in the ablest Persons of a State for the publike benefit." This deliberative function was another element of what would become grouped under legislative power. Finally, the Lords was also celebrated for serving as "an excellent Screen and Bank between the Prince and People." The constituent parts were meant to check and balance one another.[19] This account of how the powers of government should be distributed across interlocking institutions reflected a distinctly Polybian theory.

But this was a risky theory for Royalists to adopt, as it placed the king on a more or less equal footing with the two Houses of Parliament. Why embrace it, then? Historians have suggested that the *Answer* mobilized "the imagery of fortune" in order to warn against future disasters, should the delicate balance of government be disturbed.[20] Its message was arguably blunter still. Leave the government as it is, the *Answer* warned, or spark a revolution that will "end in a dark equall Chaos of Confusion." The English constitution was a "splendid and excellently distinguished form of Government" because it was a bulwark against revolution.[21] Parliament was playing with fire if it forced through any changes.

Unsurprisingly, Parliamentarians were perfectly happy to run with this Polybian reading of the English constitution. One of their leading pamphleteers, Henry Parker, took the obvious step of comparing the English constitution to the Roman Republic, noting how "no defect at all could be in that popular and mixt government." He insisted that Parliament did not seek to alter the constitution, but simply recognized that "there are severall degrees of Prerogatives Royall," and wished the king to have "greater power of protection, and lesse of oppression."[22] The real question, in his mind, was not whether the king should enjoy some executive powers, but rather which ones. Other influential writers, such as the Puritan William Prynne or the clergyman Philip Hunton, similarly made the case for Parliament by painting the English constitution in explicitly Polybian colors.[23]

The fact that rival camps could lay claim to the same constitutional ideal highlights further reasons for its allure. First, to state the obvious, this ideal was remarkably elastic. There were few constraints on how one might distribute the powers of government across its constitutive parts. The monarchic element could enjoy a great many executive powers, or very few. The Polybian theory of government was like an enchanted mirror that reflected whatever constitutional balance one wished to see in it.

Another reason why both sides appealed to the same theory was its distinguished pedigree. Not only did a mixed constitution have Polybius's approval but it also received plaudits from Plato, Aristotle, Cicero, and, in more modern times, Machiavelli, along with many others. There were also some doubters, most notably the French jurist Jean Bodin, who argued that the very idea of mixed government was illogical.[24] In England, his opinion was strongly echoed by Thomas Hobbes and Robert Filmer, who lamented how "there is scarce the meanest man of the multitude but can now in these daies tell us that the government of the Kingdome of England is a Limited and Mixed Monarchy."[25] But most observers of English history reached a different conclusion. Indeed, the perception that the English constitution was mixed and balanced made the classical recommendations all the more seductive. This prestige, combined with the model's flexibility, produced a potent combination. The looming Civil War would test how far this theory could be stretched.

These powerful reasons did not prevent all English political writers from envisaging other constitutional arrangements. In part, the contrarians were moved by the stalemate that emerged after Parliament's victory in the first Civil War. By May 1746, Charles was in custody, yet still refused Parliament's demands. The war had not resolved their constitutional differences. This impasse led writers associated with the Leveller movement and the army "agitators" to push more radical proposals. In their constitutional draft, *An Agreement of the People* (November 1647), they envisaged a new regime based on the principle of unmixed popular sovereignty. They emphasized the need for electoral reform, to ensure that Parliament was more equitably representative. Most remarkable is what did not feature in their proposal: no mention was made of either a monarch or the House of Lords. Even with a lot of squinting, this was not a balanced, Polybian constitution.

The political philosophy underpinning these proposals came from a different source. Sixteenth-century theologians such as John Major had argued that all humans received from God certain inalienable natural rights, which also formed the basis of political power.[26] All legitimate governments required the consent of the ruled, and were answerable to the people: "The power of this, and all future Representatives of this Nation, is inferiour only to theirs who chuse them," wrote the authors of the *Agreement*.[27] It was a compelling argument for popular sovereignty, which future revolutionaries, including the American colonists, would put to effective use. It captured the fundamental principle of modern constitutionalism—namely, that "all men are born and remain free, and equal in rights."[28]

In 1647, however, few political observers were ready for a revolution, or even talking about one; and few were prepared to accept this modern claim of civic equality. When Leveller soldiers presented their proposal to the army grandees, the latter were appalled. Cromwell's son-in-law, Henry Ireton, objected to the Leveller demand that "every man that is an inhabitant is to be equally considered, and to have an equal voice in the election of those representers." Ireton retorted that he did not "think it a sufficient ground" that simply by virtue of "a man's being born here he shall have a share in that power that shall dispose of the lands here, and of all things here."[29] The army officers promoted an alternative constitutional draft, the *Heads of Proposal*, which retained roles for king and lords, as well as property qualifications for the electoral franchise. As it mostly sought to consolidate the legislative powers acquired during the Long Parliament, its proposals did not fully amount to a regime change nor require a revolution.

"A Revolution of Government"

The word "revolution" in the 1640s was still used mostly as an astronomical or astrological term. Its political sense was not unknown: Grimeston's translation of Polybius was reissued in 1648, suggesting an awareness of its newfound relevance.[30] But political uses could also be tied to various prophecies. In a sermon pronounced at the House of Commons in 1644, a minister suggested that "the great revolution and turning of things upside downe in these our dayes" was a sign of the apocalypse.[31] Even this direct reference to current events was not only about political change. During the Civil War, many aspects of English society were "turned upside down."

Everything changed, however, in 1649. Following a second Civil War, during which Charles, escaped from captivity, allied himself with the Scots, the army finally had enough. Colonel Thomas Pride purged Parliament of those members who still supported further negotiations with the king. The remaining Rump Parliament—so named because more than half its members had left or been expelled—put Charles on trial. Accused of treason and tyranny, he was beheaded on January 30, 1649.

Now the word "revolution" leapt to people's lips. The General Assembly of the Church of Scotland, meeting a week after Charles's execution, recognized his son as the lawful king, and prayed that God would "prevent all those calamities and confusions that the present great revolution of Affaires doth threaten these Kingdomes with."[32] Other authors adopted Polybius's turn of phrase, from the Grimeston translation, referring to "the late revolution of government" in England.[33] The journalist and government publicist Marchamont Nedham remarked more broadly in 1650 that "Governments have their Revolutions, and fatal Periods."[34]

This sudden burst of revolution talk is highly revealing. It shows how observers had a clear understanding of what a political revolution consisted of, and that, until January 1649, what they saw did not yet amount to one. If "every great revolution is a civil war," as the historian David Armitage has argued, not every civil war was a revolution.[35] But once a recognizable set of factors fell into place, contemporaries had no trouble naming a revolution.

What were these factors? The most important was regime change. In the Polybian model, "revolution" referred specifically to the moment when one form of government gave way to another. From a temporal perspective, a revolution was not a drawn-out affair. A mere few months after Charles's execution, commentators were already describing the revolution as a thing of the past ("*late* revolution"). The revolution was over almost as soon as it had begun. There were more revolutions to come in the 1650s, but, unlike in the 1790s, they were not conceived at the time as forming part of some larger, unified process that contemporaries understood as "the English Revolution." In a 1654 treatise, written after England had gone through two more forms of government, Nedham wrote of "the many great changes of Affairs and revolution*s* of Government."[36] Finally, even for defenders of the commonwealth, revolutions remained something to be avoided. They were,

Nedham wrote, "rapid Hurricanoes of fatall necessity, which blow upon our Affaires from all points of the Compasse." The revolution of 1649 was "fatal," in the sense of "fated" to occur. "There is . . . a wheeling of all things, and a Revolution of Manners as well as Times," Nedham observed. "Nor are the huge Bodies of Common-wealths exempted from the same Fate."[37]

Political observers in 1649, in sum, conceived of "revolution" very similarly to ancient political philosophers. A revolution named the passage from one regime to another (*metabolē*), a passage typically accompanied or preceded by violence (*stasis*). On top of this destructive aspect, which the English experienced intensely during the Civil War, revolution owed its negative connotation to the fear that it was doomed to recur (*anacyclosis*). When designing a new government, the best one could hope for was to avoid the curse of short-lived states, which have "their fatall periods in a very short revolution of time," Nedham cautioned.[38] Indeed, while every empire and republic was destined to fall, some collapsed sooner than others. All one could do was to postpone inevitable decay by designing a government that best withstood internal pressures—in short, by instituting a balanced constitution.

Different Constitutions, Same Constitutionalism

The new government that Nedham was defending differed significantly from the old. In early 1649, Parliament abolished both the "kingly office" and the House of Lords, proclaiming instead a "commonwealth"—the English word for *res publica*, or republic. This was the literal "revolution of government" that contemporary authors referred to. England had abandoned monarchy, however well-tempered or mixed, for a republican form of government. "The people are, under God, the original of all just power," the Rump Parliament proclaimed on January 4, 1649. The Leveller John Lilburne celebrated this phrase, but worried that the new government could still become tyrannical.[39] He continued to push for the reforms demanded in the *Agreement*.

Nedham attacked his argument head-on, accusing the Levellers of promoting "meer Democracy." Ancient writers had warned against such a dangerous regime, noting that "the passage is quick and easie from a *meere Popularity* [i.e., democracy] to *Monarchy*." Democracies encouraged licentiousness over liberty, and elevated demagogues to tyrannical power. Nedham upheld the iron law of social inequality, accusing the Levellers of ignoring the inevitable differences between "the lowest of the people" and "the richer Sort," and following the frightful example of the "Roman

Levellers" (i.e., Tiberius and Gaius Gracchus). Yet it was also in the Roman Republic that Nedham found a positive model, since there "the Multitude were never so mad as to cast off . . . the Senate, which was their standing Councell; and without which no Common-wealth can continue of any long standing." This was the model that the English commonwealth had adopted, Nedham claimed: not a messy democracy like Athens, where the people were let loose on the government, but a free state governed by a wise counsel (that is, by Parliament). Most importantly, it was a stable state that offered both freedom and protection from political changes, or, in a word, from revolution.[40]

Defenders of the new regime thus used the same arguments and logic as earlier authors who had sought to prop up the old. Both Charles's *Answer* and Nedham's *Case of the Common-Wealth* praised their respective governments for providing long-term stability. Both looked to ancient philosophers to demonstrate that these regimes were optimal. And both identified the best form of government with a well-balanced constitution, which alone could keep the next revolution at bay.

But if the English commonwealth did away with the king and House of Lords, how could it still be called well balanced? Nedham was clearly pushing the envelope, yet he could do so because the idea of a well-balanced constitution was so malleable. Already for Polybius, the monarchic element need not be a literal monarch. The Roman consuls simply inherited the powers that had once belonged to the kings. In the new English commonwealth, some of these same executive powers (such as commander in chief) were now vested in the Council of State.[41] The aristocratic part of government was Parliament itself, which like the Roman Senate remained a patrician bastion. Contrary to Leveller hopes, the electoral franchise was still restricted by property qualifications: only around 3 percent of English men were eligible to vote.[42] Still, a larger portion of the people participated in elections than served in office, so there was arguably a popular aspect to this constitution. This aspect was particularly striking compared with Continental monarchies, where very few offices were filled by election, and the people were not recognized as the ultimate source of political power. The fact that the English enjoyed rights and liberties unknown to monarchic subjects was also regarded as a democratic feature. These were some of the reasons why Nedham could still portray the commonwealth as a tempered, well-balanced government, and "the only Bank, which preserves us from the Inundations of Tyranny on the one side, and Confusion on the other."[43]

Since the regime that the ancients had praised as the most excellent could be discovered under so many guises, there were few reasons to abandon it. A further attraction of Polybian constitutionalism came from the lingering perception of human history as ever-shifting and capricious. The Levellers had provided a modern alternative to a tempered government, but no modern vision of history. Their political arguments thus remained vulnerable to the temporal criticism that "the passage is quick and easie" from democracy to the rule of one.

As it turned out, the commonwealth itself lasted a mere four years in this initial form. Cromwell and the Army Council grew impatient with the Rump Parliament, dissolving it in April 1653. There followed a short-lived experiment with a Parliament whose members were nominated by army officers for their "godliness." This Parliament of Saints (better known as Barebone's Parliament, after one of its colorful members, Praise-God Barebone) squabbled incessantly and was forced to pronounce its own dissolution after only six months.[44]

The next two governments, collectively known as the Protectorate, brought the commonwealth increasingly back in line with the old English constitution.[45] The initial Protectorate was the first English government to be established by a written constitution, the Instrument of Government (December 1653). Its most important innovation was the creation of the office of Lord Protector, naturally occupied by Cromwell. According to Nedham, by now the official publicist (if not propagandist) for the new regime, this office was created to prevent Parliament from "placing the Legislative and the Executive powers in the same persons"—namely, its own members. Keeping these powers separate, he continued, and "flowing in distinct Channels, so that they may never meet in one" constituted "a grand Secret of Liberty and good Government."[46]

Nedham has been credited with inventing, in this passage, the modern doctrine of the separation of powers.[47] It is true that Nedham phrases his point in strikingly modern terms, even if this basic division of governmental powers had already been formulated by Aristotle. But Nedham was really just expressing the flip side of Polybius's argument. If members of Parliament combined both legislative and executive powers, then "they become unaccountable for Abuses in Government," he warned. More specifically, there would be "no manner of balance or Check . . . reserved upon them."[48] Here was Polybian constitutional theory, only in reverse mode. Indeed, the very idea of checks and balances makes sense only if institutions enjoy a monopoly on the exercise of specific functions (as opposed to the entirety of a political power—e.g., all legislative power). If the Roman Senate's appropriation power serves as a check to the consuls, then obviously the consuls cannot possess this same power. As we will see with Montesquieu, his own version of this theory was quite different, and the Frenchman believed that combining legislative and executive powers was acceptable.

Nedham also highlighted a surprising precedent as evidence of his "grand Secret of Liberty":

> It was the wisdom and care of our Ancestors, so to temper the Government of our Nation in time past, that they left the Supreme Law-making Power among the People in Parliament, to sit at sometimes, and betrusted the Execution of Law, with the mysteries of Government, in the hands of a single person and his Council.[49]

One of the outstanding features of the Protectorate, then, was that it resembled the old English constitution even more closely. Earlier descriptions of the constitution, such as Charles's *Answer*, may not have used the terminology of executive and legislative powers as Nedham did. But the general idea of placing discrete powers in distinct offices, including a singular commander in chief, was not new, nor was it the experience of the Civil War and the Rump Parliament that now made it conceivable.[50] The revolution of 1649 gave political thinkers more leeway to experiment with different combinations, but the basic matrix of governmental powers and offices was one that they had inherited from classical political philosophy. Nedham concluded his text by identifying the different constituent parts still visible in the English Commonwealth:

> But here we see, our Friends have taken in the good of all the three sorts of Governments, and bound them all in one. If War be, here is the Unitive vertue (but nothing else) of *Monarchy* to encounter it; and here is the admirable Counsel of *Aristocracie* to manage it; If Peace be, here is the industry and courage of *Democracie* to improve it.

As before, the ultimate proof of this compound government lay in its resistance to revolutionary change: "the Frame of Government appears so well bounded on both sides, against Anarchie and Tyrannie."[51] If Nedham introduced "our ideal type of the pure doctrine" of the separation of powers in this text, as has been argued, he went to no lengths to emphasize its originality but rather enmeshed it in classic constitutional theory.[52]

The second version of the Protectorate, founded by another written constitution, the Humble Petition and Advice (1657), may have been what Locke had in mind when he observed that the English tended to revert back to their old constitution. Initially, members of Parliament had wished for Cromwell to assume the crown. After pondering the offer for months, he eventually declined, but accepted the proposal that he name his own successor. The net effect of this amendment was to make the Lord Protectorship hereditary, like monarchy. The Humble Petition also reestablished an "Other House," a recreation of the House of Lords. While this second house of Parliament was never fully operational during the Protectorate, its simple existence reveals how eager many politicians had become to restore their familiar institutions and offices. There were certainly dissenting views, most famously expressed in the popular 1657 pamphlet *Killing No Murder*, which insisted that Cromwell had become another tyrant who, like Charles, could be lawfully executed.[53]

Locke's assessment of the Protectorate might suggest that the English were atavistically drawn to a familiar constitutional model. But this account overlooks the equally strong attraction exerted by ancient political models on classically educated writers. Almost all republican authors of this era looked to the Roman Republic as the chief example of a "free state," and wished for the English commonwealth to become, in John Milton's words, "another *Rome* in the west." Milton particularly admired how in Rome, the "ballance [was] exactly so set, as to preserve and keep up due autoritie on either side, as well in the Senat as in the people."[54] This Polybian principle led Milton to endorse a powerful senate or Parliament of "ablest men" to counterbalance popular passions.[55] In his ideal republic, *Oceana* (1656), James Harrington laid out constitutional principles in similarly Polybian terms: "the *Common-wealth* consisteth of the *Senate proposing*, the *People resolving*, and the *Magistracy executing*: whereby partaking of the *Aristocracy* as in the *Senate*, of the *Democracy* as in the *People*, and of *Monarchy* as in the *Magistracy*, it is compleat."[56] The elegant symmetry, classical authority, and political suppleness of the well-balanced constitution made it an exceptionally attractive model for republican theorists.

Locke's observation can thus be faulted for mistaking the effect for the cause. The ancient English constitution had taken shape for an entirely different set of reasons than the English commonwealth. It was only a happy coincidence that these two visions of government could be made to align so effortlessly. At best, this coincidence fortified any attachments that seventeenth-century Englishmen felt toward their ancestral form of government, allowing them to pour new ideas into old constitutions. In other cases, it may have played only a minor role.

Indeed, for seventeenth-century writers, Roman history was often as familiar as their own. Schoolchildren learned Latin by reading Caesar's *Gallic War*, Cicero's speeches, and Sallust's and Livy's histories.

Hobbes himself worried about the influence of classical education on contemporary politics: "The Reading of the books of Policy, and Histories of the antient Greeks, and Romans," he warned, led young men to "imagine their great prosperity, not to have proceeded from the æmulation of particular men, but from the vertue of their popular forme of government."[57]

As a source for Roman history, Polybius was only one author among many, and not even the most commonly cited.[58] But his influence extended far beyond his citation index. Any author who praised the Roman Republic for its well-balanced constitution was a beneficiary of the Polybian synthesis of Greek political thought and Roman history. Later authors added important variations to this original theme, and significant differences would emerge among them. But from a *longue durée* perspective, it is the contrast between those revolutionaries who formulated arguments within the Polybian synthesis and those who rejected it, later in the eighteenth century, that stands out as the most meaningful difference for the history of revolution.

A Modern Revolution?

In a classic comparative study, the historian Crane Brinton considered the English Civil War as one of the first modern revolutions. Brinton identified numerous parallels with later revolutions: the execution of Charles I foreshadowed those of Louis XVI and Nicholas II; all three revolutions resulted in dictatorship (Cromwell, Napoleon, Stalin); even the economic situations of England, France, and Russia bore similarities.[59]

But comparisons can also be misleading. Consider the Committee of Safety that the English Army established in October 1659, as the commonwealth was collapsing, following Cromwell's death and his son's resignation. Its name invites a parallel with the French Committee of Public Safety, created in 1793, and the executive branch of the French government during the Terror. Both committees operated on the fringes of political legitimacy.[60] Was this a modern revolutionary trait, introduced by the English revolutionaries? In reality, the idea that public safety justified extralegal measures was nothing new. Cicero had expressed it most famously: "Salus populi suprema lex esto" (Let public safety be the highest law).[61] And Cicero himself had given a celebrated example of how threats to public safety could be met with extraordinary means, when as consul he denied the right of appeal (*provocatio*) to Catiline's co-conspirators. Rather than an example of the English Revolution's modernity, it serves as a reminder that both revolutions drew on classical precedents, albeit in different ways. (The Americans also established "committees of safety.")

Focusing on similarities also downplays the importance of differences. One in particular sets the English Civil War apart from the revolutions that followed 1789, and concerns the army. From Colonel Pride's Purge until General Monck's role in restoring Charles II, the army played the role of kingmaker and king breaker. But in contrast with later revolutionary bodies, the army never claimed direct political power.[62] No "dual-power" situation emerged between the victors of the civil war, the Army Council and the Council of State, as there would be between rival political bodies during the French, Russian, and Chinese revolutions.[63] Cromwell did not dismiss the Rump Parliament in the name of an alternative theory of sovereignty, as the Parisian sections did when they overthrew the French monarchy in 1792. When the army intervened in politics, it was to revise the constitution.

The reason for this difference is that, during the English Civil War and commonwealth, arguments over the future of England were not framed in revolutionary terms, as they would be after 1789. For the English, revolution was not a drawn-out process that required protection by a "revolutionary army" or a "revolutionary guard." Different groups—the Levellers, the army, the Rump Parliament, and so on—pushed rival theories of government, but there was no expectation that all parties must converge on a single consensus. "It is of unavoidable necessity, that (while the world stands) there will be divisions of Opinion," Nedham insisted.[64] Arguments about the best government for England did not presuppose that history would gradually reveal a new and improved political order.

The one exception to this general trend also offers an illuminating parallel with later revolutions: Barebone's Parliament. Many members of this Parliament were known as "Fifth Monarchy Men." Drawing on the Book of Daniel, they believed that, after the Babylonian, Persian, Greek, and Roman empires, a fifth and final empire would emerge, under the rulership of Christ. For these Puritans, human history had a clear, single direction. In this respect, they resembled modern revolutionaries, who similarly thought that history was headed toward a singular goal.[65]

The Fifth Monarchy Men were not representative of the broader historical (or even theological) outlook of other political actors, many of whom, such as Nedham, took their history lessons from classical authors. Apocalypticism also produced terrible politics. The Parliament of Saints spent months bogged down in arguments and was incapable of reaching any decision. This brief moment in the history of the English commonwealth is such an outlier that it provides limited insight into the political struggles of the day.

But the nature of the Saints' political squabbles merits attention for another reason. According to Nedham, the problem with the Fifth Monarchy Men was that they "judg[ed] all men to be carnal and Antichristian that differed in opinion from them."[66] His pluralist conception, common to political theorists from Aristotle to Madison, was antithetical to a millenarian faith. If the kingdom of God is to come, it can come only in one form and at one time. If someone disagrees with your apocalyptic prediction, not only is their opinion wrong; they become, in your eyes, "Antichristian."

This refusal to accept differences of opinion was also a characteristic of modern revolutionaries. They too believed that history was progressing toward a singular goal. Once you accept that premise, there is little room for negotiation: History cannot be headed in multiple directions at once. Anyone who disagrees with you is not only wrong; they become, in your eyes, a counterrevolutionary.

This kind of parallel has led many historians to conclude that modern revolutionaries practiced a secularized version of apocalypticism. But this is not the only, or even the correct, conclusion to draw. Modern revolutionaries reached a similar endpoint via a different route. The Enlightenment theory of progress, as we will see, was wholly distinct from Christian millenarianism. The point of this comparison is not that one caused the other but rather that one can illuminate the other. The Fifth Monarchy Men were anti-pluralist because they fervently believed in divine providence. Modern revolutionaries became anti-pluralist because they fervently believed that history was proceeding toward reason and justice. This structural similarity does not mean that these two belief systems stemmed from the same cultural origin. But it helps understand the political commitments of modern revolutionaries, for whom revolution occupied a similar place as the Second Coming of Christ. Both were gateways into a transfigured future. Modern revolutionaries thus practiced a kind of politics that was *like* the politics of religious zealots, even if they did not derive their ideas from an identical source. Ultimately, both modern revolutionaries and religious millenarians embraced a form of anti-pluralist thinking to which humans appear particularly susceptible, regardless of time or place.

CHAPTER SIX

Revolution Principles (1688–1760)

THE FIRST REVOLUTION hailed as "glorious" in England is the one that restored the Stuarts to the throne in 1660. "Before his happy Restauration," the Cambridge clergyman James Duport affirmed of Charles II, "in what sad and horrid confusions we were wrapt and involv'd . . . for which ever-glorious and wonderful revolution, as with joyful, and thankful hearts, we look up unto god this day."[1] It might seem like a mere coincidence that the same phrase was used to describe both the temporary return and the ultimate demise of the Stuart monarchy. But Duport was far from alone in hailing the Restoration as a "glorious" or "wonderful" revolution. Many writers celebrated the accession of Charles II as a "happy" or "blessed" revolution, epithets similar to those that greeted the 1688/89 revolution. These positive expressions all underscored the perceived rarity of this favorable event. They also served to contrast the Stuarts' return with the "fatal revolution" that had marked their exit. After the beheading of Charles I, "we were under an anarchy, no government at all in reality," lamented a Royalist historian in 1667, adding how "there are reckoned, during this interregnum, no less than seventeen forms of authority we were under, in the space of eleven years."[2]

There was nothing odd about describing the Stuart Restoration as a "revolution." Indeed, following common usage of the term, it was just as much a "revolution" as had been the founding of the commonwealth eleven years prior. Both ushered in new forms of government, which was the primary, political meaning of "revolution" that translators of Polybius had introduced. It was in this sense that Charles II himself used the term, referring in an address to the House of Lords to "these great Revolutions which of late have happened in that Our Kingdom, to the wonder and amazement of all the World."[3] Unless qualified by a positive modifier such as "glorious," the generic value of such "revolutions" remained mostly negative. In all but exceptional cases, revolutions were associated with disasters. Over the previous decade, wrote William Prynne, having now abandoned the Parliamentarian cause, the English had been "disquieted, vexed, oppressed, tormented with endless wars, tumults, revolutions of Governors and Governments."[4]

The Stuart Restoration was also a "revolution" in another sense—it marked a return to a point of departure. Here some might detect the astronomical meaning of the term, still prevalent at the time. But this circular motion was also part of the original concept of "revolution" in Polybius's original phrase—*politeiōn anacyclosis*, the cycle of constitutions. The Stuart Restoration was both a specific revolution, one change of government, and the completion of a full circle, the "revolution of governments." Having had just passed through no less than "seventeen forms of authority" (an idiosyncratic count, to be sure), the English were now back where they had started.

For these reasons, Charles II could reasonably inform the Convention Parliament that his return would mark a "Restoration both of King, and Peers, and People to their just, ancient and fundamental Rights"—ironically, the very claim that a different Convention Parliament would make in 1688. Indeed, at that later date, one member would insist that the tripartite nature of the English constitution, as defined by Charles I in his *Answer to the XIX Propositions*, had been confirmed by the Convention Parliament of 1660.[5] In truth, Charles II showed little interest in reviving the Polybian ideal that his father had (perhaps inadvertently) espoused. When his Lord Chancellor, Heneage Finch, addressed Parliament in 1675, he referred to the king "and *his* Three Estates"—a clear, if subtle, indication that the king was *not* one of them, but planed above the three estates, like a French monarch.[6] In 1683, following the Rye House Plot (a conspiracy to assassinate both Charles II and his brother James), the University of Oxford condemned as "false, seditious, and impious" the proposition that "the Soveraignty of *England* is in the three Estates, *viz.* King, Lords, and Commons. The King has but a coordinate power and may be overruled by other two." It then proceeded to burn books that suggested otherwise.[7]

Once it was over, the Stuarts did not dwell long on the revolution that had returned them to power. "Revolutions" were something that most people still identified with "the late Troubles," as the preceding decades of civil unrest were sometimes known.[8] What's more, as the legitimate ruler of

England, Scotland, and Ireland, Charles II had few reasons to highlight the role of a revolution in bringing him to the throne. For the rest of the Restoration, revolutions were principally seen as threats. In a speech to the House of Commons in February 1662, the king warned that "I need not tell you that there is a Republic Party still in the Kingdom, which had the courage to promise themselves another Revolution."[9] An unlikely menace in 1662, the real specter of a "republican revolution" would loom later in his reign.[10]

Classical Revolutionaries

The initial response to the revolutions that had thrown England, Scotland, and Ireland into turmoil between 1640 and 1660 was a sense of relief that they were over, and a fear that they might recur. If any further evidence was needed that revolutions produced death and disorder, the Civil War and commonwealth offered it in spades. But as the immediate trauma of those times receded into memory, others ventured a different take on the same past. Revolutions were not just something awful that happened *to* us, like hurricanes (to borrow Nedham's metaphor). They could be planned, prepared for, and carried out. This heretical thought flew against the conventional understanding of revolutions as inherently destructive. But there was, and since antiquity had been, an exception to this rule. Revolutions were a bad idea, yes—unless you were revolting against a tyrant, in which case it could be your best and only choice.

During the Restoration, concerns about tyranny weighed especially on those who feared the transformation of England into a Catholic absolute monarchy. These concerns fixated on Charles II's brother, James, then Duke of York. By 1673, it was public knowledge that James was a Catholic. Worse still, he was next in line for the throne, as Charles had no legitimate children (if plenty of illegitimate ones).

Against the backdrop of a popular frenzy known as the Popish Plot, an anti-Catholic conspiracy theory, Parliament looked for a constitutional remedy. Guided by Lord Shaftesbury, a former chancellor, members of the House of Commons introduced a bill in 1679 that sought to exclude Catholics from the line of succession. In response to this Exclusion Bill, Charles prorogued Parliament. When the same bill was introduced in the following Parliament, he dissolved that one as well, as he would the next.

Once it became evident that James's accession to the throne could not be blocked by constitutional means, his opponents contemplated a more desperate measure: revolution. In addition to plotting their actions, they sought to expose their reasons for such a drastic move. Two of these theoretical justifications of revolution have become canonical. The first is by Algernon Sidney, who paid dearly for his rebellious views. In his *Discourses concerning Government* (published posthumously in 1698), Sidney mounted a robust defense of republican government. Drawing extensively on classical examples and authorities, he also defended taking up arms against a tyrant:

> They who for the most part are the authors of great revolutions, not being so much led by a particular hatred to the man, as by a desire to do good to the publick, seldom set themselves to conspire against the tyrant, unless he be altogether detestable and intolerable, if they do not hope to overthrow the tyranny.[11]

Sidney evidently thought of revolutions as something that individuals could set into motion ("*authors* of great revolutions"), and not just the unexpected jerks of Fortune's wheel. To borrow the historian Keith Baker's distinction, Sidney already understood revolution as an "act," not just as a "fact." In this respect, he sounds distinctly modern. But on closer inspection, it is clear that his idea of revolution was still anchored in antiquity. The "great revolutions" that he had in mind were those that overthrew Pisistratus and Tarquinius Superbus, tyrants of Athens and Rome, respectively.[12]

Tyranny was in fact the one type of government that classical thinkers agreed was so evil that it could warrant a revolution. Aristotle hardly even deemed it to be a true form of government: "Tyranny . . . is the least constitutional of all governments," he pronounced in the *Politics*.[13] Sidney's argument ultimately mirrored claims that earlier English republicans had made to defend their execution of another tyrannical king. In his *Defence of the People of England* (1651), John Milton recalled how "Polybius, an historian of great authority and gravity," had celebrated the killing of tyrants in book 6:

> When princes began to [indulge] in their own lusts and sensual appetites, then [king]doms were turned into so many tyrannies, and the subjects began to conspire the death of their governors; neither were they the profligate sort that were the authors of those designs, but the most generous and magnanimous.[14]

Sidney's endorsement of this revolutionary opinion came back to haunt him in 1683. Caught up in the Rye House Plot, Sidney's unpublished *Discourses* were used against him in court, as evidence of his regicidal sympathies. He was executed, along with eleven other suspected plotters.

One suspect who avoided this fate was John Locke, who had escaped to Holland before he could be arrested. Locke was an obvious target for the royal dragnet, as he was Shaftesbury's secretary (the earl had fled England a year earlier). Had he been captured, prosecutors might have found equally incriminating evidence in his own unpublished work: the manuscript that became *Two Treatises of Government* (1690).[15]

Locke expressed his own justification of revolution in the more modern discourse of social contract theory. At the heart of his justification, however, lay the same loathsome figure as for Sidney: "Wherever law ends, tyranny begins," Locke proclaimed.[16] Because the tyrant breaks all legal bonds with his subjects, and even acts violently against them, resistance—and if necessary, revolution—is justified.

Locke's theory of revolution also exhibited certain modern facets. But the key point to recall is its ultimate purpose. When Locke noted how previous English revolutions had brought back "the old legislative of kings, lords, and commons," he was not complaining. The point of a revolution, at least in England, was not to usher in a new, better government. Rather, it was to remove a terrible government, so that the "old legislative" could be restored. The same held true for Sidney. Everyone knew under which form of government we enjoyed lasting freedom: a well-balanced constitution. You didn't need a revolution to discover that. What you needed a revolution for was to eliminate the tyrant who thwarted this time-honored goal.

Sidney's and Locke's revolutionary arguments gained notoriety in the eighteenth century, and later helped the American colonists defend their own resistance to a "tyrannical" British Empire. They failed, however, to bring about their desired revolution in the early 1680s. Upon Charles II's death, in 1685, James mounted the throne as an openly Catholic monarch. While his reign turned out to be short-lived, the events that removed him followed a different script than the one imagined by these classical revolutionaries.

1689: Rebalancing the Constitution

Towards the end of his reign, Charles II left himself open to accusations of tyrannical behavior. Judges whose political views displeased him were summarily dismissed. Charles arbitrarily detained political opponents, often moving them from jail to jail to elude appeals to habeas corpus.[17] Despite having once hailed Parliament as "so vital a Part of the Constitution of the Kingdom, and so necessary for the Government of it, that We well know neither Prince nor People can be in any tolerable Degree happy without [it]," he ruled without one for the last four years of his reign.[18] But it was his religious policies that many found most frightening. He cracked down on Protestant dissenters (who did not follow the Church of England) and loosened restrictions on Catholics. He himself converted to Catholicism on his deathbed.[19]

James perpetuated these policies, particularly those that favored Catholics. He "dispensed" many of his coreligionists from the Test Act (1673), which required that all officials reject Catholic doctrine. In the name of religious toleration, he issued a Declaration of Indulgence (1687, reissued the following year), which again relied on his dispensing power to permit Catholics and dissenters to serve in public or military office. But when he ordered every Anglican priest in the land to read the Declaration to their parishioners, seven leading bishops (including the archbishop of Canterbury) submitted a petition calling the order illegal. Furious, James sued them for libel, but the bishops were acquitted.[20] He was in the process of dismissing all officials who disagreed with his policies, in preparation for a Parliament stacked in his favor, when in June 1688, his thirty-year-old wife, the Catholic Mary of Modena, gave birth to a son.

For many of James's Anglican subjects, the sudden appearance of a male heir was the last straw. Up until then, James's religion was viewed as a passing nuisance. Next in line for the throne were his Protestant daughters from a previous marriage, Mary and Anne. The prospect of a lasting Catholic dynasty, ruling through a Bourbon-style monarchy, now filled his subjects with dread. The fact that many believed the son to be a "changeling," whisked into the birthing room in a warming pan, added insult to injury.

The birth of James Francis Edward Stuart spurred even conservative lords and commoners into action. Three weeks after the birth, seven English lords invited William of Orange to sail over from the Dutch Republic to defend the rights of his wife Mary, James's eldest daughter.[21] William used the presumed illegitimacy of the new prince to justify his intervention.

The English invitation to William was written by Algernon Sidney's brother, Henry. There was a whiff of revolutionary conspiracy to its style: "Nineteen parts of twenty of the people throughout the kingdom . . . are desirous of change," the lords assured the prince. All that the people were waiting for was a defender "to countenance their rising." We can still catch a glimpse here of the classical revolutionary mindset that Algernon Sidney and Locke had displayed during the Exclusion Crisis.[22]

But William did not wish to play the revolutionary. In his own declaration, stating the reasons for his forthcoming invasion, he posed as a traditional defender of English liberties and the "Constitution of the English Government." While denouncing James in terms reserved for tyrants, William insisted that his overriding objective was only "to have a free and lawful Parliament assembled." This constitutional focus would remain central to William's subsequent statements and actions, even after successfully landing fifteen thousand soldiers on the southeast coast of England, on November 5. This army, swelled by many deserters from James's, soon brought William to London, where in late December he issued the call for a new Parliament.[23] On January 22, another Convention Parliament gathered; less than a month later, it proclaimed William and Mary King and Queen of England, Scotland, and Ireland.

Long celebrated for being "bloodless," the Glorious Revolution that installed William and Mary has come under scrutiny of late for the violence that it did spark, particularly in Ireland and Scotland. The historian Steven Pincus has even claimed based on this reassessment that the Glorious Revolution was the "first modern revolution . . . not only because it transformed English state and society but also because, like all modern revolutions, it was popular, violent, and divisive." He further argues that these features were due to the fact that "James II had not been a defender of traditional society" but rather "a radical modernizer," a second feature of modern revolutions in this account.[24] Revolutions, it is assumed, tend to erupt when an old regime begins to undergo a transformation.

To support his argument, Pincus refers to a "theoretical standard of revolution," which he draws from political sociologists. From a historical perspective, however, this standard is questionable. The 1688 revolution was hardly the first to be "popular, violent, and divisive"—these were already aspects that Thucydides had highlighted in his description of the revolution at Corcyra. The revolutions that rattled and toppled the Roman Republic shared these characteristics as well, and Julius Caesar was the greatest modernizer the late Republic had seen.[25] Even the revolution that claimed the head of Charles I—another modernizer in the French mold—was far more violent and divisive than 1688.

In fact, precisely because James II was regarded as a dangerous modernizer who was bringing foreign methods of state building to England, his opponents perceived and portrayed themselves "not as revolutionaries demolishing the power of the crown, but as conservatives correcting revolutionary tendencies on the part of previous monarchs," as another historian argued.[26] Edmund Burke famously captured this distinction a century later, remarking that 1688 was "a revolution, not made, but prevented"—implying that the real attempt at revolution had been by James. By contrast, for the political leaders of 1688, Burke insisted that "their trust for the future preservation of the constitution was not in future revolutions."[27]

If the political leaders of 1688/89 rejected the mantle of revolutionaries, they did not deny that a revolution had occurred. Unlike the revolutions sprung by Sidney's classical heroes, however, this revolution had no clear authors beyond Fortune or "the Hand of God." Like the defenders of the Stuart Restoration nearly thirty years prior, William's supporters sought to portray this revolution as "happy" and "remarkable," all the while remaining distrustful of revolutions in general: "The Revolutions of State have been so quick and sudden of late, that all prudent Men will be cautious how they try Experiments, which are commonly dangerous and uncertain," noted one observer in 1688.[28] Revolution was still a loaded word: none of the official documents that consolidated (what historians now call) the Revolution Settlement included the word "revolution."

What the Convention Parliament much preferred to emphasize, in lieu of revolution, was continuity. Specifically, it aimed at "bringing back our Constitution to its first and purest Original, refining it from some gross Abuses, and supplying its Defects."[29] There was an interesting tension in such claims: How does one restore a constitution to its "purest Original," while also remedying its defects? This paradox was mostly papered over, as Parliament doubled down on the rhetoric of constitutional restoration. The desire to avoid any appearances of tinkering with an ancient constitution found its most striking expression in the narrative that Parliament fabricated around the king's abdication. As James had "vacated" the throne, Parliament now had the right (even the duty) to choose another occupant. This abdication narrative minimized the constitutional crisis caused by William's invasion and James's flight, and sought to reframe a revolutionary upheaval as an unusual, if ultimately regularized succession.[30]

But in the process of restoring the kingdom "to its ancient Grandeur and Renown," Parliament did in fact tinker significantly with the constitution.[31] Most importantly, it broke with the traditional line of succession by electing new monarchs to the throne, even while the previous king and his immediate successor were still alive.[32] For some writers, it was this overturning of the principle of hereditary monarchy that constituted the real "revolution" of 1689.[33] This would remain the political meaning of "revolution" that Samuel Johnson later included in his *Dictionary of the English Language*.[34]

Other restrictions imposed on these and future monarchs were also new. Before offering the throne to William and Mary, Parliament issued a "Declaration of Right," most of which was later incorporated into the better known Bill of Rights. In this Declaration, Parliament insisted that monarchs could not suspend the execution of a law (suspending power), nor could they dispense any subjects from obeying the law (dispensing power).[35] Kings and queens were also prevented from meddling in judicial affairs: "excessive bail," "excessive fines," and "cruel and unusual punishments" were all prohibited (in language that James Madison later copied nearly verbatim for the eighth amendment of the American Bill of Rights). The offer of the crown to William and Mary was not conditional on their acceptance of this Declaration, though the monarchs gave their assent to the Bill of Rights in December 1689.

This act, along with subsequent others, is rightly viewed as curtailing royal prerogative and bringing about parliamentary supremacy—the ultimate authority of Parliament over legislative affairs. Where James II, in his coronation oath, had sworn to uphold the "Laws and Customs . . . granted by ye Kings of England, [his] lawful and Religious predecessors," William and Mary were made to swear that they would rule "according to the statutes in parliament agreed on, and the laws and customs of the same."[36]

But another way to consider the constitutional reforms of 1689 is to understand them as recalibrating the overall balance of governmental powers. If these reforms mainly targeted the monarchy, that is because this was the piece of the constitutional puzzle that seemed out of place. Focusing only on this one piece, however, can lead us to overlook that the Revolution Settlement took all three constituent parts into account, and aimed for a better distribution of powers across these organs of government. As noted above, one Conventioner reminded his fellow members of Parliament that England was "a mix'd Government of *Monarchy*, *Aristocracy*, and *Democracy*," explicitly referencing Charles I's *Answer to the Nineteen Propositions*.[37]

The Glorious Revolution thus offers a clear example of how classical theories of a mixed government and a balanced constitution helped elevate the English constitution to its celebrated heights.[38] And it highlights how this achievement was accomplished by distributing governmental powers across institutions (see figure 6.1). Rather than concentrating all legislative powers in one place, the Convention Parliament granted them to different bodies, including the king, who retained a veto, and the right to summon and dissolve Parliament. Executive power was similarly shared with Lords and Commons, whose leaders would supply the king with ministers. Even the judiciary power, which was primarily vested in the people (as jurors), spilled over into the aristocratic House of Lords, which served as the highest court of appeals, and to the monarch, who retained the power to appoint judges.

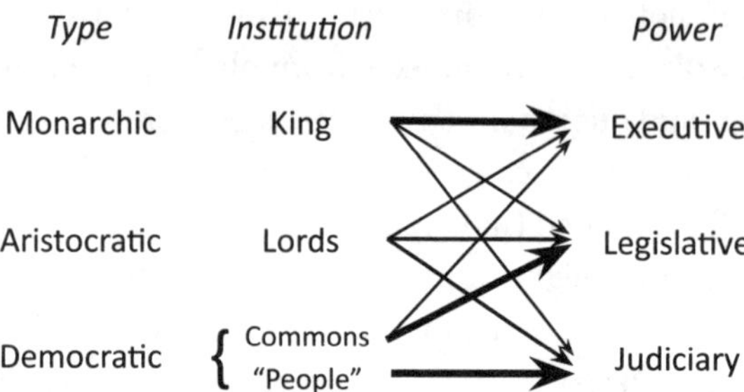

FIGURE 6.1 The balanced constitution and separation of powers.

It is in the aftermath of the Glorious Revolution, then, that we can fully appreciate the particular allure of the Polybian constitutional theory. Rather than instituting a simple one-to-one relationship between executive, legislative, and judiciary on the one hand, and monarchic, aristocratic, and democratic institutions on the other, it offered a dynamic, one-to-many design. And it was precisely this complex system that allowed for its greatest and most renowned feature—namely, the checks and balances among offices. Only by distributing governmental powers across multiple institutions could they interact in a harmonious manner.[39]

What this means historically is that, regardless of the actual reforms enacted in 1689, the English had no trouble believing that they had remained committed to (in Locke's words again) their "old legislative of king, lords and commons." The royal prerogative may have been curtailed, but the tripartite constitution remained firmly in place. Over the next century, the English and their Continental admirers would commend and praise this constitutional arrangement, which was, in Blackstone's words, "so admirably tempered and compounded, that nothing can endanger or hurt it."[40] Its virtues even outshone those of republican Rome. But these virtues were still measured in terms of maintaining the status quo, rather than advancing human progress. The Glorious Revolution thus ensured that the Polybian ideal (if not the original Polybian example) remained front and center in discussions and defenses of constitutional theory. Far from inaugurating a modern age of revolutionary change, it highlighted the powerful hold of classical thought and historical conceptions on Western political actors.

The Constitutional Consensus

The full extent of the constitutional reforms initiated in 1689 became evident only over subsequent years, as Parliament passed additional laws, and political practices established new norms. Anne was the last British monarch to veto a parliamentary bill (in 1708); she was also the last Stuart ruler. Her successor, the Hanoverian prince-elector who mounted the throne in 1714 as George I, ushered in a political sea change. Politicians from the Whig Party took over government from the Tories, some of whom had sought to install James Francis Edward Stuart as Anne's successor.

It was under the aegis of Whig political dominance that a consensus took hold over both the meaning of "the Revolution," as the events of 1688/89 were known, and the unique and unsurpassed nature of the British constitution. This consensus was often referred to as "the principles of the Revolution," or more simply "Revolution principles."[41] The very fact that a consensus existed was almost as important as its content. Many of the high-stakes arguments of the previous century often appeared as if they had been magically resolved, even when they had not.[42]

At the heart of these "Revolution principles" was the belief that the English had uncovered the secret of political stability and freedom. Already under the reign of Anne, both Whigs and Tories employed a Polybian reading of the English constitution to insist on this point. In 1701, the radical Whig John Toland happily remarked:

> All the World knows that *England* is under a free government, whose supreme legislative power is lodged in the King, Lords, and Commons, each of which have their peculiar privileges and prerogatives; no law can pass without their common authority or consent; and they are a mutual check and balance on one another's oversights or encroachments.[43]

This kind of government, he added, is known as "a mixt form" and was especially favored by Polybius. A similar appeal to Polybius and celebration of "mixt Government" also figures in Jonathan Swift's *Discourse* of the same year, where the three pure forms of government are equated with "kings, lords and Commons."[44]

An almost identical view was defended in 1701 by a Tory member of Parliament, Sir Humphrey Mackworth. He similarly applauded how the English had discovered that the "prudent distribution of power" could result in "the Just Balance of the Constitution." For Mackworth, the wisdom of this distribution lay not in granting to distinct institutions the monopoly of a particular political power, à la Montesquieu. Rather, preferring Polybius to Bodin, he argued that it was to be found in the distribution of powers across institutions and the division of sovereignty: "The Absolute, Supreme, and Legislative Authority, (which is necessary to Support all Governments against Contingencies) [is] Lodged (not in One) but in Three distinct Persons or bodies." Only divided sovereignty guaranteed that the different constituent parts could serve as "Checks one upon another."[45]

This distinctly Polybian account of the English constitution, which had been so contentious in the 1640s, had become practically banal half a century later. The essayist and Whig politician Joseph Addison gushed how:

> [He] could never read a Passage in *Polybius*, and another in *Cicero* . . . without a secret Pleasure in applying it to the *English* Constitution, which it suits much better than the *Roman*. Both these great Authors give the Pre-eminence to a mixt Government, consisting of three Branches, the Regal, the Noble, and the Popular.[46]

These classical references were soon de rigueur. The chief architect of Whig power and longest serving prime minister in British history, Sir Robert Walpole, celebrated "the perfection of our constitution," which he argued stemmed from the fact that "the monarchical, aristocratical, and democratical forms of government are mixt and interwoven . . . so as to give all the advantages of each, without subjecting us to the dangers and inconveniences of either."[47]

To highlight this "perfection" of the English constitution, political authors regularly took the Roman Republic as a point of comparison. Hence, Walpole's great Tory rival, Lord Bolingbroke, joined him in admiring how the constitution was a "mixture of monarchical, aristocratical and democratical power, blended together in one system," and in emphasizing the "triple" nature of the English state. "The best form of government must be one compounded of these three," he declared, echoing Cicero's description of a *triplex rerum publicarum*. But Bolingbroke detailed its advantages by contrasting it with the Roman precedent: "What the refinements of Roman policy could not do, hath been done in this island." While Polybius was correct in extolling the model of the Roman Republic, history taught the English that the Romans had failed to balance the constitution wisely. There was "so great a mixture of monarchical power in the Roman commonwealth" that victorious generals could dismiss the sole constraint on the consular office (its year-long term limit) and ultimately bring down the republic. "Rome triumphed, her government flourished; but her constitution was destroyed, her liberty was lost," Bolingbroke concluded. Only when measured against the yardstick of Rome did the greatness of the British model become apparent.[48]

While these comparisons always favored the English constitution over its Roman predecessor, the fundamental insight that informed these "Revolution principles" was still borrowed from Polybius. A well-balanced constitution was the result of (*a*) the distribution of governmental powers across distinct institutions, (*b*) the mixing of pure constitutional forms, and (*c*) the division of sovereign power. Or as Bolingbroke put it, "A balance of the powers, divided among the three parts of the legislature, is essential to our constitution." The secret lay not in simply mixing the three types of government together but in learning "how to fix that just proportion of each, how to hit that happy temperament of them all in one system." If successful, the result should be political harmony; if not, the cacophonous noise of revolution.[49]

At times, the belief that the English constitution had reached its most perfect expression after 1689 supported a vision of historical progress. After the troubles and revolutions of the seventeenth century, the Glorious Revolution launched a new "Augustan" age. But Bolingbroke's example shows how one could worship the English constitution without subscribing to any idea of progress whatsoever. For Bolingbroke, 1689 was a restoration. Weighing in on the debate about "whether the Revolution altered our old constitution for the better, or renewed it, and brought it back to the first principles, and nearer to the primitive institution," he leaned toward the latter. The constitution under George II was basically the same as "our old Saxon constitution." A spirit of liberty had reigned in Britain since the Romans left the island: "As far as we can look back, a lawless power, a government by will, never prevailed in Britain."[50]

This debate was not merely of antiquarian importance. If the greatness of Great Britain (as England and Scotland were known, following the 1707 Acts of Union) was not the result of a serendipitous revolution, then subsequent political thought and action should be purposefully conservative. Bolingbroke cheered the constitution, but worried whether the British could keep it. As Polybius, Cicero, Machiavelli, and others before him, he feared that corruption would destroy the liberty of British subjects, as it had in Rome. Despite his appreciation of "the Revolution," he remained suspicious of revolutions. Beware political changes that seek "to alter, without mending, the government; much less to make revolutions, and suffer by them," he advised. Revolution principles were far from revolutionary.[51]

Montesquieu's Principles: Modern Constitutionalism or Classical Theory?

The most famous statement on the English constitution was penned by a Frenchman, the baron de Montesquieu. The account he provided in *On the Spirit of Laws* (1748) proved so authoritative that even British and American writers such as Blackstone and Madison admired it. His influence on the American and French constitutions of the 1780s and 1790s was especially notable. The very structure of the US Constitution mirrors his enumeration of governmental powers, and the French Declaration of the Rights of Man defined constitutionalism according to his view.[52]

Montesquieu knew England well, having lived there for over a year, and was personally acquainted with Bolingbroke.[53] But he offered a dramatic revision of English constitutional theory, as previously formulated by Bolingbroke and others. Where the English had defined their constitution in terms of the distribution of discrete powers across multiple institutions, Montesquieu collapsed the two columns of this matrix into one. Institutions became identified with a single political power, with the result that powers became bundled and monopolized. They could no longer be spread across institutions, as the distinction between the two ceased to exist.[54]

This collapsing of function onto form is most visible in Montesquieu's choice of terms. In his lengthy chapter on the English constitution, he never once mentions "Parliament," referring instead to the legislative power (*puissance législative*). He similarly describes the monarchic office in functional terms (*puissance exécutrice*). Adopting this language, possibly from Locke, Montesquieu gained more flexibility for the many comparisons in this chapter, which devotes considerable space to political governments other than England's.[55] But its main effect was to render each power indivisible and self-contained. Strictly speaking, the legislative power, in an institutional sense, should enjoy no more and no less than the full exercise of legislative power, in a constitutional sense. The same holds true for the other two.[56]

This one-to-one identification between form and function allowed Montesquieu to make his signature argument. Theorists of the well-balanced constitution, following Polybius, had argued that the different institutions of government could "check" one another because their powers overlapped. In the Roman Republic, the Senate's decrees might have legal status, but could also be overturned by the Plebeian Assembly (or a tribune's veto). Legislative power, accordingly, was shared across these different institutions. For Montesquieu, by contrast, the greatest priority became keeping these powers separate: "All would be lost if the same man, the same body of individuals, either nobles or the people, exercised these three powers."[57]

Many scholars have noted how Montesquieu's schema was an awkward fit for England and may even have been written with a different country in mind.[58] Despite asserting that the combination of executive and legislative power destroyed liberty, Montesquieu accepted that European monarchies that combined these powers were nonetheless "moderate" (*modéré*), so long as the judicial power rested in separate hands.[59] Few English writers would have accepted this definition of liberty.[60] The criticisms leveled at James in the Bill of Rights mostly focused on his usurpations of legislative power. His dismissal of judges was seen as less problematic, and it was only in 1701, with the Act of Settlement, that the king was prohibited from removing judges without cause. In this regard, Montesquieu's argument that the independence of judicial power was key for retaining freedom seems more targeted toward his native France, where judgeships were venal offices purchased for life, and conferred nobility upon their owners. A former judge himself, Montesquieu was particularly familiar with, and proud of, this aristocratic institution.

The English did, of course, grant *some* legislative power to the monarch, as the "king-in-Parliament" formula indicated. Montesquieu did not ignore the king's legislative functions, but grafted them onto the executive power: "It must be the executive power that regulates . . . the time of the holding and duration of these assemblies." Montesquieu insisted that this particular role was essential for retaining political liberty, yet it technically violated the principle of separation. He viewed the king's power to withhold assent (i.e., to veto) in a similar light: "If the executive power does not have the right to check the enterprises of the legislative body, the latter will be despotic." Here as well, the monarch's legislative role is deemed critical for preventing despotism, yet Montesquieu reframes this veto power as part of the executive.[61]

It was precisely because Montesquieu appeared to delineate governmental powers so sharply and emphasized the clear-cut separation of their exercise that he has often been hailed as the founder of modern constitutionalism.[62] He is especially celebrated for having made republican principles palatable for modern commercial societies. But as the above examples indicate (and as jurists have long noted), Montesquieu did not actually advocate for a strict separation of powers. Madison himself recognized that Montesquieu "did not mean that these departments ought to have no PARTIAL AGENCY in, or no CONTROL over, the acts of each other."[63]

If this is the case, then, how different is Montesquieu's theory from older notions of mixed government? While he could be critical of ancient republics, there is no question that classical political thought casts a long shadow across Montesquieu's ideas.[64] What's more, in one crucial respect, Montesquieu was not a modern at all.

This classical legacy shines through in various places but is especially clear in three areas. The first is terminology. Throughout his chapter,

Montesquieu refers to institutional powers by other, suggestive names. He uses “prince” to describe the executive power, “permanent senate” in lieu of legislative power, and “the body of the people” (*le corps du peuple*) for jurors. Most notably, he approves of the division of legislative power between an aristocratic upper chamber (*corps des nobles*) and a “body of representatives” (*corps représentant*), or popular assembly. While this concession aligns his account with the actual structure of the British Parliament, it does not follow from the separation of powers doctrine. Rather, he himself characterizes it as an additional condition meant to “temper” (*tempérer*) the constitution.[65] This language hints at the outline of a tripartite constitution lurking beneath his more “modern” analysis.

It is true that Montesquieu does not explicitly describe the British government as mixed, though as one historian noted, “This is clearly a system of mixed government.” He is less hesitant when discussing other, comparable states. In a later chapter of the same book, Montesquieu uses standard mixed-government terms to describe the Roman constitution under its first kings as “monarchic, aristocratic, and popular,” and then offers it as a harmonious example of how “the three powers were distributed.” The English constitution distributed these powers differently, but the underlying principles are the same.[66]

The American framers dealt with the discrepancies between Montesquieu’s theory and the English constitution by proposing a less literal reading of the separation of powers. If this reading is correct, however, then Montesquieu was essentially restating the classical case for a balanced constitution, which distributed powers across institutions. His comments on the executive’s involvement in the legislative process are another instance of classical influence. What, then, is left of the concept of a separation of powers? Perhaps not much: one contemporary jurist dismissed it as “a sort of conceptual relic henceforth empty of content.”[67]

Finally, Montesquieu’s most important debt to older strands of political thought concerns the role of social classes in his model. As his analysis of the Venetian Republic made clear, it was not enough to assign governmental powers to different institutions. Even if there is no functional overlap among these institutions, the problem in Venice was that they “are formed of magistrates from the same body [*corps*]; this makes them nearly a single power [*puissance*].” Montesquieu alludes here to the fact that only nobles had citizenship rights in aristocratic Venice, so they alone could populate the different institutions of the state. The “body” of the nobility stands in contrast to the “body of the people,” which Montesquieu argues should instead be granted the power of judging. But if the ultimate criterion for the separation of powers is that they be entrusted to distinct *social* groups, then this is really a theory of mixed government in disguise.[68]

In fact, Montesquieu is explicit that the successful balance of political powers in a constitution is conditional on a power-sharing arrangement among social classes: "All would be lost if . . . *the same body of individuals*, either nobles or the people, exercised these three powers" (emphasis added). If the English constitution guaranteed freedom, it was not only because the powers of government were properly separated but because of the balance between the people and the nobles. On these grounds, Montesquieu would not technically have regarded the state that Madison helped found as free, since there was no formal distinction between social classes in the United States. He argued for that same reason that there was less liberty in most Italian republics (where either the common people or, as in Venice, the nobles enjoyed all three political powers) than in modern monarchies.[69] Unless the institutions tasked with exercising the different powers of government were filled by men of different social conditions, there could be no freedom.

Montesquieu thus remained committed to the two basic tenets of classical political thought: the iron law of inequality, and the belief that a good constitution must strike a balance between social groups.[70] Together, these had provided the rationale for a mixed government in the first place. But they are fundamentally opposed to the modern commitment to civic equality. "One can never leave the Romans behind," he remarked in another chapter, perhaps self-reflectively.[71] His most important contribution was a theoretical model that was so abstract that it fit neither the English constitution it was meant to explain nor future constitutions, such as the American, that claimed to embody it. By reinserting social class alongside the balance of political institutions, Montesquieu placed himself in the wake of the "judicious Polybius," whom he drew on extensively. Montesquieu even retained a classical outlook on history: England, like Rome, Sparta, and Carthage, would eventually fall, he averred, as "all human things have an end."[72]

While arguments over Montesquieu's debts to classical thinkers may divide scholars today, they did not preoccupy his eighteenth-century readers.[73] When the Genevan author Jean-Louis Delolme published his influential book on the English constitution in 1771, he showered praise on Montesquieu ("a Man of so true a genius"), and kept much of Montesquieu's terminology, referring to the monarch as the *puissance exécutive* (not *exécutrice*), and to Parliament as the *puissance legislative*. He even followed him in placing "the whole mass . . . of the Executive

Power" in one place, and in considering Parliament as the "legislative body" (*corps législatif*).[74]

But Delolme did not seek to hide that his primary theoretical model was the well-balanced constitution, or the "equilibrium between the ruling Powers of the State." The House of Commons "exerted a privilege in which consists, at this time, one of the great balances [*contrepoids*] of the Constitution"—namely, the impeachment of royal ministers; the aristocracy, represented in the House of Lords, "is destined frequently to balance the power of the People"; the king enjoys "formidable prerogatives," but they are "counterbalanced" by the "privileges of the People."[75] Delolme favorably contrasts the English constitution to classical precursors, most notably the Roman Republic, where the absence of a genuinely monarchic office fueled the ambitions of powerful men. But as with earlier writers, the point of these comparisons was to argue that the English constitution was more successful at distributing and balancing political powers, as well as social groups. The central constitutional matrix was not replaced, only reshuffled. England surpassed Rome because "all the political passions of Mankind . . . are satisfied and provided for in the English Government . . . whether we look at the Monarchical, or the Aristocratical, or the Democratical part of it."[76] Here was a constitutional theory that echoed English accounts. That it was viewed as compatible with Montesquieu's suggests that the former was not seen as striking out in a different direction.

Remember, Remember, the Fifth of November . . . 1688

The constitutional theories that proliferated after 1688 looked to the stability of the British state as proof that "the principles of the Revolution" were unmatched by any prior polity. While their authors extolled the balance maintained in the English constitution, they found its ultimate strength in what it prevented. Revolution was not merely a conceptual risk for British subjects. From the English Civil War to the Jacobite rebellion of 1745, revolution was a clear and present danger, whose consequences were known and feared. The revolution of 1688 loomed so large in English political thought because its constitutional settlement put a close to a half-century of violent and destructive revolutions.

But the English adulation of their government had consequences for how they perceived time and history as well. The vaunted stability of their constitution was not only the result of its prudent balancing of powers: it also drew strength from its perceived age. In the misty distance behind the Revolution Settlement lay the Magna Carta; beyond that, the even mistier outlines of a Saxon constitution. Not all commentators agreed on the exact genealogy of the English political system, but there was a shared sense that "English liberties" were an ancient birthright of all subjects.

For much of the eighteenth century, the English constitution thus inspired a kind of double conservatism. The revolution of 1688/89 had bequeathed England a political solution so perfect that it should be conserved at all costs. Hence the "opposition Whig" or "Country party" criticism of governmental corruption, which could undermine the system from within. But there was a more distant past that was equally imperative to conserve, one on which the present order itself depended. This was the peculiar English history that had made Britain the land of freedom, and distinguished it from the "despotic" monarchies of the Continent. These twin conservative impulses would find their most famous expression in the speeches and writings of Edmund Burke.

The conservatism that attached British subjects to their constitution could also be surprisingly radical. Indeed, some of the most daring opponents of the British establishment made good use of conservative arguments in defense of their cause. The most notorious example was John Wilkes, the member of Parliament who was arrested and tried for his excoriating criticism of then prime minister John Stuart, Earl of Bute. In issue 45 of his newspaper, the *North Briton* (April 1763), he chastised the minister for offering France excessively lenient terms in the 1763 Treaty of Paris, which brought the Seven Years' War to an end. He cloaked his attacks on Bute in strong constitutional language: "Every legal attempt of a contrary tendency to the spirit of concord will be deemed a justifiable resistance, warranted by the spirit of the English constitution," he threatened. The constitutional theory that Bolingbroke and Montesquieu had analyzed was now pressed into political action:

> The King of England is only the first magistrate of this country; but is invested by law with the whole executive power. . . . The personal character of our present amiable sovereign makes us easy and happy that so great a power is lodged in such hands; but the favourite [i.e., the prime minister] has given too just cause for him to escape the general odium.

Wilkes appealed to both the recent memory of 1688 (slyly connecting the Scottish minister to the royal house of the same surname) and the longer history of English freedom to support his charge: "The Stuart line has ever been intoxicated with the slavish doctrines of the absolute, independent, unlimited power of the crown . . . but the English nation was too spirited to suffer the least encroachment on the ancient liberties of this kingdom."[77]

Even when pushing for greater English liberties—Wilkes became a great champion for freedom of the press and parliamentary immunity—many politicians continued to look to the past. Like the parents who taught their children about the Gunpowder Plot (when Catholics nearly blew up Parliament in 1605) by chanting a nursery rhyme, British political reformers also urged their supporters to "remember, remember, the Fifth of November"—except in their case, it was November 5, 1688, the day when William of Orange landed at Torbay. When Wilkes was subsequently expelled from Parliament in 1689, his defenders formed the Society of Gentlemen Supporters of the Bill of Rights. The authority of the English constitution, as affirmed in the 1689 Bill of Rights, could be enlisted to push for political change, and to lead Great Britain back to the future.

It was this "radical conservatism" that so distinguished British reformers from their Continental allies, especially in France. In part, this discrepancy stems from the fact that the French had no equivalent of 1688 to remember. But over the course of the eighteenth century, another theory of history began to take hold among many French authors. According to this model, history was not simply the plaything of capricious Fortune, whose revolutions brought destruction and were to be feared. Instead, history marked the gradual progress of reason, and its successive revolutions elevated humanity to higher planes of social and political well-being. By the end of the century, a new generation of British dissenters and reformers also appealed to this modern doctrine of progress. But by then, the most pressing battle over the meaning of the English constitution had shifted to the thirteen American colonies. The conservative defense of English liberties was soon to be put to its most radical test.

CHAPTER SEVEN

The Last of the Polybians (1764–87)

Who could have thought . . . that the limitation of two senators for each State might perhaps be traced to the "Amphictyonick Council of Greece"?

—GILBERT CHINARD, "POLYBIUS AND THE AMERICAN CONSTITUTION"

"THE BRITISH CONSTITUTION of government as now established in his Majesty's person and family, is the wisest and best in the world," insisted James Otis in 1762.[1] This happy proclamation masked a tense political face-off. The imperial crisis initiated by the Stamp Act still lay a few years in the future, but trouble was already brewing in the Province of Massachusetts Bay. The governor had bypassed the legislature to equip a warship using public funds. Otis praised the British constitution in order to condemn the governor's acts. It was a tactic that the American colonists would hone over the coming decade.

The Americans were immensely proud of "the *inherent* natural Rights of *Englishmen*" that they enjoyed as a birthright.[2] They clung to their freedoms all the more that the neighboring French and Spanish colonists were seen as "the Slaves of arbitrary Power, Popish Caprice and Superstition."[3] So historians have long asked exactly how—and how completely—the Americans abandoned the constitutional frame that protected their rights. Did they "accompli[sh] a revolution which has no parallel in the annals of human society," as Madison later boasted? Or was this revolution ultimately more modest, reverting to Locke's "old legislative of king, lords and commons"—that is, a monarchic presidency, with upper and lower legislative chambers?[4] In short, if the Americans occasionally spoke the modern idiom of progress, were their politics and revolution still classical in style?

The English Constitution in America

When the Americans referred to revolution, they generally had a specific one in mind. "The Revolution," in the colonies as in the metropole, meant the Glorious Revolution of 1688/89. And like their British brethren, the Americans associated this revolution with the establishment of that "wisest and best" system of government, the English constitution.[5]

But it was not obvious how and where the colonies fit into this system. Every colony had its own governor, who was typically appointed by, and represented, the king. It also had its own legislative assembly, elected by landowners. These assemblies in turn usually selected a small number of their own to constitute the governor's council, which served as an upper chamber when the legislature was in session. To some extent, these colonial governments reproduced the balanced British constitution, as it had emerged after 1689. The governor stood for the king, while the assemblies represented the people: here were the monarchic and democratic elements. Because there was no aristocracy in the colonies, however, the council was rarely perceived as wholly independent or even separate from the legislative.[6]

More confusing still was how colonial governments stood in relation to Parliament. Up until 1764, this question had largely been moot. Parliament did not interfere in the government of the colonies, so their inhabitants could sing paeans to Parliament without worrying about its powers.[7] But once Parliament sought to tax the Americans, the question became vexing. A few argued that should the colonists be fairly represented in Parliament, then it could legitimately tax them.[8] This was a marginal view, however, given the challenges of sending representatives to London and maintaining contacts with constituents. The more logical solution, for the Americans, was the one proposed by the Stamp Act Congress in 1765: "The only representatives of the people of these colonies are persons chosen therein, by themselves; and . . . no taxes ever have been, or can be constitutionally imposed on them, but by their respective legislatures."[9] Needless to say, Parliament vociferously disagreed with this vision of home rule, as it asserted with the Declaratory Act of 1766: "The said colonies and plantations in America have been, are, and of right ought to be, subordinate unto, and dependent upon the imperial crown *and parliament of Great Britain*" (emphasis added).

Some Americans held the more radical position that the colonies never had been, were not, and never would be subject to the rules of Parliament. Most of the colonies had been founded during the reigns of James

I and Charles I. It could be argued, therefore, that these territories were part of the royal domain ("dominion") but not annexed to the Kingdom of England (the "realm"). Like the Crown Dependencies in the English Channel (Guernsey, Jersey, and the Isle of Man), they could be construed as the private property of the monarch, who alone had granted them charters of government. According to this logic, the colonists were free to ignore Parliament altogether.[10]

What these various positions had in common was the conviction that their resistance to Parliament's taxation and administration efforts was justified and lawful. At no point before 1776 did the colonists seek a revolution to change their form of government. It was rather in the name of their current government—as they interpreted it—that they resisted Parliament. As with the Parliamentarians in 1642 and 1688, the Americans went to war in 1775 to defend their constitutional order, not to change it. This parallel was not lost on them: "Changing the word *Stuarts* for *parliament*, and *Britons* for *Americans*, the arguments of the illustrious patriots of those times, to whose virtues their descendants owe every blessing they now enjoy, apply with inexpressible force and appositeness, in maintenance of our cause," wrote John Dickinson in 1774.[11] The American patriots, descendants of the earlier patriotic generations that resisted Charles I and James II, were once again defending their old rights and freedoms—except this time, against Parliament.

As with the Parliamentarians of the 1640s, however, this devotion to the status quo limited their options. Legitimate resistance could go only so far before it became treason. This line was unwillingly crossed when George III declared their resistance to be an "open and avowed rebellion," in August 1775.[12] Even then, Americans proved hesitant to take the last step and become revolutionaries. What would make them reject the very state whose constitution they valued so highly?

The Revolutions before the Revolution

The first Americans to become revolutionaries did so unintentionally. In May 1774, Parliament passed the Massachusetts Government Act in response to the mounting opposition in the province to previous legislation, opposition that had culminated in the Boston Tea Party (December 13, 1773). The act revoked the 1691 charter that settled the government of the province. It vastly increased the powers of the governor, who could now appoint most colonial officials. And it prevented towns from holding meetings without express permission from the governor. In response, members of the Massachusetts committees of correspondence issued a call for delegates to form a new Provincial Congress. This congress, which replaced the Massachusetts Assembly (or General Court), first met in October 1774 and assumed the powers of government for most of the province.[13]

While this new organ of government was unauthorized—and from the perspective of the British, illegal—the new congressmen did not assume the identity of revolutionaries. They continued to recognize George III as their lawful sovereign. Astute participants such as John Adams, however, could not miss the revolutionary quality of the events occurring in his province. Even before the passage of the Massachusetts Government Act, Adams had defended patriot measures in the name of "revolution principles." Just as the English writers who had developed this notion, he was referring to the principles of the Glorious Revolution. They were principles that had "been invariably applied, in support of the revolution and the present establishment, against the Stuarts, the Charleses, and the Jameses, in support of the Reformation and the Protestant religion," he explained. In this reading, American patriots defending their liberty were the rightful descendants of the English who had welcomed William of Orange. Addressing his fellow "inhabitants," Adams asserted: "If the American resistance to the act for destroying your charter, and to the resolves for arresting persons here and sending them to England for trial, is treason, the lords and commons, and the whole nation, were traitors at the revolution," that is, in 1688. Just as the Convention Parliament defended its actions as a restoration of the "true" English constitution, Adams insisted that the Massachusetts colonists wished for nothing more than their old charter and liberties. In support of his argument, he even quoted the very passage from the *Second Treatise* where Locke observes that the people have "always kept to [their] old legislative of king, lords, and commons."[14]

The Glorious Revolution thus served both as a foundation for American constitutional principles and as a model for revolutionary action. Indeed, it was largely thanks to the parallel Adams established between the Massachusetts Government Act and the Glorious Revolution that "revolution" entered patriot discourse. In July 1775, while attending the Second Continental Congress in Philadelphia, Adams confided to his Boston colleague Josiah Quincy that "a revolution seems to be in the designs of providence, as important as any that ever happened in the affairs of mankind." Tellingly, Adams did not identify the authors of this revolution; it was simply underway, much as members of Parliament in 1688 recognized that a revolution had occurred. Shortly after the first meeting of the Massachusetts Provincial Congress (to which he was a delegate), Adams wrote to Richard Henry Lee to offer guidance on how Virginia might follow Massachusetts in setting up an alternative government: "A single month is sufficient, without the least convulsion, or even animosity, to accomplish a total revolution in the government of a colony." Adams was using the term here in its technical sense of a regime change, making a point to exclude its unfavorable connotations ("without the least convulsion, or even animosity"). Seven months later, in June 1776, he was congratulating Patrick Henry for "beginning and concluding this great Revolution" by which Virginians had received their new constitution.[15] Other writers similarly recognized the "revolution" taking place in Virginia, as well as in South Carolina soon after.[16]

But only a handful of political actors or observers at the time described contemporary events in the individual colonies as "revolutions."[17] The 1775 *Essay upon Government* printed in Philadelphia affirmed "the lawfulness of revolutions," but again took the Glorious Revolution as its prime example, and did not apply the term to ongoing American events.[18] Adams alone among the Founders, and most of his contemporaries, evoked "the revolutions which are now taking place in the colonies."[19] No one was shouting, "For the Revolution!" on the streets of New York in 1776 (*pace* the musical *Hamilton*).

By June 1776, Adams had extended his diagnosis from the colonies to the continental struggle as a whole. In a famous letter to William Cushing, the chief justice of the Massachusetts Superior Court, Adams announced that Americans were "in the very midst of a revolution, the most complete, unexpected, and remarkable, of any in the history of nations." This statement does not have quite the celebratory ring often attributed to it, when read in context. Adams was in fact complaining of how this revolution caused "drudgery of the most wasting, exhausting, consuming kind, that I ever went through in my whole life."[20] "Revolutions" were still synonymous with "confusions."[21] As in 1688/89, "revolution" for Adams was a short-lived event, a brief interruption in time. Ten days before Congress issued the Declaration of Independence, Adams informed his former Harvard professor John Winthrop that a few "committees will report in a week or two, and then the last finishing strokes will be given to the politics of this revolution. Nothing after that will remain but war."[22]

Based on our common understanding of the term, it may seem surprising that Adams was the first to name the American independence movement a "revolution." But in 1776, "revolution" was not necessarily a radical idea. For Adams, it could be inherently conservative, in the sense that the Glorious Revolution had been conservative: both the American patriots and the English Protestants had launched a revolution to restore their established liberties. That Adams could have spoken of "the last *finishing* strokes . . . of this revolution" in June 1776 highlights the extent to which revolution, in his mind, was as much about continuity as change. To be a "revolutionary" in 1776—a word that did not yet exist in English—meant to stand up for the principles of a well-balanced constitution. Thanks to a century of English constitutional thought, these principles were well known. "A legislative, an executive, and a judicial power comprehend the whole of what is meant and understood by government," Adams had written to Lee. "It is by balancing each of these powers against the other two, that the efforts in human nature towards tyranny can alone be checked and restrained, and any degree of freedom preserved in the constitution."[23] If Adams could assure his Virginian friends that their political revolution was just a matter of a single month's work, it was because the model for a free constitution had already been fashioned by their fellow Britons.

Independence and a Republic . . . but a Revolution?

Of course, it was not Adams's *naming* the American Revolution that brought about the spectacular break with Great Britain in July 1776. The political coup de grâce came from a different source, Thomas Paine's famous pamphlet *Common Sense* (January 1776). Interestingly, Paine completely avoided any talk of revolution (with one exception, a passing reference to the Glorious Revolution). What Paine pushed for in his pamphlet was much more radical than anything Adams would have called "revolution." He proposed no less than ditching the well-balanced constitution that generations of American colonists had so highly praised. Or as he himself put it in an 1806 letter, he sought "to rescue man from tyranny and false systems and false principles of government." *Common Sense* was above all an explicit rejection of "the corrupt system of English government."[24]

Historians often single out Paine's criticisms of monarchy as his most remarkable attack, and for good reason: *Common Sense* convinced hitherto loyal American subjects to reject their king and embrace independence. George III had precipitated this process by proclaiming all patriots to be traitors, fit for the gallows. The full rejection of monarchy may also have been short-lived, as the American disposition for strong executive officers ran deeper than it appeared in 1776.[25]

But equally notable was Paine's frontal attack on the most sacrosanct principles of English constitutionalism. The famed balance of the British government was nothing more than an illusion, he asserted. Paine ticked off the three parts of the well-balanced constitution, before denouncing the king and lords as tyrannical. He then went further and rejected the very idea of checks and balances: "To say that the constitution of England is a *union* of three powers reciprocally *checking* each other, is farcical, either the words have no meaning, or they are flat contradictions." Paine dispensed with this hallowed constitutional ideal by means of a simple biblical quotation: "This hath all the distinctions of a house divided against itself," he sneered, referencing Mark 3:25, and (perhaps unconsciously) echoing Hobbes.[26]

And what did Paine propose in lieu of the vaunted structure of the English constitution? Not very much. In two short sentences, he sketched out a proposal for unicameral state legislatures, with next to no executive office.[27] His suggestion for a continental government was similarly vague, with most of the details to be worked out by a future convention, or "conference." Paine had no patience for the complex and delicate system of a balanced constitution: "The more simple any thing is, the less liable it is to be disordered," he retorted. This constitutional insouciance particularly grated Adams. While Paine did not use the term, his critics labeled his proposals "democratic." It was not meant as a compliment.[28]

Another feature of Paine's political statement that has attracted attention is his historical outlook. At various points, Paine voiced similar notes as the modern evangelists of progress. "Time makes more converts than reason," he announced on the opening page of his pamphlet (though his contrast between "time" and "reason" would have puzzled Turgot). The most resounding phrases appeared in the appendix, added to later editions: "We have it in our power to begin the world over again," he famously declared. "The birth-day of a new world is at hand, and a race of men, perhaps as numerous as all Europe contains, are to receive their portion of freedom from the event of a few months." Here, Paine seemed to foreshadow the kind of modern, even utopian rhetoric that we associate with the French revolutionaries, and with whom he would soon be congregating in Paris.[29]

On closer inspection, though, Paine's historical claims differed significantly from those of Enlightenment progressives. Between the sentences quoted above, he added, "A situation, *similar to the present*, hath not happened since the days of Noah until now" (emphasis added). The new world that he promised was in many respects an old one. If monarchy was an abomination, it was in large part because of what we read in the Bible: "In the early ages of the world, according to the scripture chronology, there were no kings." Paine's simple political prescriptions reflected his account of the earliest governments: "In this first parliament every man, by natural right, will have a seat." If "time hath found us" for independence, it was not because of enlightened or scientific progress, but simply because there were now enough American colonists to sustain a new country. Paine insisted that this moment could very well pass, thus acknowledging that it was not the result of any gradual historical process: "It may not always happen that our soldiers are citizens, and the multitude a body of reasonable men," he cautioned.[30]

In fact, Paine's historical and temporal claims owe less to the modern discourse of progress than to a republican focus on political timing. 1776 was America's republican moment: "Youth is the seed time of good habits, as well in nations as in individuals. It might be difficult, if not impossible, to form the Continent into one government half a century hence." For Paine, history was not leading all civilized societies toward a more rational and just future: every country simply followed its own life cycle. "The present time . . . is that peculiar time which never happens to a nation but once, viz. the time of forming itself into a government. Most nations have let slip the opportunity." The year 1776 was a once-in-a-lifetime *occasione*, to use Machiavelli's term. It had little to do with world historical progress.[31]

This republican heritage may help explain why, despite its frontal attack on the English political system, *Common Sense* was not a "revolutionary" pamphlet. Indeed, Paine expresses many of the traditional reserves *against* revolution. If in the future America cannot count on having "reasonable men" as its citizens, then it may be "a mob" that brings about regime change, for the worst. This distrust of mob violence further explains why Paine avoided the term "democracy."[32] It is also apparent in his curious reference to "Massanello," or Masaniello, the Neapolitan fisherman who in 1647 led a popular uprising against the Spanish viceroy. He subsequently became the authoritarian captain general of the city's commoners—"a king," Paine flatly asserted. Masaniello represented the threat of populist leaders who could "la[y] hold of popular disquietudes," and "collect together the desperate and the discontented," in order to "assum[e] themselves the powers of government." For Paine, the story served as a warning tale: beware the mob that elevates a demagogue to absolute power, as he will then "sweep away the liberties" of the citizens.[33]

Tellingly, Paine likely learned of this incident, directly or indirectly, from Alessandro Giraffi's *Le riuolutioni di Napoli* (The revolutions of Naples). Translated into multiple languages, including English, Giraffi's history was "instrumental in the diffusion of a more starkly political conception of 'revolution' throughout Europe."[34] Where revolution for Adams was largely synonymous with the restoration of a well-balanced constitution, as in 1688, for Paine it still evoked the disorderly and violent transition from one regime to the next. While Paine avoided any explicit discussion of democracies, his allusions to the mob and Masaniello's "revolt" made clear that he shared his contemporaries' fears of an unbridled populace. Today's Americans were virtuous, but as Paine insisted, "virtue is not hereditary." He may have cast aside classical concerns about a well-balanced constitution, but Paine was no modern progressive.

Constituting the States

By 1776, an increasing number of Americans were drawing parallels between their present moment and 1688. Dickinson's analogy between the Stuarts and Parliament was fondly quoted.[35] Few yet described current affairs as a "revolution"—the *Journals of the Continental Congress* make no mention of revolution until the end of 1777.[36] Those who did almost always drew a parallel with the Glorious Revolution. The events of 1688 offered "a precedent which is worthy of imitation. We need no other—we can have no better," argued one pamphleteer in 1776.[37]

But the more volatile and destructive meaning of "revolution" persisted as well. In an important text weighing in on the American war, the English dissenter and reformer Richard Price warned that "an important revolution in affairs of this kingdom seems to be approaching. If ruin is not to be our lot, all that has been lately done must be undone, and new measures adopted."[38] Price did not welcome this revolution, which threatened "ruin" (though he would later come around to applaud it, along with the French). Adams shared his fears. The American politician who was most eager and ready to embrace revolution in 1776 also warned against it most strongly in 1787, ventriloquizing Thucydides's horror at the incident in Corcyra. But this was not an unusual position. Alexander Hamilton, among others, shared his classical phobia, observing:

> It is impossible to read the history of the petty republics of Greece and Italy without feeling sensations of horror and disgust at the distractions with which they were continually agitated, and at the rapid succession of revolutions by which they were kept in a state of perpetual vibration between the extremes of tyranny and anarchy.[39]

Even Jefferson's unusual praise of rebellions that "refresh . . . the tree of liberty . . . from time to time with the blood of patriots and tyrants" is the exception that proves the rule, as this letter was written to protest that "our Convention has been too much impressed by the insurrection of

Massachusets [*sic*]," a reference of Shays' Rebellion.[40] Jefferson's famous phrase underscores the extent to which most other framers were indeed frightful of the potential revolution underway.

The most common explanation among American historians for these apparently contradictory views is that the framers of the 1787 constitution had grown conservative over the course of the war and the first years of the republic. The Articles of Confederation had established a weak federal government with almost no executive power; and the state constitutions were often criticized in 1787 for being "too democratic." The federal Constitution, in this analysis, is seen as a conservative attempt to curb popular participation in government, a "Thermidorian" reaction. More prosaically, the framers are slighted for privileging elite interests and turning against the people.[41]

But historians who interpret the Constitution through an economic lens often overlook how political reasons could lead to the same outcome. Acknowledging that the wealthy and the poor had distinct interests, which both had to be managed, was a central tenet of classical political thought. Failure to do so would not merely result in the redistribution of riches but could spark a revolution—precisely the worst of all political evils. It was not contradictory for men who had just staged a revolution to fear them in the future: as we have seen, the English themselves routinely celebrated "the Revolution," all the while warning against revolutions in general. This was, after all, the Polybian model. Revolutions like those of Masaniello were destructive and tyrannical and resulted in short-lived regimes. Hence, Madison's own critique of democracies as "spectacles of turbulence and contention" in *Federalist* 10. But a revolution like that of the Romans when they expelled the Tarquins, or the English when they expelled James II, was a different story. The distinction lay in the fact that these latter revolutions did not simply exchange one regime for another but put a halt to the Polybian "cycle of governments." They were revolutions to end all revolutions.

It is also important to recall that in 1776, few Americans envisaged anything like a powerful federal government. Adams objected to Paine's cursory treatment of state constitutions, but on the federal level, his own views were quite similar: "We have heard much of a continental constitution; I see no occasion for any but a congress," he wrote in his 1776 *Thoughts on Government*. Like many others, Adams assumed that politics would primarily remain a state-level affair; the federal government should have only an extremely limited jurisdiction over "war, trade, and controversies between colony and colony."[42]

The ubiquity of such views is reflected in the Articles of Confederation themselves, which do not even use the word "constitution." The political organization that it proposed was rather a "league of friendship," on the model of the ancient Greek leagues (art. 3). The decentralized organization of such leagues, which made them a good fit in 1776, would later stand out as a limitation to be overcome. In 1787, Madison criticized "the predominance of the local over the federal authority" in the Achaean League, invoking on that occasion "the authority of Polybius."[43]

Moreover, most of the states ended up adopting constitutions that were closer to Adams's "balanced" theory than to Paine's. A notorious exception was Pennsylvania, which opted for a unicameral legislature, and an executive power distributed among twelve officials, with no veto power. For some, this constitutional model proved attractive precisely because of its novelty, though others drew parallels with an imagined "ancient Saxon" constitution. In the anti-British frenzy of 1776, the well-oiled machine of English constitutionalism had lost some of its shine.[44]

The other new state constitutions, by contrast, divided legislative power between two houses, and in some cases (such as South Carolina) granted the governor or president a legislative veto. The distribution of powers among offices was also modeled on English and Roman precedents. The Massachusetts constitution (largely drafted by Adams) placed the power of appropriations in the lower chamber, as it was in Britain, and it made the governor commander in chief of military forces, as with Roman consuls. Both of these powers would find similar places in the federal Constitution.

In terms of constitutional theory, then, the principles that the framers selected in 1787 had all been clearly articulated and defended in 1776, albeit at the state level. Adams again is an illustrative case. Central to his *Thoughts on Government* was the axiom of English constitutionalism and the most important of all "Revolution principles": checks and balances. The executive power should have "a negative," or veto, over the legislative, insisted Adams, and the judiciary ought to be "a check upon both." Legislative power must also be divided between two chambers, as in Britain, and while Americans had no distinct aristocratic order, Adams argued that the upper chamber would be filled by "the most experienced, accomplished, and virtuous Men"—that is, a kind of natural aristocracy.[45] In short, the best model for state constitutions was the idealized constitution of the state they were declaring independence from.

There is little to support the view, then, that it was "a stroke of political genius" by so-called "conservatives" in 1787 to have "packaged a separation of powers as the essence of true republicanism."[46] The separation of powers—or rather the ideal of a balanced constitution, which often went by this phrase—was the most revered and commonplace principle of English constitutionalism. It was not a rhetorical trick to invoke this concept in 1787; it was an article of political faith. Most critically, it was a principle that almost all state governments (barring Pennsylvania) had either explicitly or implicitly encoded in their constitutions. The preamble to the 1776 Virginia constitution affirmed that "the legislative, executive, and judiciary department, shall be separate and distinct, so that neither exercise the powers properly belonging to the other"; the constitutions of North Carolina (1776, art. 4), Maryland (1776, art. 6), and Massachusetts (1780, art. 30) also called out this founding principle. Even the Pennsylvania constitution explicitly placed legislative and executive powers in separate offices (§ 2–3).[47]

By 1787, the excitement that some had felt (particularly in Pennsylvania) for constitutional novelty had largely faded. Even Paine ultimately turned against the Pennsylvania "democrats" for their populist (and unsuccessful) implementation of price controls.[48] Uprisings such as Shays' Rebellion clearly spooked the political and financial elites, but fears of demagoguery were what had inspired classical philosophers to develop the ideal of a balanced constitution in the first place. A certain contempt for "the mob" was baked into the principles that Adams espoused in 1776, and that found favor with most state constitution framers at that time. The main difference was that, in 1776, there was not yet a sense that a federal government designed along the same lines was needed.

Constituting the State

At the close of his *Thoughts on Government*, composed as a letter to a North Carolina colleague, Adams exclaimed, "You and I, my dear friend, have been sent into life at a time when the greatest lawgivers of antiquity would have wished to live."[49] For many of the Founders, it was an obvious parallel. Not since antiquity had there been such occasions to draw up so many constitutions for new states. Lycurgus, Solon, and Romulus, well known to them through Plutarch's *Lives*, were not simply models, they were practically contemporaries.

Many historians downplay this sense of a connection with the classical past. Perhaps in part because our own, modern education differs so greatly, we forget—or fail to recognize—how immersed in the writings of the ancients the founding generation was. Adams may have been exceptionally versed in the classics, but he was far from unusual.[50] Thomas Jefferson revered Cicero, collecting his works by the dozen, and criticized the 1776 Virginia constitution for failing to live up to the classical ideal of a balanced constitution.[51] Madison once chaired a congressional committee charged with recommending books on political thought to representatives, and selected Aristotle's *Politics* as his first choice.[52] Before he appeared as "Publius," Alexander Hamilton signed a letter as "Phocion," the Athenian statesman (and a subject of Plutarch) who was sentenced to death by a democratic mob.[53]

Such classical learning is often dismissed as "illustrative, not determinative, of thought," and "not the source of political and social beliefs."[54] As we will see, these claims are hard to justify, as the framers drew important constitutional principles, backed by ancient historical examples, from their sources. But by dismissing the importance of the classics, historians can instead celebrate the novelty of the federal Constitution. For the legal scholar Akhil Reed Amar, the ratification process gave the Constitution a democratic legitimacy unlike anything seen in antiquity: "All this was breathtakingly novel. . . . The ancient world had seen small-scale democracies in various Greek city-states and pre-imperial Rome, but none of these had been founded in fully democratic fashion."[55] In fact, there were ample ancient precedents for constitutional ratification. When the Athenians replaced their short-lived oligarchic regime, in 411 BC, they put the new constitution to a popular vote.[56] Similarly, the Twelve Tables of Roman law, while arguably closer to a bill of rights than a constitution, were approved by the Roman people.[57] The American case may have differed in scale but was hardly "breathtakingly novel." The logic behind popular ratification had less to do with modern democratic theory than with corporate governance, a political idea that can be traced back to medieval Italian jurists.[58]

This is not to say that there was nothing new under the republican sun. The very meaning of "constitution" changed in the course of the ratification debates, shifting from an account of the organs of government to the written document itself.[59] Other principles, such as judicial review, also came into being later on.

What of the constitutional contents themselves? One influential interpretation, advanced by the historian Gordon Wood, holds that 1787 marked "the end of classical politics." Wood's justification for this claim is that the American Constitution no longer rested on the balancing of "social forces" but sought instead to keep "various social interests from incorporating themselves too firmly in the government."[60] But this account misses important features of both ancient and American politics. On the ancient side, it reduces classical political thought to the balancing of social orders, ignoring how Polybius and his successors sought to balance political powers as well. The Polybian principle of checks and balances, which the English claimed to have perfected in their own constitution, focused on preventing any single *office* from acquiring excessive power. In part, this balancing act required finding an equilibrium between patrician and plebeian orders, but it also guarded against tyrannical impulses in individuals. It was as much of a political as it was a social balance.

Regarding the Americans, conversely, it is hardly the case that the framers were not preoccupied by social distinctions. In his *Defence of the Constitutions*, Adams asked, "Was there, or will there ever be, a nation, whose individuals were all equal, in natural and acquired qualities, in virtues, talents, and riches?" His reply was unambiguous: "The answer of all mankind must be in the negative." The political corollary of this observation was equally clear to Adams: there is a "natural aristocracy among mankind," which must "be considered in the institution of a government" through the creation of an upper chamber.[61]

Adams obviously did not have a literal, hereditary aristocracy in mind: witness his alarm at the Society of the Cincinnati.[62] But the theory of balanced constitutionalism did not require an actual aristocracy to be effective. For Aristotle, economic differences alone were enough. Still, Adams's full-throated defense of an aristocratic element in the balanced constitution ruffled many republican feathers. In a letter to Jefferson, Madison criticized Adams's work as containing ideas that were "unfriendly to republicanism."[63]

When it came to recognizing the deep and pervasive divisions within American society, by contrast, Madison and others were of a similar mind. At the Constitutional Convention, Madison defended longer terms for senators on the grounds that "in all civilized countries, the interest of a community will be divided. There will be debtors and creditors, and an unequal possession of property, and hence arises different views and different objects in government." Americans did not have a landed gentry, but they were not "one homogenous mass" either. Madison concluded by translating this inevitable social inequality into the terms of balanced government, as Adams before him: "This indeed is the ground-work of aristocracy; and we find it blended in every government, both ancient and modern." If the wealthier class of landowners was not protected from "all classes of people," he warned, the result would be the same as in the late Roman Republic: "An agrarian law would soon take place."[64]

In his famous *Federalist* paper no. 10, Madison suggested that the multiplication of diverse interest groups could prevent any faction from acquiring a majority. Historians such as Wood highlight this Madisonian argument to defend the originality and modernity of the American Constitution.[65] But even in this essay, we see evidence of one social division trumping all others: "Those who hold and those who are without property have ever formed distinct interests in society. Those who are creditors, and those who are debtors, fall under a like discrimination." The wealthy plantation owners of Virginia might have different interests than the financial elites of New York, but they still had more interests in common than with the poor in either state.[66]

What's more, the later, sophisticated Madisonian argument hardly featured during the Constitutional Convention. In his marathon, six-hour speech, Hamilton reduced all social groups to two: "The people are turbulent and changing; they seldom judge or determine right. Give therefore to the first class a distinct, permanent share in the government," he argued, in defense once again of the Senate.[67] He repeated this argument in more muted tones in the *Federalist Papers*, explicitly comparing the House and Senate to the "distinct and independent [Roman] Legislatures, in each of which an opposite interest prevailed; in one, the patrician; in the other, the plebeian."[68] Gouverneur Morris was more straightforward in associating the upper house of Congress with "the aristocratic body," and the lower house with "the democratic."[69] These and other comments underscore how the framers retained the iron law of social inequality doctrine, which Aristotle had outlined in the *Politics*, and which underpinned all theories of balanced government.[70] The wealthy need not be organized in a hereditary aristocracy to constitute their own defined class. Whether or not the framers explicitly identified social groups in the traditional language of mixed government, they sought to entrench them in American political institutions.

Even the fears voiced by the Americans echoed those of their ancient models. Wood suggested that Madison broke new ground when he insisted that "too much democracy . . . led not to anarchy as the classical theorists had predicted, but to a new and unprecedented kind of popular power or tyranny." But far from being "new and unprecedented," this was precisely the "tyrannical form of monarchy" that Aristotle warned could result from excessive democracy, if the people sought to "exercise despotic control over the better classes."[71]

This abiding fear of what the next revolution might bring offers perhaps the clearest sign that the framers continued to practice and profess classical politics. One of Madison's criticisms of the New Jersey Plan was that it failed to "secure the internal tranquility of the States themselves." As Adams in the preface to his *Defence*, Madison reminded the delegates that "the insurrections in Mass[achusetts] admonished all the States of the danger to which they were exposed."[72] Hamilton picked up on this theme in a *Federalist* essay entitled "The Union as a Safeguard against Domestic Faction and Insurrection." He enlisted Montesquieu on the virtues of a confederacy for preventing revolutions: "Should a popular insurrection [*sédition*] happen in one of the confederate states," the philosophe had reasoned, "the others are able to quell it."[73] Here lay one of the great advantages of a federal government, which Hamilton took pains to acknowledge was "in reality not a new idea. It has been practiced upon in different countries and ages, and has received the sanction of the most approved writers on the subject of politics." Where ancient republics had a reputation for frequent revolutions, Madison further noted how "the popular government, which was so tempestuous elsewhere, caused no disorders in the members of the Achaean republic, because it was there tempered by the general authority and laws of the confederacy."[74]

Ancient Greek confederacies in fact helped the framers resolve one of their thorniest problems of all: how to design a legislature for a federation of states. The question before them was not whether to opt for two chambers instead of one. The British model, and a century of English constitutional thought, all but ensured that they would include both an upper and a lower chamber. But how should they divvy up representation between large states such as Virginia and small ones like Rhode Island?

Historians often recount these debates as a series of plans and compromises. Edmund Randolph presented the Virginia Plan, designed by Madison, where states received proportional representation in both houses. William Paterson countered with a New Jersey Plan, in which all states had equal votes in a single legislature. Finally, the Connecticut Compromise restricted proportionality to the House, and granted equal votes in the Senate.

The problem with such narratives is that they leave out the surprising role played by ancient Greek history in these debates.[75] The delegates battled over the respective pros and cons of the Amphictyonic and Achaean leagues (or confederacies), even verbally footnoting their arguments with authoritative texts. Channeling Thucydides, they worried about containing inevitable rivalries between states: would Virginia become the new Sparta, oppressing its smaller neighbors? Would Virginia and some American Athens engulf the rest of the other states in a civil war? There were important lessons to be found in the history of both successful and unsuccessful leagues. Madison used the examples of Greek confederacies to criticize the New Jersey Plan, and to argue for a stronger federal power. His own proposal for proportional representation in both chambers may well have been defeated by Luther Martin's strategic counterexample of the "Amphictyonick Council of Greece," to which each city sent two representatives, regardless of their size, thus guaranteeing liberty for all. The final structure of the US Senate appears to be indebted to this antiquarian debate.[76]

While there were clearly important power relations at stake, the fact that these ancient Greek examples were given so much weight indicates that they were not just rhetorical embellishments. Their histories, moreover, were fresh in the delegates' minds: Adams had just provided convenient summaries in his *Defence of the Constitutions*, and recent translations of Rollin and Mably also helped refresh schoolboy memories.[77] Nor was the political potency of these classical examples limited to the shuttered rooms of the Pennsylvania State House. Madison and Hamilton invoked them at length in *The Federalist* essays to demonstrate the effectiveness of confederations, especially the Lycian and Achaean leagues, "which have best deserved, and have most liberally received, the applauding suffrages of political writers."[78] The lessons that they gleaned from these precedents extended even beyond the crucial matter of federal organization. Hamilton invoked the Achaean League in an essay on executive power, where he cited its decision to eliminate one of its two praetors as an argument for vesting executive power in a single person (a detail that he will have gleaned, directly or indirectly, from Polybius).[79]

Of course, the framers did not restrict their examples to ancient confederacies but grabbed broadly from a cornucopia of classical precedents. James Wilson defended a unitary executive by means of negative instances: the Athenian Thirty Tyrants and the Roman Decemvirs. Hamilton admired the executive power and singularity of the Roman dictator: "Every man the least conversant in Roman [hi]story, knows how often that republic was obliged to take refuge in the absolute power of a single man." Madison also justified the Senate by appealing to the classical past. Athens had only a single citizens' assembly and was in a constant state of commotion. By contrast, "history informs us of no long-lived republic which had not a senate. Sparta, Rome, and Carthage are, in fact, the only states to whom that character can be applied."[80] Madison cited a single authority on the Carthaginian senate: Polybius. It was the only time the Greek historian and political thinker would be referenced in *The Federalist Papers*.

Moderns in a State made by Ancients

In a 1940 article, the Franco-American scholar Gilbert Chinard took an earlier generation of American historians to task for overlooking the immense classical education of the framers, and its influence on their thought. He detailed the many sources that fascinated them, and the many places where these references made a difference. But there was one writer, he contended, who stood out among the pantheon of ancient thinkers: Polybius. Polybius was the hero of Adams's *Defence*, one of the most important sources on Greek and Roman political history for the framers. And Adams himself had argued that Polybius was in fact central to American political thought since the time of Independence. In the *Defence*, Adams explained, he presented authors "whose writings were in the contemplation of those who framed the American [state] constitutions," adding that "all these characters are united in Polybius."[81]

Adams's claim was not unreasonable, and his admiration of Polybius not uncommon. Benjamin Franklin was familiar with Polybius's *Histories*, and sought to purchase an edition for his son in the 1740s. While in France, Jefferson chased down multiple translations of Polybius, which he sent to American friends; he later recommended him to his nephew. Madison referred to Polybius repeatedly in his correspondence and his papers. James Monroe even quoted extensive passages from Polybius on the advantages of the Achaean League during the ratification debate in Virginia.[82]

The impact of Polybius and classical culture more broadly on the American Constitution may seem like a topic of interest only to historians. But it bears considerably on present-day political concerns as well. If the framers found in Polybius the principles for establishing a lasting government, it was because they shared his vision of history. They, too, imagined that the future threats that their constitution needed to fend off would be the same as in the past. They did not hope for or imagine a future society that differed dramatically from the present. Some may have dreamed of a time when slavery was abolished, but none believed that less offensive forms of inequality would disappear. Rather than transforming their world, they wished above all to preserve the state. To be successful, the Constitution had to subsist; it didn't need to be particularly productive. Excessive lawmaking was even viewed as a bad sign by classically minded republicans.[83]

The problem with this conception of politics is that it was soon to face its most serious challenge. What the framers did not predict was the change in how most Americans understood history, and accordingly in what they expected from government. The signs were there for them to see. Adams himself echoed the modern doctrine of progress at the start of his *Defence*, noting how "the arts and sciences, in general, during the three or four last centuries, have had a regular course of progressive improvement." This was a common theme among French and British writers, most notably the two with whom Adams's *Defence* engaged most directly. There was of course Turgot, whose letter on American governments spurred Adams to write his lengthy *Defence*, and who was perhaps the leading French proponent of the progress doctrine; and Richard Price, the addressee of Turgot's letter, who came to recognize the American Revolution as "the most important step in the progressive course of human improvement."[84] Adams became acquainted with Price during his time as ambassador to Great Britain.

But while Adams, like Turgot and Price, recognized how "inventions in mechanic arts, the discoveries in natural philosophy, navigation, and commerce, and the advancement of civilization and humanity, have occasioned changes in the condition of the world," he did not believe that historical progress would upend the art of politics. There might be "considerable improvements" in "the theory and practice of governments," but his examples showed that these improvements came from the adoption and refinement of classical principles.[85] His book did not seek to establish political science on new grounds; rather, it sought to demonstrate the lasting relevance of classical politics to a modern world.

The Constitution of 1787, built on ancient principles and English precedents, was not designed with progressive political ideas in mind. This is not to say that it makes social change impossible: clearly, that is not the case (the Civil Rights Act of 1964 offers an obvious example). But it is more likely than not to leave progressives disappointed. What the framers viewed as checks and balances appear to progressives as congressional gridlock. An oligarchic upper chamber is odious to democrats. Indeed, a constitution that balances social orders and political powers is nonsensical to those who wish to transform and equalize society. And for good cause: the primary rationale of a balanced constitution is that it thwarts change.

Retracing the constitution's genealogy is crucial, then, for recognizing that we are moderns living in a state designed by ancients. Not all Americans are "progressive" in the contemporary political sense, but even most conservatives today subscribe to the modern view of history as a slow, gradual progress toward a better society.[86] We may not agree on what "progress" means, on whether it is currently happening, or on whether we are in a period of decline. But we tend to accept a "soft" theory of progress, promoted by catchphrases about the long arc of history bending toward justice, and by built-in expectations about technological advancement.

Ironically, this modern sense of history was just starting to catch on around the time of the American Revolution, and especially the Constitutional Convention. But if it was in the air in 1787, it did not seep into the framers' conception of politics. For them, "a more perfect Union" was a constitution that prevented *disunion*, which had been the fate of many ancient and early modern confederacies.[87] For us, it has become a statement about improving the conditions of oppressed social groups, as in then-candidate Barack Obama's famous 2008 campaign speech about "a Constitution that promised its people liberty, and justice, and a union that could be and should be perfected over time."[88]

There are glints of this modern discourse scattered among the writings of the framers. Modernity was becoming fashionable, as its name suggests (modern and *la mode*—French for "fashion"—share the same semantic root). But it was still just a fad. Like many of the fads in the early American republic, it was imported. To some degree, it could be found in England, which may have been where Adams picked it up. But its hotspot was the European capital where so many new sartorial and philosophical trends originated: Paris. It was there that the modern wave of revolution would swell, crest, and crash.

Epilogue: A Tale of Two Revolutions

In 1775, Benjamin Franklin received a letter from one of his agents in Europe, Charles G. F. Dumas. Dumas, who helped to promote American interests abroad, celebrated the heightened tensions with Great Britain in excited terms: "Vices grappling with virtues! The dawn of a total revolution in the world! Seven or eight new states directed by providence to recreate the beautiful ages of Ancient Greece!"[89] While Dumas's prose is conventional, his use of "revolution" to describe the American situation, in 1775, was unusual. Even Adams was not yet calling the actions of the Continental Congress a "revolution." For the Frenchman, by contrast, it was an obvious choice of terms. As part 3 will show, the French had been using "revolution" in a positive and progressive sense since the mid-eighteenth century. A revolution, in this enlightened sense, marked the advance from one epoch of world history to the next.

While the Americans often clapped epithets onto their revolution ("mighty" or "great" were popular), they rarely thought about it as an ongoing *process* that would bring about a historic transformation. The American

Revolution might not be completed until the war was over—hence, political actors during this period sometimes referred to "the present revolution." But the events designated by this phrase were firmly in the past. The Americans had *had* a revolution: they had changed their government. As Adams put it, all that was left then was the war, which would determine whether the revolution had been successful. This understanding is on clear display in one of the earliest official documents to use the term, the *Observations on the American Revolution* (1779). Written by Gouverneur Morris, this document is notable for its sparing references to "revolution," a word which appears only on its first and last pages. In the final sentence, Morris offers thanks to God "for providential favor during the *late* revolution." Already in 1779, the American Revolution, as a political event, lay behind them.[90]

Soon, however, the Americans had to confront an uncanny event from across the Atlantic. The French proclaimed their political actions to be a "revolution" from the very start. But despite this now-familiar term and similar effects (a change in government), the French Revolution was in many respects unrecognizable to most Americans. To Adams, it offered "a spectacle so novel . . . that I have ever acknowledged myself incompetent to judge of it, as it concerned the happiness of France, or operated on that of mankind." But he did recognize that it seemed to flow from a different source: "I know that encyclopedists and economists, Diderot and d'Alembert, Voltaire and Rousseau, have contributed to this great event more than Sidney, Locke, or Hoadley, perhaps more than the American revolution."[91] In the French events, Adams recognized a set of "revolution principles" that was strikingly different from any that the Americans had expressed. Burke, who derided the "the newest Paris fashion of an improved liberty," would soon draw the same distinction in his 1790 *Reflections on the Revolution in France*.[92]

Comparisons between the American and French revolutions tend to rest on moral judgments. The Americans are praised for their moderate, measured actions, while the French are chided for utopian exuberance.[93] The evidence for these historical verdicts generally comes down to body counts. The superiority of American moderation is demonstrated by the patriotic treatment of loyalists and prisoners, compared with the French trigger-happy recourse to the guillotine.

But historians have demolished this myth of a peaceful American Revolution, which now appears just as bloody, vicious, and illiberal as the French. Some of the worst violence took place before the revolution officially occurred. Sons of Liberty enforced trade boycotts with extreme measures, publicly shaming violators, and forcing them to confess their misdeeds from beneath the gallows. Those who refused were tarred and feathered, which may sound innocuous, but was a painful form of torture. Offenders were stripped naked, and had hot pitch poured all over their bodies, causing severe burns. Others were whipped to within an inch of their lives. "Committees of safety" spied on private correspondence and suppressed loyalist newspapers and presses. French historians typically point to similar actions in France as prefiguring the Terror of 1793.[94]

Once war broke out, the violence between patriots and loyalists became even more unhinged. Many loyalists were imprisoned for their political views, often in atrocious and lethal circumstances. Like the French émigrés, some who fled to British safety had their estates confiscated and faced capital punishment, if they returned to claim them. In addition to tarring and feathering, loyalists could be forced to straddle a spiked fence rail that was carried around town for hours (euphemistically known as "rail riding"). Violence against them might be limited to sadistic shaming; it could also end with the offenders dangling at the end of a rope. Colonel Charles Lynch, whose surname became an infamous verb, was a militia officer known for his extrajudicial executions of loyalists in Virginia.[95]

The war itself was marked by more instances of horror and terror. Both sides ignored the laws of war on multiple occasions, slaughtering prisoners even after they had surrendered. American forces, on Washington's orders, razed over forty Iroquois villages, leading to the death of hundreds by starvation. Prisons could be deadlier than battlefields, with British prison ships being particularly lethal.[96]

For the most part, then, the "terrors" (as some called them at the time) of the American Revolution were not qualitatively all that different from those that marked the French. The August 1, 1793, decree by the National Convention that instructed soldiers to take no "Hanoverian" prisoners appears less unprecedented in comparison. The mass imprisonment of political suspects calls to mind similar American practices against loyalists. Even the destruction of rebel towns in the Vendée echoes the treatment of Iroquois by continental forces.[97]

The point of these comparisons is not to suggest that the French modeled themselves on the Americans. It is rather to highlight what all revolutions have in common, and what is distinctive about modern ones. The forms of violence shared by the American and French Revolutions are precisely what political writers since Thucydides had warned about. Revolutions have always been savage affairs. The English Civil War saw more death and destruction, on a per capita basis, than Britain did in World War I. Violence alone is not a helpful criterion for classifying revolutions.

It is when we descend into greater detail, however, that the particularities of modern revolutions come into view. There are some things that the democrats in Corcyra or the patriots in Virginia never did. Or rather, it is not so much what they did, but to whom they did it. What stands out in the French case, as it would in the many modern revolutions to come, is the fact that the revolutionaries went after *one another* with the same vehemence as they did their opponents. The laws used to punish émigrés and rebels were also used to prosecute political rivals. This kind of political repression was not more violent than the actions taken against overt enemies of the revolution. What was distinctive was rather the blurring of categories. Fellow revolutionaries turned into counterrevolutionaries. Rivals became enemies.

Why did the French revolutionaries target one another, while the Americans (and their English predecessors) did not? How big a difference was there between Philadelphia in 1787 and Paris in 1789? Culturally, politically, and socially, they were clearly worlds apart. But with respect to the outcomes of their respective revolutions, the most significant difference arguably lay in their understandings of "revolution." The idea of revolution that prevailed in France even before 1789 had made it an object of veneration, one that required defense and direction. Instead of marking the brief transition between regimes, revolutions opened a window in history through which society could pass into a better future. It was this Enlightenment dream that the people of France brought to life in 1789.

PART III

Modern Times

Je suis tombé par terre, c'est la faute à Voltaire.

—VICTOR HUGO, *LES MISÉRABLES* (1862)

A YEAR BEFORE his death in 1778, Voltaire wrote to Catherine the Great to applaud her political reforms in Russia. Except he used a different word: "Many other rulers are making similar changes to the laws of their countries. This revolution will stretch all the way to Rome and the inquisitorial lands. A new century will be born and you will be its creator."[1] Clearly, Voltaire did not have the classical, Polybian concept of revolution in mind here. He celebrated the innovations brought about by the tsarina, rather than warning her against the threat of historical change. And he looked forward to a future that was vastly different than the present—a new age—not just a repeat of past trends. This was not John Adams's idea of revolution. So where did it come from?

Historians often look to the French Revolution itself as the event that transformed our understanding of "revolution." The famous exchange between Louis XVI and the duc de La Rochefoucauld-Liancourt seems to capture the new meaning attached to this term. Informed of the storming of the Bastille, the king is said to have exclaimed, "It's a revolt!" to which the duc replied, "No, Sire, it's a revolution."[2]

As Voltaire's quote reminds us, however, the use of "revolution" to designate a "world-historical event," or "epoch-making cultural change" was already current before 1789.[3] To be sure, Voltaire did not associate great revolutions with mass action. In his usage, the agents of revolution were more likely to be philosophers or monarchs than crowds. The result, however, was similar: a historic break with the past, in the name of a better, fairer, and even freer future.

What caused this revolution in the history of "revolution," and when did it occur? In the late 1770s, this new meaning was still fairly recent.

Voltaire himself had regularly used the term in a classical sense earlier in his career. He concluded his 1756 *Essai sur l'histoire générale* with a mournful lament: "I have gazed upon the vast theater of revolutions that the entire Earth has witnessed since the age of Charlemagne. What did they amount to? To destruction, to the death of millions. Every great event has been a great disaster."[4] For the middle-aged Voltaire, revolutions still corresponded to the capricious and deadly turns of Fortune's wheel.

The following two chapters trace two major developments in French Enlightenment thought that made it possible for Voltaire and others to exchange a vision of revolution as devastation for one of revolution as improvement. The first was a shift in historical and political thinking that came out of the famous Quarrel of the Ancients and Moderns. Writers who championed the superiority of the moderns over the ancients put forward a theory of historical progress to buttress their claims. In their account, progress was gradual, driven by slow improvements of human reason and knowledge. This Modern perspective rejected the Ancient view of human history as chaotic and repetitive. Where the future, for the Ancients, was no more than a remixed version of the past, for the Moderns it became rife with possibility and scintillating unknowns. There may have been a touch of Christian millenarianism or golden age utopianism in the more extravagant modern visions of the future, but the mechanism for reaching this promised time was markedly different. The new and improved world of tomorrow, for the Moderns, was the direct result of gradual progress over centuries, not a Messianic interruption in human time (as in Christian apocalypticism).

This Modern, optimistic vision of human history also led French thinkers to reconsider the merits of a well-balanced government. If the goal of political thought was no longer to prevent revolutionary change, but to welcome it and even to ease its progress, then the checks and balances of a tempered constitution became a hindrance, not a help. Authors who argued strongly for the Modern idea of progress—such as the abbé de Saint-Pierre, the marquis d'Argenson, and Turgot—all attacked the classical solution and pushed for more centralized, unalloyed forms of government.

The second important shift is one that Voltaire himself was largely responsible for. He recognized that some revolutions could bring about positive change—only these were typically revolutions in culture, not governments. In his history of Louis XIV, he credited the great cultural achievements of that age to a "general revolution" that rivaled those of Periclean Athens, Augustan Rome, and the Italian Renaissance. Soon he was heralding the French Enlightenment itself as another such revolution.

It was this identification of revolution with cultural progress that allowed Voltaire and others to reintroduce the term to the political realm and flip its value. The writer Louis-Sebastien Mercier, for instance, combined this new, positive meaning of "revolution" with the modern theory of rational progress in his best-selling novel, *The Year 2440*. Here the revolution to come lay far in the future, as the inevitable result of the gradual advance of Enlightenment. As with Voltaire, the prime mover of revolution in Mercier's novel was not the crowd, but a king. Even after the people stormed back onto the stage of revolution in 1789, enlightened leaders would seek to incarnate the meaning and movement of revolutionary history.[5]

CHAPTER EIGHT

The Progress of History

WHEN CONSIDERING THE "obvious and ridiculous falsehoods" that riddled Greek myths, the philosophe and academician Fontenelle made a surprising claim: "There was also philosophy in those backwards times [*ces siècles grossiers*]," he announced in his 1686 essay "On the Origin of Fables." The minds of our distant ancestors—as those of other, non-European peoples—were no different than our own: they were simply clouded by "ignorance and barbarism." Their understanding of the world was limited and warped, but they sought to make sense of it in the same ways as we do. What another French academician, Claude Lévi-Strauss, later called *la pensée sauvage* ("savage thought") was no different, fundamentally, than modern philosophy: "How is it that this river flows incessantly, a contemplative mind must have asked in those centuries? A strange sort of philosopher, but who could have been a Descartes in our own times."[1]

Earlier Europeans confronting the strange musings of non-Western peoples had occasionally resorted to cultural relativism, in an effort to challenge the more widespread assumptions of Western supremacy. Montaigne questioned whether the cannibals of Brazil were any more "savage" than his own countrymen, who were then massacring one another in vicious religious wars.[2] But Fontenelle chose a different approach: what distinguished the "contemplative" savage from Descartes was, in a word, time: "We would be very mistaken . . . if we were surprised that Philosophy and reasoning, which for many centuries were so backwards and so imperfect, still made such slow progress today."[3] Had the primitive philosopher been born some centuries later—and, no doubt as importantly, been born French—his same curiosity might have led him to the truth.

Fontenelle's argument would be refashioned over the eighteenth century into a doctrine of historical progress. Unlike Christian millenarianism, the doctrine of progress emphasized gradual improvement rather than sudden transformation. As the philosopher Hans Blumenberg pointed out, progress entails a "relation between the quantum of time and the quality of achievement."[4] It was a matter of *chronos*, not *kairos*, to borrow the Greek contrast between different temporalities.[5] There may have been some classical and early-modern precedents to this mode of historical thinking, but it acquired its modern form and a broad base of support in the age of Enlightenment.

Fontenelle's comparison between the primitive philosopher and Descartes was intended, in part, to redeem the thinkers of the distant past or far corners of the globe. But unlike Montaigne's relativism, it also served to elevate modern Western thought above those efforts. Acknowledging similarities in mental operations between primitives and modern Europeans ultimately served as a backhanded compliment for the former.

As Europeans extended their dominance over the rest of the globe, it was the geographical implications of Fontenelle's comparison that garnered the most interest. The idea of progress served to justify Europe's "civilizing mission," as the peoples of Algeria, India, or China were left to linger in the "waiting room of history" until their primitive philosophies had matured to Cartesian levels.[6]

For his own part, Fontenelle was likely less concerned with justifying European colonization than with winning a literal academic quarrel. In 1687, Claude Perrault had read a poem at the Académie française—of which Fontenelle was a member, along with the Academy of Sciences and the Academy of Inscriptions and *Belles-lettres*—that insisted that modern Europeans had surpassed their ancient predecessors. Admirers of the classics, such as Boileau, had a fit: the serene assembly nearly came to blows, and the Quarrel of the Ancients and the Moderns took off.[7]

For the most part, the stakes of this quarrel are hard to fathom today. Defenders of the ancients were quick to recognize that the moderns had made remarkable strides in the fields of medicine and science, while defenders of the moderns agreed that in literature, rhetoric, and art, they would settle for a draw. But the historical importance of the quarrel lies precisely in how it led French academics—later followed by Idealist philosophers and Marxist revolutionaries—to rethink the very shape of history.

Indeed, the idea of progress challenged the main understanding of history that had prevailed since antiquity. Where classical authors had insisted, often pessimistically, that revolutions would remain violent and destructive "as long as the nature of mankind remains the same," as Thucydides phrased it, the "prophets of progress" promised a future that was incrementally better than the past.[8] "Better," in their view, was an objective and universal standard. All peoples were slowly advancing toward the same endpoint. Progress was epistemological, even more than technological. We might acquire airplanes, refrigerators, and telephones, but the real progress was in our minds. Slowly but surely, we would become more reasonable and reach the truth.

In the next chapter, I explore how this modern cosmology of human time led to a new idea of revolution. But before considering its effects, let us examine its emergence. How did the modern doctrine of progress come about? How did it overcome long-lasting, classical beliefs about the nature of human history? And what were its implications for political thought? As we will see, progress was a controversial idea, with as many critics as true believers. Its early adopters may well have harmed its popularity, instead of helping it. And while many in the eighteenth century remained unconvinced, a series of historical and cultural events from the 1760s to 1780s ultimately gave progress a good name. By the time the French Revolution erupted, it was hard to resist the impression that history was on the march—and for an increasing number of people, that it was headed in the right direction.

Project Progress: The Abbé de Saint-Pierre

One of Fontenelle's main allies in the Quarrel was a fellow Norman, the abbé de Saint-Pierre. The youngest son of an old aristocratic family, his religious service had little to do with faith. Unfit for military service, his Jesuit education paved the way for a career in the Church. But like many *abbés* in French intellectual circles, he spent far more time in the *salons* of cultivated Parisian aristocrats than in the pews.[9]

Remembered today for his project on perpetual peace, Saint-Pierre also articulated the first full-blown modern theory of progress. Previously, most scholars held that the human race was already in its senescence. But Saint-Pierre calculated human time differently. Assuming that a thousand years was the equivalent of one year for the human race, he declared that humanity was only seven or eight years old. At this rate, we would reach adulthood in another thirty or forty centuries.[10]

Underpinning this argument was Saint-Pierre's claim that humanity was consistently gaining in reason and had been "progressing in wisdom" since the time of Plato.[11] Saint-Pierre acknowledged that progress could be slow, and suffer setbacks from civil wars, religious superstition, or jealousy between nations. It was precisely because progress was slow—and not that time now seemed to be accelerating—that it was easy to miss. But in the long run, memory and the accumulation of learning ensured that human reason would perpetually increase.[12]

What stands out in Saint-Pierre's conception of time is not its conclusion. The adulthood of humanity lay many centuries away, even if in another essay, he foreshadowed the utopian thinker Henri Saint-Simon and declared that "we are approaching the start of the golden age."[13] Progressive thought would long remain torn between the assertion of gradual improvement and the dream that a perfect future lay just over the horizon.

A century later, when the German philosopher G.W.F. Hegel gave the theory of progress its canonical expression, he largely ignored his eighteenth-century predecessors, and instead compared the progress of reason to the Christian notion of divine providence. As we saw, many scholars still view Christianity as the main source of inspiration for the theory of historical progress. But if we return to Saint-Pierre's original formulation, it is clear that Christian ideas of time did not play a role in its genesis.[14]

Saint-Pierre was not an apocalyptic or even millenarian thinker. If the golden age of humanity—a classical motif, drawn from pagan mythology—lay ahead of us, it was not thanks to any messianic interruption of time, but rather to the gradual accumulation of knowledge and inventions on earth. Saint-Pierre may have received from the Jesuits a rosier view of human nature than the Augustinian one espoused by the Jansenists.[15] But even this cheery outlook does not translate into a theory of rational growth. Saint-Pierre's ideas were profoundly secular, in both senses of the term. They derived from debates over a secular (as opposed to spiritual) matter—namely, the relationship between ancient and modern cultural output—and they rested on a perception of human (as opposed to divine) temporality, the *saeculum*.[16]

Nor was Saint-Pierre's idea of progress providentialist, in the general Christian sense that "God intervenes in human history." The gradual improvement and accumulation of knowledge have nothing to do with a divine plan. When progress is impeded by "obstacles," there is no hidden benefit to these delays. The roadblocks on the road to "universal reason" are not part of God's plan: Saint-Pierre was no Leibnizian. When progress is impeded, that is simply a bad thing, with no hidden, redeeming merits.[17]

This Modern view of history also had major ramifications for how writers and political figures thought about revolution and government. In a Polybian universe, where history was repetitive and political change was mostly regarded as disruptive and destructive, it followed that the best form of government was one that brought about the longest stability. But once political theorists abandoned the vision of history as a directionless flow, the classical solution of designing a state to best withstand the ravages of time lost its rationale. If time was a vector extending in a single upward direction, new political solutions were needed. Temporal progress should be assisted by political reforms—that is, by progress in the political domain. If a better future beckoned, then it no longer made sense to postpone its arrival. The careful constitutional mixture of governmental powers and social classes that served as an internal system of checks and balances to prevent future revolutions began to lose its appeal.

This tight connection between historical and political thought is evident throughout Saint-Pierre's writings. There were measures we could take to ensure progress and prevent delays, he insisted. The most important action was to improve our knowledge of political science. Indeed, for Saint-Pierre the greatest differential between societies, on the scale of progress, was how much they invested in political thought. His own famous project for perpetual peace in Europe by means of a supranational arbitration court was one important step in this direction. Another was his project on "polysynody," a kind of aristocratic bureaucracy in which councils replaced ministers, and with which the regent Philippe d'Orléans briefly experimented.[18]

But perhaps Saint-Pierre's most interesting—even revolutionary—project was the one that directly challenged the traditional preference for a balanced government. He proposed filling administrative positions through a particular kind of election (*scrutin*). Groups of thirty experts, chosen by the royal ministries, would select three of their own to occupy important governmental roles; the king would then choose from among those selected. For Saint-Pierre, this plan was meant to strengthen the monarchy. There were, in his view, no limits to the power that should be granted to a rational government, which could even be despotic. The march of reason must proceed unchecked. Despite its apparent mixing of governmental forms (elsewhere he calls it an *aristo-monarchie*), his proposal was part of a larger critique of balanced government, or "divided power." Saint-Pierre claimed to be defending an undivided or "pure" form of monarchy, which remained the ultimate source of sovereignty. But with respect to government, his theory can be seen as a step in the direction of democracy.[19]

The Politics of Progress: D'Argenson and Democracy

It is precisely in that democratic direction that his friend and self-professed disciple the marquis d'Argenson pushed these ideas. D'Argenson was a school friend of Voltaire's, and a member of the Club de l'Entresol, which Saint-Pierre hosted. This club served as an important network for developing and disseminating early Enlightenment ideas. In a widely circulating manuscript entitled "To What Extent Can Democracy Be Admitted into a Monarchic Government" (1737), d'Argenson advanced a similar argument to Saint-Pierre's elections. He proposed replacing most administrative posts and offices with elected officials ("popular magistrates"). Unlike Saint-Pierre, d'Argenson called this effort by its proper name: his ambition was to create a "monarchic democracy." While the administration or government he proposed was largely democratic, he, too, insisted that sovereignty would remain "decisively" with the king.[20]

This combination, like Saint-Pierre's "aristo-monarchie," might seem like a kind of balanced constitution, but d'Argenson came out strongly against the Polybian tradition. Indeed, the opening chapter of his treatise is an explicit critique of Polybius and his ideal tripartite government (which d'Argenson saw reflected in England). Like Jean Bodin before him and Jean-Jacques Rousseau after him, d'Argenson insisted on distinguishing between sovereignty and government. Sovereignty could be monarchic and government, democratic, but this did not mean that the constitution was mixed. Both forms of government and sovereignty, respectively, should be as pure as possible. D'Argenson thus reversed the Polybian claim that all pure forms degenerate over time by countering that it was the supposedly well-balanced constitution that was, in fact, unbalanced.[21]

The recovery of democracy as a positive and desirable form of government thus took, as a first step, the rejection of the balanced constitution as a political ideal. But both of these steps rested on a wholly different understanding of human time. D'Argenson shared Saint-Pierre's "perfectionist" outlook on history: he, too, emphasized the need to renew political science in order to "perfect" the state. To assist historical progress, we must improve our own governments.[22]

Given Saint-Pierre's notoriety in Enlightenment circles, and d'Argenson's personal connections with the philosophes, one might assume that their ideas would have been well received. In fact, the generation of philosophes beginning with Voltaire and Montesquieu largely rejected the modern case for historical progress and sided with defenders of the ancients.[23] Against the modern story of gradual improvement, they advanced historical accounts that featured occasional moments of glory followed by extended periods of stagnation. Different states briefly rose to prominence at different times. The greatness of these epochs was due to not inevitable progress but sudden strokes of "genius": "There are times when in just a few years men perfect the arts and occupations they had fruitlessly been cultivating for centuries beforehand," affirmed the abbé Dubos, a prominent defender of the ancients, and one of Voltaire's historiographical models.[24] Here was *kairos* (albeit of a human kind) triumphing over *chronos*. Moreover, these moments of cultural flourishing were typically short-lived, and followed by long periods of decline, even "barbarism."[25]

Promoters of the ancients typically envisaged history as the serial displacement of a center of learning and power. The greatness of Athens under Pericles was matched only by that of Rome under Augustus, and then Italy in the Renaissance. This was a medieval commonplace, with ancient roots, known in Latin as the *translatio studii et imperii*, "the shifting of knowledge and power." Its strength was that it explained the rise, but also the fall of great civilizations. All the arts and sciences may have come from Egypt, but what was Egypt today? A desert littered with ruins. History understood as *translatio* followed the path not of progress but of perambulation. It might have a vague geographical direction, from East to West, but later centers were not necessarily better than those that came before. Many believed that Europe was still inferior to some of the great civilizations of the past. More importantly, all civilizations were impermanent. A great leader could bring back the golden age, but another age of iron lurked around the bend.[26]

Given their resistance to the modern idea of progress, the philosophes similarly rejected modern takes on political change. Commenting on Saint-Pierre's project for perpetual peace, Rousseau concluded that it would take a revolution to introduce the kind of federation the abbé proposed. Under these conditions, was it worth the risk? Rousseau himself warned that such a revolution could do more harm than the federation would prevent over time.[27] Voltaire was even blunter, mocking the abbé's zeal for "projects" and calling him "part philosopher, part lunatic."[28]

D'Argenson's ideas did not fare much better. A decade after his manuscript began to circulate, Montesquieu penned one of the most vigorous and famous defenses of the separation of powers, celebrating the English constitution that d'Argenson had snubbed. The sole mention of d'Argenson's popular magistrates in the *Encyclopédie* was negative.[29]

The Minister of Modernity: Turgot and Reason

But one philosophe picked up the torch of the Moderns and spread their historical and political arguments more successfully: Anne-Robert-Jacques Turgot. As a student, Turgot had delivered a famous lecture at the Sorbonne on the “ongoing progress of the human spirit” (1750). This text, published posthumously (in 1781), argued that the apparent confusion of human history masked an upward trend. Progress was slow, it could suffer setbacks, but in the long run we were always headed toward “ever greater perfection.”[30]

This historical vision led Turgot to consider revolutions in a new light. This different perspective is already on display in his famous *Encyclopédie* article, “Fondation” (1757). The point of a foundation, he argued, was to pursue a specific goal in perpetuity by means of an endowment. Like the well-balanced constitution, a foundation was thus designed to thwart historical change. For Turgot, this attempt to force future generations to abide by the desires of the past imposed the wishes of the dead over the living. Not only was this unnatural and undesirable but it rested on a wrong-headed understanding of history. Foundations protected their funds from the “revolutions of time,” whereas in reality, revolutions brought about changes that might make the original purpose of the foundation obsolete, even harmful. Far from being something to avoid, revolutions for Turgot were inevitable, even desirable.[31]

When he became the controller-general (i.e., minister) of finances in 1774, Turgot sketched out a proposal for the political future of France that was just as revolutionary as—and bore numerous resemblances to—Saint-Pierre’s and d’Argenson’s projects. Known as the “Memorandum on Municipalities,” and ghostwritten by his collaborator Samuel du Pont de Nemours, this proposal suggested electing “municipal assemblies,” which (like d’Argenson’s popular magistrates) would oversee administrative issues dealing with taxation, social welfare, and other local needs. Assembly members would consist of landowning citizens, with a complicated system of fractional citizenship for those earning under a minimal threshold. Above these assemblies would sit provincial ones, and at the top would be a “general municipality,” which would provide information directly to the king and his ministers about the needs of the kingdom, and help the monarch meet his budgetary requests.[32]

The creation of these elected assemblies was not presented as a counterbalance to royal power. On the contrary, Turgot adopted the language and logic of absolutism to convince the king that he would retain full decision power and could still consider himself an “absolute legislator.” An unmentioned side benefit of Turgot’s proposal is that the *parlements*—which Montesquieu had regarded as the primary check to the monarchy in the French constitution—would lose their ability to block tax increases. In theory, at least, legislative power would be entirely concentrated “in a single man,” the king.[33]

These political proposals were again keyed to a distinct historical regime. The "Memorandum" bursts with the same historical progressivism as Turgot's youthful lecture. If Louis's royal predecessors had made mistakes, it was because they were, quite literally, living in the past, and victims of historical ignorance. By adopting Turgot's proposal, the king could propel France into a better future. Within ten years, Turgot predicted, France would be unrecognizable, and infinitely superior to all other nations, past and present.[34]

Despite Turgot's claim that he sought only to strengthen the monarchy, others recognized that his plan was really a step toward democracy. When the "Memorandum" was first published in 1787, it was joined by a commentary by Jacques-Pierre Brissot, the future revolutionary leader. Brissot drew out its logical, republican conclusion—namely, that once the king was made aware of the people's needs and will, his only acceptable response would be to declare, "We wish what you wish."[35] In his own discussion of the "Memorandum," Condorcet—Turgot's close friend, collaborator, biographer, and fellow philosophe—confirmed that the plan was indeed an attempt to force the king to approve the wishes of his people. And if the role of the king was only to enact the wishes of what Condorcet was already calling, in 1786, a National Assembly, then how essential was the king?[36]

Turgot was dismissed by Louis XVI before he had the chance to submit his memorandum. But he returned to these ideas in a 1778 letter to the English reformer Richard Price, on the subject of the American Revolution. This was the letter, published in 1784, that inspired John Adams to write his *Defence of the Constitutions of the United States* (1787).[37] As we saw in chapter 7, that text offered a full-throated defense of a well-balanced constitution, and influenced the deliberations—and arguably the result—of the Constitutional Convention. If Turgot's letter was triggering for Adams, it was because he criticized the newly emancipated American states for slavishly imitating the British system of checks and balances. Turgot forcibly rejected the well-balanced constitution in favor of a single, concentrated source of power. Americans worried too much about "balancing different powers," he complained, when what the fledgling country really needed was to combine its different powers into a central body. As he had argued in his "Memorandum," dividing power led to conflicts, not to an efficient government. For Turgot, a constitution whose chief virtue lay in its capacity to delay or prevent historical change was deleterious. Instead, he sketched out a modern, progressive model of government, which privileged decisive action over compromise and balance.[38]

It is notable that in Turgot's letter to Price the role played by the monarch simply disappeared. The same hierarchy of municipal, regional, and national assemblies that he had sketched out in the "Memorandum" was now self-sufficient. The last vestige of the well-balanced constitution had vanished. Whatever the National Assembly (or its American equivalent) decided would be final. Turgot's modern democratic government now stood on the pedestal of popular sovereignty. To overturn the classical, Polybian definition of the republic, Turgot relied on the historical progressivism of the Moderns, which did not see History as a blind and meaningless sequence of events, but instead as marching slowly toward rationality. Turgot wanted modern political governments, Condorcet noted, to be "the work of reason and not, like all those that previously existed, that of chance and circumstances."[39]

Of course, his letter concerned the United States, not France. The former royal minister would not have been so rash as to suggest that France was ready for such a dramatic transformation. But he did call upon the Americans to provide a blueprint for other states: "They are the hope of the human race. They can become the model." And he secretly believed that a popular constitution was the best possible form. His own "Memorandum" had been a first step towards reforming the French constitution in this direction, but it had been foiled, alas, by his enemies. Or as Condorcet wrote, three years before the storming of the Bastille, his enemies had prevented Turgot's own "revolution" from transforming France.[40]

Perfecting the Human Race: Condorcet and the Silencing of Dissent

It fell on Condorcet to pen the most storied and studied account of progressive history before Hegel. He composed his optimistic *Outlines for a Historical Picture of the Progress of the Human Mind* (published in 1795, a year after his death) under the most inauspicious circumstances. He was on the run from the Jacobin authorities, who had already sent twenty-two Girondin ex-deputies to the guillotine on October 31, 1793. Condorcet, himself a former member of the National Convention, had witnessed first-hand the vitriolic politics of the First Republic. But even this experience did not temper his conviction that an even bigger and brighter revolution was still to come: "Everything tells us that we are approaching the era of one of the grand revolutions of the human race."[41]

While maintaining many themes and arguments of the progressive writers who preceded him, Condorcet introduced an important shift in emphasis. Where earlier theorists had insisted on the need to transform political institutions—see the abbé de Saint-Pierre's *sianse politique*—Condorcet focused on transforming the people themselves. In part, this "amelioration of the human race" would come about through scientific discoveries and new practices. But Condorcet also predicted the "real improvement of our faculties, moral, intellectual, and physical," as well as the human body. Progress was no longer simply a pedagogical project, it had become a biological one, too.[42]

The net result of this transfiguration, however, was total homogeneity. In the end, everyone should become an *homme éclairé*, a member of the "philosophical party," for it was among this class that the union of enlightenment, liberty, and virtue had already taken place. The philosophes would be the new missionaries, spreading the good news of Enlightenment to the far corners of the earth. Condorcet presented these actions as emancipatory: they should contribute to the "independence of the entire new world." But the newly independent states would still need guidance from their former masters. There was an explicit "civilizing mission" to Condorcet's gospel of liberty, one that even justified imperial violence: Europeans must "civilize or cause to disappear [*faire disparaître*]" the "savage nations" that did not progress as far as them or as quickly.[43]

Nowhere better than in Condorcet's *Outlines* do we see how the imperial and revolutionary strains of progressive historical thought grew out of the same stock. The modern doctrine of progress could be applied just as well—or just as disastrously—to a single society as it could to the world. It is when we consider its revolutionary, rather than imperial, strain, however, that we can perceive its internal logic most clearly. If Condorcet could envisage such a happy future, it was because, with time, all the profound disagreements that had marred the French Revolution and hounded him out of politics would vanish. Come the next revolution, reason would prevail. After all, disagreement was mostly a matter or error, prejudice, or superstition; as we became more and more enlightened, reason would melt away these obstacles. Then we could finally be happy, because we would all be the same.[44]

The modern doctrine of historical progress thus promoted radically different assumptions about social harmony than did the classical doctrine of historical turmoil. In the rosy modern view, deep divisions between rich and poor, urban and rural dwellers, and even different nations must eventually give way to harmonious and homogeneous relations. Condorcet still left room for political procedures (e.g., majority vote) for when collectivities are not naturally in agreement. But the antagonism of politics no longer disrupted these smooth processes, which ended up producing "unanimity."[45] The same had been true with his predecessors. Turgot's "general municipality" was to speak with one voice. The religious revolution imagined by Mercier was "peaceful and happy," with no objectors. When the revolution occurred in people's minds, they were all supposed to turn in the same direction, at the same time.

For these Moderns, the inconvertible divide between social classes that had been the premise of political thought from Thucydides and Aristotle to Nedham and Madison magically disappeared. Where harmony, for classical thinkers, was a balancing act requiring the mixing of political powers and social groups, Moderns believed that the progress of reason and justice alone would itself result in harmony. Progress would let us escape the common human sufferings, "such as have occurred and always will occur, as long as the nature of mankind remains the same," since human nature would change.[46] Already among educated people, no one questioned the laws of gravity. Come the next revolution, no one would question the truth of enlightened politics. Or rather, if they did, they deserved to meet with a swift, unforgiving fate.

CHAPTER NINE

Enlightenment Revolutions

HOW DID "REVOLUTION" become the means to usher in a new age of reason and justice? In keeping with their more classical temperament, most philosophes perpetuated a pessimistic vision of revolution. Voltaire was particularly wary, despairing in a 1760 letter to a German duchess that "everything is revolution, everything is misfortune." Even a proud republican such as Jean-Jacques Rousseau insisted that revolutions were dangerous illusions. When he famously announced, "We are approaching a state of crisis and the century of revolutions," Rousseau did not welcome this future. And in his somewhat paranoid defense of his own character, he described himself as someone "who is most allergic to revolutions and plotters of every sort."[1]

More fire-breathing philosophes also steered clear from fomenting revolution. The baron d'Holbach, sometimes regarded as the most "radical" French Enlightenment author, constantly thundered against its horrors. Indeed, one of his main accusations against priests was that they caused repeated and destructive revolutions. In addition to being "bloody," d'Holbach regularly qualified revolutions as "horrible," "terrible," "continuous," and "fatal," placing them on the same level as "seditions, religious wars, and regicides."[2] Other members of his notorious salon shared these anti-revolutionary views. In a refutation of their mutual friend Helvétius, Diderot criticized him for downplaying the risks of revolution. In fact, Helvétius would not have disagreed, since (like Rousseau) he argued that revolutions were more likely to enslave, than to emancipate, a people.[3]

(Enlightened) Cultural Revolution

There was, however, a different kind of revolution that Enlightenment authors looked upon much more favorably. Generally referred to in the singular, this revolution was conducted not in the streets but in people's minds and habits; it was a "revolution in manners [*mœurs*]," or "in minds [*esprits*]." Historians have paid less attention to this other revolution, sometimes even dismissing it as a "so-called revolution."[4] But it was arguably the most important development for the concept of revolution in the eighteenth century.

Where did this concept of a world-historical, "cultural" revolution come from? There are some early examples in Montesquieu's *Spirit of Laws* (1748), but the most influential instance was Voltaire's *Siècle de Louis XIV* (1751). A founding text of Enlightenment historiography, Voltaire's work identified revolution as its primary focus: he would explore, he wrote in the introduction, "the general revolution that must serve as a lasting testament to the true glory of our country." But this revolution was cultural, even if it also touched the state; it took place in "our arts, our minds, our manners, as in our government." It stood in stark contrast to the political revolutions that Voltaire discussed in the book, most notably the "almost unheard of revolution" that led to the beheading of Charles I in 1649.[5]

It is sometimes said that it took the French Revolution to retrospectively identify the English Civil War as a revolution. In fact, a French historian had already described it as one in a late seventeenth-century book that Louis XVI studied closely during the French Revolution.[6] The events of 1642–49 fell into the well-known genre of "history of revolutions in *X*." By contrast, the peaceful, epochal "revolution" in French culture that Voltaire identified during the reign of Louis XIV marked a major innovation in the intellectual history of revolution. The double meaning of "revolution" in this work was not evidence of indecisiveness on Voltaire's part, but rather reflects his repurposing of a political concept in a different, cultural register.[7]

Voltaire continued to deploy both meanings of "revolution" in his subsequent historical works. The most important of these was the *Essai sur les mœurs et l'esprit des nations* (*Essay on the Manners and the Spirit of Nations*, 1756). Here again he did not ignore the petty revolutions that made up most of political history: "In governments, all is revolution," he pronounced, echoing his friend d'Argenson. But in keeping with the title of his book and the promise made to his late partner Emilie du Châtelet, Voltaire paid more attention to "the spirit, manners, and practices of important nations." And it was in this cultural sphere that he called attention to the most memorable revolutions. Particularly remarkable were religious revolutions, such as the emergence and spread of Islam, "the greatest and swiftest revolution ever seen on earth." The Protestant Reformation was equally revolutionary, in a way that foreshadowed how the philosophes would describe the Enlightenment itself. Voltaire credited Luther and Henry VIII with bringing about "a revolution in people's minds." To a considerable degree, the Reformation was the main theater of revolution in the *Essai*.[8]

Voltaire's account of religious upheavals fit a broader Enlightenment pattern that defined historical change in revolutionary terms. In the "Preliminary Discourse" to the *Encyclopédie*, d'Alembert compared the advent of the "new science" in the seventeenth century to a successful revolution against a despotic ruler. In this analogy, Descartes was the leader of rebel forces who established a fairer and more prosperous government through a "spectacular revolution." Unlike the frequent and often cyclical revolutions of governments, this revolution in philosophy brought about lasting, meaningful change.[9]

Another historical turning point that received the cultural revolutionary treatment was the Renaissance. For Rousseau, after centuries of scholastic barbarity, "it took a revolution to restore common sense," which is what occurred when the Ottomans took Constantinople, sending Greeks and forgotten manuscripts into Italy. D'Alembert echoed this claim, calling the fall of the Byzantine Empire "a revolution that changed the face of the earth." While both of these authors still associated revolution with catastrophe (the fall of Constantinople), the abbé Raynal, some twenty years later, transposed the real revolution of the Renaissance to people's minds. Where history for Polybians was the unhappy sequence of "fortune's revolutions," the philosophes reconfigured history as a series of happy revolutions in thought, art, culture, and commerce.[10]

Not all of these historical revolutions were universally positive. Voltaire acknowledged that the fall of the Western Roman Empire had caused a revolution in culture as devastating as the physical decay of Rome itself. Another revolution devastated Chinese civilization in the seventeenth century. This catastrophic sense of revolution was also common in works on natural history, such as Charles Bonnet's *La palingénésie philosophique* (1769). Natural revolutions literally changed the face of the earth, through earthquakes, floods, and volcanic eruptions.[11]

Throughout the 1750s, this lingering sense of potential devastation haunted the positive meaning attributed to "revolution" by the philosophes.

D'Alembert and Diderot both warned of future revolutions that could bring another Dark Age. The best hope for politics, Diderot concluded, was to wish not for an immortal state but for "the one that would last the longest and most peacefully." The Polybian solution remained attractive.[12]

But Voltaire soon came to abandon the fear that cultural revolutions could be catastrophic—particularly when the culture in question was his own, and the revolution was the Enlightenment. Starting in the late 1750s, Voltaire began continuously referring in his letters to the "great revolution of the human spirit" currently underway. By the mid-1760s, he was dating the advent of this revolution with some precision: it had begun twelve years before, Voltaire wrote to Helvétius in 1765. Other letters similarly pointed to a start date of the early 1750s—that is, when the first volumes of the *Encyclopédie* were published, and when some of Voltaire's major historical works appeared. He sometimes compared this revolution to the Reformation, though his own had the advantage of being entirely peaceful. It had begun in France but was rapidly spreading across Europe.[13]

Coming from the author who had mercilessly mocked optimism in his satirical novel *Candide* (1759), this sunny outlook may surprise. But the late 1750s had marked the nadir of the Enlightenment's fortunes. In 1759, the Parisian *parlement* condemned Helvétius's book *De l'esprit* to flames, while the Royal Council withdrew the printing permission for the *Encyclopédie*. At the time, the future did not look like it belonged to philosophy, and d'Alembert's pessimism seemed averred.

By contrast, the mounting successes of the philosophes' royal and ideological allies in the 1760s and 1770s caused a sea change in their perception of history. The Seven Years' War (concluded in 1763) consolidated massive French losses overseas but brought about a period of peace on the continent. These were also the years of the duc de Choiseul's ascendancy over French politics, both domestic and foreign, so the philosophes had a friend and supporter in the highest place. Turgot's appointment to the ministry in 1774 made them even giddier.[14]

Now the rapid gains of the Enlightenment seemed here to stay. By 1773, Voltaire even voiced a more favorable view of Saint-Pierre, expressing second thoughts about his plan for perpetual peace.[15] Nor was he alone in looking on the bright side of history. Many other authors joined in propagating his "revolutionary" narrative of the Enlightenment. Where earlier authors had crafted an Enlightenment narrative based on the "philosophical spirit" pervading European culture, this updated narrative idolized the philosophes themselves, and their earth- (or heaven-) shattering texts.[16] In a 1762 letter to his mistress, Sophie Volland, Diderot boasted that the completion of the *Encyclopédie* would cause an intellectual revolution.[17] Like many others, he credited Voltaire for having instigated this revolution in minds all across Europe, though Voltaire, with his usual false modesty, honored Diderot as the true ringleader.[18]

Questions of paternity aside, there was a general assessment among the philosophical party of the late Enlightenment that they had collectively transformed French minds (*esprits*) and culture (*mœurs*) for the better. By the late eighteenth century, this boast had become a commonplace. A host of lesser-known philosophes repeated the claim that the Enlightenment marked a "happy revolution" in human history.[19] Even the future revolutionary radical Jean-Paul Marat, in 1785, evoked the "glorious revolution" that had started with Fontenelle and was only now bearing its full philosophical fruits.[20]

Revolution from Above: Enlightened Dictators

But there was more—more revolution, that is. In addition to celebrating their past and present successes, the philosophes grew excited about an even greater revolution to come. Again, Voltaire set the tone for these expectations of a bigger and better Enlightenment: "Everything points to a revolution that cannot fail to pass," he announced in 1764; and a year later, "There will undoubtedly soon be a great revolution in people's minds."[21]

Voltaire's hopeful outlook sometimes bordered on the millenarian. The philosophes had already achieved a tremendous revolution in how people thought, yet the next revolution would be even more amazing, perhaps even leading to the end of history.[22] Throughout the late 1760s, such prophetic claims became a recurrent theme in Voltaire's letters.[23] This remarkable revolution to come was still understood as a cultural change; Voltaire was not prophesying the storming of the Bastille. Its most distinctive and novel feature was that it now seemed inevitable. The modern cosmology of time as gradual progress had taken hold of Voltaire's imagination. And given the progress already made during the Enlightenment, the next step might lead humanity beyond the reach of setbacks and dark ages. Revolution could be the gateway to a new golden age.

But the revolution to come would be different from the one led by the philosophes. To complete their efforts, it would take more than books, letters, and witty conversations. Revolution on the scale envisaged by Voltaire and his friends required political action. So they reintroduced the idea of revolution to the political sphere, as the logical conclusion of Enlightenment progress. Voltaire's correspondence again offers a helpful window on this final revolution in the meaning of "revolution." The first political revolution that Voltaire saw fit to celebrate was Chancellor Maupeou's radical reform (1771–74) of the French *parlements*, or high courts. Maupeou's attempt to replace the *parlementaires*, who had become the main opposition force to royal policies, with state-appointed officials divided public opinion in France and split the philosophes. But Voltaire came out strongly in favor, praising Maupeou's coup as a "gentle," "simple," and "peaceful" revolution. He even wrote to the chancellor himself to reassure him that enlightened minds approved of his "great revolution."[24] Voltaire was no fan of the *parlements*, which had been his bugbear during the Calas affair. But his support of Maupeou marked an important departure in his "revolutionary" commitments.[25] While there was arguably a cultural dimension to the judicial reforms, they were first and foremost a political action.

Throughout the 1770s, other political revolutions occurred in rapid succession across the continent, reinforcing the impression that European rulers were bringing about great changes. Pierre-Paul Le Mercier de la Rivière's 1767 Physiocratic treatise, *L'ordre naturel et essentiel des sociétés politiques*, inspired crowned heads from Florence to Saint-Petersburg to reform government according to a "natural order."[26] One of these monarchs, Gustav III of Sweden, established royal autocracy following a coup against the Riksdag, or Swedish Estates, in August 1772. A month later, Voltaire wrote to Frederick II to congratulate him on his nephew's "lovely revolution in Sweden," which had made him "happy to be alive."[27] He also sent a cheery letter to d'Alembert, conflating both the recent Swedish revolution and the expulsion of the Jesuits a decade earlier: "My dear philosophe, doesn't this seem like the century of revolutions, from [the expulsion of] the Jesuits to Sweden, and maybe endless more?" There were indeed many revolutions to come.[28]

Toward the end of his life, Voltaire once again expressed excitement that rulers across Europe were leading great revolutions in their states. We already saw the letter he wrote to Catherine II, crediting her with launching a new age with her political revolution. Her political reforms were still cultural, undertaken in the spirit of the Enlightenment, but the agents of revolution were now ministers and monarchs, rather than writers and philosophers. Voltaire made this new primacy of political action clear in a letter to Frederick II in 1775, where he saluted Turgot's elevation to the ministry as the "start of a great revolution."[29]

Major changes in religion, culture, and commerce were now inseparably wedded to decisive political action. To the Parisian *salonnière* Madame Du Deffand, Voltaire conveyed his high hopes for French politics following

Louis XVI's "revolution," in the same breath as his admiration for the composer Gluck. In Voltaire's political playbook, kings were now the revolutionaries, leading the overhaul of culture and society. At heart, this political outlook was not entirely new: Voltaire had already sketched out the ideal of a philosopher-king in *Zadig*. But where in 1747 that ideal had appeared as a fairytale ending, a quarter-century later it seemed to be coming true.[30]

Voltaire was not alone in envisioning political revolution in such a positive light. In his popular 1767 novel about the Byzantine general Belisarius, Jean-François Marmontel—a close friend of Voltaire, as well as a prominent literary critic and member of d'Holbach's salon—has his eponymous and philosophical hero propose various remedies for reforming the state. One of them is for the emperor Justinian (representing Louis XV) to curb luxury, which would bring about a "moral revolution," by changing public opinion through royal action. This politico-cultural revolution, which only the king could accomplish, stood in sharp contrast to the "revolutions of fortune," or vicissitudes of history, which had reduced the former general to poverty.[31] And the baron d'Holbach himself, who had fulminated against priestly revolutions at such lengths, came around in the mid-1770s to defending philosophical revolutions, so long, again, as they were promulgated by the state. Since the state controlled education, only with state support could the philosophical and "most desirable" revolution eventually come to pass, as the progress of Enlightenment extended over time.[32]

But the most remarkable description of a royal, progressive revolution is to be found in Louis-Sebastien Mercier's best-selling utopian novel, *The Year 2440* (1774). In this Rip Van Winkle story about an eighteenth-century Parisian who wakes up seven hundred years later, the narrator (like his fellow American slumberer) discovers that he, too, has missed an "important revolution." While there is a hint in this work of a past violent clash, for the most part the revolution is portrayed as peaceful. Its net effect was to overthrow Christianity and implant Enlightenment philosophy in its place. Once again, the agents of this change were political actors, and more specifically, enlightened despots. This "important revolution" had begun in Mercier's time, in Catherine's Russia. Her judicial reforms were later pursued by a literal philosopher-king in France. Like the enlightened, freed prisoners of Plato's Cave who had to be forced back down to govern those who remained, this future French ruler disdained the throne but accomplished both a great political and a great religious revolution. Politically, he gave power back to the provinces, while on the religious front, he oversaw the final death throes of Christianity. "Did this revolution"—that is, the disappearance of religion—"occur in the most peaceful and happy manner?" asks the seven-hundred-year-old slumberer. "It was the result of philosophy," comes the answer. Of course, this was not exactly how things played out with the Civil Constitution of the Clergy in 1790.[33]

A final example of how this politico-cultural sense of revolution caught on can be found in Diderot's contributions to Raynal's *Histoire des deux Indes*. The bulk of these additions were to the notorious 1780 edition, the only one that Raynal signed, and which the Parisian *parlement* condemned. Diderot's own fiery prose contributed in no small part to this edition's shock value.[34] Like Mercier, he looked forward to the revolution that would overthrow Christianity. But his political arguments were far more moderate, as Diderot, too, portrayed kings as the true revolutionaries of the day. Only they could bring about the revolution that would end slavery. And only the French king, in particular, could lead the revolution that would challenge England's maritime supremacy. Kings did not have a monopoly on revolution: former colonists, such as the Americans, also promised great revolutions. Just as the 1770 edition opened with a look backwards to the geographic revolutions of the age of discovery, the 1780 edition ended with a prophetic glance forward to the time when all European colonies would be freed by a "happy revolution." Within a decade, the French were celebrating their own "happy revolution" in the words used by the comte de Lally-Tollendal, a noble deputy and friend of Voltaire's.[35] The next revolution had arrived, right on cue.

CHAPTER TEN

The Dual Power in the French Revolution

What is the goal toward which we strive?
. . . the reign of eternal justice.

—ROBESPIERRE, "ON THE PRINCIPLES OF POLITICAL MORALITY" (1794)

LOOKING BACK TO the springtime of 1789, when preparations were underway to host the Estates General in Versailles, the marquise Henriette-Lucy de La Tour du Pin recalled an upbeat mood. She was well situated to report on the court's disposition. Her mother, who had died seven years earlier, had been a favorite of Marie-Antoinette. Lucie, as the daughter was known, followed in her footsteps as a lady-in-waiting to the queen. Her father-in-law was the lieutenant general of the royal army, and himself a deputy for the nobility at the upcoming Estates. No one at court was yet talking about a revolution, she observed, though pamphleteers had been celebrating the calling of the Estates General as a "happy revolution" since 1788.[1] The "most thoughtful courtiers," she noted, believed that France really was on the verge of a national regeneration. The king himself "shared their illusions," she added, and believed that France was nearing a new golden age.[2] Even before the deputies gathered in Versailles, this reference was fast becoming a commonplace: "Surely on these grounds the golden age will recur," an enterprising poet wrote to the king in 1789 (see also figure 10.1).[3] If this mythical motif was recycled so often over the coming years, it was because it captured the giddy sense of historical progress that hung in the air. In 1789, the French did not hesitate to embark on revolutionary change, but felt excitement for what lay ahead.

FIGURE 10.1 "L'aristocratie écrasée: espoir de l'âge d'or" (1789). Bibliothèque nationale de France.

In the first months of 1789, it was not wholly surprising that the French court still hoped for the best. While France had suffered terrible crop failures over the previous years and was on the brink of a fiscal cliff, a string of remarkable events had also taken place. In Paris, the transformation of the Palais-Royal gardens into a bustling commercial and social hub (closed off to the police) had created an electrifying and spectacular center for the spread of news and opinion.[4] Near Lyon, the Montgolfier brothers had pioneered human flight, successfully launching hot air balloons three thousand feet into the sky. One of their famous demonstrations occurred at Versailles, in 1783, in the presence of the king and queen. Versailles was also the site of experiments on the new science of electricity, whose principal discoverer, Benjamin Franklin, resided in Paris from 1776 to 1785. Franklin was part of a commission tasked by Louis XVI to investigate the wondrous claims of Franz-Anton Mesmer, who used "animal magnetism" to cure all sorts of ailments. (An Austrian, Mesmer owed some of his success in Paris to support from his compatriot Marie-Antoinette.) And the reason for Franklin's presence in Paris, the American War of Independence, was the source of much sympathy. Few expected a republican "revolution" (as the French were calling American events) to occur on French soil, but the colonists' struggle for independence struck many as the political equivalent to some of the concurrent breakthroughs in science. "He seized lightning from heaven and the scepter from a tyrant," read Turgot's famous epigram for Franklin.[5]

By the 1780s, in short, the great revolution predicted by Voltaire and others was showing signs of its imminent arrival. What no one predicted, however, was how this tremendous upheaval would be received. Many in France and across Europe welcomed the Revolution as the promised result of an enlightened age. "I see the ardor for liberty catching and spreading," enthused Richard Price in London on November 4, 1789, "a general amendment beginning in human affairs; the dominion of kings changed for the dominion of laws, and the dominion of priests giving way to the dominion of reason and conscience."[6] But these sentiments were far from universal. Price's sermon spurred Edmund Burke to pen his damning *Reflections on the Revolution in France* (1790). In France, the blowback to the Revolution came even quicker. One of the king's brothers, the future Charles X, emigrated two days after the storming of the Bastille. Many of La Tour du Pin's "most thoughtful courtiers" followed suit, along with clergymen, military officers, and moderate politicians.

But it wasn't only enemies of the Revolution who failed to converge on the significance of the momentous events underway. Self-professed revolutionaries attacked other enthusiasts, as disagreements over the correct path forward flared nonstop. The alleged progress of history in the direction of reason and justice—what Burke derided as "this new-sprung modern light"—did not deliver its most critical component: a consensus that history was indeed progressing toward reason and justice. Instead of bowing uniformly to reason, as the philosophes had prophesied, public opinion broke into pieces. Brief moments of actual or manufactured consensus—such as the king's visit to Paris after the fall of the Bastille, the festival of the Federation in July 1790, or the bizarre "kiss of Lamourette" in July 1792, when political rivals embraced at the Assembly—only perpetuated the illusion that divergent opinions could and should be reconciled.[7]

This modern illusion proved extremely enduring, lasting well after the events of 1789 challenged its accuracy. But its impact on the French Revolution extended far beyond this initial disappointment. As it turned out, political opinions did converge, just not into a single shared view. Groups, clubs, and parties formed around different political outlooks and social experiences. A plethora of newspapers sprung up, helping to channel wavering opinions into a small cluster of mainstream views.

This clustering of opinions not only underscored the fragmentation of the public at large but had an effect on government as well. The epic clashes between rival deputies in the National Assembly and Convention left a defining mark on parliamentary politics (most notably through the invention of "right" and "left"). But it was arguably between the levels of government that these ideological clashes mattered most. The French Revolution created a host of new official positions at the local, municipal, departmental, and of course national level, opening up countless opportunities for political participation. Since many of these positions had not existed previously, their functions and jurisdiction were unclear and open for negotiation (and exaggeration). The spectrum of political opinions found in the public was in this way reproduced across and within these various levels of administration. Different political strongholds came to reflect different political viewpoints. It wasn't only public opinion that was divided; state power was, too.

Nowhere was this clash between ideologically opposed power centers more evident than in Paris itself. As early as April 1789, Parisian districts were organized into discrete administrative units. During the crisis of July 11–14, the Parisian municipal government was born. Following the October days, when Louis XVI and his family were brought to the capital by a Parisian crowd, the National Assembly gathered there as well. And in February 1790, France was divided into *départments*, adding another layer of administration. Almost immediately, these different layers came into conflict, not only over matters of jurisdiction, but also over interpretations of constitutionality, sovereignty, and government.

These conflicts between local, municipal, departmental, and national magistrates were one of the main driving forces of the French Revolution. From the moment of its birth, the Paris municipality clashed repeatedly with the sixty Parisian districts (later reconstituted as forty-eight sections), culminating in the Champs-de-Mars massacre of July 17, 1791. The sections avenged themselves a year later, reclaiming the municipal government on the night of August 9–10, 1792. This "revolutionary" Paris Commune immediately turned on the Legislative Assembly, and continued to harass the National Convention (which took office that September). Their conflict reached a climax when the Commune and sections forced the Convention—at cannon-point—to expel twenty-nine Girondin deputies. Now the main standoff was between the Convention and the "federalist" departments. That conflict between national and departmental representatives played into the proclamation of revolutionary government in October 1793. Even then, old tensions reemerged, with both radical and moderate adherents of the Cordeliers Club (a former Parisian district) clashing with the Committee of Public Safety. When Robespierre and his allies were pronounced outlaws by the Convention, on Thermidor 9 (July 27, 1794), he sought refuge in his old stronghold, the Hôtel-de-Ville (or Paris City Hall). Once again, the course of the revolution would be determined by the clash between Commune and Convention.[8]

Highlighting this pattern of intragovernmental conflict does more than just provide an explanatory model for the French Revolution. It also helps identify a defining feature of modern revolutions. The sociologist and historian Charles Tilly once argued that "multiple sovereignty" was "*the* identifying feature of revolutionary situations."[9] Tilly had a different historical moment in mind: the 1917 standoff between the Russian Provisional Government and the Petrograd Soviet of Workers' and Soldiers' Deputies. Lenin had described this situation in a famous article for the Bolshevik newspaper *Pravda* in April 1917: "The highly remarkable feature of our revolution," he observed, "is that it has brought about a *dual power*." Tilly's concept of "multiple sovereignty" extended Lenin's analysis.[10]

While "highly remarkable," this was not the first time such a standoff had arisen. Lenin himself noted that the Petrograd Soviet was modeled on the 1871 Paris Commune, which had similarly confronted (and fought) the French national government, then located in Versailles. In fact, the three features that Lenin attributed to the 1871 Commune—sourcing power in "the direct initiative of the people from below, in their local areas," "the direct arming of the whole people," and "the direct rule of the people themselves"—already characterized the Paris Commune of 1792. Drawing a line between the French and Russian Revolutions, in this regard, is not about tracing ideological continuities between, say, the Jacobins and the Bolsheviks, but rather about identifying structural parallels.[11]

At various moments in the French Revolution, we can find examples of the classic "dual-power"-type clash between the Commune and the national government. Underlying these disputes was not a disagreement about sovereignty per se: after the summer of 1789, the principle of popular sovereignty was generally accepted (at least by those who remained in France). Rather, politicians clashed over how popular sovereignty should be expressed in government. Which members of the sovereign people should have a vote in elections? Should the people have veto power over legislation? And which administrative activities should be delegated to national or municipal officials, and which could be performed by the people themselves, particularly at a local level?

These were some of the questions that not only divided the French public but also pitted different levels of administration against one another. Because one of the few beliefs that all actors shared was the modern faith in historical progress, each constituency insisted that it and it alone held the correct answers to these questions.

The splintering of actual political unity, combined with a commitment to the ideal of political unity, led modern revolutionaries to view their rivals in a new light. When each party believed that it represented the vanguard of progress and had reason and justice on its side, where did that leave supporters of other parties? There are not two reasons nor two justices. When disagreements arose, as they invariably did, your political opponents could only be mistaken, perhaps even irrational. Worse still, because everyone should recognize progress when they saw it, they were likely disagreeing in bad faith. They must be seeking to block historical progress, since progress was what the revolution was delivering. In a word, they must be counterrevolutionaries.

Revolutions that embrace a modern vision of history are thus highly susceptible to the kinds of political terror that marked so many revolutions from 1789 onward. There are clearly a number of other variables that shaped their particular outcomes. But the fact that these revolutions, despite their ideological, cultural, geographical, and socioeconomic differences, tend to display similar patterns of conflict and repression, suggests that something more than historical precedent or anthropological cycles of violence must be at work.[12] The modern vision of history, when acted upon in a revolution, does not inevitably lead to political terror, but it predisposes revolutionary actors to use it.

There is a final characteristic of modern revolutions that can also be connected to the modern vision of history. It is not only at the beginning of a revolution that rival groups form and gain toeholds in government. Revolutionary groups continuously splinter, establishing new formations with new support centers. There is a whack-a-mole quality to revolutionary politics: as soon as one political rivalry subsides, another flares up. Is there no end to this perpetual division? As Robespierre and his colleagues on the Committee of Public Safety discovered, there may be only one way out. On October 10, 1793, they suspended the constitution that their own political allies had written, and which the French people had just ratified. Instead, they proclaimed a "revolutionary government." In so doing, they led France from democracy to dictatorship.

This episode in revolutionary history has received less scrutiny than it deserves. Those sympathetic to the Revolution's aims tend to accept the Jacobins' own justification—namely, that they could not reasonably hold elections during wartime. More hostile historians simply dismiss the move as a cynical power grab. But these approaches ignore the more interesting questions that the proclamation of a revolutionary government raises. Why were there so few objections at the time? And why would the nuclear option of dictatorship prove so alluring to future revolutionaries?

If we consider these questions from the vantage point of a modern historical vision, they become less perplexing. While the initial justification for revolutionary government was the ongoing war, in subsequent speeches spokesmen for the Committee of Public Safety constantly advanced a different reason. A revolutionary government was necessary to bring about the future that had been promised, but never delivered, to the French since 1789. The government would finally achieve what had eluded previous politicians and assemblies. The more rational and just future was now at hand. The government simply needed some extra time to finalize its delivery. It especially needed that time to squash all those who questioned its goals.

These speeches help us understand how the principle of popular sovereignty could be disregarded in the name of the people. This apparent contradiction disappears once we realize that these two peoples were not contemporaneous. It was in the name of a future, improved democratic government by people *Y* that the present, inferior democratic government by people *X* must be suspended.[13] A narrative of historical progress served to legitimize the suspension of political beliefs. The ready reception of this argument in the Convention—no known objections to the October 10 decree were voiced—underscores the power of this historical vision. It was the logic of prospective retrospection: once you can imagine what the government *will have accomplished* at some future date, you *will have understood* why its actions in the present are justified.

If the French Revolution looms so large in this history, it is because all the threads of modern revolution are woven together here for the first time. In addition to the predominant place of the modern historical vision, and to the extensive linguistic usage of "revolution" in a positive sense, 1789 also marked the first time that revolutionary actors described themselves and their actions as "revolutionary."[14] This self-awareness heightened expectations for historical change, and accentuated the disappointment with fellow revolutionaries who saw things differently. Because "revolution," in 1789 and beyond, retained its Enlightenment association with progress, French "revolutionaries" had a future-facing identity. To be a revolutionary meant to do something. In Keith Baker's phrase, revolution was now an act, not a fact. Over the course of this and subsequent revolutions, different "scripts" for action took shape, providing revolutionary actors with stage directions.[15]

Not everything the French revolutionaries did was new: some of their political policies extended old regime plans and practices.[16] But there are risks in attempting to understand the French Revolution through the lens of old regime politics. An earlier generation of political historians used this approach to challenge the then-dominant Marxist interpretation of the French Revolution. For these revisionist scholars, the main political problem that the revolutionaries faced was filling the "empty space" left by the king when he ceased to exercise sovereignty.[17] Where the royal will had previously sufficed to make political decisions, the will of the people was much harder to ascertain. Accordingly, in this account, the French revolutionaries became obsessed with preserving and policing a unified general will, and rejecting as counterrevolutionary anyone who opposed it.

This interpretation of revolutionary politics, offered in the context of Cold War anti-totalitarianism, has been criticized on both empirical and theoretical grounds. But its greatest weakness may lie in its preconceptions. It oddly assumes that absolute monarchy offers the best—indeed, the only—template for thinking about sovereignty. It follows from this unusual premise that sovereignty is a singular space to be occupied individually, like a throne.[18]

Still, the revisionists identified an important problem, even if their own explanation was unsatisfactory. The French revolutionaries expected consensus among the people and had a very low tolerance for disagreement. But contrary to the revisionists' claim, this expectation was not a factor of their prior experience under a royal sovereign. There were many time-tested strategies for resolving differences of opinion among a popular sovereign. There had been no expectation of consensus in the Roman Republic, or the American republic for that matter. The French insistence that everyone express the same preferences (*volonté*) was a factor not of sovereignty but of historical thought. The French revolutionaries had inherited the modern belief that, as everyone became enlightened (and who could be more enlightened than the French?), public opinion would converge around a single, rational, correct answer. There could not be any real differences of opinion because there were only true and false opinions—and the latter were illegitimate. If there was an anti-pluralist streak among the revolutionaries, it was not *la faute à Rousseau*, but *la faute à Voltaire*.

Athens on the Seine

Histories of the French Revolution often begin on May 5, 1789, when the Estates General met in Versailles for the first time in 175 years. But the historic nature of that gathering has overshadowed an earlier event that, while not as famous, proved almost as momentous. Two weeks earlier, on April 21, Parisian voters had gathered to choose representatives for an electoral assembly, which would in turn select deputies for the Third Estate. Paris was divided into sixty districts for the occasion. The plan was for eligible voters to meet in a public place (typically a church) to discuss and elect their representatives. The municipality appointed presiding officers to oversee the process.

But things did not go to plan. Some district assemblies forced a vote to replace the officials. Others insisted on drawing up a list of grievances (*cahier de doléances*), despite having been told that there was not enough time. Nor did all districts stick to their requisite number of representatives, occasionally sending more than allowed.[19]

These minor acts of resistance were nothing compared to what came next. The Parisians who participated in these assemblies—and only a small number did, as the poll tax for the franchise was quite high—enjoyed the experience. In some districts, voters continued to gather, even after their official business had concluded. Primary assemblies turned into deliberative assemblies, as Parisians immersed themselves in the novelty of debating political questions with their neighbors in a semiformal setting.

With all eyes on the exciting events underway in Versailles, these minor incidents passed largely unnoticed. But attention returned to Paris after riots broke out on July 11, in the wake of Jacques Necker's dismissal as finance minister. History books focus on what happened next: crowds made their way to the Bastille and stormed the prison. But the apparent breakdown of public order in Paris, combined with fears of a Royalist crackdown, fueled another, less celebrated burst of civic enthusiasm. Assemblies began meeting once again in every Parisian district. They had no stated authority to gather, except that their members were part of the sovereign people. They established a militia, which became the National Guard. They elected commissioners to oversee district affairs. And for the coming year they continued to hold regular meetings. It was out of this direct experience of participatory politics that French demands for democracy would arise.

For most political observers in 1789, "democracy" was a scare word.[20] It conjured up fears of anarchy, disorder, even despotism. Classical misgivings about democracy had not faded in the eighteenth century. But they were not universal. The journalist Camille Desmoulins celebrated the ancient Greek and modern American democracies as "the only government appropriate for men," before proudly concluding, "I declare myself loudly for democracy." Desmoulins would go on to play an important role in the Cordeliers district, which became a hotbed of democratic activism and theory.[21]

For its opponents and (rare) defenders alike, democracy was primarily a mode of governmental administration. This had been the marquis d'Argenson's argument: even under a monarchic sovereign, it was more effective and rational to have a democratic system for selecting administrators. The commissioners whom the Paris district assemblies elected to oversee local affairs turned d'Argenson's "popular magistrates" into a reality. Much of their work focused on maintaining public order in the districts. The collapse of old regime institutions had left a chaotic situation, which the commissioners struggled to control.[22]

But if these new officials fulfilled a previously existing function, the district assemblies were completely new. Again, classical parallels sprang to mind: some saw in the assemblies a rebirth of the Athenian *ekklesia* or the plebeian council of republican Rome. In certain districts, all inhabitants were welcomed, regardless of the poll tax; even women were occasionally admitted to assemblies. There was a visibly Rousseauist element to these gatherings, which many commented on: the people themselves were on display, as in Rousseau's ideal republican festivals (see figure 10.2). The opportunity to rub shoulders with fellow citizens, regardless of social class or even gender, evoked for some "the fraternity of the golden age":

FIGURE 10.2 A civic ceremony in the district of Saint-Etienne-du-Mont (1790). Bibliothèque nationale de France.

"In the middle of this age of iron, [France] is reborn into the infancy of the world," wrote an enthusiastic pamphleteer from the Trinité district. The assemblies were taken as another sign that the Revolution was leading France in the direction of reason and justice.[23]

So attached were the citizens (and even *citoyennes*) of Paris to these assemblies that they sent the inaugural mayor of the Paris Commune, Jean-Sylvain Bailly, to the National Assembly in March 1790 to petition the deputies to maintain them.[24] Robespierre spoke in favor: the sections were valuable instruments of surveillance, he characteristically remarked. Most other deputies were unconvinced. Mirabeau warned that making these assemblies permanent would create "sixty sovereign sections in one large body."[25] The assembly's tepid response was ominous. A few weeks later, it passed a decree reorganizing the sixty districts into forty-eight sections, and expressly forbid the new sections from holding assemblies, except for elections or civic ceremonies.[26] In response, many of the former assemblies relaunched as political clubs—most famously, the Cordeliers Club, after the Cordeliers district was merged into a larger section.

Mirabeau's identification of sovereignty as the main area of concern with the district assemblies was revealing. It pointed to a fundamental disagreement between the districts and the assembly over the relation between sovereignty and government. The Paris districts repeatedly questioned the deputies' logic and even their legitimacy, notably calling in August 1789 for the removal and prosecution of deputies whom they called "ignorant, corrupt, or suspect."[27] Their grounds for dismissal, at the time, were the assembly's desire to grant the king a legislative veto in the new constitution. Deputies argued about the kind of veto that was suitable, before settling on a "suspensive" one. The king, they decided in September, could suspend legislation for up to two legislative terms (i.e., four years). Some more-adventurous deputies had suggested giving the people a say in overturning a royal veto.[28] In this scenario, primary assemblies, such as those that the districts sought to maintain, would have the supreme (i.e., sovereign) legislative function, approving or rejecting any vetoed laws.

It was precisely this kind of legislative power that many Parisian district members wanted for their local assemblies, only more so. Why should the king rather than the people have a veto power? "I cannot conceive of a republic without a Forum . . . and without a people's veto," Desmoulins asserted in his newspaper.[29] In addition to a popular veto, outspoken members of the Cordeliers district demanded a popular right to sanction *every* decree of the National Assembly. They justified this claim in the name of democratic government: "Republicanism or democracy is government by all: to be perfect, citizens must *personally and individually* contribute to drafting the law," insisted François Robert. Robert drew extensively on Rousseau's theory of popular sovereignty, which the philosophe had famously declared cannot be delegated to representatives. The National Assembly could still *propose* laws, Robert reasoned, but only the people themselves in local assemblies could validate them.[30]

The mere existence of the Paris district assemblies thus presented a challenge to the National Assembly's own legislative power. Both sides agreed on the ultimate source of sovereignty—it lay with the French people—but not on its exercise nor its role in government. They also butted heads over its expression. In July 1789, the abbé Sieyès proposed to the National Assembly a distinction between active and passive citizens. Women, children, and anyone who paid below a certain threshold in taxes could enjoy the benefits of citizenship passively. Only those who contributed significantly to the finances of the state could be active, voting citizens.[31]

This proposal, which the assembly approved, infuriated many in the districts. It was "a decree that humiliates man himself," thundered Louis-Charles de Lavicomterie, another Cordeliers democrat.[32] The active/passive distinction cut to the heart of how popular sovereignty related to government. For opponents of the assembly's decision, it amounted to the illegitimate disenfranchisement of a majority of voting-age French men.[33]

Democrats in the Paris districts ultimately embraced a completely different political and constitutional ideal, one that was more in line with the modern faith in historical progress. The National Assembly, despite its members' enlightened rhetoric, remained committed to classical principles of constitutionalism. While they rejected Anglo-American-style bicameralism in favor of a single legislative chamber (along the lines of the radical Pennsylvania state constitution and of Rousseau), the deputies still clung to the principle of a separation of powers.[34] Article 16 of the Declaration of the Rights of Man and of the Citizen (completed in August 1789) went so far as to proclaim that "a society in which the observance of the law is not assured, nor the separation of powers defined, has no constitution at all."

This principle found little support in the more radical districts. Desmoulins rejected the Montesquieuian division of powers in favor of another model that gave more authority to the districts.[35] In a remarkable speech to the Cordeliers Club, René Girardin offered a full-throated defense of this alternative constitutional theory. Girardin was no ordinary revolutionary. The former marquis had sheltered Rousseau during the last weeks of his life at the château d'Ermenonville, where the philosophe was buried. As the editor of Rousseau's complete works, he had as good a claim as any to being his intellectual heir. In his May 29, 1791, speech, Girardin mounted a frontal attack on the assembly's constitutional principles. The distinction between legislative, executive, and judiciary powers was "chimerical," he pronounced, as sovereignty was "inalienable and indivisible." The assembly's contrary view was untenable, tyrannical even. Allowing the assembly alone to sanction the law was a form of "representative despotism."

Girardin raised the stakes in the sections' clash with the assembly. He called the views of the Cordeliers Club "the sentiment of *our revolution*." The political argument over constitutionalism and sovereignty now doubled as a fight to control the meaning of "revolution" itself. Political opponents were henceforth guilty of much greater faults than simple errors: "All those who attempt to act against the rights of man and of the citizen are accordingly perjurers, and guilty of attacks on the sovereignty of the nation and its essential constitution."[36] The lack of agreement about the true meaning of the Revolution and the proper direction of history could spell violence.

The revolutionary who was most explicit about resorting to actual violence was Jean-Paul Marat. The incendiary journalist, who spent most of the early Revolution hiding in the Cordeliers district, was notorious for his insistence of the need to chop off five to six hundred heads for the sake of liberty—a number that he repeatedly revised upwards, until it reached hundreds of thousands. Beyond the cold-blooded "enlightened" calculus behind these calls—"sacrificing six hundred heads to save three million and three hundred thousand others is a simple calculation dictated by wisdom and philosophy"—it was their target that stood out.[37] Marat did not simply denounce open enemies of the Revolution, but concentrated his ire on its leaders. Necker, Lafayette, and many of the deputies of the National Assembly were among his most-hated antagonists.[38] The real battle to save the Revolution, for Marat, was internal, to be waged among its rival champions, most of whom, barring himself, were fakes. Like the Cordeliers, Marat insisted that true authority was vested directly in the sovereign people, and could not be delegated to representatives. His adversaries were not merely wrong, they were destroying the Revolution. It was a conflict that would soon come to a head—indeed, to many heads.

A Tale of Two Communes

The districts and the National Assembly were not the only two governments in town. The town itself, the Paris Commune, was another key player in the political contest pitting proponents of democratic and representative expressions of popular sovereignty against each other. The Commune also traced its origins back to the April 21, 1789, Paris elections of Third Estate deputies. The sixty districts had chosen 407 representatives for a Paris Electoral Assembly. After they had completed their official duty, these representatives began to meet anew, unofficially, in late June. Following Necker's dismissal, they appointed a "permanent committee," which selected Bailly as mayor and Lafayette as commander of the National Guard. The Electoral Assembly was then replaced by new representatives from the districts, who eventually came to form the General Assembly (Conseil Général) of the Paris Commune.[39]

While the members of this General Assembly were drawn from the districts, their relationship swiftly turned sour. A major bone of contention, again, was the proper exercise of sovereignty. As with the National Assembly, the General Assembly insisted that its decisions expressed the will of the Parisian people. One of the assembly's influential members was Jacques Brissot, the future leader of the Girondins (or "Brissotins," as they were initially called). He was an early advocate of republican government, but not in its democratic dispensation: "French republicans don't want the pure democracy of Athens. . . . [T]hey don't want to revive the troubles that such democracies brought; they only want a government whose essential basis is representation." He made his point even more explicitly in a letter from the communal assembly to the districts: "When [a free people] has deposited its powers in the hands of its representatives, they can only obey."[40] But that was not how the districts saw it. Many insisted that the relationship should in fact be reversed, and that the communal assembly should obey the decisions made collectively at the district level. A more Athenian, participatory style of democracy was precisely what many *did* want.[41]

The face-off between the districts and the municipal government led to some of the first physical clashes between rival revolutionary powers. In one of the earliest instances, violence was only narrowly averted. After Marat had spent weeks pillorying Necker in his newspaper, *L'ami du peuple*, the criminal court of Le Châtelet issued a warrant (its second) for his arrest.[42] But the Cordeliers district contested the court's authority. On January 15, 1790, its assembly passed a resolution stating that no district resident could be imprisoned without express permission from a district commission.[43] They even questioned the legitimacy of the communal government, implying that the "true" Commune was to be found in the body politic of Parisian citizens, not at the Hôtel-de-Ville.[44]

This insurgent attitude very nearly resulted in bloodshed on January 22, 1790, when the Cordeliers district committee declared that it was taking "M. Marat under its protection." Lafayette ordered the National Guard to enforce the arrest warrant against Marat, but the Cordeliers' own contingent of guards, along with those from some other districts, refused to comply. Georges Danton, a leader of the Cordeliers district and future minister of justice, delayed Lafayette's guards, giving Marat time to flee. In the end, no one was hurt, but the standoff between the guards and the district inhabitants came close to spiraling out of control.[45]

A year and a half later, in July 1791, the outcome was very different. Another rift opened up between the (now) Paris sections and the municipal and national government over how to deal with the king's attempted escape and capture in Varennes (on June 20–21). A variety of political groups even began to clamor for a republic. But this argument over the best form of government for France was also, and more pressingly, an argument about how exactly popular sovereignty should be expressed. The Cordeliers petition of July 14 was explicit on this point: while they pressed the National Assembly to remove Louis XVI from office, they also insisted that the deputies did not have the authority to pass final judgment on his future. Only the sovereign people enjoyed this right: "Any decree that oversteps the boundaries that have been imposed on you will be struck down as invalid and seen as a most unusual attack on the rights of the sovereign, the People."[46]

The National Assembly paid little heed to these arguments and, on July 15, cleared the king of any role in his own escape. In the eyes of many Parisians, this acquittal amounted to treason. The radical journalist Jacques Hébert denounced "the traitors of the National Assembly who want to restore the crown to Gilles Capet, former king of France." On top of lamenting the assembly's decision, many section and club members viewed it as illegitimate. They continued to draw up petitions demanding that the French people be consulted. On July 17, as six thousand Parisians gathered on the Champs-de-Mars to sign another petition, the Commune struck back. The municipal assembly had given Bailly permission a few days earlier to declare martial law. Bearing the red flag that marked this declaration, Lafayette led a detachment of National Guardsmen to break up the peaceful demonstration. This time, blood was shed. Guardsmen shot at the petitioners, killing up to fifty people.[47]

The massacre on the Champs-de-Mars cast a pall over the Revolution. Like the June days of the 1848 French revolution, when National Guardsmen shot workers protesting the closure of national workshops, it tore open a rift among the revolutionaries themselves. Mutual accusations of illegitimacy and abuses of sovereignty spilled over into street fighting. There had obviously been instances of governmental repression before. The difference now was that the state, too, was on the side of the new regime. The political conflict among rival power centers, each defending exclusivist definitions of revolution and the proper exercise of sovereignty, had become violent.

The shots fired on the Champs-de-Mars set off a cycle of violence that lasted for as long as the Revolution. Historians sometimes look to this cycle itself as the explanation for revolutionary violence.[48] It is clear that feelings of rage and revenge fueled the repressions to come. But the cycle of political violence was not a mere vendetta. Political actors on all sides were also driven by the strong sense that they, and they alone, were the legitimate defenders of the Revolution. This certainty was not restricted to particular ideologies, but was shared across the political spectrum, from moderates to radicals. Ideology could sharpen political attacks and further normalize the use of force. But it does not suffice to explain why such different revolutionary groups all resorted to violence. A more structural account that considers the interplay among multiple power centers and their claims to properly express popular sovereignty is needed. As there was no recognized process to arbitrate among these respective claims, the temptation to resort to force was always high.

Technically, the Champs de Mars massacre did not pit organs of power against one another, as the petitioners were not acting in any official capacity. They were not elected representatives of the sections, and the petitions themselves, though reflecting views about sovereignty and government that originated in the districts, were drawn up by clubs. One reason why the sections were less involved than the clubs is because the National Assembly had effectively disempowered them when rejecting the districts' request to meet in regular assemblies.

The situation changed dramatically a year later. On August 9–10, 1792, armed members of the Paris sections, together with volunteer soldiers from across France (the *fédérés*), stormed the Tuileries Palace, forcing Louis XVI and his family to seek protection from the National Assembly. This "second revolution" is remembered mainly as the night the monarchy died. But there was in fact another revolution that same night, whose consequences were no less drastic. In addition to toppling the monarchy, the sections also took control of the Commune.[49]

The revolution that occurred at the Hôtel-de-Ville that night was admittedly the less dramatic of the two. As the sections prepared to give the signal for the attack on the Tuileries Palace, they spared a thought for their old adversaries in the Commune. Rejecting the distinction between active and passive citizens, a majority of the sections invited male inhabitants of age to elect a new slate of representatives to the municipal assembly. These representatives, chosen by a much broader swath of the population, gathered that very night at the Hôtel-de-Ville, in a room adjacent to where the current assembly was sitting. The next day, these new representatives, joined with others from the remaining sections, took over their predecessors' functions. They came to be known as the "insurrectionary" Commune.

France now entered into a genuine "dual-power" period. The new Commune was founded on a different conception of popular sovereignty than the National Assembly, which had been elected by only active citizens. Like its famous descendant, the Paris Commune of 1871, it was not authorized by an official act of legislation, but sprang fully armed, as it were, from the minds of the Paris sections. Accordingly, it recognized few limits on its right to exercise sovereignty in the name of Parisians. It also clashed repeatedly with the National Legislative Assembly. This assembly was on its last legs, to be replaced by a National Convention on September 22, 1792. But the arguments between national and municipal governments were sufficiently heated that their repercussions resonated for months.

Leading the charge for the Commune was Robespierre. Admired by the Parisians for his popular and populist tirades in the original National Constitutive Assembly, he had not held national office since September 1791, when a new Legislative Assembly was elected. After the August 1792 Revolution, he was chosen as a section representative to the municipal assembly, along with other future radical leaders of the Convention. He swiftly emerged as a spokesperson for the Commune, leading multiple delegations to the Legislative Assembly. Again and again, he hit the same note in his speeches. The national government should respect the sovereign will of the Parisian people and not meddle in the Commune's affairs: "The people, obliged to look after its own safety, has entrusted its well-being to its delegates. . . . [T]hose that it has personally chosen as its magistrates should enjoy the full powers of sovereignty."[50]

Robespierre honed in on an argument that was central to how the Paris Commune justified its political actions. The people of Paris had directly charged it to see to their safety, placing no limits on its authority: "'Go forth, act in my name, and I will approve everything that you will have done,'" was their message, Jean-Lambert Tallien informed the assembly, ventriloquizing Parisian citizens.[51] There was some truth to this assertion. When the sections had elected new representatives to the Paris Commune, in August 1792, many had indeed granted "unlimited powers" to these new officials.[52] The new Commune did not hesitate to use them. They set about arresting suspected counterrevolutionaries and confiscating their property. They shut down Royalist newspapers. They made residential and civic certificates obligatory for anyone seeking to leave Paris or find employment.[53] In a particularly brazen act, they appropriated four printing presses belonging to the National Assembly, claiming them for Marat.[54] And they sent commissioners out to all eighty-three French departments, as well as to the armies, establishing a national communication network. A French historian writing a few years before Lenin uncannily described this situation in terms of a dual power: "The day after August 10, it appeared that there were two powers equally qualified for speaking to the French provinces in the name of the nation."[55]

In the eyes of the Legislative Assembly, most of the Commune's actions were simply illegal. Worse still, they amounted to a misguided understanding of popular sovereignty. The assembly accordingly passed a decree calling on the Commune to justify its actions in order to "maintain the sovereignty of the people."[56] This clash between dueling conceptions of how sovereignty related to government was again pitched as an argument over the meaning of the Revolution itself. "Do you wish, gentlemen, to dishonor our beautiful Revolution, by offering to the empire the scandalous example of a commune rebelling against the general will and the law?" demanded the assembly president, Jean-François Delacroix, in response to Tallien's claims on behalf of the Commune.[57]

But these disagreements over the proper understanding of sovereignty and revolution paled in comparison with what followed. From the beginning, the Commune's mission had been one of retribution: "Sovereign people," the General Assembly announced to the city of Paris on August 11, "suspend your vengeance . . . all the guilty will perish on the scaffold."[58] The storming of the Tuileries Palace had been a gory ordeal, and Parisians simmered with rage toward the king's defenders. The Legislative Assembly cooperated to a degree with these cries for justice, establishing an extraordinary tribunal for this purpose. Though it was authorized by the national government, this "tribunal of August 17" drew its jurors entirely from the Paris sections. Convicts sentenced to death faced the guillotine, the first time this method of execution was used to punish political crimes. This court served as a blueprint for the better known revolutionary tribunal established seven months later.[59]

But the August 17 tribunal was slow in meting out justice. The Commune, which had initially released most of the prisoners arrested by the former administration, had quickly filled the prisons back up again. The municipal assembly granted itself the authority to lock up whomever it wished, without a trial, and delegated this same power to its commissioners. Their round-up operation was supervised by a municipal committee of surveillance, which worked with sectional committees to identify and arrest suspects. On September 2, this committee was reorganized, with Marat added as a member.[60]

That date is better remembered as the start of the infamous prison massacres. Alarmed by disturbing reports from the northeastern front, crowds of Parisians went from prison to prison over the course of five days, exercising summary justice on the prisoners. They were not indiscriminate: many prisoners were acquitted. But overt enemies of the Revolution—priests who refused to swear an oath to the state, aristocrats, royal guards, and suspected Royalists—were sentenced to death. Their punishment was carried out immediately, often in a gruesome manner.[61]

Marat's involvement with the surveillance committee, and his clear delight with the massacres (expressed in a letter encouraging other departments to follow the Parisian example), have long marked him as the villainous mastermind behind these executions. But it is doubtful that he played much of a direct role, if any. For one, the crowds did not go after rival revolutionaries, as Marat had been urging them to do for years. They mostly stuck with the outspoken opponents of the Revolution. The surveillance committee issued an arrest warrant for Brissot and his ally Roland, then minister of the interior, but it was not enforced.[62]

In fact, the prison massacres flowed from the democratic theory of the Cordeliers and other radical district members. Rejecting the separation of powers as absurd and illegitimate, they had insisted on democratizing the legislative process, by giving the final say on national bills to primary assemblies. These same assemblies had established commissioners to oversee the execution of laws in their own districts, again in an attempt to make democratic government coincide as much as possible with popular sovereignty. The judiciary power, long attached to the king, was harder to appropriate. Dissatisfaction with the national justice system had been brewing for a while: recall the Cordeliers' refusal to recognize the arrest warrant for Marat in 1790. Popular frustration with the August 17 tribunal was the breaking point. The next step for the Paris democrats was to take justice into their own hands. Tellingly, the overwhelming majority of victims—around two-thirds—had not been jailed for political reasons: they were petty criminals, brawlers, counterfeiters, and debtors. Judging these prisoners was a logical extension of the democratic government that Parisians had demanded and practiced since the start of the Revolution.[63]

Many historians look to the 1792 September massacres as marking the start of the Terror, a period of political repression that reached a crescendo the following year and bequeathed its name to subsequent revolutionary purges.[64] But the differences between the prison massacres and the violent retributions to come are as significant as any parallels. The Parisian crowds ultimately carried out a form of populist violence. They targeted social elites and misfits, in the name of the unitary will of the people.[65] The massacres were fairly spontaneous, and conspicuously did not rely on state institutions. By contrast, the revolutionary violence that lay ahead—both in 1793–94, and in future revolutions—was almost always carried out through official channels: special courts, military campaigns, secret police, mass imprisonments, and so forth. Its victims also differed, since they were as likely to be rival political actors as proponents of the old regime.

Populist violence, a feature of the Revolution since the storming of the Bastille, was not unique to revolutionary politics. Angry crowds had targeted tax collectors and other administrators long before 1789. Political terror, on the other hand, was a novel phenomenon, intrinsically tied to the modern idea of revolution. Enacted through formal institutions and effacing the distinction between rivals and enemies, it stemmed from confrontation among multiple power centers. It was not necessarily populist, and could even be openly anti-populist: the Champs-de-Mars massacre is a case in point, as is the "white terror" that followed the unsuccessful Prairial insurrection of 1795. More than the product of ideology or emotions, revolutionary terror was structural. It was the culmination of a battle to control the meaning of revolution.[66]

The fallout from the September massacres lasted for months. For the Girondins, it was a useful cudgel with which to bludgeon their rivals, Marat and Robespierre in chief. They were still a stinging memory in March 1793, when Danton invoked their specter to justify a new revolutionary tribunal. But due to their shocking nature, the massacres have also overshadowed the political importance of the "insurrectionary" Commune, both for the history of the French Revolution, and for the modern history of revolution more generally. We can glimpse its centrality in a speech that Robespierre delivered in November 1792 to the National Convention, in which he defended the Commune's actions against Girondin attacks. If they had done anything illegal, then their actions were "as illegal as the Revolution, as the fall of the Bastille, as illegal as liberty itself." Accordingly, everything they did was perfectly legitimate, since it was thanks to the Revolution that political legitimacy had been established in the first place. The sovereign people had overthrown the government: how could anyone object to their authorizing a new, local government in its stead? To criticize the Commune's behavior was like insisting on "a revolution without a revolution." You could not separate what happened at the Tuileries Palace from what happened at the Hôtel-de-Ville.[67]

It was a brilliant speech, which put to rest (for a while) Girondin accusations that Robespierre dreamed of dictatorship. But there was something new and daring in Robespierre's speech that passed unnoticed at the time. He gave the municipal assembly a different name, calling it the "revolutionary general assembly" (*conseil général révolutionnaire*). It was a revealing choice of words. Since July 1789, "revolution" had chiefly been an attribute of the people.[68] When the Constitutive Assembly, in

September 1791, passed an amnesty law for "actions related to the Revolution," the actions in question were not those of the lawmakers. The latter were in fact responding to Lafayette's proposal to free those detained after the king's flight and after his own suppression of the July 17 demonstration.[69] Robespierre maintained this association between revolution and the people, but now equated the actions of the section militants with those of a government body. In his retelling, politics was revolution by other means.

This subtle terminological change foreshadowed one of the most fateful twists in the history of revolution. In the mind of Robespierre and others, the leading role of revolution could be played equally well, if not better, by the government itself. If this idea undermined existing views of revolution as popular action, it was not wholly original. Robespierre was simply recasting the modern Enlightenment idea of revolution, which had been embraced by liberal deputies in the summer of 1789, before Parisian crowds stole the spotlight. Voltaire's enlightened despot now found new life in the revolutionary council.

If Robespierre could claim the mantle of revolution for the Paris municipal assembly, it was largely thanks to the democratic theory of government that had originated in the Paris districts. Just as the district assemblies pursued a one-to-one identity with the sovereign people, so too was there meant to be no daylight between the actions of the municipal assembly and the wishes of the Parisian people. The Commune ruled, in Robespierre's words, through "popular power."[70] The Committee of Public Safety would use similar logic to justify the revolutionary government a year later, with an important twist, as we will see. Still, the insurrectionary or "revolutionary" Paris Commune was not just a blip in the history of the French Revolution, but a transitional experience that opened up new possibilities for revolutionary rulers to come.

A Dictatorship out of Time

By the time Robespierre was defending the actions of the Paris Commune, he was no longer part of it. He had moved on to the National Convention, along with Marat, Tallien, Billaud-Varenne, Collot d'Herbois, and others. The epic clash between the Montagnards (so named because they sat on the top benches) and the Girondins now took place within the assembly hall itself. But this grouping of old rivals under one roof did not mark an end to the power struggles across governmental levels. Not only did they persist, but they are crucial for understanding the two main political developments of this period: the rise of political terror, and the creation of a revolutionary government.

Even when they were not in the room, the Paris Commune and sections loomed over the heated arguments between Montagnards and Girondins, as the Parisians overwhelmingly supported the former. The Girondins continued to attack the sections for misunderstanding the relationship between popular sovereignty and representative government. Pierre-Victurnien Vergniaud, a deputy from Bordeaux, told the people that they had been tricked: "The anarchists fooled you by abusing the word 'sovereignty.' They almost overthrew the republic, by leading each section to believe that sovereignty lay within it." The Girondins insisted on the indivisibility of national sovereignty, and even sought to move the Convention's seat outside of Paris.[71]

Neither group fully controlled the Convention. If the Girondins got their way on the issue of the king's trial (the Montagnards insisted that he had already been judged), they lost on the verdict (they had wanted the people to determine his punishment). Occasionally both sides were in agreement, notably on how to respond to the monarchist and Catholic uprising that broke out in the Vendée, in February 1793. And both backed the creation of a revolutionary tribunal in March 1793. But the military rout of the French army in the Austrian Netherlands that same month kicked off another cycle of political attacks, this time with deadly consequences.[72]

The general of the defeated French army, Charles-François Dumouriez, had been allied with the Girondins; he then betrayed the republic by crossing over to the Austrians. In Paris, the response to his betrayal was explosive. At the Jacobin Club, under the presidency of Marat, members drafted a circular letter, claiming that "counterrevolution is in the government, in the National Convention." It was a call for insurrection against Dumouriez's supposed Girondin supporters.[73]

At first, it seemed as though the Jacobins, Marat in particular, had overplayed their hand. In a lengthy defense of the Girondins, Marguerite-Élie Guadet, also a deputy from Bordeaux, denied any ties with Dumouriez, and concluded his peroration by reading the Jacobin letter aloud. Immediately, calls resounded for Marat's arrest. The motion was put to the vote and passed. The following day, April 13, the Convention directed the new revolutionary tribunal to hear the case.

Marat's trial kicked off what has been called the "politicians' terror."[74] Institutions that had been created to defend the Revolution against its enemies, both domestic and foreign, were used to settle scores between political rivals. But these institutions themselves contributed to the fractured landscape of political power. The juries for the revolutionary tribunal were drawn from the Paris sections. The outcome of Marat's two-day trial, on April 23–24, was foretold: he was acquitted, and carried home on the shoulders of cheering Parisians.[75]

Ultimately, Gaudet's dramatic reveal of the Jacobin letter backfired. Two days after the Convention instructed the revolutionary tribunal to hear Marat's case, the mayor of the Paris Commune, Jean-Nicholas Pache, led a delegation to the Convention. The Commune and the sections presented a petition demanding the expulsion of twenty-two Girondins who had supported Dumouriez, and were guilty of a felony "against the sovereign people." The petition was unsuccessful. But the Girondins sensed their days were numbered.[76]

Once again, they turned to institutional power for their defense. They persuaded the Convention to create a commission to supervise the decrees of the Paris Commune. Four days after its creation, on May 25, this "Commission of Twelve" had the radical journalist and deputy *procureur* for the Commune, Jacques-René Hébert, arrested. Another delegation of Parisians immediately rushed to demand his release. The president of the Convention, the Girondin Maximin Isnard, had an unfortunate response: "If national representation were to be harmed by these recurrent insurrections, I declare in the name of all of France, Paris will be annihilated. . . . [Y]ou will search the banks of the Seine to see if Paris ever existed." Both sides recognized that the dual-power situation could be resolved only by force.[77]

While the Convention and the Commune locked horns in an institutional contest, the sections dusted off the revolutionary script of August 1792. On May 31, they recalled their representatives in the Commune's general assembly, and established a new "revolutionary committee" invested with "unlimited rights" to protect public safety.[78] Then they marched once again on the Tuileries Palace, now the seat of the National Convention. First a delegation presented a petition demanding the expulsion of the twenty-two Girondins. When that was unsuccessful, they returned on June 2 with tens of thousands of National Guards and dozens of cannon, under the command of François Hanriot. After a tense standoff, the Convention ultimately agreed to place the twenty-two (plus another seven) deputies and former ministers under house arrest.[79] Four months later, most of them would be tried by the revolutionary tribunal and sentenced to death. Marat would have relished the irony, had he not himself been assassinated in July 1793.

Even before this insurrection, the Girondins had compared the sections' attempt to expel them with Colonel Pride's purge of Parliament in 1648.[80] This analogy was popular with nineteenth-century historians, and canonized by the historian Crane Brinton in his comparative study of revolutions. But Brinton also drew a parallel with another moment in revolutionary history: the storming of the Winter Palace by the Bolsheviks in October 1917. In both cases, he argued, a show of force (if not overt violence) brought a dual-power situation to a close.[81] In principle, the Convention and the Commune, along with the Paris sections, were now aligned. The democratic vision of a sovereign people, sketched out in the radical Parisian districts in 1789, could now become a reality nationwide—or at least, that was the plan.

There were certainly signs that June 2 marked the end of the conflict between rival power centers and their competing interpretations of sovereignty and government. As the Girondin deputies were being escorted out of the Tuileries on the night of June 2, the Montagnard Jacques-Alexis Thuriot proposed a motion that the Convention now focus on writing a new constitution. In record time, the Committee of Public Safety produced a draft, which Marie-Jean Hérault de Séchelles presented to the Convention on June 10, 1793. Two weeks later, it was adopted with minor revisions and distributed around the country for ratification.[82]

In many ways, the Montagnard constitution reflected the democratic principles long demanded by the Parisian districts. Its National Assembly did not have a monopoly on legislative power. The new body only "proposed" laws that the primary assemblies could approve or veto.[83] Ultimate legislative power thus remained vested as close to the sovereign people as possible. Gone, too, was any mention of the separation of powers. The National Assembly itself selected the twenty-four members of an Executive Council (Conseil Exécutif) from a list populated by the primary assemblies. The executive branch was even physically integrated into the legislative assembly: "The executive council sits with the legislative body; it has admission to, and a separate space in, its gathering place." This novel arrangement foreshadowed the parliamentarian model that gained traction in the nineteenth century.[84]

The new constitution was overwhelmingly ratified by the French people in a national referendum, and then officially celebrated on August 10, 1793, with pagan pomp in Paris. It offered a thrilling display of national consensus, which turned out, again, to be illusory.[85] Logically, the *conventionnels* should next have called for elections and gone home. Their mandate was complete. The very name of their body—a "convention"—indicated their purpose—namely, to draft a new constitution. They were not intended to be a permanent legislative body. There was a new National Assembly waiting in the wings.[86]

But there were already signs of nascent conflicts, arising from renewed disagreements about the goals of the Revolution. The popular movement itself was splintering, with a group of "enraged" Parisians (*les enragés*) pressing for greater economic relief. They helped reopen the rift between the Convention and the sections, which invaded the Tuileries again on September 5, 1793, to demand lower prices and death to grain hoarders. One of their leaders, Jacques Roux, was imprisoned, and Danton deftly had a law passed limiting the meetings of section assemblies and forbidding women from participating in political clubs. It was a betrayal of the Montagnards' most valuable allies, as the "permanence" of assemblies had been a popular demand since 1789.[87]

It was famously during this *journée* that the protesters demanded that "terror be made the order of the day."[88] Terror they would get, only not the sort they had hoped for. The Convention did not prioritize hunting down hoarders or speculators, but instead sent armies out against declared enemies of the Revolution, such as the Vendée rebels. The vast majority of those who died during the Terror would either be killed in military operations or condemned by military tribunals as outlaws.[89]

The new constitution might have offered a framework for working through these disagreements about governmental policies in a democratic fashion. A future National Assembly could have publicly debated pros and cons of different ideas, and then proposed laws for the primary assemblies to vote on. But this democratic solution never materialized. On October 10, 1793, the young Louis-Antoine Saint-Just, on behalf of the twelve-member Committee of Public Safety, announced a change of plans. Rather than calling for new elections, the committee urged the Convention to suspend the constitution. The stated reason was that France was at war, hence the new "revolutionary government" that would henceforth be in charge would last only "until peacetime." But it is fairly clear from other statements that the real threat came not from the Prussians but from the French electors themselves. The Montagnards had enjoyed a majority in the Convention since June 1793; why would they jeopardize their hold on power? What's more, the purged Girondin deputies had found new strongholds in provincial cities. Bordeaux, Lyon, Marseille, and other cities had fallen into the hands of "federalist" leaders, who challenged the central government. Once again, the illusion of consensus had shattered.[90]

Historians have not hesitated to call the revolutionary government a dictatorship.[91] In the context of 1793, this was a loaded word. The

Girondins had been accusing Robespierre of aspiring to dictatorship since spring 1792.[92] He was, in their eyes, guilty by association with Marat, who had been openly militating for a dictator for years. But Marat wanted a dictator in the classical Roman sense. In republican Rome, dictators had to be appointed (usually by a consul), and then approved by a popular vote. Their term was time limited, and they did not have absolute power while in office. Roman dictators, for instance, still had to honor a citizen's right of appeal (the *provocatio*). Marat similarly demanded specific, not unlimited, powers for his dictator: "a supreme dictator, whose powers would give him no authority to dominate, but would be unlimited to strike down the leaders of conspiracies."[93]

The revolutionary government, by contrast, was closer to a modern dictatorship. It was not authorized by the explicit consent of the people: an overwhelming majority of French citizens had just voted to establish a representative democratic republic. The decree introduced by Saint-Just included no clear sunset clause. What defined "peacetime"? As the revolutionary armies went on the offensive in spring 1794, there was no hint that the Convention would now disband. The committee members who justified this new form of government before the Convention adopted the logic and rhetoric of political guardians, just as later dictators would.[94]

But the question of what to call this regime is ultimately less interesting than the question of why it did not elicit much resistance at the time. For there is no suggestion that the French rejected the revolutionary government as illegitimate. It helped that it was familiar: at a practical level, little changed between October 9 and October 11, 1793. The danger of challenging the new government was also real: "terror" was on everyone's lips. Suppressing counterrevolutionaries, as we will see, was its raison d'être. Still, as historians of later revolutions have argued, it is a mistake to assume that repressive regimes survive on fear alone.[95] The revolutionary government may be defined as a dictatorship, but most French citizens accepted its authority.

The Committee of Public Safety certainly went out of its way over the coming months to justify the delay of elections and suspension of the 1793 constitution. Its members even appropriated claims from the Parisian districts about the democratic expression of popular sovereignty. One forceful defense of the revolutionary government came from Billaud-Varenne, now on the Committee of Public Safety, and formerly part of the insurrectionary Commune. His defense built on arguments he had already made before the August 10 revolution. At that time, he had denounced the supposedly "well-balanced" constitution for destabilizing the country. He had also singled out a different set of values that were even more important than any classical political principles: "Is there even a constitution if it fails to assure the welfare of the empire, the happiness of the people, and internal peace?" He did not answer this rhetorical question, but it underscored the great gamble of modern revolutions: some social and political goals appear so great that they can justify the rejection of a democratic order.[96]

And this was precisely the argument that he drove home in his first speech on the revolutionary government, in December 1793. Constitutional government was simply insufficient for carrying out the great work of the Revolution: establishing freedom, purifying moral conduct, and especially purging the administration of counterrevolutionaries. This punitive function, which the Paris Commune had similarly embraced, was emphasized by all committee spokespersons: the people could launch a revolution, but it took an organized administration to punish its enemies. Terror—or, as they started calling it after February 1794, justice—must take precedence over democracy.[97]

Billaud-Varenne also described the new government in terms reminiscent of the Cordeliers' theory of popular sovereignty—minus the democratic government, of course. Revolutionary government was modeled on "natural processes," and rested on interconnected principles, not separate powers. Less than two months after it was introduced, Billaud-Varenne now recast revolutionary government as a radical experiment that would serve as a "model for drafting the organic code of the constitution." The constitution of 1793 was not only suspended, it was superseded as well. The new government would be a mechanical masterpiece, with a central executive agency reaching into the farthest depths of the state. It was the modern dream of a centralized authority that would leverage the nation's powers rather than balancing them, as Turgot had urged.[98]

The revolutionary government might appear to be a contradiction in terms. Its representatives never ceased to invoke the people as their source of legitimacy, yet the people had little say in the government. In part, this apparent contradiction resulted from the Rousseauist suspicion that unvirtuous officials could subvert the will of the people.[99] Many deputies to the National Assembly and (later) National Convention had long been suspected of corruption by Parisians. A constant theme in the reports from the Committee of Public Safety, especially Robespierre's, was that they alone could be trusted to remain virtuous. L'incorruptible—Robespierre's epithet—was the hero that the Revolution needed, at least in the eyes of some. It took a dictatorship to save democracy.

But this argument worked only when considered from a temporal perspective. It took dictatorship *now* to save democracy *later*. The justification for the revolutionary government thereby changed a fundamental feature of revolution. Up until then, the time span of revolution had been clearly defined. As the Constitutive Assembly had decreed, in the last weeks of its session, "The objective of the French Revolution has been to provide the Empire with a Constitution, and thus the Revolution must end once the Constitution is completed and accepted."[100] The problem of how and when to "end" the revolution was hotly debated, yet no one suggested that it should go on indefinitely. That was precisely what the committee spokespersons now advanced.

Robespierre perfected the argument through which the modern regime of history came to justify the revolutionary political regime.[101] Like his rival Condorcet, he placed the French Revolution in a long arc of human progress, which bent toward reason and justice. But the French were not there yet: half the Revolution still lay ahead. What remained was the moral transformation of French people, which Robespierre hoped to achieve through new institutions and festivals. The French people may already be "two thousand years in advance of the rest of the human race," as the abbé de Saint-Pierre had predicted, but their temporal arms race was not yet complete.[102]

The underlying message from the committee was accordingly that a republican constitution and democratic participation were insufficiently ambitious goals for the French Revolution. Much loftier, even utopian, achievements—Robespierre spoke of "the reign of eternal justice"—were the real prizes to be won. This was how the committee justified present compromises: by promises of future happiness. The legitimacy that it claimed, in this regard, was prospectively retrospective. One had to look forward (prospectively) to the future state of affairs that the revolutionary government would bring about, in order for this coming achievement to authorize (retrospectively) the actions that had been taken to arrive there. This complex reasoning is nicely captured by the verb tense that best approximates its logic: the aptly named future perfect. Revolutionary government *will have been justified* once it delivered a perfect future.

Simply suspending the constitution and postponing elections did not silence disagreements about what this perfect future should bring. Some believed it spelled the end of Christianity, and turned the Notre-Dame de Paris cathedral into a Temple of Reason. Others demanded greater social assistance and more repressive measures against speculators. Once again, these different opinions found institutional support at different levels of government. One of the officials presiding over the Festival of Reason held at Notre-Dame in November 1793 was Pierre Gaspard "Anaxagoras" Chaumette, the *procureur* of the Paris Commune.[103] The Cordeliers Club—not an official organ of government, but where many section leaders gathered—sought to incite another insurrection in March 1794, in order to unleash even more terror against internal and foreign enemies.[104] The Convention itself splintered between "moderates" (such as Danton and Desmoulins) and extremists.

In one respect, the revolutionary government offered the perfect line of defense against these emergent conflicts. Its committees ordered the arrest of the dissidents, who would be carted off to the guillotine after abbreviated trials. The simplest answer to the lack of consensus and the jurisdictional rivalries that had plagued the Revolution from the start was force. Terror is the ultima ratio of revolutionaries.

But something was still missing. The Committee of Public Safety was a dictatorship without a dictator. The most likely candidate, Robespierre, was both unable and unwilling to play the part. He had built his career by blocking others who showed signs of dictatorial ambition. It is hard to see how he himself could have made the pivot to first consul. Ill health also prevented him from participating in meetings of the committee or the Convention for weeks on end. At the same time, only Robespierre had the personal credit to guarantee the political bill of exchange that the revolutionary government tendered. Indeed, his fall on Thermidor 9 (July 27, 1794) lay bare the missing keystone of this political edifice. There is ultimately only one way to prevent the incessant splintering of views about where the revolution should be headed. It takes a more active leader to settle the meaning of revolution and silence dissensions. Modern revolutions crave a Leviathan.[105]

PART IV

The Progress of Revolution

CHAPTER ELEVEN

Liberal Revolution and Its Discontents

"CITIZENS, THE REVOLUTION has settled on the principles with which it began: it is over." So proclaimed the consuls in their presentation of the Constitution of Year VIII (1799). While they were three in number, it was the first consul, Napoleon Bonaparte, who gained the greatest powers under the new regime. He alone could propose and ratify new laws and appoint most government officials, including all judges. How could this constitutional arrangement reflect the principles with which the Revolution began? And what did it mean for Bonaparte to declare the Revolution to be over?[1]

The answers to these questions must be sought in the years between the fall of Robespierre and the rise of Bonaparte. The Thermidorians, who brought down the former, denounced the preceding regime as a "system of Terror," devising a label that historians use to this day. They sought to stabilize the republic by means of a more conservative constitution, bringing back property qualifications and introducing a bicameral legislature. This government became known as the Directory, as it dispersed executive power among five directors.[2]

This new government was swiftly attacked on all sides. In May ("Prairial") 1795, resurgent Jacobins staged an unsuccessful insurrection to enact the constitution of 1793. Then in October ("Vendémiaire"), it was the Royalists' turn to oppose the new government: a young General Bonaparte repulsed their attack with cannon fire in front of the Eglise Saint-Roch. The ballot box proved as difficult to manage as the streets. In September ("Fructidor") 1797, the government unconstitutionally annulled the elections of Royalist deputies, deporting sixty-five of them to French Guiana.

The following year, they blocked candidacies from Jacobin sympathizers. After the Jacobins still won a majority in both chambers in 1799, the abbé Sieyès resorted to a coup d'état, which brought the Directory to an end. Bonaparte emerged as first consul, becoming consul for life in 1802 and emperor soon after.

It would be short-sighted, however, to view Napoleon's rule as a circling back—an *anacyclosis*—to the old regime. Often dismissed as a mere dictator, Napoleon in fact played a key role in perpetuating the legacy of the French Revolution, especially abroad. In 1789, the French had pursued three political objectives all at once: the protection of individual rights, the assertion of popular sovereignty, and the creation of a representative government. Each of these objectives had been missing from the old regime, and all were inscribed in the Declaration of the Rights of Man. Many articles outlined the rights that French citizens should henceforth enjoy; article 3 shifted the source of sovereignty from the king to the nation; and articles 14–16 sketched an outline of the representative government to come.[3]

As we saw in the previous chapter, the main cause of political turmoil during the first five years of the Revolution was debates over the correct exercise and expression of popular sovereignty. What exactly did it entail? Who should be entrusted to govern? Could part of the sovereign people govern itself independently from the whole? Could the people overrule their representatives? Disagreements over these questions propelled the Revolution from crisis to crisis, often resulting in violence and repression.

During the Directory, by contrast, most political problems arose around matters of government. Who were fit to serve as representatives? What was the relation between executive and legislative power? Given the serial crises around these questions, it became increasingly clear to many observers that the constitution of 1795 had not squared the circle of republican government under popular sovereignty.

The compromise that Bonaparte and his collaborators offered to the French people in 1799 is accordingly best viewed against this backdrop. The consulate, and later the empire, reshuffled the relation between sovereignty, government, and rights. As we will see, rights remained at the center of this deal, and were its most important deliverables, even if in practice the new regime did not always deliver. Nominally, their guarantees remained the same, but in much weakened form. If we imagine popular participation in representative government as a dial, the consuls turned it almost all the way down. Popular sovereignty, too, was kept to a minimum: the people could express their will only through the occasional plebiscite and heavily mediated, indirect elections and nominations.[4]

The net result of this reconfiguration was a form of politics soon to enjoy success under the name of "liberalism." This claim may seem puzzling. Histories of liberalism tend to look back to earlier philosophers, such as Locke or Montesquieu, or to the early French Revolution. If Napoleon features in these histories at all, it is generally as a villain or opponent.[5] When he is occasionally granted the moniker of "liberal," it is typically only with respect to the constitutional reforms of 1815, during his brief return to power known as the Hundred Days.[6]

But these accounts miss Napoleon's most important contribution, which was to realign the "high" enjoyment of individual rights with a "low" exercise of popular sovereignty and "low" participation in republican government. It was critical that these "low" settings never drop to a level where they were turned entirely off. Some degree of both was still necessary for the liberal deal to function. But precisely how much of each was unclear, and subsequent liberal regimes, both in Europe and in the Americas, exploited this ambiguity. In 1799, a lower level of participation in government was heralded as a necessary condition for the high enjoyment of individual rights. It was for this reason that the consuls could describe the new constitution as resting on "the true principles of representative government," and the new powers it created as "strong and stable, as they must be to guarantee the rights of citizens and the interests of the State."[7]

Bonaparte's bargain clearly falls short of contemporary democratic standards. In practice, it was an authoritarian regime, often quite ruthless in its suppression of dissidents. But its authoritarian structure was at least partially by design, and its very appeal lay in its rejection of democratic "excesses." The democratic standards that we now consider beneficial—regular elections, maximal suffrage, and robust representative government—were in 1799 viewed as disruptive, and even ill-suited to the protection of individual rights. Many histories of liberalism adopt an expansionist logic to describe its development: first religious toleration, then economic rights, and finally political freedom. But taking Bonaparte seriously adds a twist to these narratives.[8] Liberalism emerged as an attractive political position precisely because it *curtailed* political rights. It is not the case that political rights were added *later* to the liberal package, but rather that they returned as part of the equation.

At the same time, the Bonapartist regime was more than a military dictatorship, despite its origins in a coup d'état. Central to its legitimacy was its full-throated defense of "the sacred rights of property, equality, and liberty."[9] Many of the philosophers identified as the progenitors of liberal thought had similarly promoted individual rights, yet Bonaparte's version was only loosely dependent on their ideas. Unlike Hobbes, Bonaparte still insisted on the necessity of a representative government; and unlike Montesquieu, he defended popular sovereignty. Like the classical "liberal" economists before him, he celebrated property rights, but equally critical—and what truly distinguished his regime from the *ancien*—was the pledge to protect individual liberty.[10] In these regards, the question of what Bonaparte's influences were may be misplaced: his brand of liberalism was obviously a legacy of the French Revolution. The key aspect is what he left out. Bonaparte sliced through the Gordian knot of sovereignty, government, and rights that the revolutionaries had tied in 1789, preserving the core fabric of rights and leaving much of the rest on the cutting floor.

In France, Bonaparte's bargain often felt like a lousy deal. As consul and then emperor, Napoleon Bonaparte oversaw an oppressive government that silenced critics and tolerated no dissent. But the story was different abroad. The Napoleonic Empire brought many of the principles of the French Revolution—filtered through Bonaparte's liberal dispensation—to the doorsteps of Europeans, who had previously watched the Revolution from afar. These principles were primarily disseminated in the form of legal codes and constitutions for the new regimes that the French set up in their imperial domain, when they did not annex territories outright. From the early "sister republics" to Napoleon's dynastic kingdoms, these new states typically adopted the French revolutionary language of individual rights. The Batavian Republic even issued its own Declaration of the Rights of Man and of the Citizen in 1795. Those that were created before 1799, such as the Batavian, Cisalpine, Roman, Helvetic, and Neapolitan Republics, enjoyed fairly participatory forms of representative government modeled on the French constitution of 1795, which had established the Directory. After 1804, these states, along with new ones, took the form of constitutional monarchies. Even during this imperial phase, however, the protection of individual rights remained a key plank in the Napoleonic platform. The French abolished guilds and feudal privileges and introduced commercial courts. The right to individual property, in particular, enjoyed a protected status thanks to the widespread adoption of the Napoleonic Code civil (or variations thereon).[11]

The French revolutionary wars and their imperial extension thus made critical contributions to the dissemination and implementation of liberal ideas. While many Europeans initially greeted these new regimes enthusiastically, Bonaparte's self-declaration as emperor sent the pendulum swinging in a more anti-French direction. By 1812, representatives to the

Spanish cortes gathered in Cádiz could declare themselves "liberals" for resisting their French king. But as the following section shows, even those who fought Napoleon in the name of liberalism were often his unwitting beneficiaries.

The Napoleonic Empire also had major implications for the Western hemisphere, where the struggle for liberation often overshadowed the fight for liberalism. This contrast was especially stark in Haiti, where liberation from the French did not result in any significant gain of political rights. A similar story played out in Spanish America, where lasting conflicts between Royalists and independents conflated military and political roles, and kept the dials of republican government and popular sovereignty on a very low setting. But these cases showcase how a liberal defense of rights is frighteningly compatible with authoritarian government.

Liberal Revolutionaries

The first revolutionaries to call themselves "liberals" were the Spaniards who framed a constitution in 1812—or so the story goes. Gathered in the port city of Cádiz, and protected by British warships from the French troops occupying the peninsula, they sought to establish an alternative government to that of José I, known to history as Joseph Bonaparte. Although the Cádiz constitution recognized the deposed Ferdinand VII as the lawful Spanish monarch, it was still a revolutionary document, denouncing a despotic Spanish old regime, which it consigned to the past.[12]

But this was not the first modern Spanish constitution, nor were its framers the first to self-identify as liberal. Both of those firsts belong to Napoleon, who had bestowed a constitution on Spain in 1808. Ratified by a small assembly (or *cortes*) of Spanish and Spanish American notables in the town of Bayonne, this "Acte Constitutionnel de l'Espagne" is today better known as the Bayonne constitution (or statute).[13] Napoleon presented it to the Spanish people in the following terms:

> I have destroyed everything opposed to your prosperity and greatness. I have crushed the obstacles weighing on the people. I give you a liberal constitution [*une constitution libérale [je] vous donne*], and instead of an absolute monarchy, a tempered and constitutional one.[14]

The use of "liberal" in this statement is unusual. Up until this time, the adjective *libéral* had been largely synonymous, in French, with "generous." Napoleon himself was one of the first French authors to use "liberal" in the sense of promoting freedom.[15]

The connection between these two constitutions, and between Napoleonic and Spanish liberalism, in fact runs much deeper.[16] The Bayonne constitution, which provides the most direct link between them, reiterated the key "liberal" planks of Bonaparte's bargain: freedom from arbitrary detention, property rights, and freedom of the press. It established a senatorial commission to oversee "la libertad individual" (art. 40), and another for "la libertad de la imprenta" (freedom of the press; art. 45). Freedom from arbitrary searches was protected by declaring the domicile an "asilo inviolable" (art. 126). Joseph's royal oath reiterated this dedication to liberal principles: the king swore to "respect and ensure respect for individual liberty and property and to govern solely with the interest, happiness, and glory of the Spanish nation in mind" (art. 6).

All of these principles, expressions, and institutional arrangements were lifted from earlier French constitutional documents. Indeed, Napoleonic constitutions were mostly a matter of cut and paste, with "framers" simply translating and copying (often verbatim) passages from earlier texts. The main source material for these editing operations was the constitution of 1799 and its imperial revision, the Sénatus-consulte organique of May 18, 1804. The senatorial commissions created by the Bayonne constitution were replicas of those established in this 1804 constitution.[17] The prohibition of "arbitrary detention" had already featured in the 1799 constitution (art. 46), which had also used the same language of *un aisle inviolable* to protect against warrantless searches (art. 76).[18] The oath sworn by Joseph recapitulated the imperial oath, as defined in 1804 (art. 53).

None of these ideas or even the language was original, of course, and all can be traced back to earlier revolutionary legislation. The "inviolable and sacred" status of property was enshrined in article 17 of the 1789 Declaration of the Rights of Man and of the Citizen, after having been listed as one of the four rights that humans naturally enjoy in article 2. Article 7 had forbidden the dreaded *lettre de cachet*, and arbitrary detention more generally.[19] A French version of habeas corpus was codified as early as October 1789, spelling out punishments for detaining prisoners who had not been charged with a crime for more than twenty-four hours.[20] Similar provisions were included in the 1799 constitution (art. 77–82). The penal code of 1791, in an article defining the crime of arbitrary detention ("attentat contre la liberté individuelle"), had even praised individual liberty as the "essential basis of the French Constitution."[21] It was not entirely fictional, then, for Bonaparte to claim that the constitution of 1799 confirmed the "true principles" of the French Revolution, even if his regime did not live up to them.

Like most others written around this time, the Bayonne constitution had a limited impact. For the duration of Joseph's reign (1808–13), Spain was in a state of civil war, with French control of the country weak at best. All the same, some of the measures decreed at Bayonne left a significant mark. The constitution banned the Inquisition, and freedom of the press was largely granted. Thanks to the latter, and the propaganda efforts of the Crown, the "liberal" principles proclaimed at Bayonne, and by Napoleon himself in Madrid, did not pass unnoticed.[22]

When the Spanish cortes met in Cádiz, its very existence implied an opposition to France, and by extension, to French ideas. It is no wonder, then, that the commission charged with drafting the new constitution presented its project very differently than Napoleon. In a lengthy introductory report, mostly written by the deputy Agustín Argüelles, it took pains to insist that the result of its efforts was genuinely Spanish. The new constitution, the commission argued, revived "the true ideas of political and civil liberty, incessantly sustained, defended, and asserted by our ancestors in their innumerable and passionate petitions to the Cortes." In this narrative, the villains were Ferdinand and Isabella, who had trimmed the wings of the medieval cortes, and buried Spanish freedom ("la pérdida de la libertad"). They preemptively rejected any accusations that the constitution might have been inspired by foreign (read: French) models.[23]

But the Cádiz representatives may have protested too much. In its distribution of executive and legislative power, the 1812 constitution bore a strong resemblance to the French constitution of 1791. It even borrowed language from the Declaration of 1789 to affirm the sovereignty of the nation.[24] The king enjoyed a suspensive veto (one year, repeatable), but his functions were essentially reduced to the exercise of executive power.

What's more, while the arguments by the cortes about the history of representative government had some merit, many of the more specific rights outlined in the constitution had no historical precedent. Indeed, the two freedoms that were explicitly called out are individual liberty and freedom of the press. Article 172, on the executive power of the king, criminalized any "attack on individual liberty" (atentado contra la libertad individual)—precisely the language employed in the French penal code of 1791, and the focus of the senatorial commission of the Bayonne constitution. It similarly gave the government twenty-four hours to charge prisoners with a specific crime. Freedom of the press was guaranteed by article 371, in terms similar to article 11 of the French Declaration of 1789.[25] The royal oath also had the king promise to respect "the personal liberty of every individual" (art. 173). These were not relics of the medieval legacy of the cortes.

The emergence of "liberalism" as a political movement in Europe, then, was not just a reaction to Napoleonic policies, as it is often portrayed. It was a reappropriation of the very principles that Napoleon had himself promoted, if not always in good faith. The Cádiz constitution turned up the dials of popular sovereignty and representative government, though not nearly to the levels of republican France. Bonaparte's offer of individual liberty in exchange for strong participatory government proved the more palatable of revolutionary legacies, especially in countries with little history of the latter.

In the short term, the Cádiz constitution had an equally limited impact as its predecessor. It stood little chance of implementation while French troops still occupied Spain, though it would in fact be accepted by parts of the Spanish Empire. When Ferdinand VII returned to power in December 1813, he rejected the constitution and reverted to autocratic rule. The liberals staged a comeback in 1820, forcing the king to accept the 1812 constitution for three brief years (the *trienio liberal*). The staging point for their revolution was once again Cádiz, though this time its importance lay elsewhere. It was from this port that Spanish soldiers set sail for the New World, to repress the independence movements across the Atlantic. The Napoleonic wars had triggered another set of revolutions in the Americas. It was here that liberal revolutionaries would enjoy their greatest successes, and reveal their greatest limitations.

The New Atlantic Revolutions

Perhaps the clearest sign that the "age of revolutions" did not consist of a single wave, but rather of two overlapping ones—the last classical revolution in America, followed by the first modern revolution in France—is that the revolutions that rocked the Caribbean and Spanish America from 1791 onward came in the wake of 1789, not 1776. Nationality plays an important part in explaining why 1776 did not affect other European colonies in the Western hemisphere. Events in the British Empire had only a limited impact on events in the French or Spanish empires. But this reason is not entirely satisfactory, since it fails to explain the converse—namely, why the French Revolution *did* send shockwaves across the Americas.

HAITIAN LIBERATION

Nowhere was the French influence more evident than in the case of Haiti, whose independence in 1804 terrified American politicians, especially in the slave-owning South. The uprising that sparked the long process leading to emancipation, and later to independence, began in 1791. Precisely how events in France contributed to the slave insurrection that year is still debated: there is some suggestion that news of the 1789 Declaration reached the hellish plantations of Saint-Domingue (as the French colony was then called).[26] But for the next decade, the history of events in Saint-Domingue was tightly intertwined with the history of the events in France. Indeed, it is often difficult to distinguish where the Haitian Revolution begins and the French Revolution ends, at least before 1802. The abolition of slavery in Saint-Domingue, by the French commissioners Léger-Félicité Sonthonax and Etienne Polverel in late 1793, came in response to the raging struggle by enslaved people on the island. But it also led to a historic decree by the National Convention, in February 1794, abolishing slavery throughout the French Empire.

Saint-Domingue steadily became more independent in the following years, though long avoided declaring independence. After abandoning his alliance with the Spanish (who occupied the other half of the island, present-day Dominican Republic), Toussaint Louverture gradually assumed political control of Saint-Domingue. His power reached its zenith in 1801, when he took possession of the Spanish side of the island and issued a new constitution making him "governor-general for life." The constitution reaffirmed the island's status as a French colony, and its inhabitants' status as French. But it infuriated Bonaparte, who preferred to impose his own constitutions on French vassal states.

Even after 1794, the abolition of slavery had seemed uncertain. The British invaded the island in 1794, and retained a foothold there until 1798, wooing former plantation owners with the promise of restoring slavery. Louverture's rush to write a constitution in 1801 also reflected fears that the new Bonapartist regime might reverse the 1794 decree. It was these (ultimately correct) fears that led to war with France. Bonaparte initiated the hostilities in January 1802, sending a small armada to reassert control over the island, and possibly reestablish slavery. After a series of brutal engagements, a truce was negotiated, leaving the Black generals' command intact. But Louverture was betrayed, and shipped off to a cold prison in France. He died within a year.[27]

In May 1802, Bonaparte reestablished slavery in nearby Martinique, which the French had just regained from the English, as well as in Guadeloupe. Many feared that Saint-Domingue would be next. With Bonaparte's expeditionary force weakened by disease and defections, that October the Black generals revolted again. This time, they were successful. The last French troops surrendered in November 1803, and on January 1, 1804, the new commander in chief of the Black forces, Jean-Jacques Dessalines, proclaimed the independence of (the newly named) Haiti.[28]

The Haitian Revolution was a singular event in the history of revolution. It gave a particular poignancy to the idea of liberation.[29] This particularity can be overshadowed by the many features it shared with other revolutions, particularly those in the Western hemisphere. It also culminated in national liberation, understood as freedom from outside rule. This was a characteristic that it shared not only with the many Spanish American revolutions to follow but also with subsequent liberal revolutions in Europe. The *liberales* in Cádiz sought to promote individual liberties, but also to liberate their country from the French. Even in the case of the French Revolution, *liberté* possessed these multiple meanings inherited from the ancients: individual liberty, on the one hand, but also freedom from despotic or foreign rule, on the other.[30]

But it was the meaning of individual liberty that acquired a singular value with the Haitian Revolution. For the formerly enslaved people of Saint-Domingue, liberty meant above all remaining free from enslavement. The preservation of civil freedom had been one of the reasons why Louverture had pushed through the constitution of 1801, which insisted that "there cannot exist slaves on this territory, servitude is therein forever abolished. All men are born, live and die free and French" (art. 3). Dessalines's 1804 declaration of independence stressed the same point: "We must take any hope of re-enslaving us away from the inhuman government that for so long kept us in the most humiliating torpor." Independence, or national liberation, had a unique urgency for the Haitians, who sought above all to avoid a return to their former enslaved condition.

The uniqueness of the Haitian Revolution has led many historians to regard it as an originary moment, "laying the foundation for the continuing struggles for human rights everywhere."[31] Some argue that it fulfilled the ideals of the French Revolution, whereas others highlight the non-European origins of Haitian liberation.[32] These are complex questions, made even more so by an extended chronology: slavery was abolished on the island in 1793, whereas independence occurred only a decade later. Strictly speaking, the Haitian Revolution—that is, the revolution that created the state known as Haiti—refers to the events leading up to 1804, when the colony gained independence. The earlier abolition of slavery plays an important role in these events—after all, it was to preserve their liberty that Black citizens of Saint-Domingue revolted against the French—but the act of abolition per se was not a political revolution. If anything, it served to prevent revolution, as it placated the enslaved insurgents.[33]

The absence of a causal relationship between emancipation and independence becomes clearer when we consider Saint-Domingue alongside other French Caribbean colonies. The formerly enslaved Blacks on Guadeloupe, for instance, rebelled against French rule only when Napoleon reinstated slavery in 1802.[34] Up until that point, French rule was mostly viewed as emancipatory, especially when compared with that of the British, who sought to reimpose slavery when they occupied Guadeloupe in 1794.[35] It was not preordained that the French would renege on their emancipatory promises, and between 1794 and 1802, it appeared equally if not more plausible that non-Whites could enjoy full citizenship rights within the French Republic—a prospect that was painfully missing anywhere else in the Caribbean. Until 1802, France was a greater guarantor of civil freedom than any other power, possibly greater than independence. Hence Louverture's 1801 statement that "all men are born, live and die free *and French*."

Once we distinguish between the emancipatory moment of 1793 and the revolutionary moment of 1804, then a somewhat different picture of the Haitian Revolution emerges. Indeed, the protection of civil freedom above all had other, less favorable consequences. By relentlessly defending personal liberty for all inhabitants, the Haitian generals largely avoided discussions of political freedom. This pattern was already evident under Louverture, whose 1801 constitution insisted on the former, yet who forced formerly enslaved people to remain on the same plantations where they had labored as slaves. The people also had little say in their manner of government. The same 1804 decree that declared Haitian independence simply proclaimed Dessalines governor general for life. His ascension was pronounced "in the name of the people," thus maintaining democratic appearances, but the people were not consulted. As the historian David Geggus noted, "Far from being driven by 'democratic ideals,' the revolution that grew out of the slave uprising was authoritarian from beginning to end." The pursuit of civil freedom displaced the acquisition of political rights.[36]

On paper, the Haitian Revolution still retained a semblance of liberalism. As the 1801 constitution before it, the 1805 constitution affirmed legal equality, using the same terminology as the 1789 Declaration.[37] Both also borrowed from this source to assert the "sacred" status of private property.[38] And both lifted their defense against warrantless searches from well-worn French constitutional language (*un asile inviolable*).[39] The 1805 constitution went further than its 1801 predecessor by protecting religious freedom (art. 51), and closed by promising to uphold "the sacred rights of man and the duties of the citizen."

But where the Bonapartist bargain retained a modicum of representative government and popular sovereignty, the Haitian generals essentially turned these dials even further down, from low to off. The imperial crown was declared “elective not hereditary” (art. 23), but the emperor was allowed to name his successor (art. 26). Unlike the 1801 constitution, the 1805 constitution made no provisions for any representative assembly, but attributed all legislative and executive power to the emperor (art. 30). While the constitution was issued in the name of the Haitian people, the latter had no say in its ratification, or choice of their ruler.

There is only so much one can surmise from a constitution that was in force for less than two years. Dessalines was assassinated in October 1806, and his empire ended with him. His successors quarreled, dividing the island between a more autocratic (and ultimately Royalist) north, led by Henri Christophe, and a more “republican” south, under Alexander Pétion. Each half of the island issued a number of subsequent constitutions: in 1807 and 1811 for the north, and in 1816 for the south. Ten additional constitutions followed in the nineteenth century alone. Many included solemn promises to protect “the sacred, imprescriptible and inalienable rights of man,” but for the most part Haitians remained legally bound to the plantations where they had previously worked as slaves. In his northern Kingdom of Haiti, Christophe even introduced the *corvée*, a feudal practice of forced labor, which the Americans later exploited when they occupied the island in 1915–34.[40]

In some respects, the political history of Haiti after 1804 is not all that different from that of France after 1799: both feature regimes that proclaimed rights and liberal principles, but had few enforcement mechanisms in place. Machiavelli famously asked where “the guardian for freedom” was best to be found, in the people or among the elite. Many liberal revolutionaries ended up placing this guardian in an autocrat.[41] But strongmen have a poor track record of defending liberties. Bonaparte had demonstrated the possibility of promoting individual rights with little attention to popular participation in politics. Many generals in the Americas would push this program to the point where even the dial for individual rights was turned all the way down. Liberalism, too, could pave the road to serfdom.

SPANISH BONAPARTES

The abdications of Charles IV and Ferdinand VII left the Spanish Empire in a state of confusion. Unlike in the British American colonies, there had been no buildup to independence prior to 1808. Nor did all the

Spanish-American colonies leap at the prospect of liberation when it presented itself. It took decades and a series of grueling civil wars for these American territories to break free of metropolitan Spain. Some, such as Cuba and Puerto Rico, remained Spanish possessions until the very end of the nineteenth century.[42]

Faced with the vacuum of royal power, many Iberian provinces and American colonies established "councils," or *juntas*. Where the peninsular juntas ultimately joined together to establish a provisional government, which in turn summoned the Cádiz cortes, in the Americas some of the juntas became the rallying point for independence movements. This was notably the case in Venezuela, where the junta in Caracas deposed the Spanish captain general in 1810. A formal declaration of independence was issued in July 1811. Not all provinces followed suit, and in the ones that did, a civil war erupted between independent patriots and Spanish loyalists.

Even some of the loyal provinces experienced major political changes during the French occupation of Spain. Spanish Americans had sent representatives to the Cádiz cortes, and after 1812, the new constitution was implemented in the viceroyalties of Peru, Cuba, and New Spain (which included present-day Mexico, central America, and Florida).[43] States that remained loyal to Spain in 1820 experienced the *trienio liberal* as well. In this fashion, many Spanish Americans were exposed to liberal principles and practices.

But in the more rebellious parts of the Spanish Empire, it was the patriots who championed liberal ideas, inscribing them in the many constitutions that were written, scrapped, and rewritten over the coming decades. Many of these constitutions were never implemented, or lasted mere months. All the same, they provide an effective way to trace the spread of liberal revolutionary ideas throughout Spanish America. Somewhat paradoxically, these constitutions grew both more democratic and more authoritarian over time.

Nowhere is this evolution more evident than in the political trajectory of Simón Bolívar, whose name is practically synonymous with the Spanish-American independence movement. A military leader, he played a role in establishing the first Venezuelan republic in 1811. Both in their declaration, and the constitution that followed later that year, the Venezuelans portrayed themselves as the champions of "the imprescriptible rights that belong to all peoples," rights that, they argued, they had "been deprived of for more than three centuries." They enumerated these "rights of man [*derechos del hombre*]" in the eighth chapter of their constitution, drawing from both the American Bill of Rights and the 1789 French Declaration.[44]

At the same time, they imposed steep property qualifications for voters, electors, and elected representatives. To be eligible for senatorial office, a man must be at least thirty and possess property worth six thousand pesos.[45] To vote for such a man, one must be at least twenty-one and own property worth six hundred pesos (if unmarried, and living in a major town: art. 26). The political philosophy reflected in this constitution might be described as a kind of oligarchic liberalism. Its main supporters were the *criollos*, or creoles—typically wealthy, White, American-born descendants of peninsular Spaniards.[46]

In practice, these electoral rules mattered little, as the republic swiftly collapsed. Reflecting on its demise in December 1812, Bolívar blamed the government's excessive faith in "the exaggerated notion of the rights of man." He insisted that he personally was "ever faithful to the just and liberal system proclaimed by my country." But the first republic had blundered by trusting "popular elections," which had in fact prevented "a free, correct election . . . because [country dwellers] are so ignorant that they vote mechanically, while [city dwellers] are so ambitious that they turn everything into factions." Over time, Venezuelans might gain the knowledge and virtue necessary for enjoying political rights. But for now, "our fellow citizens are not yet ready to fully exercise their rights for themselves." It was pointless, Bolívar bitterly concluded, "liberating by force any town too stupid to see the value of their rights."[47]

When Ferdinand VII was restored to the Spanish throne in 1813, he renewed the military efforts to retain his American empire. His plan backfired, with more and more states declaring independence: Rio de la Plata (present-day Argentina) in 1816, Chile in 1818.[48] Following subsequent wars up and down the Andes, and the support of Haiti, Bolívar liberated Venezuela again in 1819. Two years later, a congress in the town of Cúcuta composed a new constitution for the state we refer to as "Gran Colombia." Property qualifications were retained, but lowered. Now a would-be senator only had to own property worth four thousand pesos, or a third less than in 1811. At the same time, the constitution exhibited anxieties about the exercise of popular sovereignty, which was explicitly confined to voting in primary elections (art. 10). Gone was any section outlining the "exaggerated maxims of the rights of man." In a Bonapartist vein, the constitution made up for this absence by loudly protecting individual liberty. "No one can deprive any individual of their freedom," insisted one article (art. 126), while others defined the crime of arbitrary detention (e.g., art. 164). Freedom of expression was also affirmed, albeit in the moderate vein preferred by the French ("according to the laws"; art. 156).[49]

This "liberal" constitution bore many resemblances with the Cádiz constitution, which soldiers had forced back on Ferdinand VII in 1820. The Spanish liberals wrongly assumed that, with them back in power, their colonial cousins would return to the fold of empire.[50] In fact, more countries proclaimed independence, most notably Mexico in 1824. As the new constitution drafted by the Mexicans differed only moderately from the Cádiz constitution, independence cannot have come down to the defense of individual liberties.[51] Rather, national liberation had by now become a key plank of political liberalism, often with negative consequences for the latter.

Even these liberal constitutions disappointed Bolívar. The 1821 constitution of Cúcuta limited presidential terms to four years, renewable once. In part, this limit was disappointing because the founding president was Bolívar himself. But the general also offered more principled reasons for preferring a stronger executive office. He outlined them in a preliminary discourse to the 1826 constitution of Bolivia, the last Spanish redoubt on the continent, which had been liberated in 1825 and named after its liberator. This constitution reflected Bolívar's preference: presidency for life. The general waxed lyrical in its praise:

> Under our Constitution, the President of the Republic is like the Sun, immovable at the center of the universe, radiating life. This supreme authority should be permanent, because in systems without hierarchies, a fixed point around which magistrates and citizens and men and events revolve is more necessary than in other systems. . . . For Bolivia, this point is a president for life. In him, all order originates.[52]

The main precedent that Bolívar pointed to for the presidency for life was Haiti. "His term of office is the same as that of the presidents of Haiti," he declared, suggesting that Haiti offered "triumphant proof that a president for life, with the power to choose the successor, is the most sublime innovation in the republican system." This was basically the argument that Bonaparte had made in 1799.[53] In both cases, the protection of individual liberty was presented as the true republican goal: "Civil liberty is the only true freedom," Bolívar announced.[54] This was not an idle pronouncement. The constitution enshrined "civil liberty, individual security, property, and equality before the law," along with freedom of expression, albeit (once again) "under the responsibility determined by law" (art. 144–45). The home, again, was "an inviolable asylum" (art. 147). And the 1826 constitution emancipated all remaining slaves in the land, even if, as in Haiti, it placed restrictions on their freedom of movement (art. 11, § 5).

More intriguing was the disappearance of any property qualifications in this constitution.[55] In praising Haiti, Bolívar noted, "I have chosen as the model for Bolivia the executive of the most democratic republic in the world."[56] This "democratic" language seemingly clashed with his earlier dismissal of "stupid" people. Politics may in part explain this shift: during his ultimate attempt to liberate Venezuela, Bolívar had allied himself with the mixed-race *pardos*, expanding beyond his earlier reliance on White creole elites. But there was also a Bonapartist logic to this democratization. As consul and later as emperor, Napoleon had demonstrated how popular sovereignty could be used to prop up authoritarian government. With a more powerful executive in place, the state had apparently less to fear from poorer voters.

Neither the constitutions of Gran Colombia nor those of Bolivia lasted for very long. In 1831, the former split into what is today Ecuador, Colombia, and Venezuela, while Bolivia received a new constitution at the hands of its next leader. Many more constitutions followed: Bolivia issued another ten before the end of the nineteenth century. Along with the rest of Spanish America, these republics swiftly slipped into a pattern of *caudillismo*, or rule by a powerful military leader. Unlike military dictators in the twentieth century, caudillos usually relied on constitutions to support their rule. In theory, they embraced popular sovereignty. Part of their appeal lay precisely in the fact that they could control the people while also holding the elites in check. If they often clashed with self-proclaimed liberals and embraced more traditional values, they could also promote liberal causes. The historian Natalia Sobrevilla Perea described the Peruvian caudillo Andrés de Santa Cruz as "both an authoritarian populist and a beneficent liberal."[57]

The liberal movement propelled onward by the Cádiz constitution thus found its resolution, in nineteenth-century Spanish America, in the rule of generals who sometimes paid little more than lip service to liberal principles and constitutional rights.[58] They took their cue from the great "Liberator" Simón Bolívar himself, who had pursued ever-greater executive power in the name of liberal constitutionalism. National liberation remained at the ideological heart of caudillismo, and one of the reasons why military leaders invariably filled the executive role.[59] The preeminence of liberation is obvious in many of the constitutions of this time, where it was usually asserted in the very first article: "The Colombian nation is forever and irrevocably free and independent from the Spanish monarchy" (1821); "The Mexican nation is forever free and independent from the Spanish government and from any other power" (1824); "The Bolivian Nation is forever free and independent" (1826).

Notwithstanding the centrality of national liberation, Spanish American caudillos also bore a resemblance to the French emperor who had introduced the language and principles of liberalism into the Spanish world in the first place. In both cases, military success and personal charisma solved a political problem: Who can be trusted to govern a population splintered along economic, political, regional, and (in the Americas) racial lines? In the absence of politicians who enjoyed broad support across social groups, military leaders filled the void, translating their authority into political legitimacy.[60]

Bonapartism and caudillismo thus played a similar role in modern revolutions as the well-balanced constitution did for Polybian revolutionaries. The strong leader balanced the interests of different social groups, defending (or posing as a defender of) the people, while providing sufficient liberal guarantees to win over the elites. Both the caudillo and the well-balanced constitution were considered to be desirable revolutionary outcomes, in that they protected the postrevolutionary order. But where the Polybian solution sought above all to preserve the status quo, many viewed caudillos as a genuinely "modern" solution. If the well-balanced constitution kept future revolutions at bay, the caudillo was not necessarily opposed to progress and could even claim to usher his people into a glorious future. Porfirio Díaz, who governed Mexico from 1876 until 1910, adopted as a slogan for his government *orden y progreso*, "order and progress"—a quote from the positivist and socialist Auguste Comte.[61]

Of course, many disagreed that caudillos represented the modern liberal solution. Some denounced these regimes as insufficiently liberal, and often reserved the name "liberals" for themselves. Others challenged them as insufficiently modern, sometimes in the name of socialism. The ease with which these authoritarian regimes granted and changed constitutions also began to erode their political value. While caudillismo would define Spanish American politics for most of the nineteenth century, the discontent with authoritarian liberalism would have revolutionary effects back in Europe.

A New Liberal Hope?

The delegates to the Congress of Vienna (1814-15) looked out over a continent whose political order had been entirely uprooted by Napoleon. To the greatest extent possible, they strove to undo the transformations of the previous quarter-century. But the new order that emerged from their congress was not a simple return to the ancien régime. Some remnants of the Napoleonic empire proved hard to dislodge: his Civil Code, for instance, remained in force in various German states long after he was gone.[62] The territories of the great powers—Britain, Russia, Austria, Prussia, and France—were also recalibrated in an effort to decrease the prospects of war. This balancing act, officially called the "Holy Alliance," is better known as the Metternich system, after its chief architect, the Austrian diplomat Prince Klemens von Metternich. Initially, this system had liberal pretensions, and proposed to regulate international affairs through constitutional means. Like Napoleon's own liberal regimes, it had a secondary purpose as well: to prevent future outbreaks of revolution in Europe.[63]

This last objective proved woefully unsuccessful. "In this century, revolution must be everywhere," Victor Hugo observed.[64] If this sounded like a command, it was really a description. Revolutions erupted with frequent regularity throughout Europe in the 1820s, in Spain, Portugal, Italy, Greece, Russia, and, at the end of the decade, France and Belgium. Even the most reactionary politicians knew that the revolutionary genie could not be bottled up again. Realistically, the best possible outcome was a swift response when revolution broke out. The French novelist Stendhal satirized this fatalistic mood in his novel about the 1830 French revolution, *The Red and the Black*, where the conservative comte de Rênal tips his servants extra so that they won't massacre his family during the next Terror.

In a general sense, these subsequent European revolutions were all aftershocks of 1789. The French Revolution was the catalyst that unleashed political change across Europe, and ultimately, the world. But on closer inspection, the revolutions of 1820–48 are better understood as perpetuating the liberal legacy of the Revolution, a legacy that owed much to Napoleon. Not only had his wars spread the Revolution's principles across Europe, he also passed them through a tempering filter. Few European revolutionaries who attempted to break free of Metternich's system were Jacobins. Most sought to navigate the narrow liberal path between the Scylla of military authoritarianism and the Charybdis of democratic anarchy. The young protagonist of Stendhal's novel, Julien Sorel, who epitomized the revolutionary sensibilities of his day, obsessed over Napoleon's *Mémorial de Sainte-Hélène*, and kept a portrait of the emperor under his pillow.

Outside of France, the lasting influence of Napoleonic liberalism on later revolutions can be established both directly and indirectly. Once again, the Cádiz constitution provides a crucial link. In January 1820, an army mutiny in Spain snowballed into a political revolution. The rebels forced Ferdinand VII to reinstate the 1812 constitution. Elections brought a liberal government to power, which abolished the Inquisition (again), reestablished freedom of the press, and reformed the judiciary. These had been central goals of the 1812 *liberales*, but also underpinned the Napoleonic platform, as expressed in the 1808 Bayonne constitution. For three years, Spanish representatives struggled to find the right liberal balance, arguing incessantly with one another, and calling the more progressive among them *afrancesado*, or "Frenchified." Ironically, this *trienio liberal* would be brought to a close by another French invasion, this time on behalf of the European great powers.[65]

But the Spanish uprising had already caught on elsewhere. Portuguese liberals and military officers revolted that same year, rising up against the British protectorate that governed in the name of their distant king, João VI. The latter had sailed off to Brazil in 1807 to avoid capture by Napoleon's forces, but then chose not to leave his new capital, Rio de Janeiro, in 1814. The Portuguese liberals wanted their king back, but paired this demand with another: they also wanted a constitution, modeled on Cádiz. Their 1822 version replicated the basic arrangement of the 1812 precedent, but also drew explicitly on the French constitutional tradition. Indeed, many articles included verbatim translations of the 1789 Declaration. The imprint of Napoleon's constitutional practices was also evident, notably in the metaphor of the home as an "asylum" (art. 5), or in the creation of a special court to protect the freedom of the press (art. 8). Their victory was short lived: João VI abandoned the constitution within months. But it was not forgotten, serving as a rallying cry for the liberal opposition until it was briefly reinstated in 1836.[66]

The Spanish insurgents also offered hope to liberals in Naples, in the kingdom of the Two Sicilies. Its ruler, Ferdinand I (uncle of Ferdinand VII of Spain), had been restored in 1816, having spent the previous decade in Palermo. He succeeded Joachim Murat, one of Napoleon's top generals and brother-in-law. Murat was shot by a firing squad in 1815, but many of his former officials remained in place (they were known as "Muratists"). They faced suspicions at court, however, and eventually made common cause with another opposition group, the Carbonari. This secret society, modeled on freemasonry, had emerged around Naples during Murat's reign, initially to oppose French occupation. But when Ferdinand I did not give his subjects a constitution, the Carbonari turned on him. They provided the spark for the revolution: Muratist officers, who populated the upper echelons of the army, the leadership.[67]

Faced with a widespread insurrection, Ferdinand capitulated and granted a constitution to the kingdom in July 1820. His subjects did not want just any old constitution: they, too, clamored for the 1812 Cádiz one.

Ferdinand caved in to pressure, and swore an oath to "never deprive anyone of his property and . . . respect in all other things the political liberty of the nation and the personal liberty of each individual"—the very words prescribed by the 1812 Cádiz constitution (art. 173), and an echo of the Napoleonic oath to "respect individual liberty and property, and to solely govern with a view to the interest, happiness, and glory of the nation."[68] But Ferdinand's oaths were of little value. He was soon begging Metternich for military assistance, and by March 1821 Austrian soldiers were in Naples. Despite its ephemeral success, this first Carbonari revolution offered a template for others and helped to set in motion the Risorgimento, a century-long effort to liberate and unify Italy.[69]

For the Greek and Russian revolutionaries of the 1820s, inspiration came less from Cádiz than from the French and Napoleonic legacy directly. "In my opinion, the French Revolution and Napoleon opened the eyes of the world," wrote Theodoros Kolokotronis, the commander of Greek forces fighting for independence from the Ottomans. Kolokotronis's own eyes had been opened in the Heptanese, the seven Greek islands in the Ionian Sea, which Bonaparte captured after defeating Venice in 1797. The French were soon expelled, but regained control from 1807 to 1814, when Kolokotronis resided there and had his political awakening.[70]

The fall of Napoleon triggered efforts to launch a struggle for independence, most notably by the Filiki Eteria (Society of Friends). Founded in Odessa by three Greek merchants in 1814, this secret organization borrowed its structure from the Carbonari and left adherents guessing at its leadership (many wrongly assumed Tsar Alexander I was behind it).[71] Its members communicated in code; the name given to Napoleon's family was "the Blessed."[72] Their armed insurrection began in 1821, and lasted eight years. Along the way, the Greeks issued multiple constitutions, initially adopting a Directory-style executive, and ultimately selecting the former Russian foreign minister Count Ioannis Kapodistrias as their chief executive. Each subsequent constitution added further rights provisions. Like most revolutionaries, the Greeks fell prey to infighting and civil war: even liberal revolutionaries found it hard to reach a consensus.

The Greek Revolution would likely have failed had it not been for a groundswell of enthusiasm across Europe. Here, finally, was a revolution that Metternich could not suppress. The plight of fellow Christians struggling for independence from the "cruel Turk" proved too stirring a story to ignore. Volunteers, including Lord Byron, came to fight and die on their side, until three of the great powers (Britain, France, and Russia) joined the war, securing Greek independence in 1829.

The impact of Napoleon on the Russian Decembrist Revolt of 1825 may seem more surprising, given the lingering resentment toward the emperor's 1812 campaign. Before the war, Napoleon had enjoyed some support among Russian elites. Tolstoy captured this attraction in *War and Peace*, where Pierre Bezukhov defends the emperor against aristocratic prejudices: "Napoleon is great because he rose superior to the Revolution, suppressed its abuses, preserved all that was good in it—equality of citizenship and freedom of speech and of the press—and only for that reason did he obtain power." It was the liberal platform all tied up in a Napoleonic bow. Unlike his predecessor, Alexander I was known as a Francophile, and at the start of his reign toyed with giving his people a constitution and emancipating the serfs.[73]

Between 1807 and 1812, France and Russia were allies. Following Napoleon's invasion, his star rapidly faded: even the fictional Pierre tries to shoot him in Moscow. Two years later, in 1814, it was Alexander I's turn to enter Paris, after the Sixth Coalition defeated the emperor, sending him into exile. But there was a cost to Alexander's revenge. Many of his young officers had never set foot in western Europe before, or been exposed to liberal principles. "Along with the souvenirs in their knapsacks, they carried back subversive ideas in their heads," one historian remarked.[74] As the Napoleonic threat receded into the past, Alexander's own autocratic regime appeared increasingly oppressive.

On their return from western Europe, some officers formed secret societies, again drawing on Masonic models for secrecy. They conspired to do what Alexander had not: give Russia a constitution and emancipate the serfs, among other priorities. Some even dreamt of a republic, though the general trend was toward a constitutional monarchy with civil liberties. When Alexander I died unexpectedly in 1825, they sprang into action, hoping to stage a military coup. Abandoned by its leaders, it was a dismal failure. Here as well, however, the Decembrists offered a template that later revolutionary secret societies would adopt.[75]

The liberal revolutionaries of the 1820s and later decades were eclectic in their readings and influences, looking to English political thought and American constitutionalism as much as to France. They could blend these ideas into novel combinations, often bringing in elements from their own national backgrounds.[76] Liberalism was very much a contested concept, with politicians of very different stripes claiming its mantle for themselves. But the French Revolution remained the touchstone on or against which they defined their ideals. Most liberals believed that after 1789 some sort of constitutional government and individual liberties were a sine qua non. The

French Revolution also provided them with a warning about what to avoid. They feared the unruliness of a people unprepared for freedom. They too, like Napoleon, sought to disentangle the multiple legacies of 1789.

Napoleon's importance for this moment in the history of revolution can be summarized as fourfold. Historically, it was because of Napoleon's conquests that so many Europeans experienced French revolutionary principles firsthand. Politically, he demonstrated how the different strands of the Revolution could be disaggregated and rewoven into a more "liberal" arrangement. Legally, his codes and constitutions provided a reservoir of liberal language, laws, and institutions. Socially, he showed how the military could play a transformative role in establishing constitutions. Many of the 1820s revolutionaries would look down on Napoleon personally as the "Corsican ogre." But his imperial expansion and political models constituted an essential bridge between revolutionary France and nineteenth-century Europe.

Lost Illusions

Liberal demands for a constitution reflected a real lack: after 1815, few states had one. Many Europeans, by contrast, had experienced life under a constitution, or seen what it was like in neighboring states. Imperfect as the Napoleonic constitutions were, they appeared better than nothing, especially once they were gone. The absence of a constitution accordingly served as a rallying point for revolutionaries who might not agree on much else. A constitution that guaranteed basic individual liberties—that was a liberal cause most people could get behind.

The political situation became more complicated after there was a constitution in place. This remained the case in France following the Bourbon restoration. Louis XVIII "gifted" a constitution to his subjects, which he called a charter and did not invite them to ratify. Any resemblance with revolutionary constitutions had to be studiously avoided. All the same, the Bourbon Charter granted the French a laundry list of liberal desiderata: individual liberty and freedom from arbitrary detention (art. 4), freedom of religion (art. 5), freedom of expression and of the press (art. 8), and vigorous property rights (art. 9). The French could now participate in the legislative process to a greater extent than since 1799. The charter did not open the doors to everyone: property qualifications were imposed for electors and deputies, and legislative power was shared with an upper, hereditary chamber of peers. But liberals were rarely democrats, and over the next fifteen years, the French Liberals never stopped rhapsodizing about the charter.[77]

Complicating matters further was Napoleon's last act and late transformation into a liberal icon. On March 1, 1815, the emperor landed on the Côte d'Azur, having escaped from exile on Elba. During his hundred days back in power, he asked Benjamin Constant, the head of the French Liberals and his former foe, to revise the imperial constitution. The result of Constant's effort, the Acte Additionel, looked remarkably like the 1814 charter. Of course, Napoleon insisted that his constitution be ratified by plebiscite, as was his wont. These promises and posturing that surrounded his return from exile confirmed Napoleon as the great liberal hope, "the child of the most liberal of revolutions," as Joseph Rey (another liberal, close to Constant) put it.[78]

Napoleon's encore performance met a soggy end at Waterloo, leaving the coast clear for the Bourbons. Under both Louis XVIII and his brother Charles X, liberal politicians sought above all to defend constitutional rights. That goal proved challenging, as "Ultra" Royalists viewed the charter as a revolutionary travesty. When a Bonapartist sympathizer assassinated the duc de Berry in 1820, the Ultras pounced. They reintroduced press censorship and authorized imprisonment without cause for up to three months. The electoral franchise was revised to give the wealthiest greater control of the legislature.

Even with the 1814 charter in place, then, French Liberals continued to advocate for the same rights and principles as their European brethren. The French may have remembered Napoleon more for curtailing individual liberties than for promoting them, but there were still a good many Bonapartists among the liberals.[79] When Charles X came to the throne in 1824, liberal opposition coalesced against his ultraroyalist predilections and ministers. Opposition boiled over into revolution in 1830, when Charles X attempted to roll back the charter once and for all, through a series of ordonnances. Parisians threw up barricades across the city (a revolutionary tactic that was just beginning to gain prominence), and the king fled.[80]

It is telling that the revolutionaries did not find it necessary to write a new constitution for their new regime. They simply made a few minor modifications and renamed it the Charter of 1830. It was under this July Monarchy—so named because the 1830 revolution took place in July, and because there was no other meaningful term to identify it—that the limits of liberal politics began to show. Some 1830 revolutionaries were disappointed that the new regime was not a republic. In 1832, they attempted to overthrow the government, in a failed insurrection immortalized by Victor Hugo's *Les misérables*. The new king, Louis-Philippe d'Orléans, would indeed become a drag on the monarchy, not least because of his resemblance to a pear (spotlighted in Honoré Daumier's infamous caricatures). Others were disappointed that property qualifications still limited the franchise, to which Louis-Philippe's minister François Guizot had the effective, if impolitic, response: "enrichissez-vous" (get rich).[81]

The July Monarchy serves as further evidence that liberalism was not necessarily a stepping stone toward democracy. Many liberals were dead set against higher levels of voter participation. They might have welcomed "democracy," but what they meant by this term was not universal suffrage. Rather, they recognized that administrative offices often functioned better when staffed by the people most directly concerned.[82] There was nothing contradictory, in their minds, in promoting more democratic forms of government while maintaining strict limits on the franchise.

But there was also a deeper source of discontent that surfaced soon after 1830, one that challenged the very premise of liberalism. What if individual liberties simply weren't enough? What if freedom of expression, the right to property, and the prevention of arbitrary detention did not satisfy modern political expectations? Liberalism looked a lot like a form of politics that protected and benefited the rich. In *The Leopard*, Prince Fabrizio Tomasi "saw revolution in that white tie and two black tails moving at this moment up the stairs of his own home"—that is, the evening dress of the nouveau riche mayor of Donnafugata during the Risorgimento.[83]

Liberals ultimately proved ineffective at directing the revolutionary tide. Hardly a year after Louis-Philippe's accession, silk workers in Lyon were revolting, as they would again in 1834.[84] Even some liberals now began to wonder: was this really all there was? Had the modern theory of progress peaked with the corpulent bourgeois whom Daumier also mocked? Had the excitement of the Revolution and even the empire all been for this? Was a lightly airbrushed royal charter really the last word in politics?

The greatest challenger to the liberal idea of revolution was history. Writing in the early 1830s, the poet Alfred de Musset diagnosed what he called "the sickness of the century" (*la maladie du siècle*). A generation that had grown up on stories of imperial glory and military campaigns was now told to forget these pipe dreams and *enrichissez-vous*. But they refused to believe that this was the world that their parents and grandparents had started a revolution for. Musset's generation was sick, because they were living in fake times. "Everything that was is no longer; everything that will be has not yet come. Do not look elsewhere for the source of our woes," he concluded.[85] Liberalism might have been a sufficient revolutionary program while absolutism was on the ascendant. But as the visceral reaction to the Terror faded, and the ennui of liberal politics set in, many of the young (and some of the old) craved more. They were, as Matthew Arnold phrased it, "wandering between two worlds, one dead, / the other powerless to be born."[86] Or as the historian François Hartog has written, "A gap and tension opened up between individuals' space of experience and their horizon of expectation."[87]

Discontent with liberalism was not simply a response to its belated victory. The previous decades had unleashed inflationary hopes in the future. The modern theory of progress promised a future wholly different from the world at hand. Philosophers and novelists had been busying themselves with charting the outlines of this society to come. To many liberals, these imaginative projections were little more than fevered dreams. Royalists denounced them as Jacobinism. Even those who read and consumed them questioned the likelihood that anything comparable might come to pass. But the details mattered little. Belief in a transfigured future was resilient, and found support in every technological advance. It also upended the politics of revolution, and gave rise to the greatest alternative to the liberal idea of revolution: socialism.

CHAPTER TWELVE

Revolutionary Futures

THE POLITICS OF IMAGINATION

> *In the early twentieth century, the vision of a future society unbelievably rich, leisured, orderly and efficient—a glittering antiseptic world of glass and steel and snow-white concrete—was part of the consciousness of nearly every literate person. Science and technology were developing at a prodigious speed, and it seemed natural to assume that they would go on developing.*
>
> —GEORGE ORWELL, *1984*

THE LIBERAL COMPROMISE that lifted Bonaparte to power, and that revolutionaries fought for across Spanish America and Restoration Europe, reflected a sober assessment of the French Revolution. The first republic had aimed too high, its liberal critics contended. It had chased impossible goals and made unrealistic promises. To secure rights and liberty, liberals charted a different course. Upholding moderation as their core value, they rejected the promises of popular leaders as fanciful and dangerous.[1] Instead, they pursued the true goal of a modern society, as they perceived it: the securing of individual rights, or what Benjamin Constant called "the liberty of the moderns."[2]

But this liberal politics of moderation faced a formidable challenge in the modern theory of historical progress. The belief in human improvement undergirded a variety of political agendas, but all had in common a dissatisfaction with the status quo. Liberals, once in power, often sought to tamp down further efforts that might jeopardize their own political accomplishments. This strategy clashed with the progressive certitude that more reforms were both inevitable and to be desired.

Liberals and progressives skirmished over their differences in print and in person, but the real battleground lay elsewhere. Indeed, for the history of revolution after Thermidor, the most important political arena was the imagination. For the next fifty years, those who held fast to the doctrine of progress did not dedicate much energy to devising new political theories, but rather gazed out onto the unknown expanses of the future. As other European colonizers mapped the "empty" spaces of continents, these time travelers catalogued the world to come. Their accounts could invite laughter or be dismissed as wild dreams. But they were the first settlers of the *futura incognita* that lay ahead. In the absence of other, less far-fetched descriptions of what tomorrow would bring, their stories of a reconfigured society slowly became part of the collective imagination, the "mythscape" of the future. As Orwell put it, these visions entered into "the consciousness of nearly every literate person."[3]

There were many versions of the future, but in each case the appeal depended mostly on the charms of a literal vision. Writers who could create an imaginary world that filled their readers with longing had already won half the battle of winning them over politically. As Albert Camus later remarked, "We could count on one hand those communists who came to the revolution by way of studying Marx. First you convert, then you read the Scriptures and the Fathers of the Church."[4]

For this purpose of conversion, many forward-looking tracts took the form of novels. The French socialist Etienne Cabet, whose followers went on to found ill-fated communities in the United States, presented his doctrines in the fictional *Voyage to Icaria* (1840), a land where everything was spotless, charming, and beautiful: "Everything is perfect in this happy land inhabited by men who finally deserve the title of men."[5] The British historian G.D.H. Cole would later recount how he became a socialist after reading *News from Nowhere* (1890), William Morris's Rip-van-Winkle narrative about an arts-and-crafts-inspired socialist future.[6] Painting could serve a similar purpose: the anarchist artist Paul Signac borrowed Saint-Simon's tagline—"The golden age lies not in the past, but in the future" (*L'âge d'or n'est pas dans le passé, il est dans l'avenir*)—as the subtitle for his 1893–95 painting *The Age of Harmony* (*Au temps de l'harmonie*), which depicted an idealized society on the Côte d'Azur (see figure 12.1).[7] Progressive artists recognized the persuasive power of images—verbal or pictorial—for advancing their political cause.

As Europe underwent industrial transformation, some of these prophecies acquired a veneer of plausibility. The locomotive, steel-and-glass construction, steamboats, and telegraphs, along with, eventually, electricity,

FIGURE 12.1 Paul Signac, *Au temps de l'harmonie: l'âge d'or n'est pas dans le passé, il est dans l'avenir* (1893–95). Wikimedia Commons, public domain.

the telephone, airplanes, and the automobile: were these not fragments of a fantastical future coming into focus? Liberals also celebrated industrial progress, hosting "universal expositions" in gigantic glass warehouses to show off their latest achievements and trumpet European superiority.[8] "The golden age is near at hand, we may be already there," announced the poet Maxime du Camp in a volume that celebrated steam, locomotives, and coils, among other modern inventions.[9] But for progressive revolutionaries, these industrial triumphs simply begged the question of why similar advances had not yet occurred in other realms, particularly the social. It was the same question that Robespierre had posed in 1793: The physical and political world was changing, why weren't our economic, familial, educational, urban, and political practices following suit?[10] The techno-utopian visions detailed by the prophets of progress had already proposed all sorts of ingenious ways to reorganize our lives, and yet more people were living in misery than ever before.[11] One installment of the future had arrived; more were due.

By focusing on the splendors that the future held in store rather than on the political means of acquiring them, progressive visionaries often fell back on a fairly generic political model. It hinged, of course, on the revolution to come. But then came a fundamental problem. How was their ideal future to materialize? Left to their own devices, the people were unlikely to make the right decisions, in the right order, and in a way that produced the right results. Bringing about a perfected state was not child's play, and the schemes proposed by progressive writers could be inordinately complex. Fourier went so far as to provide exact measurements for the hallways in his phalansteries.[12] And so there must be some sort of interim solution. Many concurred that a "temporary" government with full powers would be necessary to oversee the transition from the current regime to a new one.

This had, of course, been the political solution proposed by the Jacobins in October 1793. Spokesmen for the Committee of Public Safety—Saint-Just, Billaud-Varenne, and especially Robespierre—had similarly gestured toward a transfigured future when justice and equality would reign. Eventually, they weathered accusations of dictatorship, which contributed to their fall. As plans for the social organization of the future grew more elaborate, however, dictatorship began to look like an acceptable compromise. Voltaire's enlightened despots breathed again.

The cartography of the future thus produced a paradox. While progressive writers disagreed on many particulars (some, like Fourier, rejected socialism; others, especially the anarchists, opposed any centralized government), there was a widespread consensus that the future must be democratic. The doctrine of progress rested on the rise of reason and justice. Even liberals came to recognize an irresistible modern trend toward democracy in Western countries, exemplified by the United States.[13] Almost all socialist writers, insisting on equality, identified as democrats. The communist state of Icaria is "an almost pure democracy," rhapsodized Cabet. But the political form required to bring about this perfected state was anything but democratic. Icaria had been established, following an inevitable revolution, by a dictator, Icar. Like many others, Cabet sought to sweeten this political pill by calling Icar "an elected dictator."[14] This modicum of legitimacy did not veil the basic fact that this "almost pure democracy" of the future could be founded only through a dictatorship.

There were certainly many progressives who rejected this argument. Anarchists warned most loudly about the risks of dictatorship, even temporary. "All dictatorship has no objective other than self-perpetuation," insisted Mikhail Bakunin; "Freedom can be created only by freedom, by a total rebellion of the people, and by a voluntary organization of the people from the bottom up."[15] And there were socialists, such as Louis Blanc, a member of the French provisional government in 1848, who remained committed to electoral democracy even after ascending to power.[16] In fact, most of the European progressive intelligentsia looked unfavorably on the dictatorial option. The fact that Marx and the Bolsheviks after him opted for this route was neither inevitable nor representative. To suggest otherwise would be teleological, as if any utopian dreaming necessarily implied ruthless despotism.

At the same time, as I argue in this chapter, there was a thrust to modern revolutionary thought, which when combined with the widespread disappointment in actual revolutions gave dictatorship a distinctive appeal. The people often let revolutionaries down. "The Liberals . . . became in their turn the most fearful Conservatives," Alexander Herzen lamented about the 1848 revolution in France. "They discover[ed] the spectre of Socialism and [grew] pale with terror."[17] Absent "the solution" later proposed by Bertolt Brecht in his 1953 satirical poem by that name—if the people had disappointed the government, could not "the government . . . dissolve the people / And elect another?"[18]—it was the nature of government that would itself have to change.

So while it was certainly not predetermined that the first socialist revolution, in October 1917, would lead to a revolutionary dictatorship, it was a likely outcome. Marx's own conversion to this political model (detailed in the following chapter) of course contributed greatly to its success. But it was not just the result of Marx's personal influence. Nor was it the result of any particular ideology, socialist, communist, or other. The choice of dictatorship was rather a temporal shortcut, encouraged by the belief in a perfected future. By opening up the future as a space to be colonized by a just society, the modern doctrinaires of progress encouraged their followers to value the world to come so highly that they were willing to accept the temporary suspension of democratic beliefs.

This colonization metaphor ought to be taken literally, as the modern revolutionary predilection for dictatorship sprang from the same historical roots as the modern colonial imperative to subjugate non-Western societies. Both posited some future time when the (colonized) people would finally be ready for democratic self-governance. Until then, it was in their interest to be ruled by those with greater knowledge of how history and society should develop.[19]

It would be too crude to reduce this logic to "the end justifies the means," as that dictum flattens the chronological complexity of this modern bargain. The progressive democrats who settled on temporary dictatorship did so because they believed the eventual success of their plans would ultimately vindicate their choice. As the French Jacobins before them, they adopted the logic of prospective retrospection: the act of bringing a perfected future into existence would retrospectively legitimate the political arrangements that had permitted its delivery. Because this legitimation itself lay in a future moment, revolutionaries had to accept it on credit—a metaphor that Marx, unsurprisingly, was especially fond of.[20]

The Golden Age Ahead

Studies of socialist thinkers tend to focus on the specifics of their plans. For devotees, such details and their relative differences with other systems mattered greatly. But important as they are, these accounts can miss the more general effects of utopian scheming on progressive minds. Most readers could not have pinpointed the distinctive contributions of a Saint-Simon, an Enfantin, a Comte, a Fourier, an Owen, or a Cabet. They might even have comically confused them, as did the socialist schoolteacher in Gustave Flaubert's satirical novel *Bouchard et Pécuchet*:

> He exposed in fevered words his articles of faith: disarming the troops, abolition of judges, equal salaries, means by which the golden age would return, in the form of a republic, led by a dictator, a solid fellow who could keep the people in their place! Then he reached for a bottle of anisette and three glasses, to raise a toast to the hero, the immortal victim, the great Maximilien![21]

The confusion of political demands here, while amusing, is ultimately irrelevant. What drives this fictional teacher, like many real-world readers, is a "faith" that the future, whatever it may bring, will be radically different from the present. And its differences will not only be exotic: they will achieve a state of perfection, a golden age.

The confidence that a perfect world lay just around the corner was, like liberalism, another legacy of the French Revolution and the Enlightenment theory of progress. If society continued to progress toward reason and justice, there would inevitably come a time when all aspects of and people in society had become reasonable and just. The abbé de Saint-Pierre himself had asserted that social progress should culminate in a golden age.[22] Throughout the eighteenth and nineteenth centuries, other writers drew on specific features of this myth, which every schoolboy knew from Ovid's *Metamorphoses*. As in that primeval time when "good faith and rectitude flourished spontaneously without laws or judges," they envisioned a future without armies, judges, or even property.[23] Explorers found examples of what they believed to be remnants of this ideal state

FIGURE 12.2 Jean-Auguste-Dominique Ingres, *L'âge d'or* (1862). Harvard Art Museum. Wikimedia Commons, public domain.

among far-flung peoples, such as the Tahitians, described by the French admiral Bougainville and celebrated by the philosophe Diderot.[24] Here was another commonality shared by the colonization of non-Westerners and the colonization of the future: both projected onto unknown places or times familiar images and narratives from the distant past.[25]

No small part of the charm of the golden age myth lay in its sexual allure (see figure 12.2). Many progressive writers, from Fourier to Marx, predicted a sexual liberation and an end to bourgeois repression.[26] Long before Herbert Marcuse, free love was one of revolution's best selling points. The sexual promiscuity that Europeans discovered among the Pacific Islanders offered a model of how amorous relations might turn out after the revolution.

That "primitive" times could serve as a model for the "perfected" future might seem odd, even contradictory. What could the electrified, sophisticated, and more reasonable age to come share with the simple past? Here was a secular mystery that generated many different dogmas. Even before the French Revolution, the relatively unknown tax official Étienne-Gabriel

Morelly twisted the theory of gradual progress so that it pointed back to an original, communist state of nature, which he identified as the golden age: "It is only through a long series of moral errors and thousands of trials that human reason finally discovers that no situation can be happier than the state of simple nature," Morelly announced in his 1755 *Code de la nature* (a work long attributed to Diderot).[27]

Others questioned whether the golden age of humanity had ever been primitive. In a series of beautifully illustrated volumes, the Freemason and mesmerist scholar Antoine Court de Gébelin expanded on the traditional identification of Egypt as the "cradle of arts and sciences." In fact, he argued, Egypt was simply the remnant of a "primitive world" even greater in knowledge and power (see figure 12.3). It had since disappeared, like Atlantis, another one of its successor states, renowned since antiquity for its technological prowess.[28] Beliefs in a lost civilization, and related attempts to rediscover or restore it, also fueled revolutionary imaginations. As the search for a lost Atlantis typically doubled as the search for a lost *people*, this strand of classical fantasy became especially prominent among racists and "Aryanists." Alfred Rosenberg enshrined it in *The Myth of the 20th Century*, the most influential exposition of Nazism after *Mein Kampf*.[29]

Such was the prevalence of the golden age myth in socialist and progressive circles that it could appear more as a nuisance than a boon. When Saint-Simon insisted that only misguided poets had placed the golden age "during the ignorance and rudeness of early times," when it really lay in the future, one senses his frustration with the primitivist strain of socialist thought. But it was hard to overcome the special attraction of the golden age myth. As Marx himself acknowledged, "Why should not the historic childhood of humanity, its most beautiful unfolding, as a stage never to return, exercise an eternal charm?"[30]

One reason why socialist writers hesitated to abandon the "eternal charm" of the golden age was that it served so well to propagate their vision. Many commented on the imaginary powers of the myth. In his fictionalized account of a coal miners' strike, Emile Zola highlighted its effectiveness for communicating the promise of socialism to workers: "They saw there . . . the ideal city of their dreams, but now closer and almost real, with its brotherly people, its golden age of work and meals in common."[31] Fyodor Dostoevsky repeatedly called attention to the seductiveness of this myth, identifying it with a painting by Claude Lorrain, *Acis et Galathée* (see figure 12.4). In the version found in *The Adolescent* (1875), that painting comes to life in a dream that the nobleman Versilov has during

FIGURE 12.3 "Oedipus victorious over the sphinx," frontispiece of Antoine Court de Gébelin's *Monde primitif* (1784). Formerly owned by the John Adams Library (Boston Public Library). Public domain.

FIGURE 12.4 Claude Lorrain, *Acis et Galathée* (1657). Wikimedia Commons, public domain.

the Paris Commune. The vision is so beautiful and attractive that it overwhelms his knowledge that the Commune's efforts are doomed:

> The golden age—the most incredible dream of all that have ever been, but for which people have given all their lives and all their strength, for which prophets have died and been slain, without which the peoples do not want to live and cannot even die![32]

Dostoevsky himself was a repentant revolutionary, having faced a firing squad in his youth for his political idealism. Here he captures the close connection between these compelling visions of a desired future—"the most incredible dream of all that have ever been"—and the radical actions needed to obtain it: "for which people have given all their lives and all their strength." In his 1908 *Reflections on Violence*, the French revolutionary theorist Georges Sorel gave this insight a broader theoretical application, arguing that "men who are participating in great social movements always picture their coming action in the form of images of battle in which their cause is certain to triumph. . . . I propos[e] to give the name of 'myths' to these constructions."[33] For many writers, the golden age was the most powerful of such myths to drive people to revolution.

But the magnetic pull of the golden age on people's minds only exacerbated the temporal conflict that progressives faced. Marx cut to the heart of the problem in *The Eighteenth Brumaire of Louis-Napoleon Bonaparte* (1852): "The social revolution of the nineteenth century cannot draw its poetry from the past, but only from the future."[34] Marx himself refrained from describing society after social classes had been abolished, chiding those who did so as "utopian" and "crude." But importantly, he didn't have to: others had already sketched the outlines of the socialist future.[35]

There was certainly enough poetry of the future for writers to fuel their utopian dreams. The Russian novelist Nikolay Chernyshevsky found inspiration in the Fourierist vision of gleaming aluminum palaces in a fertile countryside. His book *What Is to Be Done?* (1863) caught the attention of a young Vladimir Lenin, who borrowed its title for one of his own revolutionary treatises.[36] The more that writers departed from traditional depictions of the golden age, however, the harder it was to harness the evocative power of that myth.

A solution to this temporal problem was found by the French anarchist writer Pierre-Joseph Proudhon. In his explosive tract *What Is Property?* (1840), Proudhon introduced the idea of a dialectical relationship between the ancient golden age and its future recurrence. The past had experienced "negative communism [*communauté*], called by the ancient poets the *age of gold*." But this earlier, "negative" state was merely a promise of humanity's communist future, to be achieved on a higher, "positive" level:

> If Providence placed the first human beings in a condition of equality, it was a vindication of its desires, a model that it wished them to realize in other forms [*sur d'autres dimensions*]. . . . Man has but one nature, constant and unalterable: he pursues it through instinct, he wanders from it through reflection, he returns to it through judgment; who shall say that we are not returning now?[37]

This Hegelian logic naturally appealed to Marx, who himself turned to communism after reading Proudhon, though the two later sparred mercilessly.[38] Marx's own adoption of this dialectical logic was further refined by his encounter with anthropological sources. The late prefaces by Marx and Engels to the *Communist Manifesto* (1882, 1883) highlight the "primeval common/communal ownership" of land.[39] Engels credited Lewis Morgan's *Ancient Society* (1877) for leading them to revise their historical views.[40]

Marx had been fascinated by Morgan's work, taking notes for a book project that Engels subsequently published as *The Origin of the Family, Private Property, and the State* (1884). According to Morgan, the most ancient form of society, or what he called the *gens*, had been communist and democratic. In the conclusion of his book, Morgan himself hailed the *gens* as an early indication of the ideal society to come:

> Democracy in government, brotherhood in society, equality in rights and privileges, and universal education, foreshadow the next higher plane of society to which experience, intelligence and knowledge are steadily tending. It will be a revival, in a higher form, of the liberty, equality and fraternity of the ancient gentes.[41]

Engels chose this quote to conclude his own study. How could he resist Morgan's inscription of the revolutionary slogan (*liberté, égalité, fraternité*) in his account of communism past and yet to come?

Revolutionary Dictatorship

Socialists and other progressives lived in anticipation of a better world. Most took its imminent arrival as a given. For Marx, it was inevitable that bourgeois capitalism would eventually collapse under its own contradictions. How and when this endpoint would come about were unclear, but those were minor details. It was all just a matter of time—that was the promise of historical progress.

This confidence that change was on the way had a transformative effect on politics. Viewed from one angle, this effect may seem negligible: the vast majority of progressive revolutionaries were committed democrats. But their conception of democracy was strangely anemic. Gone were any struggles between interest groups, social classes, regions, or religious faiths. Their democracy was "perfect" and "pure" (Cabet). Once social classes had been abolished, Marx and Engels reasoned, then all conflicts would disappear. Politics should become depoliticized. Come the revolution, there would be nothing left to argue about.

For anarchists like Proudhon, the end of politics meant that there would be no further need for a state: revolution meant "the negation of government."[42] Localities could administer themselves; since human nature would finally be fully realized, all of the problems with current society would vanish. Given the counterrevolutionary role of most governments at the time, this wholesale indictment of the state had considerable allure. Under pressure from anarchist rivals, Marx and Engels folded the "withering away of the state" into their own dialectical model of history.[43] As with the other good things they promised, this too would come to pass—just not immediately, as the anarchists, in their creative destruction, proposed.

The political harmony that progressives thought would prevail stood in sharp contrast with the present cacophony. The lesson that they often took from this contrast was that the people were not quite ready for the perfect democracy to come. Look what happened when the French people voted in the 1848 presidential elections, Marx grumbled: they chose another Bonaparte.[44] Progress was slow and uneven.

Revolutionary politics, accordingly, was defined by a delay. The world to come would be reasonable, just, and democratic, while the world at hand was anything but. The faith in historical progress encouraged a two-speed political solution, one for the bumpy, obstructed road ahead, and another for the smooth, clear way beyond. It was the same double pattern that Europeans projected onto their colonial holdings. Colonial subjects might eventually be capable of self-government, but for the time being, they were stuck in the "waiting room of history," a temporal limbo with different political rules and expectations. In both cases, time was the critical growth factor for rational advancement.[45]

For some Russian theorists, such as Alexander Herzen, the temporal gap between present-day Russia and the wished-for future was so great that their "backwards" country could even leapfrog over Europe and achieve a socialist society long before the rest.[46] Others sought more violent mechanisms for speeding up time. The "shock therapy" that many Russian revolutionaries believed would be most effective was the bomb.[47] They predicted that the spectacular assassination of top administrators could vault Russian consciousness into a just and democratic future. This commitment to violent action also brought revolution within the reach of everyone, including women. Vera Zasulich rose to fame after her failed assassination of a top Russian official, earning her comparisons with Charlotte Corday.[48]

Other revolutionaries preferred the less violent means of education. The secret society that staged an unsuccessful insurrection in Victor Hugo's *Les misérables* (1862) was named the Société de l'ABC, which turned out to be a clever play on words: in French, the first three letters of the alphabet sound identical to *abaissé*, or "oppressed." Many hoped that education, often starting with literacy, would eventually lift up the European masses, as it would non-Western subjects. Over time, education gave way among some to indoctrination: it was necessary, Lenin argued (quoting Karl Kautsky), to "introduce . . . socialist consciousness . . . into the proletarian class."[49] The masses were not going to radicalize themselves.

All of these efforts would eventually need to be supplemented by other institutions. Just as a heavy-handed colonial government was required to supervise the advancement of non-Western subjects, a revolutionary government would have to oversee the transition to the perfected future society. The conclusion that it was necessary to suspend democratic government—temporarily, of course—until the people were ready was another legacy of the Jacobins. After October 1793, the Committee of Public Safety had claimed to govern France, according to Robespierre, in "the spirit of revolutionary government, combined with the general principles of democracy."[50] He never called the revolutionary government a dictatorship, though as this statement makes clear, it was democratic only "in principle."

This period's close identification with (what became known as) the Terror made the legacy of revolutionary government a tricky one. Most revolutionaries promised that the revolution next time would not resort to violence to bring about its aims. As late as 1917, Lenin reassured his readers that, come the revolution, landowners and capitalists would merely be arrested "for a few weeks, to expose their frauds. . . . Upon exposing their frauds, we could release them."[51]

The clearest and most notorious blueprint for a temporary revolutionary dictatorship appeared in 1828. It was the work of Philippe Buonarotti, an Italian revolutionary descended from Michelangelo who had taken part in the "Conspiracy for Equality" of 1796. This conspiracy had been spearheaded by "Gracchus" Babeuf, a radical French journalist who after Thermidor styled himself "the tribune of the people." Buonarotti may have embroidered certain aspects of the conspiracy, but it was this work that brought Babeuf to the attention of later revolutionaries. In this regard, if it is not always a reliable description of the conspiracy or of Babeuf's actual views, it is important as a document of political theory in its own right.[52]

In Buonarotti's account, the Babouvists had sought to pick up where Robespierre had left off—namely, with the "catastrophe" of Thermidor. They promised to reinstate the constitution of 1793, but their plans were more elaborate than that. In over one hundred pages, Buonarotti detailed the Equals' proposals to bring about radical equality, plans that included the redistribution of wealth across the population, the disappearance of large towns, and a Spartan national education system. Robespierre had gestured rather vaguely to a coming "reign of eternal justice," but the Babouvists fleshed out this golden-age commonplace with concrete proposals.[53]

As the achievements to be obtained by the next revolution blossomed in number and in difficulty, their delivery schedule was also pushed back. Not holding political power, the Babouvists fretted a great deal about how they could accomplish all that they promised. More explicitly than the Jacobins, they relied on futural politics to resolve their conundrum. They argued that they could make a legitimate claim to power in the name of a future "order of equality," which would replace the present "egotistical" society.[54]

How this argument worked in practice was complex. On the one hand, the Babouvists promised a return to the 1793 constitution, which should have placed legislative authority in an elected national assembly and an executive council. On the other, they wished to push through a very ambitious agenda. Who would oversee this transition, or as they put it, "What will this authority be"? They floated a radical option: What if the group that had organized the revolution (the insurrectional committee) was "temporally invested with all the national power" in order to ensure "the complete success of the insurrection"? They recognized the danger of illegitimacy that even such a "provisional authority" might present: "Converting the insurrectional initiative into a permanent and necessarily broad power would raise suspicions that the members of the insurrectional committee were ambitious and self-interested." Such suspicions could hinder the committee "by not leaving them enough time to achieve the good they propose to do." But they also saw a danger "in not allowing those who began the work to complete it."[55] Time was of the essence: the Babouvists needed more time to finish what they'd started, but if they took too long, they might lose the people's confidence. They were leaning toward a compromise—asking the people for a decree that would "exclusively entrust" the insurrectionary committee with full political power—when they were betrayed.

Their arrest spared the Babouvists from confronting this paradox of relying on an act of popular sovereignty (a sort of plebiscite) to bypass democratic government—precisely the Bonapartist solution, except for the Babouvists it was intended to be only temporary. As it was, they never found themselves in a position where they needed to justify their present actions in the name of future outcomes. What would such a government have looked like in practice? Some members openly clamored for the dictatorship of a single man, "the most virtuous citizen."[56] Here again was the Jacobin solution to the danger of representative government: entrust power only to those recognized for their superior virtue. This option seemed too risky to others, though all agreed that turning political power over to a democratically elected government would be a mistake. The people were simply not prepared to govern themselves: "Abnormally deviated from the natural order, the people were incapable of making sound decisions, and needed an extraordinary means of replacing them." Until the people realized that they had been duped by aristocratic and monied interests, they would continue to be misled. They were just not *currently* "in a state where they could fully exercise sovereignty in an effective, rather than a fictive, manner."[57] Give us democracy, the progressives prayed, but not yet.

The progressives' delay tactic found further support from the liberals' weak endorsement of popular suffrage. In France, 1830 was the high-water mark of liberal success. The new regime pledged to protect individual freedoms and establish representative government more firmly. But the franchise remained highly restricted. What kind of democracy was this? asked the arch-revolutionary Louis-Auguste Blanqui, in 1832. Liberals prided themselves on the separation of powers, but this principle was meaningless when all the powers were controlled by a tiny elite (precisely Montesquieu's criticism of aristocratic Venice). This is neither a republic nor democracy, but "the most monstrous of tyrannies," he concluded.[58]

Blanqui sketched out the new battle lines of progressive revolutionaries. Asked to identify his profession, he declared that he was a "proletarian." The presiding judge retorted that this wasn't a profession. "Not a profession?" scoffed Blanqui. "It's the profession of the thirty million French who live off their work and are deprived of political rights." He gave another name to the tiny elite of citizens who enjoyed political rights: *bourgeois*. Recalling the word's etymology, he emphasized how these parasites sucked wealth from the countryside into luxurious cities (*bourgs*). The clash between the two groups, proletarians and bourgeois, had now intensified into "the war between rich and poor."[59] This kind of class conflict was nothing new—it had lain at the heart of revolutions since the Peloponnesian War—but the goal of politics was no longer to find a political compromise. The new solutions on the table would end class conflict once and for all. It was a goal that classical thinkers would have found delusional, and that the progressive futurists fervently pursued.

CHAPTER THIRTEEN

Revolution in Permanence

IN THE WEEKS after the February 1848 revolution in Paris, a young Frenchman with no political experience decided to run in the upcoming elections. He had participated somewhat haphazardly in the recent insurrection, stumbling upon a barricade, before joining the crowds that had stormed the Tuileries Palace. But the spectacle of the people in arms left a profound mark on him. Like all of his acquaintances (and most officials), he quickly embraced the new republican regime, and when someone suggested that he present himself for office, his imagination lit up. To garner support, he visited a variety of political clubs, covering the full ideological spectrum, but none of them clicked. Finally, a friend invited him to the intriguingly named Intelligence Club (Club de l'intelligence). He attended a session in the hopes of securing the club's nomination.

The meeting got off to a rough start. The assembled patriots could not even agree on which songs to sing. It was a sign of things to come: the discussion meandered widely. After a heated debate over whether Latin should be revived as the language of a democratic Europe, a long speech on tax distribution was shouted down (too many numbers!). A worker then took the floor to inform the audience that the Second Coming of Christ was at hand, only to be interrupted by a salesman in favor of abolishing all religions. Confusion reached its climax when another member urged the assembly to "spread the veal's head" (*étendre la tête de veau*). No one had the foggiest idea what he meant, just as they did not understand a word of the revolutionary from Barcelona who addressed the club in Spanish. When our budding politician was finally able to announce his candidacy, he was promptly expelled from the club.

This example (to which I will return shortly) illuminates how 1848 marked a turning point in how Europeans who were previously sympathetic to the liberal model of revolution came to question it. The modern faith in progress rested on the assumption that history would naturally bring about consensus: "The march of the human spirit is one and inalterable, and it does not change from time to time or place to place," announced Henri Saint-Simon.[1] But this belief was not panning out. European societies were perhaps more divided than ever, and showed few signs of resolving their differences. Even this realization did not bring about a new consensus. For some, it served to break the revolutionary spell, pushing them in a more conservative direction.[2] For others, the fault lay instead in the modest ambitions of the liberal model. These critics did not respond by rejecting revolution but by demanding more of it. In this way, the events of the 1848 revolutions played a key role in rehabilitating older ideas of revolutionary dictatorship, now under a new name: "revolution in permanence." Karl Marx's repackaging of this idea was particularly crucial, as it thereby entered into the most important current of socialist thought. Combined with his later interpretation of the 1871 Paris Commune, Marx's theory of permanent revolution provided a template for the regimes soon to become synonymous with revolution. The missing links between 1789 and 1917 are provided by 1848 and 1871.

Revolutionary Thrills and Spills

The ambitious Frenchman who sought a political career in 1848 was Frédéric Moreau, the main protagonist of Gustave Flaubert's 1869 novel, *Sentimental Education*. Flaubert's narrative is obviously a fictionalized account. There never was a Club de l'intelligence, and topics of more pressing importance than the revival of Latin were debated at the time. Realism, in these sections of the novel, gives way to satire. But Flaubert's fictional treatment is still illuminating, and has a basis in fact. Flaubert modeled aspects of Frédéric's experience on his own.[3] Like his hero, Flaubert was in Paris in 1848, and among the crowd that stormed the Tuileries Palace. And Flaubert was one of the most incisive analysts of nineteenth-century society, bringing a surgeon's eye to the political passions of his age. As the critic Edmund Wilson noted, he "was almost as close to the historians Michelet, Renan and Taine, and to the biographical critic Sainte-Beuve, as to Gautier and Baudelaire," two poets of that generation.[4]

Flaubert's description is particularly valuable for his insights on the psychology of revolutions. At the heart of this psychology lies the emotional response that revolutions can trigger. Flaubert recounts how Frédéric "trembled in the throes of a vast love, a love that was supreme and universal, like the heart of the whole of humanity beating in his breast."[5] As the satirical tone of this comment suggests, it was already a commonplace in Flaubert's time that revolutions could produce such feelings. After 1789, the modern faith in progress not only reversed, in the eyes of many, the classical fears of revolution, it also imbued revolution with gauzy feelings of universal harmony. The dream of brotherly love—"Alle Menschen werden Brüder" (All humans will be brothers) as Friedrich Schiller phrased it in his "Ode to Joy," which Beethoven put to music—was a crucial component of modern revolutions, and contributed to their appeal.[6] "If music should perish in the coming world upheaval, we must risk our lives to save the Ninth Symphony," Mikhail Bakunin told Richard Wagner after the latter conducted Beethoven's symphony in Dresden.[7] A month later, both joined the revolutionaries seeking to overthrow the Saxon government, the choral finale still on the lips of some of the rebels. The opera house where the Ninth was performed went up in flames.[8]

For Frédéric, this overflowing fellow feeling also inspired him to act, though Flaubert highlights a further motive (in addition to vanity): "It seemed to him that a wonderful dawn was about to break. Rome, Vienna, Berlin were in a state of revolt, the Austrians driven out of Venice, the whole of Europe in ferment."[9] One reason why modern revolutions elicit such strong reactions is precisely because they encapsulate a sense of historic sea change. Where history, for Polybius and other ancient writers, consisted mainly of "the vicissitudes of fortune," adherents to the modern faith of progress found the movement of history exhilarating. History was on the move, on the march, and this imagined transfiguration of time was all the more exciting in an age when many writers complained that time was standing still.[10]

Flaubert characteristically mocked such historical optimism, which in his novel culminates in a painting by Pellerin, a republican artist. The painting represented "the Republic, or Progress, or Civilization, in the figure of Jesus Christ driving a locomotive, crossing virgin forest."[11] Here was history's locomotive, indeed. Yet even this ridiculous allegory contained a hidden point. Progress had become the modern faith par excellence, shared by industrialists and revolutionaries alike. Where this locomotive was headed, no one agreed, but the impression that humanity was hurtling through history and across virgin territory was widespread.

Perhaps most insightfully, Flaubert called attention to a pernicious effect of revolutionary emotions. He alluded to a famous speech by Alfonse de Lamartine, a poet and historian who played an important, if brief, role in the Provisional Government that replaced Louis-Philippe in February 1848. Seeing protesters wave the red flag, he countered that they should rally around the tricolor flag instead (this incident was memorialized in paint as well: see figure 13.1). With rhetorical flourish, he reminded the crowd that the *bleu-blanc-rouge* of France had traveled around the world, whereas the red flag of insurrection had only gone around the Champs-de-Mars (a reference to the massacre of republican protesters in July 1791). It was supposed to be a moment of national unity. But Flaubert offered another reason for its success:

> People repeated the words of Lamartine about the red flag. . . . And they all lined up under the shadow of the flag, each side only perceiving its own color among all the others and promising itself, as soon as it was stronger, to tear down the other two.[12]

The republican consensus that emerged in spring 1848 was merely a mirage. As soon as they had a chance, the whites or the blues would crush the reds (or vice versa).

Such an opportunity soon came to pass. After the elections returned a conservative majority to the assembly, the government shut down the national workshops (*ateliers*), causing workers in Paris to revolt. Their insurrection was crushed in blood: during the so-called June Days, thousands of Parisian workers were killed and another eleven thousand deported or imprisoned.[13] Even Flaubert, who mercilessly poked fun at revolutionary naïveté, could not stomach the savagery of this repression. In a rare melodramatic scene of the novel, he depicts an imprisoned worker begging for bread, only to be shot point blank by a provincial soldier.[14]

For Flaubert, violence was indeed the inevitable resolution of revolutionary cacophony. Frédéric himself was nearly roughed up after the president of the Club de l'intelligence expelled him (they were old rivals). As soon as his revolutionary credentials were shown to be wanting, he was suspected of being a counterrevolutionary: "'*Aristo!*' barked a lout, shaking his fist at Frédéric, who rushed out into the courtyard, indignant."[15] It was a political purge, in miniature. This same president, Sénécal, would end up supporting Louis-Napoléon Bonaparte during his coup d'état of December 1851.

Flaubert's novel depicts revolutions as a modern superstition, a form of magical thinking that must be exorcized.[16] He clearly hoped that *Sentimental Education* would do the trick. Touring the devastation left by the 1871 Paris Commune and its bloody repression by national troops, Flaubert lamented to his friend Maxime du Camp that "if *A Sentimental Education* had been understood, none of this would have happened."[17] Unlike

FIGURE 13.1 H.F.E. Philippoteaux, *Lamartine devant l'Hôtel de Ville de Paris le 25 février 1848 refuse le drapeau rouge*. Wikimedia Commons, public domain. This file is made available under the Creative Commons CC0 1.0 Universal Public Domain Dedication.

earlier critics of revolutions, Flaubert had sought to reveal their inner workings. His realist aesthetic reflected his conservative politics, allowing him to peel back the romance of revolution and reveal how fraternal feelings could birth fratricidal fury.

As an exercise in political thought, Flaubert's novel was groundbreaking. As an intervention in French history, it failed miserably. *Sentimental Education* was a commercial flop, and the Commune broke out less than two years after it was published. In part, Flaubert's book had to contend with the hundreds of works that had filled the minds of nineteenth-century readers with dreams of the future, as we saw in the previous chapter. But there was something about 1848 that even he had missed. This was the way in which 1848 led to the revival of a robust theory of revolutionary dictatorship. And this revival was the work of the most influential and important revolutionary thinker of the nineteenth-century: Karl Marx.

Marx and the French Revolutions

Flaubert and Marx—whose daughter, Eleanor, translated *Madame Bovary* in 1886—may have crossed paths in Paris, as both were present in the springtime of 1848. But their respective takes on the events underway could hardly have been more different.[18]

With fortuitous timing, Marx and Engels had published the *Communist Manifesto* mere weeks before revolution broke out in Paris. These two events were unrelated—the *Manifesto* was hardly noticed when it first appeared. And the 1848 revolutions, especially the French one, which Marx chronicled obsessively, led him to dramatically revise the theory of revolution outlined in the *Manifesto*.

As befitting the genre, the *Manifesto* brilliantly boiled down European politics to a struggle between the "bourgeoisie" and "proletariat." These were the opposing blocs that Blanqui and other socialists (including Louis Blanc) had already pitted against each other in the 1830s.[19] Famously, Marx and Engels went out of their way in the *Manifesto* to praise the bourgeoisie as the revolutionary class par excellence. After all, it was the bourgeoisie that had destroyed aristocratic feudalism in 1789, and continued to transform the world at an astounding pace.[20] Marx retained from Saint-Simon and Cabet an enthusiasm for the bourgeoisie's industrial innovations, which could be appropriated for the greater good. The proletariat should, accordingly, learn from the bourgeoisie, and eventually follow its lead.

But in the *Manifesto*, the emphasis was on the "eventually." From Hegel, Marx had also retained a faith in historical progress. Everything should happen in due course. When they were writing the *Manifesto*, it still seemed to Marx and Engels that "communists" would best be served by supporting bourgeois parties. A new world could be built only after the old one had been demolished, and the bourgeoisie was the great battering ram of history. Accordingly, the last chapter of the *Manifesto* detailed the alliances that communists must forge with bourgeois parties across Europe: "In Germany, they fight with the bourgeoisie whenever it acts in a revolutionary way."[21] Proletarian revolutionaries had to get in line.

THE REVOLUTIONS OF 1848

The events that unfolded in Paris after the February insurrection led Marx to modify that conclusion. His ideas evolved gradually, through his constant reporting on French affairs for the *Neue Rheinische Zeitung*.[22] Initially, Marx seemed content to analyze the February revolution according to the two-stage model outlined in the *Manifesto*: "Only bourgeois rule tears up the material roots of feudal society and levels the ground on which alone a proletarian revolution is possible," he reiterated. The workers could not have expected to take power in the spring of 1848, as the proletariat was not yet a sufficiently mobilized or self-conscious class in France.[23]

The workers nonetheless scored some victories. They obliged the Provisional Government to acquiesce to some of their demands. These included the declaration of a republic, the proclamation of universal male suffrage, and the establishment of the Luxembourg Commission, charged with examining labor conditions. Marx did not think very highly of this commission, describing it as a "ministry of pious wishes." He also viewed the creation of national workshops as a ploy to enlist worker support for the bourgeois government. Compared with the regime to come, however, Marx still described the early months of the Provisional Government as a "Republic with social institutions."[24]

All this changed once the April elections brought a more outspokenly conservative government to power. The new assembly shut down the workshops, leading to an insurrection by the now-unemployed workers in June. Curiously, Marx interpreted the June crushing of the workers' uprising as a return of sorts to the natural order of historical class struggle: "The real birthplace of the bourgeois republic is not the *February victory*; it is the *June defeat*," he insisted.[25] The early influence wielded by the workers was a historical anomaly; in Hegelian terms, their day in the sun of History had not yet arrived. But it was precisely through their clash with the bourgeoisie that the proletarians discovered their own class identity: "Only after being dipped in the blood of the *June insurgents* did the tricolor become the flag of the European revolution—the *red flag!*"[26] History itself allowed Marx to update the revolutionary theory he and Engels had laid out previously in the *Communist Manifesto*. In defeat, the proletarians had come out of the shadows of the bourgeoisie and assumed their own identity as a revolutionary class.

Marx also consummated the break with the classical theory of revolution that sought a resolution in a well-balanced constitution. This objective was simply another instance of bourgeois ideology, he claimed: "With the *Legislative* National Assembly the phenomenon of the *constitutional republic* was completed, that is, the republican form of government in which the rule of the bourgeois class is constituted."[27] A constitution was nothing more than the instrument that the ruling party uses to stay in power: "The interpretation of the constitution did not belong to those who had made it, but only to those who had accepted it. . . . [I]ts wording must be construed in its viable meaning and . . . the bourgeois meaning was its only viable meaning." Employing a religious-legal analogy, Marx argued that interpretation was merely another means to power: "Bonaparte and the royalist majority of the National Assembly were the authentic interpreters of the constitution, as the priest is the authentic interpreter of the Bible, and the judge the authentic interpreter of the laws."[28] It was a version of the argument Hobbes had made in *Leviathan* about kings.

This hermeneutical claim, however, masked a more radical stance. By rejecting the constitution's legitimacy, Marx refused to grant that expressions of popular sovereignty should have the final word in settling political outcomes.[29] In many respects, Marx's resistance to popular elections was driven by a paradox of authoritarian power in nineteenth-century France. Plebiscites were a central pillar of support for Bonapartism.[30] For progressives, constitutional government was counterrevolutionary. Marx had to make philosophical lemonade out of historical lemons.

But Marx's impatience with popular sovereignty cannot just be chalked up to a conservative electorate. Viewing all politics through the lens of class struggle, he castigated the Second Republic as nothing other than a "bourgeois dictatorship" (*Bourgeoisdictatur*). With this expression, he meant two things: First, it designated a regime that did not hesitate to use force to impose its will and repress dissent. But the other half of the expression is equally important—politics was simply a matter of looking out for one's own class interests.

And so the ruthless defense of bourgeois interests that defined the Second Republic in Marx's eyes became a lesson in class domination. As in the past, the bourgeoisie was showing the way to conduct a successful revolution. Now that the proletariat had been fully elevated to the consciousness of its revolutionary-historical role, it should accordingly mimic the bourgeoisie in its pursuit and preservation of power. Or rather, in a more Hegelian mode, Marx argued that this was already happening:

> The *proletariat* rallies more and more around *revolutionary socialism*, around *communism*, for which the bourgeoisie has itself invented the name of *Blanqui*. This socialism is the *declaration of the permanence of the revolution* [*die Permanenz-Erklärung der Revolution*], the *class dictatorship* of the proletariat as the necessary transit point to the *abolition of class distinctions generally*.[31]

This oft-quoted passage of the *Class Struggles* marks an important turning point in the history of revolutionary thought. Where the legitimacy of postrevolutionary regimes had been thought, since 1789, to rest on popular sovereignty, here Marx proposes a different form of political authority, which derives from the *future* accomplishment of a revolutionary program. The proletariat is the one class that can legitimately rule over the others, since it is the only class destined to accomplish the true historical purpose of the revolution—"the abolition of class distinctions." Class sovereignty, which would later morph into party sovereignty, became the new source of legitimacy in this permanent model of revolution.

This passage is also noteworthy because it associates this type of revolutionary authority with a concept that would become central to Marxist thought: "the revolution in permanence," or "permanent revolution." Marx does not expound on this idea in *The Class Struggles in France* ("The scope of this exposition does not permit of developing the subject further," he explained), though the reference to Blanqui has led some commentators to seek its origin there.[32] But one does not find here, or in any other of Marx's discussions of permanent revolution (to which I will turn shortly), the Blanquist or Babouvist notion that revolutionary dictators are to be drawn from the conspiratorial group that launched the revolution in the first place.[33] Since revolutions, for Marx, are the necessary outcomes of socioeconomic contradictions, it would be illogical for him to adhere to Blanqui's model of planned insurrections. Finally, there is no indication that Marx had in mind here a dictatorship of the type Blanqui imagined—that is, an all-powerful Committee of Public Safety. As we will see, the French revolutionary practice that Marx preferred was fundamentally different.

What Marx sketches out in the *Class Struggles in France* is nonetheless much closer to the accelerated model of proletarian revolution *in the midst of* a bourgeois revolution later championed by Lenin and (even more explicitly) Trotsky than to the two-stage model of bourgeois revolution subsequently followed by proletarian revolution announced in the *Manifesto*. And this sketch was not a one-off draft. Indeed, Marx "developed the subject further" in a short piece published soon after: the famous March 1850 "Address of the Central Committee to the Communist League," cowritten with Engels. Here, the battle cry of the *Manifesto*, "Working Men of All Countries, Unite!" (also the motto of the Communist League) was updated with a more menacing one: "[The German workers'] battle-cry must be: *The Revolution in Permanence* [*Die Revolution in Permanenz*]."[34] As in the *Class Struggles in France*, Marx and Engels denounced constitutional government again as a class instrument of "the constitutional-democratic petty bourgeois." But they also added two twists to the theory of permanent revolution. The first was temporal: the revolution should be permanent in the literal sense that its actions must be of indefinite duration. Conversely, those who seek to end the revolution swiftly should be viewed with suspicion:

> While the democratic petty bourgeois want to bring the revolution to an end as quickly as possible, achieving at most the aims already mentioned, it is our interest and our task to make the revolution permanent [*die Revolution permanent zu machen*] until all the more or less propertied classes have been driven from their ruling positions, until the proletariat has conquered state power and until the association of the proletarians has progressed sufficiently far.[35]

Permanent revolution is thus once again associated with class dictatorship, even if this expression is not used in the text. Indeed, instead of the comparison with bourgeois rule found in the *Class Struggles in France*, Marx and Engels introduced a different historical parallel: "As in France in 1793, it is the task of the genuinely revolutionary party in Germany to carry through the strictest centralization."[36] They left no doubts about what it was specifically this earlier model had to offer. It was the Terror:

> Above all, during and immediately after the struggle the workers, as far as it is at all possible, must oppose bourgeois attempts at pacification and force the democrats to carry out their terroristic phrases [*terroristischen Phrasen*]. They must work to ensure that the immediate revolutionary excitement is not suddenly suppressed after the victory. . . . Far from opposing the so-called excesses—instances of popular vengeance against hated individuals or against public buildings with

> which hateful memories are associated—the workers' party must not only tolerate these actions but must even give them direction.[37]

This passage reads in part like a revenge fiction of what might have happened in spring 1848, had the Parisian workers only harassed the Provisional Government more vigorously. But it can also be read as a socialist account of 1793, with the workers in the role of the *sans-culottes*. Either way, Marx and Engels defined permanent revolution on the model of the "decisive, terroristic [*terroristisch*] action against the reaction" that characterized, in their view, the radical phase of the French Revolution. The battle cry for permanent revolution was a literal call to battle: "The workers must be armed and organized," they wrote; "The whole proletariat must be armed at once with muskets, rifles, cannon and ammunition."[38]

This fixation on French revolutionary Terror raises the question of how much Marx's ideas about revolution were determined by the events of 1848–50 and how much he was thinking about 1793. Some historians have characterized Marx and Engels's aggressive posture in the March address as a departure from the milder and more cautious attitude they had adopted at the beginning of the revolution. Jonathan Sperber argued, for instance, that "the policies [Marx] denounced in the March Address . . . were all central features of his own activities during most of 1848–49."[39] In Sperber's view, Marx became disenchanted by the failure of policies he had advocated in the *Neue Rheinische Zeitung*, and subsequently moved closer to the more radical wing of the Communist League, represented by Andreas Gottschalk (from whom Sperber suggests Marx borrowed the phrase "permanent revolution"). While Marx clearly used the 1848–50 revolution as an opportunity to think through and work out his own revolutionary theory, there is, however, plenty of evidence that he hatched his radical theory of proletarian revolution quite early on. Already in the fall of 1848, he made a strong case for provisional dictatorship and against constitutionalism, claiming that "every provisional organization of the state requires a dictatorship and an energetic dictatorship at that." He criticized the leader of the provisional government in Berlin, Ludolf Camphausen, "for not acting dictatorially, for not having immediately smashed up and eliminated the remnants of the old institutions . . . Herr Camphausen was lulling himself with constitutional dreaming."[40] In fact, the origins of Marx's theory of permanent revolution are to be discovered well *before* the revolution even broke out in 1848. In the following section, I show how it was Marx's studies of the French Revolution (conducted in 1843–44) that led him to first formulate this idea, albeit initially in a negative sense.

THE REVOLUTIONS OF 1789–93

Marx first used the expression "revolution in permanence" in 1843, and then twice more before 1850.[41] On each of these occasions, it was in the context of the French Revolution, and more specifically of the Terror. The importance of this context is particularly striking in the case of Marx's first usage of the term, in "On *The Jewish Question*." Marx introduces this notion by rapidly surveying some of the highlights of 1793:

> Certainly, in periods when the political state as such comes violently to birth in civil society, and when men strive to liberate themselves through political emancipation, the state can, and must, proceed to *abolish and destroy religion*; but only in the same way as it proceeds to abolish private property, by declaring a maximum, by confiscation, or by progressive taxation, or in the same way as it proceeds to abolish life, by the *guillotine*.[42]

While the particular references in this passage obviously point back to the Terror, Marx is also attempting here to generalize these events. They are not simply characteristics of Jacobinism, but are what happens in "periods when the political state as such is born violently out of civil society." It is in this context of violent political birth that Marx first invokes the idea of permanent revolution:

> At those times when the state is most aware of itself, political life seeks to stifle its own prerequisites—civil society and its elements—and to establish itself as the genuine and harmonious species-life of man. But it can only achieve this end by setting itself in *violent* contradiction with its own conditions of existence, by declaring a *permanent revolution* [*die Revolution für* permanent *erklärt*]. Thus the political drama ends necessarily with the restoration of religion, of private property, of all the elements of civil society, just as war ends with the conclusion of peace.[43]

Tellingly, the reference here to "permanent revolution" is unfavorable. This revolutionary phase resulted only in the restoration of the old regime. But the phrase itself invites further scrutiny. The term *permanent* is italicized in the original German text. While Marx often used italics for emphasis (including elsewhere in this passage), he may plausibly have used them here to indicate the foreign—and more specifically French, as we will see—origin of the word.[44] It was not a term Marx had used much before.[45] What might explain its sudden appearance in his lexicon is his reading of that time. Indeed, when Marx wrote "On *The Jewish Question*," he was living in Paris (Oct. 1843–Jan. 1845) and immersed in the study of the

French Revolution for the purposes of writing a (never completed) history of the National Convention.[46] He accordingly consulted Philippe Buchez and Pierre-Célestin Roux's *Histoire parlementaire de la Révolution française* (1833–38), a largely documentary history of the Revolution, told from a sympathetic, neo-Jacobin perspective.[47] And it is precisely during this time that Marx began affixing the qualifier "permanent" to revolution, notably in *The Holy Family* (published in 1845, written a year prior), where he remarks that Napoleon "*completed* the *Terror* by placing *permanent Revolution* in the *place* of *permanent war*."[48]

Here as well, "permanent revolution" is clearly assigned a negative value. There is nothing yet to indicate that Marx admired this revolutionary model. But we do see the strong connection in Marx's mind between "permanent revolution" and the Terror of 1793. What made that connection meaningful? What exactly did Marx take away from his readings? A first step toward answering this question would be to resolve the philological mystery surrounding this expression. Where did the expression "permanent revolution" come from? As we saw, scholars have suggested many different origins, though they are all mostly speculative.[49] But there is in fact a clear source for this expression, which historians have curiously overlooked, and that is in the documentary record of the French Revolution itself.[50]

While the precise expression "révolution permanente" can itself be found in the revolutionary archives, it is more useful to explore the revolutionary origins of "permanence," and more specifically of *en permanence*.[51] Indeed, this expression has a rich history in French revolutionary discourse. As we saw in chapter 10, radical Parisians had demanded "the permanence of the districts'" assemblies back in March 1790.[52] What they meant at the time was simply that the assemblies be allowed to continue meeting, instead of being dissolved now that their original role (participating in elections to the Estates General) had long passed.

Two years later, the expression reemerged, but this time with a different meaning. In 1792, France had declared war against Austria (in April), but the king had vetoed a measure establishing twenty thousand National Guardsmen outside of Paris, to protect the capital.[53] That July, the assembly declared "la patrie en danger" (the homeland [is] in danger). It was in this context that the deputy Jacques-Alexis Thuriot relayed a demand expressed by the Parisian sections (which had replaced the districts in 1790):

> Many departments have already requested that their sections meet in permanence [*La permanence des sections a déjà été demandée par*

> *plusieurs départements*]. In Paris, it is the permanence of the sections that made the Revolution; it is the permanence that must consolidate it. I demand that the Assembly decree that the situation is urgent and that the sections meet in permanence.

His measure was promptly approved by the assembly:

> The National Assembly, considering that when the homeland is in danger and when agitated movements are felt, it is important that citizens in the capital, at all times, look out for us all to ensure the execution of laws and the maintenance of public order, decrees that the situation is urgent.
>
> The National Assembly, having decreed the situation to be urgent, decrees that the assemblies of the Parisian sections will be held in permanence [*se tiendront et seront permanentes*], until otherwise indicated.[54]

Here we find a very different understanding of revolutionary "permanence," one that is much closer to Marx's later usage. To declare the *permanence des sections* meant that, instead of simply meeting on a regular basis, the forty-eight Parisian sections should keep their meeting places manned and open at all times. Practically, this amounted to mobilizing the armed citizens of Paris. The importance of this measure would become clear on August 8, when the Parisian sections voted massively in favor of overthrowing the king, and then stormed the Tuileries Palace the following night.[55] A year later, when the Section de Marseilles declared its intentions to meet *en permanence*, it expressed its lasting faith in this belief that the Revolution could be saved through popular, armed defense: "The revolutionary army and cannons will be maintained in permanence."[56] We are very close here to Marx and Engels's argument, in the March 1850 "Address," that "the workers must be armed and organized."

Can we be sure that Marx knew the revolutionary history of this term? It was certainly widely used, as simple word searches reveal: the phrase "*en permanence*" occurs in the *Archives parlementaires* over 200 times in 1792, and over 300 in 1793.[57] For the most part, this phrase was employed in reference to the Parisian sections: combinations of the terms "section(s)" and "permanent/ce" occur over 150 times in 1792, and over 200 in 1793.[58] But other revolutionary bodies could also meet "*en permanence*." As the Parisian sections were storming the Tuileries Palace, on the night of August 9–10, the Legislative Assembly declared itself to be "en séance permanente."[59]

These quantitative measures are taken from the *Archives parlementaires*, a collation of primary sources similar to the *Histoire parlementaire*, without the political editorializing. Marx, however, read the latter. Was the theme of *permanence* as prominent in these volumes? As they have also been digitized, we can again produce some numbers: volume 27, for instance, which covers the month of May 1793, contains ten mentions of "permanence," either in reference to the Parisian (or Marseillais) sections, sessions of the National Convention, or even the guillotine.[60] Indeed, the phrase *en permanence* could be applied to almost any revolutionary institution, thus indicating its potency. Georges Couthon, a member of the Committee of Public Safety, declared this committee itself to be meeting "in continual permanence."[61]

In addition to these examples from the revolutionary texts themselves, it is also worth paying attention to some of Buchez and Roux's editorial commentary. For instance, they make a point of underscoring the curious fact that the permanent session declared by the Legislative Assembly on August 10 was never lifted.[62] At a historical level, this detail might seem like a mere technicality. But it once again underscores the revolutionary symbolism captured in this phrase—and practice—of "permanence." When the going gets tough, the tough get permanent.

Finally, the revolutionary practice of declaring permanence did not die out with the first French revolution. Revolutionaries in the 1830s would similarly declare section meetings to take place *en permanence* in cases of political emergency. As Jill Harsin writes, "The calling of meetings *en permanence*" was one of "the symbols of the revolutionary period of half a century before" that the July Monarchy men self-consciously invoked, along with the *Marseillaise* and the various section names.[63] Permanence remained part of the revolutionary repertoire up until 1848. On February 24, the day Louis Philippe abdicated, the deputy Charles Lafitte proposed that the Chamber of Deputies meet *en permanence*. His motion was seconded by Etienne Armand Napoléon de Cambacérès, whose uncle Jean-Jacques-Régis de Cambacérès had been a deputy in the National Convention (before becoming consul alongside Napoleon Bonaparte). The chamber dismissed the motion, but clearly the echoes of 1792 had not died out, as subsequent uses of this phrase during the 1848 revolution indicate.[64] Not only the chamber met in permanence; in April so did the Parisian clubs.[65] The resurgence of this revolutionary memory may explain why Marx, in 1848, began considering "permanence" in a positive light, and also why other revolutionary theorists, such as Proudhon or Gottschalk, latched on to this phrase at the same time.

The history of permanence in the first French revolution also helps explain Marx's own understanding of the term. First, it's telling that in his very first use of the expression (in "On *The Jewish Question*"), permanence was something that had to be *declared*: "die Revolution für *permanent* erklärt." This corresponds to the original declaration of the "permanence of the sections" by the Legislative Assembly. Permanence is above all a speech act. Its declarative origins are still on display in the *Class Struggles in France*, where Marx describes "die *Permanenz-Erklärung der Revolution*." This may also explain why the anonymous deputy to the Frankfurt National Assembly, whom Engels quotes in the September 23, 1848, issue of the *Neue Rheinische Zeitung*, announced that the assembly, in response to Frederick William IV of Prussia's counterrevolutionary action, had issued "a *declaration of permanence* which will likely have as its consequence another very bloody *revolution*."[66] Secondly, let us remember that Marx only rarely uses the precise phrase "permanent revolution" (a point that gets lost in some English translations).[67] The "battle-cry" issued in the 1850 "Address" is rather *Die Revolution in Permanenz*. This phrase closely mirrors the French construction *en permanence*.

But the real payoff of this philological exercise is that it can illuminate Marx's own, fleeting use of the concept of permanent revolution, and in particular its connection with the Terror. Viewed through the lens of "permanence," the Terror was first and foremost a popular affair, with armed sans-culottes taking the lead. These sans-culottes could easily be substituted, in Marx's mind at least, with armed workers. The key point to note here is that, in this reading of the Terror, the major players of the time—the Jacobin Club, the National Convention, the revolutionary tribunal, and even the Committee of Public Safety—take a second seat to the Parisian sections. In other words, the model of "permanent revolution" that Marx discovered in the Terror had very little to do with the more notable revolutionary institutions and individuals of the time. This meant that Marx could still be critical of the Jacobin idolatry that continued to afflict, in his eyes, French revolutionaries in 1848, without rejecting the value of the Terror (redefined as a popular movement) for future revolutions.[68]

This is not to say that Marx assumed no central organization was needed. Permanent revolution, like the Terror, was still compatible with dictatorship and "the strictest centralization," as Marx and Engels announced in their 1850 "Address"—a line that Engels would furiously walk back in a post-Commune (1885) footnote praising local governments.[69] Class dictatorship still required some actual dictators. Buchez and Roux, for their part, gave a hearty endorsement of the "Jacobin dictators," saluting the "high morality of their political doctrine."[70] But the "class dictatorship" that Marx had in mind could also be construed as a kind of class sovereignty, since it was the armed sans-culottes who ultimately held the balance of power. "Permanence," in its 1792–93 incarnation, entailed a different center of political gravity than Blanqui's theory of revolutionary dictatorship.

The French revolutionary origins of "permanence" also highlight the central place of armed insurrection and popular violence in Marx's theory (recall "la guillotine en permanence"). Buchez and Roux presented this violence as not only necessary but wholly justified. In a preface entitled "On Terror and Fear as Social Methods" (*De la terreur et de la crainte comme méthodes sociales*), they laid out the neo-Jacobin thesis that the Terror was a result of specific "circumstances" in all its splendor: "Terror is thus sometimes obligatory; it is a duty to inflict it, though it always remains an exceptional method." It was nothing to be ashamed of, since everyone did it.[71] To this *raison d'état* logic, Marx could add his own philosophical argument that only history unveils the true and necessary processes of revolution. Since the Jacobins had had to use terror, clearly the workers would as well. By fishing the concept of permanence out from the ocean of French revolutionary discourse, Marx elevated the popular Terror to a law of revolutionary history.

AFTERLIVES OF PERMANENT REVOLUTION

If historians have not dedicated much effort to probing the origins of Marx's theory of permanent revolution, its family resemblance with Blanqui's idea of revolutionary dictatorship may be largely to blame. This resemblance even led fellow social democrats to denounce it. The German politician Eduard Bernstein, in his revisionist critique of Marxism, rejected permanent revolution as "Blanquism."[72] His accusation was all the more potent that, in 1850, Marx and Engels had indeed collaborated with Blanquists, notably to form the short-lived Universal Society of Revolutionary Communists. What's more, as we already saw, Marx himself invited this comparison by invoking Blanqui in his definition of permanent revolution in the *Class Struggles in France*, and by praising him elsewhere.[73]

But this identification was challenged in Bernstein's own time. Franz Mehring, who later published a biography of Marx, responded point by point to Bernstein, calling attention to the ways in which permanent revolution differed from Blanqui's "putschism."[74] Social democrats of this period also remained aware of the French revolutionary roots of this concept. Equally critical of Bernstein was Karl Kautsky (Engels's close collaborator), who wrote a history of the French Revolution, in which he argued that "the *sans-culottes* had to adopt ever more extreme measures; they had to declare the revolution in permanence (*revolution in permanenz*) and intensify all the more the terrorism that the war conditions had rendered necessary."[75] Engels himself drew attention to this French history, if in a somewhat roundabout way: "When later I read [Alfred] Bougeart's book on Marat, I found that in more than one respect we had only unconsciously imitated the great model of the genuine 'Ami du Peuple.'"[76] Bougeart had indeed highlighted Marat's defense of "permanence," discussing for instance his statement in favor of the "permanence de la commune" after the fall of the monarchy on August 10, 1792: since "the Commune's goal had not been achieved, the permanence of danger legitimates the permanence of its dictatorship."[77] What Engels depicted as unconscious imitation, however, was equally likely to have been conscious modeling, at least in the case of Marx.

Far from being particularly associated with Trotsky, the theory of "revolution in permanence" was well-known and accepted among most social-democratic leaders, both German and Russian.[78] Historians have suggested a tenuous connection between these debates and what would become the Bolshevik party line: "In Russia, Lenin adopted Trotsky's view when he resolved to seize power from the Provisional Government."[79] But Lenin did not wait until 1917 to adopt the theory of permanent revolution. He had already advocated for the creation of a "revolutionary-democratic dictatorship of the proletariat and the peasantry" in *Two Tactics of Social-Democracy in the Democratic Revolution* (1905).[80] Here he collapsed the orthodox two-stage model of revolution (described in the *Manifesto*) into the "permanent" one (developed after 1848):

> We must not be afraid (as is [the Menshevik Alexandr] Martynov) of a complete victory for Social-Democracy in a democratic revolution, i.e., of a revolutionary-democratic dictatorship of the proletariat and the peasantry, for such a victory will enable us to rouse Europe, and the socialist proletariat of Europe, after throwing off the yoke of the bourgeoisie, will in its turn help us to accomplish the socialist revolution.[81]

Due to Menshevik accusations that he had abandoned orthodox Marxism, and perhaps also to distance himself from Trotsky, who under the influence of Alexander Parvus began to champion the one-stage model at this same time, Lenin ended up downplaying his plans for dictatorship.[82] But there can be little doubt that Lenin, too, was drawing on Marx's theory of permanent revolution and, through Marx, on the French revolutionary example.[83] In *Two Tactics of Social-Democracy*, for instance, he quoted an 1848 article from the *Neue Rheinische Zeitung* where Marx wrote, "The whole French terrorism . . . was nothing but a plebian manner of settling accounts with the enemies of the bourgeoisie, with absolutism, feudalism, and philistinism." To be successful, Lenin argued, the revolutionaries would have to "settle accounts with tsarism in the Jacobin, or, if you like, in the plebeian way," and not fall prey to the "constitutional illusions" of the bourgeois parties.[84] Through the medium of Marx, the French rupture with the constitutional model of revolution would thus come to be consummated in the Bolshevik revolution. The "plebeian way," ironically, would lead to the replacement of popular sovereignty by party dictatorship.

The Paris Commune and the Striptease of History

Every theorist of historical progress, from the abbé de Saint-Pierre onwards, had recognized that it was uneven. In practice, this meant that progress in some places outpaced progress in others. A few states would be in the vanguard, while the rest would stagnate in the rear. This hierarchical relation also applied to Europe and its colonies.[85]

For revolutionaries, this logic of uneven progress meant that glimpses of the future could occasionally be found in the present. This was the case for states that were not on the cusp of historical progress. Marx believed that the French Revolution of 1789–93 could provide a script for the German revolutions of 1848.[86] Marx and Engels were particularly sanguine about this multispeed history in the final chapter of the *Manifesto*, where communist parties from different countries were assigned different roles in the upcoming revolutions based on the starting positions of their respective states.

But what were the more historically advanced countries to do? How could they know what lay in store? For many progressives, this was precisely where utopian imagination filled in the gaps. For hardened materialists, like Marx and Engels, this solution would not do. Only history itself could reveal what was to come. In this respect, Marx's own updating of his theory of revolution after June 1848 was not a reversal. He had never claimed to know precisely how future revolutionaries would self-organize. The next revolution would reveal crucial hints of what lay further ahead. Unlike Nature, whose veil no mortal was meant to lift (as the famous inscription on the Isis statue at Sais affirmed), History was a tease, unveiling the future bit by bit, often only to cover it up again. The key was to know how to catch a good look at what was coming.

Perhaps the greatest of revolutionary teases occurred during the short-lived Paris Commune. Marx had not been expecting another revolution so soon. Unlike the philosophes, Hegel, or the Jacobins, who thought that revolutions could be precipitated by the advancement of reason, Marx believed that history progressed at its own pace, driven not by the books of the intelligentsia (as they had to come to be called in Russia) but by the inexorable churn of socioeconomic relations. The Paris Communards, in his view, had appeared too early on the historical stage. The conditions for a proletarian revolution were not yet ripe.[87]

On this point, Marx's dire forecast proved correct. The fuse for the Commune was lit not by exacerbated tensions between capitalist proprietors and their wage laborers but by the national response to the French defeat at the hands of the Prussians. Paris had endured a horrific siege during the winter of 1870–71, and resentment toward the victorious Prussians still ran high. When the national government, which had relocated from Bordeaux to Versailles (out of wariness of the capital), sought to disarm the Parisian National Guard, it revolted, killing two generals, and rejecting the authority of the central government.[88]

News of the insurrection electrified Europe. Paris, the capital of revolution, had raised the red flag again. Would others join? Some cities in France, including Lyon and Marseille, briefly followed suit. But even in Paris, the Commune was quickly put down. The Versaillais, as the national forces were known, breached Paris's defenses, and during the "bloody week" of May 21–28, 1871, took back the city, killing over ten thousand Communards in the process.

Despite its short existence, the Commune offered revolutionary sympathizers much to sift through. In a mere two months, the Parisians had managed to create a new form of political organization. "The absolute autonomy of the Commune [should be] extended to every locality in France, guaranteeing each [locality] the entirety of its rights," the Parisian government had declared; "The autonomy of the Commune shall have as its limits only the equal right of autonomy of every other commune."[89] By insisting on the autonomy of the communes, the Parisians took aim at the national state as the highest and most authoritative level of government. It might still be necessary to maintain some sort of national coordinating body, but the Communards proposed a radical reinterpretation of popular sovereignty. Rather than recognizing the National Assembly as the proper place for the will of the people to be expressed, the Communards sought to transfer the expression of sovereignty to the municipal level: "Not only municipal administration, but the whole initiative hitherto exercised by the state was laid into the hands of the Commune," Marx marveled.[90]

For Marx, this downgrading of national government was inspirational. "The centralized state power, with its ubiquitous organs of standing army, police, bureaucracy, clergy, and judicature . . . originates from the days of absolute monarchy," he pronounced. The main purpose of the state in a bourgeois economy, as Marx had learned in June 1848, was to oppress the working class. State power, he now wrote, had become little more than "the national power of capital over labor, of a public force organized for social enslavement, of an engine of class despotism." Perhaps in an improved and more rational future, the state would simply disappear, or, as he and Engels later put it, "wither away." The promise of the Commune thus offered socialists a new argument in their rivalry with anarchist thinkers. The revolution to come could dissolve the state, as the anarchists wanted, but still retain forms of local administration.

Marx also found much to admire in the actual administration of the Commune. Members of the new government, called the Conseil de la Commune (Council of the Commune), were elected by universal male suffrage and came from the ranks of common people, unlike the deputies to the National Assembly, who mostly belonged to the propertied class. Here was a truly democratic government, one in which political power was actually vested in the people. The Commune model allowed socialists to insist that they were still democrats, despite Marx's invoking "the dictatorship of the proletariat," which anarchists pounced on.

Contrary to the French national government, the Commune also had no separate executive power, replete with ministries and bureaucracies. "The Commune was to be a working, not a parliamentary body, executive and legislative at the same time," Marx emphasized. There would be no backroom deals between deputies and ministers: the unity of will and action, long dreamed of since the time of Turgot, and briefly attempted by the Jacobin revolutionary government, was finally to be achieved.

Although it accomplished little and was probably doomed from the start, the Commune thus played a crucial role in socialist political thought. It provided nothing less than a sneak peek of the future. Not the future in the imaginative sense of utopian writers (the Commune had "no ready-made utopias to introduce *par décret du peuple*," Marx noted approvingly), but in the materialist sense of how societies could be organized in a democratic, nonoppressive manner. It revealed "that higher form to which present society is irresistibly tending," Marx concluded: "They have no ideals to realize, but to set free the elements of the new society with which old collapsing bourgeois society itself is pregnant." In the end of the old regime was a new beginning.

FROM PARIS TO PETROGRAD

The Russian word for *conseil* is *soviet*. This translation hints at the importance of the Paris Commune in Russian, and more particularly Bolshevik, revolutionary thought. Its importance was not immediately evident. Neither the memory of the Commune nor the arguments of the Bolsheviks played much of a role in the initial outbreak of revolution in February 1917. Terrible losses in the Great War and long absences from Saint Petersburg (renamed Petrograd in 1914) had made Tsar Nicholas II deeply unpopular. The revolution that ousted him had more in common with the 1848 revolutions than with 1871. As in that earlier French scenario, a hated monarch was replaced by a provisional government, which was tasked with preparing elections for a new National Assembly. This had also been the basic script of the 1905 Russian revolution, which had left Nicholas on the throne but constrained his power by means of a legislative assembly, the Duma. Nicholas had struck back in 1907, dissolving the Duma and returning to his autocratic ways. Ten years later, the revolutionaries took no chances and forced his immediate abdication.[91]

But a major difference with the liberal revolutionary script quickly appeared. In 1917, the workers and soldiers of Petrograd also formed their own council, or soviet, very much on the model of the Paris Commune (workers had also briefly formed a soviet in Saint Petersburg in 1905). The Petrograd Soviet had a strained relationship with the provisional government, neither acknowledging nor directly challenging its authority. This was the standoff that Lenin described in his essay "The Dual Power," where he compared the situation in 1917 Petrograd to that in 1871 Paris. The Petrograd Soviet, he wrote, was "a revolutionary dictatorship, i.e., a power directly based on revolutionary seizure, on the direct initiative of the people from below, and not on a law enacted by a centralised state power. . . . This power is of the same type as the Paris Commune of 1871."[92]

While the outcome of that earlier standoff might not have boded well for the Bolsheviks, Lenin leaned eagerly into this historical analogy. As Marx before him, Lenin interpreted the Commune both as "the first attempt by a proletarian revolution to smash the bourgeois state machine," and as "the political form 'at last discovered,' by which the smashed state machine can and must be replaced." In other words, the Communards had composed a new revolutionary script, one that provided a template for dismantling the old regime ("smashing the bourgeois state machine") but also for reorganizing politics. Driving this double action was the *conseil* itself, which did away with what Lenin termed "parliamentarism," by rejecting "the division of labor between the legislative and the executive." By cutting loose the ministries with their bureaucratic henchmen and turning the assembly from a "talking shop" into a "working body," the Commune had revealed "a state that is so constituted that it begins to wither away immediately, and cannot but wither away."[93]

But this ultimate disappearing act, which the anarchists had hoped to bring about immediately, would never result in a complete absence of organized bodies: "We cannot imagine democracy, even proletarian democracy, without representative institutions," Lenin retorted. Democracy itself was a political form, and the Commune showed how popular sovereignty and democratic government could be conjoined without producing a repressive state. Lenin also pushed back against those who wished to turn nation-states into mere federations of communes. "Marx was a centralist," he insisted. And he did not hide the need for the center to maintain control over the whole. The Bolsheviks could learn from the Commune how to organize a democracy; but that did not mean that they would give up on dictatorship, either:

> We are not utopians, we do not "dream" of dispensing *at once* with all administration, with all subordination. These anarchist dreams, based upon incomprehension of the tasks of the proletarian dictatorship, are totally alien to Marxism, and, as a matter of fact, serve only to postpone the socialist revolution until people are different. No, we want the socialist revolution with people as they are now, with people who cannot dispense with subordination, control, and "foremen and accountants."[94]

Lenin, like Marx, motivated the need for dictatorship by an appeal to temporality. Subordination was required *now*, because the people were not *yet* ready for communist society. But eventually they would be. Then the state would wither away, as it had already begun to, and the dictatorship will have been justified. It was the logic of the future perfect in full force.

The Bolsheviks overturned the provisional government in October 1917 in the name of giving "all power to the soviets." But the political form they introduced in its stead was a reversible figure, displaying two very different faces. Viewed from one angle, it appeared to be a vibrant democracy, where fairly autonomous communes, run by soviets, allowed the people to govern themselves directly. These soviets in turn elected representatives to councils at higher levels, culminating in the All-Russian

Congress of Soviets. It was a variation on the modern theme composed by Turgot in his "Memorandum on Municipalities." The will of the people would be filtered through layers of councils, distilling it for administrators to execute at the national level.

But as in that memorandum, there was a countervailing force sitting atop this political structure. Viewed from on high, the entire ladder of soviets was dominated by a supreme authority that could demand "subordination," and exert "control." Contrary to Turgot's model, however, where the sovereign discovered the people's will and interests by learning about them from the general assembly, in the Bolshevik model it was the Party and its own governing bodies—the Central Committee and the Politburo—that had a monopoly on the knowledge needed for governing. The Party even overlaid its own political structure on the system of soviets, with Party elections occurring at local, regional, and national levels, leading up to the Congress of the Communist Party of the Soviet Union.[95]

From this perspective, the system looked less like Turgot's modern democracy and more like Plato's republic, in that power rested in the hands of a guardian class.[96] The multiple layers of councils, by means of which information was meant to percolate up, could also serve as a military hierarchy in which commands were passed down. The Party structure similarly served to disseminate and impose the party line that was decided at the top, in keeping with Lenin's principle of "democratic centralism."

In theory, the dictatorial power at the top of this pyramid was meant to fade as the democratic elements became more established. The need for subordination and control, it was assumed, would be greatest at the start of the revolution. This was certainly the case after the October Revolution triggered a civil war that lasted nearly six years. But in practice, even after the war had ended, the Party retained a stranglehold on all policymaking. The political hierarchy could at times be useful for transmitting information up the chain, notably regarding conditions after the war. This knowledge helped to shape the New Economic Policy (or NEP), which the Party introduced to help revive the postwar economy. And the soviets could also convey the impression that the government was participatory, thereby helping to legitimize the regime and garner popular support.[97] But for the most part, governmental and party hierarchies were used to subordinate and control.

This dictatorial trend raises a final important question: Why did things turn out this way? Why did the democratic commitments of Marx's followers fall by the wayside? There is no compelling reason to doubt the sincerity of Lenin or other Social Democrats on this point. If their professed dedication to democracy was just hypocrisy, why should we accept as genuine similar statements in favor of economic equality? Why pursue one but not the other? There have been various attempts to answer this conundrum, with some pointing to problems of execution (e.g., Marx was a real democrat, but Lenin or Stalin perverted his thought), others to psychology (e.g., the USSR was destroyed by Stalin's paranoid narcissism), or to the general effects of absolute power (which, as the saying goes, corrupts absolutely).[98]

There may be elements of truth to these different accounts, but it is hard to see how they can explain why so many revolutions from 1917 onward exhibited the same pattern: a socialist movement that claimed to emancipate the masses morphs into a repressive regime overseen by a dominant political leader. Why did this narrative recur in so many different places and times? Is there something about the modern idea of revolution that drives it into the arms of a dictator?

CHAPTER FOURTEEN

Red Leviathan

AUTHORITY AND VIOLENCE

The Interpretation of all Lawes dependeth on the Authority Soveraign; and the Interpreters can be none but those, which the Soveraign . . . shall appoint.

—HOBBES, *LEVIATHAN*

IN MARCH 1881, members of the secret Russian revolutionary society Narodnaya Volya (The People's Will) assassinated Tsar Alexander II. Two years later, they attempted to kill his successor, but were caught before the bombs exploded. Their ringleader, Aleksandr Ulyanov, was sentenced to death by hanging. Aleksandr was Lenin's older brother.[1]

Lenin grew up in the shadow of his condemned sibling. While he later criticized his brother's organization for "relying on a theory which in substance was not a revolutionary theory at all," he also emphasized their exemplarity. The People's Will, he wrote in *What Is to Be Done?* (1901), was a "magnificent organization" that "should serve us as a model." Indeed, he insisted, "no revolutionary trend, if it seriously thinks of struggle, can dispense with such an organization." It was a secret, even conspiratorial society, but what else could one hope for in an autocratic state like Russia? This kind of organization, moreover, promoted a unified revolutionary theory—and "without revolutionary theory there can be no revolutionary movement." Only by uniting all members around "the most advanced theory" could a revolutionary party achieve its goals.[2]

Thirty years earlier, Fyodor Dostoevsky had made a similar point, albeit with a different intent. In his novel *Demons* (1871–72, also translated as *The Possessed*), a young revolutionary, Pyotr Verkhovensky, leads select members of a provincial town to believe that they are part of a vast conspiracy to overthrow the government. The ideologue of the group, Shigalov, informs the rest that he has completed the theory that will guide their efforts. It is long and detailed—ten evenings will be required to explain it—but it is definitive. "There can be no solution of the social problem but mine," he concludes. "Nothing can take the place of the system set forth in my book, and there is no other way out of it; no one can invent anything else."[3] As Lenin, Dostoevsky also highlighted the centrality of theory for revolutionary action, but drew attention to a different feature: the total exclusivity of a single one.

Dostoevsky's inspiration for this fictional society came from Sergey Nechayev, a Russian revolutionary who gained fame thanks to his *Catechism of a Revolutionary* (1869), which became the model of revolutionary nihilism.[4] After assassinating a co-conspirator, Nechayev went into exile, where he befriended the anarchist Mikhail Bakunin. Like Nechayev, Dostoevsky's revolutionaries would similarly kill one of their own. And where Nechayev preached "merciless destruction," Shigalov's plan called for giving "absolute liberty and unbounded power" to "10% of the population, while the remaining 90% "have to give up all individuality and become, so to speak, a herd."[5]

Nechayev, Dostoevsky's ideologue, Lenin's brother, and Lenin himself would all have disagreed about "what was to be done." Each defended a different "solution to the social problem," as Shigalov put it. Indeed, modern revolutionaries rarely saw eye to eye on what the future should bring, and even when they did, argued over how to achieve it. Their constant squabbles over whose theory was "the most advanced" stemmed from the belief that such a metric existed. They devised various tactics for justifying their proposals above others, many of which were already found in Marx. Nechayev claimed that history alone would reveal the future organization of society.[6] Shigalov threw all utopian thinkers ("Plato, Rousseau, Fourier") into the dustbin of philosophy, seeking instead to turn revolutionary theory into a science. Orthodox Marxists like Lenin fought to determine who should be the true standard bearer of revolution. Acquiring authority in the Soviet Union often meant demonstrating that you were the most faithful interpreter of an established figure—initially Marx and Engels, later Lenin himself.

But none of these tactics offered much guidance for choosing among contenders. Before the revolution, disagreements over what constituted "the most advanced theory" were generally resolved by opponents splintering off to form their own party. The history of nineteenth-century socialist thought is filled with such divisions and denunciations. Marx owed his eventual prominence in no small part to his incessant belittling of rivals.[7] Lenin carried on this tradition, quarreling in print with the likes of Eduard Bernstein and Alexandre Millerand, before splitting the Russian Social Democratic Party into Bolshevik and Menshevik factions.

After the revolution, however, the problem of deciding "what was to be done" became more delicate. Revolutionary leaders did not miraculously come to a consensus on contentious issues. Political disagreements continued to rage. Who was now to adjudicate between rivals? For the most part, modern revolutionaries took open democratic elections off the table. They sidelined or banned competing parties, leaving only a single party to rule. But even within a single party, dissension prevailed. Splintering off now meant either abdicating or contesting power. A successful revolution raises the stakes of theoretical disputes.

The Bolsheviks technically sought to settle their arguments by means of party votes. The Party became the arbiter of political differences, and the harbinger of historical progress. "None of us wants to be or can be right against the party," Trotsky observed in May 1924. "In the last analysis the party is always right. . . . [N]o one can be right against the party."[8] But who determined Party membership, and who appointed members to positions of power? This task was usually reserved for high-ranking Party members. But who in turn chose the high-ranking Party members? There was a circular logic to Party politics, which became painfully evident during leadership transitions, such as following the death of Lenin.[9]

In the end, there was a simple solution to this problem. The cycle could be broken by installing a general secretary, chairman, president, Great Helmsman, or Dear Leader at the top. In theory, the Party might still exercise control. But in practice, someone must determine Party membership, allocate positions of power, and impose consensus. And if these tasks were performed by an inner clique, someone must decide who belonged to that clique.

The near-ubiquity of this model in twentieth-century revolutions has little to do with ideology. Marxism contains little to justify the power exercised by Stalin, Mao, Castro, Pol Pot, or Ceaușescu. Nor is it plausible that such figures (among others) acceded to power merely by virtue of megalomania or other psychological disorders. Even if all revolutionary leaders truly were a deranged bunch, this phenomenon could not explain why modern revolutions so frequently empowered a single ruler, mad or not, to rule. Instead, it is the very structure of modern revolutions that calls for an authoritative ruler, someone to choose among the alternative paths ahead. Modern revolutions crave a Leviathan.

Why call this leader a Leviathan? In Hobbes's theory, the Leviathan plays a number of roles. To fulfill his obligation to provide security for the commonwealth, he must notably settle disagreements, which often comes down to fixing the meaning of words. What is the Eucharist? What is grace? In a post-Reformation world, all words were fighting ones. Quelling religious violence meant pinning down semantic content: "Hæretiques are none but private men, that stubbornly defend some Doctrine, prohibited by their lawfull Soveraigns," Hobbes warned. There was no philosophical or theological solution for settling the truthfulness of a doctrine. Authority, not truth, made the law ("Authoritas non Veritas facit Legem").[10]

A similar interpretative and political challenge confronted revolutionaries. The challenge for revolutionaries was "not merely the seizure of power, but the seizure of meaning."[11] At the heart of these struggles lay the fight to define the course of the revolution itself—"what was to be done." The Chinese dissident (and Nobel Peace Prize laureate) Liu Xiaobo identified what was at stake in this battle: "Whoever the person or whatever the thing, all that is necessary is to give it the name 'revolution' and it becomes progressive and full of righteous sentiment."[12] Revolution was the one political value to rule them all. Morality, asserted Nechayev in his *Catechism*, is simply "whatever contributes to the triumph of the revolution."[13]

The consequences of these struggles went well beyond setting the revolution's agenda. All revolutionaries seek to drape themselves in the red flag, but it isn't large enough for them all. Competing definitions of revolution are not only incompatible, they are mutually exclusive—in Shigalov's words, "There can be no solution of the social problem but mine." In 1924, the Bolsheviks could either keep the New Economic Policy (NEP) in place, or nationalize the economy, but they could not do both at once. There was only one right answer, and, as Trotsky learned the hard way, "no one can be right against the party."

The dictatorial solution for resolving political arguments was to allow a Leviathan figure to fix the meaning of "revolution," and end the inevitable disagreements about the way forward. These disagreements were inevitable, both in the general sense that Hobbes and Madison had recognized (humans do not naturally agree on many important matters), but also for the specific reason that the way forward, in a revolution, was intrinsically unclear. "We cannot give a description of socialism; what socialism will be like when its completed forms are arrived at—this we do not know, we cannot tell," Lenin acknowledged in a 1918 speech.[14] Mao would later

FIGURE 14.1 Caricature of Trotsky and other former Politburo members (being fed by a German soldier, under the heading "Vaterland"). By Boris Efimov, 1938. Used with permission from the Estate of Boris Efimov.

encourage intellectuals to let "a hundred flowers bloom" so that the Party could determine the best next steps.[15]

But there was also a darker side to the Red Leviathan. Mao's call for pluralism turned into a violent campaign of political oppression, as most "flowers" were ripped up and trampled underfoot. Whoever defined revolution "wrongly"—that is, according to an interpretation rejected by the revolutionary authority—did not simply stand in error. They also stood in the way of the revolution's true direction. Defeat in the conflict of interpretations did not just make you a loser, it made you a counterrevolutionary (see figure 14.1). Arguments over the meaning of "revolution" were often settled with a bullet in the back of the head.

Most forms of political violence that accompany revolutions are not specific to revolutionary movements. Many regimes imprison their opponents, shut down their presses, or kill them openly in civil war. Revolutionaries do not have a monopoly on political violence. But modern revolutions exhibit a peculiar pathology, which the Girondin Pierre-Victurnien Vergniaud diagnosed in his famous remark that revolutions, like Saturn, devour their children.[16] Or to paraphrase Hobbes again: only the revolutionary is a wolf to his fellow revolutionary.

This specific form of violence was directly connected to the political solution preferred by modern revolutionaries. The Red Leviathan was both the needed interpreter and the necessary executor of the law. The selection of one interpretation over another doubled as a condemnation of the unsuccessful contender. What made this condemnation lethal was the status to which it relegated the vanquished. By becoming counterrevolutionaries they joined a set of other types—émigrés, Royalists, priests, high officials from the old regime, saboteurs, reactionaries, and so forth—who openly opposed the new regime's legitimacy. It might seem preposterous to combine committed revolutionaries—a Condorcet, a Danton, a Trotsky, a Lin Biao—with determined foes. But such was the fatal beauty of this category: like "revolution," it was inherently ambiguous. As Mao remarked, "Under normal circumstances, it is easy to tell a good person from a bad person. But under special circumstances, when there are bad people behind the scenes, you may easily be deceived."[17] Anyone, it turned out, could be a counterrevolutionary. It fell on the Red Leviathan to decide who was.

The Structure of Revolutionary Authority

As the world was transfixed by the Moscow trials, Joseph Stalin was editing and contributing to the *History of the Communist Party of the Soviet Union (Bolsheviks): A Short Course* (1938). In many respects, it was time well spent: over forty million copies of this textbook would be printed, in over a dozen languages.[18] More than its reach, it was its symbolism that mattered. Where the trials removed Stalin's rivals, the *History* established him as the premier interpreter of the revolution.

Indeed, the trials and the *History* were ultimately two sides of the same coin. To secure his position as unchallenged leader of the Soviet Union, Stalin needed to bolster his status as an authority on revolutionary doctrine. In Soviet Russia, the struggle for power was a struggle to control the meaning of the revolution. Stalin was no ideological purist: he tacked and jibed as needed to throw off rivals. His goal was not to produce the most authoritative account of Marxism, but rather to cast *himself* as the most authoritative interpreter of Marxism. He needed to fashion himself as a Red Leviathan. As the revolutionary turned critic Régis Debray observed, "Lenin, Stalin, Mao, Enver Hoxha and various lesser bloodletters . . . in their salad days, started by lining up syllogisms on paper and criticizing in writing those of their neighbors. . . . Every one a man of letters, a product of the Book."[19] As the Church Fathers, the Revolutionary Fathers derived their own authority from (Marxist) scripture.

If Stalin found himself needing to shore up his authority, it was in large part because of the vacuum left by Lenin's death. While alive, Lenin had enjoyed a unique role. He did not always get his way, and sometimes wrangled bitterly with others. It took an inordinate amount of effort, for example, to convince his colleagues to sign the Brest-Litovsk treaty with the Central Powers.[20] Lenin also did a fair amount of improvising with policy. The Bolsheviks had not developed clear plans for the social, political, or even economic organization of Russia before the revolution. Many of the ideas that Lenin put forward during this period were not his own; indeed, some (such as the NEP) were not even Bolshevik ideas. But Lenin could give any policy proposal something that no one else could—a revolutionary stamp of authority. His proposals did not always carry the day; but when they did, his imprimatur ensured that they were recognized as truly "revolutionary" ideas (even if they involved surprising departures from Marxism, as in the case of the NEP).[21] Lenin could be wrong, but he could not be counterrevolutionary.

One might assume that it was Lenin's charisma that allowed him to issue such authoritative statements on revolution. That was the conclusion reached by Robert Tucker, who pointed precisely to Lenin's "exceptional powers or qualities" (using Weber's terms) as evidence for this claim.[22] But this judgment overlooks the fact that Lenin achieved his place at the head of the Bolshevik Party in a mostly rational fashion, through endless disputes and ideological skirmishes in the decade and a half before the October Revolution. It was on the grounds of these argumentative strengths and official Party votes that he established his authority.[23] What's more, it was a far more limited power than Weber's charismatic leaders enjoy, as the above examples indicate.

There was also a twist to Lenin's authority, which distinguished it, say, from Robespierre's: it was derivative. Its structure is neatly illustrated in a famous poster from 1933, which placed images of Lenin and Stalin in a sequence following pictures of Marx and Engels (figure 14.2).[24] This Russian-doll-like symbolism highlights an essential feature of revolutionary authority after 1789: it functions on the model of apostolic succession. The ultimate source of Lenin's authority was to be found in Marx. Lenin managed to impose himself as the best interpreter of Marx, but it was Marx who was ultimately the best interpreter of the Revolution.

FIGURE 14.2 "Raise higher the banner of Marx, Engels, Lenin, and Stalin!" by Gustav Klutsis (1933). Views and Re-Views. Brown Digital Repository. Brown University Library. https://repository.library.brown.edu/studio/item/bdr:89326/.

Marx, too, had waged doctrinal battles in order to secure his position, shoving aside his rivals on ideological grounds. He also had established his position in a "rational" manner: as Engels would later insist, Marx's theory was "scientific," as opposed to the "utopian" ideas of his predecessors.[25] These characterizations may appear opportunistic to us, but they are indicative of how Marxists fashioned their authority.

Lenin's relation to Marx was more complicated. When he assailed Eduard Bernstein's revisionist views, for instance, it was not only because he judged them misguided but because they represented a "distortion of Marx."[26] If political disagreements took the form of rational disputes, they were strictly bounded by Marxist orthodoxy. Some Marxist tenets were articles of faith. As Lenin wrote in a draft resolution "on the Syndicalist and Anarchist *Deviation* in our Party," Marxism "has not only been formally endorsed by the whole of the Communist International in the decisions of the Second (1920) Congress of the Comintern . . . but has also been confirmed in practice by our revolution."[27] Here we are closer to Weber's concept of traditional authority, for which "it is impossible for law or administrative rule to be deliberately created by legislation. Rules which in fact are innovations can be legitimized only by the claim that they have been 'valid of yore.'"[28] Marx's doctrine was obviously not from time immemorial, but it was still near impossible to contradict it openly without being branded a heretic.

There was accordingly a kind of "theological" structure to revolutionary authority in Soviet Russia. In making this claim, I am not suggesting that Marxist theory repurposed or secularized religious temporality, themes, or purpose.[29] Instead, I mean that the mechanism by which political authority was acquired in Marxist political culture mirrors that by which theologians establish authority on religious topics.[30] In both cases, the form of argumentation is rational (and can produce reasoned disagreements), but the premises are fixed by tradition. Furthermore, in both the Marxist and Christian traditions, there is a canon of "patristic" literature that would-be leaders must master and deploy in order to establish their own authority. Just as Calvin needed the authority of Augustine to defend his doctrine of predestination, Stalin needed that of Lenin to promote his economic doctrines.

As the above analogy suggests, revolutionary interpretations are always at risk of splitting off in heretical directions. Doctrinal borders must be policed. Hobbes insisted that it took an "Authority Soveraign" to distinguish proper interpretations from improper ones; otherwise, as Carl Schmitt observed in his elaboration of this idea, "In the absence of a pivotal authority, anybody can refer to the correctness of the content."[31] For Catholicism, the pivotal authority was the Pope, whose Curial offices, such as the Sacred Congregation of the Index or the Supreme Sacred Congregation of the Roman and Universal Inquisition (now the Congregation for the Doctrine of the Faith), had the last word on doctrinal matters. For Soviet Marxists, this authority technically resided in the Party. But after Lenin's death, it was up for grabs.

Auditioning for Dictatorship

The Party leader who was supposed to replace Lenin after his death was Leon Trotsky. Now, here was a charismatic leader: Trotsky cut a dashing figure in his military uniform, as war commissar during the Civil War; he was a gifted orator, with a reputation for intellectual brilliance; and he enjoyed Lenin's favor.[32] One of his chief rivals was Nikolai Bukharin, the editor of *Pravda*, who had replaced Lenin on the Politburo after his death and was regarded as an impressive revolutionary theorist.[33] By comparison, Stalin cut a poor figure. Lenin had turned against him and tried to warn the other Bolsheviks about his authoritarian tendencies in his *Testament*. Stalin did have some personal assets: far from being "the dreary bureaucrat that Trotsky wanted him to be," he was "a people person," and knew how to turn on the charm.[34] But in 1924, his chief advantage was bureaucratic: for the past two years, he had been the general secretary of the Soviet Communist Party.

Stalin's success in consolidating his rule is generally credited to his stacking the Party with his supporters. He also exhibited strategic brilliance, first allying himself with Bukharin against Trotsky and then turning on his ally. To this political agility corresponded ideological shape-shifting: contra Trotsky, Stalin supported Bukharin's "rightist" defense of the NEP, launched by Lenin in 1921; then, following an economic crisis in 1928, he embraced the arguments of the "Left Opposition" (which had included Trotsky, along with Lenin's old associates Lev Kamenev and Grigory Zinoviev).[35]

Marxist theory might not seem to play much of a role in Stalin's rise to the top. At one level, this is true: the little that Marx wrote about governing a postrevolutionary state was obsolete by 1924. But it would be misguided to conclude that theory and ideas did not matter. The battle to succeed Lenin largely took the form of a struggle over ideological orthodoxy. Arguments between rival contenders were not so much debates over the best way forward per se, but over the proper way to interpret Lenin's legacy.[36] Leninism was the source from which all new ideas had to spring, as it was the only untainted and certified source of revolutionary purity. When Kamenev criticized Bukharin's economic plans, he described them as "deviations from Lenin," while Bukharin's supporters responded that "the school of Bukharin is the Leninist School."[37] Stalin also engaged in this intellectual jousting, delivering a series of lectures at Sverdlov University (a school for Party cadres) that were serialized in *Pravda* and then published as *On Lenin and Leninism* (May 1924). Here he celebrated the genius of Lenin, while presenting himself as the best interpreter of the great man. Stalin also included some not-so-subtle jabs at Trotsky, attacking "communist vainglory," "pompous phrases," and "political fireworks" in a section on Bolshevik style (where he also praised "American efficiency").[38]

The problem, as Bukharin acknowledged, was that no one was in a position to adjudicate these debates: "We have no person who could say: I am sinless and can interpret Leninist teachings absolutely to a full 100 per cent."[39] Hence, it took a raw power struggle for one interpreter to outmaneuver the others. But this power struggle always doubled as an ideological clash. At a meeting of the Central Committee in October 1926, Trotsky attacked Stalin's theory of "Socialism in One Country" (as opposed to World Revolution), accusing Stalin of being "the grave digger of the revolution." Following this incident, he was expelled from the Politburo.[40]

Devouring Saturn's Children

From the French Revolution onward, controlling the meaning of the revolution involved denouncing false prophets. The last chapter of the "Short Course" includes a section "Liquidation of the Remnants of the Bukharin-Trotsky Gang of Spies, Wreckers, and Traitors to the Country."[41] Here Stalin insisted on the importance of purges for the Party: "To attain victory, the Party of the working class, its directing staff, its advanced fortress, must first be purged of capitulators, deserters, scabs and traitors." The text then quotes Comrade Stalin himself: "The Party becomes strong by purging itself of opportunist elements."[42]

In all revolutions, there are some officials and individuals who are genuinely opposed to revolutionary change. But the reason why the "counterrevolutionary" occupies such a privileged place in revolutionary politics is because the category can readily be expanded to encompass fellow revolutionaries.[43] Labeling one's opponents counterrevolutionaries is a nuclear option that lies in waiting to be deployed, if needed, in the battle to impose one's own view of the revolution. The temptation to use it is high, as there often exists no other way to demonstrate the validity (or superiority) of one interpretation over another.

This line of attack became possible after "revolution" acquired its modern, progressive meaning. Among the first accused to be tried before the French revolutionary tribunal, whose jurisdiction extended over all "counterrevolutionary activity," was Jean-Paul Marat, the radical Parisian journalist and scourge of the Girondins, who had him indicted. He was acquitted, but they would in turn be dragged before the tribunal six months later and sentenced to death.[44] Likewise, among the early victims of the Cheka—whose primary mission, as its official Russian name indicates, was to battle "counterrevolution"—were anarchists who had supported the October Revolution six months earlier.[45] This pattern continued throughout the twentieth century: in Iran, Ayatollah Khomeini sidelined his rivals within a year of consolidating power, again in the name of their alleged opposition to the revolution.[46]

All it took to tarnish fellow revolutionaries was to "prove" that they were part of a counterrevolutionary conspiracy. Where the Girondins failed to make this accusation stick on Marat, the Jacobins perfected the act, sending all sorts of rivals—Girondins, Hébertistes, and Dantonistes—to the guillotine as counterrevolutionaries. Some political opponents had genuine ideological differences with one another: both the Hébertistes and Dantonistes disagreed with the Committee of Public Safety's policies (albeit for different reasons). But even trivial differences of opinion could become an excuse for violence. Lenin's successors ultimately did not clash over deeply held, irreconcilable visions. Soon after Stalin had Trotsky removed from the Politburo, he adopted some of his policies. The battle to succeed Lenin was mainly fought over the power to control the course of the revolution. The centripetal structure of modern revolutions, which call for a Leviathan-like decision-maker, breeds struggles over power *tout court*.

Even leaders like Stalin and Mao, who established themselves as the dominant authorities on the revolution, could face challenges if they stumbled. For Stalin, the first large-scale attempt at collectivization led to a catastrophe of unprecedented proportions. Between spring 1932 and summer 1933, somewhere between 3.5 and 5 million Ukrainians died of starvation. This horrific event, known in Ukrainian as the Holomodor, has been categorized as a genocide.[47]

It also posed a political challenge for Stalin. His first five-year plan, completed in just four years in 1932, was supposed to catapult Russia into a socialist future. Instead, it was marred by this disaster, news of which even reached the West. A rival to Stalin emerged in the person of Sergei Kirov, the popular chief of Party organization in Leningrad. Stalin was suddenly in a precarious position. Obviously, his own policies could not be at fault. Something—or someone—else had to have gone wrong. This policy failure thus accelerated the process of revolutionary repression: there must have been "saboteurs" within the Party who had interfered to embarrass Stalin. After Kirov was mysteriously assassinated, Stalin began purging the Party, a process that culminated in the Great Terror of 1936–38.[48]

Failed policies similarly fueled political repression in China. The Great Leap Forward (1957–62) was meant to boost China's steel output to industrial levels. Peasants were removed from the fields to work in makeshift foundries. The results were doubly catastrophic: most of the steel was unusable, and the lack of available farmworkers led to massive food shortages. Horrific famines ensued, killing tens of millions.[49]

For Mao as well, this tragedy was politically dangerous. He had been the chief proponent of the Great Leap Forward, which partly originated in a boasting contest with Nikita Khrushchev. Other party cadres now dared to criticize the Great Helmsman openly. Mao's grip on power loosened for a number of years, as other leaders (such as Deng Xiaoping) pushed more liberal measures. But Mao soon regained his firm grip on power. The Cultural Revolution, launched with Mao's encouragement in 1966, proved exceptionally effective at eliminating his rivals and (eventually) restoring his position as uncontested leader.[50]

When modern revolutions descend into political terror, it can seem as if some sort of delirium has taken hold. Personal convictions cease to matter; political violence no longer serves any obvious purpose. "I hoped to find a meadow at the end of the road, I found a swamp," complains a disillusioned officer in *The Underdogs*, Mariano Azuela's 1915 novel about the Mexican Revolution.[51] Struggles that once appeared full of meaning over time turn into nihilistic battles.

There is, however, a method to this madness. The counterrevolutionary is a dangerously volatile category. Since anyone *can* be a counterrevolutionary, there are no limits to who actually gets labeled one. Stalin's purges began with the elimination of political rivals, then spread like wildfire through the Party and military.[52] Why stop with the ringleaders alone? The Khmer Rouge notoriously targeted anyone who wore glasses or spoke a foreign language, on the grounds that they must be "infected" with Western bourgeois ideas. Prisoners were forced to confess that they worked for the CIA as well as the KGB. The logic wasn't geopolitical, it was (counter)revolutionary.[53]

The Chinese Cultural Revolution offers perhaps the most astounding instance of counterrevolutionary repression spinning out of control. At one point, authorities launched a campaign against the shadowy "May 16 conspiracy." It is widely acknowledged today (even by official Chinese Communist historians) that this conspiracy was entirely fabricated. It nonetheless led to the arrest of over 3.5 million people.[54] Andrew Walder captured the surreal nature of violence during this time:

> Seemingly everywhere, organized militants divided into two factions that fought each other for control of schools, workplaces, and local governments. Both sides pledged loyalty to Mao and the Communist Party; both portrayed their fight as a defense of the revolution and an attack on leaders who had betrayed the cause.[55]

If the Cultural Revolution was a reductio ad absurdum of revolutionary violence, it was because the Great Helmsman had taken his hand off the rudder. Mao intentionally encouraged bureaucratic disruption, but gave no clear instructions on how to proceed: "To have a strategy for the mass movement and its 'general offensive' would have contradicted the basic premise of the Cultural Revolution: the people have to liberate themselves."[56] To liberate themselves, the people everywhere attacked others, with whom they often did not have any profound disagreement, but whom they targeted nonetheless as counterrevolutionaries. The nuclear option had produced a chain reaction. Mao was able to restore stability only by setting up "Mao Zedong Thought Study Classes," which provided a definition of revolution that everyone could (or must) agree upon, the definition outlined in his little red book.[57]

This analysis of revolutionary authority and violence may appear somewhat cynical, as if reducing revolutionary history to simple power struggles, and belittling the role of ideas and convictions. I would argue on the contrary that it highlights their central importance: if revolutionary politics is so conflictual, it is because individuals and groups strongly believe that how revolution is defined, and who has the power to define it, matter greatly.

Some historians construe the relation between political ideology and violence as "philosophical." In their view, the specific ideas that drive revolutionaries can lead them to inflict violence on their rivals.[58] But this emphasis on the *contents* of ideology may be misguided. Some of the most violent revolutionary leaders were not particularly ideological. In his biography of Pol Pot, for instance, Philip Short emphasizes the very limited familiarity with Marxism among the Khmer Rouge cadres.[59] Even among more theoretically inclined rulers, what mattered was less ideology per se then the power to set ideology. In this respect, revolutionary violence is ultimately a product of the conflict of interpretations. It is more hermeneutical than ideological. These two approaches are not necessarily incompatible, as the category of the counterrevolutionary suggests. But modern revolutions are not about ideas alone: they are about *which* ideas are chosen, and who gets to choose them. These are questions with deadly consequences.

In this regard, revolutionary-on-revolutionary violence is less the result of philosophy than of history—or, more precisely, of the modern doctrine of historical progress. Since the path between present and future is always unclear, disagreements about how to proceed are inevitable. As it is impossible to pursue two paths at once, someone has to choose which one to take. If democratic governance is not practiced as a binding method for choosing among options, then another form of decision-making is needed. Someone has to choose. In the end, there can be only one.

CONCLUSION

The Coming Revolution?

WHEN THE EASTERN European communist regimes collapsed in 1989, dissidents and observers alike were unsure how to describe what had happened. Was it a reform? A revolution? Or as Timothy Garton Ash half-joked, something in between, a "refolution"? Their hesitation reflected the history of the governments that were collapsing. These were states that descended from the great October Revolution itself, states that had institutionalized revolution. How could a revolutionary state be overthrown by a revolution?[1]

By 1989, however, many had soured on the progressive idea of revolution. It is difficult to pinpoint the exact moment when modern revolution lost its appeal. Many, especially young people, still dreamed of revolution in 1968. They might have grown disenchanted with the Soviet regime, which increasingly resembled a brutal gerontocracy. And 1968 was also the year when a sexagenarian Leonid Brezhnev ordered tanks into Czechoslovakia to crush the Prague spring, much like a sexagenarian Nikita Khrushchev, twelve years prior, had crushed an uprising in Hungary. The use of Soviet tanks in Eastern Europe, which had led many Western sympathizers to abandon the Communist Party in 1956, proved to be, by its absence, a critical factor in 1989.[2]

But in 1968, there were still other revolutionary models to admire. If Che Guevara had just been executed in Bolivia, after attempting to start an insurrection there, Fidel Castro's Cuba remained for many leftists a source of inspiration and promise. The Chinese Cultural Revolution, in which students played a leading role, also offered an appealing contrast to the gray rigidity of the Soviet Union. In 1968, for many in the West, it seemed like a revolution may well be in the offing, if not underway.[3]

Even in 1968, however, there were signs that the revolutionary wave had crested. When the philosopher Jean-Paul Sartre interviewed the young

Daniel Cohn-Bendit, a charismatic student leader, he asked him how the next revolution would proceed. The answer was rather anticlimactic: "The aim is now the overthrow of the regime. But it is not up to us whether or not this is achieved," Cohn-Bendit proclaimed. The students were waiting for the workers, who, it turned out, had their own demands, which did not match those of the students. French president Charles de Gaulle mysteriously disappeared to Germany, but then called an election in which his party won its greatest majority ever.[4]

Revolutionary fervor was further dampened a few years later by the publication of Aleksandr Solzhenitsyn's *The Gulag Archipelago*, in 1973. Westerners began to absorb the incredible costs of the Soviet regime. For many, it was the ultimate refutation of the doctrine of progress. Rather than inevitably leading to a more just and rational future, modern revolution had ushered in an age of nightmares.[5]

Over the next decade, revolution became increasingly synonymous with violence. One of the first books detailing the "killing fields" of the Khmer Rouge in Cambodia came out in 1977 in Paris. That same year saw the "German Autumn," when the Red Army Faction (also known as the Baader-Meinhof Gang) assassinated a series of bankers, industrialists, and politicians. The following year, in Italy, the Red Brigades kidnapped and executed the former Italian prime minister Aldo Moro. In France, historians and "new philosophers" embraced antitotalitarianism, as a response to past and present atrocities.[6]

The Iranian Revolution of 1979 suggested that the spark of revolution had not completely fizzled. But even that revolution, led mostly by leftists against a historically unpopular leader, inaugurated an important break. After deposing the shah, the Iranians drafted a new constitution, and submitted it to the people for ratification. Unfortunately for the leftists, the drafting process was controlled by the recently returned Ayatollah Khomenei and his allies, who used this opportunity to institute clerical rule. In many respects, and rather surprisingly, this Islamic revolutionary regime ended up resembling its Marxist counterparts. In both cases, a supreme leader determined the correct meaning of revolution and employed revolutionary guards to arrest or harass those who disagreed, all in the name of a better future. The Iranian Revolution once again highlights how the basic pattern of revolutionary politics and violence in the modern age was shaped less by specific ideologies than by arguments over the meaning of revolution itself.[7]

If the structure of Khomeni's regime bears a strong family resemblance to other modern revolutions, the use of a democratically ratified constitution to authorize this regime did mark a significant shift. Two decades earlier, Castro had similarly campaigned on the promise of restoring the liberal constitution of 1940, which the dictator Fulgencio Batista had suspended when he came to power. But this goal was abandoned almost immediately after the rebels triumphed, in favor of socioeconomic and political measures that were viewed as more pressing. Most striking about this political U-turn was that no one seems to have cared. As one historian noted, "Fidel Castro and the new Cuban leadership did not see their legitimacy dependent on restoring the Constitution of 1940 and holding elections." It would in fact be another sixteen years before the Cuban government finally adopted a new constitution (in 1976).[8]

By that time, however, constitutions had been staging a comeback. The "third wave" of democracy, beginning in Portugal in 1974, swept away military dictatorships across southern Europe, Latin America, and East Asia, replacing them with constitutional democracies. In the Philippines, in 1985, a "People Power" revolution forced Ferdinand Marcos from power, as millions of civilians peacefully protested electoral fraud in the circumferential highway around Manila. After he stepped down, his opponent Corazon Aquino was installed as president and swiftly dismantled the dictatorial regime. Revolution once again rhymed with constitution.[9]

If the Eastern European revolutionaries were still somewhat confused about what to name their political uprising, over the following decades the older, liberal revolutionary script staged a triumphant return around the world. From the "color revolutions" of the former Soviet republics to the Arab Spring, revolutions ushered in new constitutions and multiparty democracies at an impressive rate. Following the model that had proved so successful in Manila and Prague, revolutionaries relied on massive, mostly peaceful demonstrations to bring about regime change. Looking back in 2009 on the revolutions of the past twenty years, Garton Ash even identified a new era in the history of revolutions: the age of the Velvet Revolution (as the Czechoslovakian revolution had been called). Where the "1789 ideal type" revolution was "violent, utopian, professedly class-based, and characterized by a progressive radicalization," Garton Ash surmised, "the 1989 ideal type, by contrast, is nonviolent, anti-utopian, based not on a single class but on broad social coalitions, and characterized by the application of mass social pressure—'people power'—to bring the current powerholders to negotiate."[10]

At first, the Arab Spring seemed to validate Garton Ash's account that "these new-style revolutions" had replaced the bloody revolutions that preceded them. Demonstrators in Tunis and Cairo turned out en masse and forced their respective leaders to resign. "The power of people is stronger than the people in power," pronounced Wael Ghonim, one of the organizers of the Tahrir Square demonstrations that led President Hosni Mubarak, a former air chief marshal, to step down.[11]

But that momentous event turned out to be the turning point of the "new-style revolutions." As the Arab Spring spread to Libya, Bahrain, and Syria, the peaceful protests of massed civilians gave way to brutal civil wars. And in Egypt, Mubarak's resignation did not pave the way for a vibrant multiparty democracy. Instead, the Muslim Brotherhood became the majority party in the assembly, won the presidency, and sought to give the forthcoming constitution an Islamic stamp. After a year of protests, the army removed President Mohammed Morsi, violently suppressing his supporters. Morsi was replaced by retired field marshal Abdel Fattah El-Sisi, who ushered in a repressive regime not dissimilar to Mubarak's. It was, as Polybius would have appreciated, a *politeiōn anacyclosis,* a cyclical revolution of governments, from one military strongman back to another.[12]

Revolutions since 2011 have tended to be less velvet and more violent. Syria has been engulfed in a horrific civil war that has lasted over a decade. The Libyan revolution that toppled Muammar Gaddafi was fought with guns, not people power. Demonstrations in and around Maidan square in Kiev in 2014 also turned violent, with protesters ultimately toppling the government of Ukrainian president Viktor Yanukovych by force.

In retrospect, the brief heyday of nonviolent revolutions may have had less to do with the history of revolution and more with the history of nonviolence. The latter rose to prominence, as a form of political protest, during the Indian protests against the British Raj. The theories of Mahatma Gandhi inspired leaders of the US civil rights movement, most notably Martin Luther King Jr. While King did on occasion describe this movement as a "social revolution," he rejected the openly revolutionary platform of Black nationalists, such as Malcolm X. King aimed to overcome, not to overthrow.[13] These nonviolent tactics were subsequently repackaged for revolutionary action by the political scientist Gene Sharp. His recommendations, originally formulated for Burmese dissidents, helped Serbian opposition groups stage a successful, mostly nonviolent revolution against President Slobodan Milošević, who refused the results of the 2000 election. One of these groups, Otpor! (Resistance!), later trained organizers who went on to participate in revolutions in Georgia, Ukraine, Kyrgyzstan, Lebanon, and Egypt, among other places.[14]

Nonviolence is a strategy for improving a revolution's odds of success. In Sharp's version, it aims at crumbling a dictatorial regime's "pillars of support." It has little to say, however, about postrevolutionary politics. The assumption is that a successful revolution will lead "from dictatorship to democracy," to quote the title of Sharp's influential book. What that democracy will look like after the revolution, and how it should be organized, is left unaddressed.

As a political strategy, then, nonviolent revolutions, or "VR" in Garton Ash's parlance, may have departed from previous scripts for overturning an unpopular, oppressive regime. But they did not introduce any significant changes to the idea of revolution itself. Both the violent and nonviolent revolutions of the past forty years have aspired to the same outcome: a multiparty democratic constitution. Rather than marking a return to the classical model, however, these revolutions still harbor the progressive hope that open elections and democratic institutions will satisfy the people's political expectations. The Arab Spring, in this regard, bore a striking resemblance to the 1848 revolutions, as commentators observed at the time. In both cases, masses of people, in a kind of regional contagion, overthrew authoritarian governments in the name of popular will. Both events were greeted with wild bursts of enthusiasm, which proved tragically short-lived. The great displays of popular unanimity turned out to be illusions. The people may have wanted the fall of the regime, to quote the Arabic chant of 2010–11, but they did not agree on which regime should come next.[15]

This same pattern of enthusiastic booms followed by disillusioned busts can be observed in almost every revolution of the past thirty years. The optimism that greeted the Eastern European revolutions has been replaced by mounting discontent with crony capitalism and multiculturalism, leading to "democratic backsliding" and authoritarian populism.[16] The current president of the Philippines is the son of Ferdinand Marcos, who has largely airbrushed and burnished his father's violent legacy. None of the former Soviet republics are considered "free," with the overwhelming majority classified as "not free."[17]

Most of these recent revolutions did not usher in a genuine liberal democracy or capitalist economy. Perhaps for that reason, disappointment in their outcomes has been even stronger, and has reinvigorated traditionalist visions of history. If the passing of time does not bring about the general improvement of society, traditionalists counter, we should look instead to a glorified past era for models of social organization. This kind of temporal nostalgia features prominently in many populist movements around the globe today.[18]

Temporal nostalgia is of course nothing new. The materialist focus of political and economic liberalism in the nineteenth century similarly produced an ennui with bourgeois society that animated both traditionalists and progressives (recall Daumier's yawning caricatures). Francis Fukuyama has argued that liberal democracy, often regarded today as the only legitimate form of government, is not a natural fit for humans who crave recognition (*thymos*) and often bristle at equality.[19] But his theory, which considers human nature as essentially unchanging, does not account for how modern subjects experience history differently than their classical forebearers. The inevitable compromises of democratic governance do not sit easily with either progressives or traditionalists. Liberal democracy gets worn down by historical expectations or regrets.

Indeed, pessimism is the dominant mood of progressives today, just as much as traditionalists. Their political commitments are largely driven by apocalyptic fears of climate catastrophe, soaring inequality, and creeping authoritarianism.[20] But this temporal dynamic has driven modern progressive thought at least since the Congress of Vienna. Marx prophesized a socialist future against the backdrop of Manchester's "hell upon earth." To be a progressive is to believe that something should and can be done to remedy social and political ills, and that a fairer future is in reach, even if hard to grasp or against the odds (see figure 15.1). When this desired transformation does not materialize, however, progressives become increasingly pessimistic. As in Musset's time, they suffer from a *mal de siècle*, the disease of historical arrest: "Everything that will be is not yet. Do not look elsewhere for the source of our suffering."[21]

Discontent with our present world has led to a third act in the history of revolution. Just as the philosophes reclaimed "revolution" to express their vision of gradual progress, so too political leaders and pundits today have latched on to the term. Its violent undertones have largely faded from our collective memory: the word "revolution" no longer conjures up visions of gulags, famines, or political assassinations. Revolution's connotations today are indeed so positive that it has been adopted left, right, and center. Bernie Sanders titled the book for his 2016 presidential campaign *Our Revolution*, and subsequently launched an organization by the same name.[22] That same year, Emmanuel Macron also published a book simply called *Révolution* as part of his own, successful presidential campaign.[23] Shortly thereafter, Donald Trump's future press secretary, Kayleigh McEnany, chronicled and celebrated Trump's electoral victory in a book called *The New American Revolution*. In none of these books was there much discussion of past revolutions, nor any analysis of how these new political movements were revolutionary in a technical sense. The closest that any mainstream politician came to endorsing actual revolution may

FIGURE 15.1 A student sign at a pro-Palestinian protest at Stanford University, April 2024. Author's photo.

have been Trump's erstwhile campaign manager Steve Bannon, when he allegedly declared that he was a Leninist, explaining that "Lenin wanted to destroy the state, and that's my goal too. I want to bring everything crashing down, and destroy all of today's establishment."[24]

The appropriation of "revolution" by the political right is of course nothing new. Italian Fascists pioneered the adoption of revolutionary rhetoric for reactionary politics. The Nazis followed suit, proclaiming a "national revolution." To a great extent, these far-right revolutions were a response to the Bolshevik Revolution, which the Fascists and Nazis viewed with both fear and envy. Their idea of revolution no doubt warrants a separate study; I have not covered those revolutions in this book, as they emerged out of different historical traditions and tensions.[25]

Today's right-wing revolutionaries, by contrast, do not seek to challenge (or even fend off) a left-wing rival. They simply view revolution as a good in itself, a clean break from a corrupt and declining status quo. We can observe in this way how "revolution" has become oddly unmoored from its own past. Where one's degree of devotion to revolutionary ideals, during the French Revolution, is what originally produced the left/right divide, today anyone can be a revolutionary. As the ranks of "revolutionaries" are further swollen by business and tech executives, the precise political meaning of the term—regime change—is vanishing. When Sanders calls for a revolution, it is not an invocation to overthrow the constitution.

As everyone becomes a revolutionary, is anyone a revolutionary? How many political actors around the world remain committed to the modern idea of revolution, understood as a precipitating event for massive political and social change? Both in the West and beyond, die-hard revolutionaries are a dying breed. The largest "revolutionary" state today, the People's Republic of China, shows little interest in fostering revolution at home or promoting it abroad. Populist authoritarians in eastern Europe, Latin America, Asia, and elsewhere shy away from revolutionary pronouncements, preferring to slowly erode democratic norms.[26] Even the January 6 insurrectionists, who may have come the closest in American history to overturning a lawfully elected president, did not openly seek to overturn the US Constitution.

But this recovery of revolution as a positive political value, coupled with its dissociation from an actual political process, still leaves us in a bind. Many today hope to witness significant political change, be it in a leftward or rightward direction, but few endorse radical means for achieving it. This reticence will naturally be welcome to many observers, which by definition includes most people. It does not, however, mean that we are in a stable place. There is gnawing tension between our political structures and our political sensibilities. Our structures rest on constitutional theories that reflect an entirely different vision of history, inherited from antiquity. This is especially evident in the case of the American Constitution, designed according to the Polybian principle of checks and balances, in order to prevent history—in the form of revolutions—from intruding into our lives. Such a design serves the status quo and intentionally hinders swift and extensive political change—that is, precisely what constitutes progress or restoration in the eyes of many.[27] It is in this sense that we are moderns living in a world made by ancients. It is an awkward fit.

Some progressives have addressed this problem head-on. There are those who argue that the Constitution is fundamentally broken, and that we should "radically alter the basic rules of the game."[28] Others accuse it of being antidemocratic, in that it has become essentially impossible to amend.[29] To date, these criticisms have been largely shunned. But where conservatives once aligned themselves for the most part with Edmund Burke's defense of traditional institutions (as opposed to radical innovation), they, too, are losing ground to the revolutionaries on their own flank. Calls for a constitutional convention or even a "national divorce" have become increasingly common.[30] Here as well, a loose centrist majority continues to depict such proposals as absurd. But they are also symptomatic of the mismatch between our institutions and expectations.

Can this center hold? It has faced similar threats in the past. The abolitionist William Lloyd Garrison decried the Constitution as "an agreement with hell," and publicly burned a copy of it in 1854. The historian Charles Beard savaged the Constitution in 1913 for promoting elite economic interests. And in the early 1960s, Black nationalists such as Malcolm X argued in favor of splitting up the country. In each of these cases, progressive political forces clashed with institutions that struggled to respond. But compromises were eventually reached, even if in the first case it took a civil war. The Constitution was amended, it was reinterpreted, and legislation ensured that its promises of equity were upheld (with the Civil Rights Act of 1964).[31]

It is not unreasonable to hope, then, that our existing institutions can similarly address contemporary problems, and prevent popular discontent or alienation from ripping the system apart. Such hope does not necessarily rest on any doctrine of historical progress. All political societies, ancient or modern, must respond pragmatically to the challenges that crop up, and pursue their preferred outcomes. The ancients even had a specific term for this kind of practical thinking: the Greeks called it *phronesis*, which gave the Latin *prudentia*, and our own "prudence."[32] The prudent hope that we might solve specific problems, such as climate change or widening economic inequality, does not entail a belief that all problems will eventually disappear. But prudence comes with its own drawbacks: to many it can appear uninspiring and ill matched for the scale of our present challenges.

Centrists also harbor their own version of a modern progress doctrine. Everything would be so much better, centrists hold, if everyone was more reasonable. Invest in education, stay informed, trust the science—in short, *be more like us*. The problem with this line of thought is that it perpetuates the Enlightenment fallacy that human disagreement is simply a matter of ignorance or error. It ignores Madison's injunction that "as long as the reason of man continues fallible, and he is at liberty to exercise it, different opinions will be formed."[33] And it promotes, often unintentionally, a kind of "right thinking" that can be antipluralistic and orthodox.

The problem with this centrist doctrine is not only that it can be wrong—the science changes, educated people don't agree on important questions, information can be contradictory—but its claim to possess a monopoly on the truth is itself a source of polarization and alienation. Whoever challenges the "reasonable" conclusions du jour risks being shunned by the right-thinking crowd, thereby propelling them into the arms of the defiant.

If the center does not hold, how will things fall apart? The simple answer is that it is impossible to predict. As the political scientist Timur Kuran demonstrated, revolutions are defined by their complexity: small changes can have oversized effects. That is why revolutions usually take us by surprise, even if in hindsight they might seem preordained.[34]

If we cannot predict when or how another revolution might come about, however, we can turn to historical parallels for some guidance. If the political center continues to hollow out, we may find ourselves in a 1930s scenario—not 1930s Germany, but rather 1930s France. In the period known as *l'entre-deux-guerres*, French support for liberal democracy was dangerously low. Most intellectuals disdained it, regarding parliamentary politics as base and corrupt.[35] Political competition shifted to the margins, with far-left and far-right movements vying for popular and elite support. Violent demonstrations became commonplace: right-wing extremists attacked the assembly in February 1934.[36] The political situation was encapsulated in the layout of the Universal Exposition of 1937 in Paris, where the Soviet and Nazi pavilions faced off (see figure 15.2). A socialist government, the Popular Front, eventually came to power, only to collapse after thirteen months. Within three years, France would be occupied by Nazi Germany, with a fascist French government running the southern half of the country.

While many observers have drawn parallels between our current state and the rise of fascism, the French example reminds us how far-right movements do not evolve in a vacuum, but in a fierce rivalry with left and far-left alternatives.[37] This rivalry transcends national borders, with both sides drawing strength from successes elsewhere. The political dynamics of the 1930s produced a kind of perfect revolutionary storm, mixing hyperpolarized pressure systems that extended across much of the world. As with other complex systems, the ultimate direction of this storm was unpredictable.

There is little that can be done from the center in the face of a revolutionary storm. As Thucydides observed, in a revolution, "moderation [is] held to be a cloak for unmanliness; the ability to see all sides of a question, the inaptness to act on any. . . . [T]he advocate of extreme measures [is] always trustworthy; his opponent a man to be suspected."[38] So what *can* we do? If we cannot predict the course of revolutionary storms, we can hope to gain some clarity about their dynamic. It is clear, for instance, that most of the variables involved are interdependent. The relative strength of

FIGURE 15.2 Nazi and Soviet pavilions at the 1937 Universal Exposition in Paris. *La Tour Eiffel et fontaine du Trocadéro vus depuis le Palais de Chaillot à Paris* (1937). Séeberger frères / Centre des monuments nationaux. This file is made available by Licence Ouverte 1.0.

a political movement on the far right will also be a factor in the strength of a countervailing force on the far left. The success of the Bolshevik Revolution bolstered not only communist and socialist efforts in other countries but also the political fortunes of the far right.[39] Backlash is the force that whips a revolutionary storm into a frenzy. The establishment of a Soviet republic in Munich in 1919 contributed to the growth of far-right movements there, including the future Nazi party.[40]

This is the historical lesson that should give would-be revolutionaries pause. Revolutionary victories, on the left or on the right, are often short-lived and can ultimately produce the opposite outcome than the one desired. The only certainty about the revolution to come is that it will not turn out as planned. The injustices and problems that we face in the present can seem unbearable, and entrusting their solution to a clunky, often disappointing constitutional process, unconscionable. Revolution may appear as the only moral solution. There's just one problem: it can end up making everything worse.

Of course, simply *wanting* a revolution does not one make. The blogosphere can be ablaze with calls for radical change, but in the absence of external factors, these calls are unlikely to be heeded. As I noted at the start of this book, social scientists have long insisted that revolutions are mainly the result of socioeconomic conflicts, not ideas.[41] While I think they underestimate the role of ideas, they are right to emphasize the importance of material hardships. No one expects a revolution in Switzerland.

But perhaps the greatest revolutionary threat today is the one that dares not speak its name. The past 250 years have conflated revolution in our minds with large crowds, peaceful or violent, overcoming an unpopular autocrat. Yet not all revolutions are so brazen. As Polybius reminded us, sometimes regime change is nearly imperceptible: there is *metabolē*, but no *stasis*. The phenomenon of democratic backsliding fits this kind of silent revolution perfectly. Democratically elected leaders can corrode democratic institutions in a slow-moving coup. Serious rivals are declared ineligible to run; independent agencies are brought to heel; even the media and business are made to bend the knee. The regime shifts seamlessly from democracy to dictatorship. There are no mobs storming buildings, no banners or rallying cries. Business goes on as usual, students graduate from college, crops are harvested. Our biggest fear should be that no one even notices the revolution to come.

ACKNOWLEDGMENTS

This book has been, in every sense, a labor of love. It has certainly been laborious. I first gave a paper on the subject back in 2010. But despite kicking this book around for some fourteen years, it has been a genuine pleasure to work on. In part, it's allowed me to explore times and places that I was not familiar with (justifying my mostly flippant claim that eighteenth-century France is a great launchpad for raiding other centuries). But it's also a project that has allowed me to interact with so many fascinating and brilliant colleagues in other fields, and to have accumulated a great number of debts along the way.

Over the past decade and a half, I've presented parts of this book to audiences at the Humanities Center of California State University at Chico, Cambridge's Trinity Hall History Society, the Mellon Sawyer Seminar on Political Will at Cornell, City University of New York's Intellectual and Cultural History Seminar, the Institute of French Cultural Studies and the History department at Dartmouth, Harvard's Colloquium on Intellectual History, New York University's Berlin Center, the Davis Center for Historical Studies at Princeton (twice, at a ten year interval, which perhaps merits a dishonorable mention), Sorbonne Université, Sciences Po Paris, Stanford's Political Theory and History of Political Thought workshops, the "Pamphlets and Patrons" research group at Trier University, University of Oregon's European Studies Lecture Series, University of Lausanne's History department, "The Just City" European Research Council research project at the University of Zürich, and Yale's European Studies Council. I am extremely indebted to my hosts and to the comments and questions from attendees at these events. Special thanks to Elizabeth Anker, David Armitage, David A. Bell, Jason Frank, Paul Friedland, Stefanos Geroulanos, Peter Gordon, Natalie Hester, Troy Jollimore, Béla Kapossy, Larry Kritzman, Adam Lebovitz, Johanna Lenne-Cornuez, Darrin McMahon, Steven Pincus, Camille Robcis, Daniel Rodgers, Jerrold Seigel, Benjamin Straumann, Damien Tricoire, Richard Wolin, and Isser Woloch. I am also grateful to the participants of the *Scripting Revolution* conference that Keith Baker and I organized at Stanford in 2011, and the authors who contributed to the subsequent volume.

For this book more than any other, I have benefited greatly from the erudition of friends, colleagues, and students. I am particularly grateful to

Frederick Clark, Joshua Cohen, David Como, Brian Coyne, Rowan Dorin, Ronald Egan, Paul Friedland, Anthony Grafton, Anna Grzymala-Busse, Kinch Hoekstra, Melissa Lane, Adam Lebovitz, Daniel Lee, Antoine Lilti, Novia Jichu Liu, Alison McQueen, (the alas late) John Merriman, Noah Millstone, Samuel Moyn, Jack Rakove, Sophie Rosenfeld, Gabriella Safran, Debra Satz, Edward Shen, Sophie Smith, Céline Spector, Alexander Statman, Laura Stokes, Benjamin Straumann, Lisa Surwillo, Natasha Wheatley, and Caroline Winterer, as well as the anonymous reviewers of my *Journal of the History of Ideas* article on Polybius, and the readers for Princeton University Press. In listing these debts, I can only think about all the others that I am undoubtedly overlooking—mea culpa.

I owe particularly heavy debts to Keith M. Baker, whose *Marat* book has occupied the same gestational cycle as mine, and from whose wines and wisdom I have drunk profusely over the decades; David A. Bell, who has been encouraging and advising this project ever since it began; Jonathan Gienapp, for characteristic brilliance about the American Revolution and constitutionalism; David Hewett, with whom I read Polybius book 6 line by line in ancient Greek; Darrin McMahon, a great partner for intellectual history and rye whiskey; Bernadette Meyler, for morning constitutionals and insights on the Constitution; Josh Ober, who in true peripatetic spirit answered my questions about Greek political thought during our dog walks; Steve Sawyer, for endless debates about the French Revolution over *vin naturel*; and Jake Soll, for his *esprit* and spirits.

Special thanks as well to Priya Nelson, *éditrice extraordinaire*, who has been a wonderful reader and thought partner as I pulled this book together; Rob Tempio, for conversations going back a decade; and Emma Wagh and the remarkable editorial team at Princeton University Press.

My family has helped me lug this book around from Palo Alto to Paris, and Seaford to Florence. It was in a conversation with Zoë that the key argument of the book suddenly became apparent; she also came up with the final title. You have been my favorite conversation partner since that first night in Williams Hall. Charlie and Eloise have developed a dangerous habit of breaking into Italian revolutionary songs, much to the surprise of any nearby Italians. And I take this opportunity to formally apologize to Ms. Jody for the guillotine drawings in kindergarten. Grandmère and grandpère, thanks for still reading and discussing everything I send you; Jenny, for always knowing what to say, and what drink to pair it with. I started thinking about this book during walks with Teddy, our Keeshond; I finished writing it while walking our Great Pyrenees, Aimee. I choose not to read into the fact that Keeshonden were the revolutionary dogs of Holland, and Great Pyrenees, the royal dogs of Louis XIV.

Over the past decade, I have had the great pleasure to teach a course on the history of revolutions to rising high-school juniors and seniors, as part of the Stanford Summer Humanities Institute. This intensive three-week summer program has allowed and forced me to clarify my arguments time and time again under the friendly fire of brilliant young minds. It is to them that this book is dedicated.

Parts and early versions of this book have appeared in *French Historical Studies*, *History & Theory*, *Journal of the History of Ideas*, and in the edited volumes *Scripting Revolution* (Stanford University Press, 2015), *The Scaffold of Sovereignty* (Columbia University Press, 2017), and *Power and Time* (University of Chicago Press, 2020). Thanks to my editors and coeditors, and especially Keith Baker, Zvi Ben-Dor Benite, Stefanos Geroulanos, Nicole Jerr, and Natasha Wheatley. And special thanks to Charlie Edelstein for artistic guidance and design of the cover.

ABBREVIATIONS

Editions for classical works are to Loeb unless otherwise indicated.

Aesch., *PV*	Aeschylus, *Prometheus Bound*
AP	*Archives parlementaires de 1787 à 1860*, French Revolution Digital Archive, Stanford Libraries, https://frda.stanford.edu/
App., *B Civ.*	Appian, *Civil War*
Arist.	Aristotle
	Ath. Pol. *Athenian Constitution*
	Nic. Eth. *Nicomachean Ethics*
	Pol. *The Politics*, translated by H. Rackham
ARTFL	University of Chicago ARTFL-FRANTEXT database of French-language texts, https://artfl-project.uchicago.edu/content/artfl-frantext
Augustine, *De civ. D.*	*De civitate Dei*
Cic.	Cicero
	Brut. *On Brutus*
	Cat. *On Catiline* (*In Catilinam*)
	De orat. *On the Orator* (*De oratore*)
	Inv. *On Invention* (*De inventione*)
	Leg. *On the Laws* (*De legibus*)
	Off. *On the Offices* (*De officiis*)
	Rep. *On the Republic* (*De re publica*)
D	Voltaire, *Correspondences*
EEBO	Early English Books Online, on the ProQuest Platform, https://proquest.libguides.com/eebopqp

Encyclopédie Diderot and d'Alembert's *Encyclopédie, ou Dictionnaire raisonné des sciences, des arts et des métiers*

EVANS Early American imprints, Series I, Evans, 1639–1800, Readex, https://www.readex.com/products/early-american-imprints-series-i-evans-1639-1800

FOUNDERS Founders Online, National Archives and Records Administration and University of Virginia Press, https://founders.archives.gov

GG *Geschichtliche Grundbegriffe*

Hdt. Herodotus, *Histories*

Hes., *Op.* Hesiod, *Works and Days*

HP P.-J.-B. Buchez and P.-C. Roux's *Histoire parlementaire de la Révolution française*

Livy, *AUC* Livy, *History of Rome* (*Ab urbe condita*)

Lucr. Lucretius, *On the Nature of Things* (*De rerum natura*)

M. Aur., *Med.* Marcus Aurelius, *Meditations*

MEGA *Karl Marx, Friedrich Engels Gesamtausgabe*

NEWBERRY Newberry French Pamphlets, https://publications.newberry.org/frenchpamphlets/

Ov., *Met.* Ovid, *The Metamorphoses*

Pl. Plato, *Complete Works*, edited by John M. Cooper

- *Ap.* *Apology*
- *Criti.* *Critias*
- *Leg.* *Laws*
- *Plt.* *Statesman* (*Politicus*)
- *Resp.* *Republic*
- *Ti.* *Timaeus*

Plut. Plutarch, *Lives*

- *Aem.* Aemilius Paulus
- *Cat. Mai.* Cato the Elder
- *Lyc.* Lycurgus

Num. Numa

Marc. Marcellus

Per. Pericles

Pub. Publicola

Rom. Romulus

Sol. Solon

Polyb. Polybius, *Histories*, translated by Evelyn S. Shuckburgh

Reg. Lat. Vatican Apostolic Library

Sall. Sallust

Cat. *The Catilinarian Conspiracy*

Iug. *Jugurthine War*

Sen., *Ep.* Seneca, *Moral Epistles*

Soph., *Ant.* Sophocles, *Antigone*

Tac., *Ann.* Tacitus, *Annals*

Thuc. Thucydides, *The Peloponnesian War*, translated by Richard Crawley

Vat. Lat. Biblioteca apostolica vaticana

Vir., *Aen.* Virgil, *Aeneid*

Xen. Xenophon

Ath. Pol. *Constitution of the Athenians*

Hell. *Hellenica*

NOTES

Notes to Introduction

1. I traced this joke (which I have reformulated here) back to the Broadway play by Willie and Eugene Howard *Ballyhoo of 1932*, performed that year: see Cullen, Hackman, and McNeilly, *Vaudeville Old & New*, 1:525.

2. Quoted in Rubenstein, *Leon Trotsky*, 136.

3. On the relation between historical cosmologies and political theory, see notably: Hartog, *Regimes of Historicity*; C. Clark, *Time and Power*; D. Edelstein, Geroulanos, and Wheatley, *Power and Time*. A pioneering work to explore this connection is John G. A. Pocock's *The Machiavellian Moment.*

4. John Adams, in *Works*, 4:287.

5. Adams is directly translating Thucydides in this passage (see chapter 1 and Thuc. 3.81–84): see *Works*, 4:285.

6. M. Aur., *Med.* 68. See also Koselleck, "Historical Criteria," 46.

7. See chapters 2 and 3 (on Polybius), and 7 (on the American founding).

8. See chapter 4.

9. See chapter 4.

10. Hartog, *Chronos*, 221. On the idea of progress and Western imperialism: Chakrabarty, *Provincializing Europe.*

11. See chapters 8 and 9.

12. Condorcet, *Esquisse*, esp. the "Neuvième époque."

13. Kant, "Was ist Aufklärung?" (1784) in Schmidt, *What Is Enlightenment?*, 58. See also David Bell, "New Social History."

14. Le Mercier de La Rivière, *L'ordre naturel.*

15. Darnton, "*Philosophes* Trim the Tree."

16. César Dumarsais, "Philosophe," *Encyclopédie*, 12:510.

17. Diderot, "Droit naturel," *Encyclopédie*, 5:116.

18. Diderot, *Le neveu de Rameau*, 74; (modified) translation from *Rameau's Nephew*, 43.

19. Arist., *Pol.* 6.1318b.

20. *Federalist*, no. 10 (James Madison), 55.

21. On the "enemy of the human race" (*hostis humani generis*) in Enlightenment and revolutionary thought: D. Edelstein, *Terror of Natural Right.*

22. Baker, *Inventing the French Revolution.*

23. Sewell, *Logics of History*, chap. 8.

24. See chapter 10.

25. See Lenin, "The Dual Power," *Pravda*, April 9, 1917, in *Anthology*, 301–4.

26. For Constant: "Liberty of Ancients" (1819). For Marx: *Eighteenth-Brumaire.*

27. On Hercules, see notably Lynn Hunt's "Imagery of Radicalism." On female allegories: Gutwirth, *Twilight of the Goddesses.*

28. In general: Harold Parker, *Cult of Antiquity*; Mossé, *L'antiquité*; Fichtl, *La radicalisation*; Baker, *Jean-Paul Marat*.

29. Condorcet, *Outlines*, 231; *Esquisse*, 240. Robespierre: "Nous voulons, en un mot, remplir les voeux de la nature," in "Rapports sur les principes de morale politique," Feb. 5, 1794, in *Œuvres* 10:352. I discuss these naturalizing trends in greater depth in *The Terror of Natural Right* and *On the Spirit of Rights*. On Robespierre and Cato, see notably David P. Jordan's *The Revolutionary Career of Maximilien Robespierre*.

30. See chapter 11.

31. Constant, "Liberty of Ancients." On liberalism and the military: Isabella, *Southern Europe*.

32. Chateaubriand, *Mémoires d'outre-tombe*, 1:213; Tomasi di Lampedusa, *Leopard*, 28 (translation modified).

33. See chapter 12.

34. C. Clark, *Revolutionary Spring*.

35. See chapter 12.

36. Dostoevsky, *Possessed*, 402. See chapter 13.

37. Some of the arguments in this section draw on the introduction that Keith M. Baker and I wrote for our coedited volume *Scripting Revolution*.

38. Skocpol, *States and Social Revolutions*, 25.

39. Marx, *German Ideology*, 37–38, 64. On the unusual status of this text: Carver, "German Ideology."

40. See e.g., Erikson and Wlezien, "Leading Economic Indicators."

41. See respectively, B. Moore, *Social Origins of Dictatorship*; Skocpol, *States and Social Revolutions*; Goldstone, *Revolution and Rebellion*; Pincus, *1688*. For a related criticism to the one voiced here, see notably John Foran's "Theories of Revolution Revisited."

42. Sewell, *Capitalism*.

43. North and Weingast, "Constitutions and Commitment."

44. Grewal, "Political Theology of Laissez-Faire"; D. Edelstein, *Spirit of Rights*, chap. 5; Soll, *Free Market*.

45. On Belle Époque inequality: Piketty, *Capital*. On the reception of Marx in the late nineteenth century: Billington, *Fire in the Minds*. For Lenin: *What Is to Be Done?*; see also chapter 13 below.

46. On revolutionary thresholds: Kuran, "Now out of Never."

Chapter One

1. Thuc., 1.24.5; see Ober, *Political Dissent*, 70–79; more generally, Connor, *Thucydides*, 32–36. On chaos theory and revolution: Kuran, "Now out of Never."

2. Thuc., 1.23.6 (on the real cause of the war), 3.82.1 (on political alignments during the war); see also Arist., *Pol.* 4.1302a.

3. La Harpe, *Du fanatisme*, 9. See also White, *When Words Lose*, chap. 3.

4. Thuc., 3.81.5 (on unprecedented violence), 3.82.7 and 3.84.3 (on the overturning of laws, honor, and family ties), 3.82.4–5 (on the reversal of meaning and values), 3.84.2 (on human nature), 3.82.3 (on revolutionary contagion). See Connor, *Thucydides*, 95–105 (esp. on language and violence); J. Price, *Thucydides and Internal War*, chap. 1. For Hobbes: Slomp, "Hobbes, Thucydides," 577–78.

5. Thuc., 3.44.4 (on the contrast between justice and interests), 3.53.1 (on the problem of impartiality: the trial of the Plataeans), 5.84.1–116.4 (on the self-interested behavior of states: the Melian dialogue).

6. Thuc., 3.82.8 (on *philothymos* and *archē*), 3.82.4 (on *sophrosyne*), 3.82.7 and 3.83.3 (on oaths and contracts), 3.82.8 (on *pleonexíā*). For Hobbes, the nonenforceability of contracts was a crucial feature of the state of nature: see *Leviathan* 1.14.

7. "New" to the extent that, for Thucydides, the Peloponnesian War marked a break with an archaic, "simpler" (*euēthēs*) time in Hellenic history: see 3.83.1. Thucydides describes Corcyra as the "first" revolution (3.85.1), no doubt implying that it was the first time that a revolution unleashed such passions and violence. There had, of course, been earlier revolutions, most famously at Athens: see Ober, *Athenian Revolution*.

8. Thuc., 3.82.2 (on the constancy of human nature), 3.82.8 (on passions), 1.22.4 (on the usefulness of history).

9. For an inventory of *staseis* in classical Greece: Gehrke, *Stasis*. On the political diversity of regimes in ancient Greece: Ober, *Rise and Fall*, 40.

10. Hdt., 3.80.6.

11. On the appropriation of this term by the revolutionary Sun Yat-Sen: Chen, "Revolution," 17–18. I am indebted to my Stanford colleague Ronald Egan for sharing his "Notes on the *Classic of Changes, Geming* 革命, and the Mandate of Heaven 天命" (personal communication, Jan. 30, 2021), and to my former Stanford Summer Humanities Institute student Edward Chen for his paper "On the Use of 革命 (*Geming*, Revolution) in Historical Discourses" (class paper, July 2019).

12. *I Ching*, 254; (modified) translation from Chen, "Revolution," 16.

13. "The Speech of Tang," in Legge, *Shoo King*, 173. See also Kern, Goldin, and Pines, *Ideology of Power*.

14. "The Speech at Muh," in Legge, *Shoo King*, 304.

15. Needham and Ronan, *Shorter Science and Civilisation*, 1:144 (on the Naturalists' doctrine); quoting the *Shiji*, or *Records of the Grand Historian*.

16. Mencius, *Mencius*, bk. 8, pt. B, §14; 196.

17. Thuc., 1.18.1. After they overthrew the oligarchic government of the Five Hundred, the Athenians came close in Thucydides's view to a blended constitution: see 8.97.2 (and below). See E. Harris, "Constitution."

18. On Spartan fears of revolution: e.g., Thuc., 5.34.2.

19. A Corinthian ambassador points to the Athenian predilection for making innovations (*neōteropoiéō*) as evidence they cannot be trusted: Thuc., 1.70.2. Thucydides often uses this term or the related verb *neōterízō* as a synonym for revolution: see e.g., 1.102.3, 1.115.2, 3.72.1, 3.82.1, 4.41.3, and passim. See also Hdt., 1.210.3, and chapter 3.

20. Arist., *Pol.* 2.1270b20. Note that Aristotle also criticized the Spartan regime at length: see *Pol.* 2.1269b–70b. More generally: Fritz, *Mixed Constitution in Antiquity*; Nippel, *Mischverfassungstheorie*.

21. Plut., *Per.* 11.3.

22. Thuc., 2.65.12, quoted and discussed in Kagan, *Fall*, viii. "Faction" here translates *stasis*: on the importance of this term, see below. See also Thuc., 2.65.7, on the rise of ambition (*philothymia*) and personal profit (*kérdos*) after the death of Pericles.

23. Teegarden, *Death to Tyrants!*

24. Xen., *Hell.* 2.3.21 (seizing property), 2.3.24 (Critias's speech). More generally: Krentz, *Thirty at Athens.*

25. Pl., Letter VII (p. 1647). Both men died at the Battle of Munychia, when the democratic exiles overpowered the Thirty: see Xen., *Hell.* 2.4.19.

26. Pl., *Ap.* 32c–d.

27. Brickhouse and Smith, *Trial and Execution*; Ober, "Trial of Socrates."

28. Pl., *Resp.* 5.462a. See Pradeau, *Platon et la cité*; Shear, *Polis and Revolution.*

29. Pl., *Resp.* 8.546a (for quote), 8.555d (on oligarchies), 8.562d (on democracies), 8.566d–e (on demagogues). For the Peisistratos parallel: Hoekstra, "Athenian Democracy," 23n24.

30. A point often lost on modern theorists of revolution: see e.g., Skocpol, *States and Social Revolutions.*

31. Plut., *Sol.* 27.6–7; see also Hdt., 1.30.1–1.32.9. More generally, see McMahon, *Happiness.*

32. Pl., *Leg.* 693d.

33. Aristotle also recommended that the power of judging be extended to all citizens: "There should be some men who are able to govern and who render this service to the state either continuously or in turn. And there remain the classes which we happen to have defined just before [i.e., poorer citizens], the deliberative class and the one that judges the claims of litigants" (*Pol.* 4.1290a–b).

34. Arist., *Pol.* 5.1307a10 ("a good blend"), 4.1296a10 (on factions), bk. 6 (in general, on the different ways of blending democracy and oligarchy). More generally: F. Miller, *Nature, Justice, and Rights*, chap. 7. On the problematic concept of a "middle class": see Ober, *Mass and Elite*, 27–30.

35. *Pol.* 4.1290a (my emphasis). See also 3.1277a ("the state consists of unlike persons").

36. *Pol.* 3.1280a.

37. *Pol.* 5.1301b. See also *Nic. Eth.* 5.1131b20–1133b15. More generally, see Modrak, "Virtue, Equality, and Inequality"; McMahon, *Equality*, 107–8.

38. Hdt., 3.80.6.

39. Arist., *Pol.* 5.1301b.

40. Arist. *Pol.* 5.1302a.

41. Marx and Engels, *Communist Manifesto*, chap. 1.

42. See e.g., Shklar, "Liberalism of Fear," 23; see also Manent, *Intellectual History of Liberalism*, chap. 3. More generally, see Rawls, *Political Liberalism*, 146–50 (and the idea of a proto-liberal *modus vivendi*).

43. Kymlicka, *Multicultural Citizenship*, 80.

44. See Rosenblatt, *Lost History of Liberalism*, chap. 1.

45. *Pol.* 4.1292a.

46. *Pol.* 3.1281a (on sovereignty); see also 3.1278b, 4.1299a; and 4.1297b–98a (on the three governmental powers). See Mulgan, "Aristotle's Sovereign"; C. Johnson, "Hobbesian Conception of Sovereignty"; Ober, *Athenian Revolution*, 120; Hoekstra, "Athenian Democracy"; Lane, "Popular Sovereignty."

47. *Pol.* 6.1318a.

48. Plut., *Lyc.* 5.7. Cf. also Xen., *Ath. Pol.* 10.1–2.

49. Plut., *Rom.* 13.5. On the Roman Republic, and the idea of balancing a constitution, see the following chapter.

50. See *Catalogue of the John Adams Library*.

51. John Adams, preface to *Defence of the Constitutions*, in *Works*, 4:285.

52. Thuc., 3.82.1 (p. 199). See also the Loeb Classical Library translation by Charles Forster Smith: "To such excesses of savagery did the revolution go" (Thucydides, *Peloponnesian War*, 2:143); and Rex Warner's translation in *History of the Peloponnesian War* (223).

53. Thucydides, *Eight Bookes*, 187 ("So cruell was this Sedition"). Adams's library contained *Thucydidis "De bello Peloponnesiaco" libri octo*, edited by Henri Estienne and John Hudson (at 216).

54. See e.g., *Dictionnaire de l'Académie française* (1694), s.v. "sedition": "Emotion populaire, souslevement contre la puissance légitime." Tellingly, the 1798 edition replaces "légitime" with "établie." See also S. Johnson, *Dictionary* (1755), s.v. "sedition": "A tumult; an insurrection; a popular commotion; an uproar."

55. S. Johnson, *Dictionary*, s.v. "seditious" and "seditiousness."

56. Livy, *AUC* 2.44.9; see also 4.9.3, 5.6.10, and passim.

57. See Hansen, "Stasis," 124–29, quote at 126. See also Manicas, "War, Stasis"; Ober, *Athenian Revolution*; Armitage, *Civil War*. And see App., *B Civ*. 1.0.2, 1.0.5, 1.4.27, 1.7.55, 1.7.60 and passim.

58. Pl., *Resp*. 5.470c–d.

59. Pl., *Resp*. 8.545d. Thucydides had already employed *metabole* to signify regime change: see e.g., 6.17.3, 6.59.2, 7.55.2, 8.75.2, and 8.98.1.

60. Smith, "Language of 'Political Science.'"

61. Arist., *Pol*. 5.1301a20, 5.1301b5 (on the connections between *stasis* and *metabolē*), and 5.1303a15 (on *metabolē* without *stasis*, 385). For some other modern translations, see e.g., Aristotle, *Politics*, 147 ("revolutions in regimes"); *Complete Works*, 2:2066 ("revolution in states").

62. Livy, *AUC* 3.33.1. See also Cic., *Rep*. 1.64 (he also uses *commutationum*, from *commutatio*: 1.45, 2.9, 2.57).

63. Aristotle, *Aristotelis "Politicorum" libri octo* (1872), 1292b, 1296a, 1301a (pp. 399, 421, 495; on mutation); 1296a, 1319b (pp. 421, 473; on sedition). See Dunbabin, "Reception and Interpretation"; Schütrumpf, *Earliest Translations*; Koselleck, "Historical Criteria," 667–68; Smith, "Language of 'Political Science.'"

64. Aristotle, *"Politicorum" libri octo commentarii*, fol. 70, 63: "de causis de mutationum rerumpublicarum; seditiones et discordie ciuium." Translation completed in 1437, posthumously published in 1469 (Schütrumpf, *Earliest Translations*, 28). See Hankins, "Exclusivist Republicanism."

65. See e.g., Aristotle, *"De republica,"* bk. 5, chap. 1; *Aristotelis "Politicorum" libri octo*, (1637), 2:234–35.

66. Aristotle, *"Le livre de politiques,"* bk. 5, chap. 1, vol. 1, fol. 157: "des transmutations et corruptions et salvations des policies." Modern edition in Menut, "Maistre Nicole Oresme," 202 (on transmutations), 265 (on sedition). See Schütrumpf, *Earliest Translations*, 25.

67. Aristotle, *"Les politiques" d'Aristote*, esp. 267–69. New editions came out in 1576, 1600, and 1668. For the Italian, see *Gli otto libri*, fol. 97 and passim. See also *"Trattato dei governi."* On Segni's vocabulary, Rachum, *"Revolution,"* 30.

68. Aristotle, *Aristotles "Politiques,"* 241 A, 241 D.

69. Aristotle, *Treatise on Government*, 116, 198, 239, 252, 254, and passim; *"La politique" d'Aristote*, 2:1–3 and passim.

70. According to the *Catalogue of the John Adams Library*, he owned the Ellis translation (15). Adams was 43 when this edition was published, and had already referred to Aristotle's constitutional theory in 1774 (*Novanglus*, no.1). See Ryerson, *John Adams's Republic.*

71. Salutati, *Political Writings*, 122–25: "cum status rei publicae commutatur . . . sit quam in mutationis periculum devenire. Numquam enim quisquam tantae potentiae fuit vel prudentia tam divina cui mutatio civitatis ad intentionis propositum responderet."

Chapter Two

1. The classic reference for these events (which may be fabulous): Livy, *AUC* 1.57–2.15.

2. Most importantly, see Zera S. Fink's *The Classical Republicans.*

3. See *Federalist*, nos. 16, 70 (Alexander Hamilton; for Madison's more circumspect views, see no. 18). See chapter 7 more generally.

4. Plut., *Aem.* 38.1 (on taxes), 28.11 (on Perseus's library); *Cat. Mai.* 12.4. For a more favorable Roman view of Greek culture, Plut., *Marc.* 21.5. More generally: M. Beard, *S.P.Q.R.*

5. Walbank, *Historical Commentary on Polybius*, 1:1–6. Polybius describes his friendship with the younger Scipio at 32.9–10 ("the acquaintance began in a loan of some books and the conversation about them"). See also Momigliano, "Historian's Skin."

6. Polyb., 1.1–13. On Polybius as historian, see notably Fergus Millar's "Polybius between Greece and Rome."

7. Polyb., 1.1.2 (*tyches metabolás*); see also 2.35 and Scipio's speech upon witnessing the fall of Carthage at 39.5. See Walbank, *Historical Commentary on Polybius*, 1:16–26 (on Fortune [*Tyche*] in Polybius), 1:39, and 1:647 (commenting on 6.10.7) on the inevitable decay of all things. See also Trompf, *Idea of Historical Recurrence*; Walbank, "Fortune (*Tychē*) in Polybius." The phrase "fortune's revolutions" may have been proverbial in ancient Greek; see, for instance, the saying attributed to Cleobolus (one of the Seven Sages), *Tàs tés tyches metabolàs gennaíōs peirō phérein* (You must learn to brave the changes of fortune), *Apophthegmata*,1.5.2, in F.W.A. Mullach's *Fragmenta philosophorum Graecorum* (1:219).

8. Thuc., 1.22.4. See Rood, "Polybius, Thucydides." More generally: Connor, *Thucydides*, 29–32; Fornara, *Nature of History*, 114 (on Polybius's break with Greek historiography).

9. Polyb., 1.8.

10. For two recent excellent studies of book 6, with references to the bibliography on this text: Straumann, "Leaving the State"; Loehr, "People's Moral Emotions." See also Millar, *Roman Republic*, 23–36.

11. Pl., *Plt.* 302c–e; Arist., *Pol.* 4.1289a. I leave aside the earliest form of government identified by Polybius, a kind of primitive monarchy, whose transformation into kingship marks the beginning of civilization and history: see Polyb., 6.5.

12. Pl., *Resp.* bk. 8; see also Walbank, *Historical Commentary on Polybius*, 1:6–16.

13. Arist., *Pol.* 5.1316a. Plato hints at the "cyclical" (*kúklos*) nature of all things in *The Republic* (8.546a). In some places, Aristotle also describes regime change in a linear fashion (e.g., *Pol.* 2.1286b), but much of book V serves to demonstrate how one regime can be transformed into a number of others. It is possible to detect a cycle of governments in Aristotle as well: see Ober, "Nature." However, the explicit statement that governments follow each other in a regular cycle "is found in no surviving work before Polybius": Walbank, *Historical Commentary on Polybius*, 1:644 (on 6.4.7–9.14).

14. According to the *Thesaurus linguae graecae*, the only prior recorded use of *anakúklosis* (or *anakúklesis*) may come from Pythagoras, in the context of metempsychosis (the word is used to describe the movement of a die): see *Testimonia: Part A*, P39, in Laks and Most, *Early Greek Philosophy*, 42–44. But the fragment itself, from the *Theology of Arithmetic*, attributed to Iamblichus, only dates to the fourth century AD. Plato uses the related noun *anakúklesin* (*Plt.* 269e) in reference to the perpetual movement of the cosmos, and the verb *anakúkleo* to describe the circling of the immortal soul (*Ti.* 37a). Aristotle also uses this verb in a moral sense: "Fortune often turns full circle" (*Tychas pollákis anakukleīsthai*; *Nic. Eth.* 1.1100b3). My thanks to David Hewett for sifting through these philological details.

15. Polybius does not appear to use a single term to describe these transformations, but often employs *metabolē*: see e.g., 6.4.8–12, 6.5.1, 6.9.12–13, and passim.

16. Polyb., 6.10.7 (on the combination of best aspects; see also 6.3), and 6.14 (on the Roman people). While he does not ignore the tribunes (see e.g., 6.12 or 6.16), Polybius does not discuss them in this section. On the accuracy of Polybius's description: Lintott, *Constitution*, chap. 3. Livy similarly insists on the continuity between the consuls and the kings (*AUC* 2.1).

17. Atkins, *Cicero on Politics*, 92.

18. Polyb., 6.12 (on the consuls), 6.13 and 6.16 (on the senate), 6.14 (on the people).

19. See especially M.J.C. Vile, who argues that it was only in the seventeenth century that the theory of balanced constitution "brought forth a new and different theory, the separation of powers" (*Constitutionalism*, 42). I return to this question, and Montesquieu more specifically, in chapter 6.

20. *Federalist*, no. 47, 304–5. On Montesquieu himself, see chapter 6. Madison was in large part responding to criticisms by Anti-Federalists that the US Constitution violated the separation of powers: see Kaminski and Leffler, *Federalists and Antifederalists*, 68.

21. Kramnick, editor's introduction to *Federalist Papers*, 53. See also Richard, *Founders and the Classics*, chap. 5; Bellamy, "Political Form," 455; Rakove, "Politics Indoors." I return to this question in chapters 6 and 7.

22. Montesquieu, *Spirit of Laws*, 157; *Esprit des lois*, 1:169.

23. Polyb., 6.18.7–8 (translation modified). "Equilibrium" here translates the verb *emménō*, whose meaning is closer to "fix" or "stabilize" (hence the Loeb translation: "All in fact remains *in statu quo*").

24. See e.g., in Plato: in Sparta, "owing to its being blended of the right elements and possessed of due measure, the kingship not only survived itself but ensured the survival of all else" (*Leg.* 3.691d–692a; "blended": *symmeiktos*); Aristotle: "The better the constitution is mixed, the more permanent it is" (*Pol.* 4.1297a; "mixed": *mígnumi*).

25. Polyb., 6.10.7 (the Spartan constitution is "in equilibrium and balanced" [*isorropoūn kai sygostatoūmenon*]). Plato had used *isórropo* in *Timaeus* (52e), but

in reference to the natural world. On the distinction between mixed and balanced constitutions: Nippel, *Mischverfassungstheorie*, 19n2; Straumann, *Crisis and Constitutionalism*, 152.

26. In an informative article, David Wootton proposes a contrary reading: "Polybius is still thinking of a simple balance between two equal forces, not of some complex balance between multiple forces." But Wootton, who comments only on the passage in book 6, chapter 10, does not consider the self-evidently dynamic account of how the *three* forces of the Roman Republic interact with one another in book 6, chapter 17, nor does he discuss Polybius's prophetic vision of how the republic will ultimately fall (Polyb., 6.57.6). See Wootton, "Liberty, Metaphor, and Mechanism," 223.

27. See Loehr, "People's Moral Emotions"; Polyb., 6.7–10 (for *systema*, 6.10.14).

28. For the quote: Polyb., 6.10.7. I return to Polybius's prophetic account of the fall of Rome below.

29. Polyb., 6.18.8; see also 6.10.8 (describing how kingship was "restrained" [*kōluoménes*] in Sparta).

30. "It is possible that Toland is the source of later usages of 'checks and balances,'" suggests Wootton, laying a somewhat less direct emphasis on Polybius, though he acknowledges that Toland's use of this phrase "led directly to an appeal to the authority of Polybius": "Liberty, Metaphor, and Mechanism," 244, and n106. Wootton also cites the examples from Spelman and Adams that I discuss in this paragraph. The phrase "check and balance" appeared in Civil War literature: see e.g., Fairfax, *Declaration*, 5 ("notwithstanding such an Army as this to checke and ballance them in behalf of the Kingdom and Parliament"). I could not find any earlier examples in EEBO.

31. Nedham, *True State of the Case*, 10. Nedham was familiar with Polybius, referencing book 6 in *The Case of the Common-Wealth of England Stated* (96). Wootton does not discuss this earlier source. See chapter 5 for a more detailed discussion of Nedham.

32. I.e., Polyb., 6.18.7–8.

33. Toland, *Art of Governing*, 31, 33.

34. Polybius, *Fragment*, iv.

35. Wootton argues that it was Adams who "popularized" the phrase "checks and balances": "Liberty, Metaphor, and Mechanism," 212; and see chapter 7.

36. *Federalist*, no. 51.

37. Arist., *Pol.* 3.1281a, 4.1299a; see chapter 1.

38. Polyb., 6.11–14. Machiavelli reached the same conclusion, in his rewriting of Polybius: "In one and the same city [Rome], there are the principality, the aristocrats, and the popular government" (*Discourses*, 1.2.5, p. 13).

39. Cic., *Rep.* 2.42.

40. Atkins and Young, "Polybius." See also Polyb., 6.51.2 (on the Carthaginian constitution).

41. Bodin, *Easy Comprehension of History*, 179.

42. See chapter 7.

43. Polyb., 6.47 (on customs and laws, *ethi kai nómoi*), 6.53 (on funeral rites), 6.56 (on elections and religion). See Walbank, *Historical Commentary on Polybius*, 1:741; Lintott, *Constitution*, 22–23. Aristotle had similarly called attention to the importance of customs, philosophy, and laws (*ethi, philosophia, nómoi*), but provided only a single example (the public messes of Crete and Sparta): *Pol.* 2.1263b.

44. Polyb., 6.50.3 (and for the comparison with Sparta, 6.48–50); Machiavelli, *Discorsi*, 2.3.

45. Polyb., 6.57.6; Loehr, "People's Moral Emotions," 173–76. Cf. also Polybius's similar account of the decline of the Carthaginian constitution (6.51.6).

46. The section in book 6 where Polybius discussed the origins of the Roman Republic is lost, though he does allude in one passage to the "expulsion" (*katalysin*) of the Roman kings: Polyb., 3.22.1.

47. Sall., *Iug.* 8.1. See also 41–2 (on the aftermath of the Punic Wars).

48. App., *B Civ.* 1.9.82.

49. On Cicero and Polybius: Atkins, *Cicero on Politics*, chap. 3.

50. Livy, *AUC* 4.9.3.

51. Sall., *Cat.* 39.6; see also Cic., *Cat.* 1.1.3; Livy, *AUC* 1.52.1, 4.13.6, and passim. *Novae res* was likely a translation of the Greek *neōterízō*, which could also have the sense of revolution: see e.g., Hdt., 1.210.2–3; Thuc., 1.115.2; Pl., *Resp.* 8.555d; Arist., *Pol.* 2.1262b.

52. Livy, *AUC* 6.18.3 (on Manlius's "revolutionary plans," or *novandarum rerum*), 6.20.3 ("the first man to go over from the patricians to the plebs").

53. Montesquieu, *Spirit of Laws*, e.g., 3.3.

54. Cic., *Rep.* 1.69.

55. Cic., *Rep.* 1.44–45; see also 1.69 (Loeb 69–71, 105). Straumann, *Crisis and Constitutionalism*; Atkins, *Cicero on Politics*.

56. Cic., *Rep.* 2.69; quoted in Augustine, *City of God*, 2.21.

57. Polyb., 6.10.11, 6.48.2–5. More generally, see Kurt Raaflaub's *Discovery of Freedom in Ancient Greece*.

58. See e.g., Hdt. 1.95.2. For Pericles's identification of freedom and democracy: Thuc., 2.37.1–2. *Eleutheria* is more commonly associated in Thucydides with *autonomia*: see e.g., 3.46.5. Both Aristotle and Polybius recognize, but reject, the exclusive democratic claim to freedom: see *Pol.* 5.1310a33 and Polyb., 6.57.9, respectively. Most recently, see Annelien de Dijn's *Freedom: An Unruly History*.

59. Cic., *Rep.* 1.44, 1.53 (Loeb 71, 81). On the identification of liberty and democracy, see 1.47. More generally: Arena, *Libertas*.

60. Cic., *Rep.* 1.69 (Loeb 104).

Chapter Three

1. Cic., *Rep.* 1.45: "mirique sunt orbes et quasi circumitus in rebus publicis commutationum et vicissitudinum" (Loeb 71).

2. Augustine, *City of God*, 22.12: "after passing through many different bodies" (post multas per diuersa corpora reuolutiones), English translation, 1141. See also *Oxford Latin Dictionary* (Oxford: Oxford University Press, 2012), s.v. "reuoluo."

3. "Touz jours feront li corps celestre / Selon leurs revolucions": *Roman de la rose*, Douce ms 322, ll. 17476–77 (Johns Hopkins Sheridan Libraries, Digital Library of Medieval Manuscripts, https://dlmm.library.jhu.edu/en/digital-library-of-medieval-manuscripts/). See also *Trésor de la langue*, s.v. "révolution."

4. *Romaunt of the Rose*, ll. 4354–66, fol. 84v–85r (University of Glasgow, Digitisation of Middle English Manuscripts, The Hunterian Collection, https://www.gla.ac.uk/myglasgow/library/files/special/Rose/, with modernized English spelling and

grammar). See also *Oxford English Dictionary*, s.v. "revolution (n.)," December 2023, https://doi.org/10.1093/OED/1140385503.

5. See notably Arendt, *On Revolution*, 32; Gilbert, "Revolution"; Koselleck, "Historical Criteria," 46.

6. The classical origins of this motif extend back much further. Herodotus reported that Croesus gave the following advice to Cyrus: "Disaster has been my teacher. . . . [M]en's fortunes are on a wheel [*kyklos*], which in its turning does not allow the same man to prosper [*eutychéein*, from *tyche*] forever" (Hdt., 1.207.2–3). See also Soph., *Ant.* 1158–59 ("Fortune sets upright and Fortune sinks the lucky and unlucky from day to day").

7. Boethius, *Consolation of Philosophy*, bk. 2, chap. 1, 20–22. On the parallels between Polybius's *anacyclōsis* and Fortune's wheel: Pocock, *Machiavellian Moment*, 78. See also I. Cohen, *Revolution in Science*, 58. More generally: Brendecke and Vogt, *End of Fortuna*.

8. The labels on the famous wheel of fortune illustration in the Carmina Burana manuscript at the Bavarian State Library in Munich read "regno," "regnavi," "sum sine regno," "regnabo" (I rule, I have ruled, I am without rule, I shall rule).

9. Boccaccio, *De casibus virorum illustrium*, I.7 (see also I.2, I.12, and IX.26).

10. See chapter 4.

11. Hatto, "'Revolution,'" 502; Griewank, *Der neuzeitliche Revolutionsbegriff*; Rachum, *"Revolution,"* 10, 12, 19–22, 27–28. See also Bulst et al., "Revolution (Rebellion, Aufruhr, Bürgerkrieg)."

12. Rachum, *"Revolution,"* 12–13, 27–28.

13. Machiavelli, *Prince*, chap. 26 ("in tante revoluzioni di Italia").

14. Smith, "Language of 'Political Science.'"

15. Salutati, "On Tyranny" (1400), in *Political Writings*.

16. Leonardo Bruni's translation was printed at the end of the fifteenth century as *Polybius historicus de primo bello punico* (Brixiae [Brescia]: G. Britannico, 1498). The first five books appeared as *Polybii "Historiarum" libri V*, trans. Niccolò Perotti (Rome: C. Sweynheym et A. Pannartz, 1472). On the reception history more generally: Momigliano, "Polybius's Reappearance."

17. For an earlier exception: Hankins, "Europe's First Democrat?"

18. Rucellai, *Liber de urbe Roma*, 165. Although he only alludes to the section on the Roman constitution (as opposed to the theory of *anacyclōsis*). *Contra* Dionisotti, *Machiavellerie*, 139–40. See also Black, *Machiavelli*, 134; Monfasani, "Machiavelli, Polybius," 46; J. Dymond, "Human Character." On the Orti Oricellari (or gardens), see Gilbert, "Bernardo Rucellai."

19. Aristotle, *"Politicorum" libri octo commentarii*, commentary on 3.5, fol. 42. Cf. Tuck, *Sleeping Sovereign*, 11.

20. Seyssel, *La grant monarchie*, fol.8: "mutation," "dissentiones ciuiles."

21. Pedullà, *Machiavelli in Tumult*, 43–44.

22. Machiavelli, *Discourses on Livy*, 1.2, p. 26; *Discorsi*, 25: "E questo è il cerchio nel quale girando tutte le republiche si sono governate e si governano." Machiavelli selectively paraphrases Polybius (Polyb., 6.5–9).

23. Hexter, "Seyssel, Machiavelli."

24. Monfasani, "Machiavelli, Polybius"; J. Dymond, "Human Character."

25. MS Vat. Lat. 2968, 4v: "Hic est politiarum veluti circulus." See also Reg. Lat. 1099, 15v (an illuminated manuscript).

26. Machiavelli, *Discorsi*, 1.2, 1.49, 3.3, 3.7 (on *mutazioni*); 1.10, 1.13, 1.24, 2.26, 3.26 (on *sedizione*). See Viroli, "Machiavelli"; Pasquino, "Machiavelli and Aristotle."

27. Livy, *AUC* 2.11. The story of Mucius Scaevola is also told in Plutarch's *Life of Publicola*. Machiavelli refers to it in the *Discorsi* (1.24.2 and 3.1.3). Rousseau recounts his youthful enthusiasm in *Les confessions* (38).

28. Livy, *AUC* 1.19–21; Plut., *Num.* Cf. Machiavelli, *Discorsi*, 1.11.4.

29. See e.g., Livy, *AUC* 28.44.5 (on the Carthaginians). Machiavelli mainly draws from the first ten books of Livy's *History*, but occasionally refers to later books as well: see Machiavelli, *"Discourses" of Niccolo Machiavelli*, 2:272.

30. Polyb., 1.66-88 (on the mercenary war). See Eckstein, *Moral Vision*, 125–29. Machiavelli stresses the danger of relying on mercenaries in chapter 12 of *The Prince*: "An example of the worth of ancient mercenaries is provided by the Carthaginians: they were attacked by their own mercenary troops after the first war against the Romans, despite the fact that the generals were Carthaginians" (44). In chapter 6, Machiavelli also praises Hiero of Syracuse for having "disbanded the old army and raised a new one" (22), another reference to mercenaries. Indeed, Polybius had described how Hiero dispatched with his "disaffected and mutinous" mercenaries by placing them at the front of the battle line, and allowing them to be slaughtered. He then replaced them with "citizen levies" (1.9). The books from Livy's *History* covering the first Punic War are lost (and there are very few discussions of mercenary forces in books 1–10). There are many allusions to events discussed in Polybius's first five books throughout the *Discourses*, as well: see Machiavelli, *"Discourses" of Niccolo Machiavelli*, 2:290–91.

31. In addition to the detailed description of the "cruelty and inhumanity" of the mercenaries who fought their Carthaginian employers (Polyb., 1.88), see also the problems that come from mercenaries in the Roman war with the Illyrians (e.g., Polyb., 2.7).

32. Machiavelli, *Discorsi*, 1.43 (chapter title).

33. Polyb., 6.52.

34. The Lascaris translation available in manuscript form extends only up to Polybius 6.18. He later published his translation of the middle section of book 6, on the Roman camps (see below). It is uncertain whether he translated the final third of the extracts, which return to political theory.

35. There was a codex (Pluteus LXIX) in the Laurentian Library in Florence that included extracts of book 6 in Greek: see Machiavelli, *"Discourses" of Niccolo Machiavelli*, 2:290.

36. See J. Dymond, "Human Character." Leslie Walker noted how the comparison of Rome and Sparta in the *Discorsi* (1.5–6) closely resembles Polybius's own comparison of the two in the *Histories* (6.50): see Walker's introduction to *The "Discourses" of Niccolo Machiavelli* (1:62). Indeed, Polybius already made the "Machiavellian" argument here that the Roman constitution was better suited for republics that sought to expand their territory through conquest, as opposed to republics that sought simply to remain in power over the same territory for as long as possible (see chapter 2). Walker provides a long list of other similarities here (and at 2:290–91).

37. Cf. Lintott, *Constitution*, 236–43; see also Eckstein, "Polybius and 'Machiavellianism,'" in *Moral Vision*, chap. 1. Not to belabor the point, but I am obviously drawing a distinction here with Pocock's *Machiavellian Moment*.

38. Polybius, *De militia romanorum* (*c*.1523). This translation was by Janus Lascaris, the only part of his translation of book 6 to be published.

39. Egnazio, *Le vite de gl'imperadori*.

40. Egnazio, *De Cæsaribus libri 3* (1516).

41. Egnazio, *Le vite de gl'imperadori*, n.p. (8th page of the Polybius translation): "E questo è il riuolgimento de le Republiche."

42. Rachum, *"Revolution,"* 10–28.

43. Egnazio, *Le vite de gl'imperadori*, n.p.: "nessuno meglio di voi ha inteso & veduto le cagioni de i riuolgimenti delle Republiche" (from the dedication).

44. Polybius, *Deux restes*.

45. Polybius, *Les cinq premiers livres*. Cf. Momigliano, "Polybius's Reappearance," 89.

46. Polybius, *Deux restes*, n.p.: "Voilà doncq' la reſolution des choſes publiques comme en façon de cercle."

47. *Trésor de la langue*, s.v. "résolution."

48. Polybius, *Cinq premiers livres*, fol. 287: "Voylà donq' la reuolution des polices."

49. Polybius, *Polibio "Historico" greco*.

50. Schweiger, *Handbuch der classischen Bibliographie*, s.v. "Polybius," 1:271–74. Domenichi's translation was reprinted in 1546, 1563, and 1564.

51. Polybius, *Polibio "Historico" greco*, fol. 306: "Questa è la riuolution delle Republiche quasi in un cerchio; questa è la naturale dispensatione di quelle con laquale si mutano, et si riuolgono, & di nuouo ritornano col medesimo ordine."

52. E.g., Polybius, fol. 302: "riuolutione delle republiche."

53. Musculus's edition was reprinted in Lyon (1554), Basel (1557), and Geneva (1597, 1608).

54. Polybius, *Polybii Megalopolitani "Historiarum,"* 199: "Hæc est illa politiarum reuolutio, hæc natura œconomia, secundum quam Reipublicæ status mutatur & transfertur, ac rursus in idem reuoluitur." See Hexter, "Seyssel, Machiavelli," 76n8; Momigliano, "Polybius's Reappearance," 89.

55. Polybius, *Polybii Megalopolitani "Historiarum,"* 197: "mutationes."

56. Polybius, index, s.v. "politiarum tria genera": "reuolutiones ac mutationes."

57. Polybius, *Römische "Historien,"* 328.

58. Bulst et al., "Revolution (Rebellion, Aufruhr, Bürgerkrieg)," 681–85.

59. Polybius, *De "Historie,"* 379.

60. See Van Gelderen, *Political Thought*; see also Van Gelderen's edition of contemporary tracts, collected in *The Dutch Revolt*. The earliest reference to the Dutch Revolt as a revolution that I could find is *Historical Remarques upon the Late Revolutions in the United Provinces Drawn from Their Own Papers* (1675); see also Pierre Jurieu, *Histoire du calvinisme*, 258 ("l'Europe ne vît rien dans le sîecle passé de plus considérable que cette grande révolution laquelle arriva dans les Pays bas").

61. Momigliano, "Polybius's Reappearance," 93.

62. Polybius, *Polybii Lycortæ F. Megalopolitani*, 458B: "Hic orbis est quo in sese Respublicæ reuoluuntur." See also the index, s.v. "Orbis quo Resp. reuoluuntur." More generally: Grafton and Weinberg, *I Have Always Loved*.

63. D. Giannotti, *Della repubblica fiorentina*, 20, 120: "mutazione dello Stato." On Giannotti: Pocock, *Machiavellian Moment*, 292–302; Blythe, *Ideal Government*, 297–300; Rachum, *"Revolution,"* 29–30.

64. In Cavalcanti, *Trattati overo discorsi*, quote at fol. 8: "il riuolgimento delle Republiche quasi in un cerchio col quale si sono gouvernate."

65. Le Roy, *De la vicissitude*, 14.

66. Scaino, *"La politica" di Aristotile*, fol. 148: "seditioni," "mutamenti," "riuolutioni delle citta."

67. Scaino, fol. 188, and fol. 38 (fourth discourse): "riuolutioni civili."

68. Rachum, *"Revolution,"* 40.

69. Corio, *Historia continente* (1503): "le reuolutioni de quasi tutta l'Italia." Cf. *L'historia di Milano* (1554). Discussed in Rachum, *"Revolution,"* 34 (without mention of the Polybius translations).

70. Pigna, *Historia de principi*: "riuolutione del Romano Imperio."

71. Sale, *Parafrasi delle leggi.*

72. Giorgio Benzone, writing the continuation to Pietro Marcello's *Vite de' prencipi di Vinegia*: "Tante riuolutioni di stati in Italia" (189). Marcello's work, *De uitis principum et gestis Venetorum compendium*, was originally published in 1502.

73. Nannini, *Orationi militari*, 266: "riuolutioni de gli stati."

74. Botero, *Della ragione di stato*, 96, 138: "riuolutioni degli Stati." *Contra* Rachum, *"Revolution,"* 32.

75. Spontone, *Dodici libri*, 9.5, 253: "reuolutione d'uno Stato."

76. Rachum, *"Revolution,"* 35. *Vocabolario degli Accademici*, s.v. "revoluzione": "più proprio degli stati, che d'altro."

77. For some examples of this genre: Quartiermastro, *Relatione delle rivolutioni*; G. Giannotti, *Parere di Gasparo Giannotti*; Assarino, *Delle riuolutioni di Catalogna*; Giraffi, *Le riuolutioni di Napoli*. This text went through multiple editions, and was also translated into English: see Giraffi, *Exact Historie*, and chapter 7.

78. See e.g., Greenblatt, *Swerve.*

79. See chapter 1.

Chapter Four

1. Plut., *Aem.* 27.1–2; Polyb., 39.5 (on Scipio).

2. Polyb., 1.4.1. See Walbank, "Fortune (*tychē*) in Polybius."

3. Aesch., *PV* l.510.

4. Augustine, *City of God*, 164–65; *De civ. D.* 4.18. More generally: Markus, *Saeculum*; Miano, *Fortuna.*

5. Chestnut, *First Christian Histories*, chaps. 3 and 7; McGinn, "Introduction."

6. Augustine develops this metaphor in an earlier work, *On Order [De ordine]* (1.2; p. 5).

7. Augustine: "From the evil use of free will there arose the whole series of calamities by which the human race is led by a succession of miseries from its depraved origin, as from a corrupt root, even to the ruin of the second death, which has no end" (*City of God*, 556; *De civ. D.* 13.14). As Hannah Arendt summarized, "Secular history in the Christian view remained bound within the cycles of antiquity—empires would rise and fall as in the past" (*On Revolution*, 17). See also Markus, *Saeculum*; Chestnut,

First Christian Histories; Coyle, "Augustine and Apocalyptic"; Landes, "Fear of an Apocalyptic Year"; McQueen, *Political Realism*, chap. 2.

8. Markus, *Saeculum*, chap. 1; Spiegel, "Structures of Time." On Boethius, see chapter 4.

9. Augustine, *City of God*, 1161; *De civ. D.* 22.24; quoted and discussed in Nisbet (*History of the Idea*, 54–64). Nisbet claims that Augustine's acknowledgment of past progress in book 22 "could have been written by . . . a Condorcet or Godwin in the eighteenth century" (54).

10. L. Edelstein, *Idea of Progress*.

11. Cic., *De orat.* 1.33 ("aut a fera agrestique vita ad hunc humanum cultum civilemque deducere"). Cicero may have been echoing here Theseus's speech in Euripides's *The Suppliants* (l.201–10: "He has my praise, whichever god brought us to live by rule from chaos and from brutishness, first by implanting reason, and next by giving us a tongue to declare our thoughts, so as to know the meaning of what is said").

12. Lucr., 5.330–33 ("nunc artes expoliuntur, nunc etiam augescunt"), 5.1446–47 ("nisi qua ratio vestigia monstrat").

13. Lucr., 5.1452–53 (translation modified).

14. See Blumenberg, "On a Lineage"; more generally, chapter 7.

15. Lucr., 5.1456–57 (translation modified). See Ludwig Edelstein's analysis of this passage: "This last sentence can mean only that all arts have a measure of perfection beyond which it is impossible to go; and so Lucretius cannot have believed in a general law of progress, in the continuous advance of the arts and sciences throughout the ages to come" (*Idea of Progress*, 163).

16. Cic., *Brut.* 70–71. See also Cic., *Inv.* 1.2–3.

17. Gombrich, "Debate on Primitivism," 29. See also Lovejoy and Boas, *Primitivism*.

18. As Ludwig Edelstein notes, Seneca makes the point that *knowledge* can increase indefinitely: see Sen., *Ep.* 64.7–8, and L. Edelstein, *Idea of Progress*, 169–78. Edelstein goes on to compare Seneca to Condorcet (175), but to my mind this comparison misses a critical difference, which is that progress for the moderns is never merely scientific/epistemological.

19. Hes., *Op.* 140–70. See also Ov., *Met.* 1.89–150.

20. See Arist., *Pol.* 2.1268b–69a. On *mos maiorum*, see e.g., Cic., *Off.* 1.35.

21. See e.g., Löwith, *Meaning in History*; Cohn, *Pursuit of the Millennium*. This argument remains popular: see e.g., Ackerman, *Revolutionary Constitutions*, 27; Satia, *Time's Monster*, 28.

22. Revelations 20:4–5.

23. Cohn in particular focuses on Joachim, in *Pursuit of the Millennium*.

24. Loewen, *Luther and the Radicals*, chap. 5; Haude, *In the Shadow*; Arthur, *Tailor-King*.

25. Rogers, *Fifth Monarchy Men*; Daniel 7:22–27. I return to this group in chapter 5.

26. See also Walzer, *Revolution of the Saints*; more generally, McQueen, *Political Realism*.

27. See e.g., Montaigne, "On the Education of Children," in *Essays*.

28. See chapter 10.

29. The most famous proponent of this view is Carl Becker, in *The Heavenly City of the EIghteenth-Century Philosophes*.

30. Vir., *Aen.* 6.792–93 ("aurea condet saecula").

31. Levin, *Myth of the Golden Age*; and see chapter 10.

Part II

1. Locke, *Two Treatises of Government, Second Treatise*, §223.

2. See Peter Laslett's introduction to Locke's *Two Treatises of Government.*

3. See Pocock, *Three British Revolutions.* Both Bernard Bailyn's *Ideological Origins of the American Revolution* and John Pocock's *Machiavellian Moment* already pointed to continuities between the English Civil War, the Glorious Revolution, and the American Revolution. By omission, Pocock's *Machiavellian Moment* also suggested that the French Revolution was not part of the tradition he was excavating.

4. Palmer, *Age of the Democratic Revolution*; Arendt, *On Revolution*; more recently, Armitage and Subrahmanyam, *Age of Revolutions*; Israel, *Expanding Blaze*; Klooster, *Revolutions in the Atlantic*; Motadel, *Revolutionary World*; Perl-Rosenthal, *Age of Revolutions.*

5. Brinton, *Anatomy of Revolution*; Pincus, *1688*; Scott, *Old World Ended.*

6. *Contra* Arendt: "The stage was set for revolutions in the modern sense of a complete change of society, when John Adams, more than a decade before the actual outbreak of the American Revolution, could state: 'I always consider the settlement of America as the opening of a grand scheme and design in Providence'" (*On Revolution*, 13). I offer an alternative history of this "modern sense" in chapters 8 and 9.

Chapter Five

1. T. Harris, *Restoration*; Baker, "Revolution 1.0," 192.

2. Manin, *Principles of Representative Government*, 86–88; also Post, *Medieval Legal Thought*; Elton, *Body of the Whole*; Boucoyannis, *Kings as Judges*; Grzymała-Busse, *Sacred Foundations.*

3. For a comparison of the English Parliament with continental estates: Elton, *Body of the Whole*, 20–32.

4. Aylmer, *Harborovve.* Discussed in Weston, *English Constitutional Theory.* See also Vile, *Constitutionalism*, notably 41–42; Mendle, *Dangerous Positions.*

5. Arist., *Pol.* 2.1270b20. See Blythe, *Ideal Government*, esp. chap. 3.

6. Blythe, *Ideal Government*, esp. chap. 3.

7. Seyssel, *La grant monarchie* (1519); in the seventeenth century, these judges gained the right to acquire noble status as well (creating the so-called *noblesse de robe*, as opposed to the older *noblesse d'épée*). More generally: Hexter, "Seyssel, Machiavelli."

8. Weston noted Alymer's familiarity with Polybius: *English Constitutional Theory*, 9–12. That said, the only explicit reference I found in *Harborovve* to "Poly." was on the struggle "betwixt the Romains and Carthagiens" over Sicily, which does not entail any knowledge of book 6 (marginal note, two pages after Q3).

9. Ponet, *Short Treatise*, 6; quoted and discussed in Fink, *Classical Republicans*, 22–23; see also Vile, *Constitutionalism*, 41.

10. Hayward, *Ansvver*, n.p. Discussed in Weston, "Beginnings," 142n41.

11. Polybius, *"History" of Polybius*, 287. Two further print runs/editions appeared in 1634; a second and third edition were printed in 1648 and 1673, respectively. Earlier translations of Polybius into English did not include book 6.

12. Cromartie, *Constitutionalist Revolution*, chap. 8.

13. See the "Root and Branch" petition, which sought to remove bishops from the Church of England: Cromartie, *Constitutionalist Revolution*, 256–57.

14. By contrast, a petition that suggested that the "temporal" lords in the upper chamber sit with the Commons was regarded as "horrible": see Como, *Radical Parliamentarians*, 115–16 (and 91–96 on the legislative effort to exclude the bishops from the House of Lords).

15. See Cromartie, *Constitutionalist Revolution*, 260–61.

16. *The Grand Remonstrance*, in Gardiner, *Constitutional Documents*, 206.

17. Weston, *English Constitutional Theory*, 16 (on its explicitly Polybian elements, 18); Vile, *Constitutionalism*, 43–44; Pocock, *Machiavellian Moment*, chap. 11; Mendle, *Dangerous Positions*.

18. Colepeper, *His Majesties Answer*, 17–18. Colepeper had voted for the bill of attainder against the Earl of Strafford, Charles I's close advisor: see Cromartie, *Constitutionalist Revolution*, 259 (and on the *Answer*, 265).

19. Colepeper, *His Majesties Answer*, 18–19. In his English translation of Polybius, Grimeston had used "hinder" to render the famous passage (6.18.8, featuring the verb *kōluō*) that later commentators and translators would turn into "check and balance": "the Enterprize of either of them may be mutually restrained and hindred, so as none of them can fly off, nor aduance it selfe" (Polybius, *"History" of Polybius*, 291–92). On these later translations, see chapter 3.

20. Pocock, *Machiavellian Moment*, 363. Pocock credits this imagery to Machiavelli, though the *Answer* draws directly on Polybius book 6.

21. Colepeper, *His Majesties Answer*, 22. While the *Answer* does not use the word "revolution," it clearly had this danger in mind: "this kinde of regulated Monarchie . . . is intended to draw to him such a Respect and Relation from the great Ones, as may hinder the ills of Division and Faction, and such a Fear and Reverence from the people, as may hinder Tumults, Violence, and Licenciousnesse" (18).

22. Henry Parker, *Observations*, 40 (on republican Rome), 21 (on the English constitution), 41 (on royal prerogative). See Mendle, *Dangerous Positions*, 130.

23. Prynne, *Soveraigne Povver of Parliaments*, notably the appendix; Hunton, *Treatise on Monarchie*, 25, discussed in Fink, *Classical Republicans*, 25. See Weston, *English Constitutional Theory*, 28.

24. Bodin, *Easy Comprehension of History*, 178 ("what Polybius affirmed ought . . . to seem absurd—that the sovereignty of the state was partly in the people, partly in the senate, partly in the consuls").

25. Filmer, *Anarchy*, 1, quoted in Vile, *Constitutionalism*, 42. See also Fink, *Classical Republicans*, 47–48.

26. See Skinner, *Foundations*, 2:78, and passim.

27. *An Agreement of the People for a Firme and Present Peace* (Nov. 3, 1647), in Hart and Kenyon, *Tracts on Liberty*, 4:276–85. See also Overton, *Arrow against All Tyrants*. More generally: Galligan, "Levellers"; Bejan, "Point of Equality."

28. *Declaration of the Rights of Man and of the Citizen*, art. 1. More generally: Edelstein, *Spirit of Rights*.

29. Woodhouse, *Puritanism and Liberty*, 52.

30. Hill, "Word 'Revolution,'"; T. Harris, "Did the English."

31. Gillespie, *Sermon*. See Como, "God's Revolutions"; Bucholz and Key, *Early Modern England*, 267; more generally: McQueen, *Political Realism*.

32. General Assembly of the Church of Scotland, *Reverend Brethren*, 1.

33. See e.g., Beech, *Englands Present Distempers*; see also Goodwin, *Synkrētismos*.

34. Nedham, *Case of the Common-Wealth*, title of chap. 1.

35. Armitage, "Every Great Revolution."

36. Nedham, *True State of the Case*, 4 (emphasis added).

37. Nedham, 1–2.

38. Nedham, *Case of the Common-Wealth*, 4.

39. Lilburne, *Englands New Chains Discovered*: "You have done the Nation so much right, and yourselves so much honour as to declare that the People (under God) are the original of all just Powers" (1).

40. Nedham, *Case of the Common-Wealth*, 80–81 (on democracy), 83–85 (on the multitude), 92 (on the comparison with the Roman Republic). See Zagorin, *History of Political Thought*.

41. An Act of this Present Parliament for Constituting a Counsell of State for the Comonwealth of England, art. 2: "You are hereby authorised and impoured to order and direct, all the Militias and forces both by Sea and Land of England, and Ireland, and the Dominions to them or eyther of them belonging, preserving the peace or safety thereof, and for preventing, resisting and suppressing all tumults and insurrections that shall happen to rise in them or eyther of them, or any invasions of them from abroad" ("February 1649").

42. Elton, *Body of the Whole*," 32.

43. Nedham, *Case of the Common-Wealth*, 88. Cf. Colepeper, *His Majesties Answer*, on the House of Lords: "an excellent Screen and Bank between the Prince and People" (19). *His Majesties Answer* had also stated that "the good of Democracy is Liberty" (18), a classical argument found notably in Aristotle's *Politics* (5.1310a); see also Hunton, *Treatise on Monarchie*.

44. I return to this brief experiment in the following section.

45. Woolrych, *Commonwealth to Protectorate*.

46. Nedham, *True State of the Case*, 10. On the Instrument of Government, see notably Vile's *Constitutionalism and the Separation of Powers* (52–53). Nedham had previously insisted that "Freedom consists in a due and orderly Succession of the Supreme Assemblies," drawing a comparison between Parliament and Roman plebeian assemblies. But the new position of Lord Protector demanded a different justification (*Excellencie of a Free-State*, 19). Although this text was published in 1656, it is a collection of earlier pieces that Nedham had published in *Mercurius Politicus*. The description of freedom cited here was first published in 1651.

47. In this text, Vile claims, "we find the doctrine of the separation of powers standing on its own feet, claiming to be the only true basis for a constitutional government" (*Constitutionalism*, 52).

48. Nedham, *True State of the Case*, 10. This passage is notable for its use of this expression in a constitutional sense: see Wootton, "Liberty, Metaphor, and Mechanism"; see also the discussion in chapter 2.

49. Nedham, *True State of the Case*, 11. Cf. Vile, who contends that Nedham's argument in this text "was almost completely stripped of the paraphernalia of mixed government" (*Constitutionalism*, 55).

50. Again, my reading is opposed here to Vile, who claims that "the execution of the King, and the abolition of the House of Lords, destroyed the institutional basis of the theory of mixed government, and any justification of the new constitution which was to be framed for England would have to rest upon a different theoretical basis" (*Constitutionalism*, 53).

51. Nedham, *True State of the Case*, 51–52.

52. Vile, *Constitutionalism*, 55.

53. Allen, *Killing Noe Murder*. The second Protectorate also dramatically raised the property qualifications of English voters: see Bucholz and Key, *Early Modern England*, 272. On the Humble Petition: Cromartie, *Constitutionalist Revolution*, 273.

54. Milton, *Readie & Easie Way*, 22, 57. On Milton: Fink, *Classical Republicans*, 95; Armitage, Himy, and Skinner, *Milton and Republicanism*. See also Nedham, *Excellencie of a Free-State*, 23.

55. "The ground and basis of every just and free government (since men have smarted so oft for committing all to one person) is a general Councel of ablest men, chosen by the people to consult of publick affairs from time to time for the common good" (Milton, *Readie & Easie Way*, 44).

56. Harrington, *Commonwealth of Oceana*, 15. On Harrington and Polybius: Fink, *Classical Republicans*, 81, 155, and passim; Pocock, *Machiavellian Moment*, 387, and passim.

57. Hobbes, *Leviathan*, 2.29.

58. Nedham cites Polybius book 6 in *Case of the Common-Wealth of England* (96), but the anecdote he refers to is actually found in book 8 (the poisoning of Aratus: Polyb., 8.14).

59. Brinton, *Anatomy of Revolution*.

60. Especially, in the French case, after the suspension of the constitution, in October 1793: see chapter 9.

61. Cic., *Leg*. 3.8.

62. Cromartie, *Constitutionalist Revolution*, 272.

63. I discuss Lenin's "dual power" theory, and its application to the French Revolution, in chapter 10.

64. Nedham, *Case of the Common-wealth*, 99.

65. Rogers, *Fifth Monarchy Men*; Capp, *Fifth Monarchy Men*.

66. Nedham, *True State of the Case*, 18.

Chapter Six

1. Duport, *Three Sermons*, n.p. See Tim Harris, *Restoration* and "Did the English," 28.

2. Fage, *Cosmography*, 48.

3. Charles II, *Two Gracious Letters*, n.p.

4. Prynne, *First and Second Part*, 90–91.

5. "Proposals Humbly Offered to the Lords and Commons in the present Convention, for Settling of the Government, &c.," in *Collection of Papers Relating to the Present Juncture*, n.p. I could not find any reference to *His Majesties Answer* in the proceedings of the 1660 Parliament. It is possible that the enthusiastic member of Parliament was extrapolating from Charles's letter.

6. Speech of Oct. 13, 1675 ("To establish a right Understanding between Himself [the king] and his Three Estates, and between the Estates themselves . . ."), in *History and Proceedings of the House of Commons*, 235 (see also 202).

7. University of Oxford, *Judgment and Decree*, 3, 7. See Goldie, "English System of Liberty."

8. See e.g., R.B., *Wars in England*. On the "late Troubles": Corporation Act (1661), in Kenyon, *Stuart Constitution*, 351. More generally: Tim Harris, "Did the English," 29.

9. "The King's Particular Speech to the Commons Alone," Feb. 28, 1662, in *History and Proceedings of the House of Commons*, 52.

10. See also the April 13, 1675, speech by Finch to both Houses of Parliament: "A Difference in Matters of State wou'd gratify our Enemies too . . . that hope to see, and practice to bring about Revolutions in the Government," in *History and Proceedings of the House of Commons*, 204.

11. Sidney, *Discourses concerning Government*, 1.19, p. 186.

12. "The histories of Greece, Sicily, and Italy shew that all those who made themselves tyrants in several places, did it by the help of the worst, and the slaughter of the best" (Sydney, 1.19). Baker, *Inventing the French Revolution*, 206.

13. *Pol.* 4.1293b; Hansen, "Mixed Constitution," 519. Cicero expresses a similar view about the unconstitutionality of tyranny (*Rep.* 2.48). The Athenian assembly passed a law legalizing (even mandating) tyrannicide: see Teegarden, *Death to Tyrants!*

14. Milton, *Defence of the People*, 132. In the original Latin (*Defensio pro populo Anglicano*, 1651), Milton quotes the Casaubon translation: *Polybii Lycortae F. Megalopolitani* (456D = Polyb. 6.7.9). Sidney also lists Polybius among "all the ancient Grecians, Italians, and others, who asserted the natural freedom of mankind" (*Discourses concerning Government*, 1.5, p. 18).

15. See Peter Laslett's introduction to Locke's *Two Treatises of Government*; see also Ashcraft, *Revolutionary Politics*.

16. Locke, *Two Treatises of Government, Second Treatise*, §202.

17. Kenyon, *Stuart Constitution*, 392–93.

18. "The King's Letter from Breda to the House of Commons" and "The Commons Reply," in *History and Proceedings of the House of Commons*, 3. The Commons did not pass up on the chance to quote this line back to Charles in its response.

19. Tapsell, *Personal Rule*.

20. Pincus, *1688*, chap. 7.

21. Tim Harris, *Revolution*.

22. "Invitation to William," in E. N. Williams, *Eighteenth-Century Constitution*, 8–10. On the Sidney brothers' relationship: Scott, "Unfinished Family Business."

23. "Declaration of Reasons" and "Directions for Electing the Convention," in E. N. Williams, *Eighteenth-Century Constitution*, 10–16, 18–19; see also Tim Harris, *Revolution*.

24. Pincus, *1688*, 33 (on revolutions and modernization), quotes at 474–75. Tim Harris also insists on Scottish and Irish dimensions in *Revolution*.

25. Syme, *Roman Revolution.*

26. E. N. Williams, *Eighteenth-Century Constitution*, 3.

27. See Burke, "Speech on the Army Estimates of 1790, and on the French Revolution," in *Writings and Speeches*, 292 ("not made"), and *Reflections on the Revolution*, 27 ("not in future revolutions"). See Bourke, *Empire and Revolution*, 613–25 (esp. 621–22).

28. "Proposals Humbly Offered to the Lords and Commons in the Present Convention, for Settling of the Government, &c.," "A Protestant Precedent Offer'd to the Bishops for the Exclusion of K. *James* the Second," and "A Letter to a Member of the Convention," in *Collection of Papers Relating to the Present Juncture.* More generally: Baker, "Revolution 1.0," 194.

29. "Proposals Humbly Offered to the Lords and Commons."

30. Tim Harris, *Revolution*, chap. 7.

31. "An Answer to the Desertion Discuss'd," in *Collection of Papers Relating to the Present Juncture.* There is a lively debate among historians over the extent to which the Glorious Revolution altered the English constitution. For a summary of the literature: Cox, "Glorious Revolution."

32. Tim Harris, *Revolution*, chap. 8.

33. See e.g., [Cary and Atwood?], *Answer to Mr. Molyneux*, 109, 121.

34. S. Johnson, *Dictionary* (1766), s.v. "Revolution": "Change in the state of a government or country. It is used among us . . . for the change produced by the admission of king William and queen Mary" (third definition).

35. Edie, "Revolution."

36. "Coronation Oaths (Old and New), 1685 and 1689," in E. N. Williams, *Eighteenth-Century Constitution*, 37. See Selinger, *Parliamentarism*; Lieberman, "Mixed Constitution," 321–24; Goldsworthy, *Parliamentary Sovereignty*, chap. 2.

37. "Proposals Humbly Offered to the Lords and Commons," in *Collection of Papers Relating to the Present Juncture.*

38. *Contra* Vile, who argues that these two theories are "logically quite distinct" from each other, and suggests that the separation of powers doctrine gradually eclipsed ideas of mixed government: see *Constitutionalism*, 36, and passim. I return to this point below.

39. Lieberman, "Mixed Constitution," 325–31.

40. Blackstone, introduction to *Commentaries on the Laws*, §2; 1:51.

41. Kenyon, *Revolution Principles.*

42. Ayres, *Classical Culture*, 5; Lieberman, "Mixed Constitution," 319.

43. Toland, *Art of Governing*, 31.

44. Swift, *Discourse*, 9. Adams would quote extensively from this text (including this passage) in his *Defence of the Constitutions* (1.4; in *Works*, 4:383).

45. Mackworth, *Vindication*: "To the Right Honourable the Lords Spiritual and Temporal," n.p,, and chap. 1 (2–3); see Vile, *Constitutionalism*, 75–76.

46. Joseph Addison, *Spectator*, no. 287 (Jan. 29, 1712), quoted in Ayres, *Classical Culture*, 9–10.

47. Quoted in Fink, *Classical Republicans*, 189. Blackstone echoed this description in the introduction to his *Commentaries on the Laws*: §2 (quoting Cicero on the "triple" constitution), 1:50–51; on the "mutual check" of the three "constituent parts"

of Parliament, see 1.2.2 (p. 155). More generally: Goldie, "English System of Liberty," 40–41; Lieberman, "Mixed Constitution," 318.

48. Bolingbroke, *Dissertation upon Parties*, letter 13, 125 ("mixture"), 127 ("best form," with reference to Tac., *Ann.* 4.33), 128–29 ("refinements," "monarchical power"), letter 11, 107 ("Rome triumphed"). Blackstone quotes the same Tacitus passage, and makes a similar observation about the superiority of the English over the Roman constitution: *Commentaries on the Laws*, §2, 1:50. In addition to the studies cited above, see also: Kramnick, *Bolingbroke and His Circle*; Skjönsberg, *Persistence of Party.*

49. Bolingbroke, *Dissertation upon Parties*, 96 ("balance of powers"), 127 ("happy temperament"). See also Mackworth: "The Three several Powers Vested in the King, Lords and Commons, are like the Three Perfect Conchords in Musick, which being exactly Tun'd to one another, upon proper Instruments, make admirable Harmony; but if you stretch any one String, beyond its proper pitch, you put all out of Tune, and destroy the whole Consort" (*Vindication*, 6).

50. Bolingbroke, *Dissertation upon Parties*, letter 9, 82 ("altered"), letter 16, 154 ("Saxon constitution"), letter 12, 114 ("lawless power"). See Spadafora, *Idea of Progress*, 16.

51. Bolingbroke, *Dissertation upon Parties*, letter 12, 116.

52. See art. 1, § 1; art 2, § 1; and art. 3, § 1 of the US Constitution. For the French Declaration, see art. 16: "Any society in which the guarantee of rights is not secured, nor the separation of powers determined, has no constitution."

53. Shackleton, "Montesquieu, Bolingbroke" and *Montesquieu.*

54. Montesquieu, *Esprit des lois*, 11.6, 1:168–79; *Spirit of Laws*, 156–66. For a survey of some of the debates surrounding Montesquieu's political thought: Dijn, "Was Montesquieu a Liberal." More generally: Spector, *Montesquieu*; Craiutu, *Virtue for Courageous Minds*, chap. 2.

55. On Montesquieu and Locke: Vile, *Constitutionalism*, 83, 94; Derathé, in Montesquieu, *Esprit des lois*, 1:476–78.

56. This was essentially the same argument that Nedham had made regarding the division of executive and legislative powers during the Protectorate: see chapter 5.

57. Montesquieu, *Spirit of Laws*, 157 (translation modified); *Esprit des lois*, 1:169. On the place of "bodies" here, see below. See also Derathé, in *Esprit des lois*, 1:475.

58. See Vile, *Constitutionalism*; Hansen, "Mixed Constitution," 511–12.

59. See "When legislative power is united with executive power in a single person or in a single body of the magistracy, there is no liberty," and "In most kingdoms in Europe, the government is moderate because the prince, who has the first two powers, leaves the exercise of the third to his subjects": Montesquieu, *Spirit of Laws*, 157; *Esprit des lois*, 1:169.

60. It is somewhat ambiguous whether the "moderate" monarchies that Montesquieu describes are also free. He provides a second definition of how the combination of powers can destroy liberty ("Nor is there liberty if the power of judging is not separate from legislative power and from executive power": Montesquieu, *Spirit of Laws*, 157; *Esprit des lois*, 1:169), but it is unclear whether this definition is supplemental to the first or can stand alone. As we will see, Montesquieu later grants *greater* liberty to the moderate monarchies than to Italian republics. In this regard,

he appears to endorse a gradated concept of liberty (i.e., some states are more free than others).

61. Montesquieu, *Spirit of Laws*, 162; *Esprit des lois*, 1:174. Cf. Locke, who stated more straightforwardly that in some governments the executive "has also a share in the legislative" (*Two Treatises of Government, Second Treatise*, §151).

62. See e.g., Rahe, *Montesquieu*; Pangle, *Theological Basis*.

63. *Federalist*, no. 47 (Madison), 304; and see the discussion (and comparison with Polybius) in chapter 2. See also Derathé, in Montesquieu, *Esprit des lois*, 1:475–76.

64. Russo, "Youth of Moral Life"; and E. Nelson, *Greek Tradition*, chap. 5. On the ways in which Montesquieu departs from a standard Polybian account: Spector, "Pouvoir contre pouvoir."

65. "Among the three powers of which we have spoken, that of judging is in some fashion, null. There remain only two; and . . . they need a power whose regulations temper them" (Montesquieu, *Spirit of Laws*, 160; *Esprit des lois*, 1:173).

66. Montesquieu, *Spirit of Laws*, 11.12, p. 170; *Esprit des lois*, 1:183. Vile, *Constitutionalism*, 91 ("clearly a system"). More generally: Derathé, in *Esprit des lois*, 1:477 ("Il ne me paraît pas du tout sûr que Montesquieu n'ait pas été un partisan de l'État mixte ni que son interprétation de la constitution anglaise ne soit pas orientée en ce sens"); Lieberman, "Mixed Constitution," 336; Craiutu, *Virtue for Courageous Minds*, 36–40; Spector, "Pouvoir contre pouvoir."

67. Pimentel, "Le sanctuaire vide," 121.

68. Montesquieu, *Spirit of Laws*, 11.6, p. 158; *Esprit des lois*, 1:170. See Bellamy, "Political Form," 444; for a different interpretation: Cotta, "Montesquieu."

69. See his assertion that "in the Italian republics, where the three powers are united, there is less liberty than in our monarchies" (Montesquieu, *Spirit of Laws*, 11.6, p. 157; *Esprit des lois*, 1:169). He recognizes that the powers may still be vested in separate political institutions, but because the same social class or "body" (the nobility or the people) controls all institutions, there is no actual separation.

70. "In a state there are always some people who are distinguished by birth, wealth, or honors; but if they were mixed among the people and if they had only one voice like the others, the common liberty would be their enslavement" (Montesquieu, *Spirit of Laws*, 11.6, p. 160; *Esprit des lois*, 1:172); see also chapter 1. Aristotle had suggested that the wealthier citizens should fulfill executive functions (magistracies), while the people exercised legislative and judicial power (*Pol.* 4.1290a–b). Montesquieu agreed on the judicial power but rejected the suggestion that the people enjoy legislative power, countering that this was the "great vice" of ancient republics (160).

71. Montesquieu, *Spirit of Laws*, 11.13, p. 172 (translation modified); *Esprit des lois*, 1:185.

72. See Montesquieu, *Spirit of Laws*, 4.8, p. 39, and passim (on Polybius), and 11.6, 166 ("an end"); *Esprit des lois*, 1:45 and 1:179. More generally on Polybius: Guelfucci, "Polybe et Montesquieu"; Spector, "Pouvoir contre pouvoir."

73. Lieberman, "Mixed Constitution," 336.

74. De Lolme, *Constitution of England*, 2.18, p. 305 (on Montesquieu), 2.1, p. 139 (on executive power), 2.3, p. 154 (on the legislature). Some of the material in the English translation (including the praise of Montesquieu) is missing from the original French edition, and was added later by Delolme: see Lieberman, introduction

to *Constitution of England*, xx. For the French original: De Lolme, *Constitution de l'Angleterre*, chap. 11, p. 114 (on executive power), chap. 12, p. 131 (on the *corps législatif*). See also Lieberman, "Mixed Constitution," 336–40; McDaniel, "Jean-Louis Delolme."

75. See respectively, for the English, De Lolme, *Constitution of England*, 2.1, p. 139 (equilibrium), 1.3, p. 44 (Commons), 2.3, p. 158 (Lords), 2.10, p. 193 (prerogatives); and for the French, *Constitution de l'Angleterre*, chap. 11, p. 113 ("l'équilibre entre les Pouvoirs qui gouvernent"); chap. 2, p. 28 (*contrepoids*); chap. 13, p. 140 ("balancer souvent le pouvoir du Peuple"); chap. 17, p. 174 (*contre-balancées*). This is not an exhaustive list. See also Lieberman, introduction to *Constitution of England*, xiii–xiv; Wootton, "Liberty, Metaphor, and Mechanism," 235–36.

76. De Lolme, *Constitution of England*, chap. 2.18, p. 313 (not in the original French).

77. Wilkes, *North Briton*, 266–28. See Cash, *John Wilkes*; Thomas, *John Wilkes*, chap. 7.

Chapter Seven

1. Otis, *Vindication of the Conduct*, 20.

2. Elisha Williams, *Essential Rights and Liberties*, 65. I discuss American rights regimes in *On the Spirit of Rights*.

3. *All Canada*, 3–4.

4. *Federalist*, no. 14 (Madison), 145; Locke, *Two Treatises of Government, Second Treatise*, §223.

5. Greene, *Negotiated Authorities*, 90 (and chap. 4 more generally); Pincus, *Heart of the Declaration*.

6. Bailyn, *Origins of American Politics*, esp. 21–24; Greene, *Negotiated Authorities*, chap. 7.

7. See e.g., Mayhew, *Discourse Concerning Unlimited Submission*: during the Civil War, Parliament had taken "a most righteous and glorious stand, made in defence of the natural and legal rights of the people" (44).

8. Otis, *Rights of the British Colonies*, 90.

9. Stamp Act Congress, "Declaration of Rights and Grievances" (1765), no. 5. See also E. Nelson, *Royalist Revolution*, 30.

10. E. Nelson, *Royalist Revolution*, 35–36; see also Kammen, "Meaning of Colonization"; Greene, *Negotiated Authorities*, 31.

11. Dickinson, *Constitutional Power of Great-Britain*, 368–70; discussed in E. Nelson, *Royalist Revolution*, 61.

12. George III, "Proclamation for Suppressing Rebellion," 1775.

13. R. Brown, *Revolutionary Politics in Massachusetts*.

14. John Adams, "Novanglus," in *Works*, no. 1, 4:15–16 (on "revolution principles"), no. 3, 4:33 (on "treason"), no. 6, 4:83 (for Locke).

15. John Adams to Josiah Quincy (July 29, 1775), in *Works*, 9:361; John Adams to Richard Henry Lee (Nov. 15, 1775), in *Works*, 4:186; John Adams to Patrick Henry (June 3, 1776), in *Works*, 9:386. Adams's importance in adopting and disseminating "revolution" has oddly been missed by previous historians: see e.g., Rachum,

who states that before February 1776, "nobody even dared openly to use the word 'independence,' let alone 'revolution'" (*"Revolution,"* 200).

16. Braxton, *Address to the Convention*, 8; Drayton, *Charge*, 1.

17. This claim rests on surveys of databases, including EVANS and FOUNDERS.

18. Also discussed in Wood's *Creation of the American Republic* (24).

19. John Adams to Nathanael Greene (June 22, 1776), in *Works*, 9:402.

20. John Adams to William Cushing (June 9, 1776), in *Works*, 9:391. Adams subsequently described the revolution (which, by 1777, he already dubbed "American") as "great" and "remarkable": see e.g., John Adams to Abigail Adams (July 3, 1776) and John Adams to William Gordon (April 8, 1777) on "American Revolution" (FOUNDERS).

21. John Adams to Nathanael Greene (June 22, 1776): "I hope that when we get a little over the confusions arising from the revolutions which are now taking place in the colonies, and get an American Constitution formed, something will be done" (*Works*, 9:403); see also John Adams to Jonathan Mason (July 18, 1776): "The confusions in America, inseparable from so great a revolution in affairs, are sufficient to excite anxieties in the minds of young gentlemen just stepping into life" (*Works*, 9:422–23).

22. John Adams to John Winthrop (June 23, 1776), in *Works*, 9:410.

23. John Adams to Richard Henry Lee (Nov. 15, 1775), in *Works*, 4:186.

24. Quoted in Foner, *Tom Paine*, 75.

25. See E. Nelson, *Royalist Revolution*.

26. Paine, *Common Sense*, 5. Foner, *Tom Paine*, 76; see also Rosenfeld, *Common Sense*, chap. 4; J. Clark, *Thomas Paine*, chap. 4; and Lebovitz, introduction to *Colossus*. Hobbes had used the same biblical verse to criticize "an opinion received of the greatest part of England, that these Powers [of sovereignty] were divided between the King, and the Lords, and the House of Commons" (*Leviathan*, 2.18).

27. "Let the assemblies be annual, with a president only. The representation more equal, their business wholly domestic, and subject to the authority of a Continental Congress" (Paine, *Common Sense*, 30).

28. Paine, 4. See e.g., Inglis, *True Interest of America*, 15, 53, 70.

29. Paine, *Common Sense*, introduction ("time," n.p.), 70 ("power" and "birthday"). For this "progressive" reading, see notably Craig Nelson's *Thomas Paine*.

30. Paine, *Common Sense*, 30 ("scripture"), 3 ("parliament"), 35 ("time"), 70 ("multitude"). On Paine's biblical references, see Eric Nelson's *Hebrew Republic*. I discuss the broader phenomenon of "natural republicanism" in *The Terror of Natural Right*.

31. Paine, *Common Sense*, 40. On republican timing, see especially Pocock's *Machiavellian Moment*.

32. Paine, *Common Sense*, 70. For an alternative argument that republicanism and democracy "were used interchangeably": W. Adams, *First American Constitutions*, 106.

33. Paine, *Common Sense*, 33.

34. Como, "God's Revolutions," 46. For the English version of *Le riuolutioni di Napoli*: Giraffi, *Exact Historie*. John Adams owned a 1663 edition of Howell's translation: see *Catalogue of the John Adams Library*, 103. For other sources: J. Clark, *Thomas Paine*, 155n158.

35. See e.g., Cumings, *Sermon Preached in Billerica*.

36. The first allusion I could find was in a report calling for the officer of a new Canadian Battalion to "prepare them for Effecting a Revolution, wherever the United States shall deem such a Measure Expedient" (Dec. 1777): *Journals of the Continental Congress*, 9:987.

37. *Alarm*, 3.

38. R. Price, *Nature of Civil Liberty*, 62.

39. John Adams, preface to *Defence of the Constitutions*, in *Works*, 4:285; *Federalist*, no.9 (Hamilton), 118.

40. Jefferson to William Stephen Smith (Nov. 13, 1787) (FOUNDERS). See more generally: Richards, *Shays's Rebellion*.

41. This trend extends back to Charles Beard's famous study, *An Economic Interpretation of the Constitution of the United States* (1913). More recently: Bouton, *Taming Democracy*; Holton, *Unruly Americans*. It also features prominently in Taylor's *American Revolutions* (chap. 10). For a critique of this historiography: E. Nelson, *Royalist Revolution*, 149. For the Thermidor reference: Morison and Commager, *Growth*, 1:277.

42. John Adams, *Thoughts on Government*, in *Works*, 4:208.

43. James Madison to Thomas Jefferson (Oct. 24, 1787) (FOUNDERS).

44. See esp., Lebovitz's *Colossus*, and his discussion of Demophilus's *Genuine Principles of the Ancient Saxon, or English Constitution*. The 1777 Georgia constitution also provided for only one legislative chamber, though its members elected an "executive council" (similar to the older colonial governments). When it became a state in 1777, Vermont opted for a Pennsylvania-style assembly.

45. This passage, from an earlier version of *Thoughts on Government*, is found in his letter to William Hooper (March 27, 1776) (FOUNDERS). On the aristocratic ideal of the senate in state constitutions, see also Wood's *Power and Liberty* (37). More generally: Rakove, *Revolutionaries*, chap. 4.

46. Taylor, *American Revolutions*, 361.

47. See Rakove, "Montesquieu's 'Influence' on Madison."

48. Foner, *Tom Paine*, chap. 6.

49. John Adams, *Thoughts on Government*, in *Works*, 4:200.

50. For helpful surveys: Chinard, "Polybius"; Gummere, *American Colonial Mind*, esp. chap. 10; Richard, *Founders and the Classics* and *Greeks & Romans*; Ricks, *First Principles*.

51. "An elective despotism was not the government we fought for; but one . . . in which the powers of government should be so divided and balanced among several bodies of magistracy, as that no one could transcend their legal limits, without being effectually checked by the others" (Jefferson, *State of Virginia*, 195); Madison quoted this passage in *Federalist*, no. 48. See Leonard, "Jefferson's Constitutions." On Cicero: Jefferson, *Literary Commonplace Book*, 160. Jefferson could also be critical of his generation's constant appeals to classical authorities: see Onuf and Cole, introduction to *Thomas Jefferson*.

52. Richard, *Founders and the Classics*, 140.

53. Hamilton, *Letter from Phocion*; see Sellers, "Constitutional Thought."

54. Bailyn, *Ideological Origins*, 26.

55. Amar, *America's Constitution*, 8. For a similar claim about the novelty of the American constitution: Loughlin, *Against Constitutionalism*.

56. See the *Athenian Constitution*, possibly composed by Aristotle: "This then was the constitution drawn up by the Hundred elected by the Five Thousand. These proposals were carried by the multitude [*tou plēthous*], being put to the vote by Aristomachus" (*Ath. Pol.* 32.1). The author uses *epikurōu*, which Liddell, Scott, and Jones's *Greek-English Lexicon* translates as "confirm, sanction, ratify." Thucydides discusses this same episode: "The Athenians . . . deposed the Four Hundred and voted [*epsēphísanto*] to hand over the government to the Five Thousand": Thuc., 8.97 (*psēphízō*, "to vote"). See also Teegarden, *Death to Tyrants!*, 25–27.

57. See Livy, *AUC* 3.34.5–6: "Laws of the Ten Tables were passed by the Assembly of Centuries."

58. Ciepley, "U.S. Government a Corporation?"; on the connection to Italian jurists, Bartolus and Baldus de Ubaldi in particular: D. Edelstein, "Rousseau, Bodin."

59. Gienapp, *Second Creation*.

60. Wood, *Creation*, 606; see also *Power and Liberty*, 95. Wood has considerably softened his earlier argument: "The American revolutionaries exploited all of these classical ideas in their creation of the United States," he asserted in 2010. "They established mixed constitutions in emulation of ancient Rome": Wood, "Prologue," 24.

61. J. Adams, *Works*, 4:392, 397; Adams likely borrowed the phrase "natural aristocracy" (which he uses repeatedly) from Harrington: see *Works*, 4:413; Harrington, *Commonwealth of Oceana*, e.g., 26, 183.

62. Adams derided the "new order of Knights" as "the deepest Project of Evil which has yet been laid," in a letter to Samuel Osgood (April 9, 1784) (FOUNDERS).

63. James Madison to Thomas Jefferson (June 6, 1787) (FOUNDERS). See Sheehan, *Mind of James Madison*. Madison objected to the creation of "artificial distinctions, such as kings & nobles," merely for the sake of creating balance (32).

64. Madison, June 26, in Farrand, *Records of the Federal Convention*, 1:422 (Madison's notes, which do not include the reference to aristocracy), 1:431 (for Robet Yates's account). Mary Bilder found that Madison had replaced the sheet containing this speech when revising his notes. The vision of the Senate that he presented here, she comments, "to some delegates, may have had awkward parallels to the House of Lords" (*Madison's Hand*, 102–3). Chinard also discusses this passage in "Polybius" (51). Madison may have made a similar point on June 6: "All civilized Societies would be divided into different Sects, Factions, & interests, as they happened to consist of rich & poor" (Farrand, *Records of the Federal Convention*, 1:135), but this speech, too, was replaced in his notes, and may have been written much later: see Bilder, *Madison's Hand*, 73, 199. See Rakove, "Politics Indoors."

65. See also Conniff, "Obsolescence." In fact, while it was not his first choice, Rousseau had proposed precisely the same remedy as Madison to the problem of factions: "If there are partial societies [in a state], then one should multiply their number and maintain them on an equal standing [*en prévenir l'inégalité*], as did Solon, Numa, and Servius," he wrote in *The Social Contract* (2.3), in *Œuvres complètes*, 3:372. See D. Williams, *Rousseau's "Social Contract,"* 76.

66. *Federalist*, no. 10 (Madison), 124.

67. Hamilton, June 19, in Farrand, *Records of the Federal Convention*, 1:299.

68. *Federalist*, no. 34 (Hamilton); discussed in Chinard, "Polybius," 55.

69. Gouverneur Morris, July 2, in Farrand, *Records of the Federal Convention*, 1:512; discussed in Lovejoy, "Theory of Human Nature" (Morris "recognized only two permanently opposed forces in politics, the rich and the poor": 58–59).

70. See also Chinard's conclusion: "It is clear that in the opinion of several delegates, the executive represented the monarchical power, the senate the aristocratical" ("Polybius," 51). On Aristotle, see Richard Gummere's "Classical Ancestry of the Constitution" (*American Colonial Mind*, 175–76); on the iron law of social inequality, see chapter 1.

71. Wood, *Power and Liberty*, 98; Arist., *Pol.* 4.1292a.

72. Madison, June 19, in Farrand, *Records of the Federal Convention*, 1:318.

73. *Federalist*, no. 9 (Hamilton), quoting Montesquieu, *Spirit of Laws*, 9.1; p. 132.

74. *Federalist*, no. 18 (Madison), paraphrasing Mably, *Observations sur l'histoire*, 263–64, translated as *Observations on the Greeks*, 226–27 (on the excellence of the Achaean League). On ancient Greek federations: Mackil, *Creating a Common Polity*.

75. See Gummere, *American Colonial Mind*, 179–84; Lehmann, "Greek Federalism."

76. For Madison, see June 19, in Farrand, *Records of the Federal Convention*, 1:319; for Martin (of Maryland), June 28, 1:459 ("All the Ancient and Modern Confedns. and Leagues were as equals notwithstanding the vast disproportions in size and wealth"), citing Charles Rollin. Rollin had written a propos the Amphictyonic league: "Each city sent two deputies, and in consequence had two votes in the council; and that without distinction, or the more powerful having any prerogative of honour of pre-eminence over inferior states in regard to the suffrages; the liberty upon which these people valued themselves, requiring that every thing should be equal amongst them" (*Ancient History*, 10.1.2.8; 3:526). See Chinard's remark: "Who could have thought, unless such positive texts were produced, that the limitation of two senators for each State might perhaps be traced to the 'Amphictyonick Council of Greece'?" ("Polybius," 49); and see John Adams, *Defence of the Constitutions*, in *Works*, 4:509.

77. Adams discusses the Achaean (or Achaian) and Amphictyonic confederacies: see *Defence of the Constitutions*, in *Works*, 4:498–505, and 4:509 (respectively); Montesquieu, the Lycian: *Spirit of Laws*, 9.3.

78. *Federalist*, no. 16 (Hamilton), 152.

79. *Federalist*, no. 70 (Hamilton): "We have seen that the Achaeans, on an experiment of two Praetors, were induced to abolish one" (403). On the decision to switch to a single *strategos*: Polyb., 2.43. Rollin also notes this detail (*Ancient History*, 16.3.2; 5:404).

80. For Wilson: June 1, in Farrand, *Records of the Federal Convention*, 1:74; *Federalist*, no. 70 (Hamilton), 402; no. 63 (Madison), 371. See Gummere, *American Colonial Mind*, 184–90; Sellers, *American Republicanism*; Lebovitz, "Dictatorship in the American Founding."

81. John Adams, *Defence of the Constitutions*, in *Works*, 1:434, quoted in Chinard, "Polybius," 43; see also Richard, *Founders and the Classics*, 139; Sellers, *American Republicanism*, chap. 9. Arnaldo Momigliano called Polybius "one of the founding fathers of the USA," in "The Historian's Skin" (77).

82. See Benjamin Franklin to William Strahan (Nov. 28, 1747); Thomas Jefferson to George Wythe (Dec. 13, 1786) and Thomas Jefferson to Peter Carr (Aug. 10, 1787);

James Madison, "Additional Memorandums on Ancient and Modern Confederacies," Nov. 1787, and James Madison to Thomas Jefferson (Oct. 24, 1787) (FOUNDERS). For Jefferson, see also Gummere, *American Colonial Mind*, 174; for Monroe, Kaminski et al., *Ratification of the Constitution*, 1105, quoted in Chinard, "Polybius," 53.

83. Some political scientists accordingly refer to the "status quo bias" in the American Constitution: see e.g., Gilens and Page, "Testing Theories," 573. Republican political thinkers cautioned against changing the laws by making too many new ones: see e.g., Machiavelli, *Discourses*, 1.2; Rousseau, *Social Contract*, 3.11, 4.1. According to Aristotle, the demagogue disrupts the constitution by convincing the assembly to pass new laws: see *Pol.* 4.1292a.

84. On Turgot, see chapter 8. R. Price, *Importance of the American Revolution*, 6. Adams read an English translation of Turgot's letter in this work, to which it was appended. See also Haraszti, *John Adams*.

85. See e.g., "The checks and balances of republican governments have been in some degree adopted at the courts of princes": John Adams, preface to *Defence of the Constitutions*, in *Works*, 4:283. Cf. also Hamilton, who in *Federalist* no. 9 exclaims that "the science of politics . . . has received great improvement. The efficacy of various principles is now well understood, which were either not known at all, or imperfectly known to the ancients." The first two examples that he provides of these modern improvements, however, are oddly Polybian: "The regular distribution of power into distinct departments; the introduction of legislative balances and checks," 119.

86. See, for instance, William Buckley's 1955 mission statement for the *National Review*: "It is the job of centralized government (in peacetime) to protect its citizens' lives, liberty and property. All other activities of government tend to diminish freedom and hamper progress. . . . The competitive price system is indispensable to liberty and material progress" ("Our Mission Statement"). More recently, see David Brooks: "If you look at the American conservative tradition . . . you don't see people trying to revert to some past glory. Rather, they are attracted to innovation and novelty, smitten with the excitement of new technologies" ("What Happened").

87. See Amar, *America's Constitution*, chap. 1.

88. Obama, "More Perfect Union."

89. Charles-Guillaume-Frédéric Dumas to Benjamin Franklin (June 30, 1775): "Les vices aux prises avec les vertus! Le crépuscule d'une révolution totale dans le monde! Sept ou huit Etats nouveaux appellés par la Providence à nous retracer les beaux âges de l'ancienne Grece!" (FOUNDERS). For other, slightly later French examples calling American events a "revolution": Rachum, *"Revolution,"* chap. 9.

90. G. Morris, *Observations*. There is also one reference to "the revolution of England"—i.e., 1688.

91. John Adams to the Inhabitants of Providence, R.I. (April, 30 1798), in *Works*, 9:184 ("spectacle so novel"); and John Adams to Richard Price (April 19, 1790), in *Works*, 9:563.

92. Burke begins his analysis by emphasizing how he belongs "to more clubs than one, in which the constitution of this kingdom, and the principles of the glorious Revolution are held in high reverence; and I reckon myself among the most forward in my zeal for maintaining that constitution and those principles in their utmost purity and vigour" (*Reflections on the Revolution*, 4, 25 [on Paris fashion]).

93. See, classically: Arendt, *On Revolution*; most recently: Chirot, *You Want a Revolution?*

94. For the American case: Jasanoff, *Liberty's Exiles*; Hoock, *Scars of Independence*, esp. chap. 4; Taylor, *American Revolutions*, 107–9, 216–19. Compare with French accounts of the leadup to the Terror: Tackett, *King Took Flight* and *Coming of the Terror*.

95. These examples are all found in Hoock's *Scars of Independence* and Taylor's *American Revolutions*. On the French émigré experience: Simonin, *Déshonneur dans la République*.

96. Taylor, *American Revolutions*, 245 (on execution of prisoners, by both American and British forces), 256 (on Sullivan's expedition against the Iroquois); Hoock, *Scars of Independence*, 250–64 (on the Paoli massacre), 213–21 (on prison ships), chap. 9 (on Iroquois villages).

97. For the French examples: David Bell, *First Total War*; D. Edelstein, *Terror of Natural Right*.

Part III

1. Letter of October 28, 1777 (D20862): "Plusieurs princes font le même changement dans les lois de leur pays. Cette révolution s'étendra jusqu'à Rome et jusqu'aux pays d'inquisition. C'est un siècle nouveau qui va naître et dont vous aurez été la créatrice."

2. Hannah Arendt stated this thesis most baldly: "The modern concept of revolution, inextricably bound up with the notion that the course of history suddenly begins anew . . . was unknown prior to the two great revolutions at the end of the eighteenth century"(*On Revolution*, 28). See also Hunt, *Politics, Culture, and Class*, 34. More critically: Baker, *Inventing the French Revolution*; Sewell, "Historical Events."

3. As Baker notes, the duc was not even using the term in this sense: "Liancourt was perhaps telling Louis XVI that the form of French government had been transformed before his very eyes. But in this case, Liancourt needed only to draw on the conventional use of the term 'revolution' to do so" (*Inventing the French Revolution*, 218).

4. "J'ai parcouru ce vaste théâtre des révolutions que la terre entière a éprouvées depuis le temps de Charlemagne; à quoi ont-elles abouti: A la destruction, à des millions d'hommes égorgés. Tout grand événement a été un grand malheur" (*Essay sur l'histoire générale*, chap. 211, 7:142). Voltaire subsequently revised this passage in later editions.

5. David Bell, *Men on Horseback*.

Chapter Eight

1. Fontenelle, *L'origine des fables*, 296: "faussetés manifestes et ridicules . . . Il y a eu de la philosophie même dans ces siècles grossiers. . . . D'où peut venir cette rivière qui coule toujours, a dû dire un contemplatif de ces siècles-là? Etrange sorte de philosophe, mais qui aurait peut-être été un Descartes dans ce siècle-ci."

2. Montaigne, "Des cannibales," in *Essays* (1580).

3. Fontenelle, *L'origine des fables*, 307: "On auroit grand tort . . . d'être surpris que la Philosophie & la maniere de raisonner ayent été pendant un grand nombre de Siécles très grossieres, & très imparfaites, & qu'encore aujourd'hui les progrès en soient si lents."

4. Blumenberg, "On a Lineage," 6.

5. Hartog, *Chronos*.

6. Chakrabarty, *Provincializing Europe*, 8–9.

7. On Fontenelle's own role in the Quarrel of the Ancients and the Moderns: Fumaroli, "Les abeilles." The central role of the Quarrel in the history of the idea of progress was famously emphasized by Auguste Comte in his *Cours de philosophie positive* (4:235); for this reference: L. Edelstein, *Idea of Progress*, xvi–xvii. The Quarrel (and Comte's judgment) is also a starting point for J. B. Bury in *The Idea of Progress* (109); see also Blumenberg, *Legitimacy*, 33. More recently: Statman, *Global Enlightenment*. On the Quarrel and competing ideas of history: Norman, *Shock of the Ancient*.

8. Thuc., 3.82.2. For this phrase: Haraszti, *John Adams*.

9. On Saint-Pierre's friendship with Fontenelle: Rouvillois, *L'invention du progrès*.

10. Saint-Pierre, "Observasions sur le progrèz," 11: 275, 310. On Saint-Pierre, see notably: Keohane, *Philosophy and the State*; Spector, "Who Is the Author"; Dornier, *La monarchie éclairée*.

11. Saint-Pierre, "Observasions sur le progrèz," 275–76: "a cause des avantajes que nous donent la Tradition orale & la Tradition écrite & inprimée"; "le progrèz du janre humain vers la sajesse en vint deux siècles."

12. Saint-Pierre, 313. Reinhart Koselleck has argued that the dominant temporal sense in the eighteenth century was "acceleration," but Saint-Pierre's emphasis on the slow pace of progress does not fit that thesis: see "Historical Criteria."

13. Saint-Pierre, *Projet pour perfectionner*, 231 ("nous touchons . . . au comencement de l'age d'or"). See also: "Les Poëtes ont feint l'âge d'or du tems de Saturne & de Rée . . . ils ont feint folement que cet âge a été le premier," whereas in fact "l'Histoire, la Filosopfie & l'experience nous aprenent tout le contraire" (225). Cf. Saint-Simon, *De la réorganisation*, 112 (he discusses Saint-Pierre extensively in this work).

14. Hegel, *Philosophy of History*, 12–16. For this reason, Löwith places particular importance on Hegel in his secularizing account of the origins of progress (*Meaning in History*, chap. 3, esp., e.g., 57). More generally: Bourke, *Hegel's Global Revolutions*. See also chapter 4.

15. Palmer, *Catholics and Unbelievers*. On the impact of Christianity on ideas of revolution, see chapter 3.

16. Markus, *Saeculum*.

17. Saint-Pierre, "Observasions sur le progrèz," 277, 284. For the quote: Guyatt, *Providence*, 3. Saint-Pierre corresponded with Leibniz about his project for perpetual peace.

18. Saint-Pierre argued that we could even "faire en moins de 150 ans un progrèz dix fois plus grand au bonheur du Janre humain" ("Observasions sur le progrèz," 291–92); he recommended changes in "la Sianse [i.e., *science*] du Gouvernemant" (291). See Dornier, *La monarchie éclairée*, chap. 5.

19. On elections: Saint-Pierre, "Projet de règlement sur le scrutin," in *Projet pour perfectionner*, 128–97. On the revolutionary nature of his plans: "Ce plan est si grand, qu'il faut être bien hardi pour en entreprendre l'execution" (187). Against the balanced constitution: "fonction & autorité [de gouverner] qui ne devoient jamais se partajer"

("Observations politiques sur le gouvernement des rois de France," in *Ouvrajes*, 9:17–18). For his warning against "un État dans lequel l'Autorité suprême êst partajée": "Observasions sur les quatre principaux défauts du gouvernement d'Angleterre," in *Ouvrajes*, 11:149. On despotic power: "Quand le pouvoir est uni à la raizon il ne sauroit jamais être trop grand, & trop despotique pour la plus grande utilite de la Société" (*Projet pour perfectionner*, 203–4) and "Nous n'avons donq à dezirer . . . pour augmenter la felicité de notre Patrie . . . que la despoticité & l'autorité du Ministère aille toujours en augmentant" ("Reflexions morales et politiques sur la vie de Charles XII, roi de Suede," in *Ouvrajes*, 9:379). More generally: Keohane, *Philosophy and the State*, 370–76 (373 on *aristo-monarchie*); Kaiser, "Abbé de Saint-Pierre" (619 on mixed government). The history of democracy sketched out in this section is indebted to Stephen Sawyer; see notably "The Forgotten Democratic Tradition of Revolutionary France."

20. D'Argenson's work, "Jusques où la démocratie peut être admise dans le gouvernement monarchique," was posthumously published as *Considérations sur le gouvernement ancien et présent de la France* (1764). Quotes from Jainchill, *"Considérations sur le gouvernement."* On balanced constitutions: "La puissance tribunitienne chez les Romains, le droit des communes et des parlements chez les Anglais, celui des états nationaux, provinciaux, ou de remontrances chez nous, tous ces remèdes ne sont que des maux; ils partagent la puissance publique, tandis qu'elle doit être une et décidée" (84); on despotism, 78, and Jainchill's introduction (60). See also Rosanvallon, "History of the Word"; Sawyer, "Forgotten Democratic Tradition." On the club: Childs, *Political Academy in Paris*.

21. Jainchill, *"Considérations sur le gouvernement."* 76: "Il est humainement impossible d'empêcher que tôt ou tard l'un des trois gouvernements ne gagne sur les autres." In both Saint-Pierre's and d'Argenson's critiques, we can detect echoes of Jean Bodin's famous definition of sovereignty in *Les six livres de la république* (1576). Bodin had similarly argued that the Aristotelian/Polybian tradition was based on a misconception: far from being a perfect mixture of three governmental forms, the Roman Republic was really a democracy (*République*, 1.2). See Lee, *Popular Sovereignty*.

22. Jainchill, *"Considérations sur le gouvernement."* 83: "la science qu'on appelle politique"; "perfectionner le dedans d'un État de tous les degrés de perfection dont il est susceptible."

23. Russo, *Styles of Enlightenment*; D. Edelstein, *Enlightenment*; Cavarzere, *Historical Culture*.

24. Dubos, *Réflexions critiques*, 2:175–220 (174 for quote: "Il arrive des jours où les hommes portent en peu d'années jusqu'à un point de perfection surprenant les arts et les professions qu'ils cultivoient presque sans aucun fruit depuis plusieurs siècles"). For similar ideas: Voltaire, *Siècle de Louis XIV*, chap. 1; d'Alembert, "Discours préliminaire," *Encyclopédie*, 1:i–liii. See also Hunt, *Measuring Time, Making History*, chap. 2. On genius in the Enlightenment: McMahon, *Divine Fury*, chap. 3.

25. See d'Alembert: "La barbarie dure des siecles, il semble que ce soit notre élément; la raison & le bon goût ne font que passer" ("Discours préliminaire," *Encyclopédie*, 1:xxxiii). See Pocock, *Barbarism and Religion*.

26. Well before Hegel, it was already commonplace to describe the movement of history from East to West: see Voltaire, *Essay sur l'histoire générale*; Bailly, *Lettres sur l'origine*. On the *translatio*, notably: Curtius, *European Literature*, 29–30, 384–85; see also Levin, *Myth of the Golden Age*.

27. "On ne voit point de ligues fédératives s'établir autrement que par des révolutions: & sur ce principe, qui de nous oseroit dire si cette ligue Européenne est à désirer ou à craindre? Elle feroit peut-être plus de mal tout-d'un-coup qu'elle n'en préviendroit pour des siècles": Rousseau, "Jugement sur le projet de paix perpétuelle," in *Œuvres complètes*, 3:600. See Spector, "Plan for Perpetual Peace."

28. Voltaire to Frederick II, Jan. 26, 1740 (D2149), and to the comte d'Argental, Sept. 8, 1752 (D5011): "homme moitié filosofe et moitié fou." Saint-Pierre had sent Voltaire a rather condescending letter in 1739: "Destinez le reste de votre vie non plus à divertir les dames d'esprit et d'autres anfans, songez à instruire les hommes" (D2085).

29. Montesquieu, *Spirit of Laws*, 11.6 (see chapter 6). See the article "Vingtième, imposition," by Damilaville and Diderot (falsely attributed to Boulanger), in *Encyclopédie*, 17:881.

30. Turgot: "La masse totale du genre-humain, par des alternatives de calme et d'agitations, de biens et de maux, marche toujours, quoiqu'à pas lents, à une perfection plus grande" (*Œuvres posthumes*, 52–92, quote at 53–54). W. Nelson, *Time of Enlightenment.*

31. Turgot: "assigner un fond ou une somme d'argent, pour être employée à perpétuité à remplir l'objet que le fondateur s'est proposé"; "révolutions du tems sur les richesses publiques"; "Le tems amene de nouvelles révolutions, qui font disparoître l'utilité dont elle pouvoit être dans son origine, & qui peuvent même la rendre nuisible" ("Fondation," *Encyclopédie*, 7:72–74)

32. See Turgot, *Œuvres posthumes.* See especially Cavanaugh, "Turgot" (on Turgot's familiarity with d'Argenson's treatise, 48n65). See also Baker, *Condorcet*, 202–14; Vardi, *Physiocrats.*

33. Turgot: "S[a] M[ajesté] peut donc se regarder comme un législateur absolu" ("Memorandum on Municipalities," in *Œuvres posthumes*, 7) See also Condorcet, *Vie de M. Turgot*, "Tout devoit y être l'ouvrage d'un seul homme," 119; see also 112, 122 (for his discussion of Turgot's plan, 112–51), and in particular: "Dans une constitution ainsi formée le voeu général de la Nation seroit le seul obstacle à l'autorité qui, toujours tranquille & assurée, ne verroit plus . . . aucun Corps intermédiaire" (122). See also Cavanaugh, "Turgot," 48 (on his opposition to Montesquieu).

34. Turgot: "Ils se sont trompés quelquefois. Ils l'ont été souvent par l'ignorance de leur siècle"; "Dans dix ans d'ici, sa nation ne serait pas reconnaissable. . . . [E]lle serait infiniment au-dessus de tous les autres peuples qui existent et qui ont existé." Turgot returns to this point in conclusion: "Enfin, au bout de quelques années, V[otre] M[ajesté] aurait un peuple neuf, et le premier des peuples" ("Memorandum on Municipalities," 98).

35. See "Observations d'un républicain sur ces mémoires et en général sur le bien qu'on doit attendre de ces administrations dans les monarchies," in Turgot, *Œuvres posthumes*, 101 (for quote: "Nous voulons ce que vous voulez").

36. Condorcet, *Vie de M. Turgot*, 119 ("La générosité qui porteroit à leur [the representatives] laisser le soin de prononcer sur leurs intérêts ne seroit qu'une cruauté hypocrite"), 122 ("Il [the king] feroit à sa Nation un bien éternel, mais qu'il ne pouvait le faire sans sacrifier une partie de l'autorité Royale"), 123 ("Assemblée nationale"). See also Cavanaugh ("Turgot," 50), who underscores important differences between Turgot's emphasis on popular will and the Physiocratic desire for a "legal despot" (see esp. 43–44).

37. See esp., Lebovitz, *Colossus*. See also Aldridge, "John Adams Confronts Turgot." The second edition of Adams's work included a subtitle: "Against the Attack of Mr. Turgot in His Letter to Dr. Price, Dated the Twenty-Second day of March, 1778."

38. See Turgot, "Lettre au Dr. Price sur les constitutions américaines," in *Œuvres de Turgot*, 5:532–40: e.g., "Je vois dans le plus grand nombre [of state constitutions] l'imitation sans objet des usages de l'Angleterre. Au lieu de ramener toutes les autorités à une seule, celle de la nation, l'on établit des corps différens" (534–35); "On s'occupe à balancer ces différens pouvoirs," when what the fledgling country really needed was "une fusion de toutes les parties, qui n'en fasse qu'un corps un, et homogene" (535–36); "Tout ce qui établit différens corps [est] une source de divisions" (535).

39. "[Turgot] vouloit que cette institution fût l'ouvrage de la raison, & non, comme toutes celles qui ont existé jusqu'ici, celui du hasard & des circonstances" (Condorcet, *Vie de M. Turgot*, 120). See also, in Turgot's letter, "Ce peuple nouveau situé si avantageusement pour donner au monde l'exemple d'une constitution où l'homme jouisse de tous ses droits, exerce librement toutes ses facultés, et ne soit gouverné que par la nature, la raison et la justice, saura-t'il former une pareille constitution?" ("Lettre au Dr. Price," 534). Turgot also evokes "des Républiques fondées sur l'égalité de tous les citoyens" ("Lettre au Dr. Price," 535).

40. Turgot to Price: "Il est l'espérance du genre humain. Il peut en devenir le modèle" ("Lettre au Dr. Price," 539). Turgot's enemies "devoient triompher & empêcher une révolution qui, en faisant le bonheur de la France, eût contribué par un grand exemple à celui de toutes les nations" (Condorcet, *Vie de M. Turgot*, 111). On Turgot's preference for democracy: Condorcet, *Vie de M. Turgot*, 216; Cavanaugh, "Turgot," 47.

41. Condorcet, *Outlines*, 19; *Esquisse*, 19. On this text, see notably: Baker, *Condorcet*; Rothschild, *Economic Sentiments*; D. Williams, *Condorcet and Modernity*; Sonenscher, "Sociability"; W. Nelson, *Time of Enlightenment*.

42. Condorcet, *Outlines*, 319 (tenth epoch); *Esquisse*, 330. See, more generally: Ozouf, *L'homme régénéré*.

43. Condorcet, *Outlines*, 15 ("this union having once taken place in the whole enlightened class of men"), 323 (enlightened missionaries), 321 ("independence," "cause to disappear"); *Esquisse*, 15 ("réunion"), 334–35, 332. On the idea of a "philosophical party": Comsa et al., "French Enlightenment Network," 530.

44. See e.g., "Will not every nation one day arrive at the state of civilization attained by those people who are most enlightened, most free, most exempt from prejudices, as the French, for instance, and the Anglo-Americans?" (Condorcet, *Outlines*, 317; *Esquisse*, 328).

45. See the discussion of majority voting: "Each individual may enter into a previous engagement to comply with the will of the majority, which by this engagement becomes unanimity" (Condorcet, *Outlines*, 232 [ninth epoch]; *Esquisse*, 241).

46. Thuc., 3.82.2, and chapter 1.

Chapter Nine

1. Voltaire to Princess Louise of Saxe-Gotha-Altenburg, Aug. 20, 1760 (D9158): "Tout est révolution, tout est malheur." Rousseau on the illusion of revolutions: oppressed peoples who seek to "overthrow the yoke" of tyranny, "s'éloignent d'autant plus de la liberté," and thus "leurs révolutions les livrent presque toûjours à des

séducteurs qui ne font qu'aggraver leurs chaînes" ("Dédicace," *Discours sur les origines de l'inégalité*, in *Œuvres complètes*, 3:113). In a particularly Polybian vein, he recommended to the Poles a constitution that would avoid "tout changement vif et brusque et le danger des revolutions" (*Considérations sur le gouvernement de Pologne* [1771], in *Œuvres complètes*, 3:1028). On the "century of revolutions": *Emile*, bk. 3, in *Œuvres complètes*, 4:468. Rousseau added: "Tout ce qu'ont fait les hommes, les hommes peuvent le détruire." *Contra* Rachum, who suggests that Rousseau here is revealing "his uneasiness in discussing such a weighty and sensitive subject," but implies that Rousseau actually favored revolution: see *"Revolution,"* 172–74. See also Spector, *Rousseau*, 167. On his own character: "l'homme du monde qui porte un plus vrai respect aux loix, aux constitutions nationales, et qui a le plus d'aversion pour les révolutions et pour les ligueurs de toute espéce" (*Rousseau juge de Jean-Jacques, Dialogues* [1776], "Les anglois," in *Œuvres complètes*, 1:935).

2. On priests and revolution—"Ce flambeau secoué par le fanatisme, l'imposture & la Tyrannie, ne fit qu'allumer des passions cruelles, des fureurs inextinguibles, des discordes fatales, & produire des révolutions sanglantes": d'Holbach, *La contagion sacrée*, 1:75. See also *Théologie portative*, 23; *Histoire critique*, 26. On revolutions as "affreuses," "terribles," "continuelles," and "fatales": *Histoire critique*, 26; *Système de la nature*, 1:30, 223, 269, 432, 2:75; *Système social*, 31, 234, 308, 638; *La morale universelle*, 1:216, 2:49, 220. On revolutions as seditions, etc.: *Théologie portative*, 23. For a "radical" reading of d'Holbach: Israel, *Democratic Enlightenment* and *Revolution of the Mind*, 4. But as Alan C. Kors pointed out in his classic study, d'Holbach's politics were fairly conservative (*D'Holbach's Coterie*).

3. "Faut-il sacrifier aux hasards d'une révolution le bonheur de la génération présente pour le bonheur de la génération à venir?": Diderot: *Réfutation d'Helvétius* (1774), in *Œuvres complètes*, 2:346. Diderot is commenting here on section 2, chapter 15 of *De l'homme*, which does not contain any discussion of revolution. In fact, Helvétius had written that "le caractere des peuples change donc. Mais dans quel moment ce changement se fait-il le plus sensiblement appercevoir? Dans les momens de révolution où les peuples passent tout-à-coup de l'état de liberté à celui de l'esclavage" (*De l'homme*, 280). On Diderot's politics in the prerevolutionary decade: Tricoire, "Diderot."

4. One important exception is Keith Baker, in *Inventing the French Revolution* (213–14). See also Mailhos, "Le mot 'révolution,'" 90. For the "so-called" quote: Rachum, *"Revolution,"* 171. Jonathan Israel, in *A Revolution of the Mind*, does not distinguish between references to a revolution in culture, which the philosophes generally praised, and to political revolutions, which they generally condemned (at least before the 1770s: see below). Leora Auslander adopts the idea of a "cultural revolution" in her study, but uses it in a very different sense: see *Cultural Revolutions*.

5. Montesquieu discusses the "great revolutions" in the realm of commerce: *Spirit of Laws*, 21.1, 21.8. Voltaire: "la révolution générale qui doit servir de marque éternelle à la véritable gloire de notre patrie"; "dans nos arts, dans nos esprits, dans nos mœurs, comme dans notre gouvernement" (*Siècle de Louis XIV*, 1:4); "[Charles I] s'engagea dans une guerre civile, qui lui fit perdre enfin le trône & la vie sur un échafaut, par une révolution presque inouïe" (*Siècle de Louis XIV*, 1:27. In his correspondence, Voltaire also described his focus in this work as the "general revolution": see D4295, D5049, D5084.

6. J.C.D. Clark, for instance, argued that François Guizot's 1826 *Histoire de la révolution d'Angleterre* was "the first to apply the term 'revolution' to the Civil War": *Revolution and Rebellion*, 37. In fact, Pierre-Joseph d'Orléans published his *Histoire des révolutions d'Angleterre depuis le commencement de la monarchie* over a century earlier, in 1689. This history was reprinted around 20 times. D'Orléans related the history of the English Civil War in book 9 (vol. 3). He referred to these events repeatedly as "la révolution que j'écris" (3:223, 238, 248), and described the fall and death of Charles I as "une révolution dont il n'y avait point encore eu d'exemple" (3:269), and again as "la plus universelle & la plus étonnante révolution qu'elle [l'Angleterre] eût encore vue" (3:432); quotes from the 1787 edition. On Louis XVI's reading: Campan, *Vie privée de Marie-Antoinette*, 2:217; see also Hanet-Cléry, *Journal*, 159.

7. See Goulemot, *Le règne de l'histoire*, chap. 4. Cf. "Voltaire's handling of 'revolution' is therefore at best indecisive": Rachum, *"Revolution,"* 170. On Voltaire's historiography more generally: Pocock, *Barbarism and Religion*, vol. 2; Pierse, *Voltaire Historiographer*.

8. Voltaire, *Essai sur les mœurs*: "Tout est révolution dans les gouvernements" (chap. 32, *Œuvres complètes*, 22:465); cf. d'Argenson, "Tout est révolution dans ce monde" (Jainchill, *"Considérations sur le gouvernement,"* 81). On Voltaire's historiography: "l'esprit, les mœurs, [et] les usages des nations principales" ("Avant-propos," in *Œuvres complètes*, 22:3). On Islam: "la plus grande et la plus prompte révolution que nous connaissions sur la terre" (chap. 5; *Œuvres complètes*, 22:97). On Luther: "cette grande révolution dans l'esprit humain" (chap. 128; *Œuvres complètes*, 25:413). On Henry VIII, "la révolution qu'il fit dans les esprits de ses peuples" (chap. 118; *Œuvres complètes*, 25:210). On the Reformation more generally: "Tout a été révolution depuis le seizième siècle, en Ecosse, en Angleterre, en Allemagne, en Suède, en Dannemarck, en Hollande, en Suisse et en France" (chap. 137; *Œuvres complètes*, 26A:76). See also the rise of Genghis Khan: "Une révolution qui n'avait point d'exemple, [qui] donnait une nouvelle face à la plus grande partie de l'Asie" (chap. 57; *Œuvres complètes*, 23:367). More generally: Mailhos, "Le mot 'révolution'"; Hunt, *Measuring Time, Making History*.

9. Baker: "To the extent that Enlightenment historiography took as its object world history—the history of human civilization as a whole—the revolutions it identified as dynamic processes of transformation had universal implications. They were not merely local events, but phenomena of world historical significance" (*Inventing the French Revolution*, 213). D'Alembert: "On peut le [Descartes] regarder comme un chef de conjurés, qui a eu le courage de s'élever le premier contre une puissance despotique & arbitraire, & qui en préparant une révolution éclatante, a jetté les fondemens d'un gouvernement plus juste & plus heureux qu'il n'a pû voir établi" ("Discours préliminaire," *Encyclopédie*, 1:xxvi).

10. Rousseau: "Il falloit une revolution pour ramener les hommes au sens commun"; "La chute du trône de Constantin porta dans l'Italie les débris de l'ancienne Grece" (*Discours sur les sciences et les arts* [1750], in *Œuvres complètes*, 3:6). Rousseau also described the different stages of early human existence as revolutions in the *Discours sur l'inégalité* (*Œuvres complètes*, 3:167, 171, 187). D'Alembert: "une de ces révolutions qui font prendre à la terre une face nouvelle" ("Discours préliminaire," *Encyclopédie*, 1:xx). Raynal: "une grande révolution dans les esprits" (*Histoire* [1776], 132). On commercial revolutions, see the opening of Raynal's *Histoire* (1776):

"une révolution dans le commerce, dans la puissance des nations, dans les mœurs, l'industrie et le gouvernement de tous les peuples" (1). See F. Clark, *Dividing Time*.

11. On Rome: "révolution . . . dans les esprits" (*Essai sur les mœurs*, chap. 12, *Œuvres complètes*, 22:227); and on China, "une révolution plus complète que celle de Gengis-Kan et de ses petits-fils" (chap. 195, *Œuvres complètes*, 26C:286). On natural revolutions: M. Miller, *Natural History of Revolution*.

12. See, respectively, d'Alembert, "Discours préliminaire," *Encyclopédie*, 1:xxxiii; Diderot, "Encyclopédie," *Encyclopédie*, 5:637; Diderot, "Citoyen," *Encyclopédie*, 3:489 ("celui qui dure le plus long-tems & le plus tranquillement").

13. Voltaire: "grande révolution dans l'esprit humain," letter to Denis Diderot, January 8, 1758 (D7570). See also, that same year, D7579 and D7584. Letter to Helvétius: "Il s'est fait depuis douze ans une révolution dans les esprits," June 26, 1765 (D12660). On the timing of this revolution, see D7570, D14211, D14363, D14981, D15163, D15377, and D15499. Comparing the peaceful revolution of the Enlightenment to the Reformation: see D15490, D17249. The Enlightenment revolution spreading throughout Europe: see D12660, D13139, D13437, D13588, D13437, D14363, D14447, D14728, D14738, D14793, D15228, and D15255.

14. David Bell, *Cult of the Nation*; C. Jones, *Great Nation*. Voltaire and Choiseul exchanged 90 letters between 1759 and 1776.

15. "Mais, je l'avouerai, je formai des souhaits / Pour que cet art si beau ne s'exerçât jamais, / Et qu'enfin l'équité fît régner sur la terre / L'impraticable paix de l'abbé de Saint-Pierre" (Voltaire, *La Tactique*; a critique of the comte de Guibert). The poem was first sent to the abbé de Voisenon, an author and diplomat: see Voltaire's letter of Nov. 19, 1773 (D18638). See also *Œuvres de 1773*, vol. 75A of *Œuvres complètes*. On Guibert and Voltaire: Pichichero, *Military Enlightenment*.

16. D. Edelstein, *Enlightenment*.

17. "Cet ouvrage produira sûrement avec le tems une révolution dans les esprits": letter of September 26, 1762, *Lettres à Sophie Volland*, ed. A. Babelon (Paris: Gallimard, 1950), 2:8–9 [ARTFL].

18. Diderot, *Salon de 1767*, 85: "Je ne dis pas que le philosophe Voltaire par exemple, s'occupe en vain à démontrer la vérité et à démasquer l'erreur, car je dirais une grande sottise et la révolution qu'il a produite dans les esprits d'un bout de l'Europe à l'autre déposerait contre moi." Frederick II also credited Voltaire with having led "cette révolution qui se fit au dix-huitième siècle dans l'esprit humain" (letter of April 24, 1767; D14162). Voltaire improbably denied all intellectual involvement: "Je n'ai assurément aucune part dans cette révolution qui s'est faite depuis quelques années dans l'esprit humain. Ce n'est pas ma faute si ce siècle est éclairé, si la raison a pénétré jusque dans des cavernes" (letter to d'Argental, Sept. 26, 1766, D13588). See also Voltaire's 1758 letter to Diderot (D7570), where Voltaire credits him with launching the revolution ("on vous en a monsieur la principale obligation").

19. See Jean-Baptiste-Claude Delisle de Sales: "Depuis un demi-siecle, il paroît s'être formé une heureuse révolution dans l'esprit national," a revolution that he credits to "les philosophes." He also calls it the "heureuse révolution qui s'est opérée dans les esprits" (*De la philosophie*, xxii, 58). Voltaire and Delisle de Sales corresponded in the 1770s, and Voltaire defended him during his trial and imprisonment. See also Antoine-Léonard Thomas, a French academician: "Depuis un demi-siècle, il s'est fait parmi nous une espèce de révolution" (*Essai sur les éloges*, 169).

20. Marat: “glorieuse révolution que Fontenelle avoit commencée, et qui auroit enfin amené le siècle de la vraie philosophie” (*Eloge de Montesquieu*, 77). On Marat’s prerevolutionary career: Baker, *Jean-Paul Marat.*

21. Voltaire to Bernard Louis Chauvelin: “Tout ce que je vois jette les semences d’une révolution qui arrivera immanquablement” (April 2, 1764, D11807); Voltaire to Elie Bertrand: “Il se fera sans doute un jour une grande révolution dans les esprits” (March 26, 1765, D12503). See also Keith Baker: “The Enlightenment itself was a profound revolution. . . . Lived as a process of cultural transformation, it was already separating past from present and reorienting expectations toward the future” (*Inventing the French Revolution*, 214).

22. “Soyez très sûr qu’il se ferait alors une grande révolution dans les esprits et qu’il suffirait de deux ou trois ans pour faire une époque éternelle,” Voltaire wrote to his friend Damilaville in 1766 (D13449); for a more ironic take: Voltaire to d’Alembert, D17446 (1771). See also Charles Bonnet: “Notre monde a été apparemment sous la forme de ver ou de chenille: il est à présent sous celle de chrysalide: la dernière révolution lui fera revêtir celle de papillon” (*La palingénésie philosophique*, 262). See Mailhos, “Le mot ‘révolution,’ ” 84.

23. See Voltaire’s letters: D13235, D13607 (1766); D14102, D14185 (1767); and D14752, D15228, D15242 (1768).

24. On “la révolution des parlements,” see D17295, D17382, D17434, D17437, and D17827. See also: “les esprits les mieux faits trouvaient la grande révolution que vous avez faitte aussi nécessaire que difficile” (Voltaire to Maupeou, Nov. 22, 1772, D18033). More generally: Echeverria, *Maupeou Revolution.*

25. I did find one earlier example of a purely political revolution that found favor with Voltaire. In the *Essai sur les moeurs,* Voltaire wrote, “Il n’y a point d’exemple d’une révolution si juste, si subite, et si tranquille” as the condemnation and disposal of a Danish tyrant in the 1500s (chap. 119; *Œuvres complètes*, 25:244). But as with seventeenth-century English examples, what’s notable here is how Voltaire repeatedly qualifies the revolution in a positive manner (“so fair . . . so peaceful”).

26. Neill, “Quesnay and Physiocracy”; Vardi, *Physiocrats*; Carvalho, *La physiocratie.*

27. Barton, “Gustav III of Sweden,” 3–4. Letter to Frederick II: “belle révolution de Suede” that “donne envie de vivre” (Sept. 15, 1772, D17911).

28. See Roberts, *Age of Liberty*; Barton, “Gustav III of Sweden,” 11–13. Voltaire to d’Alembert: “Mon cher philosophe, ce siècle cy ne vous parait-il pas celui des révolutions, à commencer par les jesuites et à finir par la Suède, et peut être à ne point finir?” (Sept. 16, 1772, D17913).

29. For Voltaire’s letter to Catherine, see the introduction to part 3 (and D20862). See also: “Je vous réponds que de la mer glaciale jusqu’à Venise il n’y a pas un homme d’état aujourd’hui qui ne pense en philosophe. Il s’est [fait] dans les esprits une plus grande révolution qu’au seizième siècle. Celle de ce 16ème siècle a été turbulente, la nôtre est tranquile” (Voltaire to François Louis Allamand, June 17, 1771, D17249). On Turgot: “Il y a surtout un monsieur Turgot qui serait digne de parler avec votre majesté. Les prêtres sont au désespoir. Voilà le commencement d’une grande révolution” (Voltaire to Frederick II, Aug. 10, 1775, D19599).

30. Voltaire to Madame du Deffand: “Il me paraît que vous autres parisiens vous allez voir une grande et paisible révolution dans votre gouvernement et dans votre

musique. Louis 16 et Gluk vont faire de nouveaux Français" (July 28, 1774, D19051); see also Voltaire to Madame du Deffand (August 12, 1774, D19075). See the conclusion to *Zadig*: "L'empire jouit de la paix, de la gloire et de l'abondance: ce fut le plus beau siècle de la terre; elle était gouvernée par la justice et par l'amour" (143).

31. Marmontel, *Bélisaire*, 181, 193, 25 (on "révolutions de la fortune"): "C'est donc au luxe qu'il faut s'en prendre; c'est par lui que doit commencer la révolution dans les moeurs"; "c'est elle, dit Bélisaire, qui, sans gêne et sans violence, remet chaque chose à sa place; et c'est d'elle qu'il faut attendre la révolution dans les mœurs"; "Cette révolution vous paroît difficile; elle dépend de la volonté et de l'exemple du souverain." On Marmontel and this novel, see notably Kors's *D'Holbach's Coterie* (124–29).

32. "Le gouvernement seul peut faire régner dans un état les vertus générales et les mœurs publiques. C'est du temps et du progrès des lumieres que l'on peut attendre cette révolution si desirable dans les esprits des maîtres de la terre": D'Holbach, *La morale universelle*, 3:66.

33. On the start of the revolution: "Le point lumineux a [*sic*] parti du fond du nord; . . . c'est une femme qui a commencé cette importante révolution. Alors la justice a parlé par la voix de la nature, souveraine législatrice, mère des vertus et de tout ce qui est bon sur la terre"; "La révolution s'est opérée sans efforts, et par l'héroïsme d'un grand homme. Un roi philosophe, digne du trône puisqu'il le dédaignoit, plus jaloux du bonheur des hommes que de ce fantôme de pouvoir, redoutant sa postérité et se redoutant lui-même"; "'Cette révolution s'est faite de la manière la plus paisible et la plus heureuse?' 'Elle a été l'ouvrage de la philosophie'" (Mercier, *Deux mille quatre cent quarante*, 77, 291, 101–2 [on the peaceful revolution]). See Darnton, *Forbidden Best-Sellers*, 126 (on the allusion to violence); Rufi, *Le rêve laïque*; Lilti, "Le philosophe utopique."

34. See in particular his direct address to Louis XVI, using the informal *tu*: Raynal, *Histoire* (1780), 4.18, 1:469–75. English translation available in Diderot, *Political Writings*, 171–73. See Duchet, *Diderot*.

35. On the revolution that would overthrow Christianity: Raynal, *Histoire* (1780), 6.13; 2:58. On slavery: "Pour renverser l'édifice de l'esclavage . . . à quel tribunal porterons-nous la cause de l'humanité, que tant d'hommes trahissent de concert? Rois de la terre, vous seuls pouvez faire cette révolution"; "Et puisse avant que je meure, cette grande révolution déja commencée, s'achever à la suite de quelquesunes des réformes que j'ai indiquées" (Raynal, *Histoire* [1780], 11.24 [3:203–5], 13.58 [3:508]); on colonial revolutions, 18.18 (4:390) and 18.44 (4:412); on the happy revolution, 19.15 (4:706). Lally-Tollendal: "l'heureuse révolution qui se prépare sera consommée," June 9, 1789, *AP*, 8:83. Many of the *cahiers de doléance* also used this phrase.

Chapter Ten

1. See e.g., *Le Moniteur*, no. 4 (1788), 1 (Newberry), most likely written by Guilaume Saige. See also Garrett, "*Moniteur* of 1788."

2. "Les gens graves se contentaient de parler de la destruction de tous les abus. La France, disaient-ils, allait se régénérer. Le mot de *Révolution* n'était pas proféré. Celui assez osé pour le prononcer aurait passé pour un fou. . . . C'est ce qui explique comment tant de gens honnêtes et purs, et parmi eux le roi lui-même, le premier à

partager leurs illusions, espéraient, à ce moment, qu'on allait entrer dans un âge d'or": La Tour du Pin, *Journal d'une femme*, 8.6, 1:160.

3. Bezassier, *La muse patriotique*, 1: "Il est sûr qu'en ces lieux l'âge d'or va renaître."

4. Philippe d'Orléans, owner of the Palais-Royal, installed the arcades and stores in 1781–84; a private space, it was off-limits to the police. See McMahon, "Birthplace of the Revolution"; C. Jones, *Paris*, chap. 6.

5. See Darnton, *Mesmerism*. Turgot's Latin epigram read: "Eripuit coelo fulmen sceptrumque tirannis."

6. R. Price, *Discourse*, 50.

7. See Keith M. Baker, "Public Opinion as Political Invention," in *Inventing the French Revolution*; Darnton, *Kiss of Lamourette*; Rosenfeld, *Common Sense*. Burke, *Reflections on the Revolution*, 75.

8. See C. Jones, *Fall of Robespierre*.

9. Tilly, *From Mobilization to Revolution*, 191, emphasis added. See also: "A revolutionary situation begins when a government previously under the control of a single, sovereign polity becomes the object of effective, competing, mutually exclusive claims on the part of two or more distinct polities" (191). Tilly also builds on the work of Peter H. Amann ("Revolution"). See also Brinton, *Anatomy of Revolution*, 132–37.

10. Lenin, "The Dual Power," *Pravda*, April 9, 1917; in *Anthology*, 301. See also Arno Mayer: "Revolution at once springs from and feeds on the collapse of the state's undivided and centralizing sovereignty and its dissolution into several centers of competing power or impotence" (*Furies*, 6).

11. Lenin, "Dual Power," 301–4.

12. See e.g., A. Mayer, *Furies*.

13. Lenin would make this same argument (with respect to Marx) in *The State and Revolution* (5.2; in *Anthology*, 372–73).

14. Baker, "Revolution 1.0."

15. Baker, *Inventing the French Revolution*, 211; Baker and Edelstein, *Scripting Revolution*.

16. See Tocqueville, *Ancien Régime*.

17. Claude Lefort draws explicitly on Kantorowicz's *The King's Two Bodies* (1957) in "The Logic of Totalitarianism" (303). See also Steinmetz-Jenkins, "Claude Lefort." François Furet drew on Lefort's argument (without citing him) in *Interpreting the French Revolution*. On Furet's debt to Lefort: Moyn, "Intellectual Origins."

18. With Stephen Sawyer, I offer a more extended criticism of the revisionist position: D. Edelstein and Sawyer, "Sovereignty and Government."

19. This account of the Parisian districts draws particularly on the following: Rose, *Making of the Sans-Culottes*; Genty, "Pratique et théorie"; Rosanvallon, *Society of Equals*, chap. 1; Burstin, *Une révolution à l'œuvre*; Andress, "Neighborhood Policing."

20. On "democracy" as a scare word, see e.g., Brissot: "Le mot démocratie, est un épouvantail dont les fripons se servent pour tromper les ignorans" (*Plan de conduite*, 21). More generally: Rosanvallon, "History of the Word."

21. Desmoulins, *La France libre* (1789), 68, 70; Hammersley, *French Revolutionaries*; Leuwers, *Camille et Lucile Desmoulins*.

22. On democracy as administration: Sawyer, "Forgotten Democratic Tradition"; Rosanvallon, "History of the Word." On maintaining public order: Andress, "Neighborhood Policing."

23. On the parallel with the forum, see e.g., Desmoulins: "Nous n'avons point de place publique assez grande, mais nos districts y suppléent & remplissent bien mieux l'objet de la tribune & du *Forum*" (*Révolutions de France et de Brabant*, no. 17 [March 22, 1790], 166). On the opening of the assemblies to all inhabitants: Rose, *Making of the Sans-Culottes*, 50–53, 62–63 (on women). On the festivals: Jason Frank, *Democratic Sublime*; Tackett, *Glory and the Sorrow*. On golden age fraternity: *Adresse de la Commune de Paris*, 8–11; for the "age of iron" quote: Prévost de Saint-Lucien, *Plan d'organisation*, 1–2; both texts quoted in Rose, *Making of the Sans-Culottes*, 61, 73; and see Burstin, *Révolution à l'œuvre*, 95–96. On the myth of the golden age in French revolutionary thought and print culture, see my *Terror of Natural Right*.

24. "Ces sections ont émis un vœu qu'elles m'ont chargé de vous apporter. . . . Ce vœu est la permanence des districts dans les assemblées formées régulièrement chaque mois" (March 22, 1790, *AP*, 12:333). Another supporter of the "permanence des districts" was Marat: see e.g., *L'ami du peuple*, no. 132 (June 13, 1790), no. 147 (June 28, 1790), no. 176 (July 29, 1790), no. 493 (June 18, 1791), no. 608 (Nov. 24, 1791). See also Burstin, *Une révolution à l'œuvre*, 102–4, 125.

25. "Demander la permanence des districts, c'est vouloir établir soixante sections souveraines dans un grand corps, où elles ne pourraient qu'opérer un effet d'action et de réaction capable de détruire notre constitution" (May 3, 1790, *AP*, 12:381).

26. "Décret relatif à l'organisation de la municipalité de Paris" (May 21, 1790), title 1, art. 11 and 19, in *Collection générale des decrets*, 2:415–50. The decree was signed into law by Louis XVI on June 27, 1790. See Burstin, *Une révolution à l'œuvre*, 141–46.

27. See the petition by the district of Palais-Royal, read at the National Assembly by Lally-Tollendal on Aug. 31, 1789 (*AP*, 8:512). Recall movements persisted through July 1791: Rose, *Making of the Sans-Culottes*, 131.

28. See the (very Rousseau-inspired) proposal by Jean-Baptiste Salle to have the electoral assemblies vote a vetoed law up or down, by an *appel à la nation*: *AP*, 8:529 (Sept. 1, 1789). Salle also couched his proposal in terms of sovereignty: "Government is not sovereignty. . . . [W]hen the people of Athens, Sparta, Rome, etc., exercised sovereignty, that is, passed laws . . . they were wise" (530–31). On the debate over the veto: Blackman, *1789*, 188–214.

29. Desmoulins, *Révolutions de France et de Brabant*, no. 17 (March 22, 1790), 166.

30. Robert, *Le Républicanisme adapté*, 87 ("Le républicanisme ou la démocratie est le gouvernement de tous: pour être parfait, il faut que tous les citoyens concourent *personnellement et individuellement* à la confection de la loi"); see also: "L'assemblée nationale ne doit porter que des loix provisoires, sujettes à la sanction nationale" (110).

31. July 20–21, 1789, *AP*, 8:259. On Sieyès's theory of citizenship and representation, see notably Friedland, *Political Actors* (155–64).

32. Lavicomterie, *Les droits du peuple*, 156. See also Desmoulins: this distinction "tu[e] la liberté et l'esprit d'égalité . . . je mets tout à coup hors de la révolution douze à quinze millions d'hommes, qui se demandent où est cette égalité des droits politiques qu'on leur promettoit" (*Discours sur la situation politique*, 25). Armand-Joseph Guffroy: "J'ai dit que l'orgueilleuse distinction de citoyens actifs et passifs étoit un germe sûr d'esclavage" (*Le Franc en vedette*, 18). See also Burstin, *Une révolution à l'œuvre*, 126–27.

33. Rosanvallon, *Le sacre du citoyen* and *La société des égaux*.

34. See Lebovitz, *Colossus*.

35. "On a souvent parlé des trois pouvoirs qui devaient se balancer dans un bon gouvernement. Ces trois pouvoirs, à mon avis, sont l'assemblée nationale, les municipalités, & les districts": Desmoulins, *Révolutions de France et de Brabant* no.17 (March 22, 1790), 166. See also Soboul, *Sans-Culottes*, 101.

36. Girardin, *Discours sur la nécessité*, 14–16 ("Tous ceux qui tenteroient d'agir contre les droits de l'homme et du citoyen, seroient par conséquent parjures, et criminels d'attentat à la souveraineté de la nation et à sa constitution essentielle"). See J. Miller, *Rousseau*; Rose, *Making of the Sans-Culottes*, 127; Hammersley, *French Revolutionaries*, 47–48. For a contrary view: Monnier, *Républicanisme*, 62.

37. See Marat, *L'ami du peuple*, no. 142 (Aug. 3, 1790), 8 (for quote: "Sacrifier six cent têtes pour en sauver trois millions trois cent mille, est un calcul tout simple que dicte la sagesse & la philosophie"); no. 356 (Jan. 30, 1790), 100,000 heads; no. 471 (May 27, 1791), 500,000 heads. More generally: Baker, *Jean-Paul Marat*.

38. See e.g.: "Il n'est pas étrange que les plus mortels ennemis du peuple siègent dans l'assemblée nationale" (Marat, *L'ami du peuple*, no. 383 [Feb. 26, 1791], 1).

39. Details in Rose, *Making of the Sans-Culottes*, 48–60.

40. Brissot, "Ma profession de foi" (July 1791): "Les républicains de France ne veulent point la démocratie pure d'Athènes. . . . Ils ne veulent donc point ressusciter les troubles que ces démocraties entraînoient; ils ne veulent qu'un gouvernement dont la représentation soit la base essentielle" (partially quoted in Rosanvallon, "History of the Word," 144). Letter from the Commune, Oct. 15, 1789: "Lorsqu'ils [les peuples libres] ont déposé leurs pouvoirs entre les mains de leurs Représentants, ils ne savent plus qu'obéir" (quoted in Genty, "Pratique et théorie," 12).

41. Hammersley: the districts "insisted that sovereignty should be held and exercised by the citizens gathered in the district assemblies" (*French Revolutionaries*, 13); and see Rose, *Making of the Sans-Culottes*, 72; Genty, "Pratique et théorie," 9.

42. Marat himself describes this incident in *L'ami du peuple*, no. 93 (Jan. 10, 1790). A first warrant for his arrest had already been issued in October. See *HP*, 4:290–95; Baker, *Jean-Paul Marat*. The Cordeliers was not the only district that resisted the Châtelet's jurisdiction: see Burstin, *Une révolution à l'œuvre*, 130–33.

43. "Nul décret ou ordre, quel qu'en soit la nature, tendant à priver un citoyen de sa liberté, ne serait mis à exécution dans le territoire du district, sans qu'il n'eut été revêtu du *visa* des cinq commissaires" (*HP*, 4:294). The Cordeliers had already passed a resolution in October 1789 stating that it would protect "all authors in its jurisdiction, and will defend them with all its power": see Horn, *Making of a Terrorist*, 21.

44. "On ne doit qu'applaudir aux districts qui soutiennent que ces décrets ou ordres ne doivent être exécutés qu'après avoir été visés par des commissaires honorés à cet effet du choix de *la véritable commune* jusqu'à ce que le grand oeuvre de la régénération française soit tellement accompli" (*HP*, 4:294).

45. *HP*, 4:295 (for quote).

46. On the demands for a republic: see e.g., the Cordeliers' *Adresse à la nation* (July 12, 1791), in Mathiez, *Le Club des Cordeliers*, 97. There were similar republican demands by Brissot and Danton (Mathiez, 97n3); see also Rose, *Making of the Sans-Culottes*, 132; Tacket, *King took Flight*; Hammersley, *French Revolutionaries*, 50. On the role of the sovereign, see the Cordeliers' petition of July 9: "Il n'appart[ient] qu'à la nation de prononcer sur cet étrange événement" (quoted in Mathiez, *Le Club des Cordeliers*, 87). On the Cordeliers' petition of July 14: "Tout décret, qui ne se renfermeroit pas

dans les bornes qui vous sont prescrites, seroit frappé de nullité et auroit en même tems le caractère du plus étrange attentat aux droits du Souverain, le Peuple" (quoted in *Le Club des Cordeliers*, 113).

47. For the assembly's decision: *AP*, 28:335 (July 15), and 28:374 (July 16). For Hébert: *Grande colère du Père Duchesne contre les traîtres de l'Assemblée nationale*, no. 63 (July 16, 1791), in Brunet, *Le Père Duchesne*, 87. On the massacre itself: Andress, *Massacre*.

48. See A. Mayer, *Furies*; Wahnich, *Liberté ou la mort*; see also Duong, *Virtues of Violence*.

49. Rudé, *Crowd*, 95–113; Reinhard, *Chute de la royauté*; Burstin, *Une révolution à l'œuvre*, 403–14.

50. Aug. 12, 1792, *AP*, 48:79: "Le peuple, forcé de veiller lui-même à son propre salut, a pourvu à sa sûreté par des délégués. . . . Il faut que ceux qu'il a choisis lui-même pour ses magistrats aient toute la plénitude de pouvoir qui convient au souverain." See Tackett, *Coming of the Terror*, 195–97. The "insurrectionary" Commune included two other future members of the Committee of Public Safety, Billaud-Varenne and Collot d'Herbois; Jean-Lambert Tallien, who as a *conventionnel* led the repression of Bordeaux; and Marat.

51. Aug. 31, 1792, *AP*, 49:144: "Allez, agissez en mon nom, et j'approuverai tout ce que vous aurez fait." This speech was possibly written by Robespierre: a nineteenth-century historian claimed to have seen a version (since burned) with edits in Robespierre's hand. See Mortimer-Ternaux, *Histoire de la Terreur*, 3:175n1.

52. See *HP*, 17:410–11; Braesch, *Commune du 10 août*, chap. 3.

53. See Tallien's August 31 speech to the assembly, justifying all the actions: *AP*, 49:144.

54. Mortimer-Ternaux, *Histoire de la Terreur*, 3:89.

55. Brasech, *Commune du 10 août*, 374 ("Il apparut, au lendemain du 10 août, qu'il y avait en France deux pouvoirs également qualifiés pour parler à la province au nom de la nation").

56. On the illegality of the Commune's actions: René-Pierre Choudieu, speech of Aug. 30, 1792, in *AP*, 49:111. The decree was proposed that same day by Pierre-Joseph Cambon: "L'Assemblée nationale, voulant assurer le maintien de la souveraineté du peuple, décrète que les commissaires provisoires, représentants de la Commune de Paris, justifieront des pouvoirs qu'ils ont reçus du peuple composant les sections de cette ville" (49:111).

57. Aug. 31, 1792, *AP*, 49:145: "Voudriez-vous, Messieurs, déshonorer notre belle Révolution, en donnant à tout l'empire le scandale d'une commune rebelle à la volonté générale, à la loi?"

58. Proclamation of Aug. 11, 1792, quoted in Braesch, *Commune du 10 août*, 350.

59. Boulant, *Le tribunal révolutionnaire*, chap. 1.

60. Braesch, *Commune du 10 août*, 350–73.

61. See Caron, *Les massacres de septembre*; Bluche, *Septembre 1792*; Wahnich, *Liberté ou la mort*; Tackett, *Coming of the Terror*, chap. 8.

62. Braesch, *Commune du 10 août*, 518–20; Tackett, *Coming of the Terror*, 199. The circular letter, *Circulaire adressée le 3 Septembre par le comité de surveillance de la Commune, aux départements*, has been reproduced in various places, notably:

Peltier, *Dernier tableau de Paris*, 372; and discussed in Caron, *Les massacres de septembre*, 289–96.

63. Caron, *Les massacres de septembre*: 95–99, 304 (on the identity and breakdown of the victims); 435 (on the connection with popular sovereignty). See also Soboul: "During the rising of September 1792, the people took control of the administration of justice, as an essential aspect of their sovereignty" (*Sans-Culottes*, 131–32).

64. Tackett adopts Georges Lefebvre's label of "the first terror" in *Coming of the Terror* (192–93); see Lefebvre, *French Revolution*, 1:241. This connection was already common in the nineteenth century, as Mortimer-Ternaux's *Histoire de la Terreur* makes clear.

65. See e.g., Mudde, "Populist Zeitgeist" (on general will, 543); Müller, *What Is Populism?* For populism in the French Revolution: Rousselière, "Popular Sovereignty"; Baker, *Jean-Paul Marat*.

66. On the white terror: H. Brown, *Ending the French Revolution*, 127. On emotions in the Terror, see notably: Reddy, *Navigation of Feeling*, esp. chap. 6; Linton, *Choosing Terror*; Andress, "Jacobinism as Heroic Narrative."

67. Speech to the National Convention, Nov. 5, 1792, *AP*, 53:158–65 (quotes at 160–61).

68. For the period 1789–91, *peuple* was the third-most-commonly associated word with *révolution*. Data produced thanks to the collocation function of ARTFL's PhiloLogic search engine: see https://artflsrv03.uchicago.edu/philologic4/archparl/.

69. Decree of Sept. 14, 1791, *AP*, 30:632 ("faits relatifs à la Révolution"); see Lafayette's decree, adopted the day before: *AP*, 30:621.

70. *AP*, 53:164.

71. For Vergniaud: speech to the National Convention, March 13, 1793, *AP*, 60:165: "Les anarchistes t'ont trompé par l'abus qu'ils ont fait du mot Souveraineté. Peu s'en est fallu qu'ils n'aient bouleversé la République, en faisant croire à chaque section que la souveraineté résidait dans son sein"; see also Soboul, *Sans-Culottes*, 131. On the proposal to move the capital, see Armand Gensonné's speech to the National Convention of April 20, 1793 (*AP*, 63:17).

72. I discuss these events at greater length in *Terror of Natural Right* (chap. 3).

73. For the text of the letter: *AP*, 61:637: "La contre-révolution est dans le gouvernement, dans la Convention nationale." For a more detailed account of these incidents: David Bell, *First Total War*; Baker, *Jean-Paul Marat*.

74. Linton, *Choosing Terror*, chap. 6 (though her chronology is somewhat different: see 174).

75. Baker, *Jean-Paul Marat*.

76. Petition read before the National Convention on April 15, 1793, *AP*, 62:132–34. As in July 1791, the Parisians insisted that the Convention put the question to the departments.

77. Speech to the National Convention on May 25, 1793, *AP*, 65:320: "Si par ces insurrections toujours renaissantes il arrivait qu'on portât atteinte à la représentation nationale, je vous le déclare, au nom de la France entière, Paris serait anéanti. . . . on chercherait sur les rives de la Seine si Paris a existé."

78. See Tourneux, *Procès-verbaux de la Commune*, 138; the name was chosen on June 1, 1793 (150). On this insurrection: Rudé, *Crowd*, chap. 8; Slavin, *Making of an Insurrection*; Tackett, *Coming of the Terror*, 270–76; Alpaugh, *Non-violence*, chap. 5.

79. Decree of June 2, 1793, *AP*, 65:708.

80. See Gaudet, speech to the Convention on May 17, 1793, *AP*, 65:38; Brissot, writing to his constituents on May 27, 1793: "C'est cette purgation du colonel Pride . . . qu'on veut renouveler dans la Convention" (*AP*, 65:399). See Sydenham, *Girondins*, 173.

81. Brinton, *Anatomy of Revolution*, 127–37. Brinton also draws on Lenin's dual-power argument in his analysis, though focuses on different groups (e.g., the Convention vs. the Jacobin Club).

82. For Thuriot: decree of June 2, 1793, *AP*, 65:708. For the initial presentation of the constitution: *AP*, 66:257–64; for the final version: *AP*, 67:143–50.

83. See arts. 53, 58–60 (in part, popular approval depended on tacit consent). By comparison, the "Girondin" constitution that Condorcet had presented in February 1793 attributed "l'exercice *plein et entier* de la puissance législative" to the legislative body (title 7, § 2, art 1; *AP*, 58:617; emphasis added). The people could still challenge a law, however: see title 8, "De la censure du peuple" (619). For an interesting comparison of the two constitutions: Mathiez, "La constitution de 1793." On Condorcet's constitution: Rosanvallon, *La démocratie inachevée*; Urbinati, *Representative Democracy*, chap. 6.

84. On the executive: art. 75: "Le Conseil exécutif réside auprès du Corps législatif; il a l'entrée et une place séparée dans le lieu de ses séances." Cf. Selinger (*Parliamentarism*), who sees this kind of integration as a later development. Condorcet's constitution maintained executive and legislative powers more separately: see esp. title V, § 3, art. 2 (*AP*, 58:608).

85. See Soboul, *Mouvement populaire*, 56 ("l'unanimité factice").

86. I discuss the ratification festival and reasons for suspending the constitution in greater detail in *The Terror of Natural Right* (chap. 4).

87. Soboul, *Mouvement populaire*, chap. 3; Burstin, *Une révolution à l'œuvre*, 619–21.

88. On this phrase: Martin, *Violence et révolution*.

89. See Greer, *Incidence of the Terror*; Mari, *Mise hors de la loi*; Martin, *Violence et révolution*; D. Edelstein, *Terror of Natural Right*, chap. 3.

90. Already on August 11, Robespierre had spoken out against holding elections: see speech in *Œuvres* (10:65). Billaud-Varenne acknowledged the threat posed by the "administrateurs fédéralistes des départements" in his *Rapport . . . sur un mode de gouvernement provisoire & révolutionnaire* (7).

91. See e.g., Palmer, *Twelve Who Ruled*; Soboul, *Mouvement populaire*, 179.

92. See the accusations made by Brissot and Guadet at the Jacobin Club on April 25, 1792: in Aulard, *La Société des Jacobins*, 526–36.

93. Marat, *L'ami du peuple*, no. 634 (April 19, 1792): "un dictateur suprême, dont les pouvoirs soient circonscrits de manière que sans autorité pour dominer, il en est une illimitée pour abattre les chefs des conspirateurs." Marat first called for a dictator in July 1790: *L'ami du peuple*, no. 177, 8. Rousseau described the office of dictator in the *Social Contract* (4.6). On the original Roman model: Lintott, *Constitution*; Baehr and Richter, *Dictatorship in History and Theory*; Fichtl, *La Radicalisation de l'idéal républicain*; Baker, *Jean-Paul Marat*.

94. Dahl, *Democracy and Its Critics*, chap. 4.

95. See e.g., Stephen Kotkin's introduction to *Magnetic Mountain* (1–25).

96. Billaud-Varenne, *Discours*, 4: "A-t-on une constitution, quand elle est insuffisante pour assurer la prospérité de l'empire, le bonheur du peuple, et la paix dans l'intérieur?"

97. Billaud-Varenne, *Mode de gouvernement provisoire*, 2–5. On the importance of revolutionary government: e.g., Saint-Just, original Oct. 10 speech: "Citoyens, tous les ennemis de la République sont dans son gouvernement" (*AP*, 76:313); Robespierre, December 25 speech on "the principles of revolutionary government," in *Œuvres*, 10:276; decree introduced by Billaud-Varenne in his second speech on revolutionary government (April 20, 1794): the Convention "fera triompher la République democratique, et qu'elle punira ses ennemis" (*Théorie du gouvernement démocratique*, 24). On the rhetorical shift from "terror" to "justice": D. Edelstein, *Terror of Natural Right*, chap. 5.

98. Billaud-Varenne, *Mode de gouvernement provisoire*, 5 (on the natural process and three principles); 9 (on the organic code: "modèle pour la rédaction du code organique de la constitution"); 6, 8 (on the mechanics).

99. On this suspicion: D. Edelstein and Sawyer, "Sovereignty and Government."

100. Decree of Sept. 14, 1791, *AP*, 30:632: "L'objet de la Révolution française a été de donner une Constitution à l'Empire, et qu'ainsi la Révolution doit prendre fin au moment où la Constitution est achevée et acceptée."

101. See Hartog, *Regimes of Historicity*; C. Clark, *Time and Power*.

102. Robespierre, "Rapports sur des idées religieuses et morales avec les principes républicains, et sur les fêtes nationales," May 7, 1794, in *Œuvres*, 10:442–65 (quote at 444).

103. Aulard, *Culte de la raison*. On the economic demands during this period: Gross, *Fair Shares for All*.

104. See Soboul, *Mouvement populaire*, 321–38.

105. David A. Bell, "Waiting for Caesar in France," in *Men on Horseback*, 91–132. More generally: McPhee, *Robespierre*. On Thermidor 9: C. Jones, *Fall of Robespierre*.

Chapter Eleven

1. Constitution of 22 frimaire year VIII (Dec. 13, 1799), arts. 41 and 44. The French text of the proclamation reads, "La Révolution est fixée aux principes qui l'ont commencée: elle est finie." See notably: Velley, "Une constitution trop 'vivante'?"

2. See Baczko, *Ending the Terror*; H. Brown, *Ending the French Revolution*; Jainchill, *Reimagining Politics*; Belissa and Bosc, *Le Directoire*.

3. See e.g., Lyons, *Napoleon Bonaparte*; Gueniffey, *Bonaparte*; David Bell, *Napoleon*.

4. See e.g., Lyons, *Napoleon Bonaparte*, chap. 6; Dwyer, "'Citizen Emperor.'"

5. See, esp., Rosenblatt, *Lost History of Liberalism*, chap. 2. See also Bertier de Sauvigny, "Liberalism, Nationalism and Socialism"; Siedentop, "Two Liberal Traditions"; Manent, *Intellectual History of Liberalism*; Vierhaus, "Liberalismus"; Mehta, *Liberalism and Empire*; Dijn, *French Political Thought*; Ryan, *Making of Modern Liberalism*; Duncan Bell, "What Is Liberalism?"

6. See notably: Lyons, *Napoleon Bonaparte*, chap. 19. See also Hazareesingh, *Legend of Napoleon*. In *Reimagining Politics*, Jainchill describes the constitution of 1799 in terms of "liberal authoritarianism," a term he borrows from Howard Brown (*Ending the French Revolution*, part 3).

7. See "Proclamation des consuls," in Constitution of 22 frimaire. More generally: Woloch, *Napoleon and His Collaborators*; Gueniffey, *Bonaparte*, chap. 24; David Bell, *Napoleon*; Colley, *Gun*.

8. See e.g., Francis Fukuyama, who in *Liberalism and Its Discontents* acknowledges Napoleon's contribution to liberalism, but focuses on property rights. On the "retreat" of Cold War liberals from a more progressive project: Moyn, *Liberalism against Itself*.

9. "Proclamation des consuls," in Constitution of 22 frimaire.

10. The French enjoyed property rights (albeit of a different nature) before the French Revolution: see e.g., Blaufarb, *Great Demarcation*.

11. See notably: Palmer, *Age of the Democratic Revolution*; Doyle, *Oxford History*, chap. 15; Acemoglu et al., "Consequences of Radical Reform"; Oddens, Jacobs, and Rutjes, *Political Culture*; Planert, *Napoleon's Empire*.

12. See Rodriguez O., "Hispanic Revolution" and *True Spaniards*, esp. chap. 5; Eastman and Sobrevilla Perea, *Rise of Constitutional Government*; Breña, "Cádiz Liberal Revolution."

13. See notably: Sarasola, "Primera constitución española." Sarasola suggests that Hugues-Bernard Maret (who drew up constitutions for other "sister republics") also drafted the Bayonne constitution. See also Adelman, "Iberian Passages"; Ternavasio, "Impact of Spanish Constitutionalism"; Colley, *Gun*, 184–85.

14. Bonaparte, "Proclamation": "Tout ce qui s'opposait à votre prospérité et à votre grandeur, je l'ai détruit; les entraves qui pesaient sur le peuple, je les ai brisées; une constitution libérale vous donne, au lieu d'une monarchie absolue, une monarchie tempérée et constitutionnelle."

15. For an earlier use, see the "Proclamation du Général en Chef Bonaparte," 19 Brumaire year VIII (Nov. 10, 1799): "Les idées conservatrices, tutélaires, libérales, sont rentrées dans leurs droits par la dispersion des factieux qui opprimaient les Conseils, et qui, pour être devenus les plus odieux des hommes, n'ont pas cessé d'être les plus méprisables"; quoted in Bertier de Sauvigny ("Liberalism, Nationalism and Socialism," 151), who notes that this proclamation was likely written by P.-J.-G. Cabanis. See also Jainchill, *Reimagining Politics*, chap. 5 (who notes that Constant had adopted the term in this political sense in 1796).

"Liberal," in its political meaning, entered the *Dictionnaire de l'Académie française* only in 1835. Emile Littré's 1873 dictionary provides a few earlier examples from Mme de Staël and Chateaubriand: see *Dictionnaire de la langue française*, s.v. "libéral." The use of "liberal" in the expression "liberal arts" or "liberal education" (phrases which were also common in French) is unrelated to the emergence of the term's political meaning, as these expressions were direct translations from Latin (*studia liberalia, artes liberales*). The French use of "liberal" in this political sense was likely influenced by earlier English usage: see Rosenblatt, *Lost History of Liberalism*, chap. 1. Tellingly, when Burke's *Reflections* were translated into French in 1790, the translator rendered "This idea of a liberal descent" as "Cette idée d'une transmission glorieuse": see *Réflexions sur la révolution*, 65.

16. See Colley, *Gun*: "Because of his invasion of the Iberian peninsula, and because of the complex repercussions of his Bayonne Statute, Napoleon helped to foster the spread of written constitutions into the length and breadth of South America" (193).

17. Art. 60 created a "commission sénatoriale de la liberté individuelle"; art. 64, a "commission sénatoriale de la liberté de la presse." On these commissions: Sibalis, "Arbitrary Detention"; Le Quang, "La Commission sénatoriale."

18. This phrase had in fact already featured in the 1795 constitution, art. 395 ("La maison de chaque citoyen est un asile inviolable"), whose wording repeated that of Condorcet's 1793 constitutional proposal (see title X, § 6, art. 14, in *AP*, 58:623, Feb. 16, 1793).

19. Article 7 reads, "No man may be accused, arrested or detained except in the cases determined by the Law, and following the procedure that it has prescribed. Those who solicit, expedite, carry out, or cause to be carried out arbitrary orders must be punished."

20. "Décret sur la réformation de quelques points de la jurisprudence criminelle," in *AP*, 9:394; Oct. 9, 1789.

21. Code pénal, pt. 2, title 1, § 3, art. 19, in *AP*, 31:332; Sept. 25, 1791.

22. See Sarasola, "Primera constitución española"; Adelman, "Iberian Passages," 72; Breña, "Cádiz Liberal Revolution," 100n13; Colley, *Gun*.

23. See Agesta, *Discurso preliminar*, 70, 76. A French translation of this preliminary report was more readily available: see Commission des Cortès, "Rapport," viii, xxii. (A second French translation was published in 1823.) On this report: Busaall, "Constitution politique"; see also Hamnett, "Medieval Roots."

24. *Constitución política de la monarquía española* (Cádiz: Imprenta real, 1812): "La soberanía reside esencialmente en la Nación," art. 3; cf. "Le principe de toute souveraineté réside essentiellement dans la nation" (1789 Declaration, art. 3). See also Herr, "Constitution of 1812."

25. Both included a final legalist caveat: compare "following the restrictions and the responsibility established by the laws" (art. 371) with "except in cases where this liberty is abused, as in cases determined by the law" (1789 Declaration, art. 11).

26. Popkin, *You Are All Free*, 17–18.

27. See Hazareesingh, *Black Spartacus*; David Bell, "The Spartacus of the Caribbean," in *Men on Horseback*, 133–70.

28. See notably: Girard, "Napoléon Bonaparte." See also Dubois, *Avengers*.

29. See esp., Getachew, "Universalism."

30. See e.g., Raaflaub, *Discovery of Freedom*.

31. Dubois, *Avengers*, 7; see also Buck-Morss, *Hegel*; Getachew, "Universalism."

32. See e.g., Robin Blackburn: "African values and concepts animated the liberation wars" in (*American Crucible*, 199). Contrast Lynn Hunt: "Without the initial declaration [of the Rights of Man and of the Citizen], the abolition of slavery in 1794 would have remained inconceivable" (*Inventing Human Rights*, 166).

33. See Popkin, *You Are All Free*.

34. Dubois, *Colony of Citizens*.

35. Friedland, "Every Island."

36. Geggus, "Caribbean," 97, 100.

37. 1801 constitution: "La loi y est la même pour tous, soit qu'elle punisse, soit qu'elle protège" (art. 5); cf. 1805 constitution: "La loi est une pour tous, soit qu'elle

punisse, soit qu'elle protège" (art. 4); cf. the 1789 Declaration: the law "doit être la même pour tous, soit qu'elle protège, soit qu'elle punisse" (art. 6). See also 1806 constitution, art. 5.

38. 1801 constitution: "La propriété est sacrée et inviolable" (art. 13); 1805 constitution: "La propriété est sacrée" (art. 6); cf. the 1789 Declaration: "La propriété étant un droit inviolable et sacré" (art. 17). See also 1806 constitution, art. 8.

39. 1801 constitution: "La maison de toutes personnes est un asile inviolable" (art. 63); 1805 constitution: "La maison de tout citoyen est un asile inviolable" (General Dispositions, art. 6); cf. 1795 constitution: "La maison de chaque citoyen est un asile inviolable" (art. 359), rephrased slightly in the 1799 constitution, art. 76. Given that the 1795 constitution also concluded with a section "General Dispositions," it is likely that the Haitian framers had this text as their model. This article reappeared in subsequent Haitian constitutions as well (e.g., 1806 constitution, art. 24).

40. See Dubois, *Haiti.*

41. Machiavelli, *Discourses*, 1.5.

42. Rodríguez O., *True Spaniards*, chap. 2.

43. See Rodríguez O., Sobrevilla Perea, "Cádiz Constitution."

44. *Venezuelan Declaration of Independence*. More generally: Lynch, *Simón Bolívar*. On the 1811 constitution: Lynch, *Spanish American Revolutions*, 197; D. Edelstein, *Spirit of Rights*, 205.

45. Art. 49. At the time, one peso was equal to one dollar. For comparison's sake, Thomas Jefferson estimated the value of Monticello at $6,300 in 1800: see Thomas Jefferson Foundation, "Cost of Monticello," The Jefferson Monticello, https://www.monticello.org/site/research-and-collections/cost-monticello.

46. Simon, *Ideology of Creole Revolution.*

47. Simón Bolívar, *The Cartagena Manifesto*, in *El Libertador*, 3–7.

48. Adelman, "Iberian Passages."

49. On the 1826 constitution of Cúcuta: Lynch, *Simón Bolívar*, 201–4.

50. See Lynch, *Spanish American Revolutions*, 335–40; Rodríguez O., *Independence of Spanish America*, 194–95; Kinsbruner, *Independence in Spanish America*, 89.

51. See Rodríguez O., *True Spaniards*; Colley, *Gun*, 191. For the Mexican constitution of 1824: *Constitutive Acts of the Mexican Federation* (Mexico, 1824).

52. Bolívar, *El Libertador*, 56–57.

53. Simon, *Ideology of Creole Revolution*, 114.

54. Bolívar, *El Libertador*, 61.

55. To be a citizen, Bolivians needed to be 21 years old (or married), literate, and employed, but not as a "domestic servant" (art. 13)—the same exclusion found in the French 1793 constitution.

56. Bolívar, *El Libertador*, 57.

57. Sobrevilla Perea, *Caudillo of the Andes*, 9–13 (on constitutionalism and contrast with military dictators), 126 (for quote); see also Lynch, *Caudillos in Spanish America*, 407–8 (on balancing class interests).

58. Breña, "Cádiz Liberal Revolution," 95.

59. Sobrevilla Perea, *Caudillo of the Andes*, 13 (on Bolívar as a model), 9 (on national liberation).

60. See Bell's *Men on Horseback*, on charisma, and similarities between Napoleon and Bolívar. On the role of military officers in the promotion of liberal ideas in Europe, see also Maurizio Isabella's *Southern Europe in the Age of Revolutions*.

61. See Garner, *Porfirio Diaz*. This same quote features today on the Brazilian flag.

62. See Arvind and Stirton, "Explaining the Reception."

63. See Nakhimovsky, *Holy Alliance*. More generally: Vick, *Congress of Vienna*; Lok, *Europe against Revolution*.

64. Hugo, *Les misérables*, 635: "Il faut en ce siècle que la Révolution soit partout."

65. See Coverdale, *Basque Phase*, chap. 3; Alonso, "Cádiz Reprised."

66. See Paquette, *Imperial Portugal*; Rivero, "Portuguese Uprising of 1820"; Isabella, *Southern Europe*, 146–61.

Art. 17 of the 1822 constitution (on "the free communication of thoughts") directly translates art. 11 of the 1789 Declaration; art. 2 draws on arts. 4–5; art. 4, on art. 7; art. 6, on art. 17; art. 9, on art. 6; art. 12, on art. 6; and art. 26, on art. 3. The Portuguese preamble also borrows heavily from the 1789 preamble: compare "intimately convinced [*intimamente convencidas*] that the public misfortunes, which have so oppressed and still oppress them, had their origin in the contempt of the citizen's rights [*no desprezo dos direitos do cidadão*], and in the forgetfulness [*no esquecimento*] of the fundamental laws of the Monarchy" with the French, "believing that the ignorance, neglect, or contempt [*l'ignorance, l'oubli ou le mépris*] of the rights of man are the sole cause of public calamities and of the corruption of governments."

67. See Romani, *Neapolitan Revolution*, 26 (on the Francophilia of the revolution's Muratist leader, Gen. Guglielmo Pepe). See also Rath, "Carbonari"; Billington, *Fire in the Minds*; Stites, *Four Horsemen*, chap. 3; Isabella, *Southern Europe*, 192–97.

68. For the Napoleonic oath, see art. 6 of the Bayonne constitution, and art. 53 of the 1804 constitution.

69. Schneid, "War and Revolution."

70. Mazower, *Greek Revolution*, epigraph to chap. 1 for quote. See also Isabella, *Southern Europe*, 205–17.

71. Billington, *Fire in the Minds*, 134.

72. Mazower, *Greek Revolution*, 11.

73. Tolstoy, *War and Peace*, 21. Yarmolinsky, *Road to Revolution*, chap. 2. See also Stites, *Four Horsemen*, chap. 5; Nakhimovsky, *Holy Alliance*.

74. Yarmolinsky, *Road to Revolution*, 21.

75. Stites, *Four Horsemen*, chap. 5.

76. Sotiropoulos, *Liberalism after the Revolution*.

77. Rosanvallon, *La monarchie impossible*; Craiutu, *Liberalism under Siege*.

78. Rey, *Adresse à l'Empereur*, 9, quoted in Billington, *Fire in the Minds*, 135. See also Lyons, *Napoleon Bonaparte*, chap. 19.

79. Alexander, *French Revolutionary Tradition*.

80. Traugott, *Insurgent Barricade*.

81. See notably François Furet's *Revolutionary France, 1770–1880*.

82. Sawyer, *Demos Rising*.

83. Tomasi di Lampedusa, *Leopard*, 75.

84. C. Clark, *Revolutionary Spring*, 52–63.

85. Musset, *La confession*, 23.

86. Arnold, "Grande Chartreuse," st. l, ll. 85–86. More broadly: Yack, *Longing for Total Revolution*; Fritzsche, *Stranded in the Present*.

87. Hartog, *Regimes of Historicity*, 73, referencing Koselleck, "Modernity."

Chapter Twelve

1. See Craiutu, *Virtue for Courageous Minds*.

2. Constant, "Liberty of Ancients."

3. Duncan Bell, "Mythscapes" and *Dreamworlds of Race*. For the Orwell quote, see the epigraph to this chapter (*1984*, 148).

4. Camus, *L'homme révolté*, 125n1: "On compterait sur les doigts de la main les communistes qui sont venus à la révolution par l'étude du marxisme. On se convertit d'abord et on lit ensuite les Ecritures et les Pères." This theme of an "irrational" conversion to the revolution is common in the secondary (especially Anglo-American) literature on revolutionary history: see for instance, Edmund Wilson's assessment of "the purely emotional character of [Mikhail Bakunin's] rebellion," in *To the Finland Station* (279). More generally: Manuel, *Prophets of Paris*.

5. Cabet, *Voyage en Icarie*, 56.

6. W. Morris, *News from Nowhere*; Cole, *William Morris*, 1.

7. See Saint-Simon, *De la réorganisation*, 112. On this text, see notably Frank Manuel's *New World of Henri Saint-Simon* (172–79). On Signac: A. Dymond, "Politicized Pastoral."

8. See e.g., Union centrale des arts décoratifs and Musée des arts décoratifs, *Le Livre des expositions*.

9. Du Camp, *Les chants modernes*, quote at 47.

10. "Rapports sur des idées religieuses."

11. C. Clark, *Revolutionary Spring*, 33–51.

12. See Fourier, *Utopian Vision*; Beecher, *Charles Fourier*.

13. See Sawyer, *Demos Rising*.

14. Cabet, *Voyage en Icarie*, 38–39.

15. Bakunin, "Critique," 332.

16. Gerçek, "'Social Question.'"

17. Quoted in Berlin, "Russia and 1848," 3.

18. Brecht, "The Solution," ll. 9–11.

19. See Chakrabarty, *Provincializing Europe*.

20. See e.g., Marx, *Class Struggles in France*, 55.

21. Flaubert, *Bouvard et Pécuchet*, 191.

22. See Saint-Pierre, *Projet pour perfectionner*, 231; see also chapter 8.

23. Ov., *Met.* 1.89–90: "vindice nullo, sponte sua, sine lege fidem rectumque colebat."

24. See Bougainville, *Voyage autour du monde*; Diderot, *Supplément au voyage*. More generally: Grell and Michel, *Primitivisme*.

25. Grafton, *New Worlds, Ancient Texts*.

26. See e.g., Fourier, *Utopian Vision*, 52 and passim; Pilbeam, *Saint-Simonians*; Heckert and Cleminson, *Anarchism & Sexuality*; Marx and Engels, *Communist Manifesto* (on the abolition of marriage: "The Communists might possibly be

reproached . . . that they desire to introduce, in substitution for a hypocritically concealed, an openly legalised community of women"), chap. 2.

27. Morelly, *Code de la nature*, 120 (same page for golden age). Engels discusses Morelly in *Socialism: Utopian and Scientific* (1880), chap. 1.

28. See e.g., Pl., *Criti.* 108d–121c; Sprague de Camp, *Lost Continents*.

29. More generally: D. Edelstein, "Hyperborean Atlantis."

30. Marx, *Foundations of the Critique of Political Economy* (or *Grundrisse*, 1857–58), in Marx and Engels, *Reader*, 246.

31. Zola, *Germinal*, 1328; cf. also: "Et les idées semées par Étienne poussaient, s'élargissaient dans ce cri de révolte. C'était l'impatience devant l'âge d'or promis" (1292).

32. Dostoevsky, *Adolescent*, 466–67. See also Peace, "Dostoyevsky." This same vision features in the famous chapter of *The Possessed* [*Demons*], "Stavrogin's Confession," which was excised from the original edition: see Joseph Frank, *Miraculous Years*, 488–92.

33. Sorel, *Reflections on Violence*, 20. See Roth, *Cult of Violence*; Stanley, *Sociology of Virtue*.

34. Marx and Engels, *Reader*, 597.

35. See e.g., Stedman Jones, "Religion."

36. Chernyshevsky, *Vital Question*, e.g. 378; Lenin, *What Is to Be Done?* See notably: Paperno, *Chernyshevsky*; Joseph Frank, *Through the Russian Prism*, 187 (and on Lenin, 199–200). See also Stites, *Revolutionary Dreams*, 26–28.

37. Proudhon, *What Is Property?*, 268, 56; *Qu'est-ce que la propriété?*, 293, 41–42. On Proudhon, see notably: Cole, *Socialist Thought*; Noland, "History and Humanity"; Beecher, *Writers and Revolution*, chap. 7.

38. See e.g., Tucker, *Philosophy and Myth*, 107–8; Stedman Jones, *Karl Marx*.

39. Marx and Engels, *Reader*, 472.

40. For instance, Engels amended the famous statement in the *Manifesto* that "the history of all hitherto existing society is the history of class struggles," adding a footnote in the 1888 edition: "That is, of all *written* history" (Marx and Engels, *Reader*, 473). Before written history, the note goes on, "village communities were found to be, or to have been the primitive form of society everywhere from India to Ireland."

41. Morgan, *Ancient Society*, 552; Engels, *Origin of the Family*.

42. Proudhon, *L'idée générale*, 112.

43. Bloom, "'Withering Away.'"

44. Marx, *Eighteenth Brumaire*, in Marx and Engels, *Reader*, 594–617.

45. Chakrabarty, *Provincializing Europe*.

46. See Berlin, "Russia and 1848"; see also Verhoeven, "'Une Révolution Vraiment Scientifique,'" 203.

47. Verhoeven, *Odd Man Karakozov*.

48. See Siljak, *Angel of Vengeance*; Patyk, *Written in Blood*.

49. Lenin, *What Is to Be Done?*, in *Anthology*, 28.

50. Robespierre, "On the Principles of Political Morality" (Feb. 5, 1794), in *Œuvres*, 10:353.

51. Lenin, "Enemies of the People," in *Anthology*, 306.

52. Buonarotti, *Conspiration pour l'égalité*. On the Babouvists, see notably: Dommanget, *Sylvain Maréchal, l'égalitaire*; Rose, *Gracchus Babeuf*; Billington, *Fire in the Minds*. Laura Mason has recently questioned many of Buonarotti's assertions, in *The Last Revolutionaries*. See more generally: Baehr and Richter, *Dictatorship in History*.

53. Buonarotti, *Conspiration pour l'égalité*, 109, 215, 221, 238.

54. Buonarotti, 9–11.

55. Buonarotti, 134, 200, 93, 201, 202.

56. Buonarotti, 138.

57. Buonarotti, 133.

58. Blanqui, *Défense*, 9. More generally: Hutton, *Cult of the Revolutionary*. Blanqui's argument echoes Montesquieu's criticism of the Venetian Republic, in the famous chapter on the English constitution: the separation of powers does not exist when they are all controlled by the same social group. See Montesquieu, *Spirit of Laws*, 11.6; see also chapter 5.

59. Blanqui, *Défense*, 4, 5, 7.

Chapter Thirteen

1. Saint-Simon, *De la réorganisation*, 79: "La marche de l'esprit humain est une et inaltérable et ne varie point selon les temps ou les lieux."

2. See e.g., Klein, "Baudelaire and Revolution."

3. See F. Brown, *Flaubert*, chap. 10. Flaubert arrived in Paris on February 23, the very day that Guizot resigned and that troops fired on the crowd gathered beneath the Ministry of Foreign Affairs. Flaubert was subsequently "among the first to enter" the Tuileries Palace, when it was stormed by a crowd the following day (210).

4. Wilson, "Politics of Flaubert," 72. See also Terdiman, *Discourse/Counter-discourse*, chap. 4; Jonsson, *Brief History*; Beecher, *Writers and Revolution*, chap. 10. On revolutionary emotions: Reddy, *Navigation of Feeling*.

5. Flaubert, *Sentimental Education*, 272; *L'education sentimentale*, 427.

6. Schiller, *An die Freude*; this line is from the postrevolutionary, 1808 revision.

7. Quoted in Aldred, *Bakunin*, 27.

8. Newman, *Life of Richard Wagner*, 2:49–53, 83 (on the choral), and passim.

9. Flaubert, *Sentimental Education*, 276; *L'education sentimentale*, 432.

10. See chapter 12. More generally: Koselleck, "Historical Criteria."

11. Flaubert, *Sentimental Education*, 278; *L'education sentimentale*, 432.

12. Flaubert, *Sentimental Education*, 273; *L'education sentimentale*, 428.

13. See notably: Smith Robertson, *Revolutions of 1848*; Sperber, *European Revolutions*; C. Clark, *Revolutionary Spring*, 557–68 (on the June Days).

14. Flaubert, *Sentimental Education*, 312; *L'education sentimentale*, 470.

15. Flaubert, *Sentimental Education*, 287 (translation modified); *L'education sentimentale*, 442 (and for the episode at the Club de l'intelligence more generally, 436–42).

16. On Flaubert's comparison of socialism to magic, see his letter of Nov. 13, 1879, to Maxime du Camp: "La Magie croit aux transformations immédiates par la vertu des formules, exactement comme le socialisme. Ni l'un ni l'autre ne tiennent compte du temps et de l'évolution fatale des choses," in *Correspondance*, 8:275.

17. Du Camp, *Souvenirs littéraires*, 2:328: "Si on avait compris *L'Education sentimentale*, rien de tout cela ne serait arrivé." See P. Brooks, *Flaubert in the Ruins*.

18. See Terdiman, *Discourse/Counter-discourse*, chap. 4. On Marx more generally, see notably: Sperber, *Karl Marx*; Stedman Jones, *Karl Marx*; Heinrich, *Karl Marx*.

19. Stedman Jones, *Karl Marx*, 234; on Blanqui, see chapter 12.

20. See e.g., Berman, *All That Is Solid*.

21. Marx and Engels, *Communist Manifesto*, chap. 4. See e.g., S. Moore, "Marx and Lenin."

22. Engels published these articles posthumously under the title *The Class Struggles in France, 1848 to 1850* (1895). On this work, and the role of historiography in the development of Marx's revolutionary theory: Krieger, "Marx and Engels"; Seigel, *Marx's Fate*; Hayes, "Marx's Analysis."

23. Marx, "Class Struggles in France." See also: "The French working class had not attained this level; *it was still incapable of accomplishing its own revolution*" (emphasis added). For pagination purposes, I provide page references to the MEGA edition, as well as the original German citation when the wording matters: *Die Klassenkämpfe in Frankreich* (here, chap. 1, 127).

24. Marx, *Die Klassenkämpfe in Frankreich*, chap. 1, 136.

25. Marx, chap. 1, 136. See also: "So swiftly had the march of the revolution ripened conditions that the friends of reform of all shades . . . were compelled to group themselves around the banner of the most extreme party of revolution, around the *red flag*" (chap. 3, 190–91). See Seigel, *Marx's Fate*, 206–13.

26. Marx, *Die Klassenkämpfe in Frankreich*, chap. 1, 140.

27. Marx, chap. 3, 168. On Marx and Engels's anticonstitutional perspective during the 1848–50 revolutions, see also Engels's "The Campaign for the German Imperial Constitution," which comes down very strongly against the constitutional model, in Day and Gaido, *Witnesses to Permanent Revolution* (7–8). This rejection of purely "political" solutions to social inequality can be traced back to Marx's early arguments about human emancipation (notably in "On the Jewish Question"): see Seigel, *Marx's Fate*, chap. 4.

28. Marx, *Die Klassenkämpfe in Frankreich*, chap. 3, 169.

29. See Marx's criticism of the *Volkskultus* and his claim that "the real people," as opposed to "the imaginary" ones, were merely "representatives of the different classes." ("Es war dies ihr *Volkskultus*. Statt ihres *eingebildeten* Volkes brachten die Wahlen das *wirkliche* Volk ans Tageslicht, d.h. Repräsentaten der verschiedenen Klassen" [chap. 1, 135]). Note, however, that Marx also criticizes the bourgeois "Party of order" for suspending universal suffrage (at the end of chap. 3).

30. On Napoleon I's plebiscites, see chapter 11. His nephew Napoleon III continued this tradition, holding plebiscites in 1851 (to confirm his coup d'état) and in 1852 (to confirm his imperial position).

31. "Das *Proletariat* immer mehr um den *revolutionairen Socialismus*, um den *Communismus*, für den die Bourgeoisie selbst den Namen *Blanqui* erfunden hat. Dieser Socialismus ist die *Permanenz-Erklärung der Revolution*, die *Klassendictatur* des Proletariats als nothwendiger Durchgangspunkt zur *Abschaffung der* Klassenunterschiede *überhaupt*" (Marx, *Die Klassenkämpfe in Frankreich*, chap. 3, 192).

32. See, for instance, Billington: "In propounding this doctrine, [Marx] drew close to Blanqui, whose ideas would also provide fortification for Lenin at a later

time" (*Fire in the Minds*, 282). In his biography of Marx, David McLellan reads the reference to Blanqui literally, suggesting that Marx genuinely is describing "the revolutionary socialism of Blanqui" (*Karl Marx*, 239). On Blanqui, see notably Patrick H. Hutton's *Cult of the Revolutionary Tradition*. I am grateful to Biliana Kassabova for conversations about Blanqui's unpublished manuscripts.

33. On Marx's familiarity with Buonarotti: B. Brown, "French Revolution," esp. 423–24.

34. English translation (modified) from the Marx/Engels Internet Archive. For the original, see Marx and Engels, *Ansprache der Zentralbehörde*, 254–63. On this work, see notably Michael Löwy's *Theory of Revolution in the Young Marx* (149–52).

35. Marx and Engels, *Ansprache der Zentralbehörde*, 258.

36. Marx and Engels, 262.

37. Marx and Engels, 259.

38. Marx and Engels, 260.

39. Sperber, *Karl Marx*, 252. This was also McLellan's assessment (*Karl Marx*, 233).

40. Marx, "Crisis and the Counter-revolution." Lenin cites this passage in *Two Tactics of Social-Democracy*, in the epilogue: *Lenin Anthology* (142). The Nov. 23, 1848, issue of the *Neue Rheinische Zeitung* evokes the "Organ der in Permanenz erklärten Revolution"; see also the Jan. 13, 1849, article on the Hungarian War, which refers to "die Revolution in Permanenz."

41. Day and Gaido, *Witnesses to Permanent Revolution*, 3. Tucker had already indexed these three early uses in his *Marx-Engels Reader*; see also Guérin, *La lutte des classes*, 1:5–9.

42. English translation from the *Marx-Engels Reader* (36; emphasis in original). Original: Marx, *Zur Judenfrage*, in MEGA, pt. 1, vol 2, pp. 150–51.

43. English translation from the *Marx-Engels Reader* (36; emphasis in original). Original: Marx, *Zur Judenfrage*, in MEGA, pt. 1, vol 2, p. 151.

44. For instance, in the preceding pages of *Zur Judenfrage*, Marx italicizes the words "bourgeois," "citoyen," and "Guillotine" (this last example comes from the quotation above).

45. I was able to locate only one prior use, in a May 12, 1842, *Rheinische Zeitung* article. My thanks to Adrian Daub for his comments on the German usage of *permanent*.

46. See Sperber, *Karl Marx*, chap. 4. On Marx's interest in French revolutionary history: B. Brown, "French Revolution," esp. 422 onward; Furet, *Marx*; Löwy, "Poetry of the Past"; Mah, "French Revolution."

47. Marx cites Buchez and Roux in "On *The Jewish Question*" and in *The Holy Family* (respectively, vols. 28 and 31–32 of the *Histoire parlementaire*). See MEGA, pt. 1, vol. 2, p. 159, and vol. 4, p. 122. He may also have read Etienne Cabet's *Histoire populaire de la Révolution française, de 1789 à 1830*. On Marx's other readings, see also: B. Brown, "French Revolution," 422–24; Furet, *Marx*, 20.

48. "Er *vollzog* den *Terrorismus*, indem er an die Stelle der *permanenten Revolution* den *permanenten Krieg setzte*." In MEGA, pt. 1, vol. 4, 125–26 (my translation).

49. Billington traces the term back to German Illuminists in *Fire in the Minds of Men*. I. Bernard Cohen has suggested that Proudhon may have been at the origin of this phrase (*Revolution in Science*, 274).

50. Michael Löwy suggested a related genealogy for Marx's expression: "It may be . . . that the phrase comes directly from Jacobin usage. During moments of revolutionary crisis the Jacobin Club would declare itself assembled 'en permanence'—in permanent session" (*Politics*, 8n20). While Löwy was on the right track, this historical reference is inexact: the origins of this expression are not to be found with the Jacobin Club, but rather with the Parisian sections. I outline below why this distinction matters and can help us to better comprehend what Marx had in mind when referring to "revolution in permanence." Guérin's mostly forgotten *La lutte des classes*, to which Löwy's article directed my attention, also establishes a connection between permanent revolution and the Terror, though the author is mainly concerned with demonstrating the emergence of a "proletariat" class during the French Revolution.

51. In a spring 1793 treatise dealing with constitutional matters, Jean-Baptiste-Moïse Jollivet, a former member of the Legislative Assembly, used it to warn against the dangers of weakening central political authority: "Then society would truly have no social aspect; it would be in perpetual and permanent revolution" (*Principes fondamentaux*, 665, annex to April 12, 1793 session). See also *Adresse du conseil général permanent du département de l'Orne, à ses concitoyens*, read at the beginning of the July 8, 1793, session of the National Convention, which summoned Frenchmen to be "continuously on guard against ill-wishers; since, to maintain you in a permanent state of revolution, of license and of anarchy, they will use all sorts of tricks" (*AP*, 68:396).

52. See speech by Bailly to the assembly, March 22, 1790, *AP*, 12:333; discussed in chapter 10.

53. See C. Jones, *Great Nation*, 459.

54. July 25, 1792, *AP*, 47:143. This episode is also recounted in the *Histoire parlementaire* (*HP*, 16:179).

55. See chapter 10.

56. "L'armée révolutionnaire et les canons vont être en permanence" (*AP*, 74:593).

57. Results obtained by a string search for "en permanence" in the *AP* (https://frda.stanford.edu/) and reporting results by frequency per year. Exact numbers: 223 and 344. Some of the metadata on the volumes is erroneous, however, so exact numbers are provided only to give a general order of magnitude.

58. Results obtained through a proximity search at the sentence level for "section* permanen*" and reporting results by frequency per year (https://frda.stanford.edu/). Exact numbers: 169 and 232, but see qualifier in preceding note.

59. *HP*, 17:23.

60. See e.g., "La guillotine est en permanence à Lyon" (May 15, 1793; *HP*, 27:18). This term also features frequently in Etienne Cabet's *Histoire populaire de la Révolution française*: in vol. 3, which deals with years 1792–94, there are 14 mentions of "permanence."

61. *HP*, 32:197 ("en permanence continuelle"). Marx cites from this volume in *The Holy Family*.

62. "Ce fut la dernière du corps législatif; et c'est ici qu'il faut remarquer que la séance fut toujours considérée comme permanente depuis le 10 août. La permanence prononcée dans la nuit du 9 au 10 ne fut point levée. Les journaux du temps, le *Moniteur*, portent constamment en tête de leurs comptes-rendus: *Suite de la séance permanente du 10 août*. C'est donc à tort que presque tous les historiens ont écrit que la permanence avait cessé dans le mois d'août" (*HP*, 17:17–18).

63. See Harsin, *Barricades*, 16–17 and passim. My thanks to Biliana Kassabova for this reference.

64. This event is described in numerous histories of 1848: e.g., Lermina, Faure, and Spoll, *Histoire anecdotique illustrée*, 236–37 (for a fairly detailed account); 188, 271, 328, 337 (for some other examples).

65. Detail mentioned in Edward Stillingfleet Cayley's *European Revolutions of 1848* (1:97). My thanks to Isser Woloch for bringing this to my attention.

66. *Neue Rheinische Zeitung*, no. 110 (Sep. 23, 1848). In MEGA, pt. 1, vol. 7, p. 737 (my translation). Marx, *Zur Judenfrage*, 151 ("On *The Jewish Question*"); Marx, *Die Klassenkämpfe in Frankreich*, chap. 3, 192.

67. See for instance, the translation of the March 1850 "Address of the Central Committee," which concludes with "Their battle-cry must be: *The Permanent Revolution*."

68. Hence, I disagree with Michael Löwy, who assumes that when Marx refers to the Terror, he has in mind "the Jacobin model of 1793." But *permanence* was not a Jacobin concept at all: it was in fact the Jacobin-dominated National Convention that abolished the permanence of the sections on September 5, 1793. See Löwy, "Poetry of the Past," 122. On the Convention: D. Edelstein, *Terror of Natural Right*, 139.

69. See Tucker, in Marx and Engels, *Reader*, 510n4: "It must be recalled today that this passage is based on a misunderstanding."

70. *HP*, 31:313: "haute moralité de leur doctrine politique." They go on to add: "Vaincus dans leur propre conscience par l'équité évidente des principes jacobins, les malhonnêtes gens de tous les partis tremblaient à cette heure [Feb. 1794] devant la droiture, devant la franchise et devant la fermeté du pouvoir qui les [i.e., the dictators] proclamait."

71. "La terreur est donc quelquefois obligatoire; c'est un devoir d'y recourir, mais elle reste toujours un moyen expectionnel. . . . [C]e n'est pas la révolution française qui la première a eu recours aux moyens de la terreur; elle n'a fait, en cela, qu'imiter ce qu'on avait fait mille fois avant elle" (*HP*, 20:vi–vii).

72. See *The Preconditions of Socialism and the Tasks of Social Democracy* (1899), discussed in Day and Gaido, *Witnesses to Permanent Revolution*, 16–18.

73. Day and Gaido, *Witnesses to Permanent Revolution*, 11–12. On this organization, and Marx's dealings with Blanquists in 1850: Lattek, *Revolutionary Refugees*, 52–57.

74. See Franz Mehring, "The Revolution in Permanence" (1889), in Day and Gaido, *Witnesses to Permanent Revolution*, 457–63.

75. See Karl Kautsky, "The Sans-Culottes of the French Revolution" (1889), in Day and Gaido, *Witnesses to Permanent Revolution*, 541. This text constitutes a chapter in his longer history, *Die Klassengegensätze von 1789*; a French translation was also published: *La lutte des classes* (quote at 85).

76. Engels, "Marx and the *Neue Rheinische Zeitung* (1848–49)," in Day and Gaido, *Witnesses to Permanent Revolution*, 14.

77. Alfred Bougeart: "Le but de la commune n'est pas complètement atteint, la permanence du danger légitime la permanence de sa dictature" (*Marat*, 97).

78. Note also that Socialist Revolutionaries (SRs) were similarly debating this theory around the same time: see Perrie, "Socialist Revolutionaries."

79. Day and Gaido, *Witnesses to Permanent Revolution*, 54.

80. See Service, *Lenin*, 173–74.

81. Lenin, *Collected Works*, 9:82.

82. For Trotsky, too, the relation between permanent revolution and the French Terror was still evident: see his praise of Jacobinism in *Results and Prospects*, chap. 3.

83. According to one source, David Riazanov, Lenin "knew [the 1850 March circular address] by heart" and "used to delight in quoting" it (*Karl Marx*, chap. 5), also referenced in Guérin, *La lutte des classes*, 1:473n14. Day and Gaido similarly note that this address "was destined to play a central role in all the debates over the class character and political alliances of the Russian revolution in 1903–7" (*Witnesses to Permanent Revolution*, 9).

84. Lenin, *Two Tactics*, 58; also in *Anthology*, 132. Lenin again quotes from *The Class Struggle in France* in the conclusion to *Two Tactics of Social-Democracy*: "The workers do not expect to make deals; they are not asking for petty concessions. What they are striving towards is ruthlessly to crush the reactionary forces, i.e., to set up a *revolutionary-democratic dictatorship of the proletariat and the peasantry*" (*Two Tactics*, 113). See also Lenin's article "On Constitutional Illusions" (*Collected Works*, 25:196–210). See more generally: Skilling, "Permanent or Uninterrupted Revolution."

85. See Chakrabarty, *Provincializing Europe*; Satia, *Time's Monster*.

86. See e.g., in Marx and Engels, "Address of the Central Committee" (also in *Ansprache der Zentralbehörde*, 262).

87. See Stedman Jones, *Karl Marx*, 501.

88. On the Commune, see notably: Deluermoz, *Le crépuscule des révolutions*; Merriman, *Massacre*; Eichner, *Paris Commune*.

89. Commune de Paris, "Déclaration au peuple français."

90. Marx, "Third Address." Subsequent quotes in this section are from this same source.

91. See in general: Pipes, *Russian Revolution*; Fitzpatrick, *Russian Revolution*.

92. Lenin, "The Dual Power," in *Collected Works*, 24:38–41. On the place of the Commune in Bolshevik thought, see notably: Billington, *Fire in the Minds*; Pipes, *Russian Revolution*, 362–64; Harison, "Paris Commune of 1871"; Bergman, "Paris Commune."

93. Lenin, *State and Revolution*, chap. 3 ("Experience of the Paris Commune of 1871: Marx's Analysis"), 437 ("smash," "at last discovered"), 429 ("parliamentarism"), 428 ("talking shop"), 407 ("wither away").

94. Lenin, 429 ("representative institutions"), 434 ("centralist"), 430 ("anarchist dreams").

95. Harding, *Leninism*.

96. Dahl, *Democracy and Its Critics*, chap. 4.

97. Kotkin, *Magnetic Mountain*.

98. See most recently: Chirot, *You Want a Revolution?*

Chapter Fourteen

1. Service, *Lenin*.

2. Lenin, *What Is to Be Done?* (1901), in *Anthology*, 85, 19–20. See also Harding, *Lenin's Political Thought*, esp. chap. 7.

3. Dostoevsky, *Possessed*, 402. On Dostoevsky's own revolutionary experiences: Joseph Frank, *Years of Ordeal*.

4. On Nechayev: Patyk, *Written in Blood*. See also Camus, *L'homme révolté*, 186, 206–9.

5. Nechayev, *Catechism*, no. 6; Dostoevsky, *Possessed*, 403.

6. "The revolutionary despises all doctrines and refuses to accept the mundane sciences, leaving them for future generations. He knows only one science: the science of destruction" (Nechayev, *Catechism*, no. 3).

7. See Stedman Jones, *Karl Marx*.

8. Quoted in Rubenstein, *Leon Trotsky*, 136. Orwell probably remembered this line: "Whatever the Party holds to be truth, *is* truth," O'Brien tells Winston Smith in *1984* (249).

9. See S. Cohen, *Bukharin*. I return to the situation after Lenin's death below.

10. Hobbes, *Leviathan*, chap. 42; 5:920 ("Hæretiques"; original pagination, 317); chap. 26, 4:431 (*Authoritas*; original pagination, 317). See also Pettit, *Made with Words*, chap. 8.

11. See Bonnell, *Iconography of Power*, 1.

12. Xiaobo, "That Holy Word, 'Revolution,'" 310.

13. Nechayev, *Catechism*, no. 4 (translation modified).

14. Lenin, "Speech against Bukharin's Amendment to the Resolution on the Party Programme" (March 18), in *Collected Works*, 27:147, quoted and discussed in Lasky, *Utopia and Revolution*, 50. See also Buber, *Paths in Utopia*, 115.

15. See Schram, "Mao Tse-Tung's Thought"; Spence, *Search for Modern China*, 536–43.

16. "Il a été permis de craindre que la Révolution, comme Saturne dévorant successivement tous ses enfants, n'engendrât enfin le despotisme avec les calamités qui l'accompagnent," March 13, 1793, *AP*, 60:162.

17. Quoted in MacFarquhar and Schoenhals, *Mao's Last Revolution*, 254 (possibly apocryphal).

18. See Brandenberger and Zelenov, introduction to *Stalin's Master Narrative*. See also Service, *History of Modern Russia*, 236–38; Conquest, *Great Terror* (on the Moscow trials).

19. Debray, *Praised Be Our Lords*, 11.

20. See Service, *Lenin*, chap. 20.

21. "It was asserted that the Bolsheviks were equipped with scientific knowledge of what needed to be done. . . . Lenin claimed unrivaled correctness for his ideology and was uninhibited in aspiring to indoctrinate the whole society with his prescriptions" (Service, 354).

22. Robert C. Tucker, "Lenin and Revolution," in Lenin, *Anthology*, lvii. Weber, *Economy and Society*. See also Kimmel, *Revolution*, 33–36; Collins, "Weber."

23. See e.g., Service, *Lenin*, pt. 2.

24. See Pisch, *Personality Cult of Stalin*, 183; more generally: Bonnell, *Iconography of Power*.

25. Engels, *Socialism*.

26. Lenin, *The State and Revolution*, in *Anthology*, 347.

27. Lenin, "On the Syndicalist and Anarchist Deviation in our Party," March 16, 1921, in *Anthology*, 497, emphasis added.

28. Weber, *Economy and Society*, 227.

29. This is a common thesis in studies of Marxism: see Tucker, *Philosophy and Myth*; Stites, *Revolutionary Dreams*; Halfin, *Stalinist Confessions*; Gregor, *Totalitarianism and Political Religion*, chap. 4.

30. By "mirrors," too, I do not mean that it necessarily has a religious origin, only that there is a structural analogy. My use of political theology here thus differs from Carl Schmitt's, for whom "all significant concepts of the modern theory of the state are secularized theological concepts" (*Political Theology*, 36).

31. Schmitt, 33.

32. See Service, *Trotsky*, chap. 31.

33. See S. Cohen, *Bukharin*, 215.

34. Montefiore, *Stalin*, 36, 48.

35. See Kotkin, *Paradoxes of Power*, 425 (on Stalin's role as general). See also S. Cohen, *Bukharin*, 214; Fitzpatrick, *Russian Revolution*, chap. 4.

36. See Tumarkin, *Lenin Lives!*, 122.

37. Quoted in S. Cohen, *Bukharin*, 218, 221.

38. Stalin, *Foundations of Leninism*, chap. 9.

39. Quoted in S. Cohen, *Bukharin*, 224.

40. See Kotkin, *Paradoxes of Power*, 555–58 (on "Socialism in One Country"), 615 (on the 15th Party Congress).

41. Stalin, *History*, 346.

42. Stalin, 360–61. More generally: Werth, *La terreur*.

43. One of the first uses of the term "contre-révolution" at the National Assembly was in reference to the troops of émigrés massing under the command of the Prince de Condé: see July 28, 1790, *AP*, 17:400. There were sporadic uses of this term before.

44. Godfrey, *Revolutionary Justice*; Baker, *Jean-Paul Marat*.

45. See Avrich, *Russian Anarchists*, 189.

46. Arjomand, *Turban and the Crown*, 154–63.

47. Naimark, *Stalin's Genocides*.

48. See Conquest, *Great Terror*; Werth, *La terreur*; Applebaum, *Gulag*; Kotkin, *Waiting for Hitler*.

49. Dikötter, *Mao's Great Famine*.

50. For the Khrushchev anecdote and Mao's loss of prestige: Dikötter, *Mao's Great Famine*, 14. More generally: MacFarquhar and Schoenhals, *Mao's Last Revolution*.

51. Azuela, *Underdogs*, 70. More generally: Benjamin, *La Revolución*.

52. See e.g., Montefiore, *Stalin*, chaps. 18–19.

53. Short, *Pol Pot*, chaps. 9 and 11.

54. See MacFarquhar and Schoenhals, *Mao's Last Revolution*, chap. 13.

55. Walder, *Fractured Rebellion*, 1.

56. MacFarquhar and Schoenhals, *Mao's Last Revolution*, 161.

57. MacFarquhar and Schoenhals, 240; see also Cook, *Mao's Little Red Book*.

58. See e.g., A. Mayer, *Furies*. More generally, see the classic thesis of Jacob Talmon, *The Origins of Totalitarian Democracy*.

59. Short, *Pol Pot*, 65–66.

Conclusion

1. Garton Ash, *Magic Lantern.*

2. Kuran, "Now out of Never."

3. For the interest in Cuba: e.g., Debray, *Revolution in the Revolution?* On the Chinese influence in 1968: Wolin, *Wind from the East.*

4. Interview originally published in *Le nouvel observateur* (May 20, 1968); English translation by B. R. Brewster: Sartre and Cohn-Bendit, "Jean Paul Sartre Interviews." More generally: Seidman, *Imaginary Revolution.*

5. See e.g., Christofferson, *French Intellectuals.*

6. Ponchaud, *Cambodge année zéro*; more recently: Short, *Pol Pot.* On the Red Brigades: Orsini, *Anatomy of the Red Brigades.* One of the early antitotalitarian works of the so-called *nouveaux philosophes* was Bernard-Henri Lévy's *La barbarie à visage humain.* François Furet's *Penser la Révolution française* was published in 1978.

7. See Arjomand, *Turban for the Crown.*

8. Pérez-Stable, *Cuban Revolution*, 53, 59, 74 (quote).

9. See the classic work by Samuel P. Huntington, *The Third Wave.* On the Philippines: e.g., Claudio, *Taming People's Power.*

10. Garton Ash, "Velvet Revolution."

11. Ghonim, *Revolution 2.0.*

12. Kirkpatrick, *Into the Hands.*

13. For Malcolm X, see notably "Message to the Grassroots." King uses the phrase "social revolution" in his "Letter from Birmingham Jail."

14. Sharp, *From Dictatorship to Democracy.* See also his earlier work, *The Politics of Nonviolent Action.* See also Rosenberg, "Revolution U"; Paulson, "Case Study: Serbia"; Popovic, *Blueprint for Revolution.*

15. Weyland, "Arab Spring"; Toska, "Multiple Scripts."

16. See e.g., Lindberg, "Nature of Democratic Backsliding."

17. Data from Freedom House: https://freedomhouse.org/explore-the-map?type=fiw&year=2023/. In 2023, Ukraine, Moldova, and some small states in the Caucasus were described as "partly free."

18. See Van Prooijen et al., "Make It Great Again."

19. This was already the thesis presented in part 5 of Francis Fukuyama's *End of History and the Last Man.* More recently, see his *Liberalism and Its Discontents.*

20. See e.g., Solnit, *Hope in the Dark.*

21. See chapter 11 (for the Musset quote). On a similar theme: Planinc, *Regenerative Politics.*

22. Sanders, *Our Revolution*; see also his *Guide to Political Revolution* and his political movement, "Our Revolution," whose mission (as stated on the original website) is to "reclaim democracy for the working people of our country by harnessing the transformative energy of the 'political revolution.'" (Action Network, "Our Revolution," accessed Aug. 6, 2024, https://actionnetwork.org/groups/our-revolution).

23. For the English translation: Macron, *Revolution.*

24. Radosh, "Steve Bannon."

25. See notably Mosse, *Fascist Revolution*, esp. chap. 4.

26. See Scheppele, "Rule of Law"; Müller, *What Is Populism?*; Levitsky and Ziblatt, *How Democracies Die.*

27. Gilens and Page, "Testing Theories," 573 (on status quo).

28. Doerfler and Moyn, "Constitution Is Broken."

29. Grewal and Purdy, "Original Theory of Constitutionalism."

30. See e.g., Talev, "Two Americas Index."

31. See H. Mayer, *All on Fire* (Garrison); C. Beard, *Economic Interpretation*; Malcolm X, "Message to the Grassroots."

32. See e.g., Arist., *Nic. Eth.* 6.1140b21–22.

33. *Federalist*, no. 10.

34. Kuran, "Now out of Never."

35. Judt, *Past Imperfect*.

36. See e.g., Millington, "Trump, Fascism."

37. See Steinmetz-Jenkins, *Did It Happen Here?*

38. Thuc., 3.82.4–5.

39. Hobsbawm, *Age of Extremes*.

40. M. Jones, *Founding Weimar*.

41. See the introduction.

BIBLIOGRAPHY

Acemoglu, Daron, Davide Cantoni, Simon Johnson, and James A. Robinson. "The Consequences of Radical Reform: The French Revolution." *American Economic Review* 101, no. 7 (2011):3286–307.

Ackerman, Bruce. *Revolutionary Constitutions*. Cambridge, MA: Harvard University Press, 2019.

Adams, John. *The Works of John Adams*. 10 vols. Boston, MA: Little, Brown and Co., 1856.

Adams, Willi Paul. *The First American Constitutions: Republican Ideology and the Making of the State Constitutions in the Revolutionary Era*. Translated by Rita and Robert Kimber. Lanham, MD: Rowman and Littlefield, 2001.

Adelman, Jeremy. "Iberian Passages: Continuity and Change in the South Atlantic." In Armitage and Subrahmanyam, *Age of Revolutions*, 59–82.

Adresse de la Commune de Paris dans ses soixante sections, à l'Assemblée Nationale. Paris, 1790.

Agesta, Luis Sánchez, ed. *Discurso preliminar a la constitución de 1812*. Madrid: Centro de Estudios Constitucionales, 1989.

The Alarm: or, An Address to the People of Pennsylvania. Philadelphia, 1776.

Aldred, Guy A. *Bakunin*. Glasgow: Strickland, 1940.

Aldridge, A. Owen. "John Adams Confronts Turgot." *Studies in Eighteenth-Century Culture* 30 (2001):91–104.

Alexander, R. S. *Re-writing the French Revolutionary Tradition: Liberal Opposition and the Fall of the Bourbon Monarchy*. Cambridge: Cambridge University Press, 2003.

All Canada in the Hands of the English. Boston: B. Mecom, 1760. Evans.

Allen, William [pseud.]. *Killing Noe Murder: Briefly Discoursed in Three Quæstions*. [Dutch Republic], 1657. EEBO.

Alonso, Gregorio. "Cádiz Reprised: The Liberal Triennium in Spain and Spanish America, 1820–1823." In Eastman and Sobrevilla Perea, *Rise of Constitutional Government*, 245–63.

Alpaugh, Micah. *Non-violence and the French Revolution: Political Demonstrations in Paris, 1787–1795*. Cambridge: Cambridge University Press, 2014.

Amann, Peter H. "Revolution: A Redefinition." *Political Science Quarterly* 77, no. 1 (1962):36–53.

Amar, Akhil Reed. *America's Constitution: A Biography*. New York: Random House, 2006.

Andress, David. "Jacobinism as Heroic Narrative: Understanding the Terror as the Experience of Melodrama." *French History and Civilization* 5 (2014):6–23.

———. *Massacre at the Champs de Mars: Popular Dissent and Political Culture in the French Revolution*. London: Boydell, 2000.

———. "Neighborhood Policing in Paris from Old Regime to Revolution: The Exercise of Authority by the District de Saint-Roch, 1789–1791." *French Historical Studies* 29, no. 2 (2006):231–60.

Applebaum, Anne. *Gulag: A History of the Soviet Camps*. London: Penguin Books, 2012.

Archives parlementaires de 1787 à 1860, recueil complet des débats législatifs & politiques des chambres françaises. Edited by J. Mavidal, E. Laurent, et al. Paris: Librairie administrative de P. Dupont, 1862–. https://sul-philologic.stanford.edu/philologic/archparl/.

Arena, Valentina. *Libertas and the Practice of Politics in the Late Roman Republic*. Cambridge: Cambridge, University Press, 2012.

Arendt, Hannah. *On Revolution*. 1963; New York: Penguin Books, 1977.

Aristotle. *Aristotelis "Politicorum" libri octo*. Translated by Hermann Conring. Helmstedt, [Saxony]: Jacob Lucis, 1637.

——. *Aristotelis "Politicorum"libri octo*. Translated by William of Moerbeke, edited by Franz Susemihl. Leipzig: B. G. Teubneri, 1872.

——. *Aristotles "Politiques," or "Discourses of Government."* London: Adam Islip, 1598.

——. *The Complete Works of Aristotle*. Revised Oxford translation, edited by Jonathan Barnes. Princeton, NJ: Princeton University Press, 1984.

——. *"De republica qui politicorum dicuntur" libri VIII*. Translated by Joachim Périon. Paris: J. L. Tiletanum, 1543.

——. *Gli otto libri della "Republica"* [sic]*, che chiamono "Politica" di Aristotile*. Translated by Antonio Brucioli. Venice: A. Brucioli, 1547.

——. *"La politique" d'Aristote*. Translated by Jean-François Champagne. Paris: A. Bailleul, 1797.

——. *"Le livre de politiques" d'Aristote*. Translated by Nicole Oresme. Paris: Antoine Vérard, 1489.

——. *"Les politiques" d'Aristote* . . . Translated by Louis Le Roy. Paris: Vascosan, 1568.

——. *"Politicorum" libri octo commentarii* . . . Translated by Leonardo Bruni, edited by Jacques Lefèvre d'Etaples. Paris: Henri Estienne, 1506.

——. *The Politics*. Translated by Carnes Lord. Chicago: University of Chicago Press, 1984. [Cited as *Politics*.]

——. *The Politics*. Translated by H. Rackham. Cambridge, MA: Harvard University Press, 1932. [Cited as *Pol.*]

——. *"Trattato dei governi" di Aristotile*. Translated by Bernardo Segni. Florence: Lorenzo Torrentino, 1549.

——. *A Treatise on Government*. Translated by William Ellis. London: T. Payne, 1778.

Arjomand, Saïd. *The Turban and the Crown: The Islamic Revolution in Iran*. Oxford: Oxford University Press, 1988.

Armitage, David. *Civil War: A History in Ideas*. New York: Knopf, 2017.

——. "Every Great Revolution Is a Civil War." In Baker and Edelstein, *Scripting Revolution*, 57–68.

Armitage, David, Armand Himy, and Quentin Skinner, eds. *Milton and Republicanism*. Cambridge: Cambridge University Press, 1985.

Armitage David, and Sanjay Subrahmanyam, eds. *The Age of Revolutions in Global Context, c. 1760–1840*. New York, Palgrave Macmillan, 2010.

Arnold, Matthew. "Stanzas from the Grande Chartreuse." 1855. The Poetry Foundation. https://www.poetryfoundation.org/poems/43605/stanzas-from-the-grande-chartreuse.

Arthur, Anthony. *The Tailor-King: The Rise and Fall of the Anabaptist Kingdom of Muenster*. New York: St. Martin's, 2011.

Arvind, T. T., and Lindsay Stirton. "Explaining the Reception of the Code Napoleon in Germany: A Fuzzy-Set Qualitative Comparative Analysis." *Legal Studies* 30, no. 1 (2010):1–29.

Ashcraft, Richard. *Revolutionary Politics and Locke's "Two Treatises of Government."* Princeton, NJ: Princeton University Press, 1986.

Assarino, Luca. *Delle riuolutioni di Catalogna libri due*. Bologna: Giacomo Monti, 1645.

Atkins, Jed. *Cicero on Politics and the Limits of Reason*. Cambridge: Cambridge University Press, 2013.

Atkins, Jed W., and Carl E. Young. "Polybius and the Compound Constitution." In *Reading Texts on Sovereignty: Textual Moments in the History of Political Thought*, edited by Stella Achilleos and Antonis Balasopoulos, 25–32. London: Bloomsbury, 2021.

Augustine. *The City of God against the Pagans*. Edited and translated by Robert W. Dyson. Cambridge: Cambridge University Press, 1998.

———. *On Order [De ordine]*. Translated by Silvano Borruso. South Bend, IN: St. Augustine's, 2007.

Aulard, François-Alphonse, ed. *La Société des Jacobins: Recueil de documents pour l'histoire du club des Jacobins de Paris*. vol. 3. Paris: Jouaust, 1892.

———. *Le culte de la raison et le culte de l'Être suprême (1793–1794)*. Paris: Alcan, 1892.

Auslander, Leora. *Cultural Revolutions: Everyday Life and Politics in Britain, North America, and France*. Berkeley: University of California Press, 2009.

Avrich, Paul. *The Russian Anarchists*. Princeton, NJ: Princeton University Press, 1967.

Aylmer, John. *An Harborovve for Faithfull and Trevve Subiectes*. London: John Day, 1559. EEBO.

Ayres, Philip. *Classical Culture and the Idea of Rome in Eighteenth-Century England*. Cambridge: Cambridge University Press, 1997.

Azuela, Mariano. *The Underdogs*. Translated by E. Munguia Jr. 1915; New York: Signet, 1996.

Baczko, Bronislaw. *Ending the Terror: The French Revolution after Robespierre*. Translated by Michel Petheram. Cambridge: Cambridge University Press, 1994.

Baehr, Peter, and Melvin Richter, eds. *Dictatorship in History and Theory: Bonapartism, Caesarism, and Totalitarianism*. Cambridge: Cambridge University Press, 2004.

Bailly, Jean-Sylvain. *Lettres sur l'origine des sciences*. Paris: Debure, 1777.

Bailyn, Bernard, *The Ideological Origins of the American Revolution*. 1967; Cambridge, MA: Harvard University Press, 1992.

———. *The Origins of American Politics*. New York: Alfred A. Knopf, 1968.

Baker, Keith. *Condorcet: From Natural Philosophy to Social Mathematics*. Chicago: University of Chicago Press, 1975.

———. *Inventing the French Revolution*. Cambridge: Cambridge University Press, 1990.

———. *Jean-Paul Marat*. Chicago: University of Chicago Press, forthcoming.

———. "Revolution 1.0." *Journal of Modern European History* 11, no. 2 (2013):187–219.

Baker, Keith M., and Dan Edelstein, eds. *Scripting Revolution: A Historical Approach to the Comparative Study of Revolutions*. Stanford, CA: Stanford University Press, 2015.

Bakunin, Mikhail. "Critique of the Marxist Theory of the State." In *Statism and Anarchy* (1873), in *Bakunin on Anarchy*, edited and translated by Sam Dolgoff. New York: Knopf, 1972. Marxists' Internet Archive. https://www.marxists.org/reference/archive/bakunin/works/1873/statism-anarchy.htm.

Barton, H. Arnold. "Gustav III of Sweden and the Enlightenment." *Eighteenth-Century Studies* 6, no. 1 (1972):1–34.

Beard, Charles. *An Economic Interpretation of the Constitution of the United States.* New York: Macmillan, 1913.

Beard, Mary. *S.P.Q.R.: A History of Ancient Rome.* New York: Liveright, 2015.

Becker, Carl. *The Heavenly City of the Eighteenth-Century Philosophes.* 1932; New Haven, CT: Yale University Press, 2003.

Beech, William. *A View of Englands Present Distempers Occasioned by the Late Revolution of Government in this Nation.* London: William Raybould, 1650. EEBO.

Beecher, Jonathan. *Charles Fourier: The Visionary and His World.* Berkeley: University of California Press, 1986.

——. *Writers and Revolution: Intellectuals and the French Revolution of 1848.* Cambridge: Cambridge University Press, 2021.

Bejan, Teresa. "What Was the Point of Equality?" *American Journal of Political Science* 66, no. 3 (2022):604–16.

Belissa, Marc, and Yannick Bosc. *Le Directoire: La république sans la démocratie.* Paris: La Fabrique, 2018.

Bell, David A. *The Cult of the Nation in France.* Cambridge, MA: Harvard University Press, 2001.

——. *The First Total War: Napoleon's Europe and the Birth of Modern Warfare.* Boston, MA: Houghton Mifflin, 2007.

——. "For a New Social History of the Enlightenment: Authors, Readers, and Commercial Capitalism." *Modern Intellectual History* 20, no. 2 (2023):663–87.

——. *Men on Horseback: The Power of Charisma in the Age of Revolution.* New York: Farrar, Straus, and Giroux, 2020.

——. *Napoleon: A Concise Biography.* Oxford: Oxford University Press, 2015.

Bell, Duncan. *Dreamworlds of Race: Empire and the Utopian Destiny of Anglo-America.* Princeton, NJ: Princeton University Press, 2020.

——. "Mythscapes: Memory, Mythology, and National Identity." *British Journal of Sociology* 54, no. 1 (2003):63–81.

——. "What Is Liberalism?" *Political Theory* 42, no. 6 (2014):682–715.

Bellamy, Richard. "The Political Form of the Constitution: The Separation of Powers, Rights, and Representative Democracy." *Political Studies* 44 (1996):436–56.

Benjamin, Thomas. *La Revolución: Mexico's Great Revolution as Memory, Myth, and History.* Austin: University of Texas Press, 2000.

Bergman, Jay. "The Paris Commune in Bolshevik Mythology." *English Historical Review* 129, no. 541 (2014):1412–41.

Berlin, Isaiah. "Russia and 1848." In *Russian Thinkers.* London: Hogarth, 1978.

Berman, Marshall. *All That Is Solid Melts into Air: The Experience of Modernity.* London: Verso Books, 1983.

Bertier de Sauvigny, G. "Liberalism, Nationalism and Socialism: The Birth of Three Words." *Review of Politics* 32, no. 2 (1970):147–66.

Bezassier, J. D. *La muse patriotique*. Paris, 1789. Newberry.

Bilder, Mary. *Madison's Hand: Revising the Constitutional Convention*. Cambridge, MA: Harvard University Press, 2015.

Billaud-Varenne. *Discours de M. Billaud-Varenne, sur les mesures à prendre pour sauver la patrie*. Paris, Imprimerie de Patriote françois, 1792. Newberry.

——. *Rapport . . . sur la théorie du gouvernement démocratique*. Paris: Convention Nationale, 1794.

——. *Rapport . . . sur un mode de gouvernement provisoire & révolutionnaire*. Paris: Imprimerie des régies nationales, an II [1793].

Billington, James H. *Fire in the Minds of Men: Origins of the Revolutionary Tradition*. New York: Basic Books, 1980.

Black, Robert. *Machiavelli*. London: Routledge, 2013.

Blackburn, Robin. *The American Crucible: Slavery, Emancipation and Human Rights*. London: Verso Books, 2011.

Blackman, Robert H. *1789: The French Revolution Begins*. Cambridge: Cambridge University Press, 2019.

Blackstone, William. *Commentaries on the Laws of England*. Oxford: Clarendon, 1768.

Blanqui, Louis-Auguste. *Défense du citoyen Louis Auguste Blanqui devant la Cour d'assises*. Paris: Auguste Mie, 1832.

Blaufarb, Rafe. *The Great Demarcation: The French Revolution and the Invention of Modern Property*. Oxford: Oxford University Press, 2016.

Bloom, Solomon F. "The 'Withering Away' of the State." *Journal of the History of Ideas* 7, no. 1 (1946):113–21.

Bluche, Frédéric. *Septembre 1792, logiques d'un massacre*. Paris: R. Laffont, 1986.

Blumenberg, Hans. *The Legitimacy of the Modern Age*. Translated by Robert M. Wallace. Cambridge: MIT Press, 1983.

——. "On a Lineage of the Idea of Progress." Translated by E. B. Ashton. *Social Research* 41, no. 1 (1974):5–27.

Blythe, James M. *Ideal Government and the Mixed Constitution in the Middle Ages*. Princeton, NJ: Princeton University Press, 1992.

Boccaccio, Giovanni. *De casibus virorum illustrium*. c. 1350.

Bodin, Jean. *Method for the Easy Comprehension of History*. Translated by Beatrice Reynolds. New York: Columbia University Press, 1945.

Boethius, Anicius Manlius Severinus. *The Consolation of Philosophy*. Oxford: Oxford University Press, 1999.

Bolingbroke, Henry St. John. *A Dissertation upon Parties* (1733–34). In *Political Writings*, edited by David Armitage. Cambridge: Cambridge University Press, 1997.

Bolívar, Simón. *El Libertador: Writings of Simón Bolívar*. Edited by David Bushnell, translated by Frederick H. Fornoff. Oxford: Oxford University Press, 2003.

Bonaparte, Napoléon. "Proclamation, Au camp impérial de Madrid, 7 décembre 1808." In *Œuvres de Napoléon Bonaparte*, 4:179. Paris: Panckoucke, 1822. ARTFL.

Bonnell, Victoria. *Iconography of Power: Soviet Political Posters under Lenin and Stalin*. Berkeley: University of California Press, 1999.

Bonnet, Charles. *La palingénésie philosophique*. 1769. ARTFL.

Botero, Giovanni. *Della ragione di stato: Libri dieci*. Turin: Gio. Dominico Tarino, 1596.

Boucoyannis, Deborah. *Kings as Judges: Power, Justice, and the Origins of Parliaments*. Cambridge: Cambridge University Press, 2021.

Bougainville, Louis Antoine de. *Voyage autour du monde*. Edited by Michel Bideaux and Sonia Faessel. 1771; Paris: Presses de l'Université de Paris-Sorbonne, 2001.

Bougeart, Alfred. *Marat, l'ami du peuple*. Paris: Libraire internationale, 1865.

Boulant, Antoine. *Le tribunal révolutionnaire: Punir les ennemis du peuple*. Paris: Perrin, 2018.

Bourke, Richard. *Empire and Revolution: The Political Life of Edmund Burke*. Princeton, NJ: Princeton University Press, 2015.

——. *Hegel's Global Revolutions*. Princeton, NJ: Princeton University Press, 2023.

Bouton, Terry. *Taming Democracy: "The People," the Founders, and the Troubled Ending of the American Revolution*. Oxford: Oxford University Press, 2007.

Braesch, Frédéric. *La Commune du 10 août 1792*. Paris: Hachette, 1911.

Brandenberger, David, and Mikhail Vladimirovich Zelenov. Introduction to *Stalin's Master Narrative: A Critical Edition of the "History of the Communist Party of the Soviet Union (Bolsheviks): Short Course,"* edited by Brandenberger and Zelenov. New Haven, CT: Yale University Press, 2019.

Braxton, Carter. *An Address to the Convention of the Colony of Ancient Dominion of Virginia*. Philadelphia: John Dunlap, 1776. EVANS.

Breña, Roberto. "The Cádiz Liberal Revolution and Spanish American Independence." In *New Countries: Capitalism, Revolutions, and Nations in the Americas, 1750–1870*, edited by John Tutino, 71–104. Durham, NC: Duke University Press, 2017.

Brendecke, Arndt, and Peter Vogt, eds. *The End of Fortuna and the Rise of Modernity*. Berlin: De Gruyter, 2017.

Brickhouse, Thomas C., and Nicholas D. Smith, eds. *The Trial and Execution of Socrates: Sources and Controversies*. New York: Oxford University Press, 2002.

Brinton, Crane. *The Anatomy of Revolution*. Rev. ed. 1938; New York: Knopf Doubleday, 1965.

Brissot, Jacques-Pierre. "Ma profession de foi sur la monarchie et sur le républicanisme." In *Recueil de quelques écrits, principalement extraits du "Patriote françois."* Paris: Bureau du Patriote françois, 1791.

——. *Plan de conduite pour les députés du peuple aux États-Généraux de 1789*. April 1789. NEWBERRY.

Brooks, David. "What Happened to American Conservatism?" *Atlantic*, December 8, 2021. https://www.theatlantic.com/magazine/archive/2022/01/brooks-true-conservatism-dead-fox-news-voter-suppression/620853/.

Brooks, Peter. *Flaubert in the Ruins of Paris: The Story of a Friendship, a Novel, and a Terrible Year*. New York: Basic Books, 2017.

Brown, Bruce. "The French Revolution and the Rise of Social Theory." *Science & Society* 30, no. 4 (1966):385–432.

Brown, Frederick. *Flaubert: A Biography*. Cambridge, MA: Harvard University Press, 2006.

Brown, Howard. *Ending the French Revolution: Violence, Justice, and Repression from the Terror to Napoleon*. Charlottesville: University of Virginia Press, 2006.

Brown, Richard. *Revolutionary Politics in Massachusetts: The Boston Committee of Correspondence and the Towns, 1772–1774*. Cambridge, MA: Harvard University Press, 1970.

Brunet, Charles, ed. *Le Père Duchesne d'Hébert, ou Notice historique et bibliographique sur ce journal*. Paris: Libraire de France, 1859.

Buber, Martin. *Paths in Utopia*. 1950; Syracuse, NY: Syracuse University Press, 1996.

Buchez, P.-J.-B., and P.-C. Roux, eds. *Histoire parlementaire de la Révolution française*. 40 vols. Paris: Paulin, 1834–38.

Bucholz, Robert, and Newton Key. *Early Modern England, 1485–1724*. London: Wiley-Blackwell, 2009.

Buckley, William. "Our Mission Statement." *National Review*, November 19, 1955. https://www.nationalreview.com/1955/11/our-mission-statement-william-f-buckley-jr/.

Buck-Morss, Susan. *Hegel, Haiti, and Universal History*. Pittsburgh, PA: University of Pittsburgh Press, 2009.

Bulst, Neithard, Jörg Fisch, Reinhart Koselleck, and Christian Meier. "Revolution (Rebellion, Aufruhr, Bürgerkrieg)." In *GG*, 5:653–788.

Buonarotti, Philippe, ed. *Conspiration pour l'égalité dite de Babeuf, suivie du procès auquel elle donna lieu, et des pièces justificatives*. Brussels: Librairie romantique, 1828.

Burke, Edmund. *Reflections on the Revolution in France*. Edited by W. Alison Phillips and Catherine Beatrice Phillips. Cambridge: Cambridge University Press, 1912.

———. *Réflexions sur la révolution de France*. Paris: Laurent fils, 1790.

———. *The Writings and Speeches of Edmund Burke*. Vol. 4. Oxford: Oxford University Press, 2015.

Burstin, Haim. *Une révolution à l'œuvre: Le faubourg Saint-Marcel (1789–1794)*. Paris: Champ Vallon, 2005.

Bury, J. B. *The Idea of Progress: An Inquiry into Its Origin and Growth*. London: Macmillan, 1920.

Busaall, Jean-Baptiste. "Constitution politique de la Monarchie espagnole, promulguée à Cadix, le 19 mars 1812." *Jus politicum* 9 (2013). http://juspoliticum.com/uploads/pdf/JP9-Busaall_CoCadix-corr.pdf.

Cabet, Etienne. *Voyage en Icarie*. 1840; Paris: Bureau Populaire, 1845.

Campan, Madame. *Mémoires sur la vie privée de Marie-Antoinette*. 3 vols. Paris: Baudouin frères, 1823.

Camus, Albert. *L'homme révolté*. Paris: Gallimard, 1951.

Capp, B. S. *The Fifth Monarchy Men: A Study in Seventeenth-Century English Millenarianism*. London: Faber, 1972.

Caron, Pierre. *Les massacres de septembre*. Paris: Maison du livre français, 1935.

Carvalho, Thérence. *La physiocratie dans l'Europe des Lumières*. Le Kremlin-Bicêtre, France: Mare et Martin, 2021.

Carver, Terrell. "'The German Ideology' Never Took Place." *History of Political Thought* 31, no. 1 (2010):107–27.

[Cary, John, and William Atwood?] *An Answer to Mr. Molyneux, His Case of Ireland's Being Bound by Acts of Parliament in England, Stated. . . .* London: Rich. Parker, 1698. EEBO.

Cash, Arthur H. *John Wilkes: The Scandalous Father of Civil Liberty*. New Haven, CT: Yale University Press, 2006.

Catalogue of the John Adams Library in the Public Library of the City of Boston. Boston, MA: John Adams Library, 1917.

Cavalcanti, Bartolomeo. *Trattati overo discorsi di M. Bartolomeo Caualcanti sopra gli ottimi reggimenti delle republiche antiche et moderne. Con un discorso di M. Sebastiano Erizo gentil'huomo vinitiano de gouerni ciuili.* . . . Venice, 1571.

Cavanaugh, Gerald J. "Turgot: The Rejection of Enlightened Despotism." *French Historical Studies* 6, no. 1 (1969):31–58.

Cavarzere, Marco. *Historical Culture and Political Reform in the Italian Enlightenment.* Oxford University Studies in the Enlightenment, 2020:09. Liverpool: Liverpool University Press, 2020.

Cayley, Edward Stillingfleet. *The European Revolutions of 1848.* 2 vols. London: Smith, Elder, 1856.

Chakrabarty, Dipesh. *Provincializing Europe: Postcolonial Thought and Historical Difference.* Rev. ed. Princeton, NJ: Princeton University Press, 2009.

Charles II. *His Majesties Two Gracious Letters.* . . . Edinburgh: Christopher Higgins, 1660. EEBO.

Chateaubriand, François-René de. *Mémoires d'outre-tombe.* 3 vols. 1849; Paris: Poche, 1973.

Chen, Jianhua. "Revolution: From Literary Revolution to Revolutionary Literature." In *Words and Their Stories: Essays on the Language of the Chinese Revolution*, edited by Ban Wang, 15–32. Leiden: Brill. 2011.

Chernyshevsky, Nikolay. *A Vital Question, or What Is to Be Done?* Translated by Nathan Haskell Dole and S. S. Skidelsky. New York: Thomas Y. Crowell, 1886.

Chestnut, Glenn F. *The First Christian Histories.* Macon, GA: Mercer University Press, 1986.

Childs, Nick. *A Political Academy in Paris, 1724–1731: The Entresol and Its Members.* Oxford: Voltaire Foundation, 2000.

Chinard, Gilbert. "Polybius and the American Constitution." *Journal of the History of Ideas* 1, no. 1 (1940):38–58.

Chirot, Daniel. *You Say You Want a Revolution? Radical Idealism and Its Tragic Consequences.* Princeton, NJ: Princeton University Press, 2020.

Christofferson, Michael Scott. *French Intellectuals against the Left: The Antitotalitarian Moment of the 1970s.* New York: Berghahn Books, 2004.

Ciepley, David. "Is the U.S. Government a Corporation? The Corporate Origins of Modern Constitutionalism." *American Political Science Review* 111, no. 2 (2017):418–35.

Clark, Christopher. *Revolutionary Spring: Europe Aflame and the Fight for a New World, 1848–1849.* New York: Crown, 2023.

——. *Time and Power: Visions of History in German Politics.* Princeton, NJ: Princeton University Press, 2019.

Clark, Frederick. *Dividing Time: The Invention of Historical Periods in Early Modern Europe.* Chicago: University of Chicago Press, forthcoming.

Clark, J.C.D. *Revolution and Rebellion.* Cambridge: Cambridge University Press, 1986.

——. *Thomas Paine: Britain, America, and France in the Age of Enlightenment and Revolution.* Oxford: Oxford University Press, 2018.

Claudio, Lisandro E. *Taming People's Power: The EDSA Revolutions and Their Contradictions.* Manila: Ateneo de Manila University Press, 2013.

Cohen, I. Bernard. *Revolution in Science.* Cambridge, MA: Harvard University Press, 1985.

Cohen, Stephen F. *Bukharin and the Bolshevik Revolution: A Political Biography, 1888–1938*. Oxford: Oxford University Press, 1980.

Cohn, Norman. *The Pursuit of the Millennium: Revolutionary Millenarians and Mystical Anarchists of the Middle Ages*. New York: Oxford University Press, 1970.

Cole, G.D.H. *Socialist Thought: The Forerunners (1789–1850)*. Vol. 1 of *A History of Socialist Thought*. London: MacMillan, 1953.

———. *William Morris as a Socialist*. London: William Morris Society, 1960.

Colepeper, John. *His Majesties Answer to the XIX. Propositions of Both Houses of Parliament*. London: Robert Barker, 1642. EEBO.

Collection générale des decrets rendus par l'Assemblée Nationale. 17 vols. Paris: Baudoin, 1789–94. ARTFL.

A Collection of Papers relating to the Present Juncture of Affairs in England. London, 1688. EEBO.

Colley, Linda. *The Gun, the Ship, and the Pen: Warfare, Constitutions, and the Making of the Modern World*. New York: Liveright, 2021.

Collins, Randall. "Weber and the Sociology of Revolution." *Journal of Classical Sociology* 1, no. 2 (2001):171–94.

Commission des Cortès. "Rapport de la commission des Cortès, chargée de présenter le projet de constitution." In *Constitution politique de la monarchie espagnole*, translated by E. Nunez de Taborda, v–xxiii. Paris: Firmin Didot, 1814.

Commune de Paris. "Déclaration au peuple français." April 19, 1871. Bibliothèque nationale de France, Gallica. https://gallica.bnf.fr/.

Como, David. "God's Revolutions." In Baker and Edelstein, *Scripting Revolution*, 41–56.

———. *Radical Parliamentarians and the English Civil War*. Oxford: Oxford University Press, 2018.

Comsa, Maria Teodora, Melanie Conroy, Dan Edelstein, Chloe Summers Edmondson, and Claude Willan. "The French Enlightenment Network." *Journal of Modern History* 88, no. 3 (2016):495–534.

Comte, Auguste. *Cours de philosophie positive*. 6 vols. Paris: Rouen frères, 1830–42.

Condorcet, Marquis de. *Esquisse d'un tableau historique des progrès de l'esprit humain*. Paris: Agasse, 1795.

———. *Outlines of a Historical View of the Progress of the Human Mind*. London: Johnson, 1795.

———. *Vie de M. Turgot*. London, 1786.

Conniff, James. "On the Obsolescence of the General Will: Rousseau, Madison, and the Evolution of Republican Political Thought." *Western Political Quarterly* 28, no. 1 (1975):32–58.

Connor, W. R. *Thucydides*. Princeton, NJ: Princeton University Press, 1984.

Conquest, Robert. *The Great Terror: Stalin's Purge of the Thirties*. 1968; New York: Random House, 2018.

Constant, Benjamin. "The Liberty of Ancients Compared with That of Moderns" (1819). In *Political Writings*, edited and translated by Biancamaria Fontana, 309–28. Cambridge: Cambridge University Press, 1988.

Cook, Alexander C., ed. *Mao's Little Red Book: A Global History*. Cambridge: Cambridge University Press, 2014.

Corio, Bernardino. *Historia continente da lorigine di Milano. . . .* Milan: Giovanni Giacomo e fratelli da Legnano, 1503.

———. *L'historia di Milano volgarmente scritta. . . .* Venice: Giovanni Maria Bonelli, 1554.

Cotta, Sergio. "Montesquieu, la séparation des pouvoirs, et la Constitution fédérale des Etats-Unis." *Revue internationale d'histoire politique et constitutionelle* 1 (1951):225–47.

Coverdale, John F. *The Basque Phase of Spain's First Carlist War*. Princeton, NJ: Princeton University Press, 1984.

Cox, Gary W. "Was the Glorious Revolution a Constitutional Watershed?" *Journal of Economic History* 72, no. 3 (2012):567–600.

Coyle, J. Kevin. "Augustine and Apocalyptic: Thoughts on the Fall of Rome, the Book of Revelation, and the End of the World." *Florilegium* 9 (1987):1–34.

Craiutu, Aurelian. *Liberalism under Siege: The Political Thought of the French Doctrinaires*. Lanham, MD: Lexington Books, 2003.

———. *A Virtue for Courageous Minds: Moderation in French Political Thought, 1748–1830*. Princeton, NJ: Princeton University Press, 2012.

Cromartie, Alan. *The Constitutionalist Revolution: An Essay on the History of England, 1450–1642*. Cambridge: Cambridge University Press, 2006.

Cullen, Frank, with Florence Hackman and Donald McNeilly. *Vaudeville Old & New: An Encyclopedia of Variety Performers in America*. New York: Routledge, 2007.

Cumings, Henry. *A Sermon Preached in Billerica on the 23d of November 1775*. Worcester, [MA]: I. Thomas, 1776.

Curtius, Ernst Robert. *European Literature and the Latin Middle Ages*. Princeton, NJ: Princeton University Press, 1948.

Dahl, Robert. *Democracy and Its Critics*. New Haven, CT: Yale University Press, 1989.

Darnton, Robert. *The Forbidden Best-Sellers of Pre-revolutionary France*. New York: W.W. Norton, 1996.

———. *The Kiss of Lamourette*. New York: Norton, 1990.

———. *Mesmerism and the End of the Enlightenment in France*. Cambridge, MA: Harvard University Press, 1968.

———. "The *Philosophes* Trim the Tree of Knowledge." Chapter 5 in *The Great Cat Massacre*. New York: Vintage, 1985.

Day, Richard B., and Daniel Gaido. *Witnesses to Permanent Revolution: The Documentary Record*. Leiden: Brill, 2009.

Debray, Régis. *Praised Be Our Lords: A Political Education*. Translated by John Howe. London: Verso Books, 2007.

———. *Revolution in the Revolution? Armed Struggle and Political Struggle in Latin America*. Translated by Gregory Elliott. 1967; London: Verso Books, 2017.

Declaration of the Rights of Man and of the Citizen. French National Assembly, 1789.

Delisle de Sales, Jean-Baptiste-Claude. *De la philosophie de la nature*. Amsterdam: Arkstee et Merkus, 1770. ARTFL.

De Lolme, Jean-Louis. *Constitution de l'Angleterre*. Rev. ed. 1771; Amsterdam: E. Van Harrevelt, 1774.

———. *The Constitution of England*. Edited by David Lieberman. Indianapolis, IN: Liberty Fund, 2007.

Deluermoz, Quentin. *Le crépuscule des révolutions, 1848–1871*. Paris: Seuil, 2012.

Demophilus [pseud.]. *The Genuine Principles of the Ancient Saxon, or English Constitution*. Philadelphia, PA: Robert Bell, 1776.

Desmoulins, Camille. *Discours sur la situation politique de la nation*. Paris, [October] 1791.

——. *La France libre*. [Paris], 1789.

Dickinson, John. *An Essay on the Constitutional Power of Great-Britain over the Colonies in America*. Philadelphia, 177. EVANS.

Diderot, Denis. *Le neveu de Rameau*. Paris: GF, 1983.

——. *Lettres à Sophie Volland*. Edited by A. Babelon. Paris: Gallimard, 1950. ARTFL.

——. *Œuvres complètes*. Paris: Garnier, 1875. ARTFL.

——. *Political Writings*. Edited and translated by John Hope Mason and Robert Wokler. Cambridge: Cambridge University Press, 2012.

——. *Rameau's Nephew*. Edited by Marian Hobson, translated by Kate E. Tunstall and Caroline Warman. Cambridge: Open Book, 2016.

——. *Salon de 1767*. Edited by J. Seznec and J. Adhemar. Oxford, Clarendon, 1963. ARTFL.

——. *Supplément au voyage de Bougainville*. 1776. In *Œuvres philosophiques*, 445–516. Paris: Garnier, 1998.

Diderot, Denis, and Jean le Rond d'Alembert, eds. *Encyclopédie, ou Dictionnaire raisonné des sciences, des arts et des métiers*. ARTFL ed., edited by Robert Morrissey and Glenn Roe. 1751–72; Chicago: University of Chicago: ARTFL Encyclopédie Project, 2022. http://encyclopedie.uchicago.edu/.

Dijn, Annelien de. *Freedom: An Unruly History*. Cambridge, MA: Harvard University Press, 2020.

——. *French Political Thought from Montesquieu to Tocqueville*. Cambridge: Cambridge University Press, 2008.

——. "Was Montesquieu a Liberal Republican?" *Review of Politics* 76, no. 1 (2014):21–41.

Dikötter, Frank. *Mao's Great Famine: The History of China's Most Devastating Catastrophe, 1958–1962*. New York: Walker, 2010.

Dionisotti, Carlo. *Machiavellerie: Storia e fortuna di Machiavelli*. Turin: Einaudi, 1980.

Doerfler, Ryan, and Samuel Moyn. "The Constitution Is Broken and Should Not Be Reclaimed." *New York Times*, August 19, 2022. https://www.nytimes.com/2022/08/19/opinion/liberals-constitution.html.

Dommanget, Maurice. *Sylvain Maréchal, l'égalitaire*. Paris: Spartacus, 1950.

Dornier, Carole. *La monarchie éclairée de l'abbé de Saint-Pierre: Une science politique des Modernes*. Oxford University Studies in the Enlightenment. Liverpool: Liverpool University Press, 2020.

Dostoevsky, Fyodor. *The Adolescent*. Translated by Richard Pevear and Larissa Volokhonsky. New York: Knopf, 2003.

——. *The Possessed*. Translated by Constance Garnett. New York: Barnes and Noble Classics, 2005.

Doyle, William. *The Oxford History of the French Revolution*. Rev. ed. Oxford: Oxford University Press, 2002.

Drayton, William. *A Charge, on the Rise of the American Empire*. N.p., 1776. EVANS

Dubois, Laurent. *Avengers of the New World: The Story of the Haitian Revolution.* Cambridge, MA: Harvard University Press, 2004.

———. *A Colony of Citizens: Revolution and Slave Emancipation in the French Caribbean, 1787–1804.* Chapel Hill: University of North Carolina Press, 2004.

———. *Haiti: The Aftershocks of History.* New York: Henry Holt, 2012.

Dubos, Jean-Baptiste. *Réflexions critiques sur la poésie et la peinture.* 3 vols. Paris: Mariette, 1733.

Du Camp, Maxime. *Les chants modernes.* Paris: Michel Levy, 1855.

———. *Souvenirs littéraires.* 2 vols. Paris: Hachette, 1906.

Duchet, Michèle. *Diderot et "L'histoire des deux Indes," ou, L'écriture fragmentaire.* Paris: A.-G. Nizet, 1978.

Dunbabin, Jean. "The Reception and Interpretation of Aristotle's *Politics*." In *The Cambridge History of Later Medieval Philosophy*, edited by Norman Kretzmann, Anthony Kenny, and Jan Pinborg, 721–37. Cambridge: Cambridge University Press, 1982.

Duong, Kevin. *The Virtues of Violence: Democracy against Disintegration in Modern France.* Oxford: Oxford University Press, 2020.

Duport, James. *Three Sermons Preached in St. Maries Church in Cambridg[e] . . . .* N.p., 1676. EEBO.

Dwyer, Philip. "'Citizen Emperor': Political Ritual, Popular Sovereignty and the Coronation of Napoleon I." *History* 100, no. 1 (2015):40–57.

Dymond, Anne. "A Politicized Pastoral: Signac and the Cultural Geography of Mediterranean France." *Art Bulletin* 85, no. 2 (2003):353–70.

Dymond, Jeffrey. "Human Character and the Formation of the State: Reconsidering Machiavelli and Polybius 6." *Journal of the History of Ideas* 82, no. 1 (2021):29–50.

Eastman, Scott, and Natalia Sobrevilla Perea, eds. *The Rise of Constitutional Government in the Iberian Atlantic World: The Impact of the Cádiz Constitution of 1812.* Tuscaloosa: University of Alabama Press, 2015.

Echeverria, Durand. *The Maupeou Revolution: A Study in the History of Libertarianism; France, 1770–1774.* Baton Rouge: Louisiana State University Press, 1985.

Eckstein, Arthur M. *Moral Vision in the "Histories" of Polybius.* Berkeley: University of California Press, 1995.

Edelstein, Dan. *The Enlightenment: A Genealogy.* Chicago: University of Chicago Press, 2010.

———. "Hyperborean Atlantis: Jean-Sylvain Bailly, Madame Blavatsky, and the Nazi Myth." *Studies in Eighteenth Century Culture* 35 (2006):267–91.

———. *On the Spirit of Rights.* Chicago: University of Chicago Press, 2018.

———. "Rousseau, Bodin, and the Medieval Corporatist Origins of Popular Sovereignty." *Political Theory* 50, no. 1 (2021):142–68.

———. *The Terror of Natural Right: Republicanism, the Cult of Nature, and the French Revolution.* Chicago: University of Chicago Press, 2009.

Edelstein, Dan, Stefanos Geroulanos, and Natasha Wheatley, eds. *Power and Time: Temporalities in Conflict and the Making of History.* Chicago: University of Chicago Press, 2020.

Edelstein, Dan, and Stephen Sawyer. "Sovereignty and Government in the French Revolution." Unpublished MS.

Edelstein, Ludwig. *The Idea of Progress in Classical Antiquity*. Baltimore, MD: Johns Hopkins Press, 1967.

Edie, Carolyn A. "Revolution and the Rule of Law: The End of the Dispensing Power, 1689." *Eighteenth-Century Studies* 10, no. 4 (1977):434–50.

Egnazio, Giovanni Battista. *Ioannis Baptistæ Egnatij Veneti de Cæsaribus libri 3 à dictatore Cæsare ad Constantinum Palæologum*. . . . Venice: Aldo Manuzio, 1516.

——. *Le vite de gl'imperadori* [sic] *romani di monsignore Egnatio, nuovamente dalla lingua latina tradotte alla volgare, con due fragmenti de "L'historia" di Polibio, della diversità delle republiche tradotti dalla greca alla volgar lingua*. Venice: Francesco Marcolino, 1540.

Eichner, Carolyn J. *The Paris Commune: A Brief History*. New Brunswick, NJ: Rutgers University Press, 2022.

Elton, Geoffrey. *"The Body of the Whole Realm": Parliament and Representation in Medieval and Tudor England*. Charlottesville: University of Virginia Press, 1969.

Engels, Friedrich. *The Origin of the Family, Private Property and the State*. Translated by Alick West and Dona Torr. London: Lawrence and Wishart, 1943.

——. *Socialism: Utopian and Scientific*. Translated by Edward Aveling. 1882; New York: Cosimo Classics, 2008.

Erikson, Robert S., and Christopher Wlezien. "Leading Economic Indicators, the Polls, and the Presidential Vote." *PS: Political Science and Politics* 41, no. 4 (2008):703–7.

An Essay upon Government. Philadelphia, 1775.

Fage, Robert. *Cosmography; or, A Description of the Whole World*. London, 1667. EEBO.

Fairfax, Thomas. *A Declaration of His Excellency Sir Thomas Fairfax* . . . . London: George Whittington, 1647.

Farrand, Max, ed. *The Records of the Federal Convention of 1787*. 3 vols. New Haven, CT: Yale University Press, 1911.

"February 1649: An Act of This Present Parliament for Constituting a Counsell of State for the Comonwealth of England." In *Acts and Ordinances of the Interregnum, 1642–1660*, edited by C. H. Firth and R. S. Rait, 2–4. London, 1911. British History Online, http://www.british-history.ac.uk/no-series/acts-ordinances-interregnum/pp2-4.

Fichtl, Ariane V. *La radicalisation de l'idéal républicain: Modèles antiques et la Révolution française*. Paris: Classiques Garnier, 2021.

Filmer, Robert. *The Anarchy of a Limited or Mixed Monarch*. London, 1648.

Fink, Zera S. *The Classical Republicans: An Essay on the Recovery of a Pattern of Thought in Seventeenth-Century England*. Chicago: Northwestern University Press, 1945.

Fitzpatrick, Sheila. *The Russian Revolution*. Oxford: Oxford University Press, 2008.

Flaubert, Gustave. *Bouvard et Pécuchet*. 1881 [posthumous]; Paris: GF, 1966.

——. *Correspondance*. 12 vols. Paris: L. Conard, 1926–54.

——. *L'education sentimentale*. Edited by Gisèle Séginger et al. In *Œuvres complètes*, vol. 4. Paris: Pléiade, 2021.

——. *Sentimental Education*. Translated by Helen Constantine, edited by Patrick Coleman. Oxford: Oxford University Press, 2016.

Foner, Eric. *Tom Paine and Revolutionary America*. Updated ed. New York: Oxford University Press, 2005.

Fontenelle, Bernard Le Bovier de. *De l'origine des fables* (1686). In *Œuvres de Fontenelle*, vol. 4. Paris: Salmon, 1825.

Foran, John. "Theories of Revolution Revisited: Toward a Fourth Generation?" *Sociological Theory* 11, no. 1 (1993):1–20.

Fornara, Charles W. *The Nature of History in Ancient Greece and Rome*. Berkeley: University of California Press, 1983.

Fourier, Charles. *The Utopian Vision of Charles Fourier: Selected Texts on Work, Love and Passionate Attraction*. Edited and translated by Jonathan Beecher and Richard Bienvenu. Boston, MA: Beacon, 1971.

Frank, Jason. *The Democratic Sublime: On Aesthetics and Popular Assembly*. Oxford: Oxford University Press, 2021.

Frank, Joseph. *Dostoevsky: The Miraculous Years, 1865–1971*. Vol. 4. Princeton, NJ: Princeton University Press, 1995.

———. *Dostoevsky: The Years of Ordeal, 1850–1859*. Princeton, NJ: Princeton University Press, 1987.

———. *Through the Russian Prism: Essays on Literature and Culture*. Princeton, NJ: Princeton University Press, 1990.

Friedland, Paul. "Every Island Is Not Haiti: The French Revolution in the Windward Islands." In *Rethinking the Age of Revolutions: France and the Birth of the Modern World*, edited by David A. Bell and Yair Mintzker, 41–79. Oxford: Oxford University Press, 2018.

———. *Political Actors: Representative Bodies and Theatricality in the Age of the French Revolution*. Ithaca, NY: Cornell University Press, 2002.

Fritz, Kurt von. *The Theory of the Mixed Constitution in Antiquity*. New York: Columbia University Press, 1954.

Fritzsche, Peter. *Stranded in the Present: Modern Time and the Melancholy of History*. Cambridge, MA: Harvard University Press, 2004.

Fukuyama, Francis. *The End of History and the Last Man*. New York: Free Press, 2006.

———. *Liberalism and Its Discontents*. New York: Macmillan, 2022.

Fumaroli, Marc. "Les abeilles et les araignées." In *La querelle des Anciens et des Modernes*, edited by Anne-Marie Lecoq, 8–218. Paris: Gallimard, 2001.

Furet, François. *Interpreting the French Revolution*. Translated by Elborg Forster. Cambridge: Cambridge University Press, 1981.

———. *Marx and the French Revolution*. Translated by Deborah Kan Furet. Chicago: University of Chicago Press, 1988.

———. *Penser la Révolution française*. Paris: Gallimard, 1978.

———. *Revolutionary France, 1770–1880*. Translated by Antonia Nevill. Oxford: Blackwell, 1992.

Galligan, Denis J., ed. *Constitutions and the Classics: Patterns of Constitutional Thought from Fortescue to Bentham*. Oxford: Oxford University Press, 2015.

———. "The Levellers, the People, and the Constitution." In *Constitutions and the Classics*, 122–51.

Gardiner, Samuel Rawson, ed. *The Constitutional Documents of the Puritan Revolution, 1625–1660*. Oxford: Clarendon, 1906.

Garner, Paul. *Porfirio Diaz*. New York: Routledge, 2014.

Garrett, Clarke W. "The *Moniteur* of 1788." *French Historical Studies* 5, no. 3 (1968):263–73.

Garton Ash, Timothy. *The Magic Lantern: The Revolution of '89 Witnessed in Warsaw, Budapest, Berlin, and Prague*. New York: Knopf, 1990.

———. "Velvet Revolution: The Prospects." *New York Review of Books*, December 3, 2009.

Geggus, David. "The Caribbean in the Age of Revolution." In Armitage and Subrahmanyam, *Age of Revolutions*, 83–100.

Gehrke, Hans-Joachim. *Stasis: Untersuchungen zu den inneren Kriegen in den griechischen Staaten des 5. und 4. Jh. v. Chr.* Munich: Beck, 1985.

General Assembly of the Church of Scotland. *Reverend Brethren*. Edinburgh: Evan Tyler, 1649. EEBO.

Genty, Maurice. "Pratique et théorie de la démocratie directe: L'exemple des districts parisiens (1789–1790)." *Annales historiques de la Révolution française* 57 (1985):8–24.

George III. "A Proclamation for Suppressing Rebellion and Sedition." London, 1775.

Gerçek, Salih Emre. "The 'Social Question' as a Democratic Question: Louis Blanc's *Organization of Labor*." *Modern Intellectual History* 20, no. 2 (2023):388–416.

Geschichtliche Grundbegriffe: Historisches Lexikon zur politisch-sozialen Sprache in Deutschland. 8 vols. Edited by Otto Brunner, Werner Conze, and Reinhart Koselleck. Stuttgart: Klett-Cotta, 1972–97.

Getachew, Adom. "Universalism after the Post-colonial Turn: Interpreting the Haitian Revolution." *Political Theory* 44, no. 6 (2016):821–45.

Ghonim, Wael. *Revolution 2.0: The Power of the People Is Greater than the People in Power; A Memoir*. Boston, MA: Houghton Mifflin Harcourt, 2012.

Giannotti, Donato. *Della repubblica fiorentina*. 1531; Venice: Gio. Gabbriel Hertz, 1722.

Giannotti, Gaspare. *Parere di Gasparo Giannotti scritto al signor Giulio Cesare Catelmi, sopra il ristretto delle reuoluzioni del reame di Cipri*. Frankfurt [?], 1633.

Gienapp, Jonathan. *The Second Creation: Fixing the American Constitution in the Founding Era*. Cambridge, MA: Harvard University Press, 2018.

Gilbert, Felix. "Bernardo Rucellai and the Orti Oricellari: A Study on the Origin of Modern Political Thought." *Journal of the Warburg and Courtauld Institutes* 12 (1949):101–31.

———. "Revolution." In *Dictionary of the History of Ideas*, edited by Philip Weiner, 4:152–67. New York: Scribner's, 1973–74.

Gilens, Martin, and Benjamin Page. "Testing Theories of American Politics: Elites, Interest Groups, and Average Citizens." *Perspectives on Politics* 12, no. 3 (2014):564–81.

Gillespie, George. *A Sermon Preached before the Honourable House of Commons at Their Late Solemne Fast Wednesday*. N.p., March 27, 1644. EEBO.

Giraffi, Alessandro. *An Exact Historie of the Late Revolution in Naples and of Their Monstrous Successes*. Translated by James Howell. London: R. Lowndes, 1650.

———. *Le riuolutioni di Napoli*. Venice: Baba, 1647.

Girard, Philippe. "Napoléon Bonaparte and the Emancipation Issue in Saint-Domingue, 1799–1803." *French Historical Studies* 32, no. 4 (2009):587–618.

Girardin, René. *Discours sur la nécessité de la ratification de la loi par la volonté générale*. Paris: Creuset, 1791.

Godfrey, James L. *Revolutionary Justice: A Study in the Organization and Procedures of the Paris Tribunal, 1793–1795*. Chapel Hill: University of North Carolina Press, 1951.

Goldie, Mark. "The English System of Liberty." In *The Cambridge History of Eighteenth-Century Political Thought*, edited by Goldie and Robert Wokler, 40–78. Cambridge: Cambridge University Press, 2006).

Goldstone, Jack A. *Revolution and Rebellion in the Early Modern World*. Berkeley: University of California Press, 1991.

Goldsworthy, Jeffrey. *Parliamentary Sovereignty: Contemporary Debates*. Cambridge: Cambridge University Press, 2010.

Gombrich, E. H. "The Debate on Primitivism in Ancient Rhetoric." *Journal of the Warburg and Courtauld Institutes* 29 (1966):24–38.

Goodwin, John. *Synkrētismos; or, Dis-satisfaction Satisfied: In Seventeen Sober and Serious Queries, Tending to Allay the Discontents, and Satisfie the Scruples, of Persons Dis-satisfied about the Late Revolution of Government in the Common-Wealth*. . . . London: J. Macock, 1653. EEBO.

Goulemot, Jean Marie. *Le règne de l'histoire: Discours historiques et révolutions, XVIIe–XVIIIe siècle*. Paris: Albin Michel, 1996.

Grafton, Anthony. *New Worlds, Ancient Texts: The Power of Tradition and the Shock of Discovery*. Cambridge, MA: Harvard University Press, 1992.

Grafton, Anthony, and Joanna Weinberg. *"I Have Always Loved the Holy Tongue": Isaac Casaubon, the Jews, and a Forgotten Chapter in Renaissance Scholarship*. Cambridge, MA: Harvard University Press, 2011.

Greenblatt, Stephen. *The Swerve: How the World Became Modern*. New York: Random House, 2011.

Greene, Jack P. *Negotiated Authorities: Essays in Colonial Political and Constitutional History*. Charlottesville: University of Virginia Press, 1994.

Greer, Donald. *The Incidence of the Terror during the French Revolution: A Statistical Interpretation*. Cambridge, MA: Harvard University Press, 1935.

Gregor, A. James. *Totalitarianism and Political Religion: An Intellectual History*. Stanford, CA: Stanford University Press, 2012.

Grell, Chantal, and Christian Michel, eds. *Primitivisme et mythes des origines dans la France des Lumières, 1680–1820*. Paris: Presses de l'Université de Paris-Sorbonne, 1989.

Grewal, David. "The Political Theology of Laissez-Faire: From Philia to Self-Love in Commercial Society." *Political Theology* 17, no. 5 (2016):417–33.

Grewal, David Singh, and Jedediah Purdy. "The Original Theory of Constitutionalism." *Yale Law Journal* 127 (2018):664–705.

Griewank, Karl. *Der neuzeitliche Revolutionsbegriff: Entstehung und Entwicklung*. Weimar, Germany: Hermann Böhlaus Nachfolger, 1955.

Gross, Jean-Pierre. *Fair Shares for All: Jacobin Egalitarianism in Practice*. Cambridge: Cambridge University Press, 2003.

Grzymała-Busse, Anna. *Sacred Foundations: The Religious and Medieval Roots of the European State*. Princeton, NJ: Princeton University Press, 2023.

Guelfucci, Marie-Rose. "Polybe et Montesquieu: Aspects d'une réflexion sur le pouvoir." *Anabases* 4 (2006):125–39.

Gueniffey, Patrice. *Bonaparte, 1769–1802*. Translated by Steven Rendall. Cambridge, MA: Harvard University Press, 2015.

Guérin, Daniel. *La lutte des classes sous la première république*. 2 vols. Paris: Gallimard, 1946.

Guffroy, Armand-Joseph. *Le Franc en vedette, ou, Le porte-voix de la vérité, sur le tocsin*. Paris, [February] 1790.

Gummere, Richard M. *The American Colonial Mind and the Classical Tradition: Essays in Comparative Culture*. Cambridge, MA: Harvard University Press, 1963.

Gutwirth, Madelyn. *The Twilight of the Goddesses: Women and Representation in the French Revolutionary Era*. New Brunswick, NJ: Rutgers University Press, 1992.

Guyatt, Nicholas. *Providence and the Invention of the United States, 1607–1876*. Cambridge: Cambridge University Press, 2007.

Halfin, Igal. *Stalinist Confessions: Messianism and Terror at the Leningrad Communist University*. Pittsburgh, PA: University of Pittsburgh Press, 2009.

Hamilton, Alexander. *A Letter from Phocion to the Considerate Citizens of New-York on the Politics of the Day*. New York: Loudon, 1784.

Hamilton, Alexander, John Jay, and James Madison. *The Federalist Papers*. Edited by Isaac Kramnick. London: Penguin Books, 1987.

Hammersley, Rachel. *French Revolutionaries and English Republicans: The Cordeliers Club, 1790–1794*. London: Boydell, 2005.

Hamnett, Brian. "The Medieval Roots of Spanish Constitutionalism." In Eastman and Sobrevilla Perea, *Rise of Constitutional Government*, 19–41.

Hanet-Cléry, Jean Baptiste C. *Journal de ce qui s'est passé à la tour du Temple, pendant la captivité de Louis XVI*. Paris: Michaud, 1823.

Hankins, James. "Europe's First Democrat? Cyriac of Ancona and Book 6 of Polybius." In *For the Sake of Learning: Essays in Honor of Anthony Grafton*, edited by Ann Blair and Anja-Silvia Goeing, 2:692–710. Leiden: Brill, 2016.

———. "Exclusivist Republicanism and the Non-monarchical Republic." *Political Theory* 38, no. 4 (2010):452–82.

Hansen, Mogens Herman. "The Mixed Constitution versus the Separation of Powers: Monarchical and Aristocratic Aspects of Modern Democracy." *History of Political Thought* 31, no. 3 (2010):509–31

———. "Stasis as an Essential Aspect of the Polis." In *An Inventory of Archaic and Classical Poleis*, edited by Hansen and Thomas Heine Nielsen, 124–29. Oxford: Oxford University Press, 2005.

Haraszti, Zoltán. *John Adams and the Prophets of Progress*. Cambridge, MA: Harvard University Press, 1952.

Harding, Neil. *Leninism*. Durham, NC: Duke University Press, 1996.

———. *Lenin's Political Thought*. Durham, NC: Duke University Press, 1977.

Harison, Casey. "The Paris Commune of 1871, the Russian Revolution of 1905, and the Shifting of the Revolutionary Tradition." *History and Memory* 19, no. 2 (2007):5–42.

Harrington, James. *The Commonwealth of Oceana*. London: Pakeman, 1656.

Harris, Edward M. "The Constitution of the Five Thousand." *Harvard Studies in Classical Philology* 93 (1990):243–80.

Harris, Tim. "Did the English Have a Script for Revolution?" In Baker and Edelstein, *Scripting Revolution*, 25–40.

———. *Restoration: Charles II and His Kingdoms, 1660–1685*. London: Penguin Books, 2006.

———. *Revolution: The Great Crisis of the British Monarchy, 1685–1720*. London: Penguin Books, 2007.

Harsin, Jill. *Barricades: The War of the Streets in Revolutionary Paris, 1830–1848*. New York: Palgrave Macmillan, 2002.

Hart, David M., and Ross Kenyon, eds. *Tracts on Liberty by the Levellers and Their Critics (1638–1660)*. 7 vols. Indianapolis, IN: Liberty Fund, 2014–18.

Hartog, François. *Chronos: L'occident aux prises avec le temps*. Paris: Gallimard, 2020.

———. *Regimes of Historicity: Presentism and Experiences of Time*. Translated by Saskia Brown. New York: Columbia University Press, 2015.

Hatto, Arthur. "'Revolution': An Enquiry into the Usefulness of an Historical Term." *Mind* 58 (1949):495–516.

Haude, Sigrun. *In the Shadow of "Savage Wolves": Anabaptist Münster and the German Reformation during the 1530s*. Boston, MA: Humanities, 2000.

Hayes, Peter. "Marx's Analysis of the French Class Structure." *Theory and Society* 22, no. 1 (1993):99–123.

Hayward, John. *An Ansvver to the First Part of a Certaine Conference, concerning Succession*. London: Waterson and Burbie, 1603. EEBO.

Hazareesingh, Sudhir. *Black Spartacus: The Epic Life of Toussaint Louverture*. London: Penguin Books, 2020.

———. *The Legend of Napoleon*. London: Granta, 2004.

Heckert, Jamie, and Richard Cleminson, eds. *Anarchism & Sexuality: Ethics, Relationships and Power*. New York: Routledge, 2011.

Hegel, G.W.F. *The Philosophy of History*. Translated by J. Sibree. New York: Dover, 1956.

Heinrich, Michael. *Karl Marx and the Birth of Modern Society: The Life of Marx and the Development of His Work*. Translated by Alexander Locascio. New York: Monthly Review, 2019.

Helvétius, Claude Adrien. *De l'homme*. London: Société Typographique, 1773.

Herr, Richard. "The Constitution of 1812 and the Spanish Road to Parliamentary Monarchy." In *Revolution and the Meanings of Freedom in the Nineteenth Century*, edited by Isser Woloch, 65–102. Stanford, CA: Stanford University Press, 1996.

Hexter, Jack H. "Seyssel, Machiavelli, and Polybius VI: The Mystery of the Missing Translation." *Studies in the Renaissance* 3 (1956):75–96.

Hill, Christopher. "The Word 'Revolution.'" In *A Nation of Change and Novelty*, 82–101. London: Routledge, 1990.

Historical Remarques upon the Late Revolutions in the United Provinces Drawn from Their Own Papers. London: Tho. Newcomb, 1675.

The History and Proceedings of the House of Commons. Vol. 1. London: Richard Chandler, 1742.

Hobbes, Thomas. *Leviathan*. Edited by Noel Malcolm. In *The Clarendon Edition of the Works of Thomas Hobbes*, vols. 3–5. Oxford: Clarendon, 2012.

Hobsbawm, Eric. *The Age of Extremes: 1914–1991*. London: Abacus, 1995.

Hoekstra, Kinch. "Athenian Democracy and Popular Tyranny." Chapter 1 in *Popular Sovereignty in Historical Perspective*, edited by Richard Bourke and Quentin Skinner. Cambridge: Cambridge University Press, 2016.

d'Holbach. *Histoire critique de Jésus-Christ ou analyse raisonnée des Évangiles*. N.p., 1770. ARTFL.

———. *La contagion sacrée, ou Histoire naturelle de la superstition*. N.p., 1768.

———. *La morale universelle, ou, Les devoirs de l'homme fondés sur sa nature*. 3 vols. Amsterdam: M.M. Rey, 1776. ARTFL.

———. *Système de la nature ou, Des loix du monde physique du monde moral*. London, 1771. ARTFL.

———.*Système social ou principes naturels de la morale et de la politique avec un examen de l'influence du gouvernement sur les mœurs*. 1773. Paris: Fayard, 1994. ARTFL.

———. *Théologie portative, ou, Dictionnaire abrégé de la religion chrétienne*. London, 1768. ARTFL.

Holton, Woody. *Unruly Americans and the Origins of the Constitution*. New York: Hill and Wang, 2007.

Hoock, Holger. *Scars of Independence: America's Violent Birth*. New York: Crown, 2017.

Horn, Jeff. *The Making of a Terrorist: Alexandre Rousselin and the French Revolution*. Oxford: Oxford University Press, 2020.

Hugo, Victor. *Les misérables*. Paris: Pléiade, 1951.

Hunt, Lynn. "The Imagery of Radicalism." In *Politics, Culture, and Class*, 87–119.

———. *Inventing Human Rights*. New York: Norton, 2007.

———. *Measuring Time, Making History*. Budapest: Central European University Press, 2008.

———. *Politics, Culture, and Class in the French Revolution*. Berkeley: University of California Press, 1984.

Huntington, Samuel P. *The Third Wave: Democratization in the Late Twentieth Century*. Norman: University of Oklahoma Press, 1991.

Hunton, Philip. *A Treatise on Monarchie*. London: John Bellamy, 1643.

Hutton, Patrick H. *The Cult of the Revolutionary Tradition: The Blanquists in French Politics*. Berkeley: University of California Press, 1981.

I Ching: Book of Changes. Translated by James Legge. New York: Bantam, 1986.

Inglis, Charles. *The True Interest of America Impartially Stated, in Certain Strictures on a Pamphlet Intitled Common Sense*. Philadelphia, PA: James Humphreys, 1776. EVANS.

Isabella, Maurizio. *Southern Europe in the Age of Revolutions*. Princeton, NJ: Princeton University Press, 2023.

Israel, Jonathan. *Democratic Enlightenment*. Oxford: Oxford University Press, 2011.

———. *The Expanding Blaze: How the American Revolution Ignited the World, 1775–1848*. Princeton, NJ: Princeton University Press, 2017.

———. *A Revolution of the Mind*. Princeton, NJ: Princeton University Press, 2009.

Jainchill, Andrew, ed. *"Considérations sur le gouvernement," a Critical Edition, with Other Political Texts*. Oxford University Studies in the Enlightenment, 2019:05. Liverpool: Liverpool University Press, 2019.

——. *Reimagining Politics after the Terror: The Republican Origins of French Liberalism*. Ithaca, NY: Cornell University Press, 2008.

Jasanoff, Maya. *Liberty's Exiles: American Loyalists in the Revolutionary World*. New York: Knopf, 2011.

Jefferson, Thomas. *Jefferson's Literary Commonplace Book*. Edited by D. L. Wilson. Princeton, NJ: Princeton University Press, 1989.

——. *Notes on the State of Virginia*. London: John Stockdale, 1785.

Johnson, Curtis. "The Hobbesian Conception of Sovereignty and Aristotle's Politics." *Journal of the History of Ideas* 46, no. 3 (1985):327–47.

Johnson, Samuel. *A Dictionary of the English Language*. 2 vols. London, 1755. https://johnsonsdictionaryonline.com/.

——. *A Dictionary of the English Language*. 2 vols. London: A. Millar, 1766.

Jollivet, Jean-Baptiste-Moïse. *Principes fondamentaux du régime social comparés avec le plan de Constitution*. In *AP*, 61:644–66.

Jones, Colin. *The Fall of Robespierre: 24 Hours in Revolutionary Paris*. Oxford: Oxford University Press, 2021.

——. *The Great Nation*. London: Penguin Books, 2003.

——. *Paris: The Biography of a City*. London: Penguin Books, 2006.

Jones, Mark. *Founding Weimar: Violence and the German Revolution of 1918–1919*. Cambridge: Cambridge University Press, 2016.

Jonsson, Stefan. *A Brief History of the Masses: Three Revolutions*. New York: Columbia University Press, 2008.

Jordan, David P. *The Revolutionary Career of Maximilien Robespierre*. Chicago: University of Chicago Press, 1985.

Journals of the Continental Congress. Washington: Government Publishing Office, 1774–.

Judt, Tony. *Past Imperfect: French Intellectuals, 1944–1956*. Berkeley: University of California Press, 1994.

Jurieu, Pierre. *Histoire du calvinisme et celle du papisme mises en parallèle, ou Apologie pour les réformateurs, pour la Réformation et pour les réformés*. Rotterdam: R. Leers, 1683.

Kagan, Donald. *The Fall of the Athenian Empire*. Ithaca, NY: Cornell University Press, 1987.

Kaiser, Thomas. "The Abbé de Saint-Pierre, Public Opinion, and the Reconstitution of the French Monarchy." *Journal of Modern History* 55, no. 4 (1983):618–43.

Kaminski, John P., and Richard Leffler, eds. *Federalists and Antifederalists: The Debate over the Ratification of the Constitution*. Rev. ed. Lanham, MD: Madison House, 1998.

Kaminski, John P., Gaspare J. Saladino, Richard Leffler, Charles H. Schoenleber, and Margaret A. Hogan, eds. *The Documentary History of the Ratification of the Constitution*. Digital ed. Charlottesville: University of Virginia Press, 2009–. American History Collection, Rotunda. https://rotunda.upress.virginia.edu/founders/FGEA.

Kammen, Michael. "The Meaning of Colonization in American Revolutionary Thought." *Journal of the History of Ideas* 31, no. 3 (1970):337–58.

Kautsky, Karl. *Die Klassengegensätze von 1789: Zum hundertjährigen Gedenktag der grossen Revolution*. Stuttgart: Dietz, 1889.

——. *La lutte des classes en France en 1789*. Translated by Edouard Berth. Paris: G. Jacques, 1901.

Kenyon, John Philipps. *Revolution Principles: The Politics of Party, 1689–1720*. Cambridge: Cambridge University Press, 1977.

——. *The Stuart Constitution, 1603–1688*. Rev. ed. Cambridge: Cambridge University Press, 1986.

Keohane, Nannerl O. *Philosophy and the State in France*. Princeton, NJ: Princeton University Press, 1980.

Kern, Martin, Paul Goldin, and Yuri Pines, eds. *Ideology of Power and Power of Ideology in Early China*. Leiden, Netherlands: Brill, 2015.

Kimmel, Michael S. *Revolution, a Sociological Interpretation*. Philadelphia, PA: Temple University Press, 1990.

King, Martin Luther, Jr. "Letter from Birmingham Jail." Philadelphia: American Friends Service Committee, May 1963.

Kinsbruner, Jay. *Independence in Spanish America: Civil Wars, Revolutions, and Underdevelopment*. Albuquerque: University of New Mexico Press, 2000.

Kirkpatrick, David D. *Into the Hands of the Soldiers: Freedom and Chaos in Egypt and the Middle East*. New York: Penguin Books, 2019.

Klein, Richard J. "Baudelaire and Revolution: Some Notes." *Yale French Studies* 39 (1967):85–97.

Klooster, Wim. *Revolutions in the Atlantic World: A Comparative History*. New ed. New York: New York University Press, 2018.

Kors, Alan C. *D'Holbach's Coterie*. Princeton, NJ: Princeton University Press, 1976.

Koselleck, Reinhart. "Historical Criteria on the Modern Concept of Revolution." In *Futures Past*, translated by Keith Tribe, 43–57. New York: Columbia University Press, 2004.

——. "Modernity and the Planes of Historicity." In *Futures Past*, 3–20.

Kotkin, Stephen. *Magnetic Mountain: Stalinism as a Civilization*. Berkeley: University of California Press, 1997.

——. *Stalin*. Vol. 1, *Paradoxes of Power, 1878–1928*. New York: Penguin Books, 2014.

——. *Stalin*. Vol. 2, *Waiting for Hitler, 1929–1941*. New York: Penguin Books, 2017.

Kramnick, Isaac. *Bolingbroke and His Circle: The Politics of Nostalgia in the Age of Walpole*. Ithaca, NY: Cornell University Press, 1968.

Krentz, Peter. *The Thirty at Athens*. Ithaca, NY: Cornell University Press, 1982.

Krieger, Leonard. "Marx and Engels as Historians." *Journal of the History of Ideas* 14, no. 3 (1953):381–403.

Kuran, Timur. "Now out of Never: The Element of Surprise in the East European Revolution of 1989." *World Politics* 44, no. 1 (1991):7–48.

Kymlicka, Will. *Multicultural Citizenship: A Liberal Theory of Minority Rights*. Oxford: Clarendon, 1995.

La Harpe, Jean-François de. *Du fanatisme dans la langue révolutionnaire*. Paris: Migneret, 1797.

Laks, André, and Glenn W. Most, eds. and trans. *Early Greek Philosophy*. Vol. 4, *Western Greek Thinkers*. Pt. 1. Cambridge, MA: Loeb/Harvard University Press, 2016.

Landes, Richard. "The Fear of an Apocalyptic Year 1000: Augustinian Historiography, Medieval and Modern." *Speculum* 75, no. 1 (2000):97–145.

Lane, Melissa. "Popular Sovereignty as Control of Office-Holders: Aristotle on Greek Democracy." Chapter 2 in *Popular Sovereignty in Historical Perspective*, edited by Richard Bourke and Quentin Skinner. Cambridge: Cambridge University Press, 2016.

Lasky, Melvin J. *Utopia and Revolution*. Chicago: University of Chicago Press, 1976.

La Tour du Pin, Henriette-Lucy de. *Journal d'une femme de cinquante ans, 1778–1815*. 2 vols. Paris: Chapelot, 1914.

Lattek, Christine. *Revolutionary Refugees: German Socialism in Britain, 1840–1860*. New York: Routledge, 2006.

Lavicomterie, Louis-Charles de. *Les droits du peuple sur l'Assemblée nationale*. Paris, 1791.

Lebovitz, Adam. *Colossus: Constitutional Theory in America and France, 1776–1799*. Princeton, NJ: Princeton University Press, forthcoming.

———. "Dictatorship in the American Founding." *Journal of American Constitutional History*, August 2024.

Lee, Daniel. *Popular Sovereignty in Early Modern Constitutional Thought*. Oxford: Oxford University Press, 2016.

Lefebvre, Georges. *The French Revolution*. Translated by Elizabeth Moss Evanson. 2 vols. London: Routledge and Kegan Paul, 1962–64.

Lefort, Claude. "The Logic of Totalitarianism." In *The Political Forms of Modern Society: Bureaucracy, Democracy, Totalitarianism*, edited and translated by John Thompson, 273–91. Cambridge: Polity, 1986.

Legge, James, ed. and trans. *The Shoo King*. Vol. 3 of *The Chinese Classics*, 5 vols. Hong Kong: Hong Kong University Press, 1960.

Lehmann, Gustav Adolf. "Greek Federalism, the Rediscovery of Polybius, and the Framing of the American Constitution." In *Federalism in Greek Antiquity*, edited by Hans Beck and Peter Funke, 512–23. Cambridge: Cambridge University Press, 2015.

Le Mercier de La Rivière, Pierre-Paul. *L'ordre naturel et essentiel des sociétés politiques*. London, 1767.

Lenin, Vladimir Ilyich. *Collected Works*. Translated by Abraham Fineburg and Julius Katzer. Moscow: Progress, 1962. Marxists' Internet Archive. https://www.marxists.org/archive/lenin/works/1905/tactics/index.htm.

———. "The Dual Power." *Pravda*, April 9, 1917. In *Lenin Anthology*, 301–4.

———. *The Lenin Anthology*. Edited by Robert C. Tucker. New York: Norton, 1975.

———. *The State and Revolution*. In *Collected Works*, vol. 25. Marxists' Internet Archive. https://www.marxists.org/archive/lenin/works/cw/pdf/lenin-cw-vol-25.pdf.

———. *Two Tactics of Social-Democracy*. In *Collected Works*, vol. 9.

———. *What Is to Be Done?* In *Essential Works of Lenin*, edited by Henry M. Christman, 53–176. New York: Dover, 1987.

Leonard, Gerald. "Jefferson's Constitutions." In Galligan, *Constitutions and the Classics*, 369–88.

Le Quang, Jeanne-Laure. "La Commission sénatoriale de la liberté individuelle face aux mesures de haute police (1804–1814): Loi intégrée, loi contournée?" *Annales historiques de la Révolution française* 394, no. 4 (2018):79–104.

Lermina, Jules, Émile Faure, and Edouard-Accoyer Spoll, *Histoire anecdotique illustrée de la révolution de 1848*. Paris: Pache et Defaux, 1868.

Le Roy, Loys. *De la vicissitude ou variété des choses en l'univers*. N.p., 1575.

Leuwers, Hervé. *Camille et Lucile Desmoulins: Un rêve de république*. Paris: Fayard, 2018.

Levin, Harry. *The Myth of the Golden Age in the Renaissance*. Bloomington: Indiana University Press, 1969.

Levitsky, Steven, and Daniel Ziblatt. *How Democracies Die*. New York: Crown, 2018.

Lévy, Bernard-Henri. *La barbarie à visage humain*. Paris: Grasset, 1977.

Liddell, Henry George, and Robert Scott. *A Greek-English Lexicon*. Revised and augmented throughout by Sir Henry Stuart Jones with the assistance of Roderick McKenzie. Oxford: Clarendon, 1940. https://logeion.uchicago.edu/.

Lieberman, David. "The Mixed Constitution and the Common Law." In *The Cambridge History of Eighteenth-Century Political Thought*, edited by Mark Goldie and Robert Wokler, 317–46. Cambridge: Cambridge University Press, 2006.

Lilburne, John. *Englands New Chains Discovered; or, The Serious Apprehensions of a Part of the People, in Behalf of the Commonwealth*. London, 1649. EEBO.

Lilti, Antoine. "Le philosophe utopique." In *L'héritage des Lumières: Ambivalences de la modernité*, 321–37. Paris: Seuil, 2019.

Lindberg, Staffan I. "The Nature of Democratic Backsliding in Europe." Carnegie Europe, July 24, 2018, https://carnegieeurope.eu/2018/07/24/nature-of-democratic-backsliding-in-europe-pub-76868.

Linton, Marisa. *Choosing Terror: Virtue, Friendship, and Authenticity in the French Revolution*. Oxford: Oxford University Press, 2013.

Lintott, Andrew. *The Constitution of the Roman Republic*. Oxford: Oxford University Press, 1999.

Locke, John. *Two Treatises of Government*. Edited by Peter Laslett. Cambridge: Cambridge University Press, 1988.

Loehr, Regina M. "The People's Moral Emotions in Polybius' Cycle of Constitutions." *Classical Philology* 116 (2021):155–82.

Loewen, Harry. *Luther and the Radicals*. Waterloo, ON: Wilfrid Laurier University, 1974.

Lok, Matthijs. *Europe against Revolution: Conservatism, Enlightenment, and the Making of the Past*. Oxford: Oxford University Press, 2023.

Loughlin, Martin. *Against Constitutionalism*. Cambridge, MA: Harvard University Press, 2022.

Lovejoy, Arthur. "The Theory of Human Nature in the American Constitution and the Method of Counterpoise." In *Reflections on Human Nature*, 37–65. 1961; Baltimore, MD: Johns Hopkins Press, 2020.

Lovejoy, Arthur, and George Boas. *Primitivism and Related Ideas in Antiquity*. Baltimore, MD: Johns Hopkins University Press, 1935.

Löwith, Karl. *Meaning in History: The Theological Implications of the Philosophy of History*. Chicago: University of Chicago Press, 1949.

Löwy, Michael. "The Poetry of the Past." *New Left Review* I/177 (1989):111–24.

———. *The Politics of Combined and Uneven Development: The Theory of Permanent Revolution*. 2nd ed. 1981; Chicago: Haymarket Books, 2010.

———. *The Theory of Revolution in the Young Marx*. Leiden, Netherlands: Brill, 2003.

Lynch, John. *Caudillos in Spanish America, 1800–1850*. Oxford: Clarendon, 1992.

——. *Simón Bolívar: A Life*. New Haven, CT: Yale University Press, 2006.

——. *Spanish American Revolutions*. New York: Norton, 1986.

Lyons, Martyn. *Napoleon Bonaparte and the Legacy of the French Revolution*. New York: St. Martin's, 1994.

Mably, Gabriel Bonnot de. *Observations on the Greeks*. London, 1776.

——. *Observations sur l'histoire de la Grèce*. Geneva: Compagnie des libraires, 1766.

MacFarquhar, Roderick, and Michael Schoenhals. *Mao's Last Revolution*. Cambridge, MA: Harvard University Press, 2006.

Machiavelli, Niccolo. *Discorsi sopra la prima deca di Tito Livio*. 2 vols. Edited by Francesco Bausi. In *Edizione nazionale delle opere di Niccolò Machiavelli*. Rome: Salerno, 2001.

——. *The "Discourses" of Niccolo Machiavelli*. 2 vols. Edited and translated by Leslie Walker. 1950; London: Routledge, 1975.

——. *Discourses on Livy*. Translated by Julia Conaway Bondanella and Peter Bondanella. New York: Oxford University Press, 1997. [Cited as *Discourses on Livy*.]

——. *Discourses on Livy*. Translated by Harvey C. Mansfield and Nathan Tarcov. Chicago: University of Chicago Press, 1996. [Cited as *Discourses*.]

——. *Il Principe*. Edited by Mario Martelli. Vol. 1 of *Edizione nazionale delle opere di Niccolò Machiavelli*. Rome: Salerno, 2006.

——. *The Prince*. Translated by Russell Price, edited by Quentin Skinner. Cambridge: Cambridge University Press, 1988.

Mackil, Emily. *Creating a Common Polity*. Berkeley: University of California Press, 2013.

Mackworth, Humphrey. *A Vindication of the Rights of the Commons of England*. London: J. Nutt, 1701.

Macron, Emmanuel. *Revolution*. Translated by Jonathan Goldberg and Juliette Scott. Melbourne: Scribe, 2017.

Mah, Harold. "The French Revolution and the Problem of German Modernity: Hegel, Heine and Marx." *New German Critique* 50 (1990):3–20.

Mailhos, G. "Le mot 'révolution' dans l'*Essai sur les mœurs* et la correspondance de Voltaire." *Cahiers de lexicologie* 13, no. 2 (1968):84–93.

Malcolm X. "Message to the Grassroots" (November 1963). In *Malcolm X Speaks*, edited by George Breitman, 3–17. 1965; New York: Grove Weidenfeld, 1990.

Manent, Pierre. *An Intellectual History of Liberalism*. Translated by Rebecca Balinski. Princeton, NJ: Princeton University Press, 1995.

Manicas, Peter T. "War, Stasis, and Greek Political Thought." *Comparative Studies in Society and History* 24, no. 4 (1982):673–88.

Manin, Bernard. *The Principles of Representative Government*. Cambridge: Cambridge University Press, 1997.

Manuel, Frank. *The New World of Henri Saint-Simon*. Cambridge, MA: Harvard University Press, 1956.

——. *The Prophets of Paris*. Cambridge, MA: Harvard University Press, 1962.

Marat, Jean-Paul. *Eloge de Montesquieu*. Libourne, France: G. Maleville, 1883. ARTFL.

Marcello, Pietro. *Vite de' prencipi di Vinegia*. Translated by Ludovico Domenichi. Venice: Plinio Pietrasanta, 1557.

Mari, Eric de. *La mise hors de la loi sous la Révolution française (18 mars 1793—an III): Une étude juridictionnelle et institutionnelle*. Paris: Librairie générale de droit et de jurisprudence, 2015.

Markus, Robert. *Saeculum: History and Society in the Theology of St Augustine*. Cambridge: Cambridge University Press, 1989.

Marmontel, Jean-François. *Bélisaire*. Paris: Merlin, 1767. ARTFL.

Martin, Jean-Clément. *Violence et révolution: Essai sur la naissance d'un mythe national*. Paris: Seuil, 2006.

Marx, Karl. *The Class Struggles in France*. 1895; London: Electric Book, 2001.

———. "The Class Struggles in France, 1848 to 1850: Part I, The Defeat of June, 1848." Marxists' Internet Archive. https://www.marxists.org/archive/marx/works/1850/class-struggles-france/ch01.htm.

———. "The Crisis and the Counter-revolution." *Neue Rheinische Zeitung*, no. 102 (September 14, 1848). Marxists' Internet Archive. http://www.marxists.org/archive/marx/works/1848/09/12.htm#102.

———. *Die Klassenkämpfe in Frankreich 1848 bis 1850*. In *Karl Marx, Friedrich Engels Gesamtausgabe*, by Marx and Engels, pt. 1, vol. 10. Berlin: Dietz Verlag, 1977.

———. *The Eighteenth-Brumaire of Louis-Napoleon Bonaparte* (1852). Translated by Saul K. Padover. Marxists' Internet Archive. https://www.marxists.org/archive/marx/works/1852/18th-brumaire/.

———. *The German Ideology*. Edited by C. J. Arthur. New York: International, 1970.

———. "On *The Jewish Question*" (written 1843; published February 1844). Marxists' Internet Archive. https://www.marxists.org/archive/marx/works/1844/jewish-question/.

———. "Third Address [The Paris Commune]." In *The Civil War in France* (1871). Marxists' Internet Archive. https://www.marxists.org/archive/marx/works/1871/civil-war-france/.

———. *Zur Judenfrage*. In MEGA, pt. 1, vol. 2.

Marx, Karl, and Friedrich Engels. "Address of the Central Committee to the Communist League" (London, March 1850). Marxists' Internet Archive. https://www.marxists.org/archive/marx/works/1847/communist-league/1850-ad1.htm.

———. *Ansprache der Zentralbehörde des Bundes der Kommunisten vom März 185*. In MEGA, pt. 1, vol. 10.

———. *The Holy Family; or, Critique of Critical Criticism: Against Bruno Bauer and Company* (1845). Chapter 6.3, "Critical Battle against the French Revolution." Marxists' Internet Archive. https://www.marxists.org/archive/marx/works/1845/holy-family/ch06_3_c.htm.

———. *Karl Marx, Friedrich Engels Gesamtausgabe*. 65 vols. Berlin: Dietz, 1975–.

———. *Marx-Engels Reader*. Edited by Robert C. Tucker. New York: Norton, 1972.

Mason, Laura. *The Last Revolutionaries: The Conspiracy Trial of Gracchus Babeuf and the Equals*. New Haven, CT: Yale University Press, 2022.

Mathiez, Albert. "La constitution de 1793." *Annales historiques de la Révolution française* 30 (1928):497–521.

———. *Le Club des Cordeliers pendant la crise de Varennes, et le massacre du Champ de Mars*. Paris: H. Champion, 1910.

Matthieu, Pierre. *Histoire des derniers troubles de France*. 1594; Lyon, 1604.

——. *Historia delle riuolutioni di Francia*. Translated by A. Senesi. Venice: Bartolomeo Fontana, 1624.

Mayer, Arno. *The Furies: Violence and Terror in the French and Russian Revolutions*. Princeton, NJ: Princeton University Press, 2000.

Mayer, Henry. *All on Fire: William Lloyd Garrison and the Abolition of Slavery*. New York: W. W. Norton, 2008.

Mayhew, Jonathan. *A Discourse concerning Unlimited Submission and Non-resistance to the Higher Powers*. Boston, MA, 1750. Evans.

Mazower, Mark. *The Greek Revolution: 1821 and the Making of Modern Europe*. New York: Penguin Books, 2021.

McDaniel, Iain. "Jean-Louis Delolme and the Political Science of the English Empire." *Historical Journal* 55, no. 1, (2012):21–44.

McEnany, Kayleigh. *The New American Revolution: The Making of a Populist Movement*. New York: Simon and Schuster, 2018.

McGinn, Bernard. "Introduction: Joachim of Fiore in the History of Western Culture." In *A Companion to Joachim of Fiore*, edited by Matthias Riedl, 1–19. Leiden, Netherlands: Brill, 2018.

McLellan, David. *Karl Marx: His Life and Thought*. New York: Harper and Row, 1973.

McMahon, Darrin M. "The Birthplace of the Revolution: Public Space and Political Community in the Palais-Royal of Louis-Philippe-Joseph D'Orléans, 1781–1789." *French History* 10, no. 1 (1996):1–29.

——. *Divine Fury: A History of Genius*. New York: Basic Books, 2013.

——. *Equality: The History of an Elusive Idea*. New York: Basic Books, 2023.

——. *Happiness: A History*. New York: Grove, 2006.

McPhee, Peter. *Robespierre: A Revolutionary Life*. New Haven, CT: Yale University Press, 2012.

McQueen, Alison. *Political Realism in Apocalyptic Times*. Cambridge: Cambridge University Press, 2018.

Mehta, Uday S. *Liberalism and Empire: A Study in Nineteenth-Century British Liberal Thought*. Chicago: University of Chicago Press, 1999.

Mencius. *Mencius*. Translated by D. C. Lau. London: Penguin Books, 1970.

Mendle, Michael. *Dangerous Positions: Mixed Government, the Estates of the Realm, and the Answer to the XIX Propositions*. Tuscaloosa: University of Alabama Press, 1985.

Menut, Albert Douglas, ed. "Maistre Nicole Oresme: *Le Livre de politiques d'Aristote*." *Transactions of the American Philosophical Society* 60, no. 6 (1970):1–392.

Mercier, Louis Sebastien. *L'an deux mille quatre cent quarante*. London, 1774. ARTFL.

Merriman, John. *Massacre: The Life and Death of the Paris Commune of 1871*. New Haven, CT: Yale University Press, 2014.

Miano, Daniele. *Fortuna: Deity and Concept in Archaic and Republican Italy*. Oxford: Oxford University Press, 2018.

Millar, Fergus. "Polybius between Greece and Rome." In *Greek Connections: Essays on Culture and Diplomacy*, edited by John T. A. Koumoulides, 1–18. Notre Dame, IN: University of Notre Dame Press, 1987.

——. *The Roman Republic in Political Thought*. Hanover, NH: University Press of New England, 2002.

Miller, Fred. *Nature, Justice, and Rights in Aristotle's Politics*. Oxford: Clarendon, 1995.

Miller, James. *Rousseau: Dreamer of Democracy*. New Haven, CT: Yale University Press, 1984.

Miller, Mary Ashburn. *A Natural History of Revolution: Violence and Nature in the French Revolutionary Imagination, 1789–1794*. Ithaca, NY: Cornell University Press, 2011.

Millington, Chris. "Trump, Fascism, and French History." *Tocqueville 21*, January 29, 2021. https://tocqueville21.com/le-club/trump-fascism-and-french-history/.

Milton, John. *A Defence of the People of England*. Amsterdam, 1692. EEBO. Posthumous English translation of *Defensio pro populo Anglicano*.

———. *Defensio pro populo Anglicano*. London, 1651.

———. *The Readie & Easie Way to Establish a Free Commonwealth*. London, 1660. EEBO.

Modrak, Deborah K. W. "Virtue, Equality, and Inequality in Aristotle's *Politics*." In *Democracy, Justice, and Equality in Ancient Greece*, edited by G. Anagnostopoulos and G. Santas, 243–56. Cham, Switzerland: Springer, 2018.

Momigliano, Arnaldo. "The Historian's Skin." In *Essays in Ancient and Modern Historiography*, 67–78. 1977; Chicago: University of Chicago Press, 2012.

———. "Polybius's Reappearance in Western Europe." In *Essays in Ancient and Modern Historiography*, 79–98. 1977; Chicago: University of Chicago Press, 2012.

Monfasani, John. "Machiavelli, Polybius, and Janus Lascaris: The Hexter Thesis Revisited." *Italian Studies* 71, no. 1 (2016):39–48.

Monnier, Raymonde. *Républicanisme, patriotisme et Révolution française*. Paris: Harmattan, 2005.

Montefiore, Simon Sebag. *Stalin: The Court of the Red Tsar*. New York: Vintage, 2003.

Montesquieu. *De l'esprit des lois*. Edited by Robert Derathé. Rev. ed. 1748; Paris: Classiques Garnier, 2011.

———. *On the Spirit of the Laws*. Edited by and translated by Anne M. Cohler, Basia Carolyn Miller, and Harold Samuel Stone. Cambridge: Cambridge University Press, 1989.

Moore, Barrington. *Social Origins of Dictatorship and Democracy: Lord and Peasant in the Making of the Modern World*. Boston, MA: Beacon, 1966.

Moore, Stanley. "Marx and Lenin as Historical Materialists." *Philosophy & Public Affairs* 4, no. 2 (1975):171–94.

Morelly, Étienne-Gabriel. *Code de la nature*. Edited by François Villegardelle. 1755; Paris: Paul Masgana, 1841.

Morgan, Lewis. *Ancient Society; or, Researches in the Lines of Human Progress from Savagery, through Barbarism to Civilization*. New York: Henry Holt, 1907.

Morison, Samuel Eliot, and Henry Steele Commager. *The Growth of the American Republic*. New York: Oxford University Press, 1942.

Morris, Gouverneur. *Observations on the American Revolution*. Philadelphia, PA: Styner and Cist, 1779.

Morris, William. *News from Nowhere*. Boston, MA: Roberts Bros., 1890.

Mortimer-Ternaux, Louis. *Histoire de la Terreur, 1792–1794*. 8 vols. Paris: Michel Levy, 1863.

Mossé, Claude. *L'antiquité dans la Révolution française*. Paris: Albin Michel, 1989.

Mosse, George L. *The Fascist Revolution: Toward a General Theory of Fascism.* 1999; Madison: University of Wisconsin Press, 2022.

Motadel, David, ed. *Revolutionary World: Global Upheaval in the Modern Age.* Cambridge: Cambridge University Press, 2021.

Moyn, Samuel. *Liberalism against Itself: Cold War Intellectuals and the Making of Our Times.* New Haven, CT: Yale University Press, 2023.

———. "On the Intellectual Origins of François Furet's Masterpiece." *Tocqueville Review/La revue Tocqueville* 29, no. 2 (2008):1–20.

Mudde, Cas. "The Populist Zeitgeist." *Government and Opposition* 39, no. 3 (2004):541–63.

Mulgan, R. G. "Aristotle's Sovereign." *Political Studies* 18 (1970):518–22.

Mullach, F.W.A. *Fragmenta philosophorum Graecorum*, 3 vols. Paris: Didot, 1860.

Müller, Jan-Werner. *What Is Populism?* Philadelphia: University of Pennsylvania Press, 2016.

Musset, Alfred de. *La confession d'un enfant du siècle.* 1836; Paris: GF, 1993.

Naimark, Norman. *Stalin's Genocides.* Princeton, NJ: Princeton University Press, 2010.

Nakhimovsky, Isaac. *Holy Alliance: Liberalism and the Politics of Federation.* Princeton, NJ: Princeton University Press, 2024.

Nannini, Remigio. *Orationi militari.* Venice: Gabriel Giolito de' Ferrari, 1557.

Nechayev, Sergey Genadievich. *The Revolutionary Catechism.* Marxists' Internet Archive. https://www.marxists.org/subject/anarchism/nechayev/catechism.htm.

Nedham, Marchamont. *The Case of the Common-Wealth of England Stated.* London: E. Blackmore and B. Lowndes, 1650. EEBO.

———. *The Excellencie of a Free-State; or, The Right Constitution of a Common-Wealth.* Edited by Blair Worden. 1656; Indianapolis, IN: Liberty Fund, 2011.

———. *A True State of the Case of the Commonwealth. . . .* London: Thomas Newcomb, 1654. EEBO.

Needham, Joseph, and Colin A. Ronan. *The Shorter Science and Civilisation in China.* Cambridge: Cambridge University Press, 1978.

Neill, Thomas P. "Quesnay and Physiocracy." *Journal of the History of Ideas* 9, no. 2 (1948):153–73.

Nelson, Craig. *Thomas Paine: Enlightenment, Revolution, and the Birth of Modern Nations.* London: Penguin Books, 2007.

Nelson, Eric. *The Greek Tradition in Republican Thought.* Cambridge: Cambridge University Press, 2004.

———. *The Hebrew Republic: Jewish Sources and the Transformation of European Political Thought.* Cambridge, MA: Harvard University Press, 2010.

———. *The Royalist Revolution: Monarchy and the American Founding.* Cambridge, MA: Harvard University Press, 2014.

Nelson, William Max. *The Time of Enlightenment: Constructing the Future in France, 1750 to Year One.* Toronto: University of Toronto Press, 2020.

Newman, Ernest. *The Life of Richard Wagner.* 2 vols. New York: Knopf, 1946.

Nippel, Wilfried. *Mischverfassungstheorie und Verfassungsrealität in Antike und Früher Neuzeit.* Stuttgart: Klett-Cotta, 1980.

Nisbet, Robert A. *History of the Idea of Progress.* New York: Basic Books, 1980.

Noland, Aaron. "History and Humanity: The Proudhonian Vision." In *The Uses of History. Essays in Intellectual and Social History*, edited by Hayden White, 59–106. Detroit, MI: Wayne State University Press, 1968.

Norman, Larry. *The Shock of the Ancient: Literature and History in Early Modern France*. Chicago: University of Chicago Press, 2011.

North, Douglass C., and Barry R. Weingast. "Constitutions and Commitment: The Evolution of Institutions Governing Public Choice in Seventeenth-Century England." *Journal of Economic History* 49, no. 4 (1989):803–32.

Obama, Barack. "A More Perfect Union." Speech delivered at the Constitution Center in Philadelphia. "Transcript: Barack Obama's Speech on Race," March 18, 2008, https://www.npr.org/templates/story/story.php?storyId=88478467.

Ober, Josiah. *The Athenian Revolution: Essays on Ancient Greek Democracy and Political Theory*. Princeton, NJ: Princeton University Press, 1999.

———. *Mass and Elite in Democratic Athens: Rhetoric, Ideology, and the Power of the People*. Princeton, NJ: Princeton University Press, 1989.

———. "Nature, History, and Aristotle's Best Possible Regime." In *Aristotle's "Politics": A Critical Guide*, edited by T. Lockwood and T. Samaras, 224–43. Cambridge: Cambridge University Press, 2015.

———. *Political Dissent in Democratic Athens: Intellectual Critics of Popular Rule*. Princeton, NJ: Princeton University Press, 2008.

———. *The Rise and Fall of Classical Greece*. Princeton, NJ: Princeton University Press, 2015.

———. "The Trial of Socrates as a Political Trial: Explaining 399 BCE." In *Political Trials: Interdisciplinary Perspectives*, edited by Jens Meierhenrich and Devin O. Pendas, 65–87. Cambridge: Cambridge University Press, 2016.

Oddens, Joris, Erik Jacobs, and Mart Rutjes, eds. *The Political Culture of the Sister Republics, 1794–1806: France, the Netherlands, Switzerland, and Italy*. Amsterdam: Amsterdam University Press, 2015.

Onuf, Peter S., and Nicholas P. Cole, eds. *Thomas Jefferson, the Classical World, and Early America*. Charlottesville: University of Virginia Press, 2011.

d'Orléans, Pierre-Joseph. *Histoire des révolutions d'Angleterre depuis le commencement de la monarchie*. 1689; Paris, Compagnie des Libraires, 1787.

Orsini, Alessandro. *Anatomy of the Red Brigades: The Religious Mind-Set of Modern Terrorists*. Translated by Sarah J. Nodes. Ithaca, NY: Cornell University Press, 2011.

Orwell, George. *1984*. Oxford: Oxford University Press, 2021.

Otis, James. *The Rights of the British Colonies Asserted and Proved*. Boston, MA: Edes and Gill, 1764.

———. *A Vindication of the Conduct of the House of Representatives of the Province of the Massachusetts-Bay*. Boston, MA, 1762. EVANS.

Overton, Richard. *An Arrow against All Tyrants*. London, 1646. EEBO.

Ozouf, Mona. *L'homme régénéré: Essais sur la Révolution française*. Paris: Gallimard, 1989.

Paine, Thomas. *Common Sense: Addressed to the Inhabitants of America*. Philadelphia, [PA]: R. Bell, 1776. EVANS.

Palmer, R. R. *The Age of the Democratic Revolution*. 2 vols. Rev. ed. 1964; Princeton, NJ: Princeton University Press, 1994.

——. *Catholics and Unbelievers in 18th Century France*. Princeton, NJ: Princeton University Press, 1939.

——. *Twelve Who Ruled*. Princeton, NJ: Princeton University Press, 1941.

Pangle, Thomas L. *The Theological Basis of Liberal Modernity in Montesquieu's "Spirit of the Laws."* Chicago: University of Chicago Press, 2010.

Paperno, Irina. *Chernyshevsky and the Age of Realism: A Study in the Semiotics of Behavior*. Stanford, CA: Stanford University Press, 1988.

Paquette, Gabriel B. *Imperial Portugal in the Age of Atlantic Revolutions: The Luso-Brazilian World, c.1770–1850*. Cambridge: Cambridge University Press, 1998.

Parker, Harold T. *The Cult of Antiquity and the French Revolutionaries*. Chicago: University of Chicago Press, 1937.

Parker, Henry. *Observations upon Some of His Majesties Late Answers and Expresses*. London, 1642. EEBO.

Pasquino, Pasquale. "Machiavelli and Aristotle: The Anatomies of the City." *History of European Ideas* 35, no. 4 (2009):397–407.

Patyk, Lynn E. *Written in Blood: Revolutionary Terrorism and Russian Literary Culture, 1861–1881*. Madison: University of Wisconsin Press, 2017.

Paulson, Joshua. "Case Study: Serbia, 1996–2000." In *Sharp's Dictionary of Power and Struggle: Language of Civil Resistance in Conflicts*, edited by Gene Sharp, 10–33. New York: Oxford University Press, 2012.

Peace, Richard. "Dostoyevsky and 'The Golden Age,'" *Dostoyevsky Studies* 3 (1982):61–78.

Pedullà, Gabriele. *Machiavelli in Tumult*. Translated by Patricia Gaborik and Richard Nybakken. Cambridge: Cambridge University Press, 2018.

Peltier, J. *Dernier tableau de Paris, ou Récit historique de la Révolution du 10 août*. London, 1794. NEWBERRY.

Pérez-Stable, Marifeli. *The Cuban Revolution: Origins, Course, and Legacy*. Rev. ed. New York: Oxford University Press, 1999.

Perl-Rosenthal, Nathan. *The Age of Revolutions and the Generations Who Made It*. New York: Basic Books, 2024.

Perrie, Maureen. "The Socialist Revolutionaries on 'Permanent Revolution.'" *Soviet Studies* 24, no. 3 (1973):411–13.

Pettit, Philip. *Made with Words: Hobbes on Language, Mind, and Politics*. Princeton, NJ: Princeton University Press, 2008.

Pichichero, Christy. *The Military Enlightenment*. Ithaca, NY: Cornell University Press, 2017.

Pierse, Síofra. *Voltaire Historiographer: Narrative Paradigms*. Oxford: Voltaire Foundation, 2008.

Pigna, Giovan Battista. *Historia de principi di Este*. Ferrara, Italy: Francesco Rossi, 1570.

Piketty, Thomas. *Capital in the Twenty-First Century*. Translated by Arthur Goldhammer. Cambridge, MA: Harvard University Press, 2014.

Pilbeam, Pamela M. *Saint-Simonians in Nineteenth-Century France: From Free Love to Algeria*. London: Palgrave Macmillan, 2014.

Pimentel, Carlos Miguel. "Le sanctuaire vide: La séparation des pouvoirs comme superstition juridique?" *Pouvoirs* 102 (2002):119–31.

Pincus, Steven. *The Heart of the Declaration: The Founders' Case for an Activist Government*. New Haven, CT: Yale University Press, 2016.

——. *1688: The First Modern Revolution*. New Haven, CT: Yale University Press, 2009.

Pipes, Richard. *The Russian Revolution*. New York: Vintage, 1991.

Pisch, Anita. *The Personality Cult of Stalin in Soviet Posters, 1929–1953: Archetypes, Inventions and Fabrications*. Acton: Australian National University Press, 2016.

Planert, Ute, ed. *Napoleon's Empire: European Politics in Global Perspective*. Basingstoke, UK: Palgrave Macmillan, 2016.

Planinc, Emma. *Regenerative Politics*. New York: Columbia University Press, 2024.

Plato. *Complete Works*. Edited by John M. Cooper. Indianapolis, IN: Hackett, 1997.

Pocock, John G. A. *Barbarism and Religion*. 6 vols. Cambridge: Cambridge University Press, 2001–15.

——. *The Machiavellian Moment: Florentine Political Thought and the Atlantic Republican Tradition*. 1975; Princeton, NJ: Princeton University Press, 2016.

——, ed. *Three British Revolutions: 1641, 1688, 1776*. Princeton, NJ: Princeton University Press, 1980.

Polybius. *Cinq premiers livres des "Histoires" de Polibe Mégalopolitain*. Translated by Louis Maigret. Paris: Estienne Groulleau, 1552.

——. *De "Historie" vanden aller voortreffelycsten oude histori schryver Polybius Megalopolitanus*. . . . Translated by Johannes Vennekool. Rotterdam: Pieter van Waesberghe, 1640.

——. *De militia romanorum et castrorum metatione liber ex Polybii "Historiis" excerptus*. Translated by Janus Lascaris. Paris: Pierre Gromors, *c*.1523.

——. *Deux restes du sixiesme livre de Polybe*. . . . Translated by Louis Maigret. Paris: J. Longis et V. Sertenas, 1545.

——. *A Fragment out of the Sixth Book of Polybius*. Translated by Edward Spelman. London: J. Bettenham, 1743.

——. *Histories*. Translated by Evelyn S. Shuckburgh. New York. Macmillan, 1889.

——. *The "History" of Polybius the Megalopolitan*. . . . Translated by Edward Grimeston. London: Nicholas Okes, 1633.

——. *Les cinq premiers livres des "Histoires" escriptes par Polybe Mégalopolitain*. Translated by Louis Maigret. Paris: Galiot du pré, 1542.

——. *Polibio "Historico" greco*. . . . Translated by Lodovico Domenichi. Venice: Gabriel Giolito de Ferrari, 1545.

——. *Polybii Lycortæ F. Megalopolitani "Historiarum" libri qui supersunt*. Edited and translated by Isaac Casaubon. Paris: H. Drouardum, 1609.

——. *Polybii Megalopolitani "Historiarum" libri priores quinque*. . . . Translated by Wolfgang Musculus. Basel, Switzerland: Per J. Hervagium, 1549.

——. *Römische "Historien" des Weisiste Warhafftigsten vnnd hochberhümpten Geschichtschreibers Polybij*. Translated by Wilhelm Xylander. Basel, Switzerland: Henricpetri, 1574.

Ponchaud, François. *Cambodge année zéro*. Paris: Julliard, 1977.

Ponet, John. *A Short Treatise of Politique Povver; and of the True Obedience Which Subjects Owe to Kings, and Other Civill Governours . . . Published in the Raigne of Queene Mary, 1556*. London, 1642. EEBO.

Popkin, Jeremy D. *You Are All Free: The Haitian Revolution and the Abolition of Slavery*. Cambridge: Cambridge University Press, 2010.

Popovic, Srdja. *Blueprint for Revolution: How to Use Rice Pudding, Lego Men, and Other Nonviolent Techniques to Galvanize Communities, Overthrow Dictators, or Simply Change the World*. Translated by Matthew Miller. New York: Random House, 2015.

Post, Gaines. *Studies in Medieval Legal Thought: Public Law and the State, 1100–1322*. Rev. ed. Princeton, NJ: Princeton University Press, 2016.

Pradeau, Jean-François. *Platon et la cité*. Paris: Presses Universitaires de France, 2010.

Prévost de Saint-Lucien, Roch-Henri. *Plan d'organisation de l'assemblée des trois cents représentants de la Commune de Paris*. Paris: Cellot, 1789. NEWBERRY.

Price, Jonathan. *Thucydides and Internal War*. Cambridge, MA: Harvard University Press, 2001.

Price, Richard. *A Discourse on the Love of Our Country*. London: Cadell, 1789.

——. *Observations on the Importance of the American Revolution*. London: T. Cadell, 1785.

——. *Observations on the Nature of Civil Liberty, the Principles of Government, and the Justice and Policy of the War with America*. Philadelphia, PA: Dunlap, 1776. Originally published in London.

Proudhon, Pierre-Joseph. *L'idée générale de la Révolution au dix-neuvième siècle*. Paris: Garnier frères, 1851.

——. *Qu'est-ce que la propriété?* Vol. 1 of *Œuvres complètes de P.-J. Proudhon*. Paris: Garnier, 1849.

——. *What Is Property?* Translated by Donald R. Kelley and Bonnie G. Smith. Cambridge: Cambridge University Press, 1993.

Prynne, William. *The First and Second Part of the Signal Loyalty and Devotion of Gods True Saints and Pious Christians*. London: T. Childe, 1660. EEBO.

——. *The Soveraigne Povver of Parliaments and Kingdomes Divided into Foure Parts*. London: Michael Sparke, Sen., 1643. EEBO.

Quartiermastro, Giovanni Pietro Rubbini. *Relatione delle rivolutioni delli regni di Boemia et Ungaria*. Bologna: heredi di Bartolomeo Cochi, 1621.

Raaflaub, Kurt. *The Discovery of Freedom in Ancient Greece*. Chicago: University of Chicago Press, 2004.

Rachum, Ilan. *"Revolution": The Entrance of a New Word into Western Political Discourse*. Lanham, MD: University Press of America, 1999.

Radosh, Ronald. "Steve Bannon, Trump's Top Guy, Told Me He Was 'a Leninist.'" *Daily Beast*, August 22, 2016. https://www.thedailybeast.com/steve-bannon-trumps-top-guy-told-me-he-was-a-leninist.

Rahe, Paul A. *Montesquieu and the Logic of Liberty*. New Haven, CT: Yale University Press, 2009.

Rakove, Jack. "Montesquieu's 'Influence' on Madison: Some Problems, Some Puzzles." In *Montesquieu: A Philosopher for the Early American Republic*, edited by Celine Spector and Hugo Toudic. Oxford Enlightenment Studies. Liverpool: Liverpool University Press, forthcoming.

——. "Politics Indoors and Out-of-Doors: A Fault Line in Madison's Thinking." In *The Cambridge Companion to "The Federalist,"* edited by Rakove and Colleen Sheehan, 370–99. Cambridge: Cambridge University Press, 2020.

——. *Revolutionaries: A New History of the Invention of America*. Boston, MA: Houghton Mifflin Harcourt, 2010.

Rath, R. John. "The Carbonari: Their Origins, Initiation Rites, and Aims." *American Historical Review* 69, no. 2 (1964):353–70.

Rawls, John. *Political Liberalism*. Rev. ed. New York: Columbia University Press, 2005.

Raynal, Guillaume Thomas François. *Histoire philosophique et politique des établissements et du commerce des Européens dans les deux Indes*. 1770; The Hague, 1776. ARTFL.

——. *Histoire philosophique et politique des établissements et du commerce des Européens dans les deux Indes*. 5 vols. Geneva: Jean-Leonard Pellet, 1780.

R.B. *The Wars in England, Scotland and Ireland, or, An Impartial Account of all the Battels, Sieges, and Other Remarkable Transactions, Revolutions and Accidents, Which Have Happened from the Beginning of the Reign of King Charles I, in 1625, to His Majesties Happy Restauration, 1660*. London: Nath. Crouch and John How, 1681. EEBO.

Reddy, William M. *The Navigation of Feeling: A Framework for the History of Emotions*. Cambridge: Cambridge University Press, 2001.

Reinhard, Marcel. *La chute de la royauté: 10 août 1792*. Paris: Gallimard, 1969.

Rey, Joseph. *Adresse à l'Empereur*. Paris: Emery, 1815.

Riazanov, David. *Karl Marx and Frederick Engels: An Introduction to Their Lives and Work* (written 1927, published 1937). Marxists' Internet Archive. http://www.marxists.org/archive/riazanov/works/1927-ma/ch05.htm.

Richard, Carl J. *The Founders and the Classics: Greece, Rome, and the American Enlightenment*. Cambridge, MA: Harvard University Press, 1994.

——. *Greeks & Romans Bearing Gifts: How the Ancients Inspired the Founding Fathers*. Lanham, MD: Rowman and Littlefield, 2008.

Richards, Leonard L. *Shays's Rebellion: The American Revolution's Final Battle*. Philadelphia: University of Pennsylvania Press, 2002.

Ricks, Thomas. *First Principles: What America's Founders Learned from the Greeks and Romans and How That Shaped Our Country*. New York: HarperCollins, 2020.

Rivero, Angel. "The Portuguese Uprising of 1820: A Forgotten Atlantic Revolution." In *The Traditions of Liberty in the Atlantic World: Origins, Ideas and Practices*, edited by Francisco Colom González and Rivero, 155–68. Leiden, Netherlands: Brill, 2015.

Robert, François. *Le républicanisme adapté à la France*. Paris, 1790.

Roberts, Michael. *The Age of Liberty: Sweden 1719–1772*. Cambridge: Cambridge University Press, 1986.

Robespierre, Maximilien. *Œuvres de Maximilien Robespierre*. 10 vols. Edited by Société des études robespierristes. Ivry, France: Phénix éditions, 2000.

Rodriguez O., Jaime E. "The Hispanic Revolution: Spain and America, 1808–1826." *Ler Historia* 57 (2009). https://doi.org/10.4000/lerhistoria.1848.

——. *The Independence of Spanish America*. Cambridge: Cambridge University Press, 1998.

——. *"We Are All Now the True Spaniards": Sovereignty, Revolution, Independence and the Emergence of the Federal Republic of Mexico, 1808–1824*. Stanford, CA: Stanford University Press, 2012.

Rogers, P. G. *The Fifth Monarchy Men*. Oxford: Oxford University Press, 1966.

Rollin, Charles. *The Ancient History of the Egyptians, Carthaginians, Assyrians, Babylonians, Medes and Persians, Macedonians and Grecians*. 7 vols. London, 1780.

Romani, George T. *The Neapolitan Revolution of 1820–1821*. Evanston, IL: Northwestern University Press, 1950.

Rood, Tim. "Polybius, Thucydides, and the First Punic War." In *Imperialism, Cultural Politics, and Polybius*, edited by Christopher Smith and Liv Mariah Yarrow, 50–67. Oxford: Oxford University Press, 2012.

Rosanvallon, Pierre. "The History of the Word 'Democracy' in France." Translated by Philip J. Costopoulos. *Journal of Democracy* 6, no. 4 (1995):140–54.

——. *La démocratie inachevée*. Paris: Gallimard, 2000.

——. *La monarchie impossible: Les chartes de 1814 et de 1830*. Paris: Fayard, 1994.

——. *La société des égaux*. Paris: Seuil, 2011.

——. *Le sacre du citoyen*. Paris: Gallimard, 1992.

——. *The Society of Equals*. Translated by Arthur Goldhammer. Cambridge, MA: Harvard University Press, 2013.

Rose, R. B. *Gracchus Babeuf: The First Revolutionary Communist*. Stanford, CA: Stanford University Press, 1978.

——. *The Making of the Sans-Culottes: Democratic Ideas and Institutions in Paris, 1789–92*. Manchester: Manchester University Press, 1983.

Rosenberg, Tina. "Revolution U." *Foreign Policy*, February 17, 2011. http://foreignpolicy.com/2011/02/17/revolution-u-2/.

Rosenblatt, Helena. *The Lost History of Liberalism: From Ancient Rome to the Twenty-First Century*. Princeton, NJ: Princeton University Press, 2018.

Rosenfeld, Sophia A. *Common Sense: A Political History*. Cambridge, MA: Harvard University Press, 2011.

Roth, Jack J. *The Cult of Violence: Sorel and the Sorelians*. Berkeley: University of California Press, 1980.

Rothschild, Emma. *Economic Sentiments: Adam Smith, Condorcet, and the Enlightenment*. Cambridge, MA: Harvard University Press, 2001.

Rousseau, Jean-Jacques. *Les confessions*. Paris: Gallimard, 1973.

——. *Œuvres complètes*. 5 vols. Edited by Bernard Gagnebin and Marcel Raymond. Paris: Pléiade/Gallimard, 1964.

Rousselière, Geneviève. "Can Popular Sovereignty Be Represented? Jacobinism from Radical Democracy to Populism." *American Journal of Political Science* 65, no. 3 (2021):670–82.

Rouvillois, Frédéric. *L'invention du progrès, 1680–1730*. Paris: CNRS éditions, 2011.

Rubenstein, Joshua. *Leon Trotsky: A Revolutionary's Life*. New Haven, CT: Yale University Press, 2011.

Rucellai, Bernardo. *Liber de urbe Roma*. Florence: Allegrini, Pisini, 1770.

Rudé, George. *The Crowd in the French Revolution*. Oxford: Oxford University Press, 1959.

Rufi, Enrico. *Le rêve laïque de Louis-Sébastien Mercier: Entre littérature et politique*. Oxford: Voltaire Foundation, 1995.

Russo, Elena. *Styles of Enlightenment*. Baltimore, MD: Johns Hopkins University Press, 2007.

——. "The Youth of Moral Life: The Virtue of the Ancients from Montesquieu to Nietzsche." In *Montesquieu and the Spirit of Modernity*, edited by David Carrithers and Patrick Coleman, 101–23. Oxford: Voltaire Foundation, 2002.

Ryan, Alan. *The Making of Modern Liberalism*. Princeton, NJ: Princeton University Press, 2012.

Ryerson, Richard Alan. *John Adams's Republic: The One, the Few, and the Many*. Baltimore, MD: Johns Hopkins University Press, 2016.

Saint-Pierre, abbé de. "Observasions sur le progrèz continuël." In *Ouvrajes de politique*, 11:257–316.

———. *Ouvrajes de politique*. 14 vols. Rotterdam: J.-D. Beman, 1733–40.

———. *Projet pour perfectionner le gouvernement des États*. Vol. 3 in *Ouvrajes de politique*. 1733.

Saint-Simon, Henri. *De la réorganisation de la société européenne*. Paris: Egron, 1814.

Sale, Valerio. *Parafrasi delle leggi di m. Valerio Sali bascianese oue discorrendo da i principij, & dalle riuolutioni de gli stati . . . .* Venice: Gio. Battista Guerra fratelli, 1580.

Salutati, Coluccio. *Political Writings*. Edited by Stefano U. Baldassarri, translated by Rolf Bagemihl. Cambridge, MA: I Tatti Library, 2014.

Sanders, Bernie. *Guide to Political Revolution*. New York: Henry Holt, 2017.

———. *Our Revolution: A Future to Believe In*. New York: Thomas Dunne, 2016.

Sarasola, Ignacio Fernández. "La primera Constitución española: El Estatuto de Bayona." *Revista de derecho* 26 (2006):89–109.

Sartre, Jean-Paul, and Daniel Cohn-Bendit. "Jean-Paul Sartre Interviews Daniel Cohn-Bendit." Translated by B. R. Brewster. *Verso Blog*, May 16, 2018. https://www.versobooks.com/blogs/3819-jean-paul-sartre-interviews-daniel-cohn-bendit.

Satia, Priya. *Time's Monster*. Cambridge, MA: Harvard University Press, 2019.

Sawyer, Stephen. *Demos Rising: Regulatory Power and the Birth of the Democratic Social Contract, 1810–1850*. Chicago: University of Chicago Press, forthcoming.

———. "The Forgotten Democratic Tradition of Revolutionary France." *Modern Intellectual History* 18, no. 3 (2020):629–57.

Scaino, Antonio. *"La politica" di Aristotile ridotta in modo di parafrasi . . . .* Rome: Case del popolo romano, 1578.

Scheppele, Kim Lane. "The Rule of Law and the Frankenstate: Why Governance Checklists Do Not Work." *Governance* 26, no. 4 (2013):559–62.

Schiller, Friedrich. *An die Freude*. Rev. ed. 1785; 1808. In *Gesammelte Werke: Berliner Ausgabe*, 1:168–70. Berlin: Aufbau, 1980.

Schmidt, James, ed. and trans. *What Is Enlightenment? Eighteenth-Century Answers and Twentieth-Century Questions*. Berkeley: University of California Press, 1996.

Schmitt, Carl. *Political Theology: Four Chapters on the Concept of Sovereignty*. Translated by George Schwab. 1922; Chicago: University of Chicago Press, 2005.

Schneid, Frederick C. "War and Revolution in the Age of the Risorgimento, 1820–1849." In *The Projection and Limitations of Imperial Powers, 1618–1850*, edited by Schneid, 196–217. Leiden, Netherlands: Brill, 2012.

Schram, Stuart R. "Mao Tse-Tung's Thought from 1949 to 1976." In *The People's Republic, Part 2: Revolutions within the Chinese Revolution, 1966–1982*, vol. 15 of *The Cambridge History of China*, edited by Roderick MacFarquhar and John K. Fairbank, 23–33. Cambridge: Cambridge University Press, 1991.

Schütrumpf, Eckart. *The Earliest Translations of Aristotle's "Politics" and the Creation of Political Terminology*. Paderborn, Germany: Wilhelm Fink, 2014.

Schweiger, F.L.A. *Handbuch der classischen Bibliographie*. 3 vols. Leipzig, 1830–34.

Scott, Jonathan. *How the Old World Ended: The Anglo-Dutch-American Revolution, 1500–1800*. New Haven, CT: Yale University Press, 2019.

———. "Unfinished Family Business: Algernon Sidney's Arguments with Henry Hammond, Sir William Temple, Henry Sidney, Charles II, and the Public Executioner." *Seventeenth Century* 31, no. 4 (2016):391–410.

Seidman, Michael M. *The Imaginary Revolution: Parisian Students and Workers in 1968*. New York: Berghahn Books, 2004.

Seigel, Jerrold. *Marx's Fate*. Princeton, NJ: Princeton University Press, 1978.

Selinger, William. *Parliamentarism: From Burke to Weber*. Cambridge: Cambridge University Press, 2019.

Sellers, M.N.S. *American Republicanism: Roman Ideology in the United States Constitution*. Basingstoke, UK: Macmillan, 1994.

———. "The Constitutional Thought of Alexander Hamilton." In Galligan, *Constitutions and the Classics*, 354–68.

Service, Robert. *A History of Modern Russia from Nicholas II to Vladimir Putin*. Cambridge, MA: Harvard University Press, 1997.

———. *Lenin*. London: Macmillan, 2000.

———. *Trotsky: A Biography*. Cambridge, MA: Harvard University Press, 2009.

Sewell, William H., Jr. *Capitalism and the Emergence of Civic Equality in Eighteenth-Century France*. Chicago: University of Chicago Press, 2021.

———. "Historical Events as Transformations of Structures: Inventing Revolution at the Bastille." *Theory and Society* 25, no. 6 (1996):841–81.

———. *Logics of History: Social Theory and Social Transformation*. Chicago: University of Chicago Press, 2005.

Seyssel, Claude de. *La grant monarchie de France*. Paris: Regnault Chauldiere, 1519.

Shackleton, Robert. *Montesquieu: A Critical Biography*. Oxford: Oxford University Press, 1961.

———. "Montesquieu, Bolingbroke, and the Separation of Powers." *French Studies* 3, no. 1 (1949):25–38.

Sharp, Gene. *From Dictatorship to Democracy: A Conceptual Framework for Liberation*. 1993; Boston, MA: Albert Einstein Institution, 2003.

———. *The Politics of Nonviolent Action*. 3 vols. Boston, MA: Peter Sargent, 1973.

Shear, Julia L. *Polis and Revolution: Responding to Oligarchy in Classical Athens*. Cambridge: Cambridge University Press, 2011.

Sheehan, Colleen A. *The Mind of James Madison: The Legacy of Classical Republicanism*. Cambridge: Cambridge University Press, 2015.

Shklar, Judith. "The Liberalism of Fear." In *Liberalism and the Moral Life*, edited by Nancy L. Rosenblum, 21–38. Cambridge, MA: Harvard University Press, 1989.

Short, Philip. *Pol Pot: Anatomy of a Nightmare*. New York: Macmillan, 2006.

Sibalis, Michael D. "Arbitrary Detention, Human Rights and the Napoleonic Senate." In *Taking Liberties: Problems of a New Order from the French Revolution to Napoleon*, edited by Howard Brown and Judith Miller, 166–84. Manchester: Manchester University Press, 2002.

Sidney, Algernon. *Discourses concerning Government*. Edited by Thomas G. West. 1698; Indianapolis, IN: Liberty Fund, 1996.

Siedentop, Larry. "Two Liberal Traditions" (1979). In *French Liberalism from Montesquieu to the Present Day*, edited by Raf Geenens and Helena Rosenblatt, 15–35. Cambridge: Cambridge University Press, 2012.

Siljak, Ana. *Angel of Vengeance: The "Girl Assassin," the Governor of St. Petersburg, and Russia's Revolutionary World*. New York: St. Martin's, 2008.

Simon, Joshua. *The Ideology of Creole Revolution: Imperialism and Independence in American and Latin American Political Thought*. Cambridge: Cambridge University Press, 2017.

Simonin, Anne. *Le déshonneur dans la République: Une histoire de l'indignité, 1791–1958*. Paris: Grasset, 2008.

Skilling, H. Gordon. "Permanent or Uninterrupted Revolution: Lenin, Trotsky, and Their Successors on the Transition to Socialism." *Canadian Slavonic Papers* 5 (1961):3–30.

Skinner, Quentin. *The Foundations of Modern Political Thought*. 2 vols. Cambridge: Cambridge University Press, 1978.

Skjönsberg, Max. *The Persistence of Party: Ideas of Harmonious Discord in Eighteenth-Century Britain*. Cambridge: Cambridge University Press, 2021.

Skocpol, Theda. *States and Social Revolutions: A Comparative Analysis of France, Russia, and China*. Cambridge: Cambridge University Press, 1979.

Slavin, Morris. *The Making of an Insurrection: Parisian Sections and the Gironde*. Cambridge, MA: Harvard University Press, 1986.

Slomp, Gabriella. "Hobbes, Thucydides and the Three Greatest Things." *History of Political Thought* 11, no. 4 (1990):565–86.

Smith, Sophie. "The Language of 'Political Science' in Early Modern Europe." *Journal of the History of Ideas* 80, no. 2 (2019):203–26.

Smith Robertson, Priscilla. *Revolutions of 1848*. Princeton, NJ: Princeton University Press, 1952.

Soboul, Albert. *Mouvement populaire et gouvernement révolutionnaire en l'an II (1793–1794)*. Paris: Flammarion, 1973.

———. *The Sans-Culottes: The Popular Movement and Revolutionary Government, 1793–94*. Translated by Remy Inglis Hall. Garden City, NY: Doubleday, 1972.

Sobrevilla Perea, Natalia. "The Cádiz Constitution in the Atlantic World" (June 9, 2016). In *Oxford Research Encyclopedia in Latin American History*. Oxford: Oxford University Press, 2024. https://doi.org/10.1093/acrefore/9780199366439.013.35.

———. *The Caudillo of the Andes: Andrés de Santa Cruz*. Cambridge: Cambridge University Press, 2011.

Soll, Jacob. *Free Market: The History of an Idea*. New York: Basic Books, 2022.

Solnit, Rebecca. *Hope in the Dark: Untold Histories, Wild Possibilities*. 2004; Chicago: Haymarket Books, 2016.

Sonenscher, Michael. "Sociability, Perfectibility and the Intellectual Legacy of Jean-Jacques Rousseau." *History of European Ideas* 41, no. 5 (2015):683–98.

Sorel, Georges. *Reflections on Violence*. Edited and translated by Jeremy Jennings. Cambridge: Cambridge University Press, 1999.

Sotiropoulos, Michalis. *Liberalism after the Revolution: The Intellectual Foundations of the Greek State, c. 1830–1880*. Cambridge: Cambridge University Press, 2022.

Spadafora, David. *The Idea of Progress in Eighteenth-Century Britain*. New Haven, CT: Yale University Press, 1990.

Spector, Céline. *Montesquieu: Liberté, droit et histoire*. Paris: Michalon, 2010.

——. "The Plan for Perpetual Peace: From Saint-Pierre to Rousseau." *Journal of the History of European Ideas* (2011). https://doi.org/10.1016/j.histeuroideas.2011.07.010.

——. "Pouvoir contre pouvoir: La constitution mixte dans *L'Esprit des lois*." Unpublished MS.

——. *Rousseau*. Cambridge, UK: Polity, 2019.

——. "Who Is the Author of the *Abstract of Monsieur l'Abbé de Saint-Pierre's "Plan for Perpetual Peace"*? From Saint-Pierre to Rousseau." *History of European Ideas* 39, no.3 (2013):371–93.

Spence, Jonathan D. *The Search for Modern China*. New York: Norton, 1999.

Sperber, Jonathan. *The European Revolutions, 1848–1851*. Cambridge: Cambridge University Press, 2005.

——. *Karl Marx: A Nineteenth-Century Life*. New York: Norton, 2013.

Spiegel, Gabrielle. "Structures of Time in Medieval Historiography." *Medieval History Journal* 19, no. 1 (2016):21–33.

Spontone, Ciro. *Dodici libri del governo di stato*. Verona: Gio. Battista Pigozzo, 1599.

Sprague de Camp, L. *Lost Continents: The Atlantis Theme in History, Science, and Literature*. New York: Dover, 1970.

Stalin, Joseph. *Foundations of Leninism*. Moscow: Foreign Languages: 1953.

——. *History of the Communist Party of the Soviet Union (Bolsheviks)*. New York: International, 1939. Marxists' Internet Archive. https://www.marxists.org/reference/archive/stalin/works/1939/x01/.

Stamp Act Congress. "Declaration of Rights and Grievances." New York, 1765.

Stanley, John. *The Sociology of Virtue: The Political and Social Theories of George Sorel*. Berkeley: University of California Press, 1981.

Statman, Alexander. *A Global Enlightenment: Western Progress and Chinese Science*. Chicago: University of Chicago Press, 2023.

Stedman Jones, Gareth. *Karl Marx: Greatness and Illusion*. Cambridge, MA: Harvard University Press, 2016.

——. "Religion and the Origins of Socialism." In *Religion and the Political Imagination*, edited by Ira Katznelson and Stedman Jones, 171–89. Cambridge: Cambridge University Press, 2010.

Steinmetz-Jenkins, Daniel. "Claude Lefort and the Illegitimacy of Modernity." *Journal for Cultural and Religious Theory* 10, no. 1 (2009):102–17.

——, ed. *Did It Happen Here? Fascism in America*. New York: Norton, 2024.

Stendhal. *The Red and the Black*. Translated by Catherine Slater. Oxford: Oxford University Press, 2009.

Stites, Richard. *The Four Horsemen: Riding to Liberty in Post-Napoleonic Europe*. Oxford: Oxford University Press, 2014.

——. *Revolutionary Dreams: Utopian Vision and Experimental Life in the Russian Revolution*. Oxford: Oxford University Press, 1989.

Straumann, Benjamin. *Crisis and Constitutionalism*. New York: Oxford University Press, 2016.

——. "Leaving the State of Nature: Polybius on Resentment and the Emergence of Morals and Political Order." *Polis* 37 (2020):9–43.

Swift, Jonathan. *A Discourse of the Contests and Dissensions between the Nobles and Commons of Athens and Rome, with the Consequences They Had upon Both Those States*. London: John Nutt, 1701.

Sydenham, M. J. *The Girondins*. London: Athalone, 1961.

Syme, Ronald. *The Roman Revolution*. Rev. ed. 1939; Oxford: Oxford University Press, 2002.

Tackett, Timothy. *The Coming of the Terror in the French Revolution*. Cambridge, MA: Harvard University Press, 2015.

——. *The Glory and the Sorrow: A Parisian and His World in the Age of the French Revolution*. Oxford: Oxford University Press, 2021.

——. *When the King Took Flight*. Cambridge, MA: Harvard University Press, 2004.

Talev, Margaret. "Two Americas Index: 20% Favor a 'National Divorce,'" *Axios*, March 16, 2023. https://www.axios.com/2023/03/16/two-americas-index-national-divorce.

Talmon, Jacob. *The Origins of Totalitarian Democracy*. 2 vols. London: Secker and Warburg, 1952.

Tapsell, Grant. *The Personal Rule of Charles II, 1681–85*. Woodbridge, UK: Boydell, 2007.

Taylor, Alan. *American Revolutions: A Continental History, 1750–1804*. New York: Norton, 2016.

Teegarden, David. *Death to Tyrants! Ancient Greek Democracy and the Struggle against Tyranny*. Princeton, NJ: Princeton University Press, 2013.

Terdiman, Richard. *Discourse/Counter-discourse: The Theory and Practice of Symbolic Resistance in Nineteenth-Century France*. Ithaca, NY: Cornell University Press, 1985.

Ternavasio, Marcela. "The Impact of Spanish Constitutionalism in the Río de la Plata." In Eastman and Sobrevilla Perea, *Rise of Constitutional Government*, 133–49.

Thomas, Antoine-Léonard. *Essai sur les éloges*. Paris, 1773. ARTFL.

Thomas, Peter D. G. *John Wilkes: A Friend to Liberty*. Oxford: Oxford University Press 2011.

Thucydides. *Eight Bookes of the "Peloponnesian Warre" Written by Thucydides*. Translated by Thomas Hobbes. London, 1629.

——. *The Peloponnesian War*. Translated by Richard Crawley. In *The Landmark Thucydides*, edited by Robert B. Strassler. New York: Free Press, 1996. [Cited as Thuc.]

——. *The Peloponnesian War*. Translated by Charles Forster Smith. Loeb Classical Library. Cambridge, MA: Harvard University Press, 1920. [Cited as *Peloponnesian War*.]

——. *Thucydidis de "Bello Peloponnesiaco" libri octo*. Edited by Henri Estienne and John Hudson. Amsterdam: R. and J. Wetstenios and Gul. Smith, 1731.

Tilly, Charles. *From Mobilization to Revolution*. New York: Random House, 1978.

Tocqueville, Alexis de. *The Ancien Régime and the French Revolution*. Translated by Arthur Goldhammer. Cambridge: Cambridge University Press, 2011.

Toland, John. *The Art of Governing by Partys*. London: Bernard Lintott, 1701.

Tolstoy, Leo. *War and Peace*. Translated by Amy Mandelker. Oxford: Oxford University Press, 2010.

Tomasi di Lampedusa, Giuseppe. *The Leopard*. Translated by Archibald Colquhoun. 1958; New York: Pantheon, 2007.

Toska, Silvana. "The Multiple Scripts of the Arab Revolutions." In Baker and Edelstein, *Scripting Revolution*, 325–44.

Tourneux, Maurice, ed. *Procès-verbaux de la Commune de Paris*. Paris, 1894.

Traugott, Mark. *The Insurgent Barricade*. Berkeley: University of California Press, 2010.

Trésor de la langue française. Trésor de la Langue Française informatisé. http://atilf.atilf.fr/.

Tricoire, Damien. "Diderot and the Ideal of Paternalistic Monarchy: An Enlightenment Struggle against Moral Decay and for Political Harmony." *Journal of the History of European Ideas* (2024). https://doi.org/10.1080/01916599.2024.2319387.

Trompf, G. W. *The Idea of Historical Recurrence in Western Thought: From Antiquity to the Reformation*. Berkeley: University of California Press, 1979.

Trotsky, Leon. *Results and Prospects* (1906). Marxists' Internet Archive. http://www.marxists.org/archive/trotsky/1931/tpr/rp03.htm.

Tuck, Richard. *The Sleeping Sovereign*. Cambridge: Cambridge University Press, 2016.

Tucker, Robert C. *Philosophy and Myth in Karl Marx*. London: Routledge, 1961.

Tumarkin, Nina. *Lenin Lives! The Lenin Cult in Soviet Russia*. Cambridge, MA: Harvard University Press, 1997.

Turgot, Anne-Robert-Jacques. *Œuvres de Turgot et documents le concernant*. Edited by Gustave Schelle. 5 vols. Paris: Alcan, 1913–23.

———. *Œuvres posthumes de M. Turgot, ou Mémoire de M. Turgot sur les administrations provinciales*. Lausanne, Switzerland, 1787.

Union centrale des arts décoratifs and Musée des arts décoratifs. *Le livre des expositions universelles, 1851–1989*. Paris: Edition des arts décoratifs, 1983.

University of Oxford. *The Judgment and Decree of the University of Oxford Past in Their Convocation July 21, 1683, against Certain Pernicious Books*. Oxford, 1683. EEBO.

Urbinati, Nadia. *Representative Democracy: Principle and Genealogy*. Chicago: University of Chicago Press, 2006.

Van Gelderen, Martin. *The Dutch Revolt*. Cambridge: Cambridge University Press, 1992.

———. *The Political Thought of the Dutch Revolt, 1555–1590*. Cambridge: Cambridge University Press, 1992.

Van Prooijen, Jan-Willem, Sabine Rosema, Axel Chemke-Dreyfus, Konstantina Trikaliti, and Rita Hormigo. "Make It Great Again: The Relationship between Populist Attitudes and Nostalgia." *Political Psychology* 43 (2022):951–68.

Vardi, Liana. *The Physiocrats and the World of the Enlightenment*. Cambridge: Cambridge University Press, 2012.

Velley, Serge. "Une constitution trop 'vivante'? Heurs et malheurs de la constitution du 22 frimaire an VIII (13 décembre 1799)." *Napoleonica: La revue* 33, no. 1 (2019):51–66.

Venezuelan Declaration of Independence and Constitution. N.p.: Longman, 1812.

Verhoeven, Claudia. *The Odd Man Karakozov: Imperial Russia, Modernity, and the Birth of Terrorism*. Ithaca, NY: Cornell University Press, 2009

——. "'Une Révolution Vraiment Scientifique': Russian Terrorism, the Escape from the European Orbit, and the Invention of a New Revolutionary Paradigm." In Baker and Edelstein, *Scripting Revolution*, 199–212.

Vick, Brian E. *The Congress of Vienna: Power and Politics after Napoleon*. Cambridge, MA: Harvard University Press, 2014.

Vierhaus, Rudolf. "Liberalismus." In *GG*, 3:741–85.

Vile, M.J.C. *Constitutionalism and the Separation of Powers*. Indianapolis, IN: Liberty Fund, 1998.

Viroli, Maurizio. "Machiavelli and the Republican Ideal of Politics." In *Machiavelli and Republicanism*, edited by Gisela Bock, Quentin Skinner, and Maurizio Viroli, 143–71. Cambridge: Cambridge University Press, 1990.

Vocabolario degli Accademici della Crusca (1612). Accademici della Crusca. http://www.lessicografia.it/index.jsp.

Voltaire. *Voltaire's Correspondences*. Edited by Theodore Besterman. Electronic Enlightenment, www.e-enlightenment.com.

——. *Essay sur l'histoire générale, et sur les mœurs et l'esprit des nations, depuis Charlemagne jusqu'à nos jours*. 7 vols. [Geneva: Cramer], 1756.

——. *Le siècle de Louis XIV*. 2 vols. Berlin: C.-F. Henning, 1751.

——. *Œuvres complètes de Voltaire*. 205 vols. Oxford: Voltaire Foundation, 1968–2022.

——. *Zadig*. Paris: Gallimard, 1999.

Wahnich, Sophie. *La liberté ou la mort: Essai sur la terreur et le terrorisme*. Paris: La Fabrique, 2003.

Walbank, Frank W. "Fortune (*Tychē*) in Polybius." In *A Companion to Greek and Roman Historiography*, edited by John Marincola, 325–31. Oxford: Blackwell, 2007.

——. *A Historical Commentary on Polybius*. 3 vols. Oxford: Clarendon, 1957–79.

Walder, Andrew G. *Fractured Rebellion: The Beijing Red Guard Movement*. Cambridge, MA: Harvard University Press, 2009.

Walzer, Michael. *The Revolution of the Saints: A Study in the Origins of Radical Politics*. Cambridge, MA: Harvard University Press, 1965.

Warner, Rex. *History of the Peloponnesian War*. London: Penguin Books, 1972.

Weber, Max. *Economy and Society: An Outline of Interpretive Sociology*. 2 vols. Edited by Guenther Roth and Claus Wittich, translated by Ephraim Fischoff, Hans Gerth, A.M. Henderson, Ferdinand Kolegar, C. Wright Mills, Talcott Parsons, Max Rheinstein, and Edward Shils. 1922; Berkeley: University of California Press, 1978.

Werth, Nicolas. *La Terreur et le désarroi: Staline et son système*. Paris: Perrin, 2007.

Weston, Corinne. "Beginnings of the Classical Theory of the English Constitution." *Proceedings of the American Philosophical Society* 100, no. 2 (1956):133–44.

——. *English Constitutional Theory and the House of Lords, 1556–1832*. New York: Columbia University Press, 1965.

Weyland, Kurt. "The Arab Spring: Why the Surprising Similarities with the Revolutionary Wave of 1848?" *Perspectives on Politics* 10, no. 4 (2012):917–34.

White, James Boyd. *When Words Lose Their Meaning: Constitutions and Reconstitutions of Language, Character, and Community*. Chicago: University of Chicago Press, 1985.

Wilkes, John. *The North Briton*. Rev. ed. Dublin: John Mitchell, 1764.

Williams, David. *Condorcet and Modernity*. Cambridge: Cambridge University Press, 2004.

———. *Rousseau's "Social Contract": An Introduction*. Cambridge: Cambridge University Press, 2013.

Williams, Elisha. *The Essential Rights and Liberties of Protestants*. Boston, MA: S. Kneeland and T. Green, 1744.

Williams, E. Neville. *The Eighteenth-Century Constitution: Documents and Commentary*. Cambridge: Cambridge University Press, 1960.

Wilson, Edmund. "The Politics of Flaubert." In *The Triple Thinkers: Twelve Essays on Literary Subjects*, 72–87. 1938; New York: Noonday, 1976.

———. *To the Finland Station*. 1940; New York: New York Review of Books, 2003.

Wolin, Richard. *The Wind from the East: French Intellectuals, the Cultural Revolution, and the Legacy of the 1960s*. Princeton, NJ: Princeton University Press, 2010.

Woloch, Isser. *Napoleon and His Collaborators: The Making of a Dictatorship*. New York: W. W. Norton, 2002.

Wood, Gordon. *The Creation of the American Republic*. Rev. ed. Chapel Hill: University of North Carolina Press, 2011.

———. *Power and Liberty: Constitutionalism in the American Revolution*. Oxford: Oxford University Press, 2021.

———. "Prologue: The Legacy of Rome in the American Revolution." In Onuf and Cole, *Thomas Jefferson*, 11–32.

Woodhouse, A.S.P., ed. *Puritanism and Liberty, Being the Army Debates (1647–9) from the Clarke Manuscripts with Supplementary Documents*. Chicago: University of Chicago Press, 1951.

Woolrych, Austin H. *Commonwealth to Protectorate*. Oxford: Clarendon, 1982.

Wootton, David. "Liberty, Metaphor, and Mechanism: 'Checks and Balances' and the Origin of Modern Constitutionalism." In *Liberty and American Experience in the Eighteenth Century*, edited by David Womersley, 209–74. Indianapolis, IN: Liberty Fund, 2006.

Xiaobo, Liu. "That Holy Word, 'Revolution.'" In *Popular Protests and Political Culture in Modern China*, rev. ed., edited by Jeffrey N. Wasserstrom and Elizabeth J. Perry, 309–24. Boulder, CO: Westview, 1994.

Yack, Bernard. *The Longing for Total Revolution: Philosophic Sources of Social Discontent from Rousseau to Marx and Nietzsche*. 1986; Berkeley: University of California Press, 1992.

Yarmolinsky, Avrahm. *Road to Revolution: A Century of Russian Radicalism*. Princeton, NJ: Princeton University Press, 1956.

Zagorin, Perez. *A History of Political Thought in the English Revolution*. London: Routledge, 1954.

Zola, Emile. *Germinal* (1894). Vol. 3 of *Les Rougon-Macquart*, edited by A. Lanoux and H. Mitterand. Paris: Gallimard, 1964.

INDEX

Page numbers in *italics* refer to figures.

A NOTE ON THE TYPE

THIS BOOK has been composed in Miller, a Scotch Roman typeface designed by Matthew Carter and first released by Font Bureau in 1997. It resembles Monticello, the typeface developed for The Papers of Thomas Jefferson in the 1940s by C. H. Griffith and P. J. Conkwright and reinterpreted in digital form by Carter in 2003.

Pleasant Jefferson ("P. J.") Conkwright (1905–1986) was Typographer at Princeton University Press from 1939 to 1970. He was an acclaimed book designer and AIGA Medalist.

The ornament used throughout this book was designed by Pierre Simon Fournier (1712–1768) and was a favorite of Conkwright's, used in his design of the *Princeton University Library Chronicle*.